INTRODUCTION

HEALTH CARE
DELIVERY

A Primer for Pharmacists

FIFTH EDITION

Edited by:

ROBERT L. McCARTHY, PhD
Dean and Professor
School of Pharmacy
University of Connecticut

KENNETH W. SCHAFERMEYER, PhD
Professor and Director
Division of Liberal Arts and Administrative Sciences
St. Louis College of Pharmacy

KIMBERLY S. PLAKE, PhD
Associate Professor
Department of Pharmacy Practice
Purdue University, College of Pharmacy

JONES & BARTLETT
LEARNING

World Headquarters
Jones & Bartlett Learning
40 Tall Pine Drive
Sudbury, MA 01776
978-443-5000
info@jblearning.com
www.jblearning.com

Jones & Bartlett Learning books and products are available through most bookstores and online booksellers. To contact Jones & Bartlett Learning directly, call 800-832-0034, fax 978-443-8000, or visit our website, www.jblearning.com.

Substantial discounts on bulk quantities of Jones & Bartlett Learning publications are available to corporations, professional associations, and other qualified organizations. For details and specific discount information, contact the special sales department at Jones & Bartlett Learning via the above contact information or send an email to specialsales@jblearning.com.

Production Credits
Publisher: David D. Cella
Acquisitions Editor: Katey Birtcher
Associate Editor: Maro Gartside
Editorial Assistant: Teresa Reilly
Senior Production Editor: Renée Sekerak
Production Assistant: Sean Coombs
Marketing Manager: Grace Richards
Manufacturing and Inventory Control Supervisor: Amy Bacus
Composition: DataStream Content Solutions, LLC
Cover Design: Kristin E. Parker
Rights and Permissions Manager: Katherine Crighton
Photo Research Coordinator: Jessica Elias
Cover Images: Assortment of multicolored pills © Radkevich Siarhei/Dreamstime.com; hundred dollar bills © Deshacam/Dreamstime.com; U.S. Supreme Court building © Jonathan Larsen/ShutterStock, Inc.; female pharmacist © Mangostock/Dreamstime.com
Printing and Binding: Malloy, Inc.
Cover Printing: Malloy, Inc.

To order this product, use ISBN: 978-1-4496-4488-8

Library of Congress Cataloging-in-Publication Data
Introduction to health care delivery : a primer for pharmacists / [edited by] Robert L. McCarthy, Kenneth W. Schafermeyer, Kimberly S. Plake.—5th ed.
       p. ; cm.
   Includes bibliographical references and index.
   ISBN-13: 978-0-7637-9088-2 (pbk.)
   ISBN-10: 0-7637-9088-5 (pbk.)
 1. Medical care—United States.   2. Pharmaceutical services—United States.   I. McCarthy, Robert L. II. Schafermeyer, Kenneth W.   III. Plake, Kimberly S.
   [DNLM: 1. Delivery of Health Care—United States.   2. Drug Industry—United States.   3. Economics, Pharmaceutical—United States.   4. Pharmaceutical Services—United States.   W 84 AA1]
   RA395.A3I567 2012
   362.1'0973—dc22
                                                                                    2011011420
6048
Printed in the United States of America
15 14 13 12   10 9 8 7 6 5 4 3 2

To my grandson, Patrick Robert McCarthy.

—Robert L. McCarthy

To my wife, Donna, for her love and the many anniversaries to come.

—Kenneth W. Schafermeyer

To my husband, Michael, whose love and support have never wavered.

—Kimberly S. Plake

Contents

Chapter 11—Home Care **295**
William W. McCloskey, Frank Marr, and Maureen A. McCarthy

Chapter 12—Informatics in Health Care **315**
Ardis Hanson, Bruce Lubotsky Levin, and David M. Scott

Chapter 15—Private Health Insurance. 375
Kenneth W. Schafermeyer and Brenda R. Motheral

Chapter 16—Government Involvement in Health Care 401
Earlene E. Lipowski and Marcus Long

Preface

When the *First Edition* was published in 1998, Professor McCarthy hoped to meet a textbook need he felt was not adequately met. As an instructor who taught healthcare delivery, systems, and policy, he had long sought a book that provided an introduction to this rapidly evolving area, but that would do so from the perspective of pharmacy. In subsequent editions, we believe that we have been true to his original intent. Over the years, as we developed new editions, we tried to be responsive to the needs of our colleagues by adding, subtracting, and changing subject matter; by providing active learning exercises; and by developing online resources for instructors and students. Given the rapidly changing nature of healthcare delivery, we have also been committed to an aggressive revision schedule; this *Fifth Edition* is being published just 13 years after the *First Edition*.

The *Fifth Edition* includes several major revisions and chapter restructures to reflect the current reality, which one might argue is the most dynamic period in American health care yet. Given the changes in health information technology and mental health care, the reader will see significant changes in the chapters exploring these important topics. Medication therapy management and the medical home appear prominently for the first time. At the request of our adopters, a comprehensive chapter on public health has once again been included. *The Patient Protection and Affordable Care Act of 2010*, the most sweeping piece of federal healthcare legislation since the passage Medicare and Medicaid in the 1960s, is addressed in detail, including a description of the pharmacy-specific provisions that have the potential to alter the way in which pharmacy is practiced and pharmacy services are reimbursed in the United States.

We hope you will find the *Fifth Edition* of *Introduction to Health Care Delivery: A Primer for Pharmacists* achieves the goals of its forebears, but also enables instructors and students of healthcare delivery to consider, more fully, how healthcare services in general—and pharmacy services in particular—are delivered. Moreover, we hope that the text and its supplementary materials—including those provided online—will facilitate thoughtful discussions among students, faculty, and practitioners about not only how health care is delivered, but how the system might be improved for all those seeking care.

This book is also accompanied by extensive student resources. To learn more, visit: http://go.jblearning.com/mccarthy5.

Contributors

Thomas E. Buckley, MPH, RPh
Assistant Clinical Professor
University of Connecticut, School of Pharmacy
Storrs, Connecticut

Suvapun Bunniran, PhD
University of Mississippi, School of Pharmacy
University, Mississippi

Aleda M. H. Chen, PharmD, MS
Assistant Professor of Pharmacy Practice
Cedarville University, School of Pharmacy
Cedarville, Ohio

Craig I. Coleman, PharmD
Associate Professor
University of Connecticut, School of Pharmacy
Storrs, Connecticut

Shane P. Desselle, BS, PhD
Associate Dean for Tulsa Programs
Professor and Chair
Department of Pharmacy: Clinical and Administrative Sciences
University of Oklahoma, College of Pharmacy
Oklahoma City, Oklahoma

Louis P. Garrison Jr, PhD
Professor for Pharmaceutical Outcomes, Research, and Policy Program
Department of Pharmacy
Adjunct Professor
Departments of Global Health and Health Services
University of Washington, School of Pharmacy
Seattle, Washington

Dana P. Hammer, PhD, MS
Director
Bracken Pharmaceutical Care Learning Center and Teaching Certificate
    Programs in Pharmacy Education
University of Washington, School of Pharmacy
Seattle, Washington

Ardis Hanson, MLS
Head
FMHI Research Library
University of South Florida
Tampa, Florida

Peter D. Hurd, PhD
Professor and Assistant to the Dean for Research
St. Louis College of Pharmacy
St. Louis, Missouri

Bruce Lubotsky Levin, DrPH, MPH
Associate Professor and Head
Graduate Studies in Behavioral Health Program
College of Behavioral and Community Sciences
University of South Florida, College of Public Health
Tampa, Florida

Earlene E. Lipowski, PhD
Associate Professor
Pharmacy Health Care Administration
University of Florida, College of Pharmacy
Gainesville, Florida

Marcus Long, MA
Vice President, Marketing and Communications
St. Louis College of Pharmacy
St. Louis, Missouri

Frank Marr, PharmD
General Manager
Walgreens Infusion Services
East Berlin, Connecticut

David J. McCaffrey III, BS, MS, PhD
Associate Professor of Pharmacy Administration and Research
Research Institute of Pharmaceutical Sciences
University of Mississippi
University, Mississippi

Maureen A. McCarthy, RPh, MBA
Clinical Pharmacist
Walgreens Infusion Services
East Berlin, Connecticut

William W. McCloskey, BA, BS, PharmD
Professor of Pharmacy Practice
Massachusetts College of Pharmacy and Health Sciences
Boston, Massachusetts

Helen Meldrum, PhD
Associate Professor of Psychology
Bentley University
Waltham, Massachusetts

Kristin B. Meyer, PharmD, CGP
Assistant Professor of Pharmacy Practice
Drake University
Des Moines, Iowa

Brenda R. Motheral, PhD
Associate Professor of Pharmacy Administration
University of Kentucky, College of Pharmacy
Lexington, Kentucky

Carol A. Ott, PharmD, BCPP
Clinical Assistant Professor of Pharmacy Practice
Purdue University, College of Pharmacy
West Lafayette, Indiana

Catherine N. Otto, PhD, MBA
Former Chair
Patient Safety Committee
American Society for Clinical Laboratory Science
Washington, District of Columbia

Ana C. Quiñones-Boex, PhD, MS
Associate Professor of Pharmacy Administration
Midwestern University, Chicago College of Pharmacy
Downers Grove, Illinois

Kyle D. Ross, PhD
Assistant Professor of Economics
Department of Economics and Finance
University of Arkansas at Little Rock
Little Rock, Arkansas

David M. Scott, MPH, PhD
Associate Professor of Pharmacy Administration
North Dakota State University, College of Pharmacy, Nursing, and Allied Sciences
Fargo, North Dakota

Jennifer L. Tebbe-Grossman, PhD
Professor of Political Science and American Studies
Massachusetts College of Pharmacy and Health Sciences
Boston, Massachusetts

Alan P. Wolfgang, MS, PhD
Associate Professor
University of Georgia, College of Pharmacy
Athens, Georgia

PART

I

SOCIAL ASPECTS OF HEALTHCARE DELIVERY

CHAPTER

1

Healthcare Delivery in America: Historical and Policy Perspectives

Jennifer L. Tebbe-Grossman

Case Scenario

The Palmers, a large, extended family, immigrated to New England in the early 1700s. In the 18th and early 19th centuries, the family and their descendants lived on farms in New England. They prospered through farming and some occasional work in small factories in nearby towns. Around 1860, family members moved to the growing cities. A number took jobs in factories; others were fortunate enough to go to high school and even college and found positions in the new professions of teaching, business, and health care. In the 20th century, some family members thrived, especially in the period of rapid economic growth after World War II. Others were barely able to make ends meet, relying at times on government programs and private charities.

One constant in the extended Palmer family is that from the time of their arrival in New England in 1740, various family members kept journals and wrote letters (and later emails or Facebook entries) recording information about their extended family members' daily lives. Suppose that in the 21st century, you have found some of these records spanning several centuries. As a future health professional, you learn about the health and disease history of the Palmer family members: what they thought caused disease and what their philosophies of health and disease were when they made their choices to seek health services; what kinds of diseases family members confronted; the differences public health improvements and technological changes made in their lives; how their health services were paid for; from whom and where they got or didn't get their health services and why; and what they thought about different healthcare policies presented by politicians and branches of government as these policies changed over time in the United States. The written or electronic record covers much of what appears in this chapter.

Based on the material in this chapter, what might you find out about the health experiences and beliefs of the Palmer family members, given their differing socio-economic backgrounds over time? What might you think about how much or how little healthcare services and their models of delivery have improved over time for American populations?

LEARNING OBJECTIVES

Upon completion of this chapter, the student shall be able to:

- Explain paradoxes of the U.S. healthcare system
- Explain health conditions in 18th- and 19th-century America in relation to disease patterns and causation theories
- Explain types of health practices and practitioners and factors explaining access to health care in 19th-century America
- Explain the various roles of government in healthcare delivery in 18th- and 19th-century America
- Explain the differences between orthodox and sectarian practitioners and their patients in relation to their perspectives on therapeutics and the delivery of health care
- Explain changes in the character, organization, and purposes of hospitals as health delivery sites from the early 19th century through the early 21st century
- Describe reforms in medical education at the turn of the 20th century and the consequences of the Flexner report of 1910
- Identify the golden age of medicine and describe what replaced it in the late 20th and early 21st centuries
- Explain the ways in which medicine and pharmacy pursued professionalization in the late 19th and 20th centuries and how these professions define themselves in the 21st century
- Explain how the factors of public health, lifestyle (diet, housing, personal hygiene), and medical practice influenced the decline of infectious diseases and increase in life expectancy at the turn of the 20th century
- Discuss the occurrences of infectious and chronic diseases in the 21st century
- Discuss the types of government policy that affected healthcare delivery in the 20th and early 21st centuries, particularly in relation to the implementation of public and private health insurance
- Discuss the implementation of Medicare and Medicaid in the 1960s, the 1973 Health Maintenance Organization Act, the 1996 Health Insurance Portability and Accountability Act, the 1997 Children's Health Insurance Program, and the 2010 Patient Protection and Affordable Care Act
- Explain the benefits and costs of the Medicare Part D Drug Plan
- Explain problems associated with incremental healthcare reform

CHAPTER QUESTIONS

1. What kinds of health beliefs did Americans hold in the 18th and 19th centuries?
2. What factors account for the decline in mortality rates and increases in life expectancy at the turn of the 20th century?
3. What were the benefits and drawbacks of the reforms in education that pharmacists and physicians implemented in the early 20th century as part of the professionalization process?
4. Who provided healthcare services for Americans and in what kinds of settings during the 18th, 19th, 20th, and 21st centuries?
5. What kinds of changes in private and public health insurance plans were considered by Americans in the past?

6. What is the potential for improved healthcare delivery in implementing patient-centered care, interdisciplinary care, and the medical home model of care?
7. How is the 2010 Patient Protection and Affordability Act characteristic of incremental healthcare reform?

INTRODUCTION

Taking a historical perspective, this chapter examines the evolution of health care and health services in the United States. Emphasis is placed on the changes in social spaces where Americans experience healthcare services—from the home, physician's office, neighborhood dispensary, or hospital—to the outpatient clinic, multigroup specialty practice, community pharmacy, or federally qualified community health center. Patterns of health and illness in the United States are examined in the context of mortality and life expectancy and the occurrence of infectious and chronic diseases. The changing social meanings of health and disease, the roles of health professionals, such as pharmacists and physicians, and the expectations of citizens as patients and consumers in an increasingly complex healthcare delivery environment are explored. Of particular concern is the context of changes in attitudes and practice toward individual and social responsibility in the delivery of healthcare services.

PARADOXES OF THE U.S. HEALTHCARE SYSTEM

The U.S. healthcare system is characterized by many paradoxes. The United States has the best, most advanced technology available—yet we have a very high rate of medical errors. There are gaps in who has access to health care, with 21.1% of persons aged 18–64 in 2009 lacking health insurance (Cohen, Martinez, & Ward 2010, p.1). Compared to other industrialized nations, the level of spending in the United States means that the country has one of the most expensive healthcare systems, especially in terms of administrative costs. The U.S. healthcare system is also fragmented in terms of how it is financed and how healthcare services are organized and delivered. The following overview highlights the paradoxes of health in America and some key components influencing the continuing crisis.

Technology

Magnetic resonance imaging systems, new diagnostics, transplant surgeries, biotechnology-based products, genetic engineering, telemedicine, new reproductive technologies, and health information technology are just a few of the rapid technologic advances that have emerged in recent years in the United States. These developments offer hopes for improved quality of life, quicker diagnoses and better treatments, and increased life expectancy. Reliance on technologic innovation also creates problems. Most Americans expect to receive only the best technical care available, which often leads to overuse of technologic advances. New technologies tend to be updated quickly, often without sufficient examination of cost and effectiveness or patient safety threat issues. While the meaningful use of electronic health records offers opportunities for cost savings, reduction in medical errors, and improved patient access and outcomes, health professionals raise concerns that in implementing electronic medical records they may lose focus on the interaction between the sick and the healer, thereby leading them to "suspend thinking, blindly accept diagnoses, and fail to talk to patients in a way that allows deep, independent probing" (Hartzband & Groopman, 2008, p. 1656; Ralston, Coleman, Reid, Handley, & Larson). While many Americans regard access to medical imaging as a sign of the superiority of the U.S. healthcare system, recent health research has focused on the avoidable public health threat that arises from investing so many resources in performing so many procedures as well as the dangers of radiation overdoses in single procedures (Bogdanich, 2010, p. A1; Lauer, 2009, pp. 842, 843). And finally, technology is not equally distributed among patient populations—significant disparities exist based on insurance status, income, and race (Weiss & Lonnquist, 2006, pp. 332–333).

Health Expenditures

The United States easily surpasses all other countries in spending, yet millions of its citizens lack adequate access to health care. In 2008, a total of $2.3 trillion, representing an increase of 4.4% from the previous year, was spent on healthcare goods and services (amounting to $7,681 per person). The federal government and health researchers pointed out that health spending growth was the slowest in 48 years, attributing this downturn as most likely connected to the economic recession (Hartman, Martin, Nuccio, & Catlin, 2010, pp. 147–149). Yet the United States also continues to spend more money for health care with the percentage of U.S. gross domestic product spent increasing from 15.9% in 2007 to 16.2% in 2008. A cost that individual households saw was in the share of personal income spent on health, which increased from 5.3% in 2001 to 5.9% in 2008 (Centers for Medicare and Medicaid Services, 2010; Hartman, Martin, Nuccio, & Catlin, 2010, pp. 147–149). The Kaiser Family Foundation also reported in 2007 that the average premium for family health coverage was $12,106 with American workers paying $3,281 of this cost (Fletcher, 2008).

According to a study comparing the United States with other developed nations, the country spends a higher share of gross domestic product on health care. The 2009 Health Care at a Glance Organization for Economic Co-Operation and Development (OECD) report compared 2007 healthcare spending of the United States (16.0%) to France (11%), Switzerland (10.8%), United Kingdom (8.4%), and Canada (10.1%). U.S. spending is higher than other developed countries in the areas of inpatient and outpatient care, as well as administrative costs, pharmaceuticals, and long-term care (OECD, 2009; Reinhardt, Hussey, & Anderson, 2004).

Health Insurance

In a 2009 Centers for Disease Control and Prevention national health interview survey, 46.3 million Americans of all ages were without health insurance. Between 2008 and 2009, there was an increase in the percentage of adults (18–64 years) lacking health insurance coverage from 19.7% to 21.1%. The survey indicated 10.9% of the 46.3 million had been without health insurance for more than 1 year. Lack of insurance varied by state, with one in five adults lacking insurance in Georgia and California, and one in four in Texas and Florida. Due to passage of health reform legislation that sought to achieve near-universal coverage, Massachusetts had a 3.7% rate of uninsured adults. Variability in the numbers of those insured across states relates to such factors as employment rates, cost of private insurance provided by employers or individual health insurance, and access guidelines for public programs such as Medicaid. Studies have shown that many Americans are uninsured for parts of the year with the numbers highest for those living in families with lower incomes. In addition, the Commonwealth Fund estimated that nearly 25 million Americans had insurance policies in 2007 but were underinsured, meaning their policies often don't cover important aspects of care including such items as preventive care health practitioner visits, prescription drug costs, medical tests, surgery or other medical procedures, or catastrophic medical conditions, and/or they usually require significant out-of-pocket payments for services (Cohen, Martinez, & Ward, 2010, p. 1; Gabel, McDevitt, Lore, Pickreign, & Whitmore, 2009; Johnson & Johnson, 2010; National Center for Health Statistics, 2009).

Health Standards

While health care in the United States is the most expensive across the globe, inadequate, improper, and even dangerous care is all too prevalent. In reports on the performance of healthcare systems internationally, the Commonwealth Fund has found that the United States "consistently underperforms on most dimensions of performance" including in areas of "access, patient safety, coordination, efficiency, and equity" (Bodenheimer, Chen, & Bennett, 2009, pp. 69, 72). Major problems for U.S. patients occur in health worker shortages and the ratio of healthcare clinicians to patients, especially in regard to physicians, nurses (including nurse practitioners), physician assistants, pharmacists, and community health and public health workers providing primary care services in rural and underrepresented areas. With increasing numbers of Americans needing primary care for chronic care services, researchers have called for such new national workforce policies as those fostering interdisciplinary and multidisciplinary care delivered in primary care settings, new financial payment systems for primary care practices and clinics, and increased education of health professionals from underrepresented population groups (Davis, Schoen, & Stremikis, 2010).

In 1999, the Institute of Medicine issued a major report, *To Err Is Human: Building a Safer Health System,* presenting data that showed 44,000 to 98,000 people die each year from medical errors, a higher number than those dying from breast cancer or auto accidents. The report outlined ways to reduce medical errors and urged Congress to create a national patient safety center. In 2005, the federal government enacted the Patient Safety and Quality Improvement Act to continue the effort to foster safety cultures in healthcare institutions. A study commissioned by the Society of Actuaries based on insurance claims data reported that medical errors and the problems that ensued from them resulted in costs of $19.5 billion to the U.S. economy in 2008 (Hobson, 2010). For the same year, the Henry K. Kaiser Foundation stated that "serious medication errors occur in the cases of five to 10 percent of patients admitted to hospitals" (Woo, Ranji, & Salganicoff, 2008, p. 1).

Those studying patient safety disagree on what progress has been made. Some argue that progress has been made in developing new adverse event reporting systems with the introduction of health information technology systems, advancing national data collection and accreditation standards, and promoting new patient safety initiatives supported by such groups as the Joint Commission and the Institute for Healthcare Improvement. Others, including Donald Berwick, an author of *To Err Is Human* and the new director of the Center for Medicare and Medicaid Services, have seen a change in awareness of medical safety but not fundamental change in the nature of the American healthcare industry (Beresford, 2010; Furukawa, Raghu, Spaulding, & Vinze, 2008;

Bosc, Dixon-Woods, Goeschel, & Pronovost, 2009; Gawande, 2010; National Healthcare Quality Report, 2009; Wachter, 2010). Berwick wanted safety responsibility relocated in "the offices and work of leaders of healthcare institutions" and "new safety initiatives … fostered by teams working at unprecedented levels of collaboration, reaching across traditional boundaries" (Berwick quoted in Beresford, 2010, p. 2). Government agencies and private foundations studying healthcare quality standards in U.S. health facilities agree that much more work is necessary to ensure safe care for the American population.

An Example: Healthcare-Associated Infections

Healthcare-associated infections were hardly discussed in the *To Err Is Human* report. Still, the 1990s saw growing concerns in healthcare facilities about antimicrobial drug-resistant nosocomial bacterial infections, including methicillin-resistant *Staphylococcus aureus*, *Clostridium difficile*, and the more recently reported multidrug-resistant NDM-producing Enterobacteriaceae (McKenna, 2010; Pitout, 2010, p. 1). The 2009 *WHO Guidelines on Hand Hygiene in Health Care* stated that "HCAI [healthcare-associated infections] concerns 5–15% of hospitalized patients and can affect 9–37% of those admitted to intensive care units (ICUs)" (p. 6). The U.S. Centers for Disease Control and Prevention reported approximately 1.7 million healthcare-associated infections and 99,000 associated deaths and cited HCAI as "one of the top-ten leading causes of death in the United States" (Agency for Healthcare Research and Quality, 2011, p. 1).

The hands of health providers and other health workers were identified as major culprits for healthcare infections. In 2000, the Centers for Disease Control and Prevention asserted that hygiene, especially hand washing, was "the single most effective way to prevent the transmission of disease" (Centers for Disease Control and Prevention, p. 1). Atul Gawande, a 2006 MacArthur fellow and research director of the Center for Surgery and Public Health at the Brigham and Women's Hospital in Boston, wrote about the hand-washing problem in *The New England Journal of Medicine* in 2004. On a tour of the Brigham and Women's Hospital with its infection-disease specialist, he learned that the biggest problem in infection control was "getting clinicians like me to do the one thing that consistently halts the spread of most infections: wash our hands" (Gawande, 2004, p. 1283).

In the United States, national guidelines for hand washing were first published by the Centers for Disease Control and Prevention in the 1980s. The 2009 *WHO Guidelines on Hand Hygiene in Health Care* defined alcohol-based hand rubbing, where available, as the standard of care for hand hygiene practices in healthcare settings with hand washing reserved for such situations as medication handling (WHO, 2009, p. 9). Yet in the first decade of the 21st century, hand-washing adherence among healthcare workers, including doctors and nurses, was not high, with "mean baseline rates ranging from 5% to 89% and an overall average of 38.7%" (WHO, 2009, p. 66).

The 2009 *National Healthcare Quality Report* notes healthcare-associated infections increased rather than declined with an increase of 8% seen in postoperative sepsis and an increase of 3.6% seen in postoperative catheter-associated urinary tract infections (*National Healthcare Quality Report 2009*, pp. 107–112). Healthcare institutions have implemented a number of interventions to address these issues (Pronovost et. al., 2006). Increasingly in the 21st century, hospitals have pursued formal hand hygiene improvement programs. For example, Massachusetts General Hospital developed an extensive hand hygiene strategy, organizing a multidisciplinary task force called Stop the Transmission of Pathogens aimed at collaboratively involving hospital employees, patients, and visitors. The program developed by the task force, "Clean Because We Care," included the recruitment and training of volunteer champions (e.g., nurses, physicians, and housekeeping staff who implemented various motivational programs). In addition, the linking of a hospital-wide hand-hygiene compliance rate of above 90% to an annual employee bonus was used to incentivize employees. In early 2009, Massachusetts General Hospital reported improvement in its compliance rates with 93% of healthcare workers washing their hands before contact with patients and 96% after contact with patients (Hooper, 2009).

Health Outcomes

Health professionals and ordinary Americans have consistently been preoccupied with the state of American health through the examination of various outcomes. A recent study comparing health outcomes in populations with diabetes, hypertension, heart disease, myocardial infarction, strokes, lung disease, and cancer in the United States and the United Kingdom concluded that "based on self-reported illnesses and biological markers of disease, U.S. residents are much less healthy than their English counterparts" (Banks, Marmot, Oldfield, and Smith, 2006, p. 2037). In this study, differences existed at all levels of socioeconomic status, although health disparities were largest for those with the least education and income. The paradox: The United States spends far more on medical care than the United Kingdom does on a per capita basis (Banks et al., 2006, p. 2037).

An often-cited statistic is that the United States ranks lower than many other nations—especially such industrialized nations as Germany, Sweden, and Canada—in terms of infant mortality rates while spending more to prevent infant deaths. In the early years of the 21st century, 43 of the 224 countries reporting infant mortality statistics had lower mortality rates than the United States (Central Intelligence Agency, 2010). Despite the 27% decline in infant mortality rates between 1990 and 2007 among all groups in the United States, there are a number of reasons to account for the United States' relatively low standing among other nations. For instance, the United States still has significant disparities in infant mortality rates based on race and ethnicity due to such factors as less access to prenatal care. In 2007, the overall infant mortality rate was 6.77 infant deaths per 1,000 live births while the rate for infants born to non-Hispanic black mothers was 13.63 deaths and 8.06 deaths for American Indian or Alaska Native mothers (Central Intelligence Agency, 2010; National Center for Health Statistics, 2009, pp. 6–7).

Programs such as "Every Child Succeeds" in Cincinnati, Ohio, have achieved success in improving infant mortality rates. In seven counties in the Cincinnati area, 8.3 of every 1,000 infants die before the age of 1 year, but for those in the "Every Child Succeeds" program, the infant mortality rate was 2.8, which is a rate that is lower than those reported in every industrialized country. Although the program enrolled 1,800 mothers, its funding allowed only one fifth of the needy women in the Cincinnati area to participate (Naik, 2006).

In another example, health officials in Dane County, Wisconsin, reported a dramatic decline between the early 1990s and 2009 in the rate of infant deaths among black mothers (fewer than 5 deaths per 1,000 live births from an average of 19 deaths), citing factors outside a medical model as an explanation. The county addressed issues affecting the well-being of mothers—their mental and physical health, social connections, and exposures to stress in their environments, including racism. In other parts of Wisconsin during the same time period, however, the black infant death rate compared to the highest rates in other parts of the United States, at more than 20 deaths per 1,000 live births (Eckholm, 2009).

Comparisons of life expectancy show similar race-based disparities. In 1900, the life expectancy in the United States for women was 51.1 years, and for men it was 48.3 years. In 2006, life expectancy for all Americans was 77.7 years—80.2 years for women and 75.1 years for men. In comparing race-based data, life expectancy for white women compared to black women was 80.6 and 76.5 years, respectively, and for white men and black men, 75.7 and 69.7 years of age. Many factors account for disparities in life expectancy, including differences in the quality of neighborhood living environments and access to preventive care services (Epstein, 2003; Kinsella, 1992, p. 1197S; U.S. Census Bureau, 2010).

According to the 2009 *National Healthcare Disparities Report*, racial, ethnic, and socioeconomic disparities have increased in the United States since the report was first issued in 2003. The 2009 report cited lack of insurance, underinsurance, and lack of access to quality care, especially for those with cancer, pneumonia, and heart failure, in explaining the differences in how various populations experience health care in the United States (*National Healthcare Disparities Report,* 2010).

Based on outcomes as measures of healthcare risks in the United States, several major concerns were highlighted in the 1st decade of the 21st century. In examining targets that the Department of Health and Human Services set in *Healthy People 2010,* the incidence of smoking among adults decreased between 1998 (24%) and 2008 (21%), but did not reach the 12% target decrease that had been set in 2000. In addition, the small progress made was threatened with recent decreases in funding for prevention efforts.

Nearly one third of Americans 20 years or older have been identified as obese in 2010. In connecting this obesity statistic to understanding the importance of decreasing the incidence of diabetes, *Healthy People* focused on this disease state and identified a baseline in 1997 of 40 cases of clinically diagnosed diabetes per 1,000 population. Unfortunately, in 2008 the rate of cases increased to 59 per 1,000 population. The *Healthy People* target of 25 cases per 1,000 population for reducing diabetes prevalence in the United States was obviously not achieved, and increased evidence-based diabetes interventions will need to be made by multidisciplinary health professionals in a variety of healthcare settings to assist in caring for these individuals. Thus, the *Healthy People 2020* plan has included the addition of the following two new goals: first, "promoting quality of life, healthy development, and healthy behaviors across life stages; and second, creating social and physical environments that promote good health" (Koh, 2010, p. 1656).

All of these existing paradoxes in the U.S. healthcare system are important to consider when reviewing the evolution of health care and the delivery of healthcare services in a variety of settings within American communities over time.

HEALTH, DISEASE, AND HEALTH PRACTITIONERS IN COLONIAL AMERICA

As different groups of European settlers arrived in the Americas in the 16th and 17th centuries, they found a variety of societies and cultures. Some of the indigenous inhabitants of North America only hunted and gathered. Other groups occupied more permanent settlements and subsisted through both agricultural production and hunting and gathering. Contrary to the belief of many Europeans that the Americas promised a new Eden of good health, Native Americans endured significantly high mortality rates. Malnutrition, violence, accidents, fungal infections, anthrax, tapeworms, tuberculosis, and syphilis were common causes of death. European settlers brought influenza—which may not have been seen previously in the Americas—and other new illnesses—including yellow fever, malaria, smallpox, and measles—against which Native Americans had no immunity. Thus, as the historian of medicine, Gerald Grob, notes, the result of early contact between Europeans and Native Americans "was a catastrophe of monumental proportions that resulted in the destruction of a large majority of the indigenous population and facilitated European domination of the Americas" (2002, p. 27).

Arriving debilitated from sea travel, settlers of England's North American colonies did not encounter an Edenic or a utopian environment. Rather, in the early years, many fell victim to malnutrition and dysentery—the consequences of poor food and insufficient clean water supplies. The colonists suffered from a wide range of endemic and epidemic infectious diseases such as yellow fever, measles, smallpox, and malaria. The British government did not implement broad public policies to address problems of health and illness or encourage the establishment of health practitioners or institutions (Cassedy, 1991). Colonial officials addressed such public health problems as garbage disposal, street maintenance, and the regulation of water supply and sanitation occasionally, and with little success in enforcement. Partially because of health emergencies (especially such epidemic outbreaks as smallpox or measles), towns and cities did become accustomed to governments enacting more extensive public health regulations. Examples included quarantines of ships arriving from areas affected by epidemic diseases, setting up isolation or pest houses, and fumigating houses where victims of smallpox or other infectious diseases had lived. Still, the medical historian James Cassedy argued that the application of these public health benefits was "so irregular, tentative, and inconsistent that the benefit to the public health must have been negligible" (1991, pp. 13–14).

When colonists became sick, they depended on various members of the community for access to the healing arts, looking as much for simple human and religious comforts as for therapeutic services. Although physicians, apothecaries, midwives, clergy, and public officials responded to individual or community health needs, it was just as common for family members or neighbors, often the females in the household, to diagnose, make medicines, and physically support the sick. Until at least 1825, women commonly depended on their female friends and relatives, and midwives when they were available, to attend to them in childbirth in their homes (Bogdan, 1992). European physicians did not look to the colonies, which had small and widely scattered populations, as locations that offered great professional or economic opportunity. Few physicians emigrated, and since medical education in the North American colonies was not considered a priority of government or private agencies, only a minority of physicians or apothecaries completed formal training. Physicians often compounded and dispensed medicines in shops next door to their medical practices. Apothecaries appeared only in small numbers as compounders, dispensers, or sometimes manufacturers and wholesalers of medicines.

In the growing colonies, all of these practitioners of the healing arts shared health beliefs that relied on a combination of folklore; mineral, plant, and vegetable herbal remedies; and magic as well as improvisation based on what they found in their environments. The colonists used health practices and medications that were common in Europe and England, such as mercury and opium preparations. They also adopted such Native American health remedies as cinchona bark, which contained quinine (Christianson, 1987; Duffy, 1993; Tannenbaum, 2002).

AMERICA IN THE 19TH CENTURY: THE HEALTHCARE ENVIRONMENT

As the nation expanded westward and its population grew in the early 19th century, Americans exhibited a local outlook on health care that was similar to their attitudes toward economic and political life. A person's health experience as a resident of a town or city on the eastern seaboard was different from the health experience of a farmer in the rural southern or midwestern areas or of an immigrant traveling west into the new territories.

Rural and Urban Health

Self-reliance was a necessity for farmers and travelers. Poverty, loneliness, exhaustion, accidents, exposure to the elements, and dangerous plant and animal life took their toll. Family members and midwives who also functioned as social healers within communities played the most important roles in caring for ordinary people in times of illness. From a beginning in the era of the American Revolution, the number of physicians who practiced medicine in their own homes and traveled to make house calls in the homes of their patients increased significantly in the 19th century in rural areas and small towns. Both midwives, or social healers, and physicians treated entire families—men, women, and children—and juggled the responsibilities of their health practices with their domestic and community responsibilities. Payment for services was in cash and often in kind, or what families produced by their labor. Many patients could not pay, however, so midwives and physicians needed to rely on other sources of income. Rural and small-town residents could request compounded and proprietary medicines through both physicians and apothecaries. They could also purchase proprietary medicines in the general store and from itinerant healers or medicine men who regularly traveled from town to town (Cassedy, 1991; Leavitt, 1995, p. 4; Ulrich, 1990; Young, 1992).

In urban areas, in the 19th century, social class largely affected a person's quality of life and access to health care. The wealthy and growing upper middle class, including those members of the Palmer family (introduced in the case scenario at the beginning of the chapter) who were well off, had servants, lived in neighborhoods that provided clean air and water, gardens and parks, and health practitioners of their choice. The lower middle classes—including skilled workers, clerks, tradesmen, and widows—could afford food and housing and occasional visits to public parks. They tried to keep their domestic spaces clean despite the unsanitary living conditions offered by tenement landlords. They could pay minimal amounts for self-dosing remedies, medicines, or doctor bills. Most major towns and cities began to provide dispensaries that offered such services as the writing of prescriptions, minor surgeries for fractures, and vaccinations for workers who could pay little or nothing at all (Rosenberg, 1974).

The working classes shared problems with the poor, including lack of such basic municipal services as garbage and sewage removal. As part of the Industrial Revolution, members of the working classes breathed air polluted by coal dust from the factories and railroads that were next to their residences. Congestion, noise, the frenetic pace of commercial life, and the accelerated influx of new waves of immigrants led to a rapid accumulation of new and old health problems, especially rising mortality rates due to infectious diseases. In addition, African Americans confronted even higher degrees of difficulty in relation to quality of life indicators because of slavery and discrimination. They experienced lack of access to health education, health facilities, and basic public health services (Byrd and Clayton, 2000; Cassedy, 1991; Hoy, 1995)

Health Values, Therapeutics, and Practitioners

Health practitioners and the general public have long disagreed about theories regarding the causes of disease and the public policies needed to address them. Some believed that supernatural forces inflicted disease because of human sin. Some believed in contagion or environmental (miasmic) theories of disease. Still others believed that the individual who did not take precautions to lead a healthful life was responsible for disease (Tesh, 1988).

Regardless of their beliefs about disease causation, most Americans generally shared the same values when it came to health, disease, and the body—that is, they looked to Galen's 2nd-century concept of humoralism. The body was an interconnected whole with a natural balance (Warner, 1997, p. 87). As Charles Rosenberg (1985) noted, "every part of the body was related inevitably and inextricably with every other. In health, the body's system was in balance; in disease, the body lost its balance and suffered disequilibrium. If health practitioners were to treat disease effectively, they needed to know about individual patients and their body's system of 'intake and outgo'" (p. 40). What could be observed empirically happening to the patient's body was therapeutically important.

Orthodox physicians (also referred to as allopathic, regular, or mainstream physicians), who had some didactic medical education or at least an apprenticeship under a practicing physician, offered their mostly middle- and upper-class patients heroic medical therapy. They adopted mostly depletive measures, whereas members of the lay public—drawing upon popular domestic medical texts and almanacs—more often employed both depletive and strengthening measures (tonics and astringents) (Horrocks, 2003). Orthodox physicians assumed an active, aggressive role whereby the patient and the family could see very visible changes in secretions and excretions in the body as a result of the physician's interventions. Using leeches, medical instruments, and a variety of drug therapies, orthodox physicians bled, purged, puked, and sweated their patients. Because cures were not often the result of a physician's care during serious illnesses, patients and families could at least share in the knowledge that they had observed the physician's efforts to do something. Rosenberg has noted the ways in which depletive drugs were used in this system:

> Drugs had to be seen as adjusting the body's internal equilibrium; in addition, the drug's action had, if possible, to alter these visible products of the body's otherwise inscrutable internal state. Logically enough, drugs were not ordinarily viewed as specifics for particular disease entities; materia medica texts were generally arranged not by drug or disease, but in categories reflecting the drug's physiological effects: diuretics, cathartics, narcotics, emetics, diaphoretics. (1985, p. 41)

Orthodox physicians competed with sectarians (also called irregulars), who offered a variety of alternative practices, cures, and remedies that were less heroic, including folk medicines, strengthening tonics, and astringents sold by both itinerant quacks and druggists. Sectarians advocated temperance from alcohol; homeopathy, the infinitesimal dose therapeutic that differed significantly from the usually higher levels of medicines required by heroic dosing (Kaufman, 1971); and regimens of fresh air, exercise, and water cures (hydropathy) taken in what Susan E. Cayleff has referred to as comfortable "cure establishments," situated in "natural surroundings" in "country settings" (1987, p. 77). In his popular *Thomson's Almanac*, Samuel Thomson vigorously attacked the orthodox physician's primary reliance on what he deemed excessive depletive measures and advocated his own medical philosophy primarily emphasizing self-treatment through the use of his regimen of herbal medicines, sweating baths, emetics, and purgatives (Haller, 2000; Horrocks, 2003, p. 120). Sylvester Graham worried about the sexual passions and advocated a vegetarian and high-fiber diet and exercise regimen that forbade spices, alcohol, tea, and coffee, in an effort to control those passions (Nissenbaum, 1980).

The commercial manufacture of proprietary medicines developed rapidly during the first half of the 19th century, replacing the functions of the domestic practitioner who formulated the family's home remedies over the hearth fire. Physicians dispensed drugs in their offices and on home visits while "pharmacists began to open stores in towns and cities to fill prescriptions for patients of physicians and to compound drugs requested by their customers" (Rothstein, 1996a, p. 376; Cowen & Kent, 1997). Gregory Higby has observed that pharmacists, as part of a shift of "allegiance from physicians to their customers," also began counter prescribing—that is, "refilling prescriptions without physician authorization, and diagnosing and treating customers" (1992, p. 5). By 1860, many Americans could buy relatively cheap commodities called patent medicines, which were manufactured in small factories, advertised in newspapers, and delivered to any town or city through improved transportation systems. As the 19th century progressed, pharmacists "sold bottles of their own or physicians' concoctions" and became retailers of the prepared drugs (Rothstein, 1996a, p. 376).

At the same time, social reformers and public officials sought to label the production and distribution of patent medicines as "quackery" and warned the consuming public that patent medicine products were dangerous and fraudulent in their claims. Reformers were unsuccessful in their efforts to pass national legislation regulating the industry until the enactment of the Pure Food and Drug Act (1906), which addressed accurate labeling. Nevertheless, such patent medicines as Lydia Pinkham's Vegetable Compound remained popular among middle-class women as a treatment for female complaints because it was seen as an "alternative to orthodox treatments they believed to be unsafe" (Cayleff, 1992, p. 317).

Americans sought out a variety of alternative therapies because they often viewed orthodox (regular) physicians as elitist practitioners who sought to monopolize health care. Many Americans accepted the egalitarian view that a variety of philosophies of healthcare practice should be available to all people. Thus, healthcare services were most commonly delivered in the home, physician's office, drugstore, and cure establishment for the middle and upper classes. The working classes and the poor did not participate in the world of these healthcare services on a regular basis because of the necessity to pay out of pocket at the moment of receiving services. Instead, when most ordinary Americans became sick, they first sought treatment from someone in their own household. They often dosed themselves with self-help remedies that they could afford in an attempt to avoid the cost of treatment from an orthodox physician or one of the many sectarian physicians (Stage, 1979).

The Rise and Transformation of the Hospital: 19th to 21st Centuries

The early 19th-century hospital had its origins in the almshouse or poorhouse, identifying it as an institution with charitable and welfare functions. Most Americans saw the almshouse and hospital as a place that protected the community from those taken in and as a place where patients usually died. Aseptic practices were not commonplace. Generally, admittance for care could be gained only if a prominent member of the community was willing to vouch for the prospective patient's moral character. Patients entering the hospital throughout most of the 19th century were those with the least resources—the "deserving" poor, with so few ties to family or community that no one could care for them. Often they were recent immigrants; however, charitable hospitals sometimes refused certain immigrant populations, particularly the Irish in eastern seaboard cities, and categorically denied admission to African Americans (Vogel, 1979).

Male and female custodial caretakers of the sick were former patients who worked for room and board or local wage-earning residents from the community who had no formal training. Distinguished members of the community served as trustees who financed the institutions, and physicians from upper-class families provided free care to patients, developing new knowledge from the treatment of the very sick (Rosenberg, 1987; Vogel, 1979).

Charitable dispensaries were used by the poor and lower classes, including the poorer members of the Palmer family mentioned in this chapter's case scenario, far more than hospitals from the late 18th century until around 1920. These autonomous, freestanding institutions were located primarily in urban, often new, immigrant neighborhoods and provided such outpatient services as prescribing medication therapies, dental work, and minor surgery. There were few employees: a steward, a house physician, and sometimes a druggist, although the house physician might also act as druggist. Later in the 19th century, established consulting physicians volunteered from the local community (Rosenberg, 1985; Starr, 1991).

Over a 50-year period after the Civil War, the number of U.S. hospitals grew from fewer than 100 to more than 6,000 general and specialty institutions including mental facilities, children's hospitals, and tuberculosis sanitariums. The new hospitals were sponsored and financed by such disparate groups as religious organizations, ethnic associations, women's groups, physician groups (including African American physician associations), and such medical sectarians as homoeopathists and eclectics.

As the 19th century drew to a close, the chiefly welfare or charitable nature of the hospital declined. Orthodox physicians and trustees sought private, paying patients from the middle and upper classes. Physicians grew to reject Galen's system of therapeutics with its heroic remedies, replacing it with an increasing acceptance of the germ theory of disease (whereby specific microorganisms were believed to be responsible for the spread of disease). Hospitals introduced new approaches to care, including the enforcement of new aseptic and antiseptic techniques; new technologic methods, including regular anesthetization in surgery and the initial medical application of X-rays; and applied nursing methods patterned on the model developed by Florence Nightingale in England (Kevles, 1997; Pernick, 1985; Reverby, 1987). Architectural designs of hospitals were planned to provide personal service in a pleasant, clean decor with comfortable furnishings.

General practitioners, as well as elite physicians, sought to admit patients to these hospitals to enhance the growth of their private medical practices. Hospitals continued to take charity patients, but the numbers decreased and these individuals received a lesser level of care. By the end of the 19th century, hospitals were well on their way in a journey from charitable guest houses to biomedical showcases, with the wealthier members of the Palmer family having the greatest access to the new technological miracles (Ludmerer, 1999; Risse, 1999, p. 4; Rosenberg, 1987, p. 47; Rosner, 1979, p. 127).

The growth of the modern hospital as an indispensable element in American health care was ensured by the 1946 National Hospital Survey and Construction Act (Hill-Burton Act) and subsequent amendments, which provided federal funding for planning and assisting in the construction of new hospitals and public health centers (Rosenberg, 1987, p. 343). While the Hill-Burton Act led to an overabundance of hospital beds with funds disproportionately going to middle-income communities, Rosenberg noted that technological innovation, increasing application of business management policies, and establishment of the principles of local initiative, state review, and federal support sharing provided for some degree of planning on a state level. Hospitals in the post–World War II era organized the financing and delivery of care around an acute disease model.

While the operation of hospitals and the conduct of medical education and research were more dependent on federal government funding, the government became more interested in pursuing service programs from the 1970s through much of the 1990s. This was particularly connected to the federal funding of Medicare and Medicaid programs beginning in the 1960s. A new emphasis also was placed on encouraging preventive health and pursuing cost-cutting and efficiency measures at the same time that hospitals struggled with the possibility of fulfilling the role of exemplary social institutions to the local community (Fox, 1993, p. 17; Litman, 1997, p. 3; Starr, 1982; Stevens, 1989, p. 364).

In the 1990s, some community hospital mergers and nonprofit to for-profit hospital conversions resulted in the maintenance of clear social missions to local communities, while others led to the closing of many community hospitals that had previously treated the poor and less well off (Bell, 1996; Blumenthal & Weissman, 2000; Cahill, 1997; Lukas & Young, 2000; Opdycke, 1999; Young, Dasai, & Lukas, 1997). In the context of thinking of the patient as a consumer, the hospital as a part of an industry sought to attract the sufficiently insured through "a patient-centered care scheme designed to achieve customer satisfaction by striving to make hospitals more pleasant, comfortable, and user friendly" (Essoyan, 2000, p. A19; La Ferla, 2000, p. 4; Risse, 1999, p. 681). Hospitals were redesigned to streamline healthcare delivery, enhancing efficiency and cost savings by using such strategies as placing patients in focused settings with a satellite pharmacy, a laboratory, and radiologic facilities, and employing "cross-trained multidisciplinary caregiving teams" (Risse, 1999, pp. 682–683).

At the turn of the 21st century, the lay public and healthcare professionals, including the physician, had confronted identity dilemmas with the use of new language in healthcare settings. When someone is sick or seeks wellness care, is he a client, patient, or consumer, and what is the connotation of the word *consumer*? Are physicians, nurses, or pharmacists health professionals, caregivers, or mere health providers (Tomes, p. 84, 2006; Risse, 1999, p. 682)? Finally, given the increasing focus on financial incentives and customer orientation, scholars, journalists, the public, health professionals, and government officials have expressed concerns about the meaning of healing and the 21st century hospital as a "a place of repairing and damaging, birthing and dying—and red tape and budgets and stress—but also a community struggling with the thorny social forces changing the world around it" (Gordon, 2010; Risse, 1999; Salamon, 2010, p. 9).

Major changes in the early 21st century in the hospital are in process. Among them are electronic record keeping and interprofessional education in the academic hospital setting as methods to improve health quality and efficiency and to reduce medical errors (including adverse drug events). In addition, the roles of primary care physicians, specialists, and hospitalists are evolving in provision of coordinated care in healthcare delivery between inpatient and outpatient settings. Concerns revolving around these changes include potential workforce shortages, the future of medical mecca academic health centers, competing specialized health facilities in the community, and financial imperatives related to private health plan and government hospital reimbursements (Berensen, Ginsburg, & May, 2006; Blue, Mitcham, Smith, Raymond, & Greenberg, 2010; Buring et al., 2009; Casalino, November, Berenson, & Pham, 2008; Crossen & Tollen, 2010; DesRoches et al., 2010; Hamel, Drazen, & Epstein, 2009; Mechanic, 2003).

One of the most discussed changes has been the effort to implement patient-centered care. This term was first introduced in 2001 as a goal for quality care in the Institute of Medicine's report, *Crossing the Quality Chasm*. In this report, patient-centered care is defined as "respectful of and responsive to individual patient preferences, needs, and values, and ensuring that patient values guide all clinical decisions" (Institute of Medicine, 2001, p. 3). Various hospitals initiated efforts to institute aspects of patient-centered care, including approaches that involved family members. In 1996, Dana Farber Cancer Institute and Brigham and Women's Hospital began a joint venture to change their paradigm of care to a patient-centered model to involve all parts of the hospital organization including "high-performing teams in which communication, collaboration, transparency, and joint decision-making" (Ponte et al., 2003, p. 84) with hospital executive leadership playing a lead role (Ponte et al., 2003).

In 2006, the American Hospital Association and the Institute for Family-Centered Care developed a tool kit that comprised a video with discussion and resource guides and self-assessment tools that could be used by patients, families, and health practitioners to improve patient care in hospitals through partnerships among the above constituencies (American Hospital Association and Institute for Family-Centerd Care, 2006). Late in the 1st decade of the 21st century, critics of patient-centered care argued for bolder meanings. Donald Berwick, president and chief executive officer of the Institute for Healthcare Improvement and appointed by President Barack Obama in 2010 as administrator of the Centers for Medicare and Medicaid Services, proposed a model for hospitals that included patient and family member participation in rounds, patient decision making on food and clothing (as allowed by health status), and patient ownership of medical records with clinicians needing to have permission to gain access to them (Berwick, 2009, p. w561). Implementation of patient-centered care has been identified as a way to prevent a fragmented healthcare experience that often occurs for patients, especially those with serious or chronic illnesses, as they need care in hospitals, other health organizations, and their homes (Epstein, Fiscella, Lesser, & Stange, 2010). Efforts to incorporate patient-centered care into the hospital clearly reflect the idea of hospitals as exemplary social institutions.

CONTINUITY AND CHANGE IN HEALTH INSTITUTIONS AND PROFESSIONS

As part of a continuing process during the early years of the 20th century, medicine and pharmacy instituted important changes in their pursuit of modern, credential-based professionalization. As self-defined members of individual professions, physicians and pharmacists sought to strengthen their positions in society by employing a variety of strategies. These professions placed new emphasis on their special expertise within their own field of study and practice: increasing the authority and purview of professional organizations, licensing and self-regulation standards; the pursuit of rigorous educational reform and professional autonomy; and a commitment to altruism that placed their clientele above any commercial concern for profit.

Medicine

Beginning in 1908, at the urging of the American Medical Association (AMA), Abraham Flexner conducted a study of medical schools sponsored by the Carnegie Foundation. He published *Medical Education in the United States and Canada* in 1910, recommending numerous changes in the focus, education, and practice of medicine in the 20th century (Flexner, 1910). The Flexner report paved the way for effectively making allopathic medicine the legally sanctioned form of practice and abandoning the apprenticeship model of medical education and the primarily commercial financing of medical schools by physician-entrepreneurs. In the early 1900s, medical educators and leaders had already reached some consensus on the direction of change as proposed in the Flexner report, and by 1930, many reforms were in place. Chiefly, these reforms included most states' acceptance that medical schools would be accredited under the control of the American Medical Association; the graduation of fewer students; and the closing of weaker medical schools with the remaining stronger institutions obtaining funding from such sources as state governments and philanthropists to pursue further discoveries in bacteriology and other biomedical sciences and to produce trained clinicians and specialists in such areas as obstetrics, cardiology, and surgery. These reforms also resulted in the reduction of the number of students admitted from the lower classes, ethnic minorities, and women. Their numbers did not reappear in any strength until the 1970s and 1980s, when the number of African Americans and women admitted to medical schools began to increase (Ludmerer, 1985; Markowitz & Rosner, 1979; Morantz-Sanchez, 1992; More, 1999; Starr, 1982). Still, in the early 21st century, "[t]he complexion of the health professions in the United States little resembles the nation's ethnic and racial composition" (Grumbach & Mendoza, 2008, p. 413) despite business arguments that there are "customer service and competitive advantages to the health industry of having a workforce that is culturally and linguistically attuned to the increasing diversity of the nation's health care consumers" (Grumbach & Mendoza, 2008, p. 414). Women have made significant inroads in the early 21st century in relation to increased admissions to medical schools, generally approaching half of students admitted annually. However, concerns have remained in relation to career advancement, sexual harassment and discrimination, fears expressed about the feminization of medicine, and the concentration of women physicians in only a few lower income medical specialty areas (Boulis, Jacobs, & Veloski, 2001; McGuire, Bergen, & Polan, 2004; Sullivan & Mittman, 2010).

Nonetheless, the medical reform of the early 20th century ushered in what John C. Burnham has termed a *golden age* in which "American physicians enjoyed social esteem and prestige along with an admiration for their work that was unprecedented in any age" (Burnham, 1982, p. 284). In post–World War II America, the biomedical model predominated in research and in areas of clinical care. An emphasis was placed on the "subcellular and molecular level, and life processes were increasingly understood in physical and chemical terms" (Ludmerer, 1999, p. 148). This golden age did not begin to be seriously challenged until the 1960s, when questions were raised both from within the profession and by the public about the physician's priestly pretension and technical performance (Burnham, 1982, p. 291).

From the 1970s through the 1990s, medical education and academic health centers came under increasing duress. Some social inequities were addressed as increasing numbers of women and minorities were admitted to medical schools and such new pedagogies as problem-based learning were widely introduced in medical school curricula to improve clinical skills. At the same time, the new managed care practice made inroads against the pursuit of academic research and the provision of "the importance to the physician's work of having sufficient time with patients" (Ludmerer, 1999, p. 383).

As the 20th century ended, physicians continued to express concern about their roles in managed care systems. They showed a willingness to treat patients in new ways; including group visits where patients with chronic illnesses, such diseases as diabetes, hypertension, and arthritis; and attend seminars led by physicians (Martinez, 2000). They also raised concerns about whether the quality of patient care and their decision-making autonomy were unduly threatened by managed care's increased emphasis on linking the number of patients whom physicians treat to their fees and salaries (Kowalczyk, 2000). Deborah A. Stone argued that the "doctor has been reconceived as an entrepreneur who is now in the business of insuring patients as well as caring for them" (1997, p. 534).

In the early 21st century, many medical schools have been making changes in the education of students to respond to evidence showing that American populations, including socially disadvantaged ones, benefit from increased primary care practices in their communities. In addition, the delivery of improved primary care reduces health spending and responds to the needs of large numbers of patients increasingly living with chronic illnesses. The patient-centered medical home model of primary care has been the chief way in which policymakers have supported efforts to expand primary care. In 1967, the concept of a medical home originally was explained by the Academy of Pediatrics and demonstrated as more effective in the delivery of good health care to children with special needs. In the intervening years a "movement" to implement the medical home developed. By 2007, health care professional organizations, national health plans, labor unions, consumer organizations, and major corporations expressed support of the medical home model.

While there is not a consensus definition of the patient-centered medical home concept, it incorporates a number of elements. Patients are whole persons rather than disease states. They are active, prepared, knowledgeable participants who work with an interdisciplinary team of caregivers that is led by a primary care physician. Over the course of lifetimes, the team coordinates patients' preventive, acute, and chronic care across settings in the healthcare system and community. The team draws upon effective information technology, including electronic health records, to support communication and quality outcomes (Colwill, 2010; Iglehart, 2008; Larson & Reid, 2010). The hope for the future is that payment will be provided based on the added value that the medical home and its practitioners provided, a combination of "fee-for-service, pay-for performance, and a separate payment for coordination and integration" (Rittenhouse & Shortell, 2009, p. 2039).

A number of demonstration projects have been funded to experiment with the patient-centered medical home model of care for the future (Kilo & Wasson, 2010; Reid et al., 2010). A single clinic multidisciplinary team practice (including a pharmacist) that is part of a group health cooperative in the Seattle, Washington, area reorganized itself along a medical home model in 2006. A 1-year study of this prototype practice showed that the clinic achieved measurable positive outcomes. In comparison to other clinics in the group health cooperative, the clinic model was able to show 29% fewer visits to the emergency room and 6% fewer hospitalizations with cost savings achieved. In addition, patients reported improvement in their experiences of care and in the quality of care they received. Health practitioners noted more job satisfaction and less burnout (Reid et al., 2010). Other medical schools have begun to implement curricular changes and to study how medical students are currently exposed to patient-centered approaches to care as they learn in hospital and ambulatory care settings (Morrison, Goldfarb, & Lanken, 2010; Saultz et al., 2010). As the 100th anniversary of the Flexner report was celebrated in 2010, medical education in the United States was once again experiencing significant transformation.

Pharmacy

As the 20th century began, pharmacists pursued several approaches in an effort to change their practice to modern credential-based professionalization. Challenges to the apprenticeship model of training pharmacists had already occurred in the 1860s and 1870s, when state universities, especially in the Midwest and West, established a pharmacy curriculum based primarily on study in the physical sciences and laboratory instruction. By the turn of the 20th century, there were more than 50 colleges and departments of pharmacy in the United States. Most, however, had minimal standards for admission and length of study, with a combination of the scientific and apprenticeship models too often providing minimal education or training.

In 1900, more than 38,000 U.S. drugstores served a population of 76 million, translating to one store per 2,000 people (Deno, Rowe, & Brodie, 1959). Few practitioners operated in individual establishments devoted exclusively to professional services. Instead, most worked in commercial enterprises—independent, druggist-owned stores or shops—that provided a variety of services and products, including soda fountains, perfumes, telephone booths, magazines, candy, and popular books. Chain drugstores, with the same ownership and the same product lines, began to appear in the early years of the 20th century and quickly expanded regionally and nationally across the United States.

In their effort to professionalize, pharmacists confronted several difficult problems. In 1915, Abraham Flexner asserted that the pharmacist was not a professional in a speech at the National Conference of Charities and Corrections in Baltimore, Maryland. Whereas the physician "thinks, decides, and orders; the pharmacist obeys—obeys of course with discretion, intelligence, and skill—yet in the end obeys and does not originate. Pharmacy, therefore, is an arm added to the medical profession, a special and distinctly higher form of handicraft, not a profession" (Flexner, 1915, p. 158). In addition, the U.S. military decided to train its enlisted soldiers to dispense medications in World War I rather than recruit and appoint pharmacists as officers. The 1922 Code of Ethics established by the American Pharmaceutical Association (currently the American Pharmacists Association, APhA) was unfortunately compatible with

Flexner's perspective. Pharmacy's primary object was "the service it can render to the public in safeguarding the handling, sale, compounding and dispensing of medicinal substances" (APA, 1922, p. 728). Ordinary Americans encountered the pharmacist as customers in the neighborhood drugstore, a commercial enterprise identified with a for-profit motive. In the 1920s, hospital pharmacy, although devalued by community druggists and often by the institutional administrations where they were located, was the area where pharmacy thrived as a "bastion of high pharmaceutical technology, art, and science" (Higby with Gallagher, 1992, p. 507).

In response to the aforementioned problems, pharmacy colleges organized their own association, the American Conference of Pharmaceutical Faculties (later renamed the American Association of Colleges of Pharmacy) in the 1920s and struggled to reach their goals of establishing more rigorous standards of education and practice. The American Association of Colleges of Pharmacy instituted the requirement of high school graduation for admission, and by 1932, it mandated 4 years of study for graduation (Deno, Rowe, & Brodie, 1959; Higby & Gallagher, 1992; Higby, 1996; Sonnedecker, 1976). Some practicing pharmacists also saw the value of education in improving their image in the community. For instance, when the consumer market for vitamins increased from $12 million to over $130 million in sales during the 1930s, pharmacists argued that purchases of these over-the-counter products should be made in drugstores rather than grocery stores because of the pharmacist's specialized knowledge and professional training (Apple, 1996).

In World War II, pharmacists were again denied a commission in the U.S. military while these were given to 1st-year medical students and nurses. Pharmacy organizations responded by contributing funding to a self-study, the 1946 *Pharmaceutical Survey*. This study made recommendations, chief of which was the expansion of the pharmacy curriculum to 6 years. The American Association of Colleges of Pharmacy proposed a 5-year program of study, with a curriculum that continued to focus on the science and technology of pharmaceutical products. Pharmacists in community drugstores in the new age of miracle drugs that followed the discovery of penicillin were relegated to a count and pour role under 1952 federal regulations and the newly promulgated American Pharmaceutical Association's Code of Ethics, which asserted that "the pharmacist does not discuss the therapeutic effects or composition of a prescription with a patient" (APhA, 1952, p. 722).

The 1960s have been defined as years of revolution in pharmacy. During this decade, ordinary community and hospital pharmacists began a push for a new identity in clinical pharmacy, where the pharmacist is the drug expert and is responsible for being a therapeutic advisor for patients and other health professionals. In another revision of the APhA Code of Ethics in 1969, the pharmacist was required to "render to each patient the full measure of his ability as an essential health practitioner" (Higby, 2002, p. 12;). For the community pharmacist, this would mean a new perception of the people that the pharmacist spoke with across their counters—going from customers to patients. A culminating point in the expression of educational reform was presented in 1975 in *Pharmacists for the Future: The Report of the Study Commission on Pharmacy* (Millis, 1975). This report called for a 6-year curriculum culminating in an entry-level doctor of pharmacy degree that was intended to provide a general education for the whole person, educating pharmacists rather than training them, and to incorporate clinical therapeutics and clerkship opportunities in healthcare workplaces (Higby, 1997; Knowlton, 2009; Worthen, 2006; APhA, 1969).

The underpinning for the new program of study and practice was the concept of *pharmaceutical care*, to be implemented in communities and such institutional settings as hospitals where pharmacists would be equal members of the healthcare team. Charles D. Hepler and Linda Strand identified pharmaceutical care as connecting the pharmacist's responsibilities with therapeutic outcomes (Hepler & Strand, 1990). While similar to the widely accepted definition, the 2004 construction states that "[P]harmaceutical care is a patient-centered practice in which the practitioner assumes responsibility for a patient's drug-related needs and is held accountable for this commitment" (Cipolle, Strand, & Morley, 2004, p. 26). This concept was a reflection on the Omnibus Budget Reconciliation Act of 1990 (OBRA), which mandated evaluation of drug therapy in the review of patient profiles and established standards of medication counseling for Medicaid patients (Higby, 2002; Elenbaas &Worthen, 2009; McGivney et. al., 2007). The 1994 Pharmacist Code of Ethics also emphasized such principles as a "covenantal" relationship between patient and pharmacist; promotion of "the good of every patient in a caring, compassionate, and confidential manner" service to "the individual, community and societal needs"; and the pursuit of "justice in the distribution of health resources" (APhA, 1994, p. 1).

Unfortunately, the bureaucratic and cost-cutting demands of third-party payers and managed care organizations greatly inhibited the ability of pharmacists to actually practice pharmaceutical care in healthcare settings (Navarro, 1999). Despite the presence of more pharmacy technicians and robotics in some cases, pharmacists spent most of their time in dispensing roles and reported dissatisfaction with their general lack of opportunities to more effectively fulfill pharmaceutical care roles. Nonetheless, some community pharmacists became more deeply involved in providing expanded pharmaceutical-care services. They documented their care for patients in computerized patient profiles to improve quality of care and to provide evidence of outcomes for compensation for pharmaceutical care services. In a project begun in 1997 in Asheville, North Carolina, for instance, community pharmacists successfully worked with patients with such chronic health problems as diabetes, hypertension, high cholesterol, and asthma, and reported positive clinical and cost-saving outcomes (Smith, Bates, Bodenheimer, & Cleary, 2010; Brock, Casper, Green, & Pedersen, 2006; Kreling, et. al., 2006). In another case, an owner of an independent drugstore in Augusta, Georgia, explained: "We are not just going to dispense your drugs … We are going to partner with you to improve your health as well" (Abelson, & Singer, 2010, p. A1).

In the 1st decade of the 21st century, pharmacists along with physicians and other health professionals have been engaged in determining their roles in the medical home model. As providers of pharmaceutical care, pharmacists had already began to articulate their roles in incorporating medication therapy management services into institutional and community settings in a major way as part of the context of the Medicare Modernization Act of 2003 and Medicare Part D (McGivney et al., 2007). In Chapter 3 of this text, Shane P. Desselle explains in detail the movement away from pharmaceutical care to medication therapy management and its potential for incorporation in medical home models of primary care in the future.

A number of demonstration projects have also documented the value of including pharmacists in the interdisciplinary care team working in the primary care medical home. A project in six Minnesota ambulatory clinics incorporated employed pharmacists who collaborated with primary care practitioners, resolved patient drug therapy problems, and contributed to reduced costs (Smith et al., 2010; Hepler, 2010).

Pharmacists, physicians, and public health professionals have argued for the place of pharmacists in the medical home of the future because of their expertise in providing services, including comprehensive therapy reviews of prescribed medications and over-the-counter or herbal products, design of adherence programs for patients with asthma, diabetes, or hypertension, personal medication care plans (lists that include actions that patients can take to keep track of managing their own medications), and recommendations for therapies that are cost-effective (American Pharmacists Association & National Association of Chain Drug Stores, 2008; Smith, et al., 2010). The 2010 Patient Protection and Affordable Care Act has embraced the notion of an expanded patient care role for pharmacists in the medical home with the possibility that community pharmacists may obtain funding for new demonstration projects (Traynor, 2010). Finally, pharmacy leaders have been involved in the Patient-Centered Primary Care Collaborative publication of the task force report, *The Patient-Centered Medical Home (PCMH): Integrating Comprehensive Medication Management to Optimize Patient Outcomes*, which supports the pharmacist role. The collaborative involves various healthcare groups, including government officials, insurance companies, and health professionals, who are committed to working together to improve the quality of health care. The report is the third in a series of reports produced by the collaborative that emphasized the need for payment reform for medication management and that "was developed to provide a framework for integrating medication management in the PCMH (patient-centered medical home) as part of the practice redesign that needs to occur when individual and group practices transform into the PCMH (Patient-Centered Primary Care Collaborative, 2010, p. 4).

Pharmacy has also seen change in the arrival of the retail clinic, which has appeared in chain pharmacies, grocery stores, and superstores that also include pharmacies. These clinics usually offer walk-in visits for convenient, lower-cost care for such acute health problems as sore throat or ear infection symptoms. Staffed by such primary care health professionals as nurse practitioners, there has generally been no formal teaming with pharmacy staff. Community-based pharmacies have also begun to offer vaccinations given by pharmacists who have acquired certification. These innovations offered possibilities for expansion of pharmaceutical care but also raised issues about constructive coordination of health care and confusion over commercial and professional healthcare roles (Farley, Devine, & Hadsall, 2007; Martin, 2010; Pollack, Gidengil, & Mehrotra, 2010).

HEALTH AND SICKNESS PATTERNS IN HISTORICAL PERSPECTIVE

Definitions of Health and Disease

Elliot Mishler notes that broader definitions of health "are neither obsolete, nor of historical and esoteric interest only," (1981, p. 3) when he refers to the World Health Organization's definition of health as a "state of complete physical, mental, and social well-being and not merely the absence of disease or infirmity" (Mishler, 1981, p. 3). In addition, Charles Rosenberg argues for not thinking in narrow constructs:

> Disease is at once a biological event, a generation-specific repertoire of verbal constructs reflecting medicine's intellectual and institutional history, an occasion of and potential legitimization for public policy, an aspect of social role and individual—intrapsychic—identity, a sanction for cultural values, and a structuring element in

doctor and patient interactions. In some ways disease does not exist until we have
agreed that it does, by perceiving, naming, and responding to it. (1992, p. xiii)

In studying healthcare delivery in the United States, how we perceive, name, and respond to health and disease and what we make the primary focus of the healthcare
system are major focuses of concern (Brandt, 1997; Tesh, 1988).

Each year the mass media reports statistics from government and research institutions
about health and disease levels, mortality and life expectancy, and causes of death
both globally and within the United States. Historians have also sought, within biomedical, cultural, social, economic, and political contexts, to account for increases in
life expectancy, declines in mortality rates, and changes in causes of death from acute
and infectious diseases to, more recently, chronic illnesses.

Health Demographics and Causes of Death

Native Americans and European settlers in the 1600s and 1700s confronted malnutrition daily, making them susceptible to endemic and epidemic infectious illnesses.
Such endemic illnesses as dysentery, malaria, and respiratory infections, with occasional epidemics, including smallpox and yellow fever, were prevalent in the 18th
century. As the 19th century progressed, people became more concerned with illnesses related to the increasing population that lived in rapidly urbanizing and indus-
trializing cities. Deaths continued to result from dysentery and respiratory infections,
but also increasingly from cholera, scarlet fever, whooping cough, measles, diphtheria, smallpox, and—above all—tuberculosis. Improvements in public health could be
noted as the 19th century ended. In particular, death rates declined—especially infant
mortality rates—and life expectancy increased, as noted earlier in this chapter (Leavitt
& Numbers, 1997).

Causes of Death and Disease

In 1900, the leading causes of death were infectious diseases, both epidemic and endemic diseases, including influenza and pneumonia, tuberculosis, gastritis, enteritis,
diphtheria, measles, scarlet fever, and whooping cough. Some chronic diseases, such
as heart and cerebrovascular disease and cancer also were among the top 10 causes of
death in the United States (Lerner & Anderson, 1963, p. 16). In the 1st decade of the
21st century, the 10 leading causes of death reported in the United States were heart
disease, cancer, stroke (cerebrovascular disease), chronic lower respiratory diseases,
accidents, Alzheimer's disease, diabetes mellitus, influenza and pneumonia, nephri-
tis, nephritic syndrome, nephrosis, and septicemia (CDC, 2009). Obviously, causes of
death were increasingly attributed to chronic illnesses both in the United States and
worldwide.

The 10-volume *Global Burden of Disease* project, edited by Christopher J. L. Murray
of Harvard University and Alan D. Lopez of the World Health Organization, estimated
that from1990 to 2020, infectious, nutritional, and childbirth–associated deaths will
decrease from 17.2 million to 10.3 million (Murray & Lopez, 1996). Noncommunicable
diseases, including unipolar major depression, ischemic heart disease, and cerebrovascular and chronic obstructive pulmonary diseases, however, will increase by 77%,
with the number of related deaths increasing from 28 million to nearly 50 million
annually (Knox, 1996a). However, critics have pointed out that developing nations
struggle with health problems and diseases linked to poverty, such as malnutrition,
dysentery, malaria, and tuberculosis (Farmer, P. 1999). With the increase in global

travel and the lack of funding for public health infrastructure, reemergent diseases, as well as AIDS, West Nile, Avian flu, and the H1N1 flu pandemic, have caused the United States to take note of the changes in patterns of infectious diseases outside its national borders and to question the capability of public health agencies to deliver appropriate services when needed within the United States (Markel, 2004; Gandy & Zumla, 2003; Garrett, 2000). In the aftermath of the terrorist attacks on September 11, 2001, the United States also became concerned about bioterrorist threats to health, including the possibility that smallpox could be used as a bioterrorist weapon (Colgrove, Markowitz, & Rosner, 2008; Rosner & Markowitz, 2006).

Factors Explaining Health Demographic Change

To understand the meaning of statistics that report declines in infant mortality rates, increases in life expectancy, declines in communicable diseases, and increases in chronic, degenerative illnesses, historians have analyzed the possible factors that account for the changing numbers and have explored public authorities' explanations for these changes. Three factors are generally cited as explanations, which are: (1) changes in standard of living or lifestyle, including improvements in personal hygiene, diet, nutrition, and housing; (2) advances in public health measures; and (3) progress in medical practice, including therapeutic interventions in the treatment of patients.

In examining the evidence, healthcare historians have found that changes in public health measures and lifestyle contributed more to health improvements than therapeutic interventions by physicians in the 19th and early 20th centuries (Leavitt & Numbers, 1997; Rothstein, 1996b). In the later half of the 19th century, cities recognized the importance of connecting the city's environment and its people's health, including improved sanitation, water supply and delivery, and refuse collection and waste removal (Melosi, 2000). In 1865, New York commissioned a report on public health and later formed a board of health with responsibilities to include enforcing sanitary regulations and controlling epidemics. By 1912, as David Rosner has noted, "garbage collection, meat and milk inspections, pure water, and sewerage systems had been installed throughout the city. Dead animals were now regularly picked up off the streets, and fire safety codes augmented stricter enforcement of housing laws" (1995, p. 15). The department of health, in its annual report, attributed "over the course of just forty-five years … a decrease of over 50 percent" in the death rate to public sanitation measures (1995, p. 15).

William Rothstein emphasizes the importance of educating the public about specific personal behaviors related to standards of living and public health:

> Until well into the 20th century, millions of Americans drank from metal drinking cups kept next to fountains for all to use, did not sterilize bottles or take other measures necessary for hygienic feeding of infants, let their children sleep in the same bed and play with siblings with contagious diseases like diphtheria and scarlet fever, purchased unrefrigerated and bacteria-laden milk and meat, used polluted wells and water supplies without boiling the water, and took baths in bathtubs after others had used the same water. These and many other similar behaviors have disappeared because the public has been educated about personal hygiene. (1996b, pp. 77–78)

At the same time, public health campaigns in the late 19th and early 20th centuries against specific diseases must be seen within the context of how health professionals, public officials, and the general public felt that disease and outsiders threatened the civic order. They often linked epidemics of infectious diseases—including small-pox, tuberculosis, bubonic plague, typhoid, and polio—to new immigrant populations. Some public health efforts focused on isolation, quarantine, and destruction of housing, often using violence to implement these policies. On the other hand, founding of ethnic and religious hospitals; the establishment of visiting and public health nursing, neighborhood clinics, and settlement houses; health advocacy programs to foster individual efforts to improve domestic hygiene; and struggles for effective public health legislation and enforcement were all examples of efforts to assist immigrants in preventive health measures, in improving the living conditions in urban housing, and in occupational safety and health on the job (Kraut, 1994; Leavitt, 1996; Ott, 1996; Tomes, 1998).

Health care historians have also discussed the role of clinical medicine and therapeutic or technological intervention in contributing to the decline of mortality rates in infectious diseases at the turn of the 20th century. Very few physician efforts, especially those who employed "heroic" measures, were helpful to patients. Such 19th century discoveries as anesthesia and X-rays were very important, but general practice physicians could often use these technological improvements in ways that caused more harm than good. The most striking example of therapeutic intervention success did not occur until the mid-20th century with the introduction of antibiotics. Historian John Parascandola has pointed out that "within a decade after penicillin was first made freely available for civilian use in the United States in 1945, antibiotics had become the most important class of drugs in the treatment of infectious disease. In 1948, antibiotics prescriptions accounted for only 1.5% of the total number written in the United States; by 1952, that figure had risen to 13.7%" (1997, pp. 108–109). Parascandola also cited a Federal Trade Commission report from 1958, which indicated a decrease of 56.4% in the total number of deaths from 1945 to 1955 for eight major diseases responsive to antibiotic therapy, versus a decline of only 8.1% for all other causes of death. In the 21st century, major public health efforts have continued to focus on when and how to implement programs using appropriate antibiotic therapy and on how to educate the public about the misuse and overuse of antibiotics, stressing the limitations of wonder drugs (Parascandola, 1997, pp. 109, 110).

Successful public health measures have often been cited to help explain some decline in infant death rates in various U.S. cities in the late 20th century. These measures included better access to stable housing and prenatal care for low-income pregnant women. Conversely, when funding decreased in a community for various programs aimed at healthy mothers and babies, infant mortality rates rose (Steinhauer, 2000). Recommendations from health professionals across disciplines for improving children's health in the beginning of the 21st century continue to include such public health measures as community and school-based clinics and education programs on diverse health populations that are public-health based and present in health professional curricula (Markel & Golden, 2004).

Chronic Illness

Since the 1920s, government agencies, biomedical health researchers, and health professionals have recognized that chronic disease must be a health policy priority in the United States (Fox, 1988). In discussing how the United States should address the fact that chronic illnesses afflict close to half the population, costing nearly $470 billion in 1990, a number of issues related to public health measures, environmental factors, standard of living, lifestyle, and therapeutic interventions are raised. Medical researchers cite such "diseases of affluence" as sedentary lifestyle, poor diet, smoking, and alcohol abuse as major causes of chronic illness (Knox, 1996b, p. A11). Other researchers documented concerns about the lack of good management of chronic disease and people's inability to receive the help they need to live on an everyday basis with chronic health conditions. Dr. Halstad R. Holman, director of an arthritis center at Stanford University, noted, "Our health care system—its structure, practices, education, and even research agendas—was developed for acute disease. We have a profound mismatch between our entire health care system and what it's structured to do and what we need it to do" (Knox, 1996b, p. A11). In the early 21st century, the United States faced a crisis in treating chronic illness far more costly than in 1990, with three fourths of the more than $2 trillion spent on health care directed toward the treatment of chronic illnesses, especially those connected to worsening health habits. Thus, the emphasis has been put on health promotion and disease prevention regardless of whether the provision of preventive care is more or less expensive (Goetzel, 2009, p. 41; Maciosek, Coffield, Edwards, Flottemesch, Goodman, & Solberg, 2006).

HEALTH POLICY OVERVIEW: 1900–1950

New Legislation in the Early 20th Century

The major hallmark of 20th-century health care was the increased role of government policy making at the local, state, and especially the federal level. During the first 2 decades of the 20th century, the federal government assumed a more vigorous role in public health, symbolized by its renaming of the Marine Hospital Service as the U.S. Public Health Service in 1912. Partially as a consequence of muckraking journalists' exposure of dangerous practices in the food and drug industries, the U.S. Congress enacted the Pure Food and Drug Act in 1906 and then significantly strengthened its oversight of this industry with more comprehensive legislation under the 1938 Federal Food, Drug and Cosmetic Act. In addressing the plight of America's poor children, many of whom lacked good nutrition and housing and were forced to work in dangerous conditions, Congress established the Children's Bureau in 1912. This legislation was followed in 1921 by the Sheppard-Towner Maternity and Infancy Act, which provided federal funding to support children's health clinics until 1929. In 1930 the National Institutes of Health and the Veterans Administration were established and the National Cancer Act in 1937 helped launch biomedical research (King, 1993; Patterson, 1987; Temin, 1980).

Public and Private Health Insurance

Twentieth-century changes in health insurance can be traced back to at least 1798, when government hospitals were established in some coastal cities to provide care for merchant seamen. In the 19th century, small numbers of Americans obtained some form of insurance against sickness primarily by gaining income protection through such groups as trade unions, fraternal organizations or their employers (Numbers, 1997, p. 277). Some purchased protection against sickness from commercial insurers. Generally, only mining and lumber companies provided actual medical benefits.

In the early 20th century, progressive reformers and labor unions began to talk about some form of government-sponsored health insurance. In 1914, workers' compensation or compulsory sickness insurance programs appeared. Operating on a state level, they generally provided cash payments for injuries or disease related to the workplace. In later decades, payments were made for medical expenses and death benefits. Employers usually purchased these programs from commercial insurers. In 1912, the American Association for Labor Legislation's Committee on Social Insurance put forward a model bill for state legislatures to consider. Until 1917, many medical leaders and associations expressed support for compulsory health insurance efforts. Opposition developed from physicians concerned about seeing their incomes decrease rather than increase. During World War I, many began to perceive social insurance proposals as un-American since the German enemy had employed compulsory insurance for industrial workers since 1883 (Numbers, 1997, pp. 269-271; Starr, 1982; Stevens, 1971).

Following the significant drops in physician and hospital income that occurred in the wake of the Great Depression, hospitals reconsidered insurance plans. In 1929, Baylor University Hospital enrolled public school teachers in a plan covering hospital costs. The American Hospital Association in 1939 approved Blue Cross insurance to cover costs of care in whichever hospital patients chose to enter. In the same year, the Blue Shield insurance plan was first approved by the California Medical Association to help cover fees physicians charged for their services. These insurance programs, which served as a third-party payment system, presented an attractive alternative to the tradition of patients paying health practitioners directly for health services. The AMA and medical associations such as the State Medical Society of Wisconsin expressed support for implementation of voluntary private insurance plans, rather than "wait for a state controlled compulsory plan" (Numbers, 1997, p. 274).

During the Franklin D. Roosevelt administration, Congress considered the Murray-Wagner-Dingall bill, which proposed to provide health care for the poor primarily through federal grants given to the states. Ultimately, this national health effort was defeated (Numbers, 1997). Private insurance, though greatly fragmented, rapidly expanded in the next 2 decades with some form of health insurance held by 51% of the civilian population" by 1951 and 737 health insurance companies selling some kind of insurance by 1959 (Stevens, p. 467, 2008; Richmond & Fein, 2005).

POST–WORLD WAR II HEALTHCARE CHANGES

In the second half of the 20th century, President Harry Truman spoke forcefully in favor of national health insurance that offered protection to all Americans (Poen, 1979). Nonetheless, legislative proposals failed largely because they evoked strong opposition from the AMA. As part of its effort to defeat the Truman proposal, the AMA undertook a $4.5 million national education campaign, warning that "national health insurance would lead to federal control of health care" (Johnson & Broder, 1996, p. 66). In the Cold War era, which was characterized by a virulent anticommunism movement, the AMA's public relations campaign equated national health insurance with socialized medicine.

In the 1950s, with support from the federal government through tax-deductibility rulings, employers and labor unions increasingly offered U.S. workers healthcare plans as part of their benefits programs. In the 1960s, the federal government established two governmental purchasing programs—Medicare and Medicaid. While a push for these programs began under the John F. Kennedy administration, President Lyndon Johnson was successful in achieving their passage with his landslide victory in the

1964 presidential election and his leadership in advancing Great Society legislation through Congress. Medicare was initially designed in two parts: Part A for hospital insurance coverage and Part B for medical care insurance including physicians and various medical services. In 1972, Medicare insurance was extended to those of any age with proven disabilities or to those with end-stage renal disease to pay for dialysis or transplant costs. Medicaid was established as a joint federal and state program to provide health care for the low-income elderly and other categories of people, including the disabled and families with children (Patel & Rushefsky, 1995; Stevens, 2008, p. 471). See Chapter 18.

Despite these incremental reforms, healthcare costs continued to rise in the 1960s and 1970s, and problems of access to services for the uninsured increased. Once again raising the possibility of a comprehensive national health policy, Senator Edward Kennedy and President Jimmy Carter launched unsuccessful attempts in the 1970s to pass such legislation as Kennedy's Health Security Act, which was designed to provide quality health care for all Americans at affordable prices (Kennedy, 1972). By 1980, the mostly private model of a healthcare system best described how most Americans were covered—that is, by private insurance programs purchased through plans offered by their employers. Coverage of the healthcare costs of only a few needy groups (e.g., veterans and the elderly) was provided through government-sponsored public insurance programs (Patel and Rushefsky, 1995, p. 25).

Prepaid Health Care, Health Maintenance Organizations, and Managed Care

While Congress did not adopt broad health insurance coverage, in 1973 it passed the Health Maintenance Organization (HMO) Act. This legislation represented a form of prepaid health coverage. Prepaid health plans were first introduced in the United States in isolated rural areas where workers needed health care in the 19th century. In the building of the Grand Coulee Dam in 1938, the highly successful Kaiser Permanente Medical Care Program initially offered healthcare services to workers employed by Henry F. Kaiser. The prepaid plan expanded its provision of comprehensive health care to workers in his steel mills and shipyards, and eventually to the general public on the West Coast and to a lesser extent in the Midwest. Unlike their strong opposition to compulsory health insurance legislative initiatives, medical organizations did not oppose Kaiser's effort because individual physicians involved in the programs economically benefitted. The 1973 Health Maintenance Organization Act required every employer with more than 25 employees that offered a health plan to include at least one HMO plan providing comprehensive medical care for a fixed fee to its enrollees. A companion bill "requiring employers to provide a basic minimum package of benefits to all their employees" (Johnson & Broder, 1996, p. 67) failed, with the AMA and the health insurance industry lobbying against the bill (Hendricks, 1993).

Rapid growth of HMOs did not become pronounced until the 1990s and a backlash against the movement developed with the public expressing concerns about access to health care and payment for services provided if a patient became very ill. In 1995, HMOs covered nearly 60 million individuals, and the less structured preferred provider organizations (PPOs) covered an additional 91 million people, including Medicare and Medicaid recipients (Anders, 1996; Blendon et al., 1998; Peterson, 1997); see Chapter 21. By 1998, 77 million Americans were enrolled in an HMO, and the number of Americans in some form of managed care had reached 135.37 million in 2010 (U.S. DHHS, 1999; Managed Care On-Line, 2010); see Chapter 17.

Renewed Efforts for National Health Insurance

As the 20th century ended, the American public experienced significant social, economic, and political changes that affected both the U.S. healthcare system and the delivery of healthcare services. In 1991, the Democratic presidential candidate, Bill Clinton, made health care a major issue in his presidential campaign, offering a step-by-step plan to achieve healthcare coverage for all Americans through his health security plan. Despite the AMA dropping its opposition to national health insurance, in 1994, Congress defeated proposals for implementing national health insurance, including President Clinton's health security plan, which was successfully lobbied against by the pharmaceutical, hospital, and health insurance industries (Hacker, 1997; White House Domestic Policy Council, 1993).

Incremental Policy Proposals

Later in the decade, however, other pieces of incremental health legislation affecting Americans' access to health care were passed. In 1996, the Health Insurance Portability and Accountability Act specified in its Title I section that employers or insurers of new employees could impose a waiting period of no more than 12 months before covering them under the employer's health plan. Title II of the Health Insurance Portability and Accountability Act addressed issues of healthcare fraud and abuse and set standards for using and disseminating health information (leading to electronic health records) to increase efficiency in the healthcare system. Congress also passed the Children's Health Insurance Program as part of the Balanced Budget Act of 1997 with the intent that it would provide health insurance for at least half of the 11 million children who lacked such coverage. In 2009, the Children's Health Insurance Program was extended by Congress with the passage of the Children's Health Insurance Program Reauthorization Act (Atchinson & Fox, 1997; Castellblanch, 1996; Goldstein, 1999; Pear, 1997; Fairbrother, Carle, Cassedy, & Newacheck, 2010).

At the beginning of the 21st century, Congress considered several bills to reduce drug prices and to expand Medicare coverage by including prescription medications. The Medicare Prescription Drug, Improvement, and Modernization Act, the largest revision of Medicare in its 38-year history, was passed in 2003. Its most important provision was Medicare Part D, which provided a voluntary prescription drug benefit program. Medicare beneficiaries could choose to enroll in the program that took effect on January 1, 2006. Many reported confusion in trying to choose a program and how to join, especially in regard to the Medicare Advantage plans offered. By June 2006, 22.5 million senior American citizens had enrolled in the program. Recent research indicated that there was an 18.4% reduction in spending on medications out of pocket by the elderly and a 12.8% increase in drug utilization as a result of the legislation (Lichtenberg & Sun, 2007; Pear, 2006; Schneeweiss et al., 2009; Yin et al., 2008); see Chapter 18.

HEALTHCARE REFORM: A CONTINUING PARADOX

Despite its outstanding achievements, a majority of Americans have repeatedly reported dissatisfaction with the U.S. healthcare system and "have favored addressing problems in the health care system since at least the mid-1980s" (Brodie, Altman, Deane, Buscho, & Hamel, 2010, p. 1127). They have thought about healthcare reform in the context of how it affects the country as a whole and how it relates to their own lives and futures. Many have expressed serious concerns about the number of uninsured or underinsured Americans and called for comprehensive reform of the U.S. healthcare system that would extend health coverage to all Americans. Others have theoretically endorsed universal health insurance yet feared the loss of their own private insurance if a comprehensive plan was established to include those without any health insurance (Blendon & Benson, 2009; Hacker, 2008; Johnson & Johnson, 2010; Sered & Fernandopulle, 2005).

Following the 2009 presidential election year where healthcare system reform was a major campaign issue, the U.S. Congress began consideration of new health legislation. With constant and often trenchant media coverage and intense partisan and sometimes volatile conflict among Democrats and Republicans, the Patient Protection and Affordable Care Act, designed to provide an additional 32 million Americans with some form of health insurance by 2018 (with the establishment of competitive health insurance exchanges in 2014), was enacted into law in March 2010 (Krugman, 2010; Mackey, 2010). President Obama said that the legislation embodied "the core principle that everybody should have some basic security when it comes to their health care" (The White House, 2010, p.1). This new reform represented incremental health reform because it did not change the fundamental structure of the U.S. healthcare system.

While the law did not include a public option whereby Americans would be provided a low-cost alternative to private health insurance—similar to the existing Medicare model—the health bill did provide a number of significant changes. Its provisions included mandating health insurance for most legal residents (reducing those uninsured from 15.6 % in 2010 to about 6% of the population by 2018); stopping insurers from imposing lifetime limits on health benefits; providing tax incentives for small businesses to provide health coverage to their employees; and imposition of new fees on large insurers to ensure that they help pay for employees' health insurance. In addition, it mandated eliminating preexisting condition clauses for children under 19 years of age beginning in 2010 and for all U.S. citizens by 2014, as well as stopping arbitrary recisions of health insurance when people file a first major claim for sickness. The act also removes barriers, especially financial ones, placed by health insurers on emergency room services; invests in education and training for an expanded health workforce; and supports pilot projects to reform Medicare and Medicaid healthcare delivery and payment. Implemented through the secretary of Health and Human Services office, various projects also include the fostering of the patient-centered medical home model and supporting the expansion of electronic health records (HealthCare. gov, 2010; Iglehart, 2010; Oberlander, 2010). The new healthcare reform legislation will be phased in between 2010 and 2015. The White House has provided a website that provides information about the health reform bill and a timeline that shows when different parts of the legislation will be implemented (http://www.whitehouse.gov/ health-care-meeting/proposal).

Given the partisan conflict that occurred during the debate over the new legislation, officials in 21 states had instituted lawsuits within the courts to fight implementation of the new healthcare law within 6 months after the act's passage. Other public officials and health policy experts hailed the new law for its potential to make health care available to more Americans, more affordable, and higher in quality (Sack, 2010a; 2010b).

Jonathan Oberlander, a professor of social medicine, health policy, and management, noted that "[E]ven with all its shortcomings, the Patient Protection and Affordable Care Act is a great leap forward for the American health care system" (Oberlander, 2010, p. 1116).

CONCLUSION

In looking at healthcare changes over time, the people of the United States have seen significant decreases in mortality rates and increases in life expectancy and some improvements in quality of life for those who live an increasingly longer life span. We have also seen that factors accounting for these changes have involved, most importantly, public health, housing, diet, and hygiene improvements, as well as therapeutic and technologic interventions. Chronic rather than infectious illnesses have become more prevalent reasons for Americans' need to access the healthcare system, although new and reemerging infectious diseases are more widespread in the 21st century than many experts expected following the discovery of miracle drugs in the mid-20th century.

The U.S. government has consistently attempted to improve access, cost, and quality of health care for American citizens chiefly through implementing incremental health reforms (Vladek, 2003). What will be the long-term effects of the most recent effort at health reform? Will the implementation of more patient-centered care in interdisciplinary medical home settings improve healthcare delivery for many Americans and find acceptance among ordinary Americans as a better way to experience health care? Will the new laws make health care more affordable and more accessible? Will the reforms decrease disparities in care among different groups of Americans? Will health outcomes for most Americans improve? The United States faces very hard economic and social choices related to healthcare delivery in national and global contexts. The need for accessible, humane health care will increase significantly as the 21st century advances.

QUESTIONS FOR FURTHER DISCUSSION

1. How will the conflict between the entrepreneurial role of health delivery organizations and the health professional's responsibility to serve the community be resolved in the future?
2. Lifestyle improvements, public health measures, and therapeutic interventions all affect health and disease patterns. How much money and effort should be devoted to these areas to address the health problems of Americans? What should the priorities be among the three areas? What roles should private and public institutions play? What roles should health professionals play?
3. To what degree is the healthcare system in crisis in the 21st century?

KEY TOPICS AND TERMS

Blue Cross
Blue Shield
Charitable hospitals
Children's Health Insurance Program
Children's Health Insurance Program Reauthorization Act
Chronic disease
Comprehensive health care
Dispensary
Flexner report
Health Insurance Portability and Accountability Act
Health Maintenance Organization Act
Heroic medical therapy
Hill-Burton Act (National Hospital Survey and Construction Act)
Humoralism
Incremental healthcare reform
Infectious disease
Medical home
Medicare
Medicare Part D
Medicare Prescription Drug, Improvement, and Modernization Act
Medicaid
Medication therapy management
Orthodox physicians
Patent medicines
Patient-centered care
Patient Protection and Affordable Care Act
Pharmaceutical care
Quackery
Sectarians
Self-dosing
Social healers

REFERENCES

Abelson, R., & Singer, N. (2010, August 14). In health shift, more patients get pharmacist's appointment. *The New York Times,* A1, A11.

Agency for Healthcare Quality and Research (2011, October). *Fact sheet: AHRQ projects to prevent healthcare-associated infections, fiscal year 2010.* Retrieved January 21, 2011 from http://www.ahrq.gov/qual/haify10.pdf

American Hospital Association and the Institute for Family-Centered Care Resource Guide. (2006). *Strategies for leadership: Patient and family-centered care.* Washington, DC: American Hospital Association and The Institute for Family-Centered Care. Retrieved January 22, 2011 from http://www.aha.org/aha/issues/Quality-and-Patient-Safety/strategies-patient centered.html

American Pharmaceutical Association. (1922). Code of ethics of the American Pharmaceutical Association. *Journal of the American Pharmaceutical Association, 11*(9), 728–729.

American Pharmaceutical Association. (1952). Code of ethics of the American Pharmaceutical Association. *Journal of the American Pharmaceutical Association, 13*(10), 721–723.

American Pharmacists Association. (1994). *Code of ethics for pharmacists.* Retrieved January 21, 2011 from http://www.pharmacist.com/AM/Template.cfm?Section=Search1&template=/CM/HTMLDisplay.cfm&ContentID=2903

American Pharmacists Association & National Association of Chain Drug Stores. (2008, March). *Medication therapy management in pharmacy practice: Core elements of an MTM service model.* Retrieved from http://www.pharmacist.com/AM/Template.cfm?Section=Home2&TEMPLATE=/CM/ContentDisplay.cfm&CONTENTID=15496

Anders, G. (1996). *Health against wealth: HMOs and the breakdown of medical trust.* Boston, MA: Houghton Mifflin.

Apple, R. D. (1996). *Vitamania: Vitamins in American culture.* New Brunswick, NJ: Rutgers University Press.

Atchinson, B. K., & Fox, D. M. (1997). From the field: The politics of the Health Insurance Portability and Accountability Act. *Health Affairs, 16*(3), 146–150.

Banks, J., Marmot, M., Oldfield, Z., & Smith, J. P. (2006, May 3). Disease and disadvantage in the United States and in England. *Journal of the American Medical Association. 295*(17), 2037–2045.

Bell, J. E. (1996, May/June). Saving their assets: How to stop plunder at Blue Cross and other nonprofits. *The American Prospect,* (26), 60–66.

Berenson, R. A., Ginsburg, P. B., & May, J. H. (2006, December 5). Hospital-physician relations: Cooperation, competition, or separation? *Health Affairs, (26)*1 [Web exclusive], W31–W42.

Beresford, L. (2009). Medical mistakes, 10 years post-op: HM and renewed emphasis on patient safety grow in tandem. *The Hospitalist, 13*(11). Retrieved from http://www.the-hospitalist.org/details/article/423625/Medical_Mistakes_10_Years_Post-Op.html

Berwick, D. M. (2009, May). What 'patient-centered' should mean: Confessions of an extremist. *Health Affairs, (28)*4, w555–w565.

Blendon, R. J., & Benson, J. M. (2009, August 27). *The New England Journal of Medicine, (361),* e13(1)–e13(4).

Blendon, R. J., Brodie, M., Benson, J. M., Altman, D. E, Levitt, L., Hoff, T., & Hugick, L. (1998, July/August). Understanding the managed care backlash. *Health Affairs, (17)*4, 80–94.

Blue, A. V., Mitcham, M., Smith, T., Raymond, J., & Greenberg, R. (2010, August). Changing the future of health professions: Embedding interprofessional education within an academic center. *Academic Medicine, (85)*8, 1290–1295.

Blumenthal, D., & Weissman, J. (2000). Trends: Selling teaching hospitals to investor-owned hospital chains: Three case studies. *Health Affairs, 19,* 158–166.

Bodenheimer, T., Chen, E., & Bennett, H. D. (2009, January/February). Confronting the growing burden of chronic disease: Can the U.S. health care workforce do the job? *Health Affairs, 28*(1), 64–74.

Bogdan, J. C. (1992). Childbirth in America, 1650–1990. In R. D. Apple (Ed.), *Women, health, and medicine in America: A historical handbook* (pp. 101–120). New Brunswick, NJ: Rutgers University Press.

Bogdanich, W. (2010, August 1). The mark of an overdose: After stroke scans, patients face serious health risks. *The New York Times,* A1, A12.

Bosk, C. L., Dixon-Woods, M., Goeschel, C. A., & Pronovost, P. J. (2009, August 8). Reality check for checklists. *The Lancet, 374* (9688), 444–445.

Boulis, A., Jacobs, J., &Veloski, J. J. (2001, October). Gender segregation by specialty during medical school. *Academic Medicine, (76)*10, S65–S67.

Brandt, A. M. (1997). The cigarette, risk, and American culture. In W. G. Rothstein (Ed.), *Readings in American health care: Current issues in socio-historical perspective* (pp. 138–150). Madison, WI: University of Wisconsin Press.

Brock, K. A., Casper, K. A., Green, T. R., & Pedersen, C. A. (2006). Documentation of patient care services in a community pharmacy setting. *Journal of the American Pharmaceutical Association, 46*(3), 378–384.

Brodie, M., Altman, D., Deane, C., Buscho, S, & Hamel, E. (2010, June). Liking the pieces, not the package: Contradictions in public opinion during health reform. *Health Affairs, 29*(6), 1125–1130.

Buring, S. M., Bhusan, A., Brazeau, G., Conway, S., Hansen, L., & Westberg, S. (2009, August). Keys to successful implementation of interprofessional education: Learning location, faculty development, and curricular themes. *American Journal of Pharmaceutical Education, (73)*4, 1–11.

Burnham, J. C. (1982, March 19). American medicine's golden age: What happened to it? *Science, 245,* 1474–1479.

Byrd, W. M., & Clayton, L. A. (2000). *An American health dilemma: A medical history of African Americans and the problem of race, beginning to 1900* (Vol. 1). New York, NY: Routledge.

Cahill, S. (1997). The Wal-Mart of hospitals. *In These Times, 21*(8), 14–16.

Casalino, L. P., November, E. A., Berenson, R. A., & Pham, H. H. (2008, September/October). Hospital-physician relations: Two tracks and the decline of the voluntary medical staff model. *Health Affairs, 27*(5), 1305–1314.

Cassedy, J. H. (1991). *Medicine in America: A short history.* Baltimore, MD: Johns Hopkins University Press.

Castellblanch, R. (1996). Legislation for sale. *In These Times, 20,* 14–16.

Cayleff, S. E. (1987). *Wash and be healed: The water-cure movement and women's health.* Philadelphia, PA: Temple University Press.

Cayleff, S. E. (1992). Self-help and the patent medicine business. In R. D. Apple (Ed.), *Women, health, and medicine in America: A historical handbook* (pp. 303–328). New Brunswick, NJ: Rutgers University Press.

Centers for Disease Control and Prevention. (2009). *Leading causes of death.* Retrieved January 21, 2011 from http://www.cdc.gov/nchs/fastats/lcod.htm

Centers for Disease Control and Prevention Media Relations. (2000, March 6). *Why is handwashing important?* Retrieved January 21, 2011 from http://www.cdc.gov/od/oc/media/pressrel/r2k0306c.htm

Central Intelligence Agency. (2009). *The CIA world factbook, 2010.* New York, NY: Skyhorse Publishing.

Christianson, E. H. (1987). Medicine in New England. In R. L. Numbers (Ed.), *Medicine in the New world: New Spain, New France, and New England* (pp. 101–153). Knoxville, TN: University of Tennessee Press.

Cohen, R. A., Martinez, M. E., & Ward, B. W. (2010, June). *Health insurance coverage: Early release of estimates from the National Interview survey, 2009.* National Center for Health Statistics: Atlanta, Georgia. Retrieved June 25, 2010 from http://www.cdc.gov/nchs/data/nhis/earlyrelease/insur201006.htm

Colgrove, J., Markowitz, G., & Rosner, D., Eds. (2008). *The contested boundaries of American public health.* New Brunswick, NJ: Rutgers University Press.

Colwil, J. M. (2010, May). A case of 'medical homelessness.' *Health Affairs, (29)*5, 1067–1070.

Cowen, D. L., & Kent, D. F. (1997). Medical and pharmaceutical practice in 1854. *Pharmacy in History, 39,* 91–100.

Crosson, F. J., & Tollen, L. A. (2010). *Partners in health: How physicians and hospitals can be accountable together.* Hoboken, NJ: Jossey-Bass Publishers.

Davis, K., Schoen, C., Stremikis, K. (2010, June). *Mirror, mirror on the wall: How the performance of the U.S. health care system compares internationally; 2010 update.* Retrieved from http://www.commonwealthfund.org/~/media/Files/Publications/Fund%20Report/2010/Jun/1400_Davis_Mirror_Mirror_on_the_wall_2010.pdf

Delaney, L. R., & Gunderman, R. B., (2008, January). Hand hygiene. *Radiology, 246*(1), 15–19.

Deno, R. A., Rowe, T. D., & Brodie, D. C. (1959). *The profession of pharmacy: An introductory textbook.* Philadelphia, PA: J. B. Lippincott.

DesRoches, C. M., Campbell, E. G., Bogeli, C., Zheng, J., Rao, S. R., Shields, A. E., . . . Jha, A. K. (2010, April). Electronic health records' limited successes suggest more targeted uses. *Health Affairs, 29*(4), 639–646.

Duffy, J. (1993). *From humors to medical science: A history of American medicine* (2nd ed.). Urbana and Chicago, IL: University of Illinois Press.

Eckholm, E. (2009, November 27). Trying to explain a drop in infant mortality. *The New York Times.* Retrieved from http://www.nytimes.com/2009/11/27/us/27infant.html?ref= infant_mortality

Elenbaas, R. M., & Worthen, D. B. (2009). Transformation of a profession: An overview of the 20th century. *Pharmacy in History, (51)*4, 151–182.

Epstein, H. (2003, October 12). Enough to make you sick? *New York Times Sunday Magazine,* pp. 75ff.

Epstein, R. M., Fiscella, K., Lesser, C. S., & Stange, K. C. (2010, August). Why the nation needs a policy push on patient-centered health care. *Health Affairs (29)*8, 1489–1495.

Essoyan, S. (2000, August 13). Hospital mixes high-tech, human touch. *Boston Globe,* p. A19.

Fairbrother, G. L., Carle, A. C., Cassedy, A., & Newacheck, P. W. (2010, July). Impact of parental job loss on children's health insurance coverage. *Health Affairs, (29)*7, 1343–1349.

Farley, J. F., Devine, J. W., & Hadsall, R. S. (2007, May/June). Professional implications of the expansion of pharmacy-based medical clinics. *Journal of the American Pharmacists Association, (47)*3, 410–414.

Farmer, P. (1999). *Infections and inequalities: The modern plagues.* Berkeley, CA: University of California Press.

Fletcher, M. A. (2008, March 24). *The Washington Post.* Retrieved from http://www.washingtonpost.com/wpdyn/content/article/2008/03/23/AR2008032301770_pf.html

Flexner, A. (1910). *Medical education in the United States and Canada* (Bulletin No. 4). New York, NY: Carnegie Foundation for the Advancement of Teaching.

Flexner, A. (1915). Is social work a profession? *Proceedings of the National Conference of Charities and Corrections.* Forty-second annual session, Baltimore, MD, May 12–19, 1915. Reprinted in March 2001 in *Research on Social Work Practice, 11*(2), 152–265.

Fox, D. M. (1988). An historical perspective: Health policy and changing epidemiology in the United States—Chronic disease in the twentieth century. In R. C. Maulitz (Ed.), *Unnatural causes: The three leading killer diseases in America* (pp. 11–31). New Brunswick, NJ: Rutgers University Press.

Fox, D. M. (1993). *Power and illness: The failure and future of American health.* Berkeley, CA: University of California Press.

Furukawa, M. F., Raghu, T. S., Spaulding, T. J., Vinze, A. (2008, May/June). Adoption of health information technology for medication safety in U.S. hospitals, 2006. *Health Affairs, 27*(3), 865–875.

Gabel, J. R., McDevitt, R., Lore, R., Pickreign, J., Whitmore, H. (2009). Trends in underinsurance and the affordability of employer coverage, 2004–2007. *Health Affairs, 28*(4), w595–w606.

Gandy, M., & Zumla, A. (2003). *The return of the white plague: Global poverty and the 'new' tuberculosis.* New York, NY: VIRSO.

Garrett, L. (2000). *Betrayal of trust: The collapse of global public health.* New York, NY: Hyperion.

Gawande, A. (2004, March 25). On washing hands. *New England Journal of Medicine, 350*(13), 1283–1286.

Gawande, A. (2010). *The checklist manifesto: How to get things right.* New York, NY: Metropolitan Books.

Goetzl, R. Z. (2009, January/February). Do prevention or treatment services save money? The wrong debate. *Health Affairs (28)*1, 37–41.

Gordon, S., Ed. (2010). *When chicken soup isn't enough: Stories of nurses standing up for themselves, their patients, and their profession.* Ithaca, NY: ILR Press.

Grob, G. N. (2002). *The deadly truth: A history of disease in America.* Cambridge, MA: Harvard University Press.

Grumbach, K., & Mendoza, R. (2008, March/April). Disparities in human resources: Addressing the lack of diversity in the health professions. *Health Affairs, (27)*2, 513–422.

Hacker, J. S. (1997). *The road to nowhere: The genesis of President Clinton's plan for health security.* Princeton, NJ: Princeton University Press.

Hacker, J. S. (2008). *The great risk shift: The new economic insecurity and the decline of the American dream.* New York, NY: Oxford University Press.

Haller, J. S., Jr. (2000). *The people's doctors: Samuel Thomson and the American botanical movement, 1790–1860.* Carbondale, IL: Southern Illinois University Press.

Hamel, M. B., Drazen, J. M., & Esptein, A. M. (2009, March 12). The growth of hospitalists and the changing face of primary care. *New England Journal of Medicine, 360*(11), 1141–1143.

Hartman, M., Martin, A., Nuccio, O., & Catlin, A. (2010, January). Health spending growth at a historic low in 2008. *Health Affairs, 29*(1), 147–155.

Hartzband P., & Groopman, J. (2008, April 17). Off the record—avoiding the pitfalls of going electronic. *New England Journal of Medicine, 358*(16), 1656–1658.

HealthCare.gov (2010, June 22). The affordable care act's new patient's bill of rights. Retrieved from http://www.healthcare.gov/news/factsheets/aca_new_patients_bill_of_rights.html

Hendricks, R. (1993). *A model for national health care: The history of Kaiser Permanente.* New Brunswick, NJ: Rutgers University Press.

Hepler, C.D. (2010, August 15). A dream deferred. *American Journal of Health-System Pharmacy, (67),* 1319–1325.

Hepler, C.D., & Strand, L. (1990). Opportunities and responsibilities in pharmaceutical care. *American Journal of Hosptial Pharmacy, (47),* 533–543.

Higby, G. J. (1992). *In service to American pharmacy: The professional life of William Procter, Jr.* Tuscaloosa, AL: University of Alabama Press.

Higby, G. J. (1996). From compounding to caring: An abridged history of American pharmacy. In C. Knowlton & R. Panna (Eds.), *Pharmaceutical care* (pp. 18–45), New York, NY: Chapman and Hall.

Higby, G. J., with Gallagher, T. C. (1992). Pharmacists. In R. D. Apple (Ed.), *Women, health, and medicine in America: A historical handbook* (pp. 489–508). New Brunswick, NJ: Rutgers University Press.

Hobson, K., (2010, August 9). Study puts cost of medical errors at $19.5 billion. *The Wall Street Journal.* Retrieved from http://blogs.wsj.com/health/2010/08/09/study-puts-cost-of-medical-errors-at-195-billion/

Hooper, D. C. (2009). Making strides in hand hygiene compliance: To 90% and beyond. Retrieved 2009. http://www.macoalition.org/Initiatives/docs/MassGeneralHospital Presentation.pdf

Horrocks, T. A. (2003). Rules, remedies, and regimens: Health advice in early American almanacs. In C. E. Rosenberg (Ed.), *Right living: An Anglo-American tradition of self-help medicine and hygiene* (pp. 112–146). Baltimore, MD: Johns Hopkins University Press.

Hoy, S. (1995). *Chasing dirt: The American pursuit of cleanliness.* New York, NY: Oxford University Press.

Iglehart, J. K. (2008, September 18). No place like home—testing a new model of care delivery. *The New England Journal of Medicine, 359*(12), 2100–2102.

Iglehart, J. K. (2010, May). Entry point. *Health Affairs, 29*(5), 758–759.

Institute of Medicine. (2000). In L. T. Kohn, J. M. Corrigan, & M. S. Donaldson (Eds.), *To err is human: Building a safer health system.* Washington, DC: National Academies Press.

Institute of Medicine. (2001). *Crossing the quality chasm: A new health system for the 21st century.* Washington, DC: National Academies Press.

Johnson, H., & Broder, D. (1996). *The system: The American way of politics at the breaking point.* Boston, MA: Little, Brown.

Johnson, N. J., & Johnson, L. P. (2010). Eds. *The care of the uninsured in America.* New York, NY: Springer.

Kaiser Family Foundation. (2010, March). Trends in health care costs and spending. Retrieved from http://www.kff.org/insurance/upload/7692_02.pdf

Kaufman, M. (1971). Homeopathy in America: The rise and fall of a medical heresy. Baltimore, MD: Johns Hopkins University Press.

Kennedy, E. M. (1972). In critical condition: The crisis in America's health care. New York, NY: Simon and Schuster.

Kevles, B. H. (1997). Medical imaging in the twentieth century. New Brunswick, NJ: Rutgers University Press.

Kilo, C. M., & Wasson, J. H. (2010). Practice redesign and the patient-centered medical home: History, promises, and challenges. *Health Affairs, 29*(5), 773–778.

King, C. R. (1993). *Children's health in America: A history.* New York, NY: Twayne.

Kinsella, K.G. (1992). Changes in life expectancy 1900–1990. *American Journal of Clinical Nutrition, 55*(6). 1196S–1202S.

Knowlton, C.H. (2009). Pharmacy practice: Where's the value proposition? *Pharmacy in History, 51*(3), 94–97.

Knox, R. A. (1996a, September 16). Changing world, changing ailments. *Boston Globe*, pp. C1–C3.

Knox, R. A. (1996b, November 13). Widespread chronic illness cited. *Boston Globe*, p. A11.

Koh, H. K. (2010, May 6). A 2020 vision for healthy people. *New England Journal of Medicine, 362*(18), 1653–1656.

Kowalczyk, L. (2000). A stretched-thin doctor draws a line. *Boston Globe*, pp. A1, C6.

Kraut, A. M. (1994). *Silent travelers: Germs, genes, and the "immigrant menace."* New York, NY: Basic Books.

Kreling, D. H., Doucette, W. R., Mott, D. A., Gaither, A., Pedersen, C. A., & Schommer, J. C. (2006). Community pharmacists' work environments: Evidence from the 2004 national pharmacist workforce study. *Journal of the American Pharmaceutical Association, 46*(3), 331–339.

Krugman, P. (2010, January 22). Do the right thing. *The New York Times*, A21.

La Ferla, R. (2000, August 13). Hospitals are discovering their inner spa. *New York Times*, sect. 9, pp. 1, 4.

Larson, E. B., & Reid, R. (2010, April 28). The patient-centered medical home movement: Why now? *Journal of the American Medical Association, (303)*16, 1644–1645.

Lauer, M. S. (2009, August 27). Elements of danger—the case of medical imaging. *New England Journal of Medicine, 361*(9), 841–843.

Leavitt, J. W. (1995). A worrying profession: The domestic environment of medical practice in mid-19th century America. *Bulletin of the History of Medicine, 69*, 1–29.

Leavitt, J. W. (1996). *Typhoid Mary: Captive to the public's health.* New York, NY: Beacon Press.

Leavitt, J. W., & Numbers, R. L. (1997). Sickness and health: An overview. In J. W. Leavitt & R. L. Numbers (Eds.), *Sickness and health in America: Readings in the history of medicine and public health* (3rd ed., pp. 3–10). Madison, WI: University of Wisconsin Press.

Lerner, M., & Anderson, O. W. (1963). *Health progress in the United States: 1900–1960.* Chicago, IL: University of Chicago Press.

Lichtenberg, F. R., & Sun, S. X. (2007, November/December). The impact of Medicare part D on prescription drug use by the elderly. *Health Affairs, 26*(6), 1735–1744.

Litman, T. J. (1997). The relationship of government and politics to health and health care—a sociopolitical overview. In T. J. Litman & L. S. Robins (Eds.), *Health politics and policy* (3rd ed., pp. 3–45). New York, NY: Delmar.

Ludmerer, K. M. (1985). *Learning to heal: The development of American medical education.* New York, NY: Basic Books.

Ludmerer, K. M. (1999). *Time to heal: American education from the turn of the century to the era of managed care.* New York, NY: Oxford University Press.

Lukas, C. V., &Young, G. J. (2000, March/April). Trends: Public hospitals, privatization and uncompensated care. *Health Affairs, 19*(2), 1–6.

Maciosek, M. V., Coffield, A. B., Edwards, N. M., Flottemesch, T. J., Goodman, M. J., & Solberg, L. I. (2006). Priorities among effective clinical preventive services: Results of a systematic review and analysis. *American Journal of Preventive Medicine, 20*(10), 1–10.

Mackey, J. (2010, August 11). The Whole Foods alternative to ObamaCare. *The Wall Street Journal,* p. A15.

Managed Care On-Line (MCOL). (2010). National HMO enrollment. National statistics. Managed care fact sheets. Retrieved from http://www.mcol.com/

Markel, H. (2004). *When germs travel: Six major epidemics that have invaded America and the fears they have unleashed.* New York, NY: Vintage Books.

Markel, H., & Golden, J. (2004, September/October). Children's public health policy in the United States: How the past can inform the present. *Health Affairs, 23*(5), 147–152.

Markowitz, G. E., & Rosner, D. (1979). Doctors in crisis: Medical education and medical reform during the progressive era, 1895–1915. In S. Reverby & D. Rosner (Eds.), *Health care in America: Essays in social history* (pp. 185–205). Philadelphia, PA: Temple University Press.

Martin, T.W. (2010, August 17). Suntan lotion, flip-flops … and flu shots. *The Wall Street Journal,* p. B1.

Martinez, B. (2000, August 21). Now it's mass medicine. *Wall Street Journal*, pp. B1, B4.

McGivney, M. S., Meyer, S. M., Duncan-Hewitt, W., Hall, D. L., Goode, J. R., & Smith, R.B. (2007, September/October). Medication therapy management: Its relationship to patient counseling, disease management, and pharmaceutical care. *Journal of the American Pharmacists Association, 47*(5), 620–628.

McGuire, L. K., Bergen, M. R., & Polan, M. L. (2004, April). Career advancement for women faculty in a U.S. school of medicine: Perceived needs. *Academic Medicine, 79*(4), 319–325.

McKenna, M. (2010). *SUPERBUG: The fatal menace of MRSA.* New York, NY: Free Press.

Mechanic, R. E . (2003, November–December). What will become of the medical mecca? Health care spending in Massachusetts. *Health Affairs, 22*(6), 131–141.

Melosi, M. V. (2000). *The sanitary city: Urban infrastructure in America from colonial times to the present.* Baltimore, MD: Johns Hopkins University Press.

Millis, J. S. (1975). *Pharmacists for the future: The report of the Study Commission on Pharmacy.* Ann Arbor, MI: Health Administration Press.

Mishler, E. G. (1981). Viewpoint: Critical perspectives on the biomedical model. In E. G. Mishler (Ed.), *Social contexts of health, illness, and patient care* (pp. 1–13). New York, NY: Cambridge University Press.

Morantz-Sanchez, R. (1992). Physicians. In R. D. Apple (Ed.), *Women, health, and medicine in America: A historical handbook* (pp. 469–487). New Brunswick, NJ: Rutgers University Press.

More, E. S. (1999). *Restoring the balance: Women physicians and the profession of medicine, 1850–1995.* Cambridge, MA: Harvard University Press.

Morrison, G., Goldfarb, S., & Lanken, P. N. (2010, February). Team training of medical students in the 21st century: Would Flexner approve? *Academic Medicine, 85*(2), 254–259.

Murray, C. J. L., & Lopez, A. D. (Eds.). (1996). *The global burden of disease: A comprehensive assessment of mortality and disability from diseases, injuries, and risk factors in 1990 and projected to 2020.* Cambridge, MA: Harvard University Press.

Naik, G. (2006, June 20). Cincinnati applies a corporate model to saving infants. *Wall Street Journal*, pp. A01, A14.

National Center for Health Statistics. (2009). *Health, United States, 2009: With special feature on medical technology.* Hyattsville, MD: U.S. Government Printing Office.

National Healthcare Disparities Report 2009. (2010, March). U.S. Department of Health and Human Services. Rockville, MD: Agency for Healthcare Research and Quality.

National Healthcare Quality Report 2009. (2010, March). U.S. Department of Health and Human Services. Rockville, MD: Agency for Healthcare Research and Quality.

Navarro, R. P. (1999). *Managed care pharmacy practice.* Gaithersburg, MD: Aspen Publications.

Nissenbaum, S. (1980). *Sex, diet, and debility in Jacksonian America: Sylvester Graham and health reform.* Westport, CT: Greenwood Press.

Numbers, R. L. (1997). The third party: Health insurance in America. In J. W. Leavitt & R. L. Numbers (Eds.), *Sickness and health in America: Readings in the history of medicine and public health* (3rd ed., pp. 269–283). Madison, WI: University of Wisconsin Press.

Oberlander, J. (2010, June). Long time coming: Why health reform finally passed. *Health Affairs, 29*(6), 1112–1116.

Opdycke, S. (1999). *No one was turned away: The role of public hospitals in New York City since 1900.* New York, NY: Oxford University Press.

Organization for Economic Cooperation and Development. (2009). *Health at a Glance: OECD Indicators.* Washington, DC: OEDC Publishing.

Ott, K. (1996). *Fevered lives: Tuberculosis in American culture since 1870*. Cambridge, MA: Harvard University Press.

Parascandola, J. (1997). The introduction of antibiotics into therapeutics. In J. W. Leavitt & R. L. Numbers (Eds.), *Sickness and health in America: Readings in the history of medicine and public health* (3rd ed., (pp. 102–112). Madison, WI: University of Wisconsin Press.

Patel, K., & Rushefsky, M. E. (1995). *Health care politics and policy in America*. Armonk, NY: M. E. Sharpe.

Patient-Centered Primary Care Collaborative. (2010). The patient-centered medical home: Integrating comprehensive medication management to optimize patient outcome. Retrieved from http://www.pcpcc.net/files/medmanagement.pdf

Patterson, J. T. (1987). *The dread disease: Cancer and modern American culture*. Cambridge, MA: Harvard University Press.

Pear, R. (1997, April 2). New health insurance rules spell out rights of workers. *New York Times*, p. A15.

Pear, R. (2006, June 11). In Texas town, patients and providers find new prescription drug plan baffling. *New York Times*, p. 30.

Pernick, M. S. (1985). *A calculus of suffering: Pain, professionalism, and anesthesia in nineteenth-century America*. New York, NY: Columbia University Press.

Peterson, M. A. (1997). Introduction: Health care into the next century. *Journal of Health Politics, Policy and Law, 22*, 291–313.

Pitout, J. D. D. (2010, August 11). The latest threat in the war on antimicrobial resistance. *The Lancet Infectious Diseases, 10*(1016), 1–2.

Poen, M. M. (1979). *Harry S. Truman versus the medical lobby: The genesis of Medicare*. Columbia, MO: University of Missouri Press.

Pollack, C. E., Gidengil, C., & Mehrotra, A. (2010, May). The growth of retail clinics and the medical home: Two trends in concert or in conflict? *Health Affairs, 29*(5), 998–1003.

Ponte, R. P., Conlin, G., Conway, J. B., Grant, S., Medeiros, C., Nies, J., … Conley, K. (2003, February). Making patient-centered care come alive: Achieving full integration of the patient's perspective. *Journal of Nursing Administration, 33*(2), 82–90.

Pronovost, P., Needham, D., Berenholtz, S., Sinopoli, D., Chu, H., Cosgrove, S., … Goeschel, C. (2006, December 28). An intervention to decrease catheter-related bloodstream infections in the ICU. *New England Journal of Medicine, 355*(26), 2725–2732.

Ralston, J. D., Coleman, K., Reid, R. J., Handley, M. R., & Larson, E. B. (2010, April). Patient experience should be part of meaningful-use criteria. *Health Affairs, 29*(4), 607–613.

Reid, R. J., Coleman, K., Johnson, E. A., Fishman, P. A., Hsu, C., Soman, M. P., … Larson, E. B. (2010, May). The group health medical home at year two: Cost savings, higher patient satisfaction, and less burnout for providers. *Health Affairs, 29*(5), 835–843.

Reinhardt, U. E., Hussey, P. S., & Anderson, G. F. (2004, May/June). U. S. health care spending in an international context. *Health Affairs, 2*(3), 10–25.

Reverby, S. M. (1987). *Ordered to care: The dilemma of American nursing, 1850–1945*. New York, NY: Cambridge University Press.

Richmond, J.B., & Fein, R. (2005). *The health care mess: How we got into it and what it will take to get out*. Cambridge, MA: Harvard University Press.

Risse, G. B. (1999). *Mending bodies, saving souls: A history of hospitals*. New York, NY: Oxford University Press.

Rittenhouse, D. R., & Shortell, S. M. (2009, May 20). The patient-centered medical home: Will it stand the test of health reform? *The Journal of the American Medical Association, 301*(19), 2038–2040.

Rosenberg, C. E. (1974). Social class and medical care in 19th century America: The rise and fall of the dispensary. *Journal of the History of Medicine and Allied Sciences, 29*(1), 32–54.

Rosenberg, C. E. (1985). The therapeutic revolution: Medicine, meaning, and social change in 19th-century America. In J. W. Leavitt & R. L. Numbers (Eds.), *Sickness and health in America: Readings in the history of medicine and public health* (2nd ed., pp. 39–52). Madison, WI: University of Wisconsin Press.

Rosenberg, C. E. (1987). *The care of strangers: The rise of America's hospital system*. New York, NY: Basic Books.

Rosenberg, C. E. (1992). Framing disease: Illness, society, and history. In C. E. Rosenberg & J. Golden (Eds.), *Framing disease: Studies in cultural history* (pp. xiii–xxvi). New Brunswick, NJ: Rutgers University Press.

Rosner, D. (1979). Business at the bedside: Health care in Brooklyn, 1890–1915. In S. Reverby & D. Rosner (Eds.), *Health care in America: Essays in social history* (pp. 117–131). Philadelphia, PA: Temple University Press.

Rosner, D. (1995). Introduction: Hives of sickness and vice. In D. Rosner (Ed.), *Hives of sickness: Public health and epidemics in New York City* (pp. 1–12). New Brunswick, NJ: Rutgers University Press.

Rosner, D. & Markowitz, G. (2006). *Are We Ready? Public Health Since 9/11*. Berkeley, CA: University of California Press.

Rothstein, W. G. (1996a). Pharmaceuticals and public policy in America: A history. In W. G. Rothstein (Ed.), *Readings in American health care: Current issues in socio-historical perspective* (pp. 375–391). Madison, WI: University of Wisconsin Press.

Rothstein, W. G. (1996b). Trends in mortality in the twentieth century. In W. G. Rothstein (Ed.), *Readings in American health care: Current issues in socio-historical perspective* (pp. 71–86). Madison, WI: University of Wisconsin Press.

Sack, K. (2010a, October 7) Judge rules health law is constitutional. *The New York Times*. Retrieved October 17, 2010 from http://www.nytimes.com/2010/10/08/health/policy/08health.html?_r=1&scp=1&sq=health%20care%20reform%20constitutional&st=cse

Sack, K. (2010b, October 15, 2010). Challenging health law, suit advances. *The New York Times*. Retrieved from http://www.nytimes.com/2010/10/15/health/policy/15health.html?scp=1&sq=challenging%20health%20law,%20suit%20advances&st=cse

Salamon, J. (2010). *Hospital: Man, Woman, Birth, Death, Infinity, Plus Red Tape, Bad Behavior, Money, God, and Diversity on Steroids*. New York: The Penguin Press.

Saultz, J. W., O'Neil, P., Gill, J. M., Biagioli, F. E., Blanchard, S., O'Malley, J. P., … Carney, P. A. (2010, June). Medical student exposure to components of the patient-centered medical home during required ambulatory clerkship rotations: Implications for education. *Academic Medicine, 85*(6), 965–973.

Schneeweiss, S., Patrick, A. R., Pedan, A., Varasteh, L., Levin, R., Liu, N., & Shrank, W.H. (2009, March/April). The effect of Medicare Part D coverage on drug use and cost sharing among seniors without prior drug benefits. *Health Affairs, 28*(2), w305–w316.

Sered, S. S., & Fernandopulle, R. (2005). *Uninsured in America: Life and death in the land of opportunity*. Berkeley, CA: University of California Press.

Smith, M., Bates, D. W., Bodenheimer, T., & Cleary, P. D. (2010, May). Why pharmacists belong in the medical home. *Health Affairs, 29*(5), 906–913.

Sonnedecker, G. (1976). *Kremer's and Urdang's history of pharmacy* (4th ed.). Philadelphia, PA: J. B. Lippincott.

Stage, S. (1979). *Female complaints: Lydia Pinkham and the business of women's medicine*. New York, NY: W. W. Norton.

Starr, P. (1982). *The social transformation of American medicine: The rise of a sovereign profession and the making of a vast industry*. New York, NY: Basic Books.

Starr, P. (1991). *The logic of health care reform (The grand rounds press)*. Knoxville, TN: Whittle Direct Books.

Steinhauer, J. (2000, February 29). High infant mortality rates in Brooklyn mystify experts. *New York Times*, pp. A1, A23.

Stevens, R. (1971). *American medicine and the public interest*. New Haven, CT: Yale University Press.

Stevens, R. (1989). *In sickness and in wealth: American hospitals in the twentieth century*. New York, NY: Basic Books.

Stevens, R. (2008). History and health policy in the United States: The making of a health care industry, 1948–2008. *Social History of Medicine, 21*(3), 461–483.

Stone, D. A. (1997). The doctor as businessman: The changing politics of a cultural icon. *The American Prospect, 22*(2), 533–556.

Sullivan, L. W. & Mittman, I. S. (2010, February). The state of diversity in the health professions a century after Flexner. *Academic Medicine, 85*(2), 246–253.

Tannenbaum, R. (2002). *The healer's calling: Women and medicine in early New England.* Ithaca, NY: Cornell University Press.

Temin, P. (1980). *Taking your medicine: Drug regulation in the United States.* Cambridge, MA: Harvard University Press.

Tesh, S. N. (1988). *Hidden arguments: Political ideology and disease prevention policy.* New Brunswick, NJ: Rutgers University Press.

Tomes, N. (1998). *The gospel of germs: Men, women, and the microbe in American life.* Cambridge, MA: Harvard University Press.

Tomes, N. (2006). Patients or health-care consumers? Why the history of contested terms matters. In Stevens, R. A., Rosenberg, C. E., & Burns, L. R. (Eds.), *History and health policy in the United States.* New Brunswick, NJ: Rutgers University Press.

Traynor, K. (2010, September 1). Pharmacy makes inroads in medical home movement. *American Journal of Health Systems Pharmacy, 67,* 1402, 1404.

Ulrich, L. T. (1990). *A midwife's tale: The life of Martha Ballard, based on her diary, 1785–1812.* New York, NY: Alfred A. Knopf.

U.S. Census Bureau. (2010). *Statistical abstract of the United States.* Washington, DC: Government Printing Office.

U.S. Department of Health and Human Services. (1999). *Health: United States 1999.* Washington, DC: Government Printing Office.

Vladek, B. (2003, January). Universal health insurance in the United States: Reflections on the past, the present, and the future. *American Journal of Public Health, 93*(1), pp. 16–19.

Vogel, M. J. (1979). The transformation of the American hospital, 1850–1920. In S. Reverby & D. Rosner (Eds.), *Health care in America: Essays in social history* (pp. 105–116). Philadelphia, PA: Temple University Press.

Wachter, R. M. (2010, January). Patient safety at ten: Unmistakable progress, troubling gaps. *Health Affairs, 29*(1), pp. 165–173.

Warner, J. H. (1997). From specificity to universalism in medical therapeutics: Transformation in the 19th-century United States. In J. W. Leavitt & R. Numbers (Eds.), *Sickness and health in America: Readings in the history of medicine and public health* (3rd ed., pp. 87–101). Madison, WI: University of Wisconsin Press.

Weiss, G. L., & Lonnquist, L. E. (2006). *The sociology of health, healing, and illness* (5th ed.). Upper Saddle River, NJ: Pearson Prentice Hall.

The White House. (2010, March 23). *Remarks by the president and vice president at signing of the health insurance reform bill.* Retrieved from http://www.whitehouse.gov/the-press-office/remarks-president-and-vice-president-signing-health-insurance-reform-bill

White House domestic policy council. (1993). *The President's Health Security Plan.* New York, NY: Times Books.

Woo, A., Ranji, U., & Salganicoff, A. (2008, May). Reducing medical errors. *Kaiser EDU.org* Retrieved from http://www.kaiseredu.org/topics_im.asp?id=137&parentID=70&imID=1

World Health Organization. (2009). WHO guidelines in hand hygiene in health care: First global patient safety challenge; clean care is safer care. Geneva, Switzerland: WHO Press.

Worthen, D. B., Ed. (2006). *The Millis study commission on pharmacy: A road map to a profession's future.* Binghamton, NY: The Haworth Press.

Yin, W., Basu, A., Zhang, J. X., Rabbani, A., Meltzer, D. O., & Alexander, G. C. (2008, February 5). The effect of the Medicare Part D prescription benefit on drug utilization and expenditures. *The Annals of Internal Medicine, 148,* 169–177.

Young, G., Dasai, K., & Lucas, C. V. (1997). Does the sale of nonprofit hospitals threaten health care for the poor? *Health Affairs, 16*(1), 137–141.

Young, J. H. (1992). *American health quackery: Collected essays.* Princeton, NJ: Princeton University Press.

CHAPTER 2

Healthcare Professionals and Interdisciplinary Care

Suvapun Bunniran and David J. McCaffrey III*

Case Scenario

Bob Jones has been a patient of WeCare Pharmacy for almost 20 years. Two months ago, he was diagnosed with stage IV lung cancer. After discussing his options with his oncologist and after careful consideration and discussions with his family Mr. Jones decided against treatment and began the process of preparing for his death. His wife, Agnes, visits the pharmacy regularly to collect prescriptions and other health-care needs for herself and her husband. On one visit, she mentions that lately Bob has been experiencing a great deal of pain and it has affected his ability to sleep as well as his mood. She says that Bob no longer wants his children and grandchildren to visit and that he barely communicates any longer because of his level of discomfort. The pharmacist empathizes with Mrs. Jones and offers to contact Bob's doctor to discuss the problem and to find a solution. Two days later someone from the pharmacy contacts Agnes Jones and informs her that a new prescription for pain medication is ready for Mr. Jones and she can pick it up at her earliest convenience.

LEARNING OBJECTIVES

Upon completion of this chapter, the student shall be able to:

- Discuss the characteristics of a profession and how professions are distinguished from other occupations
- Describe the education/training, scope of practice, and availability of various healthcare professions
- Compare and contrast multidisciplinary care and interdisciplinary care
- Recognize the various stages of the pharmacist–physician collaborative working relationship and identify strategies available to the pharmacist to establish these cooperative arrangements with physicians

*With acknowledgment to Alice M. Sapienza.

- Describe continuity of care and the medical home and the role that a pharmacist can and should play in this process
- Define quality and describe the role of interdisciplinary care in the quality movement
- Describe the three ways that healthcare quality is reported and how interested parties might use this information
- Describe how continuous quality improvement efforts influence the manner in which healthcare professionals practice
- Explain the positive and negative attributes of pay for performance
- Describe how technology would influence interdisciplinary care
- Identify quality measurements and organizations involved in collecting and disseminating this information

CHAPTER QUESTIONS

1. How it is that professions and occupations differ? Does health care constitute a special case of a profession?
2. What are the primary similarities shared between pharmacy and the other healthcare professions? Major differences?
3. How would you explain to a patient the benefits of interdisciplinary care over multidisciplinary care?
4. What are the challenges that pharmacists face when attempting to establish collaborative practice agreements with other healthcare providers?
5. How is it that a medical home will affect continuity of care?
6. What is healthcare quality to a patient, to a healthcare provider, and to a payer?
7. How might the technologies that are currently being developed change the landscape of pharmacy practice?

INTRODUCTION

Health care requires the interaction among many different providers of care and ancillary personnel. Pharmacists can and do play an important role in connecting these different providers; pharmacists also fulfill this role well because of the opportunity for interaction with the patient (e.g., the community pharmacist may see a patient as often as once per month or even more). Moreover, pharmacists have opportunities to influence the health and well-being of patients through the provision of patient-centered services (e.g., medication therapy management); however, these services rarely are provided without the pharmacist's direct interaction with other healthcare providers. As such, this chapter will present an overview about how pharmacists may work with different healthcare occupations while providing patient care. Moreover, information about many of the principle healthcare occupations with which pharmacy will interact will be presented. While this number potentially is great, the space available in the chapter is not, and as a result, the chapter will focus on the healthcare-related occupations with which pharmacy has the greatest interaction. The authors suggest that readers interested in other healthcare-related occupations visit the *Occupational Outlook Handbook* produced by the Bureau of Labor Statistics for an overview of these occupations (www.bls.gov) as well as an annual update on the healthcare occupations presented herein. The chapter will conclude with a discussion of a variety of issues affecting the pharmacy and the healthcare system currently and in the immediate future.

PROFESSIONS

While the term *professional* is used almost without thought, defining a professional in exacting terms can be quite difficult. In health care, do all providers deserve the title, "professional?" Over the years, various healthcare occupations have been considered just that—an occupation without professional status; pharmacy was one of those healthcare occupations. But exactly what are the characteristics that allow an occupation to be elevated to the level of a profession? Research as to what constitutes a profession has largely revolved around evaluating the qualities of recognized professions (e.g., law, medicine, and clergy) (Klass, 1961). While it was generally recognized that there was no one test for an occupation being a profession, occupations that were considered professions shared certain characteristics. These shared attributes have come to define which occupations society considers as professions.

While it is recognized generally that professions exist to serve society, merely providing services that the public needs and demands does not define a profession. The literature reveals five characteristics that are common to occupations considered professions; these include systematic theory and body of knowledge, professional authority and special privileges, community sanction and social utility, ethical codes and internal control, and professional culture and organizations (Buerki & Vottero, 1996). *Systematic theory and body of knowledge* is an important first distinction between the profession and the public whom it serves (Mrtek & Catizone, 1989). It results from the didactic education received in the various professional schools and continues throughout the life of the professional as he or she is required to maintain competence through continuing education. Members of professions are expected to have extensive theoretical knowledge and to use that knowledge (and the associated skill) when they provide service to society.

Professional authority and special privileges refer to the professional's ability to practice in his or her area of expertise as well as being afforded the opportunity to provide services to the public, services that the members of the public cannot presumably perform for themselves (Buerki & Vottero, 1996). The client surrenders a portion of his or her autonomy to the professional, because the client acknowledges the superior competence of the professional to do the job that the client cannot do. The client trusts the professional's judgment about which course of action will best meet the client needs.

It is believed that professions serve a socially necessary function (*social utility*) and provides a service that is of great importance to society. As such, the function of a profession is sanctioned (*community sanction*) by society in a number of different ways. The most widely recognized sanctioning is the system of licensure (Buerki & Vottero, 1996). Licenses for professions are granted by various professional boards, and these boards exist to protect society. That being said, most boards include members of society in addition to members of the profession. Another recognized community sanction is the restriction on the use of a professional title.

While society is beholden to the laws that govern the land, a profession has *ethical codes and internal control*. The professional accepts responsibility and is accountable through not only the law but also his or her profession. This is accomplished through formal and informal internal controls (e.g., codes of ethics). A profession accepts the responsibility to maintain a standard of conduct beyond the law. Despite the obvious importance of ethical codes and internal control to the value of a profession, the most difficult part about codes of ethics is enforcement. Thus the inclusion of a code of ethics as an attribute of a profession is probably the weakest part of attribute theory of professions. This is surprising somewhat given that the most effective technique for avoiding public (external) control over the profession is for the profession to maintain strong control over its members (Goode, 1957). Members of professions enjoy relative freedom from direct on-the-job supervision and from direct public scrutiny. However, when supervision does exist, the supervisor of a professional typically is a member of the same profession.

The *professional culture* is made up of values, norms, and symbols. Values are the central beliefs of a profession; the values of a profession usually include a belief in the importance and merit to society of the profession's unique expertise and a belief that the service cannot be better provided by another occupation. Another belief underlying the professions value system is the belief that the service provided is essential, in that society would suffer if the service was withdrawn. Values are the central beliefs of a profession, and norms are the accepted ways of social behavior within the profession. Symbols are often used to identify the calling of the profession. Symbols include a specific insignia, vocabulary, and dress (e.g., white lab coat).

Professions also rely upon a network of *organizations* that promote the profession and serve a number of other functions. These organizations may assist with licensure, provide continuing education, and promote a sense of collegiality. Professional organizations perform an important function for society, connecting members of the profession to one another and to other important groups, such as other professions, educational institutions, government bodies, and consumer groups. Without professional organizations, communication would be very difficult, if not impossible. Professional organizations are involved in activities that promote the interests of the profession.

Lastly, it is believed that a profession is required to render an individualized, unstandardized service directly to clients (Buerki & Vottero, 1996). Efforts made by the various healthcare professions to improve the quality of the services provided through standardization does not mean that healthcare providers do not meet this criterion. Many of the current efforts surrounding patient safety revolve around creating processes such that errors may be reduced or eliminated. This is a laudable goal; however, patients present with an almost infinite number of signs, symptoms, and personal characteristics that require that these processes be executed with the patient's best interest in mind. That best interest can only be determined by a thorough understanding of the patient's needs and wants and requires flexibility on the part of the provider to change as the patient's needs and/or wants change. The nature of health care makes the requirement of providing individualized and unstandardized service to clients seem logical; however, it may be said that healthcare providers sometimes fail to treat the patient as an individual.

Pharmacists

The profession of pharmacy has experienced a marked transformation over the past 50 years. Today's pharmacists complete more years of formal education and are much more likely to complete postgraduate training and as a result, have abilities that many do not realize and many would have never imagined would be possible. Pharmacy practice is evolving from a profession whose primary responsibility was supervising the distribution of medications to one where its members are providing medication therapy management services and advising patients on disease prevention and management (Paolini & Rouse, 2010). A complete discussion of the historical development of the profession of pharmacy as well as the current practice philosophies, roles, and responsibilities will be presented in detail in Chapter 3; however, an appreciation of the nature of collaborative relationships between healthcare providers must begin with a rudimentary understanding of the background and characteristics of one's own profession—in this case, pharmacy.

Educational Requirements

Pharmacy education has experienced many changes since its inception. Early pharmacy practitioners in the United States were trained as apprentices of experienced apothecaries. After a few years of service in these types of arrangements, the apprentice graduated and was able to practice pharmacy (Sonnedecker, 1976).

Formal university-granting education in the pharmaceutical sciences began in the late 19th century; however, at the time, no state required a pharmacy degree to practice pharmacy. In 1910, the state of New York began requiring a diploma from a recognized pharmacy school, and as a result, several states followed suit (Mrtek, 1976). At that time formal pharmacy education consisted of at least 2 years of university-based education resulting in a PhG degree (Higby, 1996). While most pharmacy schools provided the required 2 years of education, several more offered programs of 3 or even 4 years of length despite no legal or regulatory mandate to do so. A 3-year degree in pharmacy became the standard in 1925, the 4-year degree in 1932, and the 5-year degree in 1960 (Higby, 1996).

Today, a doctor of pharmacy (PharmD) is the minimum requirement for pharmacy licensure in all states. PharmD programs vary in length and structure among the various colleges/schools of pharmacy. While 2 years of preprofessional work is the minimum, some programs require 3 years of preprofessional education while others require a baccalaureate degree. Regardless of the length of the prepharmacy requirement, the final 4 years of education (or its equivalent) must be attained in a college/school of pharmacy (ACPE, 2006). Pharmacy education is a mix of didactic and experiential learning. Students spend the majority of their time in the earliest part of the curriculum in a classroom setting with some experiential learning interspersed. The later part of pharmacy curricula (typically the last year of the PharmD program) involves advanced pharmacy practice experiences exclusively. As of July 2010, there were 115 U.S.-based colleges and schools of pharmacy with accredited (full or candidate status) professional degree programs and an additional five schools with precandidate status (AACP, 2010).

To practice pharmacy in the United States, the District of Columbia, Guam, Puerto Rico or the U.S Virgin Islands, one must possess a pharmacy license. Pharmacy licensure is predicated on the successful completion of the North American Pharmacist Licensure Examination (NAPLEX). In order to sit for this exam, one must have graduated from an accredited college/school of pharmacy, or, in the case of graduates from foreign schools of pharmacy, achieve a suitable score on the Foreign Pharmacy Equivalency Examination (FPGEE) (NABP, 2010). In addition to the NAPLEX, new pharmacists must successfully complete the Multistate Pharmacy Jurisprudence Exam MPJE or a state-level equivalent law examination.

Postgraduate education and training (residencies and fellowships) are available for pharmacists. A pharmacy residency is defined as "an organized, directed, postgraduate training program in a defined area of pharmacy practice" (ASHP, 1987, p. 111) and lasts typically a minimum of 12 months. A fellowship "is a directed, highly individualized, postgraduate program designed to prepare the participant to become an independent researcher (ASHP, 1987, p. 111). While residencies are available in both the 1st and 2nd postgraduate years, a fellowship is usually sought by individuals with master's or doctoral degrees (ACCP, 2004). Additionally, it is desired that fellowship applicants have completed a residency or have equivalent clinical experience (ACCP, 2004; Kane-Gill, Reddy, Gupta, & Bakst, 2008). The match program associated with pharmacy residencies are handled primarily by the American Society of Health-System Pharmacists (ASHP). Postgraduate year 1 (PGY1) residencies are designed to enhance the general competencies of the resident in managing medication use, and as such it supports optimal medication therapy outcomes for patients (ASHP, 2010a). Residencies usually are housed in hospitals; however, the number of PGY1 residencies in other areas of pharmacy practice (e.g., community pharmacies, home care and long-term care facilities, ambulatory care settings, managed care facilities, and others) has increased significantly over the last decade. The number of pharmacists seeking PGY1 residencies has dramatically increased over the past few years (ASHP, 2009b; ASHP, 2010c). Postgraduate year 2 (PGY2) residencies are available for those who have completed a PGY1 residency and are available in ambulatory care, cardiology, critical care, drug information, emergency medicine, geriatrics, infectious diseases, informatics, internal medicine, managed care pharmacy systems, medication safety, nuclear medicine, nutrition support, oncology, pediatrics, pharmacotherapy, health-system pharmacy administration, psychiatry, and solid organ transplant (ASHP, 2010b).

Like medicine, there are varieties of specialties available for pharmacy practitioners; however, pharmacy is unique in that specialization is achieved after one is eligible to practice, not before. In pharmacy, practitioners have the ability to advance their abilities such that they can seek recognition of that training through specialization. The Board of Pharmacy Specialties (BPS) recognizes five areas of pharmacy specialization, which are nuclear pharmacy, pharmacotherapy, nutrition support pharmacy, psychiatric pharmacy, and oncology pharmacy. Beginning in 2011, the Board of Pharmacy Specialties will begin recognizing specialization in ambulatory care pharmacy (Board of Pharmacy Specialties, 2010).

Practice Environment

In spite of many advances in pharmacy practice, pharmacists continue to have the distribution of medications to patients as a primary responsibility. Along with this responsibility over distributive tasks, pharmacists serve as a valuable source of medication-related information for patients and healthcare providers. Pharmacists devote over half (55%) of their time to medication dispensing, 16% to patient care services, 14% to business/organization management, 5% to education, 4% to research, and 5% to other activities (Midwest Pharmacy Workforce Research Consortium, 2010). These proportions vary significantly based on practice setting. Pharmacists in community pharmacies can be expected to spend at least 70% of their time in dispensing-related activities. Hospital pharmacists and those reported to be engaged in other patient care roles can expect to spend less than half their time to medication dispensing. Both community and hospital pharmacists reported spending over one quarter (27%) of their time on direct patient-care activities on average (Midwest Pharmacy Workforce Research Consortium, 2010).

The number of licensed pharmacists has grown steadily over the last 10 years (**Figure 2-1**). In 2008, there were 269,900 licensed pharmacists in the United States (U.S. BLS, 2010b). Pharmacists are employed in a variety of settings including community-based practice as well as institutional-based practice. The proportion of actively practicing pharmacists working in traditional community pharmacy practice settings (independent, chain, mass merchandiser, and supermarket pharmacies) is largely unchanged (~ 54%) since 2000 (Midwest Pharmacy Workforce Research Consortium, 2010). Over three quarters (76.3%) of working pharmacists are reported to be working full-time (40 + hours per week) with an average of nearly 44 hours per week (43.8 hours) (Midwest Pharmacy Workforce Research Consortium, 2010). The rate of part-time employment among active pharmacists has increased since 2000. The proportion of pharmacists employed part time is almost 29.8% for females and 18.4% for males.

In 1990, just under one third of all practicing pharmacists were women. Currently, women represent almost half (46.4%) of the pharmacy practitioners in the United States. Minorities continue to be underrepresented in the pharmacy workforce. Census estimates in 2008 indicated that 25% of the U.S. population identified with a racial minority group; however, only 18% of pharmacists are reported to be a member of a racial minority group (HRSA Bureau of Health Professions, 2008a). This difference is even more dramatic when one considers Hispanic or Latino population. While the U.S. population is over 15% Hispanic or Latino, only 3.2% of the U.S. pharmacist population is Hispanic or Latino (HRSA, 2008a).

The supply of pharmacists is expected to be adequate to meet the demand for the foreseeable future. Despite an expected increase in demand for pharmaceuticals due in

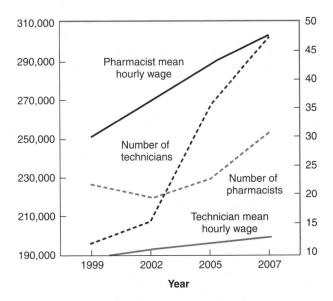

Figure 2-1 Pharmacy Staff and Mean Hourly Wage. *Source*: National Center for Health Statistics. (2010). *Health, United States, 2009: With special feature on medical technology.* Hyattsville, MD: National Center for Health Statistics.

part to growth in the elderly population and increases in science such that new thera-pies are available, it is expected that the pharmacist supply will be able to keep pace due to new schools of pharmacy and increasing enrollments (HRSA, 2008a).

Pharmacy Technicians

The presence of pharmacy technicians is commonplace in institutional and retail pharmacy settings. In fact, as pharmacy continues its progress toward more involve-ment in direct patient care, pharmacy technicians will play an important role by free-ing the pharmacist from some of his or her distributive tasks in favor of contemporary pharmacy practice roles (ASHP, 2003). The modern-day pharmacy technician in the United States grew out of the efforts of the U.S. Army to develop pharmacy specialists who could assist pharmacists with the preparation and distribution of medications to soldiers (Council on Credentialing in Pharmacy, 2003). The focus on pharmacy techni-cians increased in the late 1960s partly due to a call by the federal government for the development of a pharmacist aide curriculum in junior colleges and other educational institutions (Council on Credentialing in Pharmacy, 2003). Today, a pharmacy tech-nician is defined as "an individual working in a pharmacy [setting] who, under the supervision of a licensed pharmacist, assists in pharmacy activities that do not require the professional judgment of a pharmacist" (Pharmacy Technician Certification Board, 2010b).

Educational Requirements

State level requirements for pharmacy technicians vary greatly. Some states have estab-lished age minimums, as well as educational minimums, such as a high school diploma or its equivalent (U.S. BLS, 2010c), while others have instituted training requirements for pharmacy technicians. Currently, 39 states regulate pharmacy technicians in some manner (certification, licensure, or registration) (Council on Credentialing in Phar-macy, 2009). Of the 50 states, the District of Columbia, Puerto Rico, and Guam, 34 government bodies have established technician training requirements (NABP, 2009a); however, it is generally recognized that there is little uniformity among states regarding pharmacy technician education and training requirements (NABP, 2009c). In addition to initial training and education, some states (17) are requiring pharmacy technicians earn continuing education credits (NABP, 2009a). This requirement varies greatly in number of hours and to whom the requirement applies. For example, one state only requires continuing education credits be earned by its certified technicians. While it may be true that some states do not require technician training, it is not appropriate to conclude that pharmacy technicians in these states do not seek or receive training; it is common that pharmacy technicians receive on-the-job training (U.S. BLS, 2010c).

National certification examinations are available from the Pharmacy Technician Certi-fication Board and the Institute for the Certification of Pharmacy Technicians. Each of these bodies requires that candidates have a high school diploma or equivalent and no felony convictions or previous revocation of state certification or licensure (pharmacy or from another healthcare board). The certification examinations cover a broad range of topics related to aspects of pharmacy technician practice. For example, the Phar-macy Technician Certification Examination covers assisting the pharmacist in serv-ing patients (two thirds of the exam), maintaining medication and inventory control systems (22% of exam), and participating in the administration and management of pharmacy practice (12% of exam) (PTCB, 2010a).

Practice Environment

The number of pharmacy technicians has increased dramatically since 1999 (Figure 2-1). It is estimated that in 2008, there were 326,300 active pharmacy technicians (U.S. BLS, 2010c). Pharmacy technicians work in a variety of settings (e.g., community pharmacies, hospitals, branches of the military, mail order pharmacies); however, most (more than 75%) are employed by retail pharmacies (U.S. BLS, 2010c).

Pharmacy technicians assist pharmacists in the preparation of prescription medications (e.g., computer entry, counting medications, and labeling prescription bottles), assisting customers, and performing administrative duties within the pharmacy (e.g., record keeping, insurance claims, and prescription inventory control). Activities that explicitly would be prohibited include at a minimum, drug regimen review, clinical conflict resolution, prescriber contact concerning prescription drug order clarification or therapy modification, patient counseling, dispensing process validation, prescription transfer, and the receipt of new prescription drug orders (NABP, 2009b).

While there exists a general understanding of the nature and scope of pharmacy technician practice, the specific duties that are able to be performed by pharmacy technicians vary by state and practice setting (e.g., retail versus institutional practice) (NABP, 2009a). Each of the aforementioned duties of the pharmacy technician is performed under the direct supervision of a licensed pharmacist.

Physicians

Physicians have been the professional exemplar in health care. Physicians are concerned primarily with maintaining or restoring the health of their patients through the diagnosis and treatment of disease or injury. For pharmacy, the physician holds an important position. The physician is the healthcare provider who prescribes the most and as such, creates a great deal of demand for pharmacy products and services.

Educational Requirements

Prior to the start of the 20th century, physician education was varied. The earliest medical practitioners in what would become the United States attended informal classes and demonstrations (primarily anatomy) (Flexner, 1910). Formal medical education began in 1765, when it was proposed that a professorship in the theory and practice of medicine be established at the College of Philadelphia (Flexner, 1910). This early education focused on didactic training; however, the realization that medical education required practicum came very quickly. In fact, the earliest formal medical education resembles modern-day medical education, namely a combination of didactic and experiential learning. Over the course of some 150 years, medical education had evolved such that physicians were being trained in one of three ways, an apprenticeship system, a proprietary schools system, or a university system (Beck, 2004). As a result, many of the turn-of-the-20th-century physicians were ill equipped to provide patient care.

A major turning point in medical education in the United States was the publication of the Flexner report. In 1908, at the request of the American Medical Association (AMA), a survey of medical education was undertaken; the result of this effort was the Flexner report. The report served as a major indictment of the so-called proprietary schools. Flexner, like the AMA, believed that these schools operated more for profit than for education. The report found that these schools had loose admission standards, inadequate faculty, insufficient laboratory experiences, and poor apprenticeship programs. This report made recommendations that included minimum educational standards for admission to medical schools, a minimum length of medical school education of 4 years, and the closure (or combination with universities) of the proprietary medical schools that existed at the time (Flexner, 1910).

As a result, many medical schools closed their doors, and those that remained changed such that they met these new standards. It is interesting to find that many aspects of the present-day American medical profession and its educational processes are a direct result of the publication of the Flexner report. Today, medical education in the United States is a postbaccalaureate program that begins with 2 years of didactic study (M1 & M2) in the sciences (experiential learning is present to a lesser degree in the first 2 years of medical education) in an accredited medical school (preclinical education). During this didactic phase, it is expected that medical students will complete courses in anatomy, biochemistry, genetics, immunology, microbiology, pathology, pharmacology, physiology, and public health sciences (Liaison Committee on Medical Education, 2010). Following their didactic education, medical students (M3 & M4) begin their clerkship training. Clerkship training during these clinical years of education includes required rotations (e.g., internal medicine, surgery, pediatrics, psychiatry, obstetrics and gynecology, family medicine, and neurology) and elective rotations. With few exceptions, these 4 years of medical school are the same for all physicians. In 2010, there were 133 accredited, medical doctorate- (MD-) granting medical schools in the United States (AAMC, 2010).

An alternative educational opportunity for those interested in practicing medicine is the doctor of osteopathic medicine (DO) degree. In the United States, osteopathic medical schools have curricula that are very similar to allopathic (MD-granting) medical schools. Unlike allopathic medical schools, osteopathic medical education emphasizes hands-on diagnosis and treatment through a system of therapy known as osteopathic manipulative medicine (AACOM, 2010b, AACOM, 2010c). Additionally, advocates of osteopathic medicine point to a focus on health promotion and disease prevention in their curricula, although this is also part of allopathic medical education as well. Currently, there are 26 osteopathic medical schools in the United States (AACOM, 2010a).

Regardless of one's type of medical degree, medical licensure in the United States involves a three-step examination process (NBOME, 2010, USMLE, 2010). Medical students and graduates complete the United States Medical Licensing Examination and student and graduates of osteopathic medicine schools complete the Comprehensive Osteopathic Medical Licensing Examination. The step 1 (level 1) examination is taken typically during the second year of medical school. It assesses a student's understanding of and ability to apply scientific concepts to the practice of medicine. Specifically, areas covered on the exam include anatomy, behavioral sciences, biochemistry, microbiology, pathology, pharmacology, and physiology. The Comprehensive Osteopathic Medical Licensing Examination also includes osteopathic principles. Step 2 (level 2) exams are divided into two parts. The first part of the exam assesses clinical knowledge while the second part of the exam assesses clinical skill. The clinical knowledge examination assesses internal medicine, obstetrics and gynecology, pediatrics, preventive medicine, psychiatry, and surgery. The examination also includes emergency medicine, family medicine, and osteopathic principles. Interestingly, the assessment of clinical skills is accomplished through the use of standardized patients. Because of this fact, sites for the clinical skills exams are limited; there are five for the United States Medical Licensing Examination and one for the Comprehensive Osteopathic Medical Licensing Examination. The step 3 (level 3) exam is taken typically at the end of the first year of residency and is designed to assess a graduate's (resident's) suitability for unsupervised medical practice.

While some states allow medical school graduates to become fully licensed after a 1-year postgraduate internship, most seek a residency. A residency is a stage of graduate medical training that allows the resident to practice medicine for a prescribed period of time under the supervision of fully licensed physicians. Most residencies require 3 years of training (surgery is 5 years) (AMA, 2010a). Residents may enter a residency following the completion of an internship, or the internship might be incorporated into the residency program. Fellowship positions in subspecialties are available for physicians having already completed a residency. Medical students begin the process of deciding their futures during the M4 year. In addition to selecting their preferred sites for residency, medical students are selecting their preference for specialization. The process for selecting medical residencies is similar to that for pharmacy residencies; the student will list his or her preferred sites, and the residency sites will rank their preference for students (along with the number of residents they can house). If the process works as it is intended, students will be placed in residencies where they were a desired candidate. This process is referred to as matching. The National Resident Matching Program handles this process for residencies and fellowships.

Medical specialty certification in the United States is a voluntary process. While medical licensure continues to be the minimum requirement to be a physician in the United States, the licensure examination is not specialty specific. Board certification signifies that a physician possesses expertise in a specialty and/or subspecialty of medical practice. The American Board of Medical Specialties is the umbrella organization of 24 member boards that offer certification in more than 145 specialties and subspecialties (ABMS, 2010). In addition to the American Board of Medical Specialties, the American Board of Physician Specialties oversees 12 medical specialty boards of certification representing 18 medical specialties (ABPS, 2010). The American Osteopathic Association Bureau of Osteopathic Specialists offers certification in any of 18 specialty areas to doctors of osteopathic medicine (AOA, 2010).

Continuing medical education is required by 62 medical boards (AMA, 2010b). The number of hours needed varies by state and in some states varies by degree type (MD vs. DO) with the majority requiring between 20 and 50 hours per year (AMA, 2010b). Additionally, some states require specific continuing medical education content each license cycle (e.g., error prevention, infection control) while some states accept certificates/awards (e.g., those from the American Osteopathic Association and the American Board of Medical Specialties) as documentation of continued competence (AMA, 2010b).

Practice Environment

There has been a steady increase over the years in the number of physicians practicing in the United States (**Figure 2-2**).

Despite this increase, there continue to be fears that the rate of increase has not kept pace with the rate of increase in the U.S. population. Additionally, there are concerns

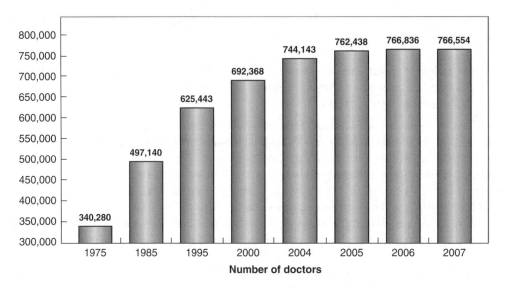

Figure 2-2 Active Doctors of Medicine. *Source*: National Center for Health Statistics. (2010). *Health, United States, 2009: With special feature on medical technology.* Hyattsville, MD: National Center for Health Statistics.

that as baby boomers begin to populate the ranks of the elderly, we may experience an even greater shortage (hyperdemand) of physicians; this increased demand is estimated to be 22% by 2020 over 2005 demand (HRSA, 2008b). This concern applies especially to primary care (**Figure 2-3**). While the number of primary care providers has increased dramatically, the largest increases in primary care providers was seen in

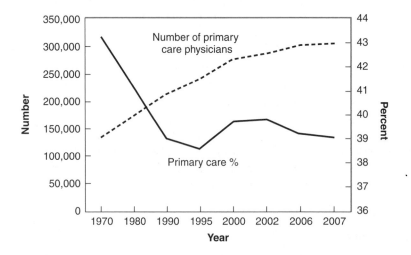

Figure 2-3 Doctors of Medicine in General Primary Care. *Source*: National Center for Health Statistics. (2010). *Health, United States, 2009: With special feature on medical technology.* Hyattsville, MD: National Center for Health Statistics.

nurse practitioners and physician assistants. The increase in the number of physicians in primary care is the result of foreign medical graduates (GAO, 2008). Specialists and subspecialists can and do provide primary care to their patients; however, the trend toward more specialists and less primary care does have implications for the future of the practice of pharmacy. As a result of increased demand for primary care, pharmacists may have an increased role in meeting the needs of patients by fulfilling their responsibilities to provide patient-centered care and, in states where it is allowed, through their expanded responsibilities in collaborative drug therapy management (ASHP, 1999).

Representation of females among the physician ranks continues to increase. In 1990, women represented only 16.9% of the physician workforce; in 2006, women accounted for 27.8% of the total physician population (AMA, 2008). Census estimates in 2006 indicated that just under 25% of the U.S. population identified with a racial minority group; however, just over 20% of physicians are reported to be a member of a racial minority group (AMA, 2008). Of that 20%, 3.5% reported being black, 5.0% Hispanic or Latino, and 12% Asian (AMA, 2008).

Nurses

Nursing represents the largest of all of the healthcare occupations. According to the American Nursing Association, nursing is "the protection, promotion, and optimization of health and abilities, prevention of illness and injury, alleviation of suffering through the diagnosis and treatment of human response, and advocacy in the care of individuals, families, communities, and populations" (American Nurses Association, 2010). As this definition would imply, currently, there are many different types of nurses. The two different entry-level types of nurses are the registered nurse (RN) and licensed vocational/practical nurse (LPN). The RN is the more advanced of the two nursing designations owing to the requirements for more education. As a result, the scope of practice for the RN is broader than that for the LPN. Oftentimes, the LPN works under the supervision of a registered nurse. In addition to the LPN and RN, nurses have the opportunities for advanced practice roles. The nurse practitioner, clinical nurse specialist, certified registered nurse anesthetist, and certified nurse midwife are all designations used by advanced practice nurses (APNs). These practitioners have prescriptive authority in most jurisdictions, and in some jurisdictions, APNs may practice independently without physician collaboration or supervision.

Educational Requirements

The educational requirements for the RN and LPN differ in scope and length. Becoming an LPN usually requires 1 year of study resulting in the issue of a diploma or certificate. The requisite education for registered nurses is as diverse as the career opportunities in nursing. There are three recognized educational pathways for those interested in being registered nurses; these are a bachelor's degree, an associate's degree, or a diploma from an approved nursing program. Nurses most commonly enter the occupation by completing an associate degree or bachelor's degree program. Prior to entering practice, graduate nurses must successfully complete the National Council Licensure Examination (NCLEX). The NCLEX is recognized by boards of nursing in all 50 states and U.S. territories. The NCLEX is divided into two separate exams; the NCLEX-RN is for registered nurses and the NCLEX-PN for vocational/practical nurses. While there are different examinations for registered nurses and for vocational/practical nurses, there is not a separate NCLEX-RN examination or passing standard for associate degree, baccalaureate degree, or diploma nursing school graduates (NCSBN, 2010). Similar to other health professions, nurses have the opportunities to specialize in any of a number of areas of nursing practice. Certification programs are available for RNs in over 20 different areas, such as ambulatory care nursing, general nursing practice, pediatric nursing, and psychiatric and mental health nursing (ANCC, 2010).

Advanced practice nurse (APN) designations require additional education above and beyond that required for licensure as an RN. APNs have at least 2 years of graduate education (e.g., master's degree); however, a new standard for qualification as an APN, that of a doctor of nursing practice, is expected to be in place by 2015 (AACN, 2006). The doctor of nursing practice is an advanced-level practice degree that focuses on the clinical aspects of nursing rather than academic research (contrast PhD in nursing). Currently, there is no indication that the move to the degree will result in an expanded practice role for advanced practice nurses. Advanced practice nurses are licensed through their respective state boards of nursing separate from RNs and LPNs. In addition to being licensed as RNs, APNs are required in some states to submit evidence of advanced education as well as evidence of certification through organizations such as the American Nurses Credentialing Center, the American Academy of Nurse Practitioners, or others (NCSBN, 2009).

The requirements for evidence of continued competence differs across states and across nurse type. Currently, 75% of states and jurisdictions require continuing competence for nurses (NCSBN, 2009). The continued competence requirements include but are not limited to continuing education, minimal practice, peer review, refresher courses, continued competency assessment, and competency examinations. Currently all states require some type of continued competence for APNs. The requirements vary by state and by APN designation but can include recertification, continuing education beyond that required for RN licensure, practice requirements, and pharmacology course work (NCSBN, 2009).

Practice Environment

There were more than 750,000 LPNs in the United Stated in 2008 (U.S. BLS, 2010a). LPNs work nights, weekends, and holidays depending on the setting in which they are employed. LPNs often assist patients with activities of daily living. As such, LPNs are often employed by nursing homes, home health care, and hospice, as well as office-based practices of physicians and hospitals. The roles that LPNs can fulfill vary by state. In 2008, there were estimated to be over 3 million licensed registered nurses in the United States (HRSA Bureau of Health Professions, 2010; U.S. BLS, 2010e). The percentage of RNs whose initial nursing education was an associate's degree was 45.4, that of a baccalaureate degree was 34.2, and a diploma in nursing, 20.4. Nurses with advanced degrees comprised 13.2% of all licensed RNs (HRSA, 2010). The majority of nurses (62.2%) work in the hospital setting (HRSA, 2010). Other notable employment opportunities for registered nurses exist within ambulatory care (10.5%) and public health (7.8%). Currently, minorities are underrepresented in the nursing population. Approximately 17% of registered nurses are reported to be a member of a minority group. While Asians are slightly overrepresented, blacks, Hispanics, and American Indians/Alaska Natives are underrepresented in comparison to population statistics.

Nursing continues to be a female-dominated profession, with only 6% of RNs reported to be male. APNs work in a variety of healthcare settings. The level of practice independence and prescriptive authority differs by state (independent practice, collaborative agreements/protocols, or practice under physician supervision) and APN designation (e.g., nurse practitioner, clinical nurse specialist, certified nurse midwife, and certified nurse anesthetist) (NCSBN, 2009).

Physician Assistants

Physician assistants' (PA) role in the health system is unique in that these providers practice medicine in a team environment under the direction of a physician. As part of their comprehensive responsibilities, PAs conduct physical exams, diagnose and treat illnesses, order and interpret tests, counsel on preventive health care, assist in surgery, and prescribe medications (AAPA, 2010a). However, the specific duties of physician assistants are determined by the supervising physician and by state law (U.S. BLS, 2010d).

Educational Requirements

Physician assistant programs began in the 1960s as an effort to address the need for assistants for physicians who would work only with physician supervision. The first program devoted to the education of physician assistants was located at the Duke University School of Medicine (Jones, 2007). As other programs have developed, each has adhered to the basic tenets that a PA would not have independent authority and the curriculum would be competency based (Jones, 2007). Today, physician assistants are educated in programs that are accredited by the Accreditation Review Commission on Education for the Physician Assistant. These programs are housed in community colleges as well as 4-year colleges and universities (Jones, 2007). Regardless of its location, the PA curriculum averages 26 months. Physician assistants are trained to diagnose and treat medical problems. As such, the PA curriculum consists of didactic instruction in the basic medical and behavioral sciences as well as experiential learning. Clinical rotations are used in the later portions of PA education. Currently, there are 149 accredited physician assistant programs in the United States (AAPA, 2010b). Like many other healthcare workers, PAs are required to complete continuing medical education (100 hours every 2 years). Additionally, PAs are retested on their clinical skills on a regular basis (every 6 years) (NCCPA, 2010).

Practice Environment

In 2008, there were almost 75,000 PAs in the United States (U.S. BLS, 2010d). The greatest percentage of PAs report being employed in a group medical practice (44.2%). Almost one quarter of all clinically practicing PAs are employed in hospitals, and 11.6% in solo physician practices. The majority of PAs (65%) are female and a predominant percentage (88.9%) are white. Minorities are underrepresented among the ranks of physician assistants with 3.9% Asian, 2.9% black, 3.6% Hispanic/Latino, and 0.6% American Indian/Alaska Native.

Other Allied Health Professionals

Table 2-1 provides a list of additional healthcare professionals pharmacists may interact with in their patient care activities.

Table 2-1 Other Allied Health Professionals

Occupation	Education	Degree(s)	Roles
Optometrists	7–9 yrs	OD	Optometrists are the primary providers of vision care. They examine eyes to diagnose vision problems, and prescribe eyeglasses and contact lenses. They diagnose diseases of the eye (e.g., glaucoma) and may have limited prescriptive authority.
Social workers	4–6 yrs	BSW, MSW	Social workers assist people by helping them cope with and solve issues in their everyday lives, such as family and personal problems and dealing with relationships. Some social workers help clients who face a disability, life-threatening disease, or a social problem, such as inadequate housing, unemployment, or substance abuse. Social workers also assist families that have serious domestic conflicts, sometimes involving child or spousal abuse.
Podiatrists	9 yrs	DPM	Podiatrists diagnose and treat disorders, diseases, and injuries of the foot and lower leg. They may prescribe medications, perform physical therapy, fit orthotics, set fractures, and perform surgery.
Dentists	6–10 yrs	DDS, DMD	Dentists diagnose and treat problems with teeth and tissues in the mouth. They may prescribe medications, perform surgery, and extract teeth.
Psychologists	6+ yrs	Specialist, MS, PhD, PsyD	Psychologists assess, diagnose, treat, and prevent mental disorders. They advise people on how to deal with problems of everyday living, including problems in the home, place of work, or community, to help improve their quality of life.
Dieticians/ nutritionists	4 yrs	BS, MS	Dietitians and nutritionists plan food and nutrition programs, supervise meal preparation, and oversee the serving of meals. Illness prevention activities occur by promoting healthy eating habits and recommending dietary modifications.
Occupational therapists	4–6 yrs	MS	Occupational therapists help patients improve their ability to perform tasks in living and working environments. They work with individuals who suffer from a mentally, physically, developmentally, or emotionally disabling condition. The goal is to help clients have independent, productive, and satisfying lives.

(continues)

Table 2-1 Other Allied Health Professionals *(continued)*

Occupation	Education	Degree(s)	Roles
Recreational therapists	4 years	BS	Recreational therapists provide activities (arts and crafts, interaction with animals, sports, games, dance and movement, drama, music, and community outings) for individuals with disabilities or illnesses to improve and maintain their physical, mental, and emotional well-being.
Physical therapists	4+ yrs	MS, DPT	Physical therapists work with patients who have limitations in their ability to move and perform functional activities. They examine patients and develop a plan using treatment techniques designed to promote the ability to move, reduce pain, restore function, and prevent disability.

Source: Data from U.S. Bureau of Labor Statistics. (2010). *Occupational Outlook Handbook* (2010–2011 ed.). Retrieved from http://www.bls.gov/oco/

COLLABORATION WITH HEALTHCARE PROVIDERS

The primary role of the pharmacist is largely focused around medication consumption (e.g., to screen for contraindications and drug–drug interactions, to serve as the physician's resource for information about medical therapies, and to provide patient education about medications) (Peterson, Albert, Amin, Patterson, & Fonarow, 2008). For high-risk disease states, pharmacists can play an ever more important role as a part of the medication management team. For example, the inclusion of a pharmacist on the multidisciplinary cardiovascular team was found to decrease medication-related errors dramatically. One research study demonstrated that when a pharmacist rounded with the intensive care unit team, there was a 66% decrease in the rate of preventable adverse drug events (Leape et al., 1999). The role of a pharmacist on a team was further cemented when LaPointe and Jollis (2003) found that over a 5-year period, a clinical pharmacist on the cardiology ward identified and corrected a significant number of medication errors (24 errors per 100 admissions). This same study also found the most common point of error occurred in the transition from the outpatient to the inpatient setting, underlining the importance for continuity of care and communication between practitioners within different organizations. Furthermore, pharmacy-led interventions have been shown to improve medication compliance in hospitalized, heart failure and postmyocardial infarction patients (Bouvy et al., 2003). Reductions in all-cause hospitalizations and medical costs as well as improved survival rates have been observed when a multidisciplinary team is engaged in patient care (Peterson, Albert, Amin, Patterson, & Fonarow, 2008).

In today's healthcare environment, there exists a call to increase both the safety and quality of services provided; this call expressly includes medication therapy. The complexity of the healthcare system makes it very difficult for one provider to be all things to all patients; in fact, many of the discussions surrounding patient safety and healthcare quality specifically mention the use of teams of healthcare providers (IOM, 1990).

In order for a pharmacist to effectively participate as a team member, he or she needs to have a fundamental understanding of his or her healthcare colleagues as well as the nuances of collaborating with other healthcare providers.

Interdisciplinary Care Versus Multidisciplinary Care

The various healthcare professionals bring much expertise to the service of the patient. However, an important distinction must be made between the types of relationships that may exist between the different healthcare providers, such as between multidisciplinary care and interdisciplinary care. *Multidisciplinary care* refers to many different professionals working for the good of the patient, albeit somewhat independently. The typical model of health care in the United States is replete with examples of multidisciplinary care. For example, a patient visiting a physician's office for an illness will likely interact with a nurse who may collect information about the patient's condition, a physician who may diagnose disease and prescribe a treatment, and after a trip to the pharmacy, a pharmacist who will dispense the medication and educate the patient on its appropriate use. While this model of care is generally recognized to lead to an improvement in outcomes, it does not take full advantage of the talents of the healthcare system. It is, at worst, a sum of the inputs from the various healthcare professionals. *Interdisciplinary care* means that the many different professionals working together for the patient's good also communicate effectively among themselves and with the patient. Teams with greater cohesiveness are associated with better clinical outcome measures and higher patient satisfaction (Grumbach & Bodenheimer, 2004).

While the importance of collaboration should not be underestimated, neither should the challenges that one faces when trying to establish collaborative relationships. Common barriers to the establishment of collaborative working relationships include boundary concerns, poor communication, power concerns, lack of trust of the other party, and poor proximity. The collaborative working relationship model (McDonough & Doucette, 2001) describes the process by which pharmacists can establish effective and productive working relationships (**Figure 2-4**). This stage model posits that pharmacists' and physicians' relationships mature as the trust, shared decision making, and interdependence between the two providers develops.

Stage 0, *professional awareness,* would best be described as the traditional pharmacist–physician working relationship. At this stage, exchanges between the pharmacist and physician are discrete and minimal. For example, a stage 0 relationship would be characterized by the pharmacist seeking refill authorization, alerting the physician to a potential or actual drug-related problem (e.g., drug–drug interaction), or discussing some other pharmacotherapy-related issue that revealed itself during dispensing. According to the model, these interactions are short in duration with no attempt to change the existing relationship. Moreover, stage 0 interactions "are considered professionally safe, routine, and defined by well-established expectations" (Brock & Doucette, 2004, p. 359).

Stage 1, *professional recognition,* involves exclusively the pharmacist's effort to establish a relationship with the physician. In stage 1, the pharmacist informs the physician of the services that the pharmacist can provide. This is an important step in the establishment of the collaborative relationship because the pharmacist's role definitions and role boundaries have been established by past experiences that the physician has had with pharmacists, including the one attempting to establish a collaborative working relationship (stage 0). The goal of this state in the model would be trust. Pharma-

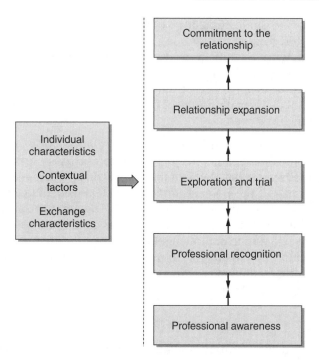

Figure 2-4 Model of Pharmacist Collaborative Working Relationships. *Source*: Brock, K. A., & Doucette, W. R. (2004). Collaborative working relationships between pharmacists and physicians: An exploratory study. *Journal of the American Pharmaceutical Association, 44*(3), 358–365.

cists are working to enhance their own attractiveness or usefulness to the physician during stage 1 interactions (Brock & Doucette, 2004).

Stage 2, *exploration and trial,* requires some low level of commitment on the part of the physician above and beyond what has been demonstrated in the first two stages; however, the pharmacist remains the primary initiator of interaction. The trial may involve the physician referring a patient or a few patients so that he or she can assess the pharmacist's ability to deliver both the quantity of services as well as the quality of the services as promised and the risks and benefits associated with being involved in the collaborative relationship.

Stage 3, *professional relationship expansion,* is the natural progression of activities undertaken in stages 1 and 2. In stage 3, the pharmacist can expect that the physician initiates the exchange; however the pharmacist can expect that the exchange efforts remain unbalanced (the pharmacist still has more responsibility as an initiator). The content of pharmacist-initiated communication continues to center on the benefits derived from the pharmacist's services as well as seeking feedback on past performance. This give-and-take exchange represents some level of commitment on the part of the physician toward the collaborative relationship; however, the pharmacist can and should expect that professional conflict will occur in this fine-tuning of the relationship.

Stage 4, *commitment to a collaborative working relationship,* is achieved when the physician is convinced that the benefits of the collaborative relationship outweigh any risks. For commitment in a relationship to exist, at the very least, the relationship needs to be relatively lengthy, consistent, and should involve a high level of input from all parties (Brock & Doucette, 2004). Commitment is most likely to be reached if there is equity in effort toward maintaining the relationship. Additionally, once commitment is achieved, work remains to be done. Failure to attend to the relationship by both parties may lead to its demise. In other words, a collaborative working relationship is a relationship in every sense of the word. Unlike earlier stages of the model, the pharmacist cannot be the sole source of relationship effort; the physician must also attend to the relationship's needs.

The success of efforts or the rapidity with which relationships are established will depend on the individuals involved. Factors found to positively influence the development of the pharmacist–physician collaboration were trustworthiness, role specification, relationship initiation, and professional interactions (Doucette, Nevins, & McDonough, 2005; Zillich, McDonough, Carter, & Doucette, 2004). As such, pharmacists must provide services that are valued by the physician and deliver on all promises made. Moreover, both parties must recognize the complementary roles of the pharmacist and physician that may result in interdependence. Lastly, frequent and meaningful interactions are important to sustain the collaborative working relationship. If the pharmacist is out of sight (or out of touch), he or she is out of mind, and there is no collaboration.

Continuity of Care

Consistent with the ideals of interdisciplinary care and collaborative work relationships is continuity of care. The days are long gone when one doctor, with the help of a nurse, provided all the health care a person needed. Now, it is not uncommon for patients to see several healthcare practitioners. They may receive care from doctors, nurses, nurse practitioners, physician assistants, pharmacists, dietitians, physical or occupational therapists, social workers, and nurse's aides. They may have several doctors, each specializing in one organ system or disease. To complicate matters, as people age they are also likely to move from one place of care to another. They may receive care in a doctor's office, hospital, rehabilitation facility, board-and-care facility, an assisted living facility, nursing home, or at home. At the end of life, they may receive hospice care. Ideally, all people involved in a person's health care, including the person receiving care, communicate and work with each other to coordinate the health care. Additionally, all interested parties (at least patient and providers) should agree on and understand the goals for health care. Then, changes in practitioners and places of care could occur smoothly, lessening the impact of care disruption. Two core concepts or aspirations of continuity are revealed by the preceding definitions. First, continuity is about the care of a single patient. As such, continuity is *not* an attribute of providers or organizations (Haggerty et al., 2003). The second element is that care is provided over time. When taken together these core elements represent a continuous care relationship, a laudable goal in health care.

Whether continuity of care represents a process or outcome remains unsettled (Christakis, 2003). Perhaps it is both, a means to an end and an end itself that can then be used similar to other intermediate outcomes in determining quality of care. However, regardless of the type of study, three types of continuity are recognized: (1) informational continuity, (2) management continuity, and (3) relational continuity. Informational continuity is considered by some to be the *sine qua non* in continuity of care; "it is the common thread linking care from one provider to another and from one healthcare event to another" (Haggerty et al., 2003, p. 1220). Information tends to center on the medical condition (disease focused), but also can include information about the patient's values and preferences (patient focused). It is believed that the importance of patient preferences increases across separate care events.

Management continuity is the consistent and coherent approach to the management of a health condition that is responsive to a patient's changing needs (Haggerty et al., 2003). In other words, it is the need for an established plan of care that meets the needs of the patient. This is believed to be particularly important in instances when a patient's case is complex or the patient suffers from chronic disease (Haggerty et al., 2003). Management continuity is achieved when care is provided in a complementary and timely manner. The use of protocols and shared management plans are evidence of management continuity of care and provide comfort to both provider and patient (Haggerty et al., 2003).

Relational continuity is also referred to as interpersonal continuity. Relational continuity represents an ongoing therapeutic relationship between a patient and one or more providers. This personal relationship between the patient and clinician is characterized by personal trust and responsibility (Saultz, 2003). As one can imagine, interpersonal continuity is believed to foster improved communication, trust, and a sustained sense of responsibility, and is associated with higher levels of satisfaction with care (Saultz & Albedaiwi, 2004). It is important to understand that strong interpersonal continuity of care is associated with improved use of preventative services, reduced hospitalizations, and lower costs of care (Saultz & Lochner, 2005).

THE MEDICAL HOME

One of the models of care currently receiving the focus of policy makers and practitioners is the medical home. Reflecting the concepts of interdisciplinary care, collaborative work relationships, and continuity of care, the medical home refers to a partnership approach in the provision of primary health care that is accessible, family centered, coordinated, comprehensive, continuous, compassionate, and culturally effective (Sia, Tonniges, Osterhus, & Taba, 2004). A medical home is patient-centered primary health care implemented to improve the patient's health across a continuum of referrals and services (Sia, Tonniges, Osterhus, & Taba, 2004). It is based on a relationship between the patient and physician, formed to improve the patient's health via open communication within a team care framework. The primary focus is to have one central clearinghouse in which all patient medication records are kept up to date, embracing the idea for shared information among healthcare professionals and thus facilitating continuity of care.

Whereas the term was used originally to describe a place—a single source of all medical information about a patient—and introduced in 1967 by the American Academy of Pediatrics, it is now a concept adopted by the numerous medical associations because it is associated with improved quality, reduced errors, and increased satisfaction (Rosenthal, 2008). Medical homes have been linked with better health, lower overall costs of care, and reductions in disparities in health. Primary care organizations, including the American Board of Family Medicine, have promoted the concept as an answer to government agencies seeking political solutions for making quality health care affordable and accessible to all Americans (Sia, Tonniges, Osterhus, & Taba, 2004).

Pharmacists can have a role in the patient-centered medical home model because it is another model requiring a team-based approach to patient care. While most conceptualizations of the medical home recognize the physician only as the primary healthcare provider, it is evident that this initiative requires a multidisciplinary approach from the entire healthcare team, including nurses, pharmacists, physicians, therapists, and other health professionals. Pharmacists should and can have a role in medication therapy management in the medical home model, as well as open shared communication with physicians. Pharmacists have been typically underused in this role, yet have great potential to demonstrate professional expertise in this model of care.

Demonstration projects have documented the value of having pharmacists as care team members by their involvement in clinical decision making, such as medication evaluations to assess medication-related problems or the failure to achieve desirable outcomes (Smith et al., 2010). Pharmacists can play important roles in optimizing therapeutic outcomes and promoting safe, cost-effective medication use for patients in medical homes, especially patients with chronic conditions (Smith et al., 2010). Barriers to medical home implementation are similar to any other model that requires change in behavior. This involves developing relationships with other professionals who are willing to work collaboratively, communicating expectations with team members, finding a patient population interested in utilizing a medical home concept, and changing reimbursement and payment policies such that it will incentivize providers to adopt a change in practice.

While the healthcare practitioners who affect the role of the pharmacist will be varied, one consistency remains the responsibility to evaluate the manner in which care is delivered and to change what is necessary to provide improved outcomes for patients. The impetus for team-based approaches to care has often been less than desired/expected outcomes associated with care. As such, it is important to understand the concept of quality in health care and the measures that interested parties use to identify quality.

DEFINING QUALITY

Quality means different things to different people and can be based on involvement, need, price, and experience. In other words, quality may mean the availability of appointment times in a physician's office; to others, it means how friendly and accommodating the staff at the organization is to the patient. Quality also may be evaluated on the basis of the diagnosis or the medication providing a cure for the patient. The Institute of Medicine (IOM) has defined *quality* as "the degree to which health services for individuals and populations increase the likelihood of desired health outcomes and are consistent with current professional knowledge" (IOM, 1990, p. 21). Another prominent definition of quality has been offered by the Agency for Healthcare Research and Quality (AHRQ), who has defined quality as "doing the right thing for the right patient, at the right time, in the right way, to achieve the best possible results" (AHRQ, 2005, p. 3).

While both definitions provide a clear picture of good quality health care, based on scientific and medical evidence, the so-called quality movement has attempted to take the specific details of a patient's life into consideration in order to improve the health and life of the patient being treated. As such, there are believed to be six components of healthcare quality (**Table 2-2**). Each of these components of quality can be influ-

Table 2-2 Components of Healthcare Quality

Effective	Providing services based on scientific knowledge to all who could benefit and refraining from providing services to those not likely to benefit.
Safe	Avoiding injuries to patients from the care that is intended to help them.
Timely	Reducing wait times and harmful delays for both those who receive and those who give care.
Patient centered	Providing care that is respectful of and responsive to individual patient preferences, needs, and values and ensuring that patient values guide all clinical decisions.
Equitable	Providing care that does not vary in quality because of personal characteristics such as gender, ethnicity, geographic location, and socioeconomic status.
Efficient	Avoiding waste, including waste of equipment, supplies, ideas, and energy.

Source: Agency for Healthcare Research and Quality (AHRQ). (2009, March). *2008 National healthcare quality & disparities reports* (AHRQ Publication No. 09-0001). Available at www.ahrq.gov/qual/qrdr08.htm

enced by every member of the healthcare team. As a result, organizations and professionals should focus their efforts to provide care that meets all of these standards in an interdisciplinary effort to achieve desired health outcomes. Unfortunately, the current state of the healthcare system frequently results in one or more of these components being unmet, so patients often struggle with inadequate quality in health care.

The six components of healthcare quality suggest the need for an interdisciplinary approach to care because it would be quite challenging for any one healthcare provider to satisfy all these quality elements for every patient under his or her care.

How Is Quality Assessed?

Although it is understood generally what quality is, how quality in health care is assessed is much less understood by healthcare providers, including pharmacists. The measures used to assess healthcare quality are used to benchmark performance. Health care quality may be measured in any of a number of ways including: (1) clinical performance measures of how well providers deliver specific services needed by specific patients (e.g., children receiving recommended immunizations); (2) assessments by patients of how well providers meet healthcare needs from the patient's perspective (e.g., do providers communicate clearly?); and (3) outcome measures (e.g., mortality rates from cancers preventable by screening) that may be affected by the quality of health care received. (AHRQ, 2009; AHRQ, 2010).

Clinical performance measures are those that are most valued from the clinician's perspective, as it is those measures that most directly influence the clinical outcomes of the patient (Kozma, Reeder, & Schultz, 1993). An example of a clinical performance measure is following standard procedures after the patient is admitted to the hospital for an acute myocardial infarction (e.g., administration of an aspirin within 24 hours of arrival). The patient's assessment of care, probably the most important to the patient as it relates to how he or she perceives his or her treatment to be, is often measured with patient report cards and quality. Lastly, the outcomes quality measures are of particular interest to researchers, policy makers, and administrators because these measures can be used to objectively review trends over time or typically take a macro perspective of how the end result was affected by some type of intervention or objectively reviewed trends over time. Varying aspects of the healthcare delivery are valuable for different reasons to different parties, depending on their perspective and the role in which they play in the patient care process. There is an abundance of quality information available and is reported in one of three ways: accreditation, report cards, and consumer ratings.

Accreditation

Healthcare organizations seek accreditation from a variety of agencies. Accreditation is the process by which certification of competency, authority, or credibility is presented to an organization. This information is used by the Centers for Medicare and Medicaid Services (CMS), third-party administrators, employers, and consumers as one component of value assessment. Medicare payments to hospitals and other facilities are contingent, among other things, on the facility meeting standards set by the Joint Commission. The Joint Commission was formed in 1952 (and was then called the Joint Commission on the Accreditation of Healthcare Organizations) under the aegis of the American Hospital Association and the American Medical Association. It not only serves as the standard accrediting body for hospitals, long-term care facilities, and other organizations, but it also participates in developing performance standards for healthcare organizations.

Much like the Good Housekeeping seal for consumer products, these performance measures serve as an indicator of quality to those unfamiliar with the healthcare organization. Possessing accreditation means that the healthcare organization has met national standards, including clinical performance measures. The Joint Commission presides over a growing, national, comparative performance measurement database that can inform its members of internal healthcare organization quality improvement activities, external accountability, pay-for-performance programs, and advance research.

Report Cards

While accreditation status is an important quality indicator, there are other quality initiatives in which organizations participate. One such effort involves the development of quality indicators and measures and providing audiences with report cards of the assessment of the organization, healthcare plan, or healthcare provider. These summary reports of key indicators are used by a variety of audiences including but not limited to consumers and employers. The National Committee for Quality Assurance (NCQA) is an entity that produces report cards for physicians and health care plans. The mission of the NCQA is "to provide information that enables purchasers and consumers of managed care to distinguish among plans based on quality" (NCQA, 2010).

Managed care organizations may seek NCQA accreditation by sharing with patients and potential clients the report cards indicating that they meet agreed-upon standards of quality. Although accreditation is voluntary, plans usually promote themselves on the basis of their grades. For example, the NCQA has developed and provides a set of measures, called the Health Care Effectiveness Data and Information Set (HEDIS), which is used by more than 90% of America's health plans to measure performance on important dimensions of care and service. **Table 2-3** contains a list of organizations

Table 2-3 Organizations Providing Quality Information

Organization type	Example of quality initiative
Managed care organizations	National Committee for Quality Assurance (NCQA)
Medicare	Medicare Health Outcomes Survey (HOS)
Inpatient setting	Joint Commission
	Hospital Quality Alliance
	Nursing Home Compare
Outpatient setting	Accreditation Association for Ambulatory Health Care
Physicians	Ambulatory Care Quality Alliance (AQA)
	National Committee for Quality Assurance (NCQA)
Pharmacies	Pharmacy Quality Alliance (PQA)

that offer some type of accreditation and/or provide quality measures specific to the type of organization.

Patient Ratings

Not only do organizations evaluate themselves using the measures that indicate quality care, but patients also evaluate these organizations. Many quality initiatives have developed surveys for patients to complete in order to rate these organizations. Many of these surveys are available on paper or on the Internet; patients rate their experience with a provider or healthcare organization. This aggregate information is subsequently published for others to see and use in evaluating potential providers and organizations. Although patient participation in this type of evaluation is not widespread, organizations continue to work to increase awareness of the patient information in the quality initiative. These websites allow for comparisons between different organizations on certain dimensions of quality of care, such as those discussed earlier. It is believed that patients will use these resources when making choices about providers or to report on their experiences with a provider. It is expected that these resources would be used as a resource for decision making much like a consumer would use product reviews on websites to evaluate product quality. Patients candidly sharing quality information about provider services are supplemented by payers finding ways to compensate these providers for good, cost-efficient care. **Table 2-4** contains a sample of organizations that collect information by patients for patient use.

The manner in which these organizations collect this type of information is through surveys, primarily. These surveys allow patients to rate their provider's performance, or the organization may examine protocols within the practice organization to determine if they meet the benchmarked standards of each item of interest. For example, the consumer assessment of healthcare providers and systems (CAHPS) program presents survey items for ambulatory-level care and facility-level care, including items related to provider communication such as "doctor respected patient's comments" and "doctor spent enough time with patient." Patients respond to the survey items and item responses are aggregated and presented in summary in the form of reports. Similarly, the Pharmacy Quality Alliance (PQA) developed measures to assess the pharmacy, the pharmacist, and the pharmacy staff (**Table 2-5**).

Table 2-4 Sample Quality Organizations Collecting Information for Patients

Organization name	Website	Description
Agency for Healthcare Research and Quality's: Consumer Assessment of Healthcare Providers and Systems	https://www.cahps.ahrq.gov	Develop standardized surveys of patients' experiences with ambulatory and facility-level care
CMS's Hospital Compare	www.hospitalcompare.hhs.gov/	Allows patients to search for information on quality care at hospitals.
CMS's Nursing Home Compare	www.medicare.gov/nhcompare	Allows consumers to search for information on quality care for Medicare and Medicaid-certified nursing homes.
Joint Commission's Quality Check	www.qualitycheck.org	Allows patients to search for accredited hospitals and other healthcare facilities.
National Committee for Quality Assurance report cards for choosing quality health care	http://www.ncqa.org	Provides information on report cards for health plans and physician groups.
U.S. News & World Report	www.usnews.com	Publishes annual rankings of America's best health plans and best hospitals.
Agency for Healthcare Research and Quality 2009 State Snapshots	http://statesnapshots.ahrq.gov	Provides state-level information from the National Healthcare Quality Report.

Table 2-5 Sample Quality Measures From Pharmacy Quality Alliance Consumer Experience Survey

In the last 12 months, if you wanted to talk to the staff at this pharmacy about your health or medicine, how often were you able to talk to staff as soon as you wanted to?

☐ Never

☐ Sometimes

☐ Usually

☐ Always

☐ I did not want to talk to staff at this pharmacy about my health or medicine in the last 12 months

In the last 12 months, how often did the staff at this pharmacy show concern for you?

☐ Never

☐ Sometimes

☐ Usually

☐ Always

IMPORTANT TRENDS AFFECTING HEALTHCARE PROFESSIONALS

Healthcare quality is a major area of focus currently within the healthcare system and requires the insight and initiative of all practitioners involved. There are five related areas that continue to receive attention and will affect the various healthcare professionals as this quality paradigm becomes the standard of practice. These areas are patient-focused care, critical pathways, continuous quality improvement (CQI), pay for performance, and technological advances.

Patient-Focused Care

Patient-focused care in a healthcare facility is

> characterized by decentralization of services, cross-training of personnel from different departments to provide basic care, interdisciplinary collaboration, various degrees of organizational restructuring, simplification and redesign of work to eliminate steps and save time, and an increased involvement of patients in their own care. (Vogel, 1993, p. 2321)

In patient-focused care, objectives include (1) improving patients' perceptions of the quality of care and staff members' job satisfaction and (2) using nonclinical and clinical staff more effectively and efficiently (Vogel, 1993).

Patient-focused care attempts to improve patient care by organizationally and physically moving selected service functions, such as basic laboratory, pharmacy, admitting/discharge, medical records, housekeeping, and material support services to patient care areas, thus effecting an organizational restructuring (Wakefield et al., 1994). In providing such care, health professionals work in teams to increase and improve communication among themselves and with the patient. In an institutional setting, it would appear that this type of care could be facilitated by organizational changes; however, in the ambulatory setting, the shift to patient-focused care will require extraordinary effort on the part of individual practitioners to collaborate with other professionals.

However, the overall theme remains the same in any setting: improving patient care and, as a result, improving outcomes requires a partnership between pharmacy professionals, doctors, patients, and payers.

Patient-focused care is a systematic and comprehensive team approach composed of multiskilled or cross-trained individuals capable of providing more of the services directly to patients. Pharmacists can be and should be key members of a multidisciplinary team who have the opportunity to assume shared responsibility for drug therapy management and patient outcomes. Pharmacists are now being trained as clinical pharmacotherapy specialists and have extensive medication-related knowledge to contribute to a team-based approach to care.

Meeting quality standards requires a culture of quality. In order to ensure quality care, a redesign of the system to support a team approach is required. Quality improvement organizations such as NCQA have developed tools and resources to assist in creating an interdisciplinary work environment in order to influence optimally patient outcomes. One of these tools, Team Strategies and Tools to Enhance Performance and Patient Safety (TeamSTEPPS) is a comprehensive set of ready-to-use materials and a training curriculum to integrate teamwork principles into any healthcare system. The Department of Defense, in collaboration with the Agency for Healthcare Research and Quality (AHRQ), developed TeamSTEPPS and has built a national training and support network called the National Implementation of TeamSTEPPS Project. This network is currently conducting training sessions throughout the country (AHRQ, 2010).

Facilitating patient-focused care requires reengineering of healthcare systems. Hammer and Champy (1993) defined reengineering as:

> The fundamental re-thinking and radical redesign of business processes to achieve dramatic improvements in critical, contemporary measures of performance, such as quality, cost, service and speed. (pp. 31–32.)

The purpose of reengineering is to achieve improved efficiencies and quality. Reengineering seeks to combine multiple jobs into one, empower workers and make them more accountable, sequence the elements of work more naturally, create greater flexibility, and blur or move organizational boundaries (Al-Shaqha & Zairi, 2000). The goals of reengineering can be met by increasing efficiency, decreasing redundancy, and eliminating waste. Extensive redesign of the basic work processes as proposed by patient-focused care advocates may result in significant changes in employee job scope, task responsibilities, professional autonomy, and reporting relationships. From the employee's perspective, such changes may be neither warranted nor welcomed. Therefore, obtaining employee buy-in and establishing appropriate incentive structures to facilitate desired changes is critical in implementing patient-focused care (Wakefield et al., 1994).

Critical Pathways

One of the ways in which to implement reengineering in pharmacy is to use the critical pathway process as a guide to reengineering procedures related specifically to the management of a patient's care. Critical pathways represent comprehensive management plans that aim to optimize and streamline patient care (Kirk, Michael, Markowsky, Restino, & Zarowitz, 1996). Critical pathways have been referred to in the medical literature by a number of different terms, including care path, care map, clinical pathway, critical path of care, case management plan, multidisciplinary action plan, collaborative care track, plan of care, clinical care plan, and care guide (Lumsdon & Hagland, 1993). These plans define key steps in the management of the patient not only to improve the quality of health care, but also to reduce resource utilization (Shane, 1995). A critical pathway is an "optimal sequencing and timing of interventions by health care professionals for a particular diagnosis or procedure, designed to minimize delays and resource utilization and maximize the quality of care" (Coffey et al., 1992, p.45).

Some of the specific goals of critical pathways include providing continuous quality improvement, decreasing service fragmentation (increasing continuity of care), optimizing cost-effectiveness of healthcare delivery, guiding the patient and family through expected treatment and progress, and increasing satisfaction of patients, families, staff, physicians, and third-party payers (Shane, 1995). Critical pathways create targeted patient outcomes and quality end points, which form a foundation for common expectations, shared responsibility, regular communication, and early problem detection and intervention among all members of the healthcare team (Coffey et al., 1992). Further, they identify specific time frames and desired outcomes associated with each care step, with the goals of minimizing delays and maximizing resource utilization (Shane, 1995). Implementation of critical pathways has reduced the use of institutional resources in caring for patients with pneumonia (Marrie et al., 2000) and has improved patient outcomes by providing a mechanism to coordinate care and to reduce fragmentation and ultimately cost (Panella, Marchisio, & Di Stanislao, 2003).

Although critical pathways are relatively new to health care, project managers in the construction and engineering fields have used them for many years. As in these other fields, critical pathways in health care are developed usually for high-volume, high-risk, or high-cost procedures. Because of increasing competition within health care, "managers have embraced critical pathways as a method to reduce variation in care, decrease resource utilization, and potentially improve healthcare quality" (Every, Hochman, Becker, Kopecky, & Cannon, 2000, p. 461). Critical pathways require organizational change such that they facilitate interdisciplinary teamwork. For example, reductions in all-cause hospitalizations and medical costs as well as improved survival rates have been observed with multidisciplinary teams (Peterson et al., 2008). The teams document pharmacologic as well as nonpharmacologic therapies, interventions, and outcomes throughout the entire course of care from admission to discharge. Critical pathways require coordinated care from everyone on the healthcare team and delineate which treatments should be done on each day of the patient's stay. Critical pathways have been shown to reduce variations in the care provided, facilitate achieving expected outcomes, decrease delays, and improve cost-effectiveness (Coffey et al., 1992).

Continuous Quality Improvement

Continuous quality improvement (CQI), also called total quality management and total quality improvement, is another mechanism in which interdisciplinary involvement is crucial. W. Edwards Deming, a statistician, introduced methods of CQI with the premise that improved quality will decrease costs because of less rework, fewer mistakes, fewer delays, and better use of people and materials. The Deming method has been incorporated into the day-to-day activities of many major companies (Gitlow & Melby, 1991). CQI enables a cross-functional, interdisciplinary team to examine processes that could or should be improved. It brings together a team of healthcare workers who know a particular procedure well and takes advantage of the fact that employees generally are more receptive to change when they are active participants in the change process.

CQI can also be viewed as a method of performance appraisal in which structures, processes, and outcomes are assessed to determine specific areas where improvement is needed. It typically follows the FOCUS-PDCA cycle (Graham, 1995):

F: Find a process to improve.

O: Organize a team that knows the process.

C: Clarify current knowledge of the process.

U: Understand sources of process variation.

S: Select the process improvement.

P: Plan the improvement.

D: Do the improvement, collect data, and analyze data.

C: Check and study the results.

A: Act to hold the gain and to improve the process further.

The PDCA cycle is used in the daily management of CQI and is used to determine the actions necessary to maintain, improve, or innovate standard methods to achieve measurable benchmarks. Inherent within CQI is the belief that it is wiser to maximize efforts to design a product or process to be right the first time and to minimize resources devoted to inspection and repair caused by poor processes (Wakefield et al., 1994). Patient-focused care builds upon previous CQI healthcare efforts by focusing on ways to improve continuity of care and by examining what, if any, changes in underlying structures and processes may be required. In a patient-focused care organization, CQI functions as a methodology for examining and improving the process of care and patient-care outcomes, regardless of internal departmental or profession-based organizational boundaries.

Pay for Performance

Pay for performance (P4P) in health care is a topic of wide discussion, especially among managed care executives, for its ability to contain costs, to improve health outcomes, and to raise the overall quality of health services. P4P has emerged as a new model built on defined measures, data collection, and public reporting that includes payment incentives aimed at quality, efficiency, and patient satisfaction (ASHP, 2009a). The focus of P4P is on value, which takes into account the relationship between quality and cost. While P4P is not a new concept, it has arrived in health care due to a convergence of events including increasing cost of care, provision of patient-centered care, the progression of evidence-based medicine, the patient safety movement, and the use of electronic data systems and the Internet.

In order to incentivize providers to provide quality care, providers are rewarded in P4P. P4P has been defined by the CMS as "quality based purchasing ... the use of payment methods and other incentives to encourage high quality and patient-focused, high value care" (CMS, 2006, p. 1). An effective P4P program should incorporate clinical quality, efficiency, and patient satisfaction. CMS and other payers are believed to be moving toward this model, as it has been demonstrated to improve quality in a cost-effective manner. P4P programs increasingly are focusing their efforts on outcome and cost-efficiency measures, rather than clinical process measures alone. The use of specific measure sets have increased drastically for outcomes, information technology, and cost efficiency, while measures for patient satisfaction and processes have maintained a similar proportion over the years. Challenges associated with adopting P4P include overcoming physician resistance, determining the necessary size of incentive pools to capture the provider's attention, and finding the resources necessary to continue funding the program (Rosenthal & Dudley, 2007).

There is evidence that P4P programs have an effect on quality. Measurement provides physicians with a new perspective on their practice and encourages change in their processes and delivery systems in order to meet program standards. Adoption of process changes in order to meet the benchmarked standards have shown that some organizations have difficulty in achieving national standards, specifically small organizations and large organizations. However, the use of national standards helps rewards programs get started (O'Kane, 2007) in order to incentivize providers to meet these standards of care. The development of national standards that are globally accepted, and consistent requirements to meet the standards are key in implementation of CQI to achieve them.

Healthcare Services and Technological Advances

Both healthcare services and the professions providing care are influenced by the introduction of new technologies. Health information technology has been shown to improve quality by increasing adherence to guidelines, enhancing disease surveillance, and decreasing medication errors (Chaundhry et al., 2006). Technological advances have made many new procedures and methods possible; for example, robotic devices automate many of the tasks associated with medication dispensing. In addition, personal digital assistants and similar handheld devices provide physicians and pharmacists with updated drug information. Moreover, the exchange of information between healthcare practitioners and the information acquisition by patients has changed exponentially when compared to past decades. The movement toward quality health care is believed also to involve the creation of interoperable transparent systems with an ultimate goal of developing an electronic health record for each patient to be used by all involved in the healthcare system.

The fragmented nature of the U.S. healthcare system includes thousands of hospitals, many thousands of healthcare professionals (e.g., physicians, nurses, and pharmacists), and many more thousands of facilities and other interested parties. This environment creates an ideal situation and incentive to incorporate technologies that can span different sites and caregivers in order to help integrate services. With the large volume of transactions in the system and the need to integrate new scientific evidence into practice and other complex information management activities, the limitations of paper-based information management are obvious (Chaundhry et al., 2006).

There is the potential for many of the key players to resist the adoption of new technologies, such as electronic health records (EHRs). While the benefits of health information technologies are clear, adapting new information systems to health care has proven difficult and rates of use have been limited. In fact, most technology applications have been created for administrative and financial transactions rather than for delivering clinical care (Chaundhry et al., 2006). Reforming the system such that incentives are provided to patients and providers is considered to be a first step toward engaging and implementing a healthcare system for all health professionals to provide better patient care. An example of incentivizing the adoption of technology-based practice changes would be e-prescribing. CMS established an incentive-disincentive program to speed the adoption of e-prescribing by Medicare providers. Beginning in 2009, CMS provided incentives for the adoption of e-prescribing for 3 years; however, beginning in 2012, CMS will add financial penalties for providers who fail to adopt e-prescribing (CMS, 2010).

In order to ensure safe medication and procedure delivery within hospitals, organizations have implemented the use of technology such as bar codes on patient admission bracelets, requiring these scans to match electronic records prior to completing procedures and medication dispensing. Electronic health records and electronic medical records have been cited as a method to increase communication between healthcare professionals and allow for continuity of care. While all these structure and process changes within the system are made to positively affect patient health outcomes, it remains the responsibility of the *professionals* in healthcare to develop and maintain methods to sustain quality health care, as it is what we have committed to when becoming professionals. It appears that today's version of interdisciplinary collaboration requires electronic systems to facilitate communication. While health information technology is one method in making this a possibility, electronic health records will only work if they are utilized to their fullest extent. Overcoming adoption barriers and utilizing the new systems to their capability are imperative to creating a fully functional system.

CONCLUSION

Interdisciplinary care is becoming more important as providing quality care becomes the gold standard for practitioners. There are a number of factors that will help ensure good quality health care (NCQA, 2007), which are:

1. Effectively utilize the best available medical research.
2. Ensure complete information exchange regarding a patient's health to other practitioners.
3. Coordinate care among multiple professionals.
4. Provide comprehensive, continuous care.
5. Pay for quality instead of volume.
6. Engage patients in their care.

Understanding the role and function of others in the healthcare system is the first step to providing collaborative interdisciplinary care. It is important to note that people are not the focus of quality; rather it is achieved through refinement of an organization's standard methods (best practices) through the use of CQI. CQI occurs through modifying standard methods as well as via system changes of structure and processes. While most of the system changes are not visible to the patient, these changes are made to provide better care.

QUESTIONS FOR FURTHER DISCUSSION

1. Consider the characteristics of a profession; in light of those characteristics, discuss pharmacy. For each of the characteristics where pharmacy does not possess or partially possesses the requirement, what remedies do you recommend?

2. Are the characteristics that have been applied historically to occupations for the purpose of defining professions relevant today? Why or why not?

3. How is it that your pharmacy education will prepare you to practice as part of a multidisciplinary team? An interdisciplinary team?

4. What are the potential benefits of engaging in collaborative practice agreements? What are the risks?

5. Collaborative practice agreements refer to the practice where healthcare providers (e.g., physicians) authorize pharmacists to perform specific activities to help patients achieve better health outcomes. In which areas of pharmacy practice would you expect most to have a collaborative practice agreement, and why?

6. People are not the focus of change; rather it is believed that developing systems that require people to provide a high quality of care through refinement of an organization's standard methods should be our focus to bring about needed change. What types of health care *system* changes can be made to facilitate establishing continuity of care and the medical home as the typical standard of care?

7. Critical pathways include providing continuous quality improvement, decreasing service fragmentation (increasing continuity of care), optimizing cost-effectiveness of healthcare delivery, guiding the patient and family through expected treatment and progress, and increasing satisfaction of patients, families, staff, physicians, and third-party payers. These pathways are typically implemented for high-volume, high-risk, or high-cost procedures. Many of the studies have demonstrated the utility of critical pathways in an institutional setting. How might this concept be applied to a community pharmacy setting?

8. Technology and the possibility of electronic health records have been repeatedly touted as the solution to eliminating the fragmentation of the healthcare system. Most of this chapter has discussed how these changes will influence practitioners. How do you think these changes will influence patients' interactions with healthcare professionals? What are the pros and cons from the patient perspective?

9. Suppose you were asked by a national pharmacy organization to increase utilization of patient-reported quality measures. Describe how you would get patients to use these services and how you would get practitioners and payers to use the results from these patient-reported measures. What influence will increased utilization of patient-reported measures have on practice?

KEY TOPICS AND TERMS

Collaborative working relationships
Continuity of care
Continuous quality improvement
Critical pathway
Health information technology
Interdisciplinary care
Medical home

Multidisciplinary care
Patient-focused care
Pay for performance
Profession
Professional
Quality of care

REFERENCES

Accreditation Council for Pharmacy Education. (2006). *Accreditation standards and guidelines for the professional program in pharmacy leading to the doctor of pharmacy degree.* Chicago, IL: Accreditation Council for Pharmacy Education.

Agency for Healthcare Research and Quality (AHRQ). (2005, September). *Guide to health care quality: How to know it when you see it* (AHRQ Publication No. 05-0088) Rockville, MD: Agency for Healthcare Research and Quality.

Agency for Healthcare Research and Quality (AHRQ). (2009, March). *2008 National healthcare quality & disparities reports* (AHRQ Publication No. 09-0001). Available at www.ahrq.gov/qual/qrdr08.htm

Agency for Healthcare Research and Quality (AHRQ). (2010, March). *2009 national healthcare quality report* (AHRQ Publication No. 10-0003). Available at www.ahrq.gov/qual/qrdr09.htm

Al-Shaqha, W. M., & Zairi, M. (2000). Reengineering pharmaceutical care: Towards a patient-focused approach. *International Journal of Health Care Quality Assurance, 13*(5), 208–217.

American Academy of Physician Assistants (AAPA). (2010a). *National physician assistant census report.* Available from http://www.aapa.org/images/stories/Data_2009/National_Final_with_Graphics.pdf

American Academy of Physician Assistants (AAPA). (2010b). *Physician assistant programs.* Retrieved from http://www.aapa.org/education-and-certification/physician-assistant-programs

American Association of Colleges of Nursing (AACN). (2006). *The essentials of doctoral education for advanced nursing practice.* Washington, DC: American Association of Colleges of Nursing.

American Association of Colleges of Osteopathic Medicine (AACOM). (2010a). *Member colleges.* Retrieved from http://www.aacom.org/people/colleges/Pages/default.aspx

American Association of Colleges of Osteopathic Medicine (AACOM). (2010b). *Osteopathic medical college information book: Entering class 2011.* Chevy Chase, MD: American Association of Colleges of Osteopathic Medicine.

American Association of Colleges of Osteopathic Medicine (AACOM). (2010c). *What is osteopathic medicine?* Retrieved from http://www.aacom.org/about/osteomed/pages/default.aspx

American Association of Colleges of Pharmacy. (2010). *Academic pharmacy's vital statistics.* Retrieved from http://www.aacp.org/about/Pages/Vitalstats.aspx

American Association of Medical Colleges. (2010). *About the AAMC.* Retrieved from https://www.aamc.org/about/

American Board of Medical Specialties (ABMS). (2010). *Specialties & subspecialties.* Retrieved from http://www.abms.org/Who_We_Help/Physicians/specialties.aspx

American Board of Physician Specialties (ABPS). (2010). *ABPS organization.* Retrieved from http://www.abpsus.org/userfiles/files/ABPS%20org.pdf

American College of Clinical Pharmacy (ACCP). (2004). *ACCP guidelines for clinical research fellowship training programs.* Lenexa, KS: American College of Clinical Pharmacy.

American Medical Association (AMA). (2008). *Physician characteristics and distribution in the U.S.* Chicago, IL: American Medical Association.

American Medical Association (AMA). (2010a). *Requirements for becoming a physician.* Retrieved from http://www.ama-assn.org/ama/pub/education-careers/becoming-physician.shtml

American Medical Association (AMA). (2010b). *State medical licensure requirements and statistics, 2010.* Chicago, IL: American Medical Association.

American Nurses Association (ANA). (2010). *What is nursing?* Retrieved from: http://www.nursingworld.org/EspeciallyForYou/StudentNurses/WhatisNursing.aspx

American Nurses Credentialing Center (ANCC). (2010). *ANCC nurse certification.* Retrieved from http://www.nursecredentialing.org/certification.aspx

American Osteopathic Association (AOA). (2010). *Physician certification overview.* Retrieved from http://www.osteopathic.org/index.cfm?PageID=ado_cert

American Society of Health-System Pharmacists (ASHP). (1999). ASHP statement on the pharmacist's role in primary care. *American Journal of Health-System Pharmacy, 56,* 1665–1667.

American Society of Health-System Pharmacists (ASHP). (2003). White paper on pharmacy technicians 2002: Needed changes can no longer wait. *American Journal of Health-System Pharmacy, 60*(1), 37–51.

American Society of Health-System Pharmacists (ASHP). (2009a). *Pay-for-performance (P4P): Evaluating current and future implications: Issues for pharmacy.* Retrieved from www.ashp.org/DocLibrary/Policy/QII/Pay-For-Performance.aspx

American Society of Health-System Pharmacists (ASHP). (2009b). *Record number of pharmacists entering residencies.* Retrieved from http://www.ashp.org/import/news/NewsCapsules/article.aspx?id=278

American Society of Health-System Pharmacists (ASHP). (2010a). *ASHP accreditation standard for postgraduate year one (PGY1) pharmacy residency programs.* Retrieved from http://www.ashp.org/s_ashp/docs/files/RTP_PGY1AccredStandard.pdf

American Society of Health-System Pharmacists (ASHP). (2010b). *ASHP accreditation standard for postgraduate year two (PGY2) pharmacy residency programs.* Retrieved from http://www.ashp.org/s_ashp/docs/files/RTP_PGY2AccredStandard.pdf

American Society of Health-System Pharmacists (ASHP). (2010c). Record numbers participate in residency match. Retrieved from http://www.ashp.org/import/news/NewsCapsules/article.aspx?id=342

American Society of Hospital Pharmacists (ASHP). (1987). Definitions of pharmacy residencies and fellowships. *American Journal of Hospital Pharmacy, 44,* 1142–1144.

Beck, A. H. (2004). The Flexner report and the standardization of medical education. *JAMA. 291*(17), 2139–2140.

Board of Pharmacy Specialties. (2010). *Current specialties.* Retrieved from http://www.bpsweb.org/specialties/specialties.cfm

Bouvy, M. L., Heerdink, E. R., Urquhart, J., Grobbee, D. E., Hoes, E. W., & Leufkens, H. G. (2003). Effect of a pharmacist-led intervention on diuretic compliance in heart failure patients: A randomized controlled study. *Journal of Cardiac Failure, 9,* 404–411.

Brock, K. A., & Doucette, W. R. (2004). Collaborative working relationships between pharmacists and physicians: An exploratory study. *Journal of the American Pharmaceutical Association, 44*(3), 358–365.

Buerki, R. A, & Vottero, L. D. (1996). The purposes of professions in society. In C. H. Knowlton, R. P. Penna (Eds.), *Pharmaceutical care* (pp. 3–17). New York, NY: Chapman and Hall.

Centers for Medicare and Medicaid Services (CMS). (2006). State Medicaid Director Letter #06-003, dated April 6, 2006.

Centers for Medicare and Medcaid Services (CMS). (2010). Electronic prescribing (eRx) incentive program. Retrieved from http://www.cms.gov/ERxIncentive/

Chaudhry, B., Wang, J., Wu, S., Maglione, M., Mojica, W., Roth, E., ... Shekelle, P. G. (2006). Systematic review: Impact of health information technology on quality, efficiency, and costs of medical care. *Annals of Internal Medicine, 144,* E-12–E-22.

Christikis, D. A. (2003). Continuity of care: Process or outcome? *Ann Fam Medicine, 1*(3), 131–133.

Coffey, R. J., Richards, J. S., Remmert, C. S., LeRoy, S. S., Schoville, R. R., & Baldwin, P. J. (1992). An introduction to critical paths. *Quality Management in Health Care, 1*(1), 45–54.

Council on Credentialing in Pharmacy. (2003). Sesquicentennial Stepping Stone Summits—Summit two: Pharmacy technicians. *Journal of the American Pharmacists Association. 43*(1), 84–92.

Council on Credentialing in Pharmacy. (2009). *Scope of contemporary pharmacy practice: Roles, responsibilities, and functions of pharmacists and pharmacy technicians.* Available at http://www.pharmacycredentialing.org/ccp/Contemporary_Pharmacy_Practice.pdf

Doucette, W. R., Nevins, J., & McDonough, R. P. (2005). Factors affecting collaborative care between pharmacists and physicians. *Research in Social and Administrative Pharmacy, 1*(4), 565–578.

Every, N. R., Hochman J., Becker, R., Kopecky, S., & Cannon, C.P. (2000). Critical pathways: A review. *Circulation, 101,* 431–435.

Flexner, A. (1910). *Medical education in the United States and Canada.* New York, NY: Carnegie Foundation.

Gitlow, H. S., & Melby, M. J. (1991). Framework for continuous quality improvement in the provision of pharmaceutical care. *American Journal of Hospital Pharmacy, 48,* 1917–1925.

Goode, W. J. (1957). Community within a community: The professions. *Am. Soc. Rev, 22*(2), 194–200.

Government Accounting Office (GAO). (2008). *Primary care professionals: Recent supply trends, projects, and valuation of services.* Available at http://www.gao.gov/new.items/d08472t.pdf

Graham, N. O. (1995). *Quality in health care: Theory, application, and evolution.* Gaithersburg, MD: Aspen Publications.

Grumbach, K., Bodenheimer, T. (2004). Can health care teams improve primary care practice? *JAMA, 291,* 1246–1251.

Haggerty, J. L., Reid, R. J., Freeman, G. K., Starfield, B. H., Adair, C. E., & McKenfry, R. (2003). Continuity of care: A multidisciplinary review. *BMJ, 327,* 1219–1221.

Hammer, D., & Champy, J. (1993). *Reengineering the corporation.* New York, NY: Harper Business.

Higby, G. J. (1996). From compounding to caring: An abridged history of American pharmacy. In C. H. Knowlton & R. P. Penna (Eds.), *Pharmaceutical care* (pp. 3–17). New York, NY: Chapman and Hall.

HRSA Bureau of Health Professions. (2008a). *The adequacy of pharmacist supply: 2004–2030.* Retrieved from ftp://ftp.hrsa.gov/bhpr/workforce/pharmacy.pdf

HRSA Bureau of Health Professions. (2008b). *The physician workforce: Projections and research into current issues affecting supply and demand.* Retrieved from ftp://ftp.hrsa.gov/bhpr/workforce/physicianworkforce.pdf

HRSA Bureau of Health Professions. (2010). *The registered nurse population: Initial findings from the 2008 national sample survey of registered nurses.* Retrieved from http://bhpr.hrsa.gov/healthworkforce/rnsurvey/initialfindings2008.pdf

Institute of Medicine. (1990). IOM. *Medicare: A strategy for quality assurance.* K.N. Lohr (Ed.). Washington, DC: National Academies Press.

Jones, P. E. (2007). Physician assistant education in the United States. *Academic Medicine, 82*(9), 882–887.

Kane-Gill, S., Reddy, P., Gupta, S. R., & Bakst, A. W. (2008). Guidelines for pharmacoeconomic and outcomes research fellowship training programs. *Pharmacotherapy, 28*(10), 269e–276e.

Kirk, J. K., Michael, K. A., Markowsky, S. J., Restino, M. R., & Zarowitz, B. J. (1996). Critical pathways: The time is here for pharmacist involvement. *Pharmacotherapy, 16,* 723–733.

Klass, A. A. (1961). What is a profession? *Canadian Medical Association Journal, 85,* 698–701.

Kozma, C. M., Reeder, C. E., & Schultz, R. M. (1993). Economic, clinical, and humanistic outcomes: A planning model for pharmacoeconomic research. *Clinical Therapeutics, 15*(6), 1121–1132.

LaPointe, N. M., & Jollis, J. G. (2003). Medication errors in hospitalized cardiovascular patients. *Archives of Internal Medicine, 163,* 1461–66.

Leape, L., Cullen, D. J., Dempsey, C. M., Burdick, E., Demanaco, H. J., Ives, E. J., & Bates, D. W. (1999). Pharmacist participation on physician rounds and adverse drug events in the intensive care unit. *JAMA, 282,* 267–270.

Liaison Committee on Medical Education. (2010). *Functions and structure of a medical school: Standards for accreditation of medical education programs leading to the M.D. degree.* Retrieved from http://www.lcme.org/functions2010jun.pdf

Lumsdon L & Hagland M. (1993). Mapping Care. *Hospital & Health Networks. 67,* 34–40.

Marrie, T. J., Lau, C.Y., Wheeler, S. L., Wong, C.J ., Vandervoort, M. K., & Feagan, B. G. (2000). A controlled trial of a critical pathway for treatment of community-acquired pneumonia. *JAMA, 283,* 749–755.

McDonough, R. P., & Doucette, W. R. (2001). A conceptual framework for collaborative working relationships between pharmacists and physicians. *Journal of the American Pharmaceutical Association, 41,* 682–692.

Midwest Pharmacy Workforce Research Consortium. (2010). *Final report of the 2009 national sample survey of the pharmacist workforce to determine contemporary demographic and practice characteristics.* Alexandria, VA: American Association of Colleges of Pharmacy.

Mrtek, R. G. (1976). Pharmaceutical education in these United States—An interpretive historical essay of the twentieth century. *American Journal of Pharmaceutical Education, 40*(4), 339–365.

Mrtek, R. G., & Catizone, C. (1989). Pharmacy and the professions. In A. I. Wertheimer, M. C. Smith (Eds.), *Pharmacy practice: Social and behavioral aspects* (pp. 23–57). Baltimore, MD: Williams and Wilkins.

National Association of Boards of Pharmacy. (2009a). *2010 survey of pharmacy law.* Mount Prospect, IL: National Association of Boards of Pharmacy.

National Association of Boards of Pharmacy. (2009b) *Model State Pharmacy Act and model rules of the National Association of Boards of Pharmacy.* Mount Prospect, IL: National Association of Boards of Pharmacy.

National Association of Boards of Pharmacy. (2009c). *Report of the Task Force on Pharmacy Technician Education and Training Programs.* Mount Prospect, IL: National Association of Boards of Pharmacy.

National Association of Boards of Pharmacy. (2010). *Foreign pharmacy graduate equivalency examination.* Retrieved from http://www.nabp.net/programs/examination/fpgee/#FPGEE

National Board of Osteopathic Medical Examiners (NBOME). (2010). *Bulletin of information.* Retrieved from http://www.nbome.org/docs/comlexBOI.pdf

National Center for Health Statistics. (2010). *Health, United States, 2009: With special feature on medical technology.* Hyattsville, MD: National Center for Health Statistics.

National Commission on Certification of Physician Assistants (NCCPA). (2010). *Certification process overview.* Retrieved from http://www.nccpa.net/CertificationProcess.aspx

National Committee for Quality Assurance (NCQA). (2010). *About NCQA.* Retrieved from http://www.ncqa.org/tabid/675/Default.aspx

National Committee for Quality Assurance (NCQA). (2007). *The essential guide to health care quality.* Washington DC: National Committee for Quality Assurance.

National Council of State Boards of Nursing (NCSBN). (2009). *2009 member board profiles.* Chicago, IL: National Council of State Boards of Nursing.

National Council of State Boards of Nursing (NCSBN). (2010). *Frequently asked questions about general NCLEX information.* Retrieved from https://www.ncsbn.org/General_FAQ.pdf

O'Kane, M. E. (2007). Performance-based measures: The early results are in. Journal of Man Care Pharm. 13(2) Suppl S-B: S3–S6.

Panella, M., Marchisio, S., & Di Stanislao, F. (2003). Reducing clinical variations with clinical pathways: Do pathways work? *International Journal of Quality Health Care, 15*(6), 509–521.

Paolini, N., & Rouse, M. J. (2010). Scope of contemporary pharmacy practice: Roles, responsibilities, and functions of pharmacists and pharmacy technicians—Executive summary. *American Journal of Health-System Pharmacy, 67,* 1030–1031.

Peterson, E. D., Albert, N. M., Amin, A., Patterson, J. H., & Fonarow, G. C. (2008). Implementing critical pathways and a multidisciplinary team approach to cardiovascular disease management. *The American Journal of Cardiology, 102* (suppl), 47G–56G.

Pharmacy Technician Certification Board. (2010a). *Exam preparation.* Retrieved from https://www.ptcb.org/AM/Template.cfm?Section=Exam_Preparation&Template=/CM/ContentCombo.cfm&NavMenuID=806&ContentID=3269

Pharmacy Technician Certification Board. (2010b). PTCB FAQs—*Pharmacy technicians.* Retrieved from https://www.ptcb.org/AM/Template.cfm?Section=Help&Template=/CM/HTMLDisplay.cfm&ContentID=3410#Pharmacy_Technicians

Rosenthal T. (2008). The medical home: Growing evidence to support a new approach to primary care. *Journal of the American Board of Family Medicine. 21*(5): 427–440.

Rosenthal, M. B., & Dudley, R. A. (2007). Pay-for-performance: Will the latest payment trend improve care? *JAMA, 297*(7), 740–744.

Saultz, J. W. (2003). Defining and measuring interpersonal continuity of care. *Annals of Family Medicine, 1*(3), 134–143.

Saultz, J. W., & Albedaiwi, W. (2004). Interpersonal continuity of care and patient satisfaction: A critical review. *Annals of Family Medicine, 2*(5), 445–451.

Saultz, J. W., & Lochner, J. (2005). Interpersonal continuity of care and care outcomes: A critical review. *Annals of Family Medicine, 3*(2), 159–166.

Shane, R. (1995). Take the first step on the critical pathway. *American Journal of Health-System Pharmacy, 52,* 1051–1053.

Sia, C., Tonniges, T. F., Osterhus, E., & Taba, S. (2004). History of the medical home concept. *Pediatrics, 113*(5), 1473–1478.

Smith, M., Bates, D. W., Bodenheimer, T., & Cleary, P. D. (2010). Why pharmacists belong in the medical home. *Health Affairs, 29*(5), 906–913.

Sonnedecker, G. (Ed.). (1976). *Kremers and Urdang's history of pharmacy* (4th ed.). Philadelphia, PA: Lippincott.

U.S. Bureau of Labor Statistics (U.S. BLS). (2010a). Licensed practical and licensed vocational nurses. *Occupational outlook handbook* (2010–11 ed.). Retrieved from http://www.bls.gov/oco/ocos102.htm

U.S. Bureau of Labor Statistics (U.S. BLS). (2010b). Pharmacists. *Occupational outlook handbook* (2010–11 ed.). Retrieved from http://www.bls.gov/oco/ocos079.htm

U.S. Bureau of Labor Statistics (U.S. BLS). (2010c). Pharmacy technicians and aides. *Occupational outlook handbook* (2010–11 ed.). Retrieved from http://www.bls.gov/oco/ocos325.htm

U.S. Bureau of Labor Statistics (U.S. BLS). (2010d). Physician assistants. *Occupational outlook handbook* (2010–11 ed.). Retrieved from http://www.bls.gov/oco/ocos081.htm

U.S. Bureau of Labor Statistics (U.S. BLS). (2010e). Registered nurses. *Occupational outlook handbook,* (2010–11 ed.). Retrieved from http://www.bls.gov/oco/ocos083.htm

U.S. Medical Licensing Examination (USMLE). (2010). Bulletin of information. Retrieved from http://www.usmle.org/General_Information/bulletin/2010/2010bulletin.pdf

Vogel DP. (1993). Patient-focused care. *American Journal of Hospital Pharmacists, 50,* 2321–2329.

Wakefield, D. S., Cyphert, S. T., Murray, J. F., Uden-Holman, T., Hendryx, M. S., Wakefield, B. J., & Helms, C. M. (1994). Understanding patient-centered care in the context of total quality management and continuous quality improvement. *The Joint Commission Journal on Quality Improvement, 20*(3), 152–161.

Zillich, A. J., McDonough, R. P., Carter, B. L., & Doucette, W. R. (2004). Influential characteristics of physician/pharmacist collaborative relationships. *Annals of Pharmacotherapy, 38,* 764–769.

The Pharmacist and the Pharmacy Profession

Shane P. Desselle

Case Scenario

Suppose you have just completed your educational degree requirements and earned your PharmD degree a few weeks ago. You are currently working 8 hours per day at WeCare Pharmacy to fulfill your internship requirements, and your appointment to take the board exam the next week is quickly approaching. You have your head buried in books and notes one Wednesday evening when suddenly it hits you, "Gosh, if I pass the NAPLEX [North American Pharmacist Licensure Examination] and jurisprudence examinations, I'll be a registered pharmacist before the end of next month!"

That weekend you make the trip back home to visit with your family for the first time since moving 5 hours away to take the job at WeCare. Your mom lovingly fires a series of questions your way: "Well, what's it like almost being a pharmacist? Is it what you thought it would be? Have you met any other pharmacists? How do they treat you at your new job? What do you do there, anyway?"

You begin to reply to your mom, one question at a time, but then become puzzled that you are not sure exactly how to answer her. In fact, you had not really thought about these things. What is pharmacy all about anyway? Do you have a pharmacist's mentality, or does such a thing exist? Did you make the right career and organizational choice? How do you meet other pharmacists in the area? How do you stay apprised of what is going on in the worlds of pharmacy and health care? And ultimately, what do you need to know and do to be the best pharmacist you can be?

LEARNING OBJECTIVES

Upon completion of this chapter, the student shall be able to:

- Identify three eras in pharmacy practice and education during the 20th century. Describe the principal forces that shaped the profession.
- Define *pharmaceutical care* and *medication therapy management*. Compare these as missions and professional mandates for pharmacy. Identify barriers to these missions and describe where the profession stands in their implementation.

- Discuss the difference between licensure and certification. Discuss opportunities for pharmacists to obtain certification. Identify other postgraduate educational opportunities for pharmacists.
- Describe roles played by professional pharmacy organizations. Identify benefits for pharmacists who join professional pharmacy organizations. Describe the mission and goals of several key professional pharmacy organizations.
- Describe the roles and functions of pharmacy technicians. Discuss the trend toward technician certification and professionalization and explain what these will mean to pharmacy practice.
- Describe how the Internet and other technological, financial, and political forces have affected pharmacy practice. Discuss advantages of and possible threats to patient safety from Internet pharmacy practice. Identify other technologies affecting contemporary pharmacy practice.
- Discuss the implications of the pharmacist workforce for practice and education. Describe factors that affect the pharmacist labor supply. Discuss estimates of the pharmacy workforce for the coming decades.

CHAPTER QUESTIONS

1. How have pharmacists' education and training and the roles they play in society evolved throughout the 20th century?
2. What is *pharmaceutical care*? What are its goals? Why did the pharmacy profession embrace it as a mission? How has pharmaceutical care evolved into the concept of medication therapy management? Which barriers might prevent pharmacists from providing optimal level of care guided by these two concepts and how might these be overcome?
3. What are the subdisciplines that constitute pharmacy education and practice? What are some of the postgraduate educational and career options in these areas?
4. What is the difference between certification and licensure? What are some areas in which pharmacists may obtain board certification?
5. What purposes do professional pharmacy organizations serve? What are some of the key organizations that shape pharmacists' practice?
6. What are some trends concerning the roles of pharmacy technicians in practice?
7. What are the advantages and disadvantages of using Internet pharmacies from a patient's perspective? What are some of the public health concerns regarding the proliferation of Internet pharmacies?
8. What types of various technologies are shaping the way that health care and medication therapy management services are being delivered and how?
9. Why is the pharmacy workforce such a critical issue to the profession? What do estimates of pharmacists' labor supply suggest?

INTRODUCTION

Chapter 2 introduced the concepts of professionalism and interdisciplinary care while briefly describing the training, expertise, and professional roles of pharmacists and some of the many healthcare professionals with whom pharmacists interact on a regular basis. This chapter examines in greater detail those same aspects of the pharmacy profession, its pharmacist members, and pharmacy education; it is divided into seven major sections.

The first section is an abridged history of the profession and the evolution of current medication use systems. This appropriately leads into the second section, a discussion of pharmacy's mission and philosophy of practice, termed pharmaceutical care, and its evolution into medication therapy management. The third section discusses current and expected future trends in practice, emphasizing pharmacist specialization and examining the various settings in which pharmacists practice. A multitude of professional organizations represent pharmacists in each of these settings, as discussed in the fourth section. The fifth section describes the roles of pharmacy technicians, now pharmacists' most important adjuncts in providing pharmaceutical care.

The sixth section examines a phenomenon pervading the delivery of medical care called cyberpharmacy, or the application of e-commerce to modern medication use systems. Other trends affecting the future of our practice are examined as well, including the projected increase in the number of prescriptions written and dispensed in the United States in the coming decades. This provides a nice segue into the seventh, very critical section of this chapter—the discussion of workforce issues. The labor supply has important implications for the future of pharmacy, including pharmacist education and training; pharmacy laws, rules, and regulations; policy regarding the use of ancillary personnel; pharmacist salaries; and, most importantly, the therapeutic outcomes of patients.

EVOLUTION OF THE PROFESSION AND MEDICATION USE SYSTEMS

Historians of pharmacy have used a variety of methods to categorize the evolution of pharmacy within the context of either waves or shifts in educational and industrial forces (Hepler, 1987), stages of professional identity (Hepler & Strand, 1990), or political shifts in the promulgation of our healthcare delivery system (Broeseker & Janke, 1998). Fortunately, there are a number of commonalities in their descriptions of the forces that have shaped our current method of practice and management of medication use systems. The approach taken here is simply to describe pharmacy practice, pharmacy education, and medication use within three distinct periods of the American 20th century leading up to today.

Before the 1940s

Pharmacy practice in the United States dates back to shortly after the country's founding. However, aside from the formation of professional associations and the first colleges of pharmacy during the 1800s, the predominant forces shaping pharmacy and medication use today took effect largely during the 20th century. Before this time, pharmacy was primarily an occupation for which its practitioners were trained via apprenticeship, much like participants in other trades. Pharmacy was considered an art that did not require theoretical knowledge and could best be learned "by daily handling and preparing the remedies in common use" (Sonnedecker, 1963, p. 204).

Without any credible standards or enforceable laws regarding the safety of therapeutic agents, the use of patent medicines was the norm. Pharmacists or apothecaries often were engaged in the wholesale manufacture and distribution of such products. The public had to rely on them to ensure that the compounds they sold were pure and unadulterated. Pharmacists came under considerable scrutiny, especially from physicians, when their increasingly profitable trade bred unscrupulous and unknowledgeable practitioners. Many of the patent medicines sold at the time were inefficacious, mislabeled, and even unsafe for consumption.

The first major piece of legislation to affect medication use in the 20th century was the Pure Food and Drug Act of 1906. Because the food and drug product industries were considered to be engaging in interstate commerce, the federal government passed this law to enable authorities to enforce penalties for certain types of misbranding and adulteration. The original statute was not particularly comprehensive or well written, however, so manufacturers, prescribers, and dispensers found many loopholes through which they could evade prosecution. Moreover, the Pure Food and Drug Act of 1906 did little to address the issue of efficacy in drug products.

Pressure continued to mount on the federal government to strengthen the food and drug laws, but unfortunately, it took a tragedy before more comprehensive measures were taken. During 1937, at least 73 deaths were attributed to ingestion of the toxic Elixir Sulfanilamide (Sonnedecker, 1963, p. 200). This scandal provided the necessary impetus for passage of the Food, Drug, and Cosmetic Act of 1938. This act afforded greater authority to the Food and Drug Administration (FDA), the federal agency charged with enforcing it, and with approving new drugs and new indications of drugs before they could be marketed in the United States. The statutes within the act and subsequent regulations issued by the FDA make it easier to enforce standards of safety and efficacy of drug products.

During the early part of the 20th century, pharmacists continued to engage in their roles as drug curators and dispensers. Interestingly, no formal legislation addressed the categorization of drugs into nonprescription and prescription products. Persons typically did not have to visit a physician if they desired a remedy for an ailment. Without such formal restrictions on dispensing, it could be argued that the pharmacist indirectly had some prescribing authority. Additionally, the pharmacist was relied on to provide advice to consumers on compounds he or she prescribed and dispensed (Hepler, 1987). Anecdotally, since pharmacists were—and still are—very accessible and visited frequently by customers, they were often the first source of entry into the healthcare system, particularly in rural areas that may have been underserved by physicians. They continued to fill this role despite a report published in 1910 by Abraham Flexner, who was appointed to study medical education, in which he contended that pharmacy was not a profession because its only responsibility was to carry out orders given by physicians. In response to this and other reports questioning the standing of pharmacy among other occupations, the American Association of Colleges of Pharmacy (AACP) commissioned a study directed by W.W. Charters. The study ultimately served as the basis for the AACP to require a 4-year baccalaureate degree program to be established by all colleges of pharmacy (Hepler, 1987).

The 1940s to the Early 1970s

The relatively brief period from the 1940s to the early 1970s brought significant changes in how health care was organized, delivered, and financed. This period has previously been described as the "era of expansion" (Relman, 1988, p. 1221). The Hospital Survey and Construction (Hill-Burton) Act of 1946 provided considerable grant monies for the renovation and expansion of existing hospitals as well as the construction of new ones, primarily in underserved inner-city and rural areas (Torrens, 1993; see Chapter 8). Continuously mounting pressure from the growing number of persons who were unable to access the healthcare system led to the passage in 1965 of the Titles XVIII and XIX amendments to the 1935 Social Security Act, which established the Medicare and Medicaid programs. The result was a significant increase in the number of persons with some type of health coverage and a dramatic rise in the utilization of medical care goods and services. The Medicaid program, in particular, resulted in a dramatic shift in the use of pharmaceuticals and significantly increased the number of prescriptions dispensed (see Chapter 18).

In contrast with the trend of expanding roles for other allied healthcare professionals during this period, pharmacists began to see their roles in medication use management diminish. Several forces were at play in bringing about these changes. First, large, wholesale apothecaries were eventually transformed into large-scale manufacturers of pharmaceutical products. Previously, the majority of products dispensed by pharmacists were the result of their compounding bulk agents. Technological advances in industrial manufacturing and pharmaceutics, coupled with the increasing number of available compounds and societal demand that medicinal products become more uniform in their composition, resulted in the ability of and desire by manufacturers to prefabricate drugs in standardized dosage forms such as elixirs, syrups, tablets, and capsules.

The most influential piece of legislation that affected the medication use process in the United States was passed in 1951. The Durham-Humphrey amendment to the Food, Drug, and Cosmetic Act created the prescription or "legend" drug, whose label was required to carry the warning, "Caution: Federal law prohibits dispensing without a prescription." The result was an entirely new class of products that pharmacists did not have the ability to dispense without written orders from a licensed prescriber. At the same time, the profession's code of ethics as derived by the American Pharmaceutical (now Pharmacists) Association stated that "The pharmacist does not discuss the therapeutic effects or composition of a prescription with a patient. When such questions are asked, he suggests that the qualified practitioner is the proper person with whom such matters should be discussed" (Buerki & Vottero, 1994, p. 93). These forces relegated the pharmacist largely to a dispenser of presynthesized drug products.

The 1940s to early 1970s period also ushered in tremendous changes in the foci of pharmacy curricula throughout the United States. As part of this reform, many baccalaureate pharmacy programs were expanded to include a 5th year. Many of the extra didactic credit hours in these curricula were devoted to the further inclusion of scientific courses. Hepler (1987) contends that the primary objective of pharmaceutical education was to legitimize faculties, curricula, and ultimately the profession itself. He argues that the pharmaceutical industry encouraged research at pharmacy schools that was oriented toward the drug product. Courses in pharmacognosy gave way to natural products and medicinal chemistry; zoology was transformed into physiology; and galenical pharmacy evolved into pharmaceutics. In addition, new disciplines, such as pharmacology, biopharmaceutics, and pharmacokinetics, were born from the melding and application of other basic sciences. An argument for inclusion of these courses into curricula is that with the proliferation of new drug discoveries, practitioners required a scientific background to interpret literature and understand the proper use of drug products that would continue to enter the market throughout the pharmacist's career.

Nevertheless, it was argued that pharmacists became "overeducated and underutilized" during this period (Hepler, 1987, p. 537). Brodie (1967) wondered if the profession had lost the mainstream of its practice. A pioneer in pharmacy, he coined the term *drug use control*, a mantle he suggested pharmacists carry to use their education to promote patient welfare in the form of drug safety. He defined this term as "that system of knowledge, understanding, judgments, procedures, skills, controls and ethics that assures optimal safety in the distribution and use of medication" (Brodie, 1967, p. 65).

The Early 1970s to the Present

The 1970s ushered in considerable concern over skyrocketing healthcare costs that were consuming an increasingly larger portion of the U.S. gross national product. The previous era in health care had resulted in the rapid perfusion of expensive new medications and technologies, professionalization and specialization of healthcare occupations, and proliferation of medical diagnoses for conditions not previously linked to biomedical origins (medicalization), such as alcoholism. Moreover, the orientation of most insurance plans in the form of indemnity rather than service benefits provided incentives for medical care providers and patients to overuse healthcare services, often resulting in duplication and a loss of continuity in the care provided.

In recent years, several measures have been taken to counter these trends. Although they had existed before that time, the Health Maintenance Organization Act of 1973 paved the way for managed care organizations to garner a larger share of the health insurance market. Perhaps even more critical was the implementation of a prospective payment system of diagnosis-related groups by the Health Care Financing Administration (now the Centers for Medicare and Medicaid Services) for Medicare patients (Pink, 1991). A diagnosis-related group is essentially a taxonomy of disease states and conditions for which patients may be admitted into a hospital. Reimbursement to hospitals for treating Medicare patients was set prospectively according to their diagnosis, regardless of the length and intensity of care. This system provided an incentive for hospitals to discharge patients quicker and sicker into other less intensive and expensive health care settings.

This period for pharmacy began with two reports that raised concerns among the entire profession. First, the Dichter Institute study, a survey commissioned by the American Pharmaceutical Association (APhA, now the American Pharmacists Association) in 1973 found that more respondents saw pharmacists as businessmen than as healthcare providers (Maine & Penna, 1996). With the rapid expansion of large, full-service chain pharmacies that sold many products besides medicines, along with a lack of knowledge of pharmacists' training and expertise, study respondents viewed pharmacists more as extensions of pharmaceutical manufacturers and wholesalers. The blame for patients' lack of awareness of the services that pharmacists could provide rested squarely on the shoulders of the profession and pharmacy academia.

The second study that generated some alarm was the Millis Commission's report in 1975, *Pharmacists for the Future: The Report of the Study Commission on Pharmacy* (Millis, 1975). This report suggested that pharmacists found themselves inadequately prepared in systems analysis and management skills and had particular deficiencies in communicating with patients, physicians, and other healthcare professionals. A subsequent report suggested inculcating more of the behavioral and social sciences into pharmacy curricula and encouraged more faculty participation and research in real problems of practice (Millis, 1976).

Before the release of these reports, the American Society of Hospital (now Health-Systems) Pharmacists had published *Mirror to Hospital Pharmacy*, which stated bluntly that pharmacy had lost its way in producing professionals, while noting that the frustration and dissatisfaction of practitioners were beginning to affect students (Hepler, 1987). The clinical pharmacy movement was created to capture the essence of the drug use control concept put forth by Brodie and to promote the pharmacist's role as therapeutic advisor. This movement brought about changes in pharmacy education and practice.

In the late 1960s, the 6-year PharmD degree was introduced, with the additional year being devoted mostly to therapeutics courses and experiential education. Throughout the 1970s, 1980s, and into the early 1990s, an increasing number of colleges of pharmacy began offering the PharmD degree, but primarily as a postbaccalaureate program. Pharmacists who completed such programs secured jobs as clinical pharmacists, primarily in hospitals where they performed fewer dispensing functions and provided more services such as pharmacokinetic dosing, therapeutic monitoring, and drug information. Eventually, colleges of pharmacy began phasing out their baccalaureate programs. In 1995, the Argus Commission of the AACP recommended the 6-year PharmD as the entry-level degree into the profession (American Association of Colleges of Pharmacy, 1996).

PHARMACEUTICAL CARE

AACP – American Association of Colleges of Pharmacy

Initial Conceptualization

Despite the strides made by the profession during the 1970s and 1980s, questions existed about pharmacy's place in society—that is, performing services just for service's sake, without actually serving the welfare of the patient, was by no means a societal mandate and did not necessarily constitute a professional role (Penna, 1990). It was argued that clinical pharmacy, in itself, maintained its focus on products and services and not on the patient. It was also becoming increasingly apparent that medicalization and the proliferated use of drugs had repercussions in addition to benefits. Studies indicating dramatic rises in adverse drug reactions, hospitalizations, and even deaths from drug misadventuring grew more common (Manasse, 1989a, p. 936; 1989b, p. 1148). Evidence also demonstrated the pervasiveness of patient nonadherence to medications (Boyd, Covington, Stanaszek, & Coussons, 1974) and its ramifications (Col, Fanale, & Kronholm, 1990).

Linda Strand and her colleagues identified eight categories of problems that could arise and result in poorer health outcomes and drug-related morbidity and mortality of patients, which included: (1) untreated indications; (2) improper drug selection; (3) subtherapeutic dosage; (4) failure to receive drugs; (5) overdosage; (6) adverse drug reactions; (7) drug interactions; and (8) drug use without indications (Strand, Cippole, Morley, Ramsey, & Lamsam, 1990). Hepler and Strand then recognized that many of these problems could be reduced or averted by pharmacists—that pharmacy's raison d'etre should be to serve society by maximizing the benefits and minimizing the untoward effects of drug therapy for patients (Hepler & Strand, 1990).

This recognition operationally defined pharmacy's mandate for the 21st century: pharmaceutical care as

> the responsible provision of drug therapy for the purpose of achieving definite outcomes that improve a patient's quality of life. These outcomes are (1) cure of a

disease, (2) elimination or reduction of a patient's symptomatology, (3) arresting or slowing of a disease process, or (4) preventing a disease or symptomatology." (Hepler & Strand, 1990, p. 539)

Hepler and Strand further delineated this concept to describe it as a process in which the pharmacist establishes a covenantal relationship with the patient in a mutually beneficial exchange. He or she cooperates with the patient and other professionals in designing, implementing, and monitoring a therapeutic plan that will produce specific outcomes, thereby performing three basic functions: (1) identifying potential and actual drug-related problems, (2) resolving actual drug-related problems, and (3) preventing potential drug-related problems (Hepler & Strand, 1990).

Implementation

By the mid-1990s, pharmaceutical care had become the rallying cry for leaders in practice, professional organizations, and academia. One can plainly see, however, that despite the many strides taken by the profession since Hepler and Strand's landmark paper, pharmaceutical care is not the pervasive modus operandi. This is not to say that most pharmacists are inadequate; indeed, the vast majority of pharmacists are well trained, hard working, caring, ethical, and competent professionals. But changing the mission and practice philosophy of an entire profession is not easy, particularly when many barriers exist. Some of these barriers include:

1. Drug product focus: Pharmacists have historically been preoccupied with dispensing drug products.
2. Service focus: Some services provided by pharmacists are distant from the patient and may be performed without regard to the resultant outcomes (e.g., pharmacokinetic dosing calculations).
3. Other healthcare professionals: Physicians, nurses, and other allied healthcare professionals may view pharmaceutical care as an infringement on their turf.
4. Lack of incentives: The current methods for paying and rewarding pharmacists center on dispensing volume, not on the care provided.
5. Logistical barriers: Many pharmacies are not designed and equipped properly to provide private consultation, disease monitoring, and dissemination of information—all key to the pharmaceutical care process.
6. Pharmacy ignorance and inertia: "The greatest barrier to pharmaceutical care is ourselves. The success of an idea requires the dedication of people who believe in it and who pledge themselves to its general acceptance and implementation" (Penna, 1990, p. 547).

The last barrier was especially significant because the term *pharmaceutical care* generated ambivalence among many pharmacists. It is difficult to blame individual practitioners for their failure to embrace this notion. For years, a considerable amount of ambiguity surrounded the concept. Pharmaceutical care represents an entire philosophy of practice; therefore, identification of the steps involved in preparing and following up on care plans, while useful, is not enough to guide pharmacists in this mission. Pharmacists' interactions with patients make up just one component of implementing an effective practice. Other things must be considered, including adequate human, financial, and technical resources, in addition to management, marketing, and legal issues. **Table 3-1** presents a more contemporary view of pharmacy care that includes

Table 3-1 Pharmaceutical Care Practice Domains

I.   Risk management
- Devise system of data collection
- Perform prospective drug utilization review
- Document therapeutic interventions and activities
- Obtain over-the-counter medication history
- Calculate dosages for drugs with a narrow therapeutic index
- Report adverse drug events to FDA
- Triage patients' needs for proper referral
- Remain abreast of newly uncovered adverse effects and drug–drug interactions

II. Patient advocacy
- Serve as patient advocate with respect to social, economic, and psychological barriers to drug therapy
- Attempt to change patients' medication orders when barriers to compliance exist
- Counsel patients on new and refill medications as necessary
- Promote patient wellness
- Maintain caring, friendly relationship with patients
- Telephone patients to obtain medication orders called in and not picked up

III. Disease management
- Provide information to patients on how to manage their disease state/condition
- Monitor patients' progress resulting from pharmacotherapy
- Carry inventory of products necessary for patients to execute a therapeutic plan (e.g., inhalers, nebulizers, glucose monitors)
- Supply patients with information on support and educational groups (e.g., American Diabetes Association, Multiple Sclerosis Society)

IV. Pharmaceutical care services marketing
- Meet prominent prescribers in the local area of practice
- Be an active member of professional associations that support the concept of pharmaceutical care
- Make available an area for private consultation services for patients as necessary
- Identify software that facilitates pharmacists' patient care-related activities

V.   Business management
- Utilize technicians and other staff to free up the pharmacist's time
- Ensure adequate work flow for efficiency in operations

Source: Copyright © 2009 by the McGraw Hill Companies. Originally published in Desselle, S.P. (2009). Pharmaceutical care as a management movement. In S.P. Desselle and D.P. Zgarrick, 2nd ed. (Eds.), *Pharmacy management: Essentials for all settings* (pp. 3–17). New York: McGraw-Hill.

these and other domains. Pharmacists must be competent in each of these areas to maximize their ability to provide effective patient-oriented services.

Medication Therapy Management

While the pharmaceutical care movement made an indelible mark on the profession, its terminology is being replaced with more contemporary language that reflects pharmacists' growing roles in the provision of public health services (Desselle and

Zgarrick, 2009, p. 3). In recognizing the morbidity and mortality resulting from medication errors as a public health problem, the profession has begun to embrace the concept of medication therapy management (MTM). MTM represents a comprehensive and proactive approach to help patients maximize the benefits from drug therapy and includes services aimed at facilitating or improving patient adherence to drug therapy, educating entire populations of persons, conducting wellness programs, and becoming more intimately involved in disease management and monitoring. Eleven professional pharmacy organizations came together to produce a white paper on the core elements of an MTM service model. The model is designed to improve collaboration among pharmacists, physicians, and other healthcare professionals; enhance communication between patients and their healthcare team; and optimize medication use for improved patient outcomes. The core elements of an MTM service model include medication therapy review, a personal medication record, a medication-related action plan, intervention and/or referral, and documentation and follow-up. **Figure 3-1** illustrates the MTM core elements service model. First the pharmacist, with assistance from properly trained staff, interviews the patient and creates a database with appropriate information, reviews the patient's medication regimen, identifies any medication-related problems, prioritizes them, and creates a plan for the patient. This may be accomplished with the assistance of other healthcare professionals to whom pharmacists may triage the patient should the need arise. The pharmacist implements a plan by creating and communicating the personal medication record and medication-related action plan while documenting all actions taken and following up with the patient.

Pharmaceutical care and MTM do not differ much in their basic tenets and core elements; i.e., becoming more proactive and taking greater responsibility for patients' medication therapy-related outcomes. The shift from pharmaceutical care to MTM reflects a more collaborative approach between the pharmacist and other healthcare providers, facilitating greater likelihood in collaborative working relationships and enhancing the likelihood of reimbursement for services. Moreover, the concept of pharmaceutical care might be criticized as pharmacy taking an overly insular individualistic approach to advancing the profession and treating patients. The MTM movement was strengthened by language in the Medicare Prescription Drug, Improvement and Modernization Act (MMA) of 2003 (public law number 108-173), which mandates payment for MTM services and proffers pharmacists as viable health professionals who may offer such services.

Reimbursement Issues

The profession has made strides to address many barriers toward advancing pharmacy practice and MTM services, but still has further to go in having pharmacists formally recognized as providers and educators who should be reimbursed for providing patient-related services. Pharmacists have long had opportunities to become certified as experts in pharmacotherapy, but recognition of those achievements outside the pharmacy profession has been problematic. In the 1990s and early 21st century, state governments aided this quest by beginning to pass legislation expanding pharmacists' scope of practice to include broader pharmacotherapeutic decision making, implementation of home healthcare services, and provision of immunizations.

Many leaders in pharmacy hailed the passage of MMA. While many of its provisions are of concern to pharmacists—particularly in regard to formulary issues, methods used to calculate payment to providers and the concentration of market power to

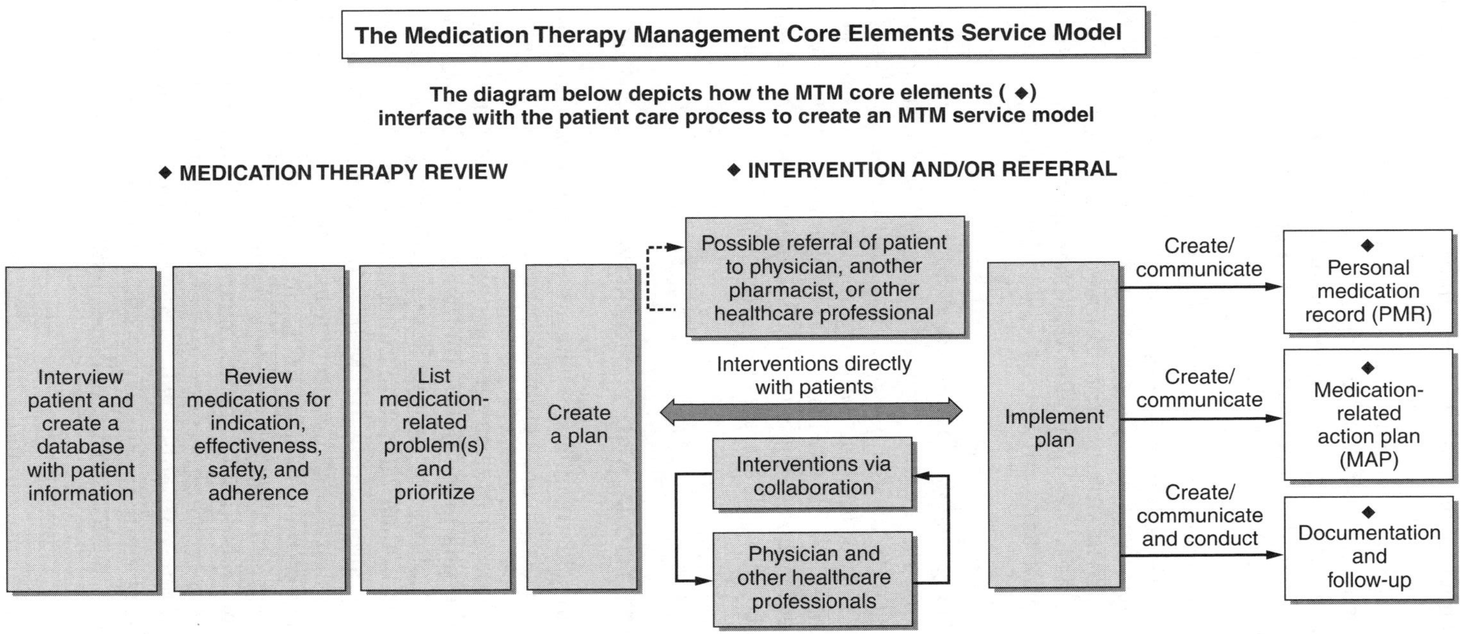

The Medication Therapy Management Core Elements Service Model

The diagram below depicts how the MTM core elements (◆)
interface with the patient care process to create an MTM service model

◆ **MEDICATION THERAPY REVIEW**

◆ **INTERVENTION AND/OR REFERRAL**

Interview patient and create a database with patient information	Review medications for indication, effectiveness, safety, and adherence	List medication-related problem(s) and prioritize	Create a plan

Possible referral of patient to physician, another pharmacist, or other healthcare professional

Interventions directly with patients

Interventions via collaboration

Physician and other healthcare professionals

Implement plan

Create/communicate → Personal medication record (PMR) ◆

Create/communicate → Medication-related action plan (MAP) ◆

Create/communicate and conduct → Documentation and follow-up ◆

Figure 3-1 Flow Chart of a Medication Therapy Management Service Model. *Source:* Used with permission. Copyright © 2008 by the American Pharmacists Association and the National Association of Chain Drug Stores Foundation. All rights reserved. MTM = medication therapy management.

health plans—the MMA is the most comprehensive federal legislation to date that recognizes the need for medication therapy management services in ambulatory care. The MMA does not strictly govern face-to-face encounters and does not mandate that such services be provided by a pharmacist, but its language does position pharmacy as a choice to fulfill a role in reducing drug-related morbidity and educating older adults on the proper pharmacologic and nonpharmacologic management of comorbid diseases. Of course, providing coverage for prescription medicines for many older adults who previously lacked such insurance also may serve to increase prescription volume and potentially boost profits for pharmacies, which could then invest additional monies into reengineering their practices to provide more patient-oriented services. To date, the implications of MMA appear to be a mixed bag for both pharmacy and patients, with additional persons being afforded drug coverage at relatively stable premiums, but with more rapid inflationary costs of prescription drugs and limited, albeit important strides made toward reimbursement of pharmacists for direct MTM involvement. Health plans often have filled the niche for MTM services to qualified beneficiaries through the use of telephone and mail services often implemented by nurses and other healthcare professionals.

Some progress also is being made in the private sector. The Asheville project featured a long-term effort supported by employers to reimburse pharmacists for providing diabetes management services to their employees. The results suggested that pharmacists could help patients in improving both short-term (Cranor & Christensen, 2003) and long-term (Cranor, Bunting, & Christensen, 2003) outcomes, while saving employers money from averted medical costs. To that end, it appears as though some patients may be willing to pay for pharmacists' services out of pocket if necessary (MacKinnnon & Mahrous, 2002).

PHARMACY PRACTICE TODAY AND TOMORROW

One might be tempted to ask, "Well, just where are we now and where are we going?" That question may not be easy to answer, but a few trends are worth noting.

First, the PharmD has replaced the baccalaureate (bachelor of science) degree as the entry-level degree in the pharmacy field. Another trend in pharmacy education is the continued efforts by colleges of pharmacy to incorporate more of the social and administrative sciences into their curricula. Colleges of pharmacy were initially slow to respond to the changes proposed by the Millis Commission. The AACP refocused its efforts to encourage a more liberal education for pharmacy students in the 1990s with its Commission to Implement Change in Pharmaceutical Education (1993; American Association of Colleges of Pharmacy, 1996). Among the issues addressed by the commission were the incorporation of specific courses and concepts related to health policy organization, communication, economic analysis, and the understanding of cultural diversity throughout the curriculum. The commission also addressed how courses should be taught, stressing multidisciplinary, problem- or service-based approaches to delivering course content to encourage problem-solving and critical-thinking skills in future practitioners.

Other trends related to pharmacy practice concern the proliferation of new and exciting areas of practice, the emergence of collaborative working relationships, expanded scope of practice agreements legislated by a number of states, the use of automated technology and technicians for dispensing functions, and shifts in the pharmacist labor supply.

Licensure Requirements

Pharmacy continues to be one of the more rewarding professions with respect to the starting salaries of its members following completion of the entry-level degree and licensure. In addition to completing the PharmD degree, prospective pharmacists must log a certain number of hours as an intern practicing under the supervision of a licensed preceptor pharmacist; the number of hours required varies across states. The graduate must also successfully complete the North American Pharmacist Licensure (NAPLEX) Examination and his or her respective state's jurisprudence examinations. When the requirements for licensure within a state have been completed, the candidate is qualified to become a registered pharmacist (RPh) who is licensed to practice in that particular state only.

Postgraduate Educational Opportunities

A choice of exciting careers awaits the pharmacy graduate. Some career paths, however, require the student to pursue postgraduate education. Master's and doctoral degree programs are offered at many colleges of pharmacy in the general areas of medicinal chemistry, pharmaceutics, pharmacology/toxicology, and social and administrative sciences, with each college tailoring its specific programs in each of these areas to student needs and faculty interests and backgrounds. Pursuing one of these degrees is ideal for the student who is interested in a career in academia, the pharmaceutical industry, government, or another setting requiring research expertise. Individuals who are interested in advancing their careers in the practice arena may seek one of any number of residencies and fellowships offered through universities, hospitals, and other healthcare providers throughout the United States.

Specialization Through Certification

Other opportunities are available to pharmacists through the process of certification. Certification is recognition by a nongovernment association or agency that an individual has completed predetermined qualifications in a field of specialized knowledge. Pharmacists may become board certified in any of the following six specialties through programs administered by the Board of Pharmacy Specialties (BPS):

1. *Oncology pharmacy.* Addresses medication therapy needs of patients with cancer. Specialists are closely involved in recognition, management, and prevention of unique morbidities associated with cancer and cancer treatment and recognition of the balance between improved survival and quality of life as primary outcome indicators.
2. *Psychiatric pharmacy.* Addresses the often complex medication therapy regimens and concomitant somatic comorbidities of patients with psychiatric disorders. The specialist is responsible for optimizing drug treatment and patient care by conducting patient assessments, recommending treatment plans, monitoring patient response, and recognizing drug-induced problems.
3. *Nutrition support pharmacy.* Addresses the care of patients who receive specialized nutrition support, including parenteral and enteral nutrition. The specialist has responsibility for promoting maintenance and/or restoration of optimal nutritional

status and designing and modifying treatment needs. He or she often functions as a member of a multidisciplinary nutrition support team.

4. *Nuclear pharmacy.* Seeks to improve and promote public health through the safe and effective use of radioactive drugs for diagnosis and therapy. A nuclear pharmacist specializes in procurement, compounding, quality assurance, dispensing, distribution, and development of radiopharmaceuticals.

5. *Pharmacotherapy.* Assumes responsibility for ensuring the safe, appropriate, and economical use of drugs in patient care. The specialist often has responsibility for direct patient care, may conduct clinical research, and serves as a primary source of drug information for other healthcare professionals.

6. *Ambulatory Care.* Beginning in 2011, the Board of Pharmacy Specialties will have begun to confer certification for candidates meeting their qualification in ambulatory care. The ambulatory care pharmacist must understand and apply skills related to pharmacists' roles in public health, develop rapport with ambulatory patients, prioritize patients' drug-related problems, apply pharmacoeconomic principles when designing a treatment plan, perform health screening, and conduct physical assessment procedures, as appropriate (BPS, 2010).

These programs are rigorous and require extensive work and study. Pharmacists may also complete other certification programs in a wide variety of areas—most notably in the management of certain disease states/conditions, such as diabetes, hypertension, and pain management. Other potential areas of focus include geriatrics, pediatrics, managed care, and management/marketing. These programs are administered by professional or health organizations, such as the American Diabetes Association, and they are often approved by the American Council on Pharmaceutical Education, though they do not indicate board certification.

Unlike licensure, certification does not give the recipient any legal privileges. It does offer the recipient many advantages, however. Aside from the implicit value of the knowledge and expertise gained, some job descriptions posted by medical care institutions require certification. In addition, third-party payers may be more likely to reimburse a board-certified specialist or reimburse such a professional for the same services at a higher rate. Board certification also represents a marketing tool that specialists can use to advocate their services. As of 2009, nearly 8,000 pharmacists had become certified through the Board of Pharmacy Specialties alone, with more than half of those certifications in pharmacotherapy (BPS, 2010).

PROFESSIONAL PHARMACY ORGANIZATIONS

A Brief History

The diversity of pharmacists' practice settings is reflected in the large number of professional pharmacy organizations. The first professional pharmacy organization, the APhA, was founded in 1852 for the purpose of establishing national standards of quality for drugs and chemicals. Its founding came in response to criticism of the pharmacy trade by physicians who threatened to regulate the profession. Shortly thereafter, the APhA developed a code of ethics for its member practitioners. During the 1900s, other professional associations developed. Some of them were offshoots from within various sections of the APhA. The number of professional organizations continues to grow as the interests and work environments of pharmacists expand.

The Purpose and Functions of Pharmacy Organizations

Professional pharmacy organizations represent a few of tens of thousands of national associations in the United States, not including state and local associations. The primary reason that these organizations exist is to serve the interests of their members. They publish position papers as well as lobby governments, other professional organizations, and private businesses on behalf of their members. Examples of issues targeted for lobbying efforts include the crafting of specific language beneficial to pharmacists in regulations proposed by federal agencies, reimbursement for cognitive services, and expansion of the scope of pharmacy practice.

Specific benefits and services that professional pharmacy organizations provide include the following:

- *Information dissemination.* Publishing of journals and newsletters to disseminate the results of pertinent studies and updates on professional practice and legal issues. Recently, associations have also initiated weekly email services and regular updates on their websites.
- *Maintenance of practitioners' competency.* Establishing codes of ethics and standards of practice, as well as providing free continuing education and professional meetings.
- *Career planning assistance.* Posting of jobs in related fields, placement of advertisements in journals by employers, and sponsorship of workshops for career advancement.
- *Financial benefits.* Providing discount rates on items such as resource materials, credit cards, and insurance policies.
- *Participation in governance.* Providing an opportunity for members to help create and revise organization policies at professional meetings and serve on committees.

Professional Organizations With Pharmacist Membership

Individual pharmacists may enroll as members of some of the organizations that directly or indirectly serve the profession.

The *American Pharmacists Association* (APhA, www.pharmacist.com) changed its name from the American Pharmaceutical Association to more accurately reflect the importance of its primary constituents: pharmacists. Arguably the most diverse pharmacy-related organization in terms of its membership, the APhA serves pharmacists in all practice settings. Headquartered in Washington, D.C., it is actively involved in lobbying the government on pharmacists' behalf. Its student organization, the Academy of Student Pharmacists, has more student members than any other professional association. The APhA publishes numerous journals and newsletters, including *Pharmacy Today*, to help students and practitioners keep abreast of current issues, and *Journal of the American Pharmacists Association*, which features research in the administrative, basic, and clinical pharmaceutical sciences. It also publishes monographs, such as those describing the MMA of 2003, which are very helpful to pharmacists.

Formerly the American Society of Hospital Pharmacists, the *American Society of Health-Systems Pharmacists* (ASHP, www.ashp.org) changed its name to reflect the evolution of hospitals into integrated delivery networks. The ASHP is a national accrediting organization for pharmacy residency and pharmacy technician training programs. It publishes numerous educational materials and handbooks, including *American Hospital Formulary System Drug Information*. It also publishes *American Journal of Health-Systems Pharmacy* and produces *International Pharmaceutical Abstracts*, a bimonthly abstracting and indexing service. The ASHP promotes guidelines, standards, and best practices in a number of pharmacy practice arenas. Its annual clinical meeting is the largest gathering of pharmacists worldwide.

Founded as the National Association of Retail Druggists, the mission of the *National Community Pharmacists Association* (NCPA, www.ncpanet.org) is to keep the business of pharmacy viable. The NCPA is the voice for America's independent community pharmacists. It provides continuing education through its publication, *America's Pharmacist.* The NCPA's Management Institute serves as a clearinghouse for up-to-date management information. The organization also affords to its members the opportunity to join ValuRite, a professional services administration organization, which provides greater purchasing power to community pharmacy owners. The NCPA administers the National Institute for Pharmacist Care Outcomes program and sponsors the NCPA Foundation, which awards grants intended to promote the profession and pharmacy care outcomes. The NCPA also publishes *NCPA Digest on CD-ROM.* The *NCPA Digest* allows independent community pharmacies to assess and compare their financial and clinical performance with indicators for other pharmacies of similar size.

The *Academy of Managed Care Pharmacy* (www.amcp.org) serves patients and the public through the promotion of wellness and rational drug therapy by the application of managed care principles. Part of its mission is the advancement of pharmacy practice in managed healthcare systems. The Academy of Managed Care Pharmacy publishes *Journal of Managed Care Pharmacy*, which highlights research on administrative issues and on the rational use of drug therapies, including cost-effectiveness and outcomes studies. This organization has been a leader in efforts to standardize formulary submissions and to improve the quality of formulary decisions made by insurers and institutions. It also provides weekly email and fax-on-demand services that keep its members informed about drug therapy and legislative issues from around the United States.

Membership in the *American College of Apothecaries* (www.acainfo.org) is open to pharmacists who own or hold shares in a pharmacy, primarily apothecary-style pharmacies with low levels of front-end merchandise. Among its publications are *Guidelines for Improving Communication in Pharmacy Practice* and *Guidelines for Marketing Your Community Pharmacy Practice.*

Founded to strengthen pharmacy's role in long-term care, the *American Society of Consultant Pharmacists* (www.ascp.com) publishes the journal, *Consultant Pharmacist,* which features articles on the results of drug utilization reviews and clinical studies, drug information, and managerial aspects of consultant pharmacy. Among its other publications is *Drug Regimen Review: A Process Guide for Pharmacists.*

Founded to advance the practice of clinical pharmacy, the *American College of Clinical Pharmacy* (www.accp.com) promotes clinical research, rational drug therapy, and fellowship training. It also publishes educational materials related to pharmacoeconomics and outcomes research. Many faculty members in departments of pharmacy practice are members of the American College of Clinical Pharmacy.

The *National Pharmaceutical Association* (www.nphanet.net) is dedicated to representing the views and ideas of minority pharmacists on critical issues affecting health care and pharmacy as well as advancing the standards of pharmaceutical care among all practitioners.

The *National Council on Patient Information and Education* (www.talkaboutrx.org) is dedicated to improving communication between healthcare professionals and patients. It also makes available the Talking About Prescriptions Planning Kit and Educate Before You Medicate promotional materials.

Organizations with Corporate Membership

Pharmacists may also be affected by or interact with other organizations of which they are not members. The members of these organizations are corporations, rather than individuals.

Formerly the National Wholesale Druggists Association, the *Healthcare Distribution Management Association* (www.healthcaredistribution.org) is the national association of full-service drug wholesalers. This organization's mission is to strengthen relations between wholesalers, their suppliers, and customers, and to sponsor and disseminate research and information on new technology and management practices for wholesalers. Full-service drug wholesalers are typically large companies involved in myriad aspects of drug distribution, including automated dispensing technologies and storage of specialty compounds.

The *Institute for Safe Medication Practices* (www.ismp.org) is the United States' only nonprofit organization devoted entirely to medication error prevention and safe medication use. It oversees a voluntary medication error-reporting system and promotes error reduction strategies to the healthcare community, policy makers, and the public.

The voice of the chain drug store industry, the *National Association of Chain Drug Stores* (www.nacds.org) is involved in numerous professional activities, including sponsoring student recruitment programs in high schools, conducting visitation programs for faculty and students to chain store headquarters operations, and awarding grant support for studies in management and administration. It posts positions for pharmacists in chain pharmacies throughout the United States on its website and, along with organizations such as the NCPA, supports the SureScripts Electronic Prescribing Network to allow for the electronic exchange of information between prescribers and pharmacies.

The *Pharmaceutical Researchers and Manufacturers of America* (www.pharma.org) is a powerful consortium of manufacturers of brand-name products that is heavily involved in supporting research and development of new drugs and pharmaceutical delivery systems.

Formerly the Nonprescription Drug Manufacturers Association (NDMA), the *Consumer Healthcare Products Association* (www.chpa-info.org) is concerned with issues relevant to makers of over-the-counter medications and encourages responsible self-medication practices by consumers. The Consumer Healthcare Products Association conducts a voluntary labeling review service for members and promotes the readability of over-the-counter product labels.

The *Generic Pharmaceutical Association* (www.gphaonline.org) represents manufacturers and distributors within the generic drug industry. The Generic Pharmaceutical

Association is dedicated to the provision of high-quality, cost-effective equivalents to brand-name prescription drugs. It provides lawmakers, government agencies, regulators, prescribers, and pharmacists with information regarding the safety, effectiveness, and therapeutic equivalence of generic medicines.

Educational and Regulatory Organizations

Some organizations provide services to pharmacists (who may or may not be members of those groups) and regulate their practice and educational requirements.

Society grants pharmacy the power of self-regulation as long as society can reap the benefits of having highly competent and moral professionals serving its interests. The *National Association of Boards of Pharmacy* (NABP, www.nabp.net) assists state boards of pharmacy in protecting the public by developing, implementing, and enforcing uniform standards. The NABP develops and administers the North American Pharmacist Licensure Examination and oversees reciprocity of licenses across states.

The *Accreditation Council for Pharmacy Education* (www.acpe-accredit.org) is a national agency that provides for the accreditation of professional degree programs in pharmacy and for the approval of providers of continuing pharmaceutical education. The Accreditation Council for Pharmacy Education is an autonomous agency whose board of directors is made up of members of the AACP, APhA, NABP, and American Council on Education.

The *American Association of Colleges of Pharmacy* (AACP) is a national organization representing the interests of pharmaceutical educators. The AACP is committed to excellence in pharmaceutical education. Both individual faculty members and schools of pharmacy constitute its membership. It publishes *American Journal of Pharmaceutical Education*, with contributions from pharmacy faculty throughout the United States, to disseminate information on course content, curricula, and innovative teaching strategies.

The mission of the *American Foundation for Pharmaceutical Education* (www.afpenet. org) is to advance and support pharmaceutical sciences education at U.S. schools and colleges of pharmacy by awarding scholarships and grants to pharmacy students and faculty.

PHARMACY TECHNICIANS

As the practice of pharmacy evolves, so do the roles of pharmacy technicians. The number of prescriptions dispensed in the United States has increased rapidly in recent years, as has the diversity of settings in which pharmacists practice. To keep up with the rising demand for pharmaceutical products and services, technicians will play a greater role in support of pharmaceutical care. This section examines pharmacy technicians, their expanding roles and responsibilities, and certification and management issues.

The Choice of a Career as a Pharmacy Technician

In 2006, approximately 285,000 pharmacy technicians were practicing in the United States (Bureau of Labor Statistics, 2010–2011) with a median hour wage of $12.32 with exact earnings dependent upon their location, practice setting, experience, and certification status. Technicians receive their training through formal educational programs at vocational or technical schools and community colleges, formal on-the-job training programs sponsored by employers, or informal on-the-job training. An increasing number of nationally accredited technician training programs exist, with the standard for accreditation by the ASHP calling for 600 hours of contact time, extending over at least 15 weeks (American Society of Hospital Pharmacists, 1993).

The jobs of pharmacy technicians were once geared toward clerical and custodial duties. Indeed, the Scope of Pharmacy Practice Project conducted in the early 1990s revealed that pharmacy technicians spent more than 26% of their time collecting, organizing, and evaluating information in assisting pharmacists to serve patients, more than 21% of their time developing and managing medication distribution and control, and a bit less than 7% of their time providing drug information and education (American Society of Hospital Pharmacists, 1994).

Pharmacy Technicians' Expanding Roles and Responsibilities

Today, pharmacy technicians are involved in far more areas of pharmacy practice. In addition to assisting with outpatient prescription dispensing, many community pharmacy technicians participate in purchasing/inventory control, billing, and repackaging products. Most hospital pharmacy technicians assist with inpatient medication dispensing, but many also prepare intravenous admixtures and engage in nonsterile compounding, repackaging, purchasing, and billing. A significant minority of the technicians surveyed indicated that they participate in educating and training other technicians.

The Scope of Pharmacy Practice Project report also provided a comprehensive classification of pharmacy technician responsibilities and activities (American Society of Hospital Pharmacists, 1994). It segmented these duties into three main function areas:

1. *Assist the pharmacist in serving patients.* Receive prescription or medication orders, obtain information from patients and from other healthcare professionals, collect data, update patient records or profiles, process the medication or prescription order, compound a medication or prescription order, provide medication to the patient, determine and obtain charges for services, communicate with third-party payers, and determine whether counseling by the pharmacist is desired.
2. *Maintain medication and inventory control systems.* Identify drugs, equipment, and supplies to be ordered, place orders, receive goods and verify their receipt against original purchase orders, place received goods into proper storage, perform nonpatient-specific distribution of pharmaceuticals (e.g., crash carts and automated dispensing systems), remove expired or recalled products, perform required inventory analyses, perform quality assurance tests on compounded medications, and repackage finished dosage forms for dispensing.
3. *Participate in the administration and management of a pharmacy practice.* Coordinate communications throughout the site, collect productivity information, participate in quality improvement activities, assist with ensuring compliance with regulatory standards, perform routine sanitation and maintenance activities, perform billing and accounting functions, and conduct staff training.

As some work environments shift further toward patient-oriented philosophies, new roles and responsibilities for technicians are emerging, including the following:

- Managing an automated pharmacy station (Jackson, Bickham, and Clark, 1998).
- Implementing a prescription assistance program for indigent patients (Mangino, Szajna, Ptachcinski, & Skledar, 1998).
- Triaging patients, processing consults, and managing follow-up appointments in a drug therapy monitoring clinic (Johnson & Yanchick, 1998).
- Monitoring drug use and disease management guidelines in a patient assessment program (Ervin, Skledar, Hess, & Ryan, 1998).
- Conducting pediatric compounding, processing emergency requisitions, emergency operating department setup, and participating in investigational drug studies during the midnight shift at a university hospital (Bedoya, Patel, Bickham, & Clark, 1998).
- Performing duties related to the provision of quality home care services (Ramirez, Jones, & Holmes, 1993).

Pharmacy Technician Education and Training

Many concerns have been raised about the need for standardization in technician training and education (American Pharmaceutical Association, 2003; Cooksey et al., 2002). In light of the changing environment of pharmacy practice, establishing a minimum knowledge and skills set for pharmacy technicians may be warranted. While most definitions of pharmacy technicians exclude the use of the term, *professional judgment*, a study by Wilson, Kimberlin, and Brushwood (2005) demonstrated that technician practice fits a model of professional expertise and that technicians use reasoning and judgment skills in their tasks. As such, pharmacy practice might be better served with some sort of technician credentialing process to optimize their contributions to pharmacy practice.

Some progress toward improving education and training for technicians has been made. In 2002, the Sesquicentennial Stepping Stones Summits, a consortium of pharmacy leaders and stakeholders, firmly established the need and potential future credential requirements of pharmacy technicians (American Pharmaceutical Association, 2003b). While stronger terminology such as *licensure* was not applied to technicians, it was agreed upon that national registration of technicians and further requirements of standardized education are essential in driving a skilled and knowledgeable workforce of future pharmacists' support personnel. More recently, ASHP began the Pharmacy Technician Initiative to advocate for state laws that require completion of ASHP-accredited pharmacy technician training and for national certification (Desselle, 2005).

Pharmacy Technician Certification

The trend toward expansion of pharmacy technicians' roles is reflected in the movement toward voluntary certification of these professionals. A certified pharmacy technician has completed requirements promulgated by either the Pharmacy Technician Certification Board or the Institute for the Certification of Pharmacy Technicians. Their rigorous examinations include questions on communication, organizational and interpersonal skills, pharmacy operations, pharmacy law, and calculations. The Pharmacy Technician Certification Board was founded jointly by the APhA, the ASHP, the Illinois Council of Health-System Pharmacists, and the Michigan Pharmacists Association. As of June 2006, more than 240,000 applicants had become certified through the Pharmacy Technician Certification Board (PTCB, 2008), up from slightly more than 48,000 in 1998 (Muenzen, Greenberg, & Murer, 1999).

Certification offers advantages to both the technician and the pharmacist. For technicians, certification may result in an increase in pay or a promotion in title. It may also bring greater job security and give the person an edge when seeking a job or changing jobs. It may also result in expanded job functions and responsibilities and—perhaps most importantly—increased satisfaction on the job. The increased confidence and satisfaction from the technician becoming certified may enhance his or her performance, thereby increasing the pharmacy's productivity. It may also decrease training time and lower the cost of on-the-job training.

Pharmacists have traditionally been reticent to allow technicians to expand their scope of practice, but this reluctance appears to be changing. Today's pharmacists are more secure in their roles and are beginning to see that certified technicians can reduce their workloads and mitigate their stress levels (Mott, Vanderpool, & Smeenk, 1998). One study indicated that pharmacists see certification as valuable toward enhancing technicians' knowledge sets, attitudes, and skills (Schmitt & Desselle, 2009).

In addition to addressing the problem of an acute shortage of pharmacists, technician certification has grown more popular because of the progress made in curricula and in the training of technicians, thanks to the development of the Model Curriculum for Pharmacy Technician Training (American Pharmaceutical Association, 2003a). Also, a majority of states have revised their pharmacy practice acts in areas related to technicians, and a number of states have liberalized their pharmacist-to-technician ratios. Finally, a few states have begun making certification a requirement for technician registration or licensure.

E-COMMERCE, INTERNET PHARMACY, AND OTHER TECHNOLOGIES

What Is Internet Pharmacy?

During the later part of the 1990s, the Internet changed the way that Americans work and play. It has contributed significantly to a booming economy and new heights in productivity never seen before in the United States.

No formal definition exists for *Internet pharmacy,* also known as *online pharmacy, cyberpharmacy,* and *e-pharmacy.* There are basically three types of Internet pharmacies. One type provides legend pharmaceuticals pursuant to a valid prescription order; it is essentially a mail-order pharmacy whose business address is in cyberspace. Upon receipt of a prescription from a physician who is not affiliated with the website, the pharmacist will fill it, mail the product to the patient, and then either bill the patient directly or bill his or her insurance company. The pioneers in this field expanded rapidly to provide many other services.

A second type of Internet pharmacy includes sites that offer free information and counseling for a fee but without the dispensing component. These businesses can be grouped with many other websites that offer health information, with or without a fee, but that are not necessarily pharmacies. While some of these sites are legitimate, such as those operated by various professional groups, others are not.

It is the third type of online pharmacy that has drawn the concern of medical professionals, government, regulatory agencies, and society at large. At these sites, consumers log on and complete a survey or questionnaire about their medical problem or make a direct request for a particular prescription drug product. The consumer may be charged a fee for completing the questionnaire, which may be returned or discounted if the physician does not issue a prescription. At legitimate sites of this kind, a physician reviews the data. Many sites, however, pretend to have licensed prescribers and pharmacists in house. They have obtained the medications illegally and are selling them to consumers at high prices without regard for the purchasers' safety.

Illegal Pharmacy Operations on the Internet

Illegal pharmacy sites pose a significant health threat to many Americans. The drugs acquired from certain Internet sources may be adulterated or perhaps even not contain the supposed active ingredient. Stopping illegal Internet pharmacy operations has been an arduous task for authorities because it is difficult to find their geographic locations. Few enforceable laws govern these types of businesses.

Issues related to Internet pharmacy include reimportation and diversion of pharmaceuticals. As prescription drugs continue to take up a larger portion of the monies spent on health care, many persons are seeking alternatives to traditional means for purchasing prescription drugs. Some, for example, try to purchase medications from pharmacies in Canada and Mexico to save money. In fact, some state governments have formed cooperatives to arrange for purchase of medications from Canadian pharmacies for state employees or for Medicaid beneficiaries. This contradicts FDA regulations; to date, the federal government has not strictly enforced those rules. There is considerable debate about the authenticity of medications acquired from Canadian Internet sites. The acquisition of drugs from legitimate Canadian operations poses little, if any threat, beyond that normally accompanying medication use without face-to-face counseling with a health professional; however, many web-based pharmacy operations use a Canadian name or domain name, but are not legally recognized Canadian pharmacies.

What Is Being Done to Curb Fraudulent Operations on the Web?

The NABP responded to illegal online sales of prescription drugs quickly by unveiling its Verified Internet Pharmacy Practice Site program in February 1999 (Paulsen, 1999). Verified Internet Pharmacy Practice Site is a voluntary program designed to certify each participating online pharmacy's ability to dispense pharmaceuticals. Certification involves documenting licensure from the appropriate state board of pharmacy, ensuring that the pharmacy meets a rigorous 19-point set of criteria, and conducting an on-site review of the pharmacy's written policies and procedures by an NABP-trained inspection team. Certified pharmacies display the Verified Internet Pharmacy Practice Site seal on the home page of their website. This seal contains a hyperlink to NABP's home page, where visitors can view information about the online pharmacy.

On a federal level, an initiative by the Clinton Administration to protect consumers from the illegal sale of pharmaceuticals over the Internet was never funded. Some states have also taken measures against illegal online prescription sales. For example, the state of Arkansas passed a law that requires any pharmacy shipping prescription drugs to a resident of the state to have at least one pharmacist licensed to practice by

Arkansas's state board (Conlan, 1999). Other states have enacted similar legislation. A few state health departments have successfully identified illegal operations and prosecuted those involved.

Perhaps the most effective means to curb patients' acquisition of medications from specious sources is to improve access to drug therapy. While not a panacea, the MMA greatly improved many seniors' ability to obtain necessary medications and will afford them the opportunity to receive expanded medication therapy management services. Additionally, manufacturers of branded drug products offer an array of medication assistance programs to qualified patients. These programs also have limitations, such as paperwork for providers and the occasional delay for patients receiving medication, but they provide access to medications for many persons in need, particularly those for whom generic or therapeutic substitution is not an option. These and other government and private sector solutions attempt to reduce the number of indigent persons without prescription drug access and will undoubtedly reduce the demand for prescription drugs from alternative sources. Pharmacists working in bricks-and-mortar operations can do their part by providing quality service to patients. Although web-based commerce is preferred—and even mandated—by payers for a certain segment of the population, pharmacists may advocate to patients that direct, face-to-face communication is optimal. One study found that information provided via ask-the-pharmacist services on the web was less than optimal, even from trusted sources (Holmes, Desselle, Nath, &Markuss, 2005). Yet another found poor readability and incomplete information for certain drugs on the websites of national chain pharmacies (Ghoshal & Walji, 2006).

Technology and Pharmacy

One thing that hardly seems to slow is the rate of technological innovation, and this includes the delivery of health care. Telemedicine is an application of clinical medicine where medical information is transferred through interactive audiovisual media for the purpose of consulting and sometimes for remote medical procedures or examinations. Telemedicine has become increasingly widespread. Breakthroughs in videoconferencing, software facilitating remote access, and electronic medical records technologies are changing the way health care is delivered and facilitating access among previously underserved populations. Handheld personal digital assistants and iPhone applications help healthcare professionals and patients manage diseases and find useful information on myriad medical conditions and drug therapies. Using these technologies, prescribers can transmit prescriptions electronically to the pharmacy. The physician can check for compliance with the patient's insurance formulary and obtain the patient's drug history for drug utilization evaluation messaging, all on the same system, before the prescription is even transmitted. Claims can even be preadjudicated before the prescription reaches the pharmacy. In such a case, the prescription will not require manual entry by pharmacy personnel.

There is an increasing availability of software aimed specifically to help pharmacists and other medical professionals document care and interventions, which may be helpful in increasing quality of care, securing reimbursement for services, and fending off costly litigation. Advances in robotics technology and automation are helpful to mail-order, health-system, and other types of pharmacies dispensing large quantities of prescription orders in order to improve work flow, increase accuracy, and manage systems.

Many other technologies will affect pharmacy and medication use systems that are beyond the scope of this chapter. Pharmacists are encouraged to embrace but also be shrewd evaluators of technology and stay abreast of current developments in the field to provide higher quality care and leverage their careers.

PHARMACY WORKFORCE

Implications of Workforce Size for Pharmacy

The final section of this chapter addresses an issue that is intrinsically tied to many of the concepts discussed throughout this text—namely, the number of pharmacists and support personnel available in the United States as measured in terms of the number of full-time equivalent (FTE) employees. Maintaining an adequate supply of pharmacists is critical on several fronts.

First, given that the number of prescriptions dispensed annually has continued to rise, an adequate number of pharmacists must be working in community settings to fulfill society's demand for cost-effective pharmaceuticals that are dispensed promptly and accurately.

Second, an adequate supply of well-trained pharmacists is essential to the provision of pharmacy care and MTM services. If the number of available FTE pharmacists is unable or minimally able to meet society's need for dispensing, it becomes that much more difficult for the profession to continue along its path of maturation from a product- to a patient-centered focus. One study revealed while the proportion of pharmacies offering any kind of pharmacy care services was increasing, only four services were offered at more than 10% of community pharmacy practices in 2004—specifically, immunizations, smoking cessation, health screening, and diabetes management (Doucette et al., 2006).

Third, an adequate workforce is required to meet the need for public safety. In recent years, medication-related errors and their resultant morbidity and mortality in the hospital setting have come under intense scrutiny. Although pharmacists are not entirely responsible for all of these errors, a number of steps can be taken to mitigate this problem. The lay press has also called attention to the lack of consistency in detecting prescription-related problems in pharmacies across the United States (CNN.com, 2007). Part of the problem is that many pharmacies are understaffed or are staffed consistently with floaters who do not have a regular site at which to practice.

Pharmacy workforce issues are also important to pharmacy's role in reforming the healthcare system (Knapp, 1994). As greater emphasis is placed on preventive care, pharmacists may be increasingly called upon to provide MTM services, as well as healthy lifestyle counseling, disease management, immunizations, and other public health initiatives, including disaster relief. Additionally, the government continues to grapple with shortages of primary care practitioners in inner-city and rural areas. One study showed that the presence of pharmacists in combination with other healthcare professionals such as nurse practitioners in rural areas suffering from a scarcity of physicians can mitigate the problem of diminished access to health care (Knapp, Paavola, Maine, Sorofman, & Politzer, 1999).

The size of the pharmacy workforce is also a source of concern for state boards of pharmacy and the academic community. State boards of pharmacy enforce regulations that affect the number and use of pharmacy technicians. Some state boards have enacted rules limiting the number of technicians who are allowed to work in direct care settings by specifying a maximum ratio of technicians to pharmacists. As mentioned previously, some boards of pharmacy have had to amend these ratios to respond to labor supply shortages.

For their part, schools of pharmacy have the responsibility for continuing to graduate an adequate number of pharmacists to meet the needs of society while maintaining the quality and integrity of their programs. The AACP, the Accreditation Council for Pharmacy Education, and individual schools must keep abreast of supply trends by region and across the United States.

Factors Affecting Pharmacist Labor Supply

As the profession continues to operate within a dynamic healthcare environment while undergoing comprehensive change, numerous forces appear poised to affect the current and future supply of pharmacists.

First, the demographic composition of pharmacists is shifting toward a greater proportion of female practitioners. Whereas the profession was once virtually all male, by 1991 approximately 32% of pharmacists were female. Women accounted for approximately 46% of the pharmacist supply in 2000 and 50% in 2003 (Gershon, Cultice, & Knapp, 2000). This trend has significant implications because childbearing women will take at least some time off for maternity leave and women are more likely than men to work part-time for child rearing or other reasons.

Another factor affecting the pharmacist labor supply is the transition from the bachelor of science to the PharmD degree as a requirement for practice. The PharmD typically adds an extra year of academic study, which at first resulted in a downturn in applications to some schools of pharmacy, although many schools are rebounding with higher numbers of applicants and often see fluctuations from year to year in applications based upon myriad factors. The increased emphasis on pharmacotherapeutics and experiential training also requires additional clinical faculty and preceptors.

Yet another factor reducing the pharmacist labor supply is the dwindling number of independent pharmacies, whose owner pharmacists tend to work more hours than employee pharmacists (Knapp, 1994).

The effects of other factors on pharmacist labor supply are less certain. Pharmacist specialization, while increasing pharmacists' competency to provide pharmaceutical care, may result in their propensity to work in nontraditional settings and reduce their supply in distributive settings. As of 2010, there were nearly 9,000 pharmacists who had acquired certification through the Board of Pharmacy Specialties, and this number is expected to grow (BPS, 2009).

Finally, two factors that directly affect the pharmacy labor supply are pharmacy technicians and automation. Certification of technicians can serve to increase their level of competence and allow these individuals to perform roles that had previously been within the pharmacist's scope of practice only. Automation and other technologies can free up time for pharmacists, allowing them to turn their attention toward patient consultative and disease management activities.

Estimates of the Pharmacist Workforce

Although leaders in the profession agree that workforce issues are important, there has been less consensus on how to measure the labor supply and, therefore, where the profession stands. A variety of methods have been used to quantify the pharmacy labor supply, including worker–population ratios, demand versus supply techniques, the relative income of pharmacists, and the internal rate of return for investing in pharmacy education (Sorkin, 1989). Data on pharmacy manpower are generated primarily from the following three sources: (1) the Pew Health Professions Commission, (2) the Bureau of Labor Statistics, and (3) the Bureau of Health Professions.

In 1995, the Pew Health Professions Commission published a report projecting a future surplus of as many as 40,000 pharmacists (Knapp, 1994). Other researchers view this report as inaccurate. Instead, the general consensus forecasts a shortage of pharmacists nationally, with some regions being extremely short of these professionals.

The most comprehensive attempt to measure and predict the future pharmacist labor supply has been the combined effort of professional associations and the BHP in creating the Pharmacy Manpower Project census database (Gershon et al., 2000). This model incorporates the change in the entry-level degree, the opening of new pharmacy schools, the influx of international pharmacy graduates, and separation rates (actuarial estimates of retirement, death, and occupational mobility). It projected a workforce of 196,011 active pharmacists in 2000 and predicts a workforce of 249,086 active pharmacists by 2020. It implies further that the ratio of active pharmacists to the general population will increase by 2020 to a level 76.7 pharmacists per 100,000 population, compared with 68.9 pharmacists per 100,000 population in 1995. The model does not consider FTE employees, however, and its primary drawback is that its definition of active pharmacists includes a potentially increasing number of practitioners who are working part-time.

Efforts are being made to track the balance of supply and demand forces of pharmacists longitudinally by making survey-based estimates of the amount of difficulty faced by employers in filling open pharmacist positions (Knapp & Livesey, 2002). As of 2001, there was considerable demand in excess of available supply, with the problem being more acute in certain states. This issue is of particular concern as patients experience a number of unmet needs in medication use (e.g., medication counseling and drug therapy monitoring) (Law, Ray, Knapp, and Balesh, 2003) and a sizable portion of pharmacists' work hours are consumed by activities not directly related to patient care (Schommer, Pedersen, Doucette, Gaither, & Mott, 2002). The projected shortage encouraged a number of new colleges/schools of pharmacy to open across the United States as a response to the unmet need.

The Pharmacy Manpower Project, a consortium of professional pharmacy organizations, has collaborated with researchers to create the Aggregate Demand Index. The Pharmacy Manpower Project seeks to collect, analyze and disseminate data on the supply of licensed pharmacists in the United States (Aggregate Demand Index, 2009). The Aggregate Demand Index reports an index from 1 to 5 for each state and for various practice settings, wherein 1 indicates a high surplus and 5 indicates a high demand for pharmacists. In September 2009, the aggregate index for the nation was 3.74, compared to 3.94 12 months prior. The reduction in this index is likely an indicator of the increasing number of accredited colleges/schools of pharmacy in the United States.

CONCLUSION

The pharmacy profession has come a long way in a little more than a century. The current pace of change, however, promises more momentous transitions over the next few decades. It is difficult to gauge exactly what pharmacy practice will be like in another century with the profession's renewed focus on patients, the continued specialization of pharmacists in specific disease states, the growing trend of pharmacy technician certification, the rapid diffusion of technology as a facilitator to the provision of care, and a shift in the composition of its workforce. It remains clear, however, that pharmacy will remain an integral part of our healthcare delivery system and an exciting career choice for its practitioners.

QUESTIONS FOR FURTHER DISCUSSION

1. How will pharmacists' roles continue to evolve over the next 10–20 years? What will be the status of pharmacy care and MTM service delivery in 20 years?
2. Should the focus on pharmacist credentialing be on general pharmacotherapy or on further specialization to create experts in managing specific disease states?
3. Why are proportionately fewer pharmacists active in professional associations at a national level compared to physicians and other healthcare professionals? How has this hindered pharmacy as a profession?
4. What is the contribution of each subdiscipline within pharmacy toward practice, education, and research?
5. Should certification of pharmacy technicians be mandated? Why or why not?
6. How can pharmacy professionals leverage the Internet and other technologies to improve patient care, enhance reimbursement, and advance our roles on interdisciplinary care teams?
7. What can be done to ensure an adequate supply of pharmacists for the future?

KEY TOPICS AND TERMS

History of pharmacy
Pharmaceutical care
Pharmacy technician
Pharmacy workforce
Professional pharmacy organizations
Technology

REFERENCES

Aggregate Demand Index. (2009). Retrieved from http://www.pharmacymanpower.com/index.html

American Association of Colleges of Pharmacy. (1996). Paper from the Commission to Implement Change in Pharmaceutical Education: Maintaining our commitment to change. *American Journal of Pharmaceutical Education, 60,* 378–384.

American Pharmaceutical Association. (2003a). Pharmacy technicians (2002): Needed changes can no longer wait [white paper]. *Journal of the American Pharmaceutical Association, 43,* 93–107.

American Pharmaceutical Association. (2003b). Sesquicentennial Stepping Stone Summits-summit two: Pharmacy technicians. *Journal of the American Pharmaceutical Association, 43,* 84–92.

American Society of Hospital Pharmacists. (1993). ASHP accreditation standard for pharmacy technician training programs. *American Journal of Hospital Pharmacy, 50,* 124–126.

American Society of Hospital Pharmacists. (1994). Summary of the final report of the Scope of Pharmacy Practice Project. *American Journal of Hospital Pharmacy, 51,* 2179–2182.

Bedoya, R., Patel, H., Bickham, P., & Clark, T. (June, 1998). *Role of the midnight pharmacy technician.* Paper presented at the ASHP Midyear Clinical Meeting, Reno, NV.

Board of Pharmacy Specialties (BPS) 2009 Annual Report. (2009). Retrieved from http://bpsweb. org/pdfs/2009_Annual_Report.pdf

Board of Pharmacy Specialties (BPS). (2010). *Specialties.* Retrieved from http://bpsweb.org/ specialties/specialties.cfm

Boyd, J. R., Covington, T. R., Stanaszek, W. F., & Coussons, R. T. (1974). Drug defaulting, part 2: Analysis of noncompliance patterns. *American Journal of Hospital Pharmacy, 31,* 485–491.

Brodie, D. C. (1967). Drug-use control: Keystone to pharmaceutical service. *Drug Intelligence, 1,* 63–65.

Broeseker, A., & Janke, K. K. (1998). The evolution and revolution of pharmaceutical care. In R. L. McCarthy (Ed.), *Introduction to health care delivery: A primer for pharmacists* (pp. 393–416). Gaithersburg, MD: Aspen.

Buerki, R. A., & Vottero, L. D. (1994). *Ethical responsibility in pharmacy practice.* Madison, WI: American Institute of the History of Pharmacy.

Bureau of Labor Statistics (2010–2011). *Occupational outlook handbook* (2008–2009 ed.). Retrieved from http://www.bls.gov/oco/ocos252.htm

CNN.com. (2007). *Don't be a victim of pharmacy errors.* Retrieved from http://articles. cnn.com/2007-10-25/health/pharmacy.errors_1_pharmacy-prescription-walgreens?_ s=PM:HEALTH

Col, N., Fanale, J. E., & Kronholm, P. (1990). The role of medication noncompliance and adverse drug reactions in hospitalizations in the elderly. *Archives of Internal Medicine, 150,* 841–845.

Commission to Implement Change in Pharmaceutical Education. (1993). Background paper II: Entry-level curricular outcomes, curricular content and educational process. *American Journal of Pharmaceutical Education, 57,* 386–399.

Conlan, M. F. (1999, May 17). It's the law. *Drug Topics, 143,* 72, 74.

Cooksey, J. A., Knapp, K. K., Walton, S. M., & Cultice, J. M. (2002). Challenges to the pharmacist profession from escalating pharmaceutical demand. *Health Affairs, 21,* 182–188.

Cranor, C. W., Bunting, B. A., & Christensen, D. B. (2003). The Asheville project: Long-term clinical and economic outcomes of a community pharmacy diabetes care program. *Journal of the American Pharmaceutical Association, 43,* 173–184.

Cranor, C. W., & Christensen, D. B. (2003). The Asheville project: Short-term outcomes of a community pharmacy diabetes care program. *Journal of the American Pharmaceutical Association, 43,* 149–159.

Desselle, S. P. (2005). Job turnover intentions among certified pharmacy technicians. *Journal of the American Pharmacists Association. 45,* 676–683.

Desselle, S. P., & Zgarrick, D. P. (2009). *Pharmacy management: Essentials for all practice settings* (2nd ed.). New York, NY: McGraw-Hill.

Doucette, W. R., Kreling, D. H., Schommer, J. C., Gaither, C. A., Mott, D. A., & Pedersen, C. A. (2006). Evaluation of pharmacy service mix: Evidence from the 2004 National Pharmacist Workforce Study. *Journal of the American Pharmacists Association, 46,* 348–355.

Ervin, K. C., Skledar, S. J., Hess, N. M., & Ryan, M. L. (June, 1998). *Expanding the scope of clinical pharmacy programs: Technician facilitated patient assessment.* Paper presented at the ASHP Midyear Clinical Meeting, Reno, NV.

Gershon, S. K., Cultice, J. M., & Knapp, K. K. (2000). How many pharmacists are in our future? The Bureau of Health Professions projects supply to 2020. *Journal of Managed Care Pharmacy, 6,* 298–306.

Ghoshal, M., & Walji, M. F. (2006). Quality of information available on retail pharmacy websites. *Research in Social and Administrative Pharmacy, 2,* 479-498.

Hepler, C. D. (1987). The third wave in pharmaceutical education: The clinical movement. *American Journal of Pharmaceutical Education, 51,* 369–385.

Hepler, C. D., & Strand, L. M. (1990). Opportunities and responsibilities in pharmaceutical care. *American Journal of Hospital Pharmacy, 47,* 533–543.

Holmes, E. R., Desselle, S. P., Nath, D. M., & Markuss, J. M. (2005). Quality analysis of consumer drug information provided through Internet pharmacies. *Annals of Pharmacotherapy, 39,* 662–667.

Jackson, M. L., Bickham, P., & Clark, T. (June, 1998). *Technician management of automation and inventory.* Paper presented at ASHP Midyear Clinical Meeting, Reno, NV.

Johnson, I., & Yanchik, J. (June, 1998). *Responsibilities of a pharmacy technician in a pharmacist-run drug therapy monitoring clinic in a primary care setting.* Paper presented at the ASHP Midyear Clinical Meeting, Reno, NV.

Knapp, K. K. (1994). Pharmacy manpower: Implications for pharmaceutical care and health care reform. *American Journal of Hospital Pharmacy, 51,* 1212–1220.

Knapp, K. K., & Livesey, J. C. (2002). The aggregate demand index: Measuring the balance between pharmacist supply and demand, 1999–2001. *Journal of the American Pharmaceutical Association, 42,* 391–398.

Knapp, K. K., Paavola, F. G., Maine, L. L., Sorofman, B., & Politzer, R. M. (1999). Availability of primary care providers and pharmacists in the United States. *Journal of the American Pharmaceutical Association, 39,* 127–135.

Law, A. V., Ray, M. D., Knapp, K. K., & Balesh, J. K. (2003). Unmet needs in the medication use process: Perceptions of physicians, pharmacists, and patients. *Journal of the American Pharmaceutical Association, 43,* 394–402.

MacKinnon, G. E., III, & Mahrous, H. (2002). Assessing consumers' interest in health care services offered in community pharmacies. *Journal of the American Pharmaceutical Association, 42,* 512–515.

Maine, L. L., & Penna, R. P. (1996). Pharmaceutical care—An overview. In C. Knowlton & R. Penna (Eds.), *Pharmaceutical care* (pp. 133–154). New York, NY: Chapman and Hall.

Manasse, H. R. (1989a). Medication use in an imperfect world: Drug misadventuring as an issue of public policy, part 1. *American Journal of Hospital Pharmacy, 46,* 929–944.

Manasse, H. R. (1989b). Medication use in an imperfect world: Drug misadventuring as an issue of public policy, part 2. *American Journal of Hospital Pharmacy, 46,* 1141–1152.

Mangino, M. H., Szajna, J. L., Ptachcinski, R., & Skledar, S. J. (June, 1998). *Role of a pharmacy technician in implementing a prescription assistance program for indigent and underinsured patients.* Paper presented at the ASHP Midyear Clinical Meeting, Reno, NV.

Millis, J. S. (1975). *Pharmacists for the future: The report of the Study Commission on Pharmacy.* Ann Arbor, MI: Health Administration Press.

Millis, J. S. (1976). Looking ahead—The report of the Study Commission on Pharmacy. *American Journal of Hospital Pharmacy, 33,* 134–138.

Mott, D. A., Vanderpool, W. H., & Smeenk, D. A. (1998). Attitudes of Ohio hospital pharmacy directors toward national voluntary pharmacy technician certification. *American Journal of Health-Systems Pharmacy, 55,* 1799–1803.

Muenzen, P. M., Greenberg, S., & Murer, M. M. (1999). PTCB task analysis identifies role of certified pharmacy technicians in pharmaceutical care. *Journal of the American Pharmaceutical Association, 39,* 857–864.

Paulsen, M. (1999). New NABP program combines criteria, inspections to certify online pharmacy quality. *Journal of the American Pharmaceutical Association, 39,* 870.

Penna, R. P. (1990). Pharmaceutical care—pharmacy's mission for the 1990s. *American Journal of Hospital Pharmacy, 47,* 543–549.

Pharmacy Technician Certification Board (PTCB). (2008). Active PTCB and State Regulations as of June 30, 2008. Retrieved January 3, 2011, from https://www.ptcb.org/AM/Template.cfm?Section=National_Statistics&Template=/CM/HTMLDisplay.cfm&ContentID=2680

Pink, L. A. (1991). Hospitals. In J. E. Fincham & A. I. Wertheimer (Eds.), *Pharmacists and the U. S. healthcare system* (pp. 158–190). Binghamton, NY: Pharmaceutical Products Press.

Ramirez, E., Jones, C. J., & Holmes, D. B. (December, 1993). *Expanding roles of the pharmacy technician in promoting quality home care services.* Paper presented at the ASHP Annual Meeting, Denver, CO.

Relman, A. S. (1988). Assessment and accountability: The third revolution in medical care. *New England Journal of Medicine, 319,* 1220–1222.

Schmitt, M. R., & Desselle, S. P. (2009). Pharmacists' attitudes toward technician certification: A qualitative study. *Journal of Pharmacy Technology, 25,* 79–88.

Schommer, J. C., Pedersen, C. A., Doucette, W. R., Gaither, C. A., & Mott, D. A. (2002). Community pharmacists' work activities in the United States during 2000. *Journal of the American Pharmaceutical Association, 42,* 399–406.

Sonnedecker, G. (1963). *Kremers and Urdang's history of pharmacy.* Philadelphia, PA: J. B. Lippincott.

Sorkin, A. L. (1989). Some economic aspects of pharmacy manpower. *American Journal of Hospital Pharmacy, 46,* 527–533.

Strand, L. M., Cippole, R. J., & Morley, P. C. (1988). Documenting the clinical pharmacist's activities: Back to basics. *Drug Intelligence and Clinical Pharmacy, 22,* 63–66.

Strand, L. M., Cippole, R. J., Morley, P. C., Ramsey, R., & Lamsam, G. D. (1990). Drug-related problems: Their structure and function. *DICP Annals of Pharmacotherapy, 24,* 1093–1097.

Tice, B., & Phillips, C. R. (2002). Implementation and evaluation of a lipid screening program in a large chain pharmacy. *Journal of the American Pharmaceutical Association, 42,* 413–419.

Torrens, P. R. (1993). Historical evolution and overview of health service in the United States. In J. S. Williams & P. R. Torrens (Eds.), *Introduction to health services* (4th ed., pp. 3–28). Albany, NY: Delmar.

Wilson, D. L., Kimberlin, C. L., & Brushwood, D.B. (2005). Exploring the professional expertise of pharmacy technicians. *Journal of Pharmacy Technology, 21,* 341-347.

The Patient

Kimberly S. Plake*

Case Scenario

Mary is a 67-year-old woman who is greatly concerned about her health. She currently has type 2 diabetes and hypertension, and she knows that she is at least 50 pounds overweight. Lately, Mary has been experiencing symptoms that do not seem to be explained by her current chronic diseases. Because she does not have insurance and has limited access to health services owing to her rural location, she decided to do some research on her symptoms before making an appointment with the physician. Mary became concerned because she found some information on the Internet that indicated that she might have early signs of arthritis. She started taking Tylenol (acetaminophen) when she saw a commercial indicating that it can be used for her symptoms. However, it did not seem to be controlling all of her pain.

Mary decided that she must go to a physician because she could no longer stand the pain. Before meeting with her physician, she talked to her neighbor, Mrs. Johnson, who suffers from arthritis. After learning of Mary's suspicions, Mrs. Johnson gave her an article about arthritis from a women's magazine. A couple of pages after the article, Mary saw an advertisement for Voltaren Gel (diclofenac topical) and planned to talk with her physician about this medication.

At her appointment, Mary asked the physician about the information she obtained from the Internet and about Voltaren Gel (diclofenac topical). In addition, she brought a list of her current symptoms. The physician, sensing that Mary would like to be an active participant in her health care, answered her questions, prompted her to provide information he thought was pertinent to her care, and then talked about her treatment options. After discussing her alternatives with her physician, Mary decided to begin taking Naprosyn (naproxen) for her arthritis and to start a weight reduction program to help treat her osteoarthritis.

*With acknowledgment to Peter L. Steere and Edward Krupat.

LEARNING OBJECTIVES

Upon completion of this chapter, the student shall be able to:

- Describe factors that influence the healthcare system's focus on the treatment of diseases rather than the prevention of them
- Identify and describe services and programs for individuals with limited financial resources or limited access to healthcare services
- Explain the impact of the Internet on patients' access to health information
- Define and explain direct-to-consumer advertising
- Compare and contrast health practitioners' opinions of direct-to-consumer advertising to those of the pharmaceutical industry
- Explain the following models of the practitioner–patient relationship and their application when interacting with patients:
  a. Szasz and Hollender's models of care
  b. Consumer model of care
  c. Patient-centered model of care
- Describe the role that patient autonomy plays in patient–practitioner relationships
- Compare and contrast the biomedical and biopsychosocial models of care
- Compare and contrast compliance and adherence
- Identify factors influencing patient adherence to therapeutic recommendations
- Explain health literacy
- Identify communication techniques that can be used regardless of patients' health literacy level
- Explain the following health behavior models:
  a. Locus of control
  b. Health belief model
  c. Theory of reasoned action
  d. Theory of planned behavior
  e. Social cognitive theory (self-efficacy)
  f. Transtheoretical model (stages of change)
- Explain patient attitudes and behavior using the models described in the chapter when presented with a patient
- Describe motivational interviewing and its use in behavioral change
- Develop an approach to facilitate behavior change and indicate the rationale for the selected approach when given a patient case

CHAPTER QUESTIONS

1. In what ways is the current crisis in healthcare financing a result of past successes of America's healthcare system?
3. How have patient expectations of and experiences in the healthcare system changed over the years?
4. How do the models of healthcare delivery address some of the classic issues of patient–practitioner relations (the balance of power, patient autonomy, and patient satisfaction)?
5. What factors influence patients' adherence to therapeutic recommendations? In which direction (more or less adherent) do you think each of these factors influence adherence?
6. How do the health behavior models help practitioners facilitate behavior change in patients?

INTRODUCTION

As reforms in health care occur, corresponding changes are also seen in patients, health professionals, and the healthcare environment. Although the healthcare system always seems to be in a state of flux, the focus remains on restoring sick patients to health. Healthcare professionals, health institutions, and insurance companies are interested in patients and their behaviors. Along with this interest is the desire to work with patients and to improve their care and satisfaction with services. This chapter explores topics related to the patient, including the shift in focus of care from acute to chronic diseases, the healthcare environment, patient expectations of care, models of care, and healthcare behaviors.

DEFINITIONS

Being a patient perhaps at one time suggested that an individual was under the care of a physician. It suggested illnesses and a process of healing and recovery. While this definition still holds true, being a patient today may mean that a person is receiving services from a pharmacist, nurse, therapist, and/or dietician, as well as from providers of therapeutic massage, acupuncture, or a variety of other complementary services.

This multidisciplinary approach is a change in—and perhaps even in some ways a return to—the manner in which individuals seeking care find services they feel are necessary for healing. This shift comes despite the fact that medical technology is, in the United States, at its highest ever level of sophistication. While the introduction of new medical technologies has certainly changed patients' expectations and experiences, just as important are the effects that the economics of this evolving system of health care will have on the United States' financial ability to provide a reasonable standard of care for every patient.

DEMOGRAPHICS

The graying of America and its far-reaching implications are exerting serious pressure on the United States' healthcare systems. The rapid acceleration in the aging of the population (according to the U.S. Census Bureau, the median age increased by nearly 8 years between 1970 and 2000) and the use of medical services by the elderly, when combined, threaten to dramatically impact the healthcare system and healthcare reimbursement programs. The first of the baby boom population (those born between 1946 and 1964) will turn 65 years of age in 2011. By 2040, it is estimated that 20% of Americans will be age 65 or older (National Center for Health Statistics, 2010). The number of oldest elderly—those older than 85 years—is projected to grow at a rapid rate from 5.8 million in 2010 to 19 million in 2050 (Vincent & Velkoff, 2010) (see **Table 4-1**).

This success at extending longevity is at least partly attributable to the United States' effective public health policy, including improvements in sanitation and nutrition and the development of immunizations. In the early 1900s, a person could expect to live 50 years (Tebbe, 1998), whereas someone born in 2006 can anticipate 77 or more years of life (National Center for Health Statistics, 2010). In the early 20th century, Americans faced then-fatal diseases such as smallpox, malaria, yellow fever, and tuberculosis (Leavitt & Numbers, 1997), which often prevented afflicted persons from living

Table 4-1 Shifts in American Population (Thousands) as of July 1 for Each Year

	2009	2006	2003	2000
Total population	307,007	298,593	290,326	282,172
5–14 years	40,583	40,410	40,971	41,097
15–44 years	126,174	125,751	124,970	124,396
45–64 years	79,379	74,612	68,523	62,402
65–84 years	33,990	32,143	31,349	30,803
85 years and older	5,631	5,063	4,574	4,271

Source: Adapted from U.S. Census Bureau.

long enough to enter the years where more chronic diseases might be expected to be present.

Because advances in technology have helped to find treatments and cures (e.g., immunizations and antibiotics) for many of the more acute forms of illness, much of the current effort in health care focuses on the management of chronic conditions. Diabetes, hypertension, cancer, human immunodeficiency virus (HIV) infections, and other long-term (lifelong), multisystem diseases have replaced scarlet fever, measles, and whooping cough as targets of the country's healthcare system. Mary, from our case scenario, is an example of this phenomenon—she has several chronic conditions to be managed.

TREATMENT VERSUS PREVENTION

The U.S. system of health care, despite significant investments and experimentation with managed care and related wellness programs, remains largely a system designed to care for the sick. An emphasis on prevention has been increasing among a variety of entities in the healthcare system, as well as the federal government through its *Healthy People* initiative (http://www.healthypeople.gov/). Among these entities, one shared goal is to improve health through the development of wellness initiatives. Nevertheless, broad-based initiatives focused on wellness and prevention have met with limited success with many individuals slow to embrace some of the suggested wellness behaviors, such as dietary and exercise recommendations. Changing consumer behavior and community responsibilities to promote wellness, despite clear messages of the dangers of not doing so, is a slow and difficult task (Knowles, 1997). Cigarette smoking, for example, has long been recognized for its ability to cause cancer and emphysema but remains a frequent behavior, despite community, state, and national efforts that apply financial and cultural pressures to stop.

In addition, compliance with positive contributors to health such as consumption of a proper diet and engaging in exercise are often seen as difficult, tedious, or simply overly mundane. The relationship between such practices and actual wellness is often too unclear for many to appreciate. As a consequence, many individuals who are at risk for sedentary lifestyle diseases often experience them.

Further, while many illnesses caused by environmental factors (e.g., poor sanitation) have been minimized in the United States, many of the current preventive practices responsible for reducing chronic disease are provided by healthcare professionals, including preventive health care, such as blood pressure screening and bone density testing. Preventive health care adds costs to the healthcare system, but the reduction in future costs (money that would otherwise be spent on more acute care) can often be accomplished by making an investment in such health measures. Ideally, such an investment would come from insurers, at-risk providers, and consumers.

PATIENTS AND THE HEALTHCARE ENVIRONMENT

Changing Needs of Society

Patient demands on America's healthcare system have been moving from an acute model of need to one in which chronic disease services are required. Because of prior investments, the healthcare system is finding it painful to shift from being largely a hospital-centered structure to one that delivers community-based care. The movement away from hospital and sickness-based care has been a struggle for many patients. Although 1946's Hospital Survey and Construction Act (Hill-Burton Act; see Chapters 1 and 6) provided funds for the creation of new healthcare facilities and promoted the concept of a hospital for every community, changes in the way and amount that hospitals are paid are now causing fewer hospitals to be available to consumers (Stuifbergen, 1999). In addition, many patients do not fully understand the movement toward wellness and realize what is expected of them in practicing healthy behaviors, so they continue to use an increasingly wellness-based healthcare system for sick services.

Patients, however, are adjusting to receiving care in new settings with new practitioners. Mail-order pharmacy, surgical centers, geriatric day care, and other programs have changed the way people access services they need. Through changes in healthcare reimbursement and the systems of care offered to patients, a slow acceptance of new models has emerged (Greeno, 1999). Outpatient surgery, for example, has replaced all but the most invasive procedures provided by hospitals. Such a shift has forced patients and families to take a more active role in postsurgical recovery and care.

Access Issues

In places where economics limits the availability of healthcare services, patients are confronted with new challenges. Although residents in rural sections of the United States (like Mary in our case scenario) have geographical issues to contend with, both rural and poor urban patients often have access to lower quality health care relative to their wealthier urban counterparts (Chan, Hart, & Goodman, 2006; Hall, Lemak, Steingraber, & Schaffer, 2008; Stuifbergen, 1999). Financial constraints and insurance coverage often impact the care the patient receives. Patients who cited financial constraints report forgoing preventive care, medical tests, and prescriptions (Schoen, Osborn, How, Doty, & Peugh, 2008).

This issue creates a paradox. When members of these communities seek out treatment for their illness, their care frequently is more emergent and expensive than if better access had been available in the first place (Greeno, 1999; Smolderen et al., 2010). Finding an appropriate set of qualified practitioners in either rural or urban settings who are willing to provide health care to the poor is very difficult (Hall et al., 2008). The differences between public and private healthcare reimbursement levels historically not only have determined the quality of care one can expect to receive, but also weigh heavily on its accessibility. For example, lower levels of payment in these communities has tended to mean health care for patients often is less readily available and of poorer quality. In the case of Mary, she delayed seeking treatment until she could no longer stand the pain. One of the reasons for her delay was that she had limited access to physicians because she lived in a rural area.

Programs for the Indigent

Because of financial constraints and lack of health insurance, individuals may not seek proper medical care or do so only when they require urgent care. To accommodate the costs of treating these patients, some states have allowed hospitals to access special funding. Other mechanisms for treating the uninsured population include free clinics and the goodwill of practitioners. To ensure access to medications and help patients and providers pay for pharmaceutical care when financial resources are limited, the Omnibus Reconciliation Act of 1990 (OBRA '90) mandated rebates from the drug manufacturing industry in exchange for coverage by Medicaid programs of their products. Further, to make drug therapies more affordable to agencies such as U.S. Public Health Service grantees and other drug-assistance programs, drug makers must discount their products or relinquish coverage of their products under Medicaid reimbursement programs for all eligible patients. Because the lack of continued access to quality drug therapy is such a critical element in the management of uninsured patients' disease, significant resources are now being applied to make such products available, including those offered by municipal, county, state, and federal government programs (outside of Medicaid), as well as by charitable organizations, private donors, and healthcare providers themselves.

Medication assistance programs, also known as patient assistance programs, are an example of programs intended to increase low-income patients' access to prescription medications. In these programs, patients who meet the eligibility criteria receive brand-name medications from pharmaceutical companies at no or very little cost. Eligibility criteria vary across programs, but often include income limitations and lack of or limited prescription insurance coverage. Although the programs provide accessibility to medications, patients may have to complete a complex application process and may have to apply to multiple programs, depending on their medication regimens (Chauncey, Mullins, Tran, McNally, & McEwan, 2006; Chisholm, Reinhardt, Vollenweider, Kendrick, & Dipiro, 2000).

PATIENTS' EXPECTATIONS: CONSUMERISM

Health care is different from most consumer products and services offered in the marketplace. When buying a car, a consumer can go to the car dealership and test drive a car before deciding to purchase it. Of course, a patient cannot test drive surgery. Instead, patients rely on health professionals to advise them about the most appropriate procedure or decision.

Although the patient may rely on health professionals' advice on appropriate decisions, consumers are becoming increasingly more active participants in the healthcare process. In the past, healthcare professionals seemed to have all the knowledge related to health and well-being. Patients visited the physician or other health professional to obtain this information. The physician would advise, and the patient would (in theory) comply.

Today, however, a wealth of information is available. Patients can watch television and learn about medications available for various conditions. They can use the Internet to find resources and information on diseases, treatments, and medications. For example,

Mary found information on arthritis through the Internet and learned of the use of Tylenol (acetaminophen) to treat this condition while watching television. Patients are becoming informed consumers. As a consequence, the dynamic of the relationship between healthcare professionals and patients is changing.

Instead of the physician telling the patient what to do, a more collaborative relationship between physician and patient is evolving. In this relationship, the patient asks questions and becomes an active participant in making healthcare decisions; in a sense, the healthcare professional and patient become partners in the care process. In some cases, the patient may actually ask the physician for a specific product or treatment for a condition based on personal research. For example, Mary went to her physician's appointment armed with specific questions about arthritis and Voltaren Gel (diclofenac topical). (The "Models of Care" section in this chapter discusses this phenomenon in more detail.)

ACCESS TO HEALTH INFORMATION

Internet

Seventy-four percent of American adults go online and 57% of American households have broadband connections (Fox & Jones, 2009). With the increased accessibility to the Internet comes an increased volume of information. Patients can obtain data on a wide variety of topics, including information about diseases, medications, and therapies. Of Internet users surveyed in a 2009 study, 61% indicated they had used the Internet to look online for health information (Fox & Jones, 2009). A recent study found that individuals with chronic disease are less likely to go online for health information, primarily due to the lack of access to the Internet (Fox & Purcell, 2010). However, 51% of American adults with at least one chronic condition had gone online to look for health information. Health information sought by individuals included information on (1) a specific condition, medical problem, or procedure; (2) prescription or nonprescription medications; (3) alternative treatments; (4) weight control; (5) exercise and fitness; (5) health insurance; (6) doctors; and (7) medical facilities (Fox & Purcell, 2010).

By using the Internet, patients like Mary can easily acquire information that is written in a layperson's terms. They can go online at any time of day or night—information is immediately available around the clock. Besides finding information, patients can identify support systems through online advocacy groups, chat rooms, and message boards (Fox & Jones, 2009; Levy & Strombeck, 2002; Sennett, 2000). Compare this ready accessibility and ease of use to the maze that must be navigated to reach many healthcare practitioners, and it is easy to see why patients might turn to the Internet for help. Health professionals are, in turn, being asked by their patients about the information they obtain from online sources. With the anticipated increase in the use of the Internet as a source for health information, patients' questions to practitioners about this information will likely become more frequent. For this reason, healthcare practitioners should be aware of how to retrieve information from the Internet as well as how to evaluate the credibility of websites.

Direct-to-Consumer Advertising

In 1997, the Food and Drug Administration (FDA) offered new guidelines for direct-to-consumer (DTC) advertising in the form of broadcast television commercials for prescription drugs (Wilkes, Bell, & Kravitz, 2000). These guidelines allowed drug man-ufacturers to advertise pharmaceutical products and their indications without stating all the risks. In such a case, the advertisement had to include a statement describing where additional information can be obtained about the medication (e.g., websites, physicians, and pharmacists).

As a consequence of the FDA's decision, television advertisements for medications have proliferated (Wilkes et al., 2000). When watching television, a patient can learn of many different products available with or without a prescription. These commer-cials range from a description of a health problem/disease to an explanation of a par-ticular brand-name product, such as Humira (adalimumab) or Lunesta (eszopiclone). In addition, print advertisements may be found in magazines and newspapers. In the chapter-opening case, Mary used information from both television and print advertise-ments. She tried to self-treat her arthritis with the Tylenol that she learned about from a television advertisement. She learned about Voltaren Gel (diclofenac topical) from a magazine advertisement. What is the impact of DTC advertising on patients? Do they pay attention to what they have seen or heard from these advertisements?

In a survey conducted in 2008, 91% of respondents recalled seeing an advertisement for a prescription medication (*USA Today,* Kaiser Family Foundation, & Harvard School of Public Health, 2008). Almost one third (32%) of these patients discussed prescription medication seen in an advertisement with their physician. Of these indi-viduals, 44% indicated that the physician prescribed the medication discussed while 54% reported that their physician recommended another medication as a result of their discussion (*USA Today* et al., 2008).

It appears that DTC advertising may be influencing consumer demand for a medication. Drugs that are heavily advertised to patients are some of the best-selling medications (General Accounting Office, 2002). Many companies advertise their products in this way as part of their strategy for dealing with an increasingly competitive marketplace—that is, in an attempt to increase the demand/market share for their products (Wilkes et al., 2000). In fact, recent studies suggest that DTC advertising increases drug utilization and sales (Dave & Saffer, 2010; General Accounting Office, 2002; Kaiser Family Foun-dation, 2003).

As with any controversial issue, both supporters and detractors of DTC advertising exist. Proponents suggest that such advertising enables consumers to become better informed by learning about new products and alternative treatment options (Kaiser Family Foundation, 2006). Critics of DTC advertising claim that this practice promotes inappropriate prescribing, strains the patient–provider relationship, increases the costs of care, and distorts the physician's professional role (Kaiser Family Foundation, 2006; Wilkes et al., 2000). Despite these concerns, it appears that DTC advertising will con-tinue in the future and be a part of the healthcare dynamic.

Self-Care

Self-health care is "a range of behavior undertaken by individuals to promote or restore health" (Dean, 1989, p. 119). In other words, it consists of actions that individuals take to treat or prevent an illness. These actions can include self-medicating with nonpre-scription products and seeking advice from family and friends.

When individuals become ill, they go through an appraisal process of their symptoms. Is it serious? Is it getting better? Is it disruptive? Depending on the results of their assessment, patients may believe that they are sick and assume the sick role. As a part of this transformation, they begin to investigate what is occurring. They may talk to friends and family members for their advice, take medication, and consult alternative health practitioners. For example, Mary talked to her friend, Mrs. Johnson, about arthritis. In addition, patients may assume a wait-and-see attitude or they may take action. When patients perceive the illness as serious or life-threatening, they might be prompted to go to the physician (Lubkin, 1990; Suchman, 1965). In the case of Mary, she did not seek attention from the physician until she could no longer stand the pain and it became disruptive to her life.

In the last several years, pharmacies and pharmacists have played a larger role in helping patients manage their self-care. Pharmacists have implemented disease management programs for a variety of chronic diseases, including diabetes (Baran et al., 1999; Nau & Ponte, 2002), hyperlipidemia (Bluml, McKenney, & Cziraky, 2000), and hypertension (Park, Kelly, Carter, & Burgess, 1996). An example of a diabetes disease management program is the Asheville project, in which pharmacists in Asheville, North Carolina, have been providing diabetes services since March 1997. The pharmacists in the 12 participating community pharmacies receive reimbursement for the cognitive services they provide to their patients. These services include patient education and training, clinical assessment, monitoring, follow-up, and referrals (Cranor & Christensen, 2003).

In addition, preventive and screening services are being implemented in pharmacies, both chain and independent. Vaccination programs to administer the influenza vaccine are commonly found in community pharmacies in most states. Similarly, many pharmacies offer diabetes and hypertension screening programs. With the success of the Asheville project, pharmacy services have grown and encompass management of chronic diseases (e.g., diabetes, hyperlipidemia, hypertension, asthma) nutrition counseling, refill reminder programs, and medication therapy management (MTM). As pharmacists become more intimately involved in patient care, learning about models of care and health behavior theory is important to improve their interactions with patients and to facilitate health behavior change.

MODELS OF CARE

Szasz and Hollender's Three Models of Care

Two physicians, Thomas Szasz and Marc Hollender (1956), described three models of patient care. These models, which are now recognized by many as the standard in the field, relate the nature of the patient's illness to the patient's capacity for meaningful dialogue and/or independent action. Each model of care is analogous to the relationship between parents and their children at different stages in their lives (infant, adolescent, and adult).

The activity–passivity model is characterized by an active practitioner and a passive patient; it is analogous to the relationship parents have with an infant child. This model of care is typically used in emergency situations, when the patient has been severely injured and is incapable of coherent communication and/or independent action (e.g., trauma, delirium, or coma). Szasz and Hollender described this form as the oldest type of practitioner–patient relationship; by definition, this model does not include much, if any, interpersonal communication. In this model, the patient is simply a recipient—the object of the practitioner's actions.

The guidance–cooperation model is used in situations in which the patient is capable of interpersonal communication and is actively involved in the relationship. Szasz and Hollender considered this form to be the most commonly used approach to care. Under this model, patients have more power of independent action than in the activity–passivity model of care, but still require professional attention and defer to medical expertise. This relationship is analogous to the relationship between parents and an adolescent child, and it typically applies to patients who are seeking help for some acute condition (e.g., infection or a broken bone).

The third model, mutual participation, applies most commonly when patients have some type of chronic disease (e.g., diabetes, heart disease, or arthritis). This model assumes that the patient and the practitioner are equally powerful and interdependent. Their mutual power comes from their relatively equal yet distinct knowledge bases; the practitioner possesses medical expertise, and the patient has personal experiences gained by living with the condition. In this way, both parties are interdependent; they share with and learn from each other to achieve an ongoing, successful treatment program. The patient and the practitioner relate to each other as two adults. For example, Mary and her physician exchanged information; her physician presented Mary with treatment options, and she made the decision as to which option she would try.

Szasz and Hollender described these three models of care as operating in a dynamic fashion, applied as the patient's situation dictates. That is, much as a parent's relationship with a child changes as the child gains independence, so, too, might a practitioner's relationship change with a patient. If a patient's condition evolves from traumatic to acute to chronic, as in an accident with enduring health effects, the practitioner's model of care would likewise evolve to accommodate these changes. Nonetheless, Szasz and Hollender acknowledged that (at least in the 1950s) the balance of power in physician–patient relations was significantly tipped toward physicians, with guidance–cooperation being the standard mode of practice, and mutual participation being least common.

As is suggested by the parent–child analogies of these models, the traditional imbalance of power has often been characterized as paternalistic (Beisecker & Beisecker, 1993; Emanuel & Emanuel, 1992; Parsons, 1951; President's Commission, 1982). However, as pointed out by Reeder (1972), societal changes beginning in the 1960s fostered a shift in this traditional imbalance, with patients becoming decreasingly deferential.

The Consumer Model of Care

Reeder suggested a consumer model of care that was eventually elaborated on by others (Haug & Lavin, 1981, 1983; Roter & Hall, 1992). The consumer model is characterized by greater patient autonomy in decision making, where the traditional authority of physicians has become increasingly challenged. As the word consumer suggests, patients are perceived as increasingly informed and skeptical buyers of medical care, whereas physicians are sellers who respond to the needs of the patient. In this conceptualization, the traditional emphasis on the physician's rights (to direct) and the patient's obligations (to follow) are essentially reversed to emphasize the patient/buyer's rights and the physician/seller's obligations. This dramatic shift in power has led some to criticize this model as going too far, by emphasizing conflict and mistrust while discrediting medical expertise.

As with most representations, the three Szasz and Hollender models and the consumer model reflect some significant proportion of reality—emphasizing the balance of power within the physician–patient relationship. This has been a popular topic, with the nature of the relationship being represented in various ways (see, for example, Childress and Siegler, 1984; Emanuel & Emanuel, 1992; Roter & Hall, 1992; and Veatch, 1972). Some observers, however, have shifted the emphasis away from issues of power and disease as the focus of the medical encounter; instead, they consider the manner in which practitioners and patients relate to each other in terms of how they define the problem at hand.

The Patient-Centered Model of Care

The patient-centered model is often contrasted with the disease-centered model of patient care (Balint, Hung, Joyce, Marinker, & Woodcock, 1970; Byrne & Long, 1976; Henbest & Stewart, 1990; Levenstein. Brown, Weston, Stewart, McCracken, & McWhinney, 1989; Mishler, 1984). In the disease-centered models, the presenting problem is understood with scientific detachment; the focus is on organic pathology and accurate diagnosis.

The patient-centered orientation shifts the focus from just the body to the person as a whole. Practitioners who adopt this model are encouraged to view the illness through the patient's eyes by considering these four key elements: (1) understanding the patient's ideas about what is wrong; (2) eliciting the patient's feelings (especially fears) about the illness; (3) assessing how the problem affects the patient's daily life; and (4) discovering what expectations the patient has regarding treatment (Weston, Brown, & Stewart, 1989). With these considerations in mind, the dialogue between practitioner and patient takes on different characteristics. Instead of the traditional closed-ended, disease-centered questions, phrased to keep the patient's responses brief and focused on pathology, a patient-centered dialogue asks open-ended questions that facilitate the patient's feedback and explore the meaning of the problem from the patient's point of view.

Consider the contrast between these two models as they are depicted in the following examples. We begin with the disease-centered interview.

> **Doctor:** Hello, Pat. What seems to be the problem that's brought you here today?
>
> **Patient:** I've been getting these stomach cramps lately, and I thought I ought to come and find out what's going on.
>
> **Doctor:** I see. How long have you been having the cramps?
>
> **Patient:** A couple of weeks.
>
> **Doctor:** Have you been constipated?
>
> **Patient:** Yes, I have.
>
> **Doctor:** How about diarrhea?
>
> **Patient:** That, too. It goes from one to the other.
>
> **Doctor:** I see. How long does the diarrhea last?
>
> **Patient:** About three days at a time.
>
> **Doctor:** And then you get constipated?
>
> **Patient:** That's right.
>
> **Doctor:** What kinds of foods have you been eating?

Patient: For a while I was eating pretty much nothing except junk food, but since this has happened I've been laying off the Big Macs, and it's still no better.

Doctor: Have you tried any self-medication?

Patient: My roommate said I ought to take Pepto-Bismol, but I decided not to.

Doctor: That's good. You shouldn't take anything unless you consult first with a doctor. Are you on any medication regimen now?

Patient: No, I'm not taking anything at all.

Doctor: Yes, I see. Well, I'll have to examine you and do some tests before I can give any definite diagnosis. It's too early to tell what it could be.

[After the examination, the doctor and patient continue their discussion]

Patient: What could it be? When will I know?

Doctor: As I said, I can't tell you anything significant without test results, but I should have something more definitive soon. The tests will rule out some possibilities and get me closer to an answer.

Patient: I guess I'll just have to wait.

Doctor: That's right. I'll have something for you soon. Is there anything else wrong that I can take care of now?

Patient: That's all for now. I'll be in touch with you soon, doc.

Now consider how a patient-centered interview with the same patient might go.

Doctor: Hi, Pat. How are you doing?

Patient: Pretty well. I'm on spring break now.

Doctor: Really? How much longer until you're done with classes?

Patient: Finals are in early May, and then I'll be back home again.

Doctor: That's good to hear. What can I do for you today?

Patient: I've been getting these stomach cramps lately, and I thought I ought to find out what's going on.

Doctor: Sounds tough. What about them have you noted?

Patient: Sometimes I get these real bad bouts of diarrhea, and sometimes I get constipated. I'm a real mess.

Doctor: It sounds as if you don't know whether you're coming or going. What do you think is the problem?

Patient: I'm not sure. For a while I was pretty much eating only junk food, but since this has happened I've been laying off the Big Macs, and it's still no better.

Doctor: So it hasn't made much of a difference? Is there anything else you've tried?

Patient: My roommate said I ought to take Pepto-Bismol, but I decided not to try it.

Doctor: I think you made a good decision. Are things going well at school? Have you been under a lot of stress?

Patient: This has been a hard semester, and I have been having a hard time keeping my grades up.

Doctor: Well, that might have something to do with it, but that's only one possibility. I'll have to examine you and do some tests before I can tell you anything for sure.

[After the examination, the discussion continues.]

Doctor: Is there anything else on your mind?

Patient: No, that's all that's on my mind for now, but I really am concerned.

Doctor: It certainly is enough to get anyone upset, but I want you to know that these kinds of symptoms are not uncommon, and, of the several possible things it could be, most are quite treatable. I hope you're not letting this ruin your life at school.

Patient: It's been tough. I run track, but this was not my idea of practicing the dash.

Doctor: I'll bet not. Well, within the next week when the tests come back, I think we'll be able to come up with a number of good suggestions. Are you comfortable with the plan of attack we've set out? Is there anything else I can do for you?

Patient: Yeah, that's all for now. I'll be in touch with you soon, doc.

If one were to assume the role of the patient while reading these brief exchanges, the first example might ring truer to most experiences with medical practitioners, whereas the second example might seem more satisfying. A review of the research strongly suggests that patients generally express greater satisfaction with their care when treated as a whole person rather than simply as a medical problem (Hall & Dornan, 1988a, 1988b).

The Biopsychosocial Model of Care

Although paternalistic disease-centered models of care may still be the norm, in recent years there has been a general movement away from these perspectives and toward the consumer- and patient-centered models. In this context, it seems appropriate to mention one more way of conceptualizing models of care that reflects this era of change. Similar to the perceived movement from disease-centered to patient-centered care, some observers have noted a broad shift in Western medicine away from the standard biomedical model and toward a more inclusive biopsychosocial model (Engel, 1978, 1979, 1980; Stroebe & Stroebe, 1995).

Thanks to its scientific roots in molecular biology, the standard biomedical model evolved to emphasize mind–body dualism; biochemical deviation became the sole basis of disease, and psychosocial matters were relegated to nonmedical status. Because the biomedical model served our purposes so well during eras in which the major killers were acute, infectious diseases (e.g., influenza, tuberculosis, and gastroenteritis), it became accepted as the standard model of patient care. As life expectancy began to increase and chronic diseases became the major killers (e.g., heart disease, cancer, and cerebrovascular disease), the scope of the biomedical model has been viewed as overly narrow and less satisfactory given our current needs. Today, psychosocial issues such as poverty, place of residence, environmental pollution, diet, exercise, and stress are recognized as increasingly significant variables in understanding what ails us. George Engel succinctly expressed the problem with the biomedical model:

> The crippling flaw of the model is that it does not include the patient and his attributes as a person, a human being. Yet in the everyday work of the physician the prime object of study is a person, and many of the data necessary for hypothesis

development and testing are gathered within the framework of an ongoing human relationship and appear in behavioral and psychological forms, namely, how the patient behaves and what he reports about himself and his life. (1978, p. 536)

The biopsychosocial model takes into account health and illness as a product of a person's physical and social context as well as his or her emotional and psychological state. Thus this model adds behavioral and other psychosocial data into the equation with biochemical processes for scientific analysis and understanding of illness. If we are to understand how individual behaviors and the meanings that people attach to their symptoms can and do affect health, we need to consider more broad-based models in treating patients.

ADHERENCE

Often health professionals refer to whether a patient is compliant to therapeutic recommendations. Compliance refers to the patient following a health professional's recommendations, or in other words, the patient complies with what a health professional tells him to do. Although the terms are often used interchangeably, adherence implies that the patient has a choice or autonomy in following a health professional's recommendations. Similar to Szasz and Hollender's models of activity–passivity and guidance–cooperation, compliance is paternal; the pharmacist represents the parent and the patient represents the child following the parent's directions. Adherence is different than a parental relationship and suggests that the patient is a participant in the decision making and adherence to a recommendation, which reflects the mutual participation model or patient-centered care.

When a patient is nonadherent, a health professional should investigate the reasons why a patient is not following recommended advice. Often, it is assumed the patient unintentionally does not follow directions, such as in the case of forgetfulness or a change in a daily schedule. Although this does commonly occur, sometimes a patient intentionally does not take a medication or adopt a healthy behavior. In 2003, the World Health Organization released a report reviewing adherence literature on a variety of disease states in both developed and developing countries. In the report, a framework was developed to describe the factors influencing patients' adherence to recommendations. The dimensions of the framework were: (1) health system, (2) social/economic, (3) condition related, (4) patient related, and (5) therapy related. A list of selected factors found to influence adherence are provided in **Table 4-2**. Some of these factors are discussed in this chapter.

CULTURAL INFLUENCE ON HEALTH

Culture is a shared system of values, beliefs, and learned patterns of behavior that specifies acceptable and nonacceptable behaviors and offers individuals guidance on dealing with aspects of life (Galanti, 2004; Halber & Halber, 2008; Loustaunau & Sobo, 1997). Culture is different in that it is dynamic and changing. It is generally passed to each succeeding generation, but it is influenced by an individual's proximity to the culture of origin, education, gender, age, and sexual preference (Loustaunau & Sobo, 1997). Aspects regarding the cultural influence on health are briefly presented in this section of the chapter. Keeping in mind that books have been written about culture

Table 4-2 Selected Factors Influencing Patient Adherence

Dimension	Factor
Health system	Patient–provider relationship
	Communication
	Access to care and treatments
Social/economic	Living conditions
	Cost of therapy/treatment
	Literacy
	Financial resources
	Availability of social support networks
Condition related	Severity of condition
	Level of disability
	Presence of comorbidities
Patient related	Knowledge
	Illness beliefs
	Self-efficacy
	Expectations of treatment
	Motivation
	Cultural beliefs
Therapy related	Complexity of treatment regimen
	Occurrence of side effects
	Duration of treatment
	Previous treatment failures
	Immediacy of treatment effects

Source: Reprinted with permission from Plake KS. Behavior Change. In: Richardson MM, Chant C, Cheng JWM, Chessman KH, Hume AL, Hutchison LC, et al., eds. Pharmacotherapy Self-Assessment Program, sixth ed. Health Promotion and Maintenance. Lenexa, Kansas: American College of Clinical Pharmacy, 2008:2.

and its influence on health, it is not feasible to detail every aspect of culture in this short section. The author recommends the reader seek resources to inform his/her own pharmacy practice.

It is important for a health professional to consider culture because it can influence a variety of patient behaviors and outcomes. First, cultural belief systems and health practices regarding health and illness can vary. Cultural or lay belief systems of health can range from the necessity of establishing equilibrium in the body to the supernatural, such as the belief that a disease is a punishment from a higher power (Galanti, 2004; Loustaunau & Sobo, 1997). From the point of view of the patient, treatment effectiveness will be influenced by the cultural beliefs regarding the illness. In addition, certain disease states, in particular those involving mental health, are stigmatized within some cultural groups and can influence individuals' help-seeking behaviors and treatment adherence. There also is a cultural influence on how diseases and symptoms are expressed to others, including health professionals. For example, emotional stresses may be expressed as physical symptoms or complaints (Galanti, 2004; Loustaunau & Sobo, 1997). In addition, some individuals will be very expressive about their symptoms while others will be stoic and reveal very little about their health status.

Specific health practices can be used by individuals to promote healing, such as the use of prayer, rituals, folk remedies, herbs, and alternative health practitioners (e.g., acupuncturists, massage therapists, and native healers) (Galanti, 2004; Loustaunau & Sobo, 1997). In addition, certain practices within the culture can impact health, such as dietary preferences. Although at first glance, this may not appear to be of much importance, advising a patient who has recently emigrated from Africa on dietary choices using examples from a typical Western/Anglo diet would not be very effective, nor would it promote adherence.

Communication patterns, both verbal and nonverbal, can vary among cultures as well. The use of idioms or slang, such as the use of "getting cold feet," can be misinterpreted and taken for their literal or cultural meanings (Galanti, 2004). Health professionals should avoid using such terminology. Nonverbal communication also can be interpreted differently across cultures (Galanti, 2004; Loustaunau & Sobo, 1997). Such behaviors include, but are not limited to, the appropriateness of touch, eye contact, personal space, facial expressions, silence, head movements, and hand and arm gestures. For example, in the United States, direct eye contact is expected by many as a sign that an individual is listening and interested. However, in some cultures, direct eye contact signals disrespect so a patient may avert his eyes to show respect and concern (Galanti, 2004).

In some cases, the use of an interpreter may be necessary when working with patients for whom English is their second language. When using an interpreter, it is recommended that he/she be fluent in both languages of interest, be trained, preferably with a medical focus, be unrelated to the patient, and never be a child, particularly the patient's child. Although it may be difficult to find an interpreter meeting these specifications, there are reasons for these guidelines. In many cultures, there are traditional gender-specific roles that each family member plays. It may be inappropriate to discuss certain topics among mixed company, such as in the case of opposite genders or with children (Galanti, 2004). As a result, the health professional's message may not be completely relayed to the patient and/or the patient may not have fully informed the interpreter and the health professional, giving an incomplete picture of the patient's health.

Health may very much be a family affair, depending on the cultural value system. At times, a large contingent of the family may attend an appointment; others may prefer a private individual appointment with a health professional. Often, there is a hierarchical approach to decision making within the healthcare context. A specific family member or head of household, such as the case of a family matriarch or patriarch, may be making the healthcare decisions for family members. As a result, these family members may play an active role in health consultations (Galanti, 2004; Loustaunau & Sobo, 1997).

HEALTH LITERACY

Navigating the healthcare system and adhering to therapeutic recommendations requires patients to be able to read and interpret prescription bottle labels, complete health insurance or informed consent forms, read and interpret nutrition information on food labels, and follow verbal or written instructions. Although literacy is an essential skill for patients in taking care of their health, it is health literacy that encompasses the skills necessary to navigate the healthcare system. Health literacy is defined as the degree to which individuals have the capacity to obtain, process, and understand basic health information and services needed to make appropriate health decisions (Ratzan & Parker, 2000). Health literacy is necessary for patients to accomplish health-related tasks so that their health can be maintained as well as improved.

Approximately 90 million Americans lack the necessary literacy skills to function in the current healthcare system (IOM, 2004). Based on the 2007 National Healthcare Disparities Report, 12% of adults have the necessary health literacy skills to manage all aspects of their health care (Agency for Healthcare Research and Quality, 2008). Although studies have indicated that there are individuals who are at an increased risk of having limited health literacy skills, limited health literacy can affect anyone irrespective of their cultural, educational, or socioeconomic backgrounds. Of importance to health professionals, patients with limited health literacy often find accessing healthcare resources difficult, which results in poorer outcomes as compared to those with higher health literacy (Berkman et al., 2004).

Although there are instruments available to identify individuals with low literacy skills, it is often impractical to use them in a high-paced healthcare environment. In most cases, these tools are used in research to measure patients' health literacy and its impact on outcomes, as well as to assess interventions. These tools include the Short-Form Test of Functional Health Literacy for Adults (S-TOFHLA) (Baker, Williams, Parker, Gazmararian, & Nurss, 1999), Rapid Estimate of Adult Literacy in Medicine (REALM) (Davis, et al., 1993), and Newest Vital Sign (NVS) (Weiss et al., 2005). All of these instruments have been used widely in the literature to assess patients' health literacy level. Recently, screening questions have been developed and validated against some of these health instruments in an attempt to quickly assess if a patient is at risk for having limited health literacy. These screening questions include: (1) "How often do you have someone help you read hospital materials?" (2) "How confident are you filling out medical forms by yourself?" and (3) "How often do you have problems learning about your medical condition because of difficulty understanding written information?" (Chew et al., 2007). Of these three questions, "How confident are you in filling out medical forms by yourself?" was the most predictive in identifying individuals with limited health literacy (Chew et al., 2007).

Although there are methods to identify individuals with limited health literacy, experts often advise adopting communication strategies that can be used for all patients, regardless of health literacy level (Paasche-Orlow & Wolf, 2007). This approach is suggested because individuals frequently try to hide their difficulty in understanding information. For many patients, it is embarrassing and so they often act as if they understand even when they do not. In most instances, it is recommended that health-related information be communicated at the fifth-grade level or lower in order to maximize the message with the majority of individuals. Most of the approaches to address health literacy involve producing patient information materials using simplified language, format, or pictograms/graphics. For example, the United States Pharmacopeia website contains many health-related pictograms (http://www.usp.org/audiences/consumers/pictograms/). In addition, Microsoft Word provides readability statistics to help guide practitioners in their efforts to provide written communication. There are a wide variety of techniques, guidelines, templates, and tools available to assist health professionals in ways to communicate with patients. These include the teach-back or show-me technique to assess patient understanding and the Ask Me 3 program (http://www.npsf.org/askme3/) to encourage patients to become active participants in the healthcare dialogue. Additional resources include the Agency for Healthcare Research and Quality (AHRQ) pharmacy health literacy center (http://pharmacy-healthliteracy.ahrq.gov/sites/PharmHealthLiteracy/default.aspx), Pfizer Clear Health Communication Initiative (http://www.pfizerhealthliteracy.com/index.html), and the MedlinePlus website (http://www.nlm.nih.gov/medlineplus/).

HEALTH BEHAVIOR MODELS

Given that there appears to be a desire to move toward a more comprehensive patient care model, healthcare professionals should be aware of how to help patients change their health behaviors and comply with recommended therapies. The following models attempt to explain and predict health behaviors and behavior change based on a variety of factors.

Locus of Control

Locus of control has it origins in Rotter's social learning theory, which states "the potential for a behavior to occur in a given situation is a function of expectancies that the behavior will lead to a particular outcome and the extent to which an outcome is valued" (AbuSabha & Achterberg, 1997, p. 1125). Although it may sound similar to some of the models discussed later in this chapter, locus of control specifically refers to whether an individual feels that attainment of a particular outcome is within his or her control or outside of it. If we think that health outcomes are within our control, we are considered to have an internal locus of control. In other words, we think that what we do (or do not do) determines the outcome of our health. If we think that outcomes are outside of our control, we are said to have an external locus of control. In other words, we believe that forces outside of our control determine health outcomes.

External locus of control can be further divided into two categories: (1) powerful others and (2) chance (AbuSabha & Achterberg, 1997; Levenson, 1974; Wallston, Wallston, & Devellis, 1978). Individuals who believe that other people, such as healthcare professionals and family members, determine health outcomes are said to have a powerful others orientation. Those with a chance orientation believe that their health outcomes and other events are attributable to fate or chance.

Health Belief Model

The health belief model is used to understand the successes and failures of health behavior change. Rosenstock and colleagues initially developed this model to explain why people practice preventive behavior, but it has since been used to explain such behaviors as compliance with drug therapy and other disease management practices (Clark & Becker, 1998; Rosenstock, 1974; Salazar, 1991).

This model focuses on the likelihood that an individual will take action or change his or her behavior. According to this model, the perceived susceptibility and severity of the disease determine the perceived threat of the disease to the individual and contribute to the likelihood of changing behavior. Susceptibility is an individual's perception of his or her risk for contracting the disease; severity is the seriousness of a disease if left untreated (Clark & Becker, 1998; Salazar, 1991).

In addition to susceptibility and severity, the perceived benefits and barriers contribute to the likelihood of taking action. Benefits are the individual's beliefs that changing the behavior will reduce the disease threat. These are weighed against the barriers to change or the negative aspects (e.g., money, effort) of such a change in behavior, which act as deterrents to behavior change. If an individual believes that he or she has a high susceptibility to a severe/serious disease, the perceived threat is high enough so he or she may see the benefits of changing behavior (Clark & Becker, 1998; Salazar, 1991). Conversely, if the susceptibility and/or severity of the disease is low, the perceived threat is low and, therefore, the behavior change may not be perceived as providing sufficient benefits. In this case, the person is unlikely to change the behavior.

Demographic (age, gender, and ethnicity), sociopsychologic (personality, social class, and peer and reference group pressure), and structural variables (knowledge about the disease and prior contact to the disease) may influence how someone perceives the susceptibility, seriousness, and threat of the disease. In addition, cues to action can influence how an individual perceives the threat of disease. These cues might include mass media campaigns, advice from others, reminder postcards from a physician, illness of a family member or friend, or a newspaper or magazine article (Clark & Becker, 1998; Salazar, 1991).

Finally, self-efficacy may play a role in the health belief model. In brief, self-efficacy or efficacy expectation pertains to a person's confidence in his or her ability to take action or change a behavior. In other words, an individual must feel competent to overcome the barriers to positive behavior change (Strecher & Rosenstock, 1997). Self-efficacy is described in more detail in the "Social Cognitive Theory" section later in this chapter.

According to the health belief model, for an obese person to lose weight, the individual would need to believe that he or she is susceptible to the negative effects of obesity as well as the possibility of severe effects from the disease. For example, for a behavior change to occur, the person needs to believe that he or she is more susceptible to suffering a cardiovascular event because of being overweight. In addition, the individual needs to believe that the cardiovascular event is serious to perceive a threat from developing the disease. The patient may see the benefits of enrolling in a weight reduction program, but if the barriers are greater than the benefits, he or she still may not take action. In addition, modifying factors, such as social support or cues to action (e.g., an obese family member having a heart attack) may influence the likelihood that the individual will actively try to lose weight. Besides the modifying factors, the person must believe in his or her ability to overcome the barriers to losing weight (self-efficacy) before he or she will attempt the weight loss regimen.

Social Cognitive Theory

Social cognitive theory, like the other theories/models discussed in this chapter, was developed to help predict behavior. Bandura identified the following two types of expectations that influence behavior: (1) outcome expectations and (2) efficacy expectations (Bandura, 1977). Outcome expectations are the individual's expectation or belief that a particular behavior will result in a particular outcome. For example, a person may believe that exercise can help him lose weight. Efficacy expectations are the individual's expectations that he or she has the ability to accomplish this behavior, such as participating in an exercise routine to lose weight.

According to social cognitive theory, the key lies in the individual's perceptions of the outcomes and efficacy in performing these behaviors—not his or her true capabilities (Clark & Becker, 1998). That is, a person might begin an exercise program to lose weight because she believes that exercise will result in a weight loss and that she can perform this activity. In addition, expectations are specific for particular behaviors (AbuSabha & Achterberg, 1997; Clark & Becker, 1998). In other words, just because a person believes that he can undertake an exercise program, it does not mean that he believes that he can decrease his caloric intake or diet. His outcome and efficacy expectations may be different for a diet as compared to an exercise program.

Efficacy expectations are learned through the following four mechanisms: (1) performance accomplishments, (2) vicarious experience, (3) verbal persuasion, and (4) physiologic state (Bandura, 1977, 1986; Clark & Becker, 1998). Performance accomplishments refer to an individual's attempt at a particular behavior that is perceived to be difficult. The experience of success in accomplishing this difficult behavior increases self-efficacy. For example, if a person fears going on a diet, yet attempts to make this lifestyle change and experiences success, then her self-efficacy will improve.

Vicarious experiences refer to the modeling of behaviors by others and the individual observing such behaviors. To improve self-efficacy, it must be seen that the model achieved success through overcoming difficulties (as compared to being easy) and the model must be similar in characteristics (gender, age) to the observer. Perhaps a friend is successful in achieving weight loss by dieting. By observing his friend's weight loss and the difficulties in succeeding in this task, a person may feel more capable of attempting this same change.

Verbal persuasion encourages the individual to continue to make attempts in behavior changes, such as a pharmacist encouraging a patient to continue or advising him or her to attempt an exercise regimen or diet. The final mechanism that influences efficacy expectations pertains to the physiologic state of the individual. High physiologic arousal, such as tension and agitation, increases the likelihood of failure. For instance, a person who feels fatigued or experiences pain after exercising may believe that he cannot accomplish the behavior.

Theory of Reasoned Action and the Theory of Planned Behavior

According to the theory of reasoned action, a determinant of a person's behavior is one's behavioral intention or the likelihood of performing the behavior. The following two factors are hypothesized to lead to an individual's behavioral intention: (1) the attitude toward performing the behavior and (2) the subjective norm associated with the behavior.

With the first factor, the likelihood of performing a behavior is influenced by the person's beliefs about the behavior and the outcome(s) associated with it. The value associated with the outcome—whether positive or negative—is another important component of one's attitude toward the behavior (Clark & Becker, 1998; Madden, Ellen, & Ajzen, 1992; Montano, Kasprzyk, & Taplin, 1997). For example, an individual who believes that losing weight is associated with positive outcomes will have a positive attitude toward the behavior change needed to lose weight.

The second factor, subjective norm, refers to what other important individuals think about the person's behavior change or of his or her desire to perform the behavior.

In other words, do others approve or disapprove of the performance of the specific behavior? As part of this evaluation of others' beliefs, the individual also is affected by his or her desire or motivation to comply with others' wishes (Clark & Becker, 1998; Madden et al., 1992; Montano et al., 1997). For example, if an individual believes that others want him to lose weight and is motivated by these beliefs or expectations, he has a positive subjective norm. Both positive attitudes and a positive subject norm will increase the likelihood of performing the behavior or carrying through on the behavioral intention.

Theory of reasoned action fails to address the issue of the person's degree of control over the behavior. Control refers to factors, both personal and external, that influence the behavior such as a workable plan, skills, knowledge, time, money, willpower, and opportunity. However, the degree of control or factors could influence both behavioral intention and the performance of a behavior. The theory of planned behavior is an extension of the theory of reasoned action in which perceived behavioral control is added to the theory of reasoned action model to address those cases in which a person does not have a high degree of control over the behavior (Clark & Becker, 1998; Madden et al., 1992; Montano et al., 1997).

Perceived behavioral control is determined by control beliefs, which refers to the presence or absence of resources for and the barriers to the performance of the behavior. In addition, the perceived power of each resource and barrier to promote or deter behavior is considered. For example, if an individual has a strong belief about the existence of resources to encourage the behavior, then she has a high perceived control over the behavior. By contrast, if an individual believes that factors can deter her from performing the behavior, such as the lack of time to exercise, the person is said to have low perceived control and is less likely to perform the behavior (Clark & Becker, 1998; Madden et al., 1992; Montano et al., 1997).

Transtheoretical Model of Change

The transtheoretical model of change was developed by Prochaska in the 1970s and 1980s to determine why the attempts to change behavior failed or succeeded. Commonly referred to as the readiness to change model, it theorizes that a patient progresses through five stages before a change in behavior, such as quitting smoking or losing weight, occurs. These stages are (1) precontemplation, (2) contemplation, (3) preparation, (4) action, and (5) maintenance (Berger, 1997; Prochaska & Velicer, 1997; Prochaska, Johnson, & Lee, 1998).

Patients in the precontemplation stage have not thought of changing a specific behavior, and such a change is not expected to occur in the foreseeable future (the next 6 months). Patients are in the precontemplation stage for a variety of reasons, including being uninformed or underinformed about the outcomes of their behaviors and/or discouraged about their ability to change because of past failures. In addition, this category includes individuals who are unwilling to change their behaviors. Individuals in this stage of change avoid talking, reading, or thinking about the needed behavior change. Often they are perceived as unmotivated and as unprepared for action-oriented intervention programs (Berger, 1997; Prochaska & Velicer, 1997; Prochaska, Johnson, & Lee, 1998).

Unlike individuals in the precontemplation stage, patients entering the contemplation stage are beginning to consider a change in their behavior and intend to make that change within the next 6 months. These individuals recognize the benefits of changing, but also realize the costs or negative aspects of behavior change. For this reason, patients may become stuck in this stage because of their ambivalence about the benefits versus the costs of change. In other words, they have no plan for action and are not entirely ready to commit to a change (Berger, 1997; Prochaska & Velicer, 1997; Prochaska, Johnson, & Lee, 1998). Commitment to making a change will not occur until the benefits of the change outweigh the barriers to the behavior change.

In the preparation stage, patients commit to a behavior change and plan to take action, usually within the next month. In many cases, they have already taken some small steps toward action within the past year and are ready to make a change. These individuals are prepared to engage in an action-oriented intervention, such as a smoking cessation program (Berger, 1997; Prochaska & Velicer, 1997; Prochaska, Johnson, & Lee, 1998).

Patients in the action stage are in the process of changing their behavior and have taken specific steps to do so over the past 6 months (Berger, 1997; Prochaska & Velicer, 1997; Prochaska, Johnson, & Lee, 1998). In the maintenance stage, individuals do not use change processes as frequently as in the action stage. Instead, they focus on triggers (e.g., environment, friends, and family) that may make them susceptible to their old habits. The goal during this stage is to prevent relapse into the old behavior. People in this stage need help to control or become aware of these triggers for relapse. Despite the temptation, patients are more confident that they will not return to their old behaviors. The maintenance stage can last anywhere from 6 months to 5 years (Berger, 1997; Prochaska & Velicer, 1997; Prochaska, Johnson, & Lee, 1998).

According to the transtheoretical model of change, interventions to change patient behavior should be specific to the patient stage. If someone is overweight and in the precontemplation stage, the desired intervention should be promoting awareness rather than enrolling him or her in a weight reduction plan, such as Weight Watchers. The weight reduction plan will not be successful for this individual because he or she has no intention to change at this point. By comparison, a person in the preparation stage is ready to make a change and has already taken small steps toward weight reduction. He or she is more likely to be successful in a weight reduction program.

Besides focusing on appropriate interventions based on the patient's stage, the healthcare professional should facilitate movement through this model. For example, if someone is in the precontemplation stage, the pharmacist should use interventions and techniques geared toward moving the patient into the contemplation stage. These interventions and techniques, which are called processes of change (**Table 4-3**), can be used to help patients move toward the action and maintenance stages of change.

Motivational Interviewing

Developed by Miller and Rollnick, motivational interviewing (MI) is a patient-centered approach to facilitate behavior change by exploring and resolving a patient's ambivalence (Miller & Rollnick, 2002). Unlike the traditional advising or persuasive approach used by health professionals, the focus of motivational interviewing is to help a patient resolve his ambivalence, which is often seen in the precontemplation and contemplation stages of change in the transtheoretical model.

In motivational interviewing, a partnership is formed between the health professional and patient. Key to using this approach is preserving the patient's autonomy while elic-

Table 4-3 Processes of Change

Process of change	Definition	Example	Stage emphasized
Consciousness raising	Increasing awareness about the causes, consequences, and cures for a problem behavior or diseases	Education, pamphlets, media campaigns	Precontemplation Contemplation
Dramatic relief	Arousing an emotional response with a subsequent reduced effect if action can be taken	Personal testimonies, media campaigns, role-playing	Precontemplation Contemplation
Self-reevaluation	Assessing one's self-image with and without unhealthy habit	Smoker assessing what it would be like to be a nonsmoker	Contemplation
Environmental reevaluation	Assessing how a behavior impacts the social environment	Smoker assessing how his or her smoking impacts spouse, children, etc.	Precontemplation Contemplation
Self-liberation	Believing that one can change and committing to the change	New Year's resolution or telling others of changes	Preparation
Counterconditioning	Substituting healthy behaviors for unhealthy ones	Nicotine replacement, fat-free foods	Action Maintenance
Stimulus control	Removing cues for unhealthy behaviors and adding prompts for healthy behaviors for easy access	Removing high-fat foods from home, keeping exercise equipment in car	Action Maintenance
Contingency management	Using rewards to encourage behavior change	Praise, group recognition, purchase of new clothes after weight loss	Action Maintenance
Helping relationships	Receiving and using support from others	Buddy systems for exercise or weight loss, family involvement in change	Action Maintenance

Source: Adapted from Schumaker, S. A., Schron, E. B, Ockene, J. K., & McBee, W. L. (Eds.). (1998). *The Handbook of Health Behavior Change* (2nd ed.). New York, NY: Springer Publishing Company, LLC.

Table 4-4 Motivational Interviewing Principles

Principle	Approach
Expressing empathy	Use of reflective listening to help the patient feel understood.
Developing discrepancy	Create cognitive dissonance by having the patient compare present behavior with his goals, making it difficult for the patient to ignore the discrepancy.
Rolling with resistance	Develop mutually negotiated solutions with the patient. Use a different strategy or approach when experiencing resistance from the patient.
Avoiding argumentation	Resist arguing with patient about discrepancies because doing so creates defensiveness and resistance in the patient, making change unlikely.
Supporting self-efficacy	Provide support and encouragement to improve the patient's confidence in changing a behavior.

Source: Adapted from Miller, W. R., & Rollnick, S. (2002). *Motivational interviewing: Preparing people for change.* New York, NY: The Guilford Press.

iting a patient's motivation, or lack thereof, to adhere to healthy behaviors or therapeutic recommendations (Miller & Rollnick, 2002). As part of the collaboration between the patient and health professional, the key principles of motivational interviewing are used; these principles are expressing empathy, developing discrepancy, rolling with resistance, avoiding argumentation, and supporting self-efficacy (see **Table 4-4**). Based on reports in the literature, the use of these motivational interviewing techniques is more effective in facilitating behavior change among patients as compared to the traditional advice-giving approach in patient care (Rubak, Sandboek, Lauritzen, & Christensen, 2005).

CONCLUSION

Patient care is currently undergoing a transition toward increased collaboration between healthcare professionals and patients. Given the increasing knowledge patients have about their health, providers will need to take a different approach to care than telling the patient what to do and expecting unquestioning compliance. Of course, not all patients are alike. They have their own unique issues and characteristics that affect their interactions with healthcare professionals as well as determine their impact on the healthcare system and the healthcare system's impact on them.

As the healthcare system continues to try to change patient health behaviors, the models, as well as the factors affecting adherence, described in this chapter provide a basis for the development of effective interventions. Through the questioning of patients, healthcare practitioners can determine patients' beliefs regarding the numerous factors that influence their behaviors. By using these models, practitioners can use the information gained from patients to target specific behaviors with specific interventions.

QUESTIONS FOR FURTHER DISCUSSION

1. Would you suggest other models of care or variations on the models discussed in this chapter, based on a pharmacist–patient interaction rather than a physician–patient interaction?
2. How do your personal experiences relate to the health behavior models discussed in this chapter?
3. Do pharmacists need to make changes in the various practice settings to improve delivery of health care to patients? Why or why not?
4. How could the health behavior models and motivational interviewing be implemented in pharmacy practice?
5. How will you adapt your communication when providing patient care to patients with limited health literacy?

KEY TOPICS AND TERMS

Activity–passivity model of patient care
Adherence
Compliance
Consumer model of care
Culture
Direct-to-consumer advertising
Guidance–cooperation model of patient care
Health literacy
Health behavior models
Motivational interviewing
Mutual participation model of patient care
Patient-centered model of care
Preventive health care

REFERENCES

AbuSabha, R., & Achterberg, C. (1997). Review of self-efficacy and locus of control for nutrition and health-related behavior. *Journal of the American Dietetic Association, 97*(10), 1122–1133.

Agency for Healthcare Research and Quality. (2008). *National healthcare disparities 2007 report.* Rockville, MD: U.S. Department of Health and Human Services.

Arias, E. (2006). United States life tables, 2003. *National Vital Statistics Reports, 54*(14), 1–6.

Baker, D. W., Williams, M. V., Parker, R. M., Gazmararian, J. A., & Nurss J. (1999). Development of a brief test to measure functional health literacy. *Patient Education and Counseling, 38*(1), 33–42.

Balint, M., Hung, J., Joyce, D., Marinker, M., & Woodcock, J. (1970). *Treatment of diagnosis: A study of repeat prescription in general practice.* Toronto, Ontario: J. B. Lippincott.

Bandura, A. (1977). Self-efficacy: Toward a unifying theory of behavioral change. *Psychological Review, 84,* 191–215.

Bandura, A. (1986). *Social foundations of thought and action.* Englewood Cliffs, NJ: Prentice-Hall.

Baran, R. W., Crumlish, K., Patterson, H., Shaw, J., Erwin, W. G., Wylie, J. D., & Duong, P. (1999). Improving outcomes of community-dwelling older patients with diabetes through pharmacist counseling. *American Journal of Health-System Pharmacists, 56,* 1535–1539.

Beisecker, A. E., & Beisecker, T. D. (1993). Using metaphors to characterize doctor–patient relationships: Paternalism versus consumerism. *Health Communications, 5,* 41–58.

Berger, B. A. (1997). *Readiness for change: Improving treatment adherence.* Durham, NC: Glaxo, Inc., and Clean Data.

Berkman, N. D., DeWalt, D. A., Pignone, M. P., Sheridan, S. L., Lohr, K. N., Lux, L., ... Bonito, A. J. (2004). *Literacy and health outcomes.* Rockville, MD: Agency for Health Care Research and Quality.

Bluml, B. M., McKenney, J. M., & Cziraky, M. J. (2000). Pharmaceutical care services and results in Project ImPACT: Hyperlipidemia. *Journal of the American Pharmaceutical Association, 40,* 157–165.

Byrne, P. S., & Long, B. E. L. (1976). *Doctors talking to patients.* London, England: Royal College of General Practitioners.

Chan, L., Hart, L. G., & Goodman, D. C. (2006). Geographic access to health care for rural Medicare beneficiaries. *Journal of Rural Health, 22*(2), 140–146.

Chauncey, D., Mullins, C. D., Tran, B. V., McNally, D., & McEwan, R. N. (2006). Medication access through patient assistance programs. *American Journal of Health-System Pharmacy, 63*(13), 1254–1259.

Chew, L. D., Griffin, J. M, Partin, M. R., Noorbaloochi, S., Grill, J. P., Snyder, A., ... VanRyn, M. (2007). Validation of screening questions for limited health literacy in a large VA outpatient population. *Journal of General Internal Medicine, 23*(5), 561–566.

Childress, J. F., & Siegler, M. (1984). Metaphors and models of doctor–patient relationships: Their implications for autonomy. *Theoretical Medicine, 5,* 17–30.

Chisholm, M. A., Reinhardt, B. O., Vollenweider, L. J., Kendrick, B. D., & Dipiro, J. T. (2000). Medication assistance reports medication assistance programs for uninsured and indigent patients. *American Journal of Health-System Pharmacy, 57*(12), 1131–1136.

Clark, N. M., & Becker, M. H. (1998). Theoretical models and strategies for improving adherence and disease management. In S. A. Shumaker, E. B. Schron, J. K. Ockene, & W. L. McBee (Eds.), *The handbook of health behavior change* (2nd ed., pp. 5–32). New York, NY: Springer.

Cranor, C. W., & Christensen, D. B. (2003). The Asheville project: Short-term outcomes of a community diabetes care program. *Journal of the American Pharmacists Association, 43*(2), 149–159.

Dave, D., & Saffer, H. (2010). *The impact of direct-to-consumer advertising on pharmaceutical prices and demand.* Cambridge, MA: National Bureau of Economic Research.

Davis, T. C., Long, S. W., Jackson, R. H., Mayeaux, E. J., George, R. B., Murphy, P. W., & Crouch, M. A. (1993). Rapid estimate of adult literacy in medicine: A shortened screening instrument. *Family Medicine, 25*(6), 391–395.

Dean, K. (1989). Conceptual, theoretical, and methodological issues in self-care research. *Social Science and Medicine, 29*(2), 117–123.

Emanuel, E. J., & Emanuel, L. L. (1992). Four models of the physician–patient relationship. *Journal of the American Medical Association, 267,* 2221–2226.

Engel, G. L. (1978). The biopsychosocial model and the education of health professionals. *Annals of the New York Academy of Sciences, 310,* 169–181.

Engel, G. L. (1979). The need for a new medical model: A challenge for biomedicine. *Science, 196,* 129–136.

Engel, G. L. (1980). The clinical application of the biopsychosocial model. *American Journal of Psychiatry, 137,* 535–544.

Fox, S., & Jones, S. (2009). *The social life of health information. Pew Internet and American Life Project.* Retrieved from http://pewinternet.org/~/media//Files/Reports/2009/PIP_Health_2009.pdf

Fox, S., & Purcell, K. (2010). *Chronic disease and the Internet. Pew Internet and American Life Project.* Retrieved from http://pewinternet.org/~/media//Files/Reports/2010/PIP_Chronic_Disease_with_topline.pdf

Galanti, G. (2004). *Caring for patients from different cultures.* Philadelphia, PA: University of Pennsylvania Press.

General Accounting Office. (2002, October). *FDA oversight of direct-to-consumer advertising has limitations.* Retrieved from http://www.gao.gov/new.items/d03177.pdf

Greeno, R. (1999). Perspectives on the evolving hospitalist model. *Managed Care Interface, 12*(4), 80–84.

Halber, K.V. & Halber, D.A. (2008). *Essentials of cultural competence in pharmacy practice.* Washington, DC: American Pharmacists Association.

Hall, A. G., Lemak, C. H., Steingraber, H., & Schaffer, S. (2008). Expanding the definition of access: It isn't just about health insurance. *Journal of Health Care for the Poor and Underserved, 19*(2), 625–638.

Hall, J. A., & Dornan, M. C. (1988a). Meta-analysis of satisfaction with medical care: Description of research done in and analysis of overall satisfaction. *Social Science and Medicine, 26,* 637–644.

Hall, J. A., & Dornan, M. C. (1988b). What patients like about their medical care and how often they are asked: A meta-analysis of the satisfaction literature. *Social Science and Medicine, 27,* 935–939.

Haug, M. R., & Lavin, B. (1981). Practitioner or patient—Who's in charge? *Journal of Health and Social Behavior, 22,* 212–229.

Haug, M. R., & Lavin, B. (1983). *Consumerism in medicine: Challenging physician authority.* Beverly Hills, CA: Sage.

Henbest, R. J., & Stewart, M. (1990). Patient-centeredness in the consultation, 2: Does it really make a difference? *Family Practice, 7,* 28–33.

Institute of Medicine (IOM). (2004). *Health literacy: A prescription to end confusion.* Washington, DC: National Academies Press.

Kaiser Family Foundation. (2003, June). *Impact of direct-to-consumer advertising on prescription drug spending.* Washington, DC: Kaiser Family Foundation.

Kaiser Family Foundation. (2006, November). *Prescription drugs: Advertising, out-of-pocket costs, and patient safety from the perspective of doctors and pharmacists.* Washington, DC: Kaiser Family Foundation.

Knowles, J. H. (1997). *Doing better and feeling worse: Health in the United States.* New York, NY: Norton Press.

Leavitt, J. W., & Numbers, R. L. (1997). Sickness and health: An overview. In J. W. Leavitt & R. L. Numbers (Eds.), *Sickness and health in America: Readings in the history of medicine and public health* (3rd ed., pp. 3–10). Madison, WI: University of Wisconsin Press.

Levenson, H. (1974). Activism and powerful others: Distinctions within the concept of internal-external control. *Journal of Personality Assessment, 38,* 377–383.

Levenstein, J. H., Brown, J. B., Weston, W. W., Stewart, M., McCracken, E. C., & McWhinney, I. (1989). Patient-centered clinical interviewing. In M. Stewart & D. Roter (Eds.), *Communicating with medical patients* (pp. 107–120). Beverly Hills, CA: Sage.

Levy, J. A., & Strombeck, R. (2002). Health benefits and risks of the Internet. *Journal of Medical Systems, 26*(6), 495–510.

Loustaunau, M. O., & Sobo, E. J. (1997). *The cultural context of health, illness, and medicine.* Westport, CT: Bergin and Garvey.

Lubkin, I. M. (1990). *Chronic illness: Impact and interventions* (2nd ed.). Sudbury, MA: Jones and Bartlett.

Madden, T. J., Ellen, P. S., & Ajzen, I. (1992). A comparison of the theory of planned behavior and the theory of reasoned action. *Personality and Social Psychology Bulletin, 18*(1), 3–9.

Miller, W. R., & Rollnick, S. (2002). *Motivational interviewing: Preparing people for change.* New York, NY: The Guilford Press.

Mishler, E. G. (1984). *The discourse of medicine: Dialectics of medical interviews.* Norwood, NJ: Ablex.

Montano, D. E., Kasprzyk, D., & Taplin, S. H. (1997). The theory of reasoned action and the theory of planned behavior. In K. Glanz, F. M. Lewis, & B. K. Rimer (Eds.), *Health behavior and health education* (pp. 85–112). San Francisco, CA: Jossey-Bass.

National Center for Health Statistics. (2004). *NCHS data on aging.* Hyattsville, MD: National Center for Health Statistics.

National Center for Health Statistics. (2010). *Health, United States, 2009: With special feature on medical technology.* Hyattsville, MD.

Nau, D. P., & Ponte, C. D. (2002). Effects of a community pharmacist-based diabetes patient-management program on intermediate clinical outcome measures. *Journal of Managed Care Pharmacy, 8*(1), 48–53.

Paasche-Orlow, M. K., & Wolf, M. S. (2007). Evidence does not support clinical screening of literacy. *Journal of General Internal Medicine, 23*(1), 100–102.

Park, J. J., Kelly, P., Carter, B. L., & Burgess, P. P. (1996). Comprehensive pharmaceutical care in the chain setting. *Journal of the American Pharmaceutical Association, NS36*(7), 443–451.

Parsons, T. (1951). *The social system.* Glencoe, IL: Free Press.

President's Commission for the Study of Ethical Problems in Medicine and Biomedical and Behavioral Research. (1982). *Making health care decisions: The ethical and legal implications of informed consent in the patient–practitioner relationship* (Vol. 1). Washington, DC: U. S. Government Printing Office.

Prochaska, J. O., Johnson, S., & Lee, P. (1998). The transtheoretical model of change. In S. A. Schumaker, E. B. Schron, J. K. Ockene, & W. L. McBee (Eds.), *The handbook of health behavior change* (2nd ed., pp. 59–84). New York, NY: Springer.

Prochaska, J. O., & Velicer, W. F. (1997). The transtheoretical model of health behavior change. *American Journal of Health Promotion, 12*(1), 38–48.

Ratzan, S.C., & Parker, R.M. (2000). Introduction. In C.R. Seldin, M. Zorn, S.C. Ratzan, R.M. Parker (Eds). *National Library of Medicine Current bibliographies in medicine: Health literacy.* NLM Pub. No. CBM 2000-1. Bethesda, MD: National Institutes of Health, United States Department of Health and Human Services.

Reeder, L. G. (1972). The patient-client as a consumer: Some observations on the changing professional–client relationship. *Journal of Health and Social Behavior, 13,* 406–412.

Rosenstock, I. M. (1974). Historical origins of the health belief model. *Health Education Monographs, 2,* 328–335.

Roter, D. L., & Hall, J. A. (1992). *Doctors talking with patients—Patients talking with doctors.* Westport, CT: Auburn House.

Rubak, S., Sandboek, A., Lauritzen, T., & Christensen, B. (2005). Motivational interviewing. *British Journal of General Practice, 55,* 305–312.

Salazar, M. K. (1991). Comparison of four behavioral theories: A literature review. *AAOHN Journal, 39*(3), 128–135.

Schoen, C., Osborn, R., How, S. K. H., Doty, M. M., & Peugh, J. (2008). In chronic condition: Experiences of patients with complex health care needs, in eight countries, 2008. *Health Affairs, 28*(1), w1–w16.

Sennett, C. (2000). Ambulatory care in the new millennium: The role of consumer information. *Quality Management in Health Care, 8*(2), 82–87.

Smolderen, K. G., Spertus, J. A., Nallamothu, B. K., Krumholz, H. M., Tang, F., Ross, J. S., Ting, H. H., Alexander, K. P., Rathore, S. S., & Chan, P. S. (2010). *JAMA, 303*(14), 1392–1400.

Strecher, V. J., & Rosenstock, I. M. (1997). The health belief model. In K. Glanz, F. M. Lewis, & B. K. Rimer (Eds.), *Health behavior and health education* (pp. 41–59). San Francisco, CA: Jossey-Bass.

Stroebe, W., & Stroebe, M. S. (1995). *Social psychology and health.* Pacific Grove, CA: Brooks/Cole.

Stuifbergen, A. (1999). Barriers and health behaviors of rural and urban persons with multiple sclerosis. *American Journal of Health Behavior, 23*(6), 415–425.

Suchman, E. A. (1965). Stages of illness and medical care. *Journal of Health and Human Behavior, 6,* 114–128.

Szasz, T., & Hollender, M. (1956). A contribution to the philosophy of medicine: The basic model of the doctor–patient relationship. *Archives of Internal Medicine, 97,* 585–592.

Tebbe, J. (1998). Health care delivery in America: Historical and policy perspectives. In R. L. McCarthy (Ed.), *Introduction to health care delivery: A primer for pharmacists* (p. 18). Gaithersburg, MD: Aspen.

United States Bureau of the Census (USBOC). (2000). Retrieved August, 2000 from www.census. gov/population/estimates/nation/intfile2-1.txt

USA Today, Kaiser Family Foundation, & Harvard School of Public Health (2008, March). *The public on prescription drugs and pharmaceutical companies: Summary and chartpack.* Washington, DC: Kaiser Family Foundation.

Veatch, R. M. (1972). Models for ethical medicine in a revolutionary age. *Hastings Center Report, 2,* 5–7.

Vincent, G. K., & Velkoff, V. A. (2010). The next four decades, the older population in the United States: 2010 to 2050. *Current Population Reports* (pp. 25–1138). Washington, DC: U.S. Census Bureau.

Wallston, K. A., Wallston, B. S., & Devellis, R. (1978). Development of the multidimensional health locus of control (MHLC) scales. *Health Education Monographs, 6,* 160–170.

Weiss, B. D., Mays, M. Z., Martz, W., Castro, K. M., DeWalt, D. A., Pignone, M. ... Hale, F. A. (2005). Quick assessment of literacy in primary care: The newest vital sign. *Annals of Family Medicine, 3*(6), 514–522.

Weston, W. W., Brown, J. B., & Stewart, M. (1989). Patient-centered interviewing. Part I: Understanding patients' experiences. *Canadian Family Physician, 35,* 147–151.

Wilkes, M. S., Bell, R. A., & Kravitz, R. L. (2000). Direct-to-consumer prescription drug advertising: Trends, impact, and implications. *Health Affairs, 19*(2), 110–128.

World Health Organization. (2003). *Adherence to long-term therapies: Evidence for action.* Geneva, Switzerland: WHO.

Drug Use, Access, and the Role of the Pharmaceutical Industry

Kyle D. Ross, Louis P. Garrison Jr., and Dana P. Hammer*

Case Scenario

MPC Pharmaceuticals is a large pharmaceutical firm that does not have a presence in the erythropoietin (EPO) market. The firm has a strong desire to be selling a drug in this area, but management is divided in terms of the strategy to best achieve this. There are two main options the firm can pursue: (1) develop a new version of EPO that is superior to any drug on the market or (2) develop a copy of a current version of EPO produced by Hemocyte, Inc. called Erystim, which was approved 14 years ago. The MPC board's last meeting on the topic was in November 2009 and a decision was reached at a meeting in July 2010.

Those on the board in favor of developing a new version of EPO like the idea of having a first-in-class drug that could command premium pricing and deliver large revenues to MPC. A new version would enjoy protection from any imitators for a number of years and could support the development of other drugs in the company. However, the drawbacks to pursuing a new EPO drug are substantial as well. One of the main disadvantages of developing a new version is that it would take many years for the drug to go from discovery to approval by the Food and Drug Administration (FDA). There is a substantial amount of clinical testing that new drugs must go through in order to gain approval by the FDA. Another drawback is that there are high costs and a high level of uncertainty when developing a new drug. Even if a drug is promising early on, there is a low probability that it will eventually be approved by the FDA for sale in the United States.

The members of the board who supported developing a copy of Erystim point to the shorter time frame and higher likelihood of success that are distinct advantages to pursuing a copy of an existing drug. They feel that there are a number of drugs in the EPO market and that by developing a copy, the firm would be able to compete by charging a lower price and thereby gaining a large market share. The downside to pursuing this strategy is that other copies can enter into the market and because EPO is a biologic, there is still a fair bit of clinical testing that must be done to gain approval by the FDA.

*With acknowledgment to Peter L. Steere and Michael Montagne.

In the end, MPC chose to pursue development of a copy of Erystim. The firm made this decision based in large part on relatively recent developments in the pharmaceutical sector. One of the largest changes affecting MPC's decision was the passage of healthcare reform in March 2010. One of the pieces of the legislation was to lower the clinical trial burden for copies of biologics. This meant that MPC's version of EPO will be able to rely on Hemocyte's clinical trial data. By doing this, MPC would be able to save on development of their version and price it at a lower price than Hemocyte's Erystim. The board also decided that this aspect of healthcare reform would make any innovative drug MPC produced less profitable, since new copies would eventually be able to rely on its clinical trial data.

Another major factor that affected MPC's decision is the emphasis on cost control they had been receiving from many major insurers in the United States. Many insurers relayed that they were not excited at the idea of covering a new, more expensive version of EPO, but they would love to have the option of adding a copy of Erystim to their formularies. MPC also felt that consumers were becoming very cost conscious, indicated in part by the rise of Internet and mail-order pharmacies. Both of these factors demonstrated to MPC that in a crowded EPO market, positioning itself to compete on price was the best decision for MPC.

Since the decision was made in July 2010 to pursue a copy of Hemocyte's drug, MPC entered into negotiations to purchase EGlobin. EGlobin is a small biotech firm that has developed a drug called Erysimilar that is a copy of Erystim. By purchasing EGlobin, MPC plans to have a copy of Erystim approved by the FDA in less than 18 months. MPC feels confident that once approved, Erysimilar will be accepted by patients and physicians as a viable substitute for Erystim. This will provide revenue for the company in a relatively short amount of time and put MPC in a desirable position in the EPO market.

LEARNING OBJECTIVES

Upon completion of this chapter, the student shall be able to:

- Discuss how consumers view drugs and their expectations of them
- Describe the role prescribers and pharmacists play in treating patients with pharmaceuticals
- Describe the steps a drug goes through in its development and approval
- Describe the four stages of clinical testing a drug can go through
- Explain how the intellectual property rights of drug manufacturers are protected
- Discuss the concerns surrounding increased globalization in drug production
- Discuss how future healthcare trends could affect both the pharmaceutical sector and pharmacists

CHAPTER QUESTIONS

1. What are the primary ways U.S. consumers choose to approach decisions about using drugs, and what are the main factors that affect their decisions?
2. What is the FDA responsible for in drug regulation and what can it not control?
3. What are the main differences between the regulation of intellectual property rights for small-molecule drugs and biologics?
4. In what ways are the jobs of pharmacists likely to be different 10 years from now, and what are the main factors driving those changes?

INTRODUCTION

Pharmaceuticals are some of the most visible treatments in medical care. Consumers possess a familiarity with them that is matched by little else in medicine. Many patients choose the drug they will consume (nonprescription drugs) or might advocate for the prescription of a particular drug from their physician. This familiarity is driven in part by the fact that many pharmaceuticals are advertised directly to consumers, and consumers then form their own opinions apart from healthcare providers. The simplicity of drugs is another aspect of drugs that contributes to the comfort patients have with drugs. For the most part, a patient puts a pill in his mouth, takes a drink of water, and swallows. For other drugs, all that is required is to inject or infuse the drug, which can often be done by the patient herself at home.

This simplicity and familiarity mask the true complexity of pharmaceuticals. There are multitudes of side effects and interactions to consider when selecting a drug for treatment. Not all drugs work the same in every patient. It is a costly and lengthy process to develop and produce new drugs, especially for new diseases, and many candidate drugs will never be approved. These and other complexities associated with pharmaceuticals can lead to friction and misunderstanding among the public, pharmaceutical firms, and healthcare providers. Patients may wonder why the drug they are taking costs so much when it is so simple and small, or why their physician has prescribed a certain medication when their friend takes a different one for the same condition. Managing these types of questions often falls to healthcare providers and particularly to pharmacists.

As shown in the MPC example, pharmaceutical firms must consider many factors when making a decision about developing new drugs. Even if a new or better drug can be developed, the market may dictate that it is not the best strategy to pursue development of a new drug. Concerns about development cost and length, regulatory approval, changes in laws, patient acceptance, and insurance reimbursement all come into play.

This chapter will explore the nature of the pharmaceutical market. It will explain and answer the questions and tensions raised previously. Included in the discussion will be the relationship between consumers and drugs, the relationship between healthcare providers and drugs, how a drug goes from an idea to a package on pharmacy shelves, the role of pharmacists in the pharmaceutical market, and how the pharmaceutical market is being changed by current trends and legislation.

DRUGS AS REMEDIES, POISONS, OR MAGICAL CHARMS

Substances that produce a change in cellular or physiologic functioning of humans are called drugs, but there is more to these chemicals than their pharmacologic activity (Montagne, 1996). Social values also affect the perception and use of drugs. Some drugs are illegal, some are highly restricted in their use, and some are readily available. The social values in the United States, for example, drive the difference in legal status of marijuana, pseudoephedrine, and naproxen sodium.

Pharmakon is the Greek term for *drug*. This term has three meanings, including remedy, poison, and magical charm. Drugs are often thought of as remedies when they alleviate symptoms or eliminate disease in patients. Drugs can be poisons at the same time. Drugs can cause unpleasant side effects while delivering therapeutic effects or cause death in an overdose. Sometimes drugs' therapeutic effects are achieved by poisoning cells in a patient, such as with chemotherapy. The fact that many patients do not know or understand how a drug works lends a sense of magic to the drug. The term *magic bullet* is sometimes used to describe drugs and was coined by Paul Ehrlich as he searched for a treatment for syphilis that would destroy the syphilis bacterium without harming the tissue of the patient (Strebhardt and Ullrich, 2008).

Manufacturers focus on a drug's therapeutic effects. They are primarily concerned with optimizing the biochemical activity, increasing the specificity, and limiting the adverse events associated with a drug. Health professionals are similarly concerned with a drug's therapeutic effects. They want to treat their patients as quickly and efficiently as possible. They will choose drugs that maximize the treatment effects and minimize the side effects for each patient. Interestingly, in some cases, the side effects of a drug can lead to alternative therapeutic indications. For example, minoxidil was developed to treat high blood pressure, but was found to grow hair as a side effect. Now minoxidil is commonly used to promote hair growth. There are a number of attributes of a drug upon which patients and consumers focus. These can include the treatment effect, adverse events, and cost. Sometimes patients may request a particular drug from their prescriber because they believe it has a desired therapeutic effect. Unwanted side effects or high costs, however, may deter patients from taking medications as prescribed by their physicians.

As science and medicine have progressed, medical and social problems have increasingly come to be defined primarily by the biologic processes that drive them. Medicalization is the idea of defining or describing problems in medical terms or treatment through medical interventions (Davis, 2006). Medicalization has led to a reduction in the social stigma surrounding many conditions such as depression, eating disorders, anxiety disorders, and attention-deficit/hyperactivity disorder. These complex conditions include social, mental, and emotional components, however, and often require treatment with nonpharmacologic therapy as well, such as counseling, diet changes, and environment changes. Medicalization can sometimes minimize the importance of nonpharmacologic treatments and prevent the use of them by patients.

The difference in beliefs and values about drugs can create tension between healthcare providers and patients. The social aspects of drugs are many times of greater importance to patients than to healthcare providers and can be the main driver of the use of a drug. Healthcare providers' understanding of these differences in beliefs can improve both the treatment and satisfaction of patients.

CONSUMER PERSPECTIVE ON DRUG USE

The end use for drugs is consumption by patients. Ambulatory consumers make the final decision about whether or not they will use a drug. Consumers have a wide range of options when it comes to deciding what drug to use to treat their particular disease or symptom. For a consumer to ultimately select a drug to use, he must be reasonably confident that taking the drug will produce the desired treatment effect with minimal side effects. If a drug does not work in the desired way, or if adverse events are greater than expected, a consumer may lose faith in the drug or lose trust in the individual who recommended the drug. The latter can create tension between patients and healthcare providers and be problematic because future recommendations may not be trusted.

Consumer Choices in Drug Use

When faced with a non–life-threatening health problem, an individual has a number of different options from which to choose. The simplest response to the health problem is to ignore it or do nothing at all. This response occurs about one third of the time. Two thirds of the time a consumer will choose to take an action to resolve the health issue that she is facing (Heller, 1992; Montagne & Basara, 1996).

When taking action, consumers most commonly choose to treat themselves, rather than see a healthcare provider. When choosing to treat themselves with a nonprescription drug or herbal remedy, consumers are influenced by a number of factors. These include personal experience, advice of friends, web-based advice, direct-to-consumer advertising, and restrictions by law. The market for nonprescription drugs is significant. U.S. consumers spent $39 billion in 2008 on nondurable medical products (Centers for Medicare and Medicaid Services, 2010c). Nondurable medical products are defined by the Centers for Medicare and Medicaid Services as nonprescription drugs and medical sundries (Centers for Medicare and Medicaid Services, 2010a). Complementary and alternative medicine (CAM), which are treatments that are not considered to be a part of conventional medicine, are also important options for consumers not choosing to use typical Western medicine. Consumers spent $33.9 billion on complementary and alternative medicines in 2007 (Nahin, Barnes, Stussman, & Bloom, 2009).

Consumers will use the medical system one fourth of the time when they decide to take action. When they visit a doctor, two thirds of consumers will leave with a prescription (National Association of Chain Drug Stores [NACDS], 2005). The market for prescription drugs is much larger than that for nonprescription drugs. In 2008, U.S. consumers spent $234.1 billion on prescription drugs, which accounted for 10% of health spending. The annual rate of expenditure increase has recently slowed from 8.7% in 2006, to 4.5% in 2007 and to 3.2% in 2008. The 2007 and 2008 annual rates of expenditure increase on prescription drugs were slower than those for overall health costs. Given that there was a 2.5% rise in prescription drug prices in 2008, actual use of prescription drugs increased less than 1% in 2008. Reasons for this slowdown include the recession, fewer new drugs, and increased safety concerns (Centers for Medicare and Medicaid Services, 2010b; 2010c).

Consumer Purchases of Drugs

Where a consumer purchases a drug will depend on a number of factors. Virtually all prescriptions are filled and purchased at or through a pharmacy. Many nonprescription drug purchases also occur at pharmacies, but these purchases account for less than half of all purchases. In 2008, 35% of nonprescription drug purchases were made in pharmacies, 29% at mass merchandisers and 21% in food stores. Online retailers, dollar stores, warehouse clubs, and other outlets accounted for 15% (Kline & Company, 2009). Convenience and price are the main factors affecting the choice of where to purchase nonprescription drugs. Pharmacies have been losing share in recent years as consumers have sought and found lower prices.

Cost is frequently an overriding factor when a consumer is choosing to purchase a drug, whether it is prescription or nonprescription. When a prescription is written, the prescription typically is covered by a patient's insurance, which usually requires a copayment (a one-time flat payment) or coinsurance (a percentage of the price) for the patient. If an individual does not have health insurance, he may choose not to fill a prescription due to high costs of the drug. The market for generic drugs is driven primarily by the fact that they are cheaper than brand-name drugs. Consumers who have insurance may be required to use generics or face higher copayments when filling a prescription. Some drugs, including many new biologic drugs, are very expensive and come with coinsurance levels that make them too costly for many patients. Avastin (bevacizumab), for example, may cost as much as $100,000 per year. The issue of out-of-pocket cost is a very important component of the decision of which drug to purchase. Healthcare providers may recommend a course of treatment, but if it is too costly for the patient, other treatments may need to be considered or it may result in the patient going untreated. If a patient is unable to afford a treatment, some manufacturers offer programs (e.g., Pfizer's free medicines for the unemployed or GlaxoSmithKline's patient assistance program) to eliminate or reduce the cost for qualifying patients.

In the example at the beginning of the chapter, MPC weighed the purchasing and reimbursement of drugs heavily in making its decision to pursue a copy of an existing drug rather than develop a new drug. MPC decided that offering a low-cost alternative was the best strategy to pursue in the EPO market due, in part, to the belief that consumers would readily purchase a lower priced version of EPO.

MPC- Model predictive control
EPO- Exclusive provider organization

HEALTH PROFESSIONALS' ROLE IN DRUG USE

Health professionals serve a guiding role for patients in treating health problems. When a person goes to a health professional, he expects a recommendation for a course of action to solve his health problem. There are many recommendations a health professional may give to an individual, including lifestyle changes, physical therapy, and surgery. One of the most common, and expected, recommendations in the United States is a prescription for drug therapy.

Prescribers

Taking a drug to remedy a health problem can be simple and satisfying for both the patient and physician. Sometimes just the act of a physician prescribing a drug for a patient can satisfy a patient. Patients will sometimes demand antibiotics for viral infections and be happy only when the prescription is written, even though the drugs will do nothing for the infection. Other times, the placebo effect is all that is needed for the patient to feel better. Most of the time, though, a physician will prescribe a drug the patient needs, and the drug will aid the patient's healing. In many of these cases, the act of prescribing a drug satisfies a patient and usually requires little follow-up by the physician.

Notable factors that affect how physicians prescribe drugs are:

- Education, especially additional training in pharmacotherapeutics and preceptors' prescribing behavior
- Promotional campaigns, especially drug advertising
- Colleagues or those health professionals who are part of the prescriber's social network
- Control and regulatory mechanisms (e.g., drug laws, formularies, triplicate prescriptions)
- Demands from patients and society (Raisch, 1990a, 1990b; Soumerai, McLaughlin, & Avorn, 1989)

Dispensers

The most common image that consumers have of pharmacists is that of the community pharmacist responsible for filling their prescriptions. In 2009, there were about 3.6 billion retail prescriptions filled in the United States, which is approximately a 12.5% increase over the 3.2 billion filled in 2004 (NACDS, 2010). While both chain and independent pharmacies earn the majority of their sales through filling prescriptions, independent pharmacies rely much more heavily on these sales than do chain pharmacies (National Community Pharmacists Association [NCPA], 2009).

As technology has developed, the need for retail pharmacists to spend their time filling prescriptions has been substantially reduced and become much more automated. This trend is also due to the rise of Internet sales and mail-order delivery of prescriptions. While the time spent physically filling prescriptions has gone down, pharmacists now must spend a greater amount of time checking and verifying more prescriptions filled by technicians and robots.

The relationship consumers maintain with their pharmacists has changed over time. While not necessarily held in the same clinical esteem as physicians, many neighborhood pharmacists were, at one time, more involved with the social and nonhealthcare aspects of their patients' lives (see Chapter 1). Over the years, as volume and regulatory pressures mounted, pharmacists were able to spend increasingly less time on activities other than filling prescriptions. Even though they are highly trained to offer valuable clinical oversight, pharmacists have become concerned that their prescription-filling responsibilities are precluding them from performing more valuable and patient-centered services (McDaniel & DeJong, 1999).

Partly in response to this dissatisfaction, the dispensing element of pharmacy practice is currently undergoing rapid change, particularly through the increase in technologies that allow pharmacists to be less involved in the manual process of counting and labeling medications. While an increase in the use and certification of pharmacy technicians has helped to remove the pharmacist from many of these technical functions, the complete drug-handling capabilities of robotics and counting equipment are also working to make pharmacies more efficient and patient centered. Similarly, while prescription writing, patient management, and billing systems were once pen and paper based, computer systems have all but replaced the paper profiles and accounting required to operate a pharmacy, and e-prescribing is becoming much more commonplace. Computer and online systems also perform sophisticated screening of potential drug-related problems, adherence monitoring, and adjudication of claims during the filling process. Medication therapy management is also something pharmacists have pursued to a greater degree as they have become eligible for reimbursement for clinical activities.

Hospitals and other institutional pharmacies seeking to better manage personnel costs while maintaining quality and improving patient safety are also paying close attention to dispensing productivity. Robotics and increased technician responsibilities for filling and preparing medication orders in the central pharmacy, as well as sophisticated dispensing technologies (such as Pyxis medication-dispensing machines) on patient care units, allow pharmacists to spend more time on reviewing, recommending, and monitoring patient therapies (see Chapter 12.)

PATH OF A PHARMACEUTICAL FROM IDEA TO PRESCRIPTION

When a new drug is available for consumers to purchase (sometimes only after receiving a prescription), it has undergone many years of experimentation, testing, and regulatory approval. Each new pharmaceutical approved for sale requires a large investment of resources, and developing new drugs is quite risky for pharmaceutical companies. As a result, new drugs are typically quite expensive. Given the significant value, life-saving potential, and potential safety issues surrounding new drugs, there is a complex regulatory, development, and distribution system for them in the United States.

Regulation of Pharmaceuticals

In the United States there are two primary systems regulating the use of drugs. One of these is the various state laws and agencies that control the practice of pharmacy and professionals. The other is the regulation of the safety and effectiveness of the drugs, which is done by the FDA. The FDA determines which drugs are allowed to be sold and prescribed in the United States and which drugs are categorized as prescription and nonprescription drugs.

There are two main acts under which the FDA controls pharmaceuticals. The first of these is the Food, Drug and Cosmetic Act, which was first passed in 1938. For the most part, the Food, Drug and Cosmetic Act directs the FDA in how it regulates traditional small-molecule drugs and hormones. This includes drugs such as acetaminophen, simvastatin, and insulin. The other act under which the FDA regulates drugs is the Public Health Service Act of 1944. It is under the Public Health Service Act that the FDA regulates drugs such as biologics that are made up of much larger molecules and are more complex than small-molecule drugs. Biologics include drugs such as bevacizumab, trastuzumab, and erythropoietin. The fact that small-molecule drugs and biologics are regulated by different acts has important consequences on the regulation of intellectual property rights for these two different types of drugs.

Once the FDA has determined a drug is safe and effective enough to be sold in the United States, it has little direct control over how the drug is actually used or prescribed, such as for non-FDA-approved (off-label) indications. A drug cannot, however, be sold or marketed in the United States until the FDA has approved it. To ensure the safety and effectiveness of pharmaceuticals and biological products, the FDA performs the following seven basic functions:

1. Approval of drugs on the basis of purity, safety, and effectiveness
2. Regulation of all labeling for prescription and nonprescription drugs
3. Regulation of advertising for prescription drugs (the Federal Trade Commission regulates nonprescription advertising)
4. Regulation of manufacturing processes of drugs and institution of recalls
5. Regulation of bioequivalence for generics and biosimilars
6. Monitoring of drugs postapproval to detect any problems with the use of drugs such as unanticipated adverse reactions (e.g., postmarketing surveillance)
7. Monitoring of the safety of the nation's blood supply (U.S. FDA [n.d. e])

The FDA can only make decisions based on the information it is given. The studies used to determine the safety of a drug are generally not large enough to detect all possible adverse events. This is one of the reasons the FDA monitors drugs after they have been approved. Sometimes companies are not wholly forthright with the information they have on their candidate drugs. One recent example of this is Glaxo-SmithKline's withholding and downplaying heart attack risks of Avandia (rosiglitazone). This is not common, however, and there are laws to try to prevent this from happening. Even the information the FDA has is not without uncertainty. There are times when the FDA has to develop its own interpretations of manufacturers' data. While the public would like the FDA to never make a mistake or miss a potential side effect of a drug, it is not always possible for the FDA to be completely sure about the benefit–risk balance of a new drug when it is released onto the market. The FDA acts in what it views as good faith for the public and strives to ensure drugs on the market are safe for consumers.

Development and Approval of a New Drug

The development of a new drug is a long and expensive process. The expected capitalized cost of a new drug is $1.2–$1.4 billion (DiMasi & Grabowski, 2007). Clinical testing alone can be expected to take between 6 and 7 years. The development of a drug can be broken into four main stages. The first of these is the discovery of new compounds or proteins. The second is the preclinical testing stage. The third is the clinical testing stage. The final stage is approval and postclinical testing. Very few products make it through all of these stages to become a drug that is prescribed and taken by a consumer.

The first stage of discovery is carried out primarily by scientists who identify compounds and proteins that have potential to be a viable drug. For every 250 candidates that go to preclinical testing, between 5,000 and 10,000 compounds are evaluated (Pharmaceutical Research and Manufacturers of America [PhRMA], 2010b). This corresponds to a rate of only 2.5–5.0% candidates moving on to preclinical testing. In preclinical testing, a company conducts tests to determine whether or not a drug is safe to test in humans. These tests are carried out through animal testing and other tests in a lab. Approximately 2.5% of the candidates in this stage make it through preclinical testing (PhRMA, 2010b). This results in less than 0.1% of potential drugs making it from discovery to entry into clinical testing (see **Table 5-1**).

discovery of new compounds or protein | preclinical testing | clinical testing | Approval Post-clinical testing

Table 5-1 Drug Development to Get One Approved Drug

Stage	Length	Patients	Number in stage
Potential candidates	Varies	NA	10,000
Preclinical testing	Varies	Animals	250
Phase I clinical trial	1 year	100 healthy volunteers	10
Phase II clinical trial	2 years	300 with target disease	6
Phase III clinical trial	3–4 years	2,000–3,000 in clinical setting	2–3
FDA approval	1 year	NA	1–2
Approved drug (Some Phase IV studies)	10–14 years	Disease population	1

Source: Adapted from Pharmaceutical Research and Manufacturers of America. (PhRMA). (2010). Pharmaceutical Industry Profile 2010. Washington, DC: PhRMA.

When a firm would like to start clinical testing of a product, it must first submit an Investigational New Drug (IND) application to the FDA's Center for Drug Evaluation and Research (small-molecule drugs) or the FDA's Center for Biologics Evaluation and Research (biologics). The firm must then wait 30 days before beginning any clinical testing to give the Center for Drug Evaluation and Research or the Center for Biologics Evaluation and Research time to review the application. There are four phases of clinical testing, three of which occur prior to product approval (U.S. FDA [n.d. b; n.d. c]).

The first phase of clinical testing is conducted through Phase I clinical trials. The goal of Phase I trials is to learn about how the drug works in humans. These trials determine the dosing range and method, document the metabolism and excretion of the drug, and identify toxicities associated with the drug. These trials are relatively small with a group of less than 100 normal, healthy volunteers and are short term (less than 1 year). On average, 60% of drugs make it through Phase I trials to the next phase (Tufts Center for the Study of Drug Development [CSDD], 2010).

Phase II trials are the second phase of clinical testing. In this phase the drug is studied in a few hundred patients diagnosed with the disease the drug is designed to treat. The goal is to study and determine the efficacy and safety of the drug in the actual patients who will be treated. These trials are longer than Phase I trials; they may take up to 2 years to complete. If the trial shows sufficient efficacy and safety, then the drug will proceed to Phase III trials. For drugs in Phase II testing, only 39% of drugs will be expected to move on to Phase III testing (Tufts CSDD, 2010).

The final preapproval step is completion of Phase III testing. Testing in this phase is much more extensive and is designed to provide strong evidence of safety and efficacy. Phase III trials typically involve a few thousand patients and can last up to few years. Subjects are randomized into control and experimental groups and treated with doses and in settings that are similar to what would be expected in the real world. Once Phase III testing has been completed, the firm can move on and submit their drug for approval to the FDA. The percentage of drugs coming out of Phase II trials that are submitted for approval after entering Phase III testing is 64% (Tufts CSDD, 2010).

Once clinical testing has been successfully completed, a firm will submit its drug to the FDA for approval. The firm does this by submitting a New Drug Application (NDA). The NDA specifies all of the relevant information about a drug, including how the drug is manufactured, how the drug acts in the body, how the drug will be marketed, labeling information, and toxicologic information. The FDA then reviews the application and gives its decision on whether or not to approve the drug. When a new drug is submitted, 85% of the time it is approved (Tufts CSDD, 2010). When approval and all phases of preapproval clinical testing are combined, only 16% of drugs that begin the testing phase will be approved by the FDA (Tufts CSDD, 2010).

Once a drug is approved, it is often not the last time the FDA will examine the drug. Many times there are Phase IV trials that are conducted after the drug is already approved. Phase IV studies continue to evaluate the safety and effectiveness of drugs and look for any side effects that may have been missed in earlier trials. They monitor large groups of patients over longer time periods than Phase I, II or III trials. A firm may also want to get a drug approved as a nonprescription, over-the-counter medication. A firm can do this through the NDA process or submit an application to switch to over-the-counter status after the drug is approved through the NDA process. If a firm would like to alter the drug's ingredients, dosage, manufacturing, or labeling, it submits a supplemental NDA to the FDA to get the changes approved. Makers of generics or biosimilars instead submit an abbreviated NDA to get their products approved with a lower clinical trial burden than the original product. The FDA will examine the bioequivalence, bioavailability, and pharmacokinetic/pharmacodynamic properties of a generic or biologic to ensure they are the same or similar to a reference product.

The high cost, long time frame, and high degree of uncertainty for drug development were all important factors in MPC deciding against developing a new version of EPO in our case scenario. The payoff in the end was simply not high enough for MPC to be willing to invest a substantial amount of time and resources into a new drug. Instead, MPC decided to go with the shorter time frame of developing a copy of an existing EPO drug.

Pricing

The pricing of drugs is not a simple process and can engender a substantial amount of ill will from patients. There are many factors that go into the pricing of a drug, including the costs of producing the drug, the drug development costs, negotiated reimbursements by a payer (e.g., a pharmacy benefit manager agrees with a manufacturer on the price it will pay), margins for wholesalers, and margins for retailers. All of these factors combine to produce the price the consumer pays for the drug. In some countries with government-sponsored health systems, patients see no or very little direct, out-of-pocket cost when they are prescribed a drug. In the United States, it depends on the nature of the individual's health insurance policy. There can be substantial differences between plans. Some policies require the individual to pay a flat copayment for a prescription medication while other policies employ a percentage-based coinsurance for each prescription. If an individual has no insurance, he is usually responsible for the full cost of a prescription.

The largest component of the cost of drugs is the resources that were devoted to the research and development of an innovative drug. Once a drug is fully developed and tested, there is relatively little cost in actually producing and providing the drug. It is for this reason that many consumers and consumer advocates criticize the prices that drug companies charge for what can be lifesaving treatments. Without sufficient revenue from drug sales, however, many companies would cease to develop new drugs.

There is always a trade-off between prices today and investment in new drugs. It is difficult for pharmacists to endure the ire of patients with regard to pricing, especially when they have little control over most of the costs. Educating patients about how drugs are priced can help to alleviate the tensions that may arise when patients are upset about the price of their prescriptions.

Pharmaceutical Marketing

Pharmaceutical firms use a variety of methods to market their products. One of the methods firms use is to meet with physicians and educate them on the merits of using their product. Another method is direct-to-consumer (DTC) advertising. The United States and New Zealand are the only countries where DTC advertising is allowed. There has been much recent debate over the benefits and pitfalls of allowing companies to market their products through advertising directly to patients. Those in favor of allowing DTC advertising note that pharmaceutical firms are selling a product and should be allowed to market in the same way that other products are marketed. Those against allowing DTC advertising often state that drugs are products with the potential for serious harm. The general public is generally ill equipped to evaluate the potential for serious harm and thus DTC advertising should be prohibited. This is not a settled question, but currently, firms are allowed to advertise their products to consumers in the United States as long as they meet the guidelines of the FDA.

Distribution

Retail pharmacies obtain their medications from drug wholesalers or from drug manufacturers directly. Drug wholesalers are firms that purchase drugs from pharmaceutical manufacturers and then distribute them to retail pharmacies. The consumers then purchases their drugs from a retailer. The retailer may be a local pharmacy, mail-order pharmacy, or Internet pharmacy. At one point, many large pharmacies were moving away from purchasing from wholesalers in favor of purchasing directly from manufacturers to avoid markups from wholesalers. This trend has been reversed recently as retailers have looked to avoid the cost of warehousing and maintaining inventory.

Pharmacy benefit managers, such as Medco Health Solutions and CVS Caremark, are companies that manage prescription drug programs for health insurers and companies that offer prescription drug coverage to their employees. Pharmacy benefit managers design formularies and negotiate prices and rebates for the drugs dispensed to customers covered under their plan. Formularies are lists of medicines and how they will be reimbursed under a prescription drug benefit contract. For example, Medco may say that Lipitor (atorvastatin) requires a $30 copayment per prescription and may have negotiated to pay Pfizer $54 per prescription. Pharmacy benefit managers are now responsible for the prescription drug programs of most U.S. consumers.

Global Aspects of Pharmaceuticals and Counterfeiting

As the world becomes more and more interconnected, global issues involving medication are becoming much more significant. There are many firms located outside the United States involved in the development, production, and testing of drugs. While there are many benefits to the increased globalization of the drug market, there are challenges and pitfalls difficult for regulatory agencies such as the FDA to guard against while preserving a robust international flow of drugs and ideas.

One important component of globalization for drugs is the production of drugs outside the United States. Drugs are allowed to be produced outside the United States and then sold as prescription medications in the United States. However, the FDA must approve the manufacturing process and plant where the drugs will be produced. Even as the FDA attempts to regulate and monitor the drugs in the United States, drugs that are not manufactured properly can still be a problem in the United States. The protection of patents is also a concern for U.S. companies. In many countries, enforcement of patents is not as strong as U.S. firms would like, and foreign companies sometimes copy and produce drugs in violation of patents. Developing countries must weigh the costs and benefits of recognizing international patents. The costs of recognizing the patents include raising the prices of drugs in the country. The benefits include adherence to international treaties and a more positive research environment for firms. This can help to preserve biodiversity and natural lands (Chang & Ross, 2009). Some firms have agreed to fund preservation projects in return for first access to new discoveries in these areas. In order to fully ensure patent enforcement, the U.S. government must also work with local governments to see that patents are enforced.

It is currently against the law to purchase prescription drugs in another country for use in the United States. There is an allowable exception:

> when 1) the intended use [of the drug] is unapproved and for a serious condition for which effective treatment may not be available domestically either through commercial or clinical means; 2) there is no known commercialization or promotion to persons residing in the U.S. by those involved in the distribution of the product at issue; 3) the product is considered not to represent an unreasonable risk; and 4) the individual seeking to import the product affirms in writing that it is for the patient's own use (generally not more than 3 month supply) and provides the name and address of the doctor licensed in the U.S. responsible for his or her treatment with the product or provides evidence that the product is for the continuation of a treatment begun in a foreign country/area. (U.S. FDA, 2010, Section 9-2)

Counterfeit drugs are a problem not only in the developing world, but in the United States as well. The World Health Organization (WHO) has estimated over 30% of drugs sold in much of the developing world are counterfeit (WHO, 2008). The problem is also large in magnitude in the United States. The Center for Medicine in the Public Interest estimated that there would be $75 billion of counterfeit drugs sales in the United States in 2010 (CMPI, 2005). The FDA is charged with stopping the sale of counterfeit drugs but has a limited budget to do so. As long as production of drugs continues outside of the United States and Internet pharmacies continue to grow, it will be difficult for the FDA to effectively halt the sale of counterfeit drugs in the United States. One recent example of counterfeit drugs is the sale through an Internet pharmacy of oseltamivir in the United States. The FDA warned about oseltamivir in June of 2010, and there is no approved generic version of oseltamivir, although the brand-name version, Tamiflu, has been approved.

Counterfeit drugs pose a substantial threat to consumers. At a minimum, consumers risk receiving no benefit from treatment when consuming drugs with no active ingredients. At worst, consumers stand to suffer adverse effects or even death from drugs with harmful and toxic chemicals in them. The use of counterfeit drugs can also be detrimental to patients' health if it delays their access to effective treatments. To help protect patients, pharmacists should know which drugs are most commonly counterfeited and be familiar with their colors, shapes, and symbols. Wholesalers may unintentionally distribute counterfeit drugs, so pharmacists stand as the final guard for patients. Pharmacists should also counsel patients to only buy from reputable pharmacies to minimize the risk of using counterfeit drugs. It will be difficult, if not impossible, to eliminate counterfeit drugs, but pharmacists can work to help their patients from falling victim.

An emerging trend in the globalization of drugs is conducting clinical trials in locations outside the United States. It is estimated that between 40 and 65% of clinical trials take place at sites outside the United States (Anand, Wang, & Whalen, 2008; Tufts CSDD, 2009). Additionally, the 20 largest pharmaceutical companies are conducting one third of clinical trials exclusively outside the United States (Cairns et al., 2009). In these cases, there would be no U.S. patients for trials of drugs that will be approved for use in the United States. Many foreign trials are conducted in western Europe, but a rapidly growing number of these trials are conducted in areas chosen for their low costs, such as Asia and South America.

There are a number of concerns with the growth of foreign trials. One is that the FDA is not equipped to inspect many foreign clinical trial sites. A Department of Health and Human Services Inspector General's report found that in 2008 the FDA inspected 1.9 percent of domestic clinical trial sites, but only 0.7% of foreign clinical trial sites. It also found that some early stage clinical trials are being conducted without Investigational New Drug application approval (Department of Health and Human Services, 2010). Another concern about the use of foreign clinical trials is that it is sometimes difficult to know how to attribute differences in patient outcomes from the various sites. The sites do not always follow the same standards, especially those located in emerging market countries. As a result, it can be difficult for the FDA to know whether a difference in the data is a result of chance, patient selection, ethnic differences, unblinding, method of observation, or treatment practices (Temple, 2009). There are certainly benefits to the increasing use of foreign clinical trial sites. One primary benefit is the inclusion of a wider number of populations than may be used in a U.S.-exclusive clinical trial. This can yield important results for different ethnic groups in the United States that are not usually included in U.S. clinical trials. As the use of foreign clinical trials continues to increase, the FDA should work towards better oversight and inspection of these sites in the future. The FDA can do this by standardizing electronic clinical trial data reporting, better monitoring and enforcement of Investigational New Drugs, and exploring new and innovative ways to oversee foreign clinical trials.

Intellectual Property Rights

Intellectual property rights (IPRs) are one of the most important components of the U.S. pharmaceutical system. IPRs are laws and regulations put into place to protect the ideas and products of innovators. Examples outside of drug development include copyrights on music and patents on inventions. IPRs have two main effects on the drug market. One is that they provide incentives for firms to innovate and develop new drugs that fight diseases. The other is that they provide power to firms to control the market for a drug and charge a higher price than firms would be able to without intellectual property protections. The United States has developed intellectual property regulations that attempt to balance these two effects by giving protections to innovators for a limited amount of time.

Innovations in pharmaceuticals need IPRs because innovations are a public good. A public good is considered such when it is used by a consumer, it is not used up, and it is available for others to use. It is different from a private good, such as a hamburger, that is used up once it is consumed. Knowledge is almost always considered a public good. When one gains knowledge, that knowledge is still available for others to gain and share. It takes a large amount of upfront investment to develop the knowledge of an innovative drug. If these innovations were not given intellectual property protections, others could take the knowledge and produce drugs without having to put up any kind of investment. The price for this new drug would be quite low and it would be very difficult for the innovating firm to make back their investment. Under these circumstances, few firms, if any, would be willing to develop new drugs. Having no new drugs would be an undesirable outcome from society's point of view.

To preserve incentives to innovate, IPR protection should last at least as long, on average, as it takes for a company to recoup its capitalized investment (Grabowski, 2008). However, if firms are given indefinite intellectual property protection, prices for drugs would likely remain very high. This scenario would result in fewer patients receiving drugs. This, too, is not a desirable outcome from society's point of view. Because of this, after a specified time period, other firms are allowed to copy and sell generic (or biosimilar) versions of the innovator's drug. The costs of producing the copies of the innovation are lower than developing the new drug, so prices are lower for the generic versions of the drug. This allows for lower costs of treatment and more patients being treated. The goal of IPRs is to preserve the incentive to innovate for firms, but not to subject consumers to high prices for too long.

In practice, the mechanisms for protecting IPRs are different for small-molecule drugs than for biologic drugs. This is due to differences in the complexity and nature of development of the two types of drugs. The primary driver of IPRs for small-molecule drugs is patent protection. Patents prevent other firms from copying an innovator's product while the patent is in force. The mechanism of IPR protection for biologic drugs is data exclusivity. Data exclusivity means that a firm can rely on the innovating firm's original clinical trial data to demonstrate the safety and effectiveness of its biosimilar (or generic) drug. The generic or biosimilar firm can then avoid having to conduct its own clinical trials (or at least it can conduct much smaller and less extensive trials). Using an innovator's clinical trial data allows for firms that are copying the innovator to save a substantial amount on developing their versions of biologic drugs by being able to avoid conducting clinical trials themselves.

It is important to note here that there is a substantial difference in copies of small-molecule drugs and biologic drugs; copies of small-molecule drugs are termed *generics*; copies of biologics are termed *biosimilars*. As mentioned earlier, small-molecule drugs are much less complex and are made up of smaller molecules than biologic drugs. They are also chemically synthesized rather than being produced by living cell lines. For example, atorvastatin (Lipitor), a small-molecule drug, has a molecular weight of 1209 daltons, while bevacizumab (Avastin), a biologic, has a molecular weight of 149,000 daltons. It is therefore realistic and possible to make identical copies of small-molecule drugs. It is nearly impossible to identically replicate a biologic drug. There will always be small differences in the copied drug and the original biologic. For these reasons, small-molecule drugs and biologics are not treated the same when it comes to regulating entry of copies of a drug.

IPRs for small-molecule drugs are regulated under the Drug Price Competition and Patent Term Restoration Act (commonly called the Hatch-Waxman Act) of 1984 (U.S. FDA [n.d. a]). The main provisions of the act are to give data exclusivity periods to innovators for 5 years after initial approval of the drug. They can also get additional 3-year periods of data exclusivity for new indications and additional 6-month periods for pediatric applications. These data exclusivity periods run concurrently with patent protection. Patents are granted for a period of 20 years and are granted at any time during a drug's development. Typically, the patent is granted many years prior to the drug being approved and launched into the market. A firm may apply to get an extension if the testing and approval process takes a long time. The patent can be extended for up to 5 years. The patent may not be in force, though, for more than 14 years after a drug is first approved. Patents are the most important form of IPR protection for small-molecule drugs, because generics are exact copies of the innovative drug and the data exclusivity period is relatively short (see **Table 5-2**).

IPRs for biologic drugs are primarily regulated under the Patient Protection and Affordable Care Act of 2010. The specific provision on biologic IPRs is the Biologics Price Competition and Innovation Act of 2009 (U.S. FDA [n.d. d]). Patent regulation of biologics is almost the same as that for small-molecule drugs; patent length is 20 years with an available 5-year extension. But patents are not as important for biologics' IPRs. This is because it is easier to work around patents given the complexity of biologics and the fact that it takes longer for biologics to be developed. The most important form of IPRs for biologics is the data exclusivity period. The data exclusivity period is 12 years in length with little opportunity for extensions. Prior to the passage of the Patient Protection and Affordable Care Act, there was no pathway for manufacturers of biosimilars to rely on the clinical trial data of the innovators. While makers of biosimilars will still have to conduct more extensive clinical trials than those of small-molecule generics, the clinical trial burden is now much lower after enactment of the Patient Protection and Affordable Care Act.

Intellectual Property Right

Table 5-2 IPR Protection for Small-Molecule and Biologic Drugs

	Small-molecule drugs	Biologic drugs
Governing act	Hatch-Waxman	PPACA
Year enacted	1984	2010
Patent length	20 years from patent application with U.S. PTO	20 years from patent application with U.S. PTO
Data-exclusivity period	5 years from FDA approval	12 years from FDA approval
New clinical trials required for generics/biosimilars?	No	Yes, but limited
Interchangeability with reference drug	Yes	Yes

PPACA = Patient Protection and Affordable Care Act; U.S. PTO = United States Patent and Trademark Office.

The implementation of a limited data exclusivity period for biologic drugs was perhaps the most important factor for MPC in deciding to pursue development of a copy of Erystim. If MPC was not able to rely on the clinical trial data of Hemocyte, it would have likely decided against developing its own copy of Erystim and against purchasing EGlobin. Relying on Hemocyte's clinical trial data was a necessity for MPC to decide to pursue a biosimilar.

FUTURE TRENDS IN THE PHARMACEUTICAL SECTOR

Advances in medicine, biology, and policy reforms, along with changing demographics will influence the pharmaceutical sector over the course of the next decade. An ever-increasing understanding of the human genome will drive both the development and selection of drugs for treatment of diseases. As the U.S. population becomes older and more obese, treating diseases such as diabetes will become more and more important. The implementation of health reform, which will increase both insurance coverage and the government's role in patient care, will force a hard look at restraining spending. All of these factors will affect the drugs that patients receive to treat disease.

Personalized medicine is one of the most quickly developing areas in drug treatment. The hope of personalized medicine is that treatment selections will be optimized for each patient given his specific individual characteristics. This will be accomplished by testing patients for factors such as genetic markers that indicate one course of treatment over another. In its fullest realization, personalized medicine will avoid unnecessary treatments and, by extension, the costs and adverse events that go along with them. There are still a number of hurdles for personalized medicine to overcome such as the limited predictive power of genomic information, and the difficulty and costs of developing highly predictive genetic tests, as well as economic barriers, including our cost-based diagnostic test reimbursement system, among others (Garrison & Austin, 2006). Currently, there are a substantial amount of research and resources devoted to realizing the promise of personalized medicine, and that should continue in the coming years. Some areas where personalized medicine has begun to be implemented are in breast cancer treatment with trastuzumab and blood clotting with warfarin. As testing is improved and costs brought down, personalized medicine will become a larger part of the treatment of many diseases, especially in oncology, in the coming decades.

Biologic drugs are also expected to become a larger portion of new pharmaceuticals in the next few decades. As much as 50% of all new drug approvals could be biologic in nature by 2015 and 71% of all new drug approvals by 2025 (BioWorld, 2009). Biologics, such as monoclonal antibodies, are a large part of new cancer treatments, and it is likely that any vaccine developed for HIV/AIDS will be a biologic. As the role of biologics increases, the number of treatments for orphan diseases is likely to increase as well. Orphan diseases are diseases that affect a very small population. In the United States, they typically affect fewer than 200,000 people. Treatments for orphan diseases are twice as likely to be classified as biologics than small-molecule drugs (Trusheim, Aitken, & Berndt, 2010). Biologics hold the promise to treat diseases that are currently untreatable and improve outcomes in those that currently are treatable. The tradeoff is that biologics often carry a high cost. For example, treatment with Avastin (bevacizumab) can be as much as $100,000 per year. As biologics assume a larger role in treatments, there will be discussion of the benefits versus the costs of using them.

Population demographics and recent government action are two other influences on the pharmaceutical sector. The U.S. population as a whole continues to become more obese and is increasingly affected by chronic diseases such as diabetes. This will make controlling these chronic diseases a high priority for physicians. As such, development of drugs to treat chronic diseases will become more important. Diabetes, for example, has 235 new medicines in development in the pharmaceutical and biotechnology sectors in the United States (PhRMA, 2010a). As for the government's role, the recently passed health reform act will lead to greater health insurance coverage across the United States. As part of this increase in coverage, there will be a greater number of individuals who are covered under government programs, such as Medicaid. For the pharmaceutical industry, this will mean that a larger number of patients may receive their drugs, but at a reduced cost.

For pharmacists, the future is likely to include less responsibility to dispense prescriptions and more responsibility in managing the decisions surrounding the course of treatments patients undergo. Prescription processing and dispensing is likely to be handled to a larger degree by pharmacy technicians, mail-order companies, and machines. This is the result of continued cost pressures in the prescription-filling industry. Pharmacists will be increasingly asked to move from prescription filling to providing expertise on drug selection and educating physicians and patients. They will also be asked to use their skills and interactions with patients to promote proper usage of medications (e.g., medication therapy management), which leads to potential improvements in patient outcomes and potential cost savings.

CONCLUSION

Drugs play a large role in the delivery of health care in the United States. It is a complex and evolving role shaped by consumers, pharmaceutical firms, and healthcare providers. Pharmacists play a vital role in linking consumers to physicians and pharmaceutical firms. Understanding this role and adjusting to changes are important tasks for pharmacists as they interact with patients. Helping patients and others understand how the pharmaceutical sector works can lead to improved patient satisfaction and outcomes. Even as the role of pharmacists evolves, patients will continue to value and seek input from pharmacists.

QUESTIONS FOR FURTHER DISCUSSION

1. Which course of action would you have recommended that MPC Pharmaceuticals take? Why?
2. Do you think the way in which drugs are developed and approved in the United States should be changed? What would you suggest to improve the process?
3. How do you think intellectual property rights should be protected for innovative drug manufacturers?
4. Do you think the FDA is able to adequately oversee foreign production of drugs and foreign clinical trials? Why or why not?
5. What do you feel the role of a pharmacist should be? Do you see the changes for the role of a pharmacist outlined in this chapter as desirable?

KEY TOPICS AND TERMS

Biologic
Biosimilar
Chain pharmacy
Clinical trial
Consumer drug use
Counterfeit drugs
Data exclusivity period
Dispenser
Drug wholesaler
Generic drug
Independent pharmacy
Intellectual property rights
Internet pharmacy
Investigational new drug
Mail-order pharmacy
Medicalization
New drug application (NDA)
Nonprescription (over the counter)
Off-label drug use
Orphan diseases
Patent
Personalized medicine
Pharmaceutical manufacturer
Pharmaceutical marketing
Pharmaceutical research and development
Pharmakon
Postmarketing surveillance
Prescriber
Prescription
U.S. drug approval process
U.S. drug development process

REFERENCES

Anand, G., Wang, S., & Whalen, J. (2008, December 1). Scrutiny grows for drug trials abroad. *The Wall Street Journal.* Retrieved from http://online.wsj.com/article/SB122809561842168089.html

BioWorld. (2009, August). *Market-leading biotechnology drugs: Blockbuster dynamics in an ailing economy.* Atlanta, GA: AHC Media, LLC.

Cairns, C., Califf, R., Glickman, S., Harrington, R., McHutchison, J., & Peterson, E. (2009). Ethical and scientific implications of the globalization of clinical research. *New England Journal of Medicine, 360*(8), 816–823.

Center for Medicine in the Public Interest (CMPI). (2005). *21st century health care terrorism: The perils of international drug counterfeiting.* Retrieved from http://www.cmpi.org/uploads/File/21st-Century-Terrorism.Report.pdf

Centers for Medicare and Medicaid Services. (2010a). *National health expenditure category definitions.* Retrieved from http://www.cms.gov/NationalHealthExpendData/downloads/quickref.pdf

Centers for Medicare and Medicaid Services. (2010b). *National health expenditures 2008 highlights*. Retrieved from http://www.cms.gov/NationalHealthExpendData/downloads/highlights.pdf

Centers for Medicare and Medicaid Services. (2010c). *Table 4: National health expenditures, by source of funds and type of expenditure: Calendar years 2003–2008*. Retrieved from http://www.cms.gov/NationalHealthExpendData/downloads/tables.pdf

Chang, Y. M., & Ross, K. D. (2009). Biodiversity, intellectual property rights and North-South trade. *Economics Bulletin, 29*(2), 992–1002.

Davis, J. E. (2006). How medicalization lost its way. *Society, 43*(6), 51–56.

Department of Health and Human Services, Office of Inspector General. (2010). *Challenges to FDA's ability to monitor and inspect foreign clinical trials*. Retrieved from http://oig.hhs.gov/oei/reports/oei-01-08-00510.pdf

DiMasi, J. A., & Grabowski, H. G. (2007). The cost of biopharmaceutical R&D: Is biotech different? *Managerial and Decision Economics, 28,* 469–479.

Garrison L. P., & Austin, M. J. F. (2006). Linking pharmacogenetics-based diagnostics and pharmaceuticals for personalized medicine: Scientific and economic challenges. *Health Affairs, 25*(5), 1281–1290.

Grabowski, H.G. (2008). Follow-on biologics: data exclusivity and the balance between innovation and competition. *Nature Reviews Drug Discovery, 7,* 479–488.

Heller, H. (1992). *Health care practices and perceptions: A consumer survey of self-medication.* Washington, DC: The Proprietary Association.

Kline & Company, Inc. (2009). *Nonprescription drugs USA 2008*. Retrieved from http://www.klinegroup.com/reports/brochures/cia6g/factsheet.pdf

McDaniel, M. R., & DeJong, D. J. (1999). Justifying pharmacy staffing by presenting pharmacists as investments through return-on-investment analysis. *American Journal of Health-Systems Pharmacists, 56,* 2230–2234.

Montagne, M. (1996). The pharmakon phenomenon: Cultural conceptions of drugs and drug use. In P. Davis (Ed.), *Contested ground: Public purpose and private interest in the regulation of prescription drugs* (pp. 253–294). New York, NY: Oxford University Press.

Montagne, M., & Basara, L. R. (1996). Consumer behavior regarding the choice of prescription and non-prescription medications. In M. C. Smith & A. I. Wertheimer (Eds.), *Social and behavioral aspects of pharmaceutical care.* Binghamton, NY: Pharmaceutical Products Press.

Nahin, R. L., Barnes P. M., Stussman B. J., & Bloom B. (2009). Costs of complementary and alternative medicine (CAM) and frequency of visits to CAM practitioners: United States, 2007. *National health statistics reports; No. 18.* Hyattsville, MD: National Center for Health Statistics. Retrieved from http://nccam.nih.gov/news/camstats/costs/nhsrn18.pdf

National Association of Chain Drug Stores Foundation (NACDS). (2005). *The chain pharmacy industry profile 2005.* Alexandria, VA: NACDS.

National Association of Chain Drug Stores Foundation (NACDS). (2010). *2010–2011 chain pharmacy industry profile.* Alexandria, VA: NACDS.

National Community Pharmacists Association (NCPA). (2009). *2009 NCPA digest, sponsored by Cardinal Health.* Alexandria, VA: NCPA.

Pharmaceutical Research and Manufacturers of America (PhRMA). (2010a). *Medicines in development for diabetes 2010 report.* Washington, DC: PhRMA. Retrieved from http://www.phrma.org/sites/phrma.org/files/attachments/Diabetes_2010.pdf

Pharmaceutical Research and Manufacturers of America (PhRMA). (2010b). *Pharmaceutical Industry Profile 2010.* Washington, DC: PhRMA.

Public Health Service Act. (1944). Retrieved from http://www.fda.gov/RegulatoryInformation/Legislation/ucm148717.htm

Raisch, D. W. (1990a). A model of methods for influencing prescribing: Part I. *DICP: Annals of Pharmacotherapy, 24,* 417–421.

Raisch, D. W. (1990b). A model of methods for influencing prescribing: Part II. *DICP: Annals of Pharmacotherapy, 24,* 537–542.

Soumerai, S., McLaughlin, T. J., & Avorn, J. (1989). Improving drug prescribing in primary care: A critical analysis of the experimental literature. *Milbank Quarterly, 67,* 268–317.

Strebhardt, K. & Ullrich, A. (2008). Paul Ehrlich's magic bullet concept: 100 years of progress. *Nature Reviews Cancer, 8,* 473–480.

Temple, R. (2009). Use of non-U.S. data in NDAs. *ASCPT special session: Regulatory considerations of using non-U.S. data in NDAs: Focus on efficacy, safety, and clinical pharmacology.* Retrieved from http://www.ascpt.org/Portals/8/docs/Meetings/2009%20Annual%20Meeting/Friday/Regulatory%20Considerations.pdf

Trusheim, M. R., Aitken, M. L., & Berndt, E. R. (2010). Characterizing markets for biopharmaceutical innovations: Do biologics differ from small molecules? *Forum for Health Economics & Policy 13*(1), Article 4. Retrieved from http://www.bepress.com/fhep/13/1/4/

Tufts Center for the Study of Drug Development. (2009). *Tufts CSDD outlook 2009.* Boston, MA: Tufts CSDD.

Tufts Center for the Study of Drug Development. (2010). *Tufts CSDD outlook 2010.* Boston, MA: Tufts CSDD.

U.S. FDA. (n.d. a). *Abbreviated new drug application (ANDA): Generics.* Retrieved from http://www.fda.gov/Drugs/DevelopmentApprovalProcess/HowDrugsareDevelopedandApproved/ApprovalApplications/AbbreviatedNewDrugApplicationANDAGenerics/default.htm

U.S. FDA. (n.d. b). *Development and approval process (CBER).* Retrieved from http://www.fda.gov/BiologicsBloodVaccines/DevelopmentApprovalProcess/default.htm

U.S. FDA. (n.d. c). *How drugs are developed and approved.* Retrieved from http://www.fda.gov/Drugs/DevelopmentApprovalProcess/HowDrugsareDevelopedandApproved/default.htm

U.S. FDA. (n.d. d). *Implementation of the Biologics Price Competition and Innovation Act of 2009.* Retrieved from http://www.fda.gov/Drugs/GuidanceComplianceRegulatoryInformation/ucm215089.htm

U.S. FDA. (n.d. e). *What we do.* Retrieved from http://www.fda.gov/AboutFDA/WhatWeDo/default.htm

U.S. FDA. (2010). Coverage of personal importations. In *Regulatory procedures manual* (Section 9-2). Silver Spring, MD: U.S. FDA. Retrieved from http://www.fda.gov/ICECI/ComplianceManuals/RegulatoryProceduresManual/ucm179266.htm

World Health Organization (WHO). (2008). *Counterfeit drugs kill.* [International Medical Products Anti-Counterfeiting Taskforce (IMPACT) brochure]. Retrieved from http://www.who.int/impact/FinalBrochureWHA2008a.pdf

Critical Issues in Public Health

Ardis Hanson, Peter D. Hurd, and Bruce Lubotsky Levin

Case Scenario

Bob is a pharmacist in a small rural town in the Midwest. He and his group of coworkers want to take charge of the public health plans for a small group of people who will live in his community, Mars. They live in an isolated community that has become fairly adept at creating a lifestyle that is self-sustaining. While satellite TV and radio keep them up to date on world events, most of the community life is centered on neighbors and the town's pharmacy. Since Bob graduated from pharmacy school a few years ago, he has been adding various pharmacy-related services to the pharmacy (including blood pressure checks and diabetes counseling), and now he feels ready to take these services to the next level. Bob wants to promote the new pharmacy services with a big splash using a public health approach. He believes that a public health approach allows him to offer additional services to improve the health of his local community. His father happens to be his boss, and although he is retired, he still watches over store details and has allocated $15,000 for a budget. What should Bob recommend?

Bob decides on a promotional program that will highlight a different pharmacy service each week. If you were in Bob's shoes, what would you do each of the next 5 weeks? What should Bob do before he implements the program? How can he identify the most important needs of his community, and how can he pick activities that will tap into the community's willingness to change and try new things? How can he identify some sure-fire successes that will help his community and also help his pharmacy?

Bob decides to apply the transtheoretical model (e.g., precontemplation, contemplation, preparation, action, and maintenance) in the public health programs (Prochaska, DiClemente, & Norcross, 1992) with the goal of moving people from precontemplation to maintenance on a number of health and prevention issues. This model helps him realize that one size will not always fit because some of the community members are ready for change and others have not even thought of doing anything different. To read about a pharmacy intervention project, see the Ashville, NC project (http://www.pharmacytimes.com/files/articlefiles/TheAshevilleProject.pdf).

LEARNING OBJECTIVES _____

Upon completion of this chapter, the student shall be able to:

• Define public health, prevention, and epidemiology
• Discuss the importance of disease prevention and health promotion in identified public health issues
• Apply public health objectives to pharmacy practice and pharmacy education
• Discuss the roles of pharmacists within public health systems
• Compare and contrast specific examples of emerging public health issues pharmacists face in clinical practice

CHAPTER QUESTIONS

1. Define the terms public health, prevention, and epidemiology.
2. What are some of the critical public health issues facing our society?
3. How has the field of public health in America changed since the 18th century?
4. How does public health differ from the practice of medicine in the United States?
5. What role can pharmacy play in public health initiatives in America?

INTRODUCTION

The purpose of this chapter is to introduce essential concepts and critical issues in public health. One of the important perspectives readers should gain from this chapter is the public health viewpoint regarding the health of people. A public health perspective focuses on groups of people, communities, and at-risk populations more than on individual patients. The concern centers on the health of the public and the interventions to improve health, such as the availability of community health clinics, local antismoking laws, restaurant health inspections, and clean-air messages. This chapter will also provide readers with public health strategies and concepts fundamental to help achieve society's interest in ensuring the conditions in which people can be healthy (IOM, 1988).

Public Health

Public health has been defined in a variety of ways, but definitions tend to include efforts to prevent disease as well as promote healthy lifestyles using health promotion and health education initiatives. Winslow (1923) defined public health as preventing disease, prolonging life, promoting health through environmental efforts (including sanitation measures), controlling communicable diseases, advocating health education through personal hygiene, organizing medical and nursing services for early diagnosis and preventive treatment of disease, and ensuring health as a right of every citizen. Rosen (1993) added that:

> Throughout human history, the major problems of health that men have faced have been concerned with community life, for instance, the control of transmissible disease, the control and improvement of the physical environment (sanitation), the provision of water and food of good quality and in sufficient supply, the provision of medical care, and the relief of disability and destitution. (p. 1)

Thus, the focus on community and social group responses to health promotion and disease prevention are central components to the definition of public health.

In a major report on the status of public health in America, *The Future of the Public's Health in the 21st Century,* the Institute of Medicine (IOM) recognized the "concept of health as a public good" and "the fundamental duty of government to promote and protect the health of the public" (Institute of Medicine, 2002, p. 1). As an independent, nonprofit organization that works outside of the government, the IOM is an arm of the National Academy of Sciences and works to provide advice to decision makers and the public in health-related areas.

Prevention has been and continues to be an important component of the IOM work. Health is seen as a primary good in society because it affects so many aspects of human potential and social capital. If public health is "... what we, as a society, do collectively to assure the conditions in which people can be healthy" (Institute of Medicine, 1988, p. 19), then social and environmental issues become part of the public health population-based agenda.

Individual Versus Population Perspectives of Health

Historically, medical care training focuses on the treatment of illness in the individual. Medical and allied medical professionals are taught to alleviate pain and suffering in an individual patient. Pharmacists are taught to provide appropriate medications for individual patients and to help individuals manage their illnesses. Public health, however, pursues a population-based, multidisciplinary approach to disease prevention and health promotion in specific at-risk populations. While disease prevention, morbidity reduction, and increased longevity do benefit individuals, public health professionals examine problems, critical issues, and diseases from a population-based perspective. Using this perspective, public health examples might include a smoking cessation program for a county school system, the reduction of morbidity from automobile accidents in newly licensed automobile drivers (adolescents between the ages of 16 and 21), and the increased longevity of a state's older (ages 65–70) population through exercise programs. As these examples show, public health initiatives are designed for targeted groups of at-risk populations and communities rather than individuals.

HISTORICAL PERSPECTIVE

The development of public health and healthcare delivery systems dates back to 18th-century Europe and late 19th-century America. Historically, public health has been an intricate combination of the sanitation, environmental, and medical sciences. As bacteriologic and immunologic advances were recognized and used to control communicable diseases, the concept of disease prevention was incorporated into public health. Eventually, public health evolved into an interdisciplinary focus on public or community health sciences that now incorporates elements from the social, political, environmental, and behavioral health sciences.

Smith (1973) illustrated this community population-based perspective in his approach to a typhus outbreak in New York City during the mid-1800s. When he noticed that more than 100 victims of typhus fever lived in the same tenement, he found their building in disrepair, a basement filled with sewage, and tenants crowded into the rooms of the building. Smith became an advocate for improved living conditions and encouraged the establishment of a citywide public health board that eventually became the New York Metropolitan Board of Health (Smith, 1973). Smith's efforts focused on the living conditions of an entire group of people that also addressed the health needs of individuals.

Polioviruses date back to before the Common Era. However, polioviruses were not described in medical records until 1789 in Underwood's *Treatise on Diseases of Children*. In 1894, over 100 cases were recorded in Rutland County, Vermont (Caverly, 1894). By 1908, epidemic poliomyelitis had become problematic throughout the United States. Flexner and Lewis (1909) hypothesized that poliomyelitis was able to replicate only in nervous tissue. By the 1940s, Sabin and Ward (1941a, 1941b) disproved Flexner's theory and traced the spread of poliomyelitis as an enteric infection. By the 1950s, Salk (1953) and Sabin (1953) had developed successful vaccines to prevent poliomyelitis. In addition, numerous interventions were developed to treat persons infected with the disease. Although typhus and polioviruses are acknowledged as enteric diseases, other methods of transmission are also important to public health.

Langmuir (1964) addressed the difficulty in determining the mode of contact for the spread of diseases. He suggested that diseases, such as diphtheria, pertussis, and influenza, might be spread both through the air and by personal contact. How diseases are spread determines the public health preparedness and response to large outbreaks of disease. Further, a public health perspective uses the experience gained during one pandemic, such as the 1918 influenza pandemic, that may allow public health professionals to detect, clarify, and understand later pandemics, such as the 2009 H1N1 pandemic. However, there is always a conflict between the need for data collection to guide thoughtful and appropriate implementation of an intervention and the immediate urgency to take some sort of preventive action.

DETERMINANTS OF HEALTH: PUBLIC HEALTH MODEL

For over 60 years, the World Health Organization has defined health as "a state of complete physical, mental and social well-being, and not merely the absence of disease or infirmity" (WHO, 1948, p. 100). Other definitions of health have emphasized life functioning or as "a state of well-being, of feeling good about oneself, of optimum functioning, or the absence of disease, and of the control and reduction of both internal and external risk factors (environment, living conditions, or personal habits) for both disease and negative health conditions" (Banta & Jonas, 1995, p. 11).

Health is more than simply the absence of disease, and public health issues help broaden the perspectives that are necessary to consider the true health of a population. Certainly, the idea of health includes the minimization of the effects of disease, both on the individual and for the population as a whole. The concept of health in today's world includes the notion of an ability to function in the roles that one desires—not simply the physical role, but also mental and social roles. In general, we think of a healthy person as one who has the ability to do things physically, mentally, emotionally, and socially. This idea of health is measured by (1) physical tests, such as exercise; (2) mental tests, like those testing awareness of person, place, and time; (3) emotional tests like those for depression; and (4) other quality-of-life assessments. A healthy society means that people are living in conditions that allow and promote physical and mental behaviors and social well-being. While safe drinking water and proper waste disposal are included in public health practice, other examples include a smoke-free eating environment, a pollution-free park, and a safe road between restaurants and home.

While there are many reasons to emphasize the public nature of health, one of the most compelling is the relationship between health and social class. Across the ages and cultures, lower social classes have consistently had lower levels of health (Braveman, Cubbin, Egerter, Williams, & Pamuk, 2010). While numerous factors can help explain this association (lack of resources, less formal education, environmental risk, dangerous occupations), the link between social class and individual health is a very strong one.

EPIDEMIOLOGY

One of the core disciplines of public health is epidemiology—the study of the factors that determine the frequency and distribution of disease in human populations. The health of a community can be examined through the collection of population-based data using surveillance systems and/or descriptive epidemiologic studies. Such data include looking at a specific group in a specific place over time. The data are used to generate hypotheses regarding cause and transmission of disease with a focus on community intervention and prevention of disease recurrence. *Incidence* and *prevalence* are both terms that are commonly used to refer to measurements of disease frequency. The incidence of a disease is the rate of new cases occurring in a population over a specific time period. The prevalence of a disease is the proportion of a population affected by a disease at a specific time.

One finds that social inequities, including socioeconomic status, gender, and race/ethnicity, are key determinants of population health (Krieger, Williams, & Moss, 1997). An epidemiologic approach can also be used in looking at diet and health, exposure to pollution and cancer, or radiation risk and birth defects. In each case, populations and data about groups are used to infer the possible causes of illness. Epidemiologic approaches also provide a framework for reporting health statistics, such as the causes of death or the prevalence of health problems. For example, *Health, United States, 2009* (National Center for Health Statistics, 2010a) reports the following statistics:

1. From 1990 to 2007, the life expectancy of American men increased by 3.5 years and the life expectancy of American women increased by 1.6 years.
2. In 2007, 17% of women and 22% of men were cigarette smokers.
3. In 2007, 67% of children 19–35 months of age received vaccinations protecting them against seven childhood infectious diseases.
4. In 2007, about 43 million people (16.6% of Americans) under 65 years of age did not have health insurance coverage.

Global and National Perspectives

When examining health and disease from global and national perspectives, two of the most important measures are mortality and morbidity. Mortality rates report the number of deaths in an area per year. Morbidity rates report the number of illnesses or cases of disease in a population over a given period of time.

Globally, WHO (2008) reports that the top five causes of deaths are heart disease, stroke, lower respiratory infections, chronic obstructive pulmonary disease, and diarrheal diseases. Differences between high-, middle-, and low-income countries are obvious. In high-income countries, chronic diseases, including diabetes and dementia, are the leading causes of death (World Health Organization, 2008). Lung infection remains the only leading infectious cause of death. In middle-income countries, chronic diseases are also major causes of death; however, two other leading causes of death are tuberculosis and road traffic accidents. In low-income countries, infectious diseases, lung infections, diarrheal diseases, HIV/AIDS, tuberculosis, and malaria are the major causes of death, as are complications in pregnancy and childbirth (World Health Organization, 2008).

According to the National Center for Health Statistics (2010a), the top five causes of death in the United States are heart disease, cancer, stroke, chronic lower respiratory diseases, and unintentional injuries. Diabetes mellitus, sixth on the list, is a major focus of medication and disease management programs for physicians and pharmacists (National Center for Health Statistics, 2010a).

Globally, WHO estimates the top five risk factors for morbidity are childhood underweight, unsafe sex, alcohol use; unsafe water, sanitation, hygiene; and high blood pressure. For high-income countries, the top five risk factors are tobacco use, alcohol use, obesity, high blood pressure, and high blood glucose. For middle-income countries, the top five risk factors are alcohol use, high blood pressure, tobacco use, obesity, and high blood glucose. For low-income countries, the top five risk factors are childhood underweight; unsafe water, sanitation, and hygiene; unsafe sex; suboptimal breastfeeding; and indoor smoke from solid fuels (World Health Organization, 2009).

From morbidity risk perspectives in the United States, leading risk factors are diabetes, hypertension, high serum cholesterol, obesity, and cigarette smoking (National Center for Health Statistics, 2010a).

Morbidity and mortality statistics are critical to gauge how effective prevention and promotion programs are in improving population health. Periodic shifts in morbidity and mortality indicate programmatic changes in health priorities and allocation of resources. There is a multitude of health risks, and each risk may be the result of a complex relationship between behavioral, social, economic, and environmental factors, as well as genetic predisposition. Each of these influences may provide an opportunity for health promotion/education, prevention, and early intervention initiatives and programs. This has expanded the focus of public health to include both the prevention of acute illnesses and the minimization of the effects of chronic diseases. This includes efforts in primary, secondary, and tertiary prevention (see the "Prevention" section in this chapter). Nevertheless, the effectiveness or outcomes of these programs are often measured over decades rather than in months or years.

HEALTH DISPARITIES

Few people would be surprised by the fact that countries differ in the quality of health and/or the quality of health care that is provided to their citizens. But the lack of equality of health within a country is also quite prevalent (Cohen, 2008; Institute of Medicine, 2002). Whether one examines health within a country or between countries, health disparities exist because of such factors as racial or ethnic differences, age, and socioeconomic status. In the United States, the Minority Health and Health Disparities Research and Education Act of 2000 defines health disparities as differences in "... the overall rate of disease incidence, prevalence, morbidity, mortality or survival rates" (Minority Health and Health Disparities Research and Education Act of 2000, p. 4). WHO defines health disparities as "Inequalities ... in health are most commonly presented as the difference in health status between socioeconomic groups, but ... inequalities in health are also described by geographic location, employment status, gender and ethnic group" (Crombie, Irvine, Elliot, & Wallace, 2005, p. 3).

Higher incidence of disease, shorter average length of life, and greater infant mortality are all indicators of health disparities for minorities when compared to whites in the general U.S. population (Braveman et al., 2010). In a recent study regarding socioeconomic disparities in health in the United States, researchers found that people with the lowest incomes and least education were also the least healthy compared to those with more education and higher incomes (Braveman et al., 2010). Of special interest in this study was that groups with intermediate income and education levels were also less healthy than the most educated and wealthy. This supports the notion that health disparities are not simply issues for those at the lowest levels of socioeconomic status.

Many factors can account for the health disparities that are found in the United States. Certainly, access to quality medical care would be one of those factors. Nevertheless, a public health approach helps us look for additional explanations: the lack of a healthy diet, no safe place to exercise or play, pollutants in the air, lead paint in the house, insects and rodents in living areas, and lack of language skills necessary to navigate a complicated healthcare system. In addition, other factors, including the lack of transportation and the lack of sensitivity to different cultural practices, further helps to explain why health disparities can be so prevalent and so difficult to resolve.

Prevention and promotion are especially critical in addressing health disparities. Alvarado, Harper, Platt, Smith, and Lynch (2009) suggested that interventions to reduce the risk factors addressed by *Healthy People 2010* objectives for all populations should have been targeted to low-income and less educated populations to have the most impact on meeting 2010 objectives (also see the *"Healthy People 2020"* section in this chapter). Further, this approach would not only reduce risk factors and chronic diseases across groups but would result in overall reduction of health disparities (Alvarado et al., 2009).

Cultural competence is an integral part of addressing health disparities. Bleidt and Coleman view cultural competency as a continuum from cultural insensitivity, through cultural awareness and cultural sensitivity, to cultural integration (2008). They emphasize that pharmacy healthcare providers need to move from cultural insensitivity, where cultural differences simply fail to be recognized, to both an awareness and sensitivity to the cultural differences that influence personal health and the provision of health care. Ideally, the healthcare provider will integrate the knowledge of other cultures into the practice of health care for the individual patient. Differences in eye contact, male/female roles, health beliefs, and healthcare practices need to be appreciated, understood, and used to optimize the provision of health care to diverse populations (Bleidt & Coleman, 2008).

CHANGING HEALTH PRIORITIES

The nature of public health problems, both in the United States and globally, has changed over the past 200 years. The variety of local public health issues (e.g., clean air, drinkable water, waste disposal) becomes global in scope rather than specific to countries or selected populations. Historically, these changes in health priorities illustrate the growth and progress of scientific knowledge in the etiology and control of disease. Further, they illustrate the gradual acceptance of health promotion and disease intervention as a public responsibility. Finally, the development of public health practice also demonstrates that a number of public health issues and problems remain unresolved; this chapter will focus on such issues as HIV/AIDS, emergency response/ preparedness/natural disasters, and the H1N1 pandemic.

HIV/AIDS

The shift in health promotion and disease prevention (and early intervention) activities from focusing on chronic rather than acute illnesses has been complicated by new public health challenges that have developed in concert with advances in new medical technologies, such as genetic-based treatments, new drug discoveries, and online monitoring systems. Infectious diseases, such as HIV/AIDS, remain a major cause of morbidity and mortality throughout the world. During the last 25 years, HIV/ AIDS has resulted in an estimated 25 million deaths globally (UNAIDS, 2008). In the United States, an estimated 1,018,428 cases of AIDS were reported from 2003 to 2007 (National Center for Health Statistics, 2010b).

The majority of new cases of HIV infection are transmitted through sexual behavior, and approximately one half of all new cases of HIV infection are among people aged 25 years and younger. However, the death rate for HIV is higher for individuals between 35 to 54 years of age than for other ages. Children younger than 13 years accounted for less than 1% of HIV/AIDS diagnoses (National Center for HIV/AIDS, Viral Hepatitis, STD, and TB Prevention, 2008). Black and Hispanic Americans have AIDS rates considerably higher than rates among Caucasian Americans. High-risk heterosexual contact also accounts for a considerable proportion of new HIV diagnoses among men of minority races/ ethnicities and among women of all races/ethnicities (National Center for HIV/AIDS, Viral Hepatitis, STD, and TB Prevention, 2008). In addition, the percentage of individuals infected due to heterosexual activity also has increased, having surpassed the percentage infected through drug injection (National Center for Health Statistics, 2010b).

HIV/AIDS is not only an epidemic in the United States, but also is a pandemic, affecting the health of populations throughout the world. In 2007, more than 33 million persons worldwide were living with HIV/AIDS. Although there were 2.7 million new HIV infections and 2 million HIV-related deaths reported globally in 2007, there has been a drop in new infections that meet or exceed the 25% target decline. However, sub-Saharan Africa accounts for 67% of all people who have HIV/AIDS and for 75% of AIDS deaths. Further, there is an increase in HIV/AIDS in Indonesia, Pakistan, Vietnam, the Russian Federation, the Ukraine, and other countries (UNAIDS, 2008).

From a public health practice perspective, pharmacists provide important community-based care. Hirsch, Rosenquist, Best, Miller, and Gilmer (2009) describe the effectiveness of pharmacist-provided medication therapy management services in treating individuals with HIV/AIDS. They specifically examined patient outcomes and pharmacy and medical costs. Outcomes included antiretroviral therapy medication regimens, use of contraindicated antiretroviral therapy regimens, occurrence of opportunistic infections, and patient adherence rates. Preliminary results found pilot pharmacy patients received more appropriate HIV treatment and were more adherent to therapy. Although costs were higher in the pilot pharmacies, the increased cost was due to nonantiretroviral therapy medications and the provision of mental health services, both of which were not provided in the nonpilot pharmacies (Hirsch et al., 2009). While medication therapy management is a term often associated with the Medicare Prescription Drug, Improvement, and Modernization Act of 2003 (and Medicare Part D), pharmacists have provided patients with assistance in managing their prescriptions for years.

Emergency Response/Preparedness/Natural Disasters

Disasters often remove one's sense of well-being and security. Whether the disaster is man made or natural, a disaster may be a cataclysmic event (such as the earthquake in Haiti in 2010) or an event with a slow-onset (such as the drought in sub-Saharan Africa, 1972 to 1993) (Gommes & Petrassi, 1996). In 2009, there were 245 global natural disasters, of which 224 were weather related (United Nations International Strategy for Disaster Reduction, 2009). Fifty-five million people were affected by natural disasters while three million were affected by man-made disasters. Between January and November 2009, 48 million people were affected by weather-related events, such as floods, hurricanes, snow, drought, and other extreme weather. Over 8,900 individuals died during weather-related events, which remain the highest risk of natural disaster with the largest numbers of affected people (United Nations, 2009). In 2009, the U.S. Federal Emergency Management Agency issued 107 emergency and disaster declarations in the United States, of which 52 were major disaster declarations (U.S. Federal Emergency Management Agency, 2010). In addition to natural and technological disasters, man-made disasters (genocide and war) continue to have a significant effect upon the public's health. The Global Internal Displacement Profile Project estimates that 25 million people were forced from their homes due to severe political, religious, ethnic, or social persecution (Global IDP Project, 2005; Office of Refugee Resettlement, 2007; Office of the United Nations High Commissioner for Refugees, 2006).

Preparedness for disasters and terrorism, a critical component of protecting the health of the public, includes identifying at-risk populations, assessing community health, and mapping local and national infrastructures. The 2006 Pandemic and All Hazards Preparedness Act refocused the research priorities of the university-based Centers for Public Health Preparedness to four areas (Institute of Medicine, 2009). The first two areas address the design and implementation of emergency preparedness training and how best to communicate accurate information in a timely manner to diverse audiences. The last two areas address the creation of sustainable community-based preparedness systems and the criteria and metrics necessary to evaluate the performance of public health emergency response systems (Institute of Medicine, 2009).

With the increase in disasters nationally and globally, pharmacists have important roles in disaster and crisis response planning by providing services at disaster sites and participating in bioterrorism detection activities (Hurd & Mount, 2008). A survey of the impact of two disasters in Toronto, Canada (one health and one a major citywide blackout) emphasized the importance of pharmacies as frontline healthcare facilities (Austin, Martin, & Gregory, 2007). In lieu of official emergency preparedness guidelines and policies, pharmacists in Toronto relied on their own experience and professional judgment as well as the experiences and professional judgments of their colleagues. Documentation systems, experience, professional judgment, and teamwork practices were determined to be indicators of successful adaptation to disasters. The interview-based study highlights the importance of leadership and advanced preparation prior to actual disasters.

Armitstead and Burton (2006) describe a certification program designed to increase urban and rural community pharmacists' knowledge of bioterrorism. The program, at the University of Kentucky College of Pharmacy, trained 142 licensed pharmacists during a 2-year period (Armitstead & Burton, 2006). In Birmingham, Alabama, the school of pharmacy assisted the state in preparing for those who had been forced out of their homes by hurricane Katrina when it was discovered that refills for prescriptions were becoming a huge problem (Hogue, Hogue, Lander, Avent, & Fleenor, 2009).

HINI Pandemic

Pandemics are considered widespread epidemics of infectious or contagious diseases that affect one or more countries or continents contemporaneously. The influenza pandemics of 1918–1919, 1957–1958, and 1968–1969 killed millions of people worldwide. The 1918–1919 influenza pandemic alone killed between 20 and 40 million people, and it is estimated that approximately one third of the world's population was infected (Frost, 1920). The public health implications of earlier influenza pandemics made the emergence of the H1N1 virus in 2009 particularly serious (Taubenberger & Morens, 2006). Within 50 days of the first reported incidence of the H1N1 virus in April, 2009, the virus had spread to over 76 countries, resulting in over 160 deaths and approximately 36,000 cases (Chawla et al., 2009). By August 2009, over 2,000 deaths had occurred and over 200,000 laboratory-confirmed cases were reported (Franco-Paredes et al., 2009). Mass media coverage of hospitalizations and deaths due to the H1N1 virus, especially among younger individuals, contributed to increased awareness of disease prevention and health promotion initiatives through infectious disease control measures and mass immunization.

During the H1N1 pandemic, the Centers for Disease Control and Prevention (CDC) issued alerts on new surveillance tools to model the spread of flu and the impact of various interventions based upon disease and affected population parameters. In addition, the CDC released information for pharmacists regarding treatment guidelines, recommendations for the use of antiviral medications, emergency authorizations for medication shipment and use, situation updates, and infection control (see www.cdc.gov/h1n1flu/ for available materials). Bhavsar, Kim, and Yu (2010), for example, describe their roles as pharmacists in the CDC's emergency preparedness and response activities during the H1N1 pandemic, which included emergency use requests for medications and use of the Strategic National Stockpile of medications.

An essential part of emergency preparedness and response is effective immunization strategies at the patient, provider, and system levels (Vlahov, Coady, Ompad, & Galea, 2007). Community-based promotion and prevention campaigns utilizing television, radio, and the Internet are one way to increase immunization levels at the patient level. Vlahov and colleagues (2007) describe additional strategies for providers. At the systems level, the most important strategy is to promote broader access to influenza vaccines and reduce missed vaccination opportunities (Vlahov et al., 2007). One critical strategy is to broaden the healthcare base to include additional healthcare providers, such as nurses and pharmacists, to provide immunizations within the community setting and greater access to vaccines.

MODELS FOR CHANGE

One of the methods to promote change is to design community interventions using theories or models that have proven helpful in creating changes in behavior, both at the individual and population level. Kotter and Cohen make it clear that the first step for successful large-scale change is creating a sense of urgency (Kotter & Cohen, 2002). Whether at the patient level or the population level, people need to feel the need to change. Without that driving force, the energy to change will be lacking (Kotter, 2008).

In public health, Prochaska, DiClemente, and Norcross (1992) developed a five-step model, the transtheoretical model, which classified individuals regarding their level of readiness in adopting a behavior change. Their first step is precontemplation, which is not giving any consideration for the need to change. People in this stage will resist change because there is no perceived need. The next stage is contemplation, thinking about change, and is followed by preparation. Action and then maintenance are the last two stages and include individuals actively engaging in a behavior change (Prochaska et al., 1992). See Chapter 4 for a description of the transtheoretical model and its role in behavior change. In a population, individuals may be in various stages of readiness. In developing interventions, one may consider programs that address the various needs of these individuals. In the case of flu vaccination programs, one would want an information program to not only effect a change from thinking that a flu shot is unnecessary to necessary, but also to offer opportunities for people to take action and receive a vaccination.

Social marketing utilizes basic marketing techniques found in advertising and applies them to social issues (Hurd, Levin, Hanson, & Lang, 2008). Pharmacy students who have taken a marketing course are familiar with the four *P*s of marketing—product, price, place, and promotion. Social marketing can use these same fundamental concepts and adapt them to a public health intervention. For flu vaccinations, the product is the vaccination, the price might be free (but would need to consider transportation costs and time away from work), the place needs to be convenient, and the promotion needs to be targeted to a specific at-risk population. For example, people without access to computers will not find web pages very helpful in a campaign to increase flu awareness. The framework that models and theories provide for public health interventions is invaluable and should be a central component of health promotion and disease prevention activities.

PREVENTION

The traditional approach to disease prevention in public health is the primary-secondary-tertiary model. Primary prevention (often operationalized in health promotion activities) refers to the avoidance of disease occurrence as well as actions taken prior to disease onset. Examples include immunizations, water fluoridation, and prospective medication review for potential interactions. Secondary prevention refers to the early diagnosis (detection) and prompt treatment (early intervention) of disease and the avoidance of disability. Examples of secondary preventive efforts include hypertension and cholesterol screening, programs that encourage self-assessment for cancers, and pharmacist review of drug use in nursing homes. Tertiary prevention refers to the limitation or reduction of disability when disease has already occurred, through rehabilitation designed to encourage recovery and prevent further problems. Examples of tertiary preventive initiatives include cardiac rehabilitation programs and occupational therapy for individuals with a variety of physical disabilities.

Institute of Medicine and the Future of Public Health

The Future of Public Health (Institute of Medicine, 1988) defined the mission of public health as "the fulfillment of society's interest in assuring the conditions in which people can be healthy" (p. 40). Thus, the focus on communities and their collective responses to health promotion and disease prevention are central components in the definition of public health. *The Future of Public Health* (Institute of Medicine, 1988) provided a guide on issues important to the health of the public, with a focus on HIV/ AIDS, toxic environmental conditions, lack of health insurance, and the relationship between public and private sector care. Although these problems may have appeared as insurmountable, *The Future of Public Health* (Institute of Medicine, 1988) stressed the capability of the U.S. public health infrastructure to effectively problem solve issues of quality of life and the provision of health care.

The follow-up report, entitled *The Future of the Public's Health in the 21st Century* (Institute of Medicine, 2003) depicted the United States as a nation still challenged by toxic environments (e.g., the Three Mile Island disaster), a large uninsured population, and by health disparities, as well as facing new challenges such as obesity, antimicrobial resistance, and bioterrorism. Further, it continued to frame public health as "… what we as a society do collectively to assure the conditions in which people can be healthy" (Institute of Medicine, 1988, p. 1).

Another IOM report, *Informing the Future: Critical Issues in Health*, continued to emphasize improvement of the nation's healthcare systems (Institute of Medicine, 2009). Nevertheless, it highlighted health as a significant component of U.S. foreign policy, with recommendations for the U.S. government to increase global health efforts over the next 4 years. In addition, *Informing the Future* (Institute of Medicine, 2009) emphasizes risk management and healthy communities. Priority areas for healthy communities include care for women's and children's health, U.S. military and veterans' health, improved HIV prevention and intervention, and implementation of electronic health (medical) records (Levin & Hanson, in press).

Although the reports mentioned in this section provide an overview of the changing public health priorities since 1980, the purpose of the Institute of Medicine reports is to provide a rationale for prioritizing public health initiatives in the United States. The *Healthy People* initiatives, discussed below, describe the nation's public health objectives and establish benchmarks to determine effectiveness.

Healthy People 2020

Tobacco use, poor diet, and physical inactivity are examples of behavioral risk factors that lead to chronic diseases. Seven of the ten leading causes of death in the United States are attributable to chronic disease. An estimated 90 million individuals in the United States are affected by chronic diseases, resulting in disability and major limitations in daily living activities (Ramsey et al., 2008). In 1979, *Healthy People* provided national objectives for promoting health and preventing disease. Preparation of the *Healthy People* report was a cooperative effort of the federal health agencies, the National Academy of Sciences' Institute of Medicine, and a federal task force on disease prevention and health promotion. The authors assessed the relative contributions of lifestyle/behavior, environment, biologic factors, and health care to health problems. They suggested that approximately 50% of U.S. mortality was due to unhealthy behavior or lifestyle choices; 20% was due to environmental factors; 20% to human biologic factors; and only 10% to issues in healthcare delivery (U. S. Department of Health, Education, and Welfare, 1979).

The report sets and monitors national health objectives and measures the impact of prevention activity for the nation. For example, *Healthy People 2010* provided general goals for 10 leading health indicators, such as tobacco use, immunizations, and overweight/obesity (U.S. Department of Health and Human Services, 2000). *Healthy People 2020* supports those three general goals (U.S. Department of Health and Human Services, 2009a), all of which have aspects that are applicable to pharmacists and to pharmacy practice.

Tobacco Use

Tobacco use and abuse is a major health risk for people across the world and is responsible for nearly 500,000 deaths in the United States annually. The *Healthy People* goal for reducing tobacco use across all ages is to increase the number of evidence-based tobacco control programs, as well as the provision of insurance coverage for evidence-based treatment of nicotine dependency. Tobacco cessation programs provided by pharmacists may offer one of the most accessible ways to improve the overall health of a community (Babb & Babb, 2003).

Historically, pharmacy has been involved in smoking cessation programs because of the interest in population health. Both pharmacy students and pharmacists have been trained to counsel in tobacco cessation programs (e.g., Dent, Harris, Noonan, 2007; Hudmon, Prokhorov, & Corelli, 2006; Williams, 2009). Adding training in evidence-based practice requires effective teaching models to increase both the pharmacist's knowledge and self-efficacy in counseling patients on this difficult behavior change. Martin, Bruskiewitz, and Chewning (2003) described a multimedia program for community pharmacists that combined home study with live training. The combination of teaching strategies, which included problem solving, modeling, rehearsal, and feedback, significantly improved participants' knowledge. In addition, 75% of attendees implemented a tobacco cessation program after course completion. One year after completing the tobacco cessation course, more than 50% of community pharmacists were still providing tobacco cessation programs (Martin, Bruskiewitz, & Chewning, 2010).

Immunizations

Healthy People also prioritizes immunizations with the objective to increase vaccination coverage levels for universally recommended vaccines for young children and for influenza and pneumococcal diseases among adults. Zhao & Luman (2010) examined the trends found in the National Immunization Survey during 2000–2008. They analyzed sociodemographic factors, including race, ethnicity, and number of siblings; family poverty status; urban, suburban, or rural status; mother's education level, marital status, and age; and number and type of vaccination providers (public or private). In addition, they noted if the children had participated in the Vaccines for Children program. The authors then described how progress has been made in meeting *Healthy People 2010* goals by eliminating vaccination coverage disparities in the use of specific vaccines and vaccine series among children in underserved communities. In particular, the focus was to reduce disparities between the urban–rural divide. Generally, the trend from 2000 to 2008 indicated a reduction in disparities among most sociodemographic groups. One noteworthy trend was a substantial decrease in disparities between children living in rural areas versus those living in suburban areas (Zhao & Luman 2010).

However, Merrill & Beard (2009) disagree and claim disparities continue. In their study, influenza vaccination levels for adults did not meet the *Healthy People 2010* objectives. Furthermore, another study also found higher levels of pneumococcal vaccination coverage only among two populations—adults 65 years of age and older and younger adults with diabetes mellitus (Jackson, Baxter, Naleway, Belongia, & Baggs, 2009).

Pharmacists play an important role in helping to achieve the objectives of increasing vaccination coverage levels. All states allow pharmacists to immunize patients; some states require certification or limit the types of immunizations to flu shots and pneumococcal vaccines while other states allow pharmacists to administer a broad range of immunizations. Studies show that in states where pharmacists are authorized to provide adult immunizations, there are a larger number of individuals who receive immunizations and an increase in immunizations in rural counties (Bearden & Holt, 2005). This results in overall better individual and community health as well as reduced morbidity and mortality (Grabenstein, 2009).

Obesity

The continuing rise in obesity among children and adults in the United States has resulted in the extension of the 2010 public health goal of reducing obesity and accompanying comorbid diseases as part of the 2020 objectives. Although overweight and obesity prevalence have increased steadily among all population groups in the United States, as of 2005–2006, approximately one third of adults, or over 72 million Americans, were obese (Ogden, Carroll, McDowell, & Flegal, 2007). Furthermore, obesity in adults and women has increased faster than obesity in children. If the current trends in obesity continue, by 2030, it is projected that over 85% of adults will be either overweight or obese, and by 2048, all American adults will be overweight or obese. The prevalence of overweight or obesity in children will double (Wang, Beydoun, Liang, Caballero, & Kumanyika, 2008). By 2030, it is estimated that treating diseases associated with obesity and overweight will cost between $860 and 950 billion (16–18%) of total U.S. healthcare costs (Wang et al., 2008).

Increased obesity is associated with increased risk for premature death, increased healthcare costs, a reduced quality of life, and increased morbidity. Diseases associated with obesity include hypertension, coronary heart disease, type 2 diabetes mellitus, and certain forms of cancer (Pan et al., 2009). Disease state management programs and medication therapy management programs are essential components of managing chronic diseases. Screenings in community pharmacies for diabetes, hypertension, and dyslipidemia resulted in improved follow-up consultations with primary care providers (Snella et al., 2006). Further, as pharmacists become part of a patient's medical home, a systematic and comprehensive provision of care model, their role in advising on choice of medication, especially for obesity treatments, will become more prominent (Schnee, Zaiken, & McCloskey, 2006). The Healthy Habits Program, a weight management pharmaceutical care service (including educational programs, nutrition counseling, and exercise), at Auburn University's Pharmaceutical Care Center, not only helped over 150 patients decrease their risk status but also established pharmacists at the center of disease prevention and health promotion activities on campus (Lloyd et al., 2007). A number of studies have examined the role of the pharmacist in weight-loss programs with positive results (Bottorff, 2007; Krska, Lovelady, Connolly, Parmar, & Davies, 2010; Malone, Alger-Mayer, & Anderson, 2005).

PHARMACY AND PUBLIC HEALTH

Public Health Workforce

Healthy People 2010 identified the public health workforce as a key component of the U.S. public health infrastructure. The public health workforce, often defined as individuals employed by local, state, and federal government health agencies, includes individuals working in academic settings who teach, train, or participate in public health research. In addition, the public health workforce also includes individuals who work in private sector healthcare delivery organizations and members of local communities (Evans & Stoddard, 1994).

The importance of the public health workforce was recognized in 1993, when a list entitled "Core Functions of Public Health" was inserted into Title III of the Health Security Act (HR 3600§3311-3312, 103rd Congress, 1993). Although the bill was defeated, it eventually resulted in the creation of a single definitive list of the 10 essential public health services (Turnock & Handler, 1997). These essential public health services include:

1. Monitor health status to identify community health problems.
2. Diagnose and investigate health problems and health hazards in the community.
3. Inform, educate, and empower people about health issues.
4. Mobilize community partnerships to identify and solve health problems.
5. Develop policies and plans that support individual and community health efforts.
6. Enforce laws and regulations that protect health and ensure safety.
7. Link people to needed personal health services and ensure the provision of health care when otherwise unavailable.
8. Assure a competent public health and personal healthcare workforce.
9. Evaluate effectiveness, accessibility, and quality of personal and population-based health services.
10. Research to provide new insights and innovative solutions to health problems (Turnock & Handler, 1997).

Interest in competencies for the public health workforce gradually emerged, and in 2001, the Council on Linkages Between Academia and Practice published its core competencies list. All competencies were mapped across the 10 essential public health services. In 2009, the council published a revised list of its 2001 core competencies for public health. The competencies, which span 8 content areas, include analytic/assessment skills, policy development/program planning skills, communication skills, cultural competency skills, community dimensions of practice skills, public health sciences skills, financial planning and management skills, and leadership and systems thinking skills (Council on Linkages Between Academia and Practice, 2009).

New competencies include the use of public health informatics practices at individual, programmatic, and business operations levels; development of continuous quality improvement strategies; assessment of health literacy; assessment of organizations for cultural competence; recognition of the ethical conduct of research; development of local, state, and federal agency partnerships; implementation of appropriate judicial and operational procedures; improvement of organizational performance through evaluation; and implementation of personal development opportunities for public health staff (Council on Linkages, 2009).

In addition to core competencies, public health leaders throughout the United States have created a credentialing system for public health workers (Cioffi, Lichtveld, Thielen, & Miner, 2003; Gebbie, 2009; Gebbie et al., 2007; Ogolla & Cioffi, 2007) as well as how best to evaluate the performance of the public health system (Scutchfield, Bhandari, Lawhorn, Lamberth, & Ingram, 2009). Part of the discussion on public health system performance is tied to the accreditation and credentialing of the public health workforce. In 2003, the National Board of Public Health Examiners was created (Gebbie et al., 2007), providing graduates of public health programs a voluntary certification examination to measure their core knowledge and skills. As the credentialing of public health workforce continues, this exam likely will become a standard requirement to work in the public health field. Thus, issues such as whether persons without a formal professional public health education should be credentialed and how to measure the competence of workers without a formal professional education will need to be resolved (Gebbie, 2009). This likely will have implications for pharmacists who work within the public health workforce, especially with the move to create practice specializations within pharmacy practice.

Changing and Expanding Roles of Pharmacy and Pharmacists

One of the telling signs of the changing role of the pharmacist in public health is the increasing interest in the combination of a PharmD degree with a master's degree in public health. As of 2010, 13 colleges of pharmacy offer this dual-degree option, and the number continues to increase (AACP, n.d.). In 2008, the American Association of Colleges of Pharmacy approved a special interest group in public health, consisting of pharmacy educators with an interest in this area. The U.S. Public Health Service has a long history of hiring pharmacists and using them in public health roles ranging from the Indian Health Service to population disease control. In 2006, the American Public Health Association adopted a policy statement on the role of the pharmacist in public health (http://www.apha.org/advocacy/policy/policysearch/default.htm?id=1338), recognizing that the role of pharmacy in public health was still developing, expanding, and being redefined as the profession adopts more public health responsibilities.

As an example of the changing role of pharmacy, consider the areas of environmental and occupational health (Harbison, Morris, & Harbison, 2008). These areas usually focus on limiting the risk for worker exposure to chemicals, regulating chemical pollutants in the environment, and the safe disposal of hazardous waste. Of specific concern is medication disposal because medications can be excreted naturally by the patient and pass through filtration plants without being removed. In the 2008–2009 annual report from the President's Cancer Panel, entitled *Reducing Environmental Cancer Risk: What We Can Do Now* (Reuben, 2010), there was specific mention of the proper disposal of pharmaceuticals and the potential cancer risk to those who consume water that has been polluted by the improper disposal of pharmaceuticals by the public. Currently there are no limits in drinking water for these kinds of chemicals. The roles for pharmacists in environmental health are just beginning to be recognized and developed, including the disposal of hazardous waste from the pharmacy and compliance with Occupational Safety and Health regulations in the pharmacy (Harbison et al., 2008).

Pharmacovigilance and Risk Management

Pharmacovigilance is another example of the expanding role for pharmacy and considered part of a broader public health perspective. Pharmacovigilance is the detection, assessment, and prevention of adverse effects, particularly long-term and short-term side effects, of pharmaceutical products within public health practice (WHO Collaborating Centre for International Drug Monitoring, 2002). The burden on the public's health due to adverse drug events is significant. In a review by the Agency for Healthcare Research & Quality (2010), adverse drug events were estimated to cause more than 770,000 injuries and deaths per year, with the cost to individual hospitals exceeding as much as $5 million. Furthermore, the toxicity of the medicines used in the treatment of HIV/AIDS may result in adverse consequences of a patient's dermatologic, hepatic, hematologic, metabolic, and neurologic systems.

Discovering adverse drug reactions is an important part of pharmacovigilance and can be done in patient populations rather than on a patient-by-patient basis. Being able to use large databases to detect adverse drug reactions early can play a very important role in the safe and effective use of medications. By developing a clear picture of the risks of a medication, the patient and provider can more accurately weigh the potential harm against the benefits of the medication. To detect adverse drug reactions that are less common, countries have begun to collaborate on the creation of databases that include enough cases to find patterns in very large groups that would be missed in smaller populations (WHO, 2002). Counterfeit drugs and drugs used in nonapproved ways are additional examples of how international cooperation can lead to a rapid response to a problem. Another area of pharmacovigilance is the drug resistance of antibiotics. Moreover, a large database of drug use can help pinpoint problem areas and areas of resistance. Researchers can examine the database, looking for patients who are having trouble using their medications. An example might include an asthma patient refilling a rescue inhaler too frequently while failing to refill a second inhaler that is designed for maintenance doses. Looking for these patterns can provide information to pharmacists in the identification and resolution of medication-related problems at a population level.

In a study of the VA Pharmacy Benefits Management Strategic Healthcare Group, the use of evidence-based practices and clinical and contracting processes/procedures to improve quality of care and patient outcomes were examined, as well as the safety, appropriateness of use, effectiveness, and cost-effectiveness of prescription drugs for veterans. The authors found that cooperation of the multidisciplinary teams involved in patient care, reliance on evidence-based practices, and a focus on continuous quality improvement resulted in improved practice and health outcomes (Sales, Cunningham, Glassman, Valentino, & Good, 2005).

Formularies and the management of medication therapy provide additional examples of the changing role of pharmacy. The drug benefits in some health insurance plans are managed by a pharmacy benefit management company. Its main purpose is to provide the prescription drug benefit, which would include processing the claim and providing the medication to the individual member, either through a local pharmacy or through the mail. The pharmacy benefit management company can operate at a much larger scale than an individual health insurance plan, resulting in a reduction in costs of providing the drug benefit. Because the emphasis is on cost savings to the insurer, strategies are offered to the insurer to reduce costs. As one of these strategies, the pharmacy benefit manager will develop formularies (lists of drugs) that are preferred in the plan. If the drugs on the formulary are used, they will be cheaper, saving money for all involved, including the patient. Formularies are covered to a greater extent in Chapter 17.

Challenges Facing Pharmacy and Public Health

There are a number of public health pharmacy areas that will offer exciting opportunities for pharmacists. Three areas of public health pharmacy that would seem to have important implications for the future are health literacy, medication compliance/adherence to medication regimens, and the nutrition/exercise component of drug therapy.

Nevertheless, there are also many challenges facing the future of public health in the field of pharmacy. There are many examples of public health approaches that have been implemented by pharmacists (Hurd et al., 2008), including community outreach, student services, and intervention training programs. The broad area of healthcare reform will offer critical opportunities for pharmacy. One significant area is the development of community health teams for transitional care, which includes discharge planning with medication therapy management services under the medical home model. Healthcare reform also provides for a grant-awarding patient safety research center for medication management therapy services. A national health workforce commission will integrate healthcare training across professional schools. Although these are important opportunities for pharmacy practice, two additional areas of public health pharmacy that have important implications for the future include health literacy and medication adherence.

Health Literacy

Health literacy is associated with literacy. In *Healthy People 2010*, health literacy is defined as the degree to which an individual can obtain, process, and understand basic health information and health services and make appropriate health decisions. Zarcadoolas, Pleasant, and Greer (2005) include a number of dimensions for health literacy, fundamental literacy, scientific literacy, civic literacy, and cultural literacy. This broader definition of health literacy can be of great impact to patients and providers. Choosing a broader focus helps underscore the fact that health literacy is not simply a problem for a patient, but rather a problem for the healthcare system and the providers working within those systems.

Because of the nature of public health and its work with underserved populations, it is critical that pharmacists address and detect health literacy problems that may interfere with the patient's health. Pharmacists can use a number of tools to improve their attempts to address issues related to health literacy. One of the simplest approaches is the use of plain language (Stableford & Mettger, 2007). Attempts to use nonjargon, easy-to-understand communication is one of the keys to addressing health literacy problems. A second approach, teach back, uses the technique of requesting the patient to explain to the health practitioner the message that the patient has received as if the patient was now the teacher (Shillinger et al., 2003). This approach can be very helpful in detecting misunderstandings, gaps in knowledge, and potentially harmful misinterpretations. Other techniques are slightly more elaborate and include Newest Vital Sign (Weiss et al., 2005), the 4 habits model (Frankel & Stein, 2001), and Ask Me 3 (Partnership for Clear Health Communication AskMe3, 2010). All of these approaches are applicable to pharmacy settings. The design of health information needs to include a consideration of the health literacy and cultural background of the target audience. The ability to use health information to make informed decisions needs to be monitored and assessed. Strengths in one area, such as fundamental literacy, may not assure strengths in scientific or mathematical areas of literacy.

Adherence to Medication Regimens

The degree to which an individual complies with a prescribed regimen (drug, diet, exercise) is often referred to as medication adherence. Medication adherence is one of the continuing public health issues in pharmacy. Patients may be prescribed the correct treatment, but they sometimes fail to fill the prescription, take the medication, or correctly dose the medication. Even those who initially adhere often fail to continue taking the drug. The role of public health pharmacy approaches in addressing this problem can have a significant effect because multifaceted approaches to adherence have shown some success through tailoring programs to individual needs, simplifying the dosages, and delivering programs over a longer period of time (Touchette & Shapiro, 2008).

There are many ways to measure compliance/adherence. In addition to asking a patient about his or her medication(s), a pharmacist also should ask what really helps him or her remember to take the medication correctly, and how they cope with the challenges of taking the medication as prescribed. One pharmacy-based measure is a pill count, basically looking at the number of pills dispensed, the frequency of dosing, and the number of pills currently in the container. A modification of this would be to predict the time when a refill should be needed and then compare the actual refill to the predicted time. Other approaches are to measure therapeutic outcomes (lowered cholesterol) or the drug level in the body (achieved a therapeutic level). All are valuable, but some are more appropriate for particular situations. In public health pharmacy, comparing refill frequency with predicted times would enable the identification of population risks for the at-risk group that is being assessed.

Nutrition/Exercise and Drug Therapy

The health problems of the U.S. population include the management of chronic disease in an aging population. The baby boomer population (born between 1946 and 1964) will continue to develop chronic diseases as they age—diseases that parallel the current causes of death in the U.S. population (heart disease, cancer, and stroke). The management of chronic diseases (including diabetes, arthritis, and others) often requires a team-based approach that includes both proper diet and adequate exercise. Public health approaches to encourage populations to eat healthy and to be active can be a part of public health pharmacy practice. Within this broad category, the pharmacist can also play a part in the management of obesity. As discussed earlier, obesity is a major public health problem facing the U.S. population at all ages (DeBate, Blunt, & Becker, 2010), and the pharmacist, as a part of the healthcare team, should play a role in helping combat this serious public health problem.

Importance of Public Health in Pharmacy

Although we may think of global public health concerns in the context of communicable diseases (such as HIV or the Ebola virus), the world population is living longer and is increasingly urbanized, challenged by poverty, and very mobile. The primary focus of future prevention and early intervention initiatives will include health, nutritional education and support, and control of infectious diseases. Adding to the disease burden of heart disease, cancer, and stroke, global public health concerns will also include depression, alcohol abuse, tobacco use, and the problems associated with the health of an aging population (Giorgianni, 2000; Levin, Hennessy, & Petrila, 2010). Healthy People (HP) 2020 objectives will affect pharmacy education and practice. Objective HP2010–1-7 recommends that pharmacy education include core competencies in health promotion and disease prevention, with an emphasis on cultural diversity. Objective HC/HIT (Health Communication and Health IT) HP2020–6 increases the number of patients involved in their own healthcare decision making. This requires the pharmacist to be more proactive and to communicate more effectively with patients regarding medication choice, use, adherence, adverse effects, and self-monitoring. Objective DSC (Disability and Secondary Conditions) HP2020–6 increases the numbers of individuals with access to health and wellness programs, which further establishes pharmacists as a critical component in medical homes and as members of extended care and community care teams. Objective DSC HP2020–13 increases the number of graduate courses in disability and health as part of public health programs, a move that pharmacy schools and colleges may parallel. Objective OA (Older Adults) HP2020–6, which increases the proportion of the healthcare workforce with geriatric certification, may provide the opportunity for a new specialization in pharmacy, much like the clinical psychiatric pharmacist.

With the push toward the adoption of a national electronic health record (Levin & Hanson, in press), two objectives for health communication and health information technology may affect pharmacy practice. In the health communication/health information technology area, objectives HP2020–11 and HP2020–12 seek to "increase the proportion of providers who use health information technology to improve individual and population health" and to "increase the proportion of providers and governmental health agencies that use advanced connectivity to optimize electronic health information exchange to improve individual and population health" (U.S. Department of Health and Human Services, 2009b, p. 1). Increased use of health information systems also will lend itself to better surveillance of health events, disease tracking, and bioterrorism preparedness. Surveillance objectives address medical safety, especially the monitoring and analysis of adverse events associated with pharmaceutical therapies in community and specialty pharmacy practice.

CONCLUSION AND IMPLICATIONS FOR PHARMACY

This chapter has covered a variety of concepts, topics, and critical issues related to public health and pharmacy. For a pharmacist thinking about implementing a public health pharmacy program in a smaller community (as in the case scenario presented at the beginning of this chapter), there are many suggestions, topics, and approaches that might be considered. Creating a sense of urgency to change, or identifying an area where that urgency is already present, will be an important key to the success of a public health pharmacy program. While pharmacists are single members of the healthcare team with lower numbers than nurses or physicians, they have the potential to make significant differences for their communities and for their patients in many areas and specialties within public health.

QUESTIONS FOR FURTHER DISCUSSION

1. How may health information technologies affect pharmacy practice?
2. What role does public health have in the education and training of physicians, nurses, pharmacists, and other providers of health care?
3. Is there a need in the research, academic, and practice areas for public health pharmacists?
4. What future public health issues will be most important to pharmacy?
5. What role can pharmacists play in the development of the assessment of health needs within a specific population?

KEY TOPICS AND TERMS

Epidemiology
Health
Health disparities
Incidence
Morbidity
Mortality
Pandemic
Prevalence
Prevention
Public health

REFERENCES

AACP (American Association of Colleges of Pharmacy). (n.d.). *Table 4, Dual degree programs. 2011–2012 pharmacy school admission requirements.* Retrieved from http://www.aacp.org/RESOURCES/STUDENT/PHARMACYFORYOU/ADMISSIONS/Pages/PSAR.aspx

Agency for Healthcare Research and Quality. (2010). *Reducing and preventing adverse drug events to decrease hospital costs.* Retrieved from http://www.ahrq.gov/qual/aderia/aderia.htm

Alvarado, B. E., Harper, S., Platt, R. W., Smith, G. D., & Lynch, J. (2009). Would achieving *Healthy People 2010*'s targets reduce both population levels and social disparities in heart disease? *Circulation. Cardiovascular Quality and Outcomes, 2*(6), 598–606.

Armitstead, J. A., & Burton, D. C. (2006). Enhanced pharmacy training for counter-terrorism and disaster response. *Journal of Telemedicine and Telecare, 12*(Suppl 1), 3–5.

Austin, Z., Martin, J. C., & Gregory, P. A. (2007). Pharmacy practice in times of civil crisis: The experience of SARS and the blackout in Ontario, Canada. *Research in Social & Administrative Pharmacy, 3*(3), 320–335.

Babb, V. J., & Babb, J. (2003). Pharmacist involvement in *Healthy People 2010. Journal of the American Pharmaceutical Association, 43*(1), 56–60.

Banta, H. D., & Jonas, S. (1995). Health and health care. In A. R. Kovner & S. Jonas (Eds.), *Jonas's health care delivery in the United States* (5th ed., pp. 11–33). New York, NY: Springer.

Bearden, D. T., & Holt, T. (2005). Statewide impact of pharmacist-delivered adult influenza vaccinations. *American Journal of Preventive Medicine, 29*(5), 450–452.

Bhavsar, T. R., Kim, H. J., & Yu, Y. (2010). Roles and contributions of pharmacists in regulatory affairs at the Centers for Disease Control and Prevention for public health emergency preparedness and response. *Journal of the American Pharmacists Association, 50*(2), 165–168.

Bleidt, B. A., & Coleman, C. A. (2008). Understanding multicultural pharmaceutical education. In B. L. Levin, P. D. Hurd, & A. Hanson (Eds.), *Introduction to public health in pharmacy* (pp. 279–294). Sudbury, MA: Jones and Bartlett.

Bottorff, M. (2006). Role of the pharmacist. *Pharmacotherapy, 26*(12 pt 2), 227S–232S.

Braveman, P. A., Cubbin, C., Egerter, S., Williams, D. R., & Pamuk, E. (2010). Socioeconomic disparities in health in the United States: What the pattern tells us. *American Journal of Public Health, 100*(suppl 1), S186–S196.

Caverly, C. S. (1894). Preliminary report of an epidemic of paralytic disease occurring in Vermont in the summer of 1894. *Yale Medical Journal, 1*, 1–5.

Chawla, R., Sharma, R. K., Madaan, D., Dubey, N., Arora, R., Goel, R., … Bhardwaj, J. R. (2009). Mitigation approaches to combat the flu pandemic. *Journal of Global Infectious Diseases, 1*(2), 117–130.

Cioffi, J. P., Lichtveld, M. Y., Thielen, L., & Miner, K. (2003). Credentialing the public health workforce: An idea whose time has come. *Journal of Public Health Management and Practice, 9*(6), 451–458.

Cohen, J. A. (2008). *Challenges and successes in reducing health disparities: Workshop summary.* Washington, DC: National Academies Press.

Council on Linkages Between Academia and Practice. (2009). *Crosswalk: Original v. tier 2 (mid tier) core competencies for public health professionals (Adopted June 2009).* Washington, DC: Council on Linkages between Academia and Practice. Retrieved from http://www.phf.org/link/Orig-v-Tier2CCs.pdf

Crombie, I., Irvine, L., Elliot, L., & Wallace, H. (2005). *Closing the health inequalities gap: An international perspective.* Dundee, Scotland: World Health Organization. Retrieved from http://www.euro.who.int/document/e87934.pdf

DeBate, R., Blunt, H., & Becker, M. A. (2010). Eating disorders. In B. L. Levin & M. A. Becker (Eds.), *A public health perspective of women's mental health* (pp. 121–141). New York, NY: Springer.

Dent, L. A., Harris, K. J., & Noonan, C. W. (2007). Tobacco interventions delivered by pharmacists: A summary and systematic review. *Pharmacotherapy, 27*(7), 1040–1051.

Evans, R. G., & Stoddard, G. L. (1994). Producing health, consuming health care. In R. G. Evans, M. L. Barer, & T. R. Marmor (Eds.), *Why are some people healthy and others not? The determinants of health of populations* (pp. 27–64). New York, NY: Aldine de Gruyter.

Flexner, S., & Lewis, P. A. (1909). The transmission of poliomyelitis to monkeys. *JAMA, 53,* 1639.

Franco-Paredes, C., Hernandez-Ramos, I., Del Rio, C., Alexander, K. T., Tapia-Conyer, R., & Santos-Preciado, J. I. (2009). H1N1 influenza pandemics: Comparing the events of 2009 in Mexico with those of 1976 and 1918–1919. *Archives of Medical Research, 40*(8), 669–672.

Frankel, R. M., & Stein, T. (2001). Getting the most out of the clinical encounter: The 4 habits model. *Journal of Medical Practice Management, 16,* 184–191.

Frost, W. H. (1920). Statistics of influenza morbidity. *Public Health Reports, 35,* 584–597.

Gebbie, K., Goldstein, B. D., Gregorio, D. I., Tsou, W., Buffler, P., Petersen, D., ... Mahan, C. (2007). The National Board of Public Health Examiners: Credentialing public health graduates. *Public Health Reports, 122*(4), 435–440.

Gebbie, K. M. (2009). Public health certification. *Annual Review of Public Health, 30,* 203–210.

Giorgianni, S. J. (2000). Understanding the burden of disease: A global perspective. *The Pfizer Journal, Global Edition, 1*(1), 1–42.

Global IDP Project. (2005). *Internal displacement: Global overview of trends and developments in 2004.* Geneva, Switzerland: Norwegian Refugee Council.

Gommes, R., & Petrassi. (1996). *Rainfall variability and drought in sub-Saharan Africa, SDdimensions.* Retrieved from http://www.fao.org/waicent/faoinfo/sustdev/EIdirect/EIan0004.htm

Grabenstein, J. D. (2009). Daily versus single-day offering of influenza vaccine in community pharmacies. *Journal of the American Pharmacists Association, 49*(5), 628–631.

Harbison, R. D., Morris, S., III, & Harbison, C. (2008). Environmental and occupational health. In B. L. Levin, P. D. Hurd, & A. Hanson (Eds.), *Introduction to public health in pharmacy* (pp. 77–99). Sudbury, MA: Jones and Bartlett.

Hirsch, J., Rosenquist, A., Best, B., Miller, T., & Gilmer, T. (2009). Evaluation of the first year of a pilot program in community pharmacy: HIV/AIDS medication therapy management for Medi-Cal beneficiaries. *Journal of Managed Care Pharmacy, 15*(1), 32–41.

Hogue, M. D., Hogue, H. B., Lander, R. D., Avent, K., & Fleenor, M. (2009). The nontraditional role of pharmacists after hurricane Katrina: Process description and lessons learned. *Public Health Rep, 124*(2), 217–223.

Hudmon, K. S., Prokhorov, A. V., & Corelli, R. L. (2006). Tobacco cessation counseling: Pharmacists' opinions and practices. *Patient Education & Counseling, 61*(1), 152–60.

Hurd, P. D., Levin, B. L., Hanson, A., & Lang, W. G., IV. (2008). Disease prevention and health promotion. In B. L. Levin, P. D. Hurd, & A. Hanson (Eds.), *Introduction to public health in pharmacy* (pp. 55–76). Sudbury, MA: Jones and Bartlett.

Hurd, P. D., & Mount, J. K. (2008). Health emergency preparedness and response. In B. L. Levin, P. D. Hurd, & A. Hanson (Eds.), *Introduction to public health in pharmacy* (pp. 321–336). Sudbury, MA: Jones and Bartlett.

Institute of Medicine. (1988). *The future of public health.* Washington, DC: Committee for the Study of the Future of Public Health, Division of Health Care Services.

Institute of Medicine. (2002). *The future of the public's health in the 21st century.* Washington, DC: National Academies Press.

Institute of Medicine. (2009). *Informing the future: Critical issues in health* (5th ed.). Washington, DC: National Academies Press. Retrieved from http://books.nap.edu/openbook.php?record_id=12709

Jackson, L. A., Baxter, R., Naleway, A. L., Belongia, E. A., & Baggs, J. (2009). Patterns of pneumococcal vaccination and revaccination in elderly and non-elderly adults: A vaccine safety datalink study. *BMC Infectious Diseases, 9,* 37.

Kotter, J. P. (2008). *A sense of urgency.* Boston, MA: Harvard Business Press.

Kotter, J. P., & Cohen, D. S. (2002). *The heart of change: Real-life stories of how people change their organizations.* Boston, MA: Harvard Business School Press.

Krieger, N., Williams, D. R., & Moss, N. E. (1997). Measuring social class in U.S. public health research: Concepts, methodologies, and guidelines. *Annual Review of Public Health, 18,* 341–378.

Krska, J., Lovelady, C., Connolly, D., Parmar, S., & Davies, M. J. (2010). Community pharmacy contribution to weight management: Identifying opportunities. *International Journal of Pharmacy Practice, 18*(1), 7–12.

Langmuir, A. D. (1964). Airborne infection: How important for public health? A historical review. *American Journal of Public Health and the Nation's Health, 54,* 1666–1668.

Levin, B. L. & Hanson, A. (in press). Mental health informatics. In N. A. Cummings & W. T. O'Donohue (Eds.), *21st century behavioral healthcare reforms: The promise of integrated healthcare.* New York, NY: Routledge (Taylor & Francis Group).

Levin, B. L., Hennessy, K. D., & Petrila, J. (2010). *Mental health services: A public health perspective* (3rd ed.). New York, NY: Oxford University Press.

Lloyd, K. B., Thrower, M. R., Walters, N. B., Krueger, K. P., Stamm, P. L., & Evans, R. L. (2007). Implementation of a weight management pharmaceutical care service. *The Annals of Pharmacotherapy, 41*(2), 185–192.

Malone, M., Alger-Mayer, S. A., & Anderson, D. A. (2005). The lifestyle challenge program: A multidisciplinary approach to weight management. *The Annals of Pharmacotherapy, 39*(12), 2015–2020.

Martin, B. A., Bruskiewitz, R. H., & Chewning, B. A. (2010). Effect of a tobacco cessation continuing professional education program on pharmacists' confidence, skills, and practice-change behaviors. *Journal of the American Pharmacists Association, 50*(1), 9–16.

Merrill, R. M., & Beard, J. D. (2009). Influenza vaccination in the United States, 2005–2007. *Medical Science Monitor: International Medical Journal of Experimental and Clinical Research, 15*(7), PH92–PH100.

Minority Health and Health Disparities Research and Education Act of 2000. Sec. 301, Title III. Retrieved from http://frwebgate.access.gpo.gov/cgi-bin/getdoc.cgi?dbname=106_cong_bills&docid=f:s1880enr.txt.pdf

National Center for Health Statistics. (2010a). *Health, United States, 2009: In brief.* Hyattsville, MD: National Center for Health Statistics. Retrieved from http://www.cdc.gov/nchs/data/hus/hus09_InBrief.pdf

National Center for Health Statistics. (2010b). *Health, United States, 2009: With special feature on medical technology.* Hyattsville, MD: National Center for Health Statistics. Retrieved from http://www.cdc.gov/nchs/data/hus/hus09.pdf

National Center for HIV/AIDS, Viral Hepatitis, STD, and TB Prevention. (2008). *HIV and AIDS in the United States: A picture of today's epidemic.* Atlanta, GA: Centers for Disease Control and Prevention.

Office of Refugee Resettlement. (2007). *Refugee arrival data: By country of origin and state of initial resettlement.* Washington, DC: U.S. Department of Health and Human Services.

Office of the United Nations High Commissioner for Refugees. (2006). *The state of the world's refugees 2006: Human displacement in the new millennium.* Oxford, England: Oxford University Press.

Ogden, C. L., Carroll, M. D., McDowell, M. A., & Flegal, K. M. (2007). Obesity among adults in the United States—No statistically significant change since 2003–2004. *NCHS Data Brief,* (1), 1–8.

Ogolla, C., & Cioffi, J. P. (2007). Concerns in workforce development: Linking certification and credentialing to outcomes. *Public Health Nursing (Boston, Mass.), 24*(5), 429–438.

Pan, L., Galuska, D. A., Sherry, B., Hunter, A. S., Rutledge, G. E., Dietz, W. H., … Balluz, L. S. (2009). Differences in prevalence of obesity among black, white, and Hispanic adults—United States, 2006–2008. *MMWR. Morbidity and Mortality Weekly Report, 58*(27), 740–744.

Partnership for Clear Health Communication AskMe3. (2010). Retrieved from http://www.npsf. org/askme3/PCHC/

Prochaska, J. O., DiClemente, C. C., & Norcross, J. C. (1992). In search of how people change: Applications to the addictive behaviors. *American Psychologist, 47,* 1102–1114.

Ramsey, F., Ussery-Hall, A., Garcia, D., McDonald, G., Easton, A., Kambon, M., … Vigeant, J. (2008). Prevalence of selected risk behaviors and chronic diseases—Behavioral Risk Factor Surveillance System (BRFSS), 39 steps communities, United States, 2005. *MMWR. Surveillance Summaries: Morbidity and Mortality Weekly Report. Surveillance Summaries/CDC, 57*(11), 1–20.

Reuben, S. H. (2010). *Reducing environmental cancer risk: What we can do now.* Washington, DC: U.S. Department of Health and Human Services, National Institutes of Health, National Cancer Institute.

Rosen, G. (1993). *A history of public health.* Baltimore, MD: The Johns Hopkins University Press.

Sabin, A. B. (1953). Present status and future possibilities of a vaccine for the control of poliomyelitis. *AMA American Journal of Diseases in Children, 86*(3), 301–310.

Sabin, A. B. & Ward, R. (1941a). The natural history of poliomyelitis. I. Distribution of virus in nervous and non nervous tissue. *Journal of Experimental Medicine, 73*(6), 771–793.

Sabin, A. B. & Ward, R. (1941b). The natural history of human poliomyelitis. II. Elimination of the virus. *Journal of Experimental Medicine, 74*(6), 519–529.

Sales, M. M., Cunningham, F. E., Glassman, P. A., Valentino, M. A., & Good, C. B. (2005). Pharmacy benefits management in the Veterans Health Administration: 1995 to 2003. *The American Journal of Managed Care, 11*(2), 104–112.

Salk, J. E. (1953). Studies in human subjects on active immunization against poliomyelitis. I. A preliminary report of experiments in progress. JAMA, *151*(13), 1081–1098.

Schnee, D. M., Zaiken, K., & McCloskey, W. W. (2006). An update on the pharmacological treatment of obesity. *Current Medical Research and Opinion, 22*(8), 1463–1474.

Scutchfield, F. D., Bhandari, M. W., Lawhorn, N. A., Lamberth, C. D., & Ingram, R. C. (2009). Public health performance. *American Journal of Preventive Medicine, 36*(3), 266–272.

Shillinger, D., Piette, J., Grumbach, K. Wang, F., Wilson, C., Daher, C., … Bindman, A. B. (2003). Physician communication with diabetic patients who have low health literacy. *Archives of Internal Medicine, 163,* 83–90.

Smith, S. (1973). *The city that was.* Metuchen, NJ: Scarecrow Reprint Corp. (Original work published 1806).

Snella, K. A., Canales, A. E., Irons, B. K., Sleeper-Irons, R. B., Villarreal, M. C., Levi-Derrick, V. E., … Nelson, A. A. (2006). Pharmacy- and community-based screenings for diabetes and cardiovascular conditions in high-risk individuals. *Journal of the American Pharmacists Association, 46*(3), 370–377.

Stableford, S., & Mettger, W. (2007). *Plain language: A strategic response to the health literacy challenge. Journal of Public Health Policy, 28,* 71–93.

Taubenberger, J. K., & Morens, D. M. (2006). 1918 influenza: the mother of all pandemics. *Emerging Infectious Diseases, 12*(1), 15–22.

Touchette, D. R., & Shapiro, N. L. (2008). Medication compliance, adherence, and persistence: Current status of behavioral and educational interventions to improve outcome. *Journal of Managed Care in Pharmacy, 146*(suppl S-d), S2–S10.

Turnock, B. J., & Handler, A. S. (1997). From measuring to improving public health practice. *Annual Review of Public Health, 18,* 261–282.

UNAIDS. (2008). *Report on the global HIV/AIDS epidemic*. New York, NY: United Nations. Retrieved from http://www.unaids.org/en/KnowledgeCentre/HIVData/GlobalReport/2008/2008_Global_report.asp

United Nations International Strategy for Disaster Reduction. (2009, December 14). 55 million people affected by extreme weather disasters in 2009. *UNISDR Press Release*, pp. 1–5. Retrieved from http://www.unisdr.org/preventionweb/files/12035_PRUNDPUNISDRWMOCopenhagen 14Dec2009.pdf

U.S. Department of Health, Education, and Welfare (1979). *Healthy people: The surgeon general's report on health promotion and disease prevention* (DHEW PHS Publication No. 79-55071). Washington, DC: Public Health Service, Office of the Assistant Secretary for Health and Surgeon General.

U.S. Department of Health and Human Services. (2000). *Healthy People 2010: Understanding and improving health* (2nd ed.). Washington, DC: U.S. Government Printing Office. Retrieved from http://www.healthypeople.gov/2010/Document/tableofcontents.htm#volume1

U.S. Department of Health and Human Services (2009a). *Healthy People 2020. Health communication and health IT*. Washington, DC: Office of Disease Prevention & Health Promotion. Retrieved from http://www.healthypeople.gov/HP2020/Objectives/TopicArea.aspx?id=25&TopicArea=Health+Communication+and+Health+IT

U.S. Department of Health and Human Services. (2009b). *Healthy People 2020: Public meetings for the 2009 draft objectives*. Washington, DC: U.S. Government Printing Office. Retrieved from http://www.healthypeople.gov/hp2020/Objectives/files/Draft2009Objectives.pdf

U.S. Federal Emergency Management Agency. (2010). *2009 federal disaster declarations*. http://www.fema.gov/news/disasters.fema?year=2009

Vlahov, D., Coady, M. H., Ompad, D. C., & Galea, S. (2007). Strategies for improving influenza immunization rates among hard-to-reach populations. *Journal of Urban Health: Bulletin of the New York Academy of Medicine, 84*(4), 615–631.

Wang, Y., Beydoun, M. A., Liang, L., Caballero, B., & Kumanyika, S. K. (2008). Will all Americans become overweight or obese? Estimating the progression and cost of the US obesity epidemic. *Obesity, 16*(10), 2323–2330.

Weiss, B. D., Mays, M. Z., Martz, W., Castro, K. M., DeWalt, D. A., Pignone, M. P., ... Hale, F. A. (2005). Quick assessment of literacy in primacy care: The newest vital sign. *Annals of Family Medicine, 3*, 514–522.

WHO Collaborating Centre for International Drug Monitoring. (2002). *The importance of pharmacovigilance*. Geneva, Switzerland: World Health Organization.

Williams, D. M. (2009). Preparing pharmacy students and pharmacists to provide tobacco cessation counseling, *Drug and Alcohol Review, 28*(5), 533–540.

Winslow, C. E. A. (1923). *The evolution and significance of the modern public health campaign*. New Haven, CT: Yale University Press.

World Health Organization. (1948). *Preamble to the constitution of the World Health Organization as adopted by the International Health Conference*, New York, NY, June 19–22, 1946.

World Health Organization. (2008). *The top ten causes of death* [Fact sheet No. 310]. Geneva Switzerland: World Health Organization. Retrieved from http://www.who.int/mediacentre/factsheets/fs310_2008.pdf

World Health Organization. (2009). *Global health risks: Mortality and burden of disease attributable to selected major risks*. Geneva, Switzerland: World Health Organization. Retrieved from http://www.who.int/healthinfo/global_burden_disease/GlobalHealthRisks_report_full.pdf

Zarcadoolas, C., Pleasant, A., & Greer, D. S. (2005). Understanding health literacy: An expanded model. *Health Promotion International, 20*(2), 195–203.

Zhao, Z., & Luman, E. T. (2010). Progress toward eliminating disparities in vaccination coverage among U.S. children, 2000–2008. *American Journal of Preventive Medicine, 38*(2), 127–137.

ORGANIZATIONAL ASPECTS OF HEALTHCARE DELIVERY

Hospitals

Catherine N. Otto and William W. McCloskey

Case Scenario

Frank is a 60-year-old retired army officer with a history of hypertension and angina. One evening he complained of a severe tightness in his chest. His wife called 911, and Frank was rushed to the emergency department at a 250-bed community hospital affiliated with a medical school. After evaluation, Frank was admitted to the cardiac care unit for treatment of an acute myocardial infarction.

While Frank was hospitalized, a pharmacist specializing in cardiology introduced herself to him as part of the medical team. The pharmacist explained that one of the drugs for hypertension he was taking before admission was not on the hospital formulary, but that he would be given a very similar medication. Frank also noticed that his medications were prepared in tiny blister packs, not in the prescription vials with which he was familiar.

Upon Frank's discharge, an individual describing himself as a pharmacy resident reviewed with Frank those medications he would be taking at home. After discharge, Frank received follow-up care at the hospital's cardiac clinic.

LEARNING OBJECTIVES

Upon completion of this chapter, the student shall be able to:

- List and describe four factors that have influenced the role and function of the modern hospital
- Summarize how hospitals have adapted to changes in financing of health care and competition
- Compare and contrast horizontal and vertical integration
- Describe how hospitals are classified
- Describe and give examples of general and specialty hospitals; federal and nonfederal government hospitals; nongovernment, not-for-profit, and investor-owned hospitals
- Discuss the three sources of managerial authority in a hospital
- Describe the purpose of hospital accreditation
- Explain the roles and responsibilities of the following professionals: pharmacy director, staff/clinical pharmacist, pharmacy technician
- Explain what unit dose distribution is and describe two advantages of its use

- Compare and contrast centralized and decentralized drug distribution systems
- Describe how automation is utilized to support drug distribution
- Identify four nondistributive pharmacy services provided by a hospital pharmacist
- Define *hospital formulary*
- Summarize the purpose of a pharmacy residency program

CHAPTER QUESTIONS

1. What are the characteristics of hospitals?
2. How have hospitals adapted to changes in the delivery of health care?
3. What types of drug distribution systems are found in hospitals?
4. What is the role of the pharmacist in providing clinical services in the hospital?

INTRODUCTION

Since their origins as charitable institutions, hospitals have adapted to a variety of social, technologic, and political forces to become the center of the healthcare delivery system. This chapter explains how hospitals have evolved over time and discusses the challenges that they face. In addition, it introduces the role of the hospital pharmacist.

HISTORICAL PERSPECTIVE

The role and function of the modern hospital are a result of hospitals' adaptations to a number of significant developments that occurred in the first half of the 20th century. The Flexner report was one of the first factors that imposed a structural change on the hospital. In 1910, Abraham Flexner, funded by the Carnegie Foundation, conducted a survey of all medical schools in the United States and Canada. His evaluation assessed their admissions requirements, curricula, and financial basis and estimated the projected need for physicians and medical schools based on the size of the population. Flexner's recommendations included reducing the number of medical schools from 150 to 31, changing their admissions requirements to a minimum of a baccalaureate degree, and incorporating the scientific method as the foundation for medical education (Meites, 1995).

After the American Medical Association adopted the recommendations of the Flexner report, medical education in the United States was transformed into a system based on the scientific method. The scientific method bases diagnosis and treatment of disease on hypothesis formulation, experimentation, and conclusions. In response, hospitals became teaching and research centers for the practice of medicine. As medical practice increasingly came to rely on scientific principles, the use of technology became ever more important to the diagnosis and treatment of disease. It followed that the hospital became a center for technological innovations developed by researchers (see Chapter 1).

Health insurance provided financial stability for hospitals. Before the advent of such insurance, individuals paid for their hospital care with their own resources. Under that financing system, many individuals went without hospital care because it was unaffordable; others who received hospital care found it difficult or impossible to pay their bills. As a consequence, hospitals were at a significant risk for incurring large debts and possibly suffering bankruptcy. Once health insurance became widespread, hospitals no longer had to assume the financial risk and potential losses when patients could not pay their bills. Health insurance created a steady cash flow to hospitals and was critical for the funding of new technologies.

Because health insurance removed the financial barriers to hospital care for patients, the demand for health care increased. That is, health care was no longer limited by the individual's ability to pay. In addition, because health insurance initially covered only inpatient care, it provided a financial incentive to admit patients to the hospital to administer tests and procedures. Many of these admissions were unnecessary—routine diagnostic evaluation could have easily been performed on an outpatient basis. However, the availability of services in the hospital, coupled with the removal of the financial risk with health insurance, increased the demand for hospital beds, hospital services, and health care in the United States.

The Hospital Survey and Construction Act of 1946 (also known as the Hill-Burton Act) is credited with expanding the infrastructure of the healthcare delivery system by creating federal funding sources to build new hospitals, expand and renovate facilities, increase bed capacity, and add emerging technology. This legislation was particularly instrumental in supporting the building of hospitals in rural areas and small cities. Although Hill-Burton was not considered to be successful, it resulted in an increase in the number of beds in many hospitals and the incorporation of new technology, such as that currently used in emergency departments and intensive care units.

Finally, there has been a change in the types of diseases that are prevalent in the U.S. population. During the first half of the 20th century, infectious diseases were the most common types of illnesses warranting healthcare interventions. Because these disease processes were acute, hospitalizations were singular events. With the advent of preventive measures (such as immunizations and antimicrobial agents) and improvement in the water supply and general sanitation, morbidity resulting from infections has declined in recent decades. As a result, chronic diseases are now the most prevalent types of disease. Thus, hospitalizations are no longer singular events. Treatment for chronic diseases requires more than hospital care; it requires a continuum of care including ambulatory, acute, and long-term care.

Each of these factors has contributed to the development and modernization of the hospital and the U.S. healthcare delivery system. Adaptations made in the past continue to affect hospitals' reactions to the social, technological, and political forces.

HOSPITALS IN THE NEW CENTURY

Impact of Diagnosis-Related Groups

Over the years, the hospital adapted its structure and function so that it could remain a viable entity in the healthcare delivery system. The 1980s and 1990s brought dramatic and continuous changes to the hospital environment. One of the first significant events hospital administrators had to contend with was the diagnosis-related group (DRG) payment mechanism for the hospitalization component (Part A) of the Medicare program. Congress instituted DRGs in 1983 as a method to control increases in Medicare spending. Although hospital administrators perceived DRGs and the other prospective payment systems to be a detriment to their facilities' financial success, DRGs actually created new incentives for hospitals and other segments of the healthcare delivery system. Efficiency, utilization review, and evaluation of diagnostic procedures for appropriateness became important—if not vital—for hospitals to survive. Under the retrospective fee-for-service payment method, providers had an incentive to perform more procedures and keep patients in the hospital as long as possible. By contrast, the prospective payment mechanism of the DRG program created new incentives that ran contrary to those under fee-for-service; hospitals were motivated to perform fewer procedures and to discharge patients as quickly as possible. In the past, patients with acute myocardial infarctions like Frank in our case scenario were often hospitalized for several weeks. Under a DRG reimbursement system, uncomplicated myocardial infarction patients are discharged after a few days because reimbursement to the hospital is independent of the services provided or the length of stay.

Hospitals adapted to the shift in the payment mechanism by unbundling—that is, separating out—the services included in the DRG payment scheme. For example, presurgical diagnostic procedures were performed on an outpatient basis instead of as a component of the hospital stay. In addition, the recovery period following surgical procedures was removed from the hospital stay by transferring the patient to a rehabilitation unit or facility. These unbundled services no longer were included in the DRG prospective payment, but were billed separately under the Medicare Part B fee schedule. Thus the Medicare DRG payment mechanism resulted in decreased lengths of stay; it reimbursed only the acute phase of the illness or surgery, leading to higher acuity of inpatients—no longer was there a mixture of patients requiring limited to complex nursing and medical care—and it provided less financial support for uncompensated hospital care—there were fewer opportunities to absorb these costs from the hospital stays requiring less complex medical care.

Competition

By the 1990s, it seemed as if all the forces that had helped to elevate the hospital to the center of the healthcare delivery system had converged to cause its failure. It was as if all of the players and components of the healthcare delivery system underwent radical changes simultaneously, leaving the hospital to adapt by modifying both its structure and its function.

First, following implementation of the DRG payment method, other prospective, capitated (i.e., the provider is paid a fixed amount per capita regardless of the type or number of services delivered) methods of financing health care began replacing the predominant retrospective, fee-for-service form of financing. Second, health insurance companies began adopting the cost-containment mechanisms used in managed care, such as using prior approval mechanisms for hospital admissions and procedures, requiring second opinions for expensive procedures, and using primary care providers as gatekeepers. As a result, the supply of specialty-care providers exceeded demand, and there was a shortage of the primary care clinicians required to implement a managed care type of financing and delivery system. Third, as competition for patients grew fiercer, hospitals began advertising on radio, television, billboards, and in newspapers. Hospitals created special services and programs for targeted populations, such as homelike birthing rooms for maternity patients instead of the aseptic hospital atmosphere of labor and delivery rooms.

Horizontal Integration

Although interhospital competition continued, hospitals began to form affiliations with one another to improve efficiency and to secure better opportunities for purchasing equipment and supplies. Affiliations were created between two or more hospitals; these hospitals combined some services and usually created managerial efficiency by employing one managerial staff for both institutions (Massachusetts Hospital Association, 1995). *Horizontal integration* is the term used to describe these types of affiliations between hospitals. Sometimes the services provided by the two affiliated hospitals were similar. Often each hospital provided one or more services not provided by the other. Frequently, a partnership was formed between a smaller community hospital and a large, urban, tertiary care hospital; the urban hospital provided sophisticated technological procedures not available in the community hospital.

Vertical Integration

In addition to integrating horizontally, hospitals began to integrate vertically. An organization is vertically integrated when it provides a continuum of services. Hospitals began to expand to offer services other than acute care, such as outpatient services, home health care, rehabilitation services, and nursing home care (Massachusetts Hospital Association, 1995). Vertically integrated hospitals did not have to depend solely on the declining revenues from acute care. For example, in the chapter-opening case study, the hospital was able to participate in Frank's care postdischarge because it had an outpatient cardiac clinic. Further, by integrating vertically, hospitals were prepared to provide managed care organizations with a variety of services.

Hospitals responded to social, political, and technological forces by integrating their acute care services with other services in the delivery of health care. Reactions to these driving forces provided an unintended benefit, as hospitals undergoing vertical integration laid the foundation of a structure for providing a continuum of care—an integrated healthcare delivery system—and perhaps the model to weather the economic storm that ensued due to the recession that began in 2008.

ECONOMIC RECESSION

Health care was not immune to effects of the recession that began in 2008, as hospitals dealt with a decline in revenue, charitable donations, and the value of their financial reserves (Health Forum, 2009). As the unemployment rate increased in 2009, hospitals saw declines in elective procedures, along with an increase in patients covered by Medicaid, programs for low-income populations, and uncompensated care. Almost all administrators (87%) responded to these changes in their organizations by cutting administrative expenses, reducing staff and services, and employing other methods to maintain viability (Health Forum, 2009).

HOSPITAL CHARACTERISTICS

Hospitals are classified by length of stay, type of service provided, and ownership. Given that these classifications are not mutually exclusive, all three categories are used to classify a hospital (Health Forum, 2009). A number of other characteristics that do not fit neatly into these three categories are also used in the literature to describe hospitals—for example, community/noncommunity hospitals, teaching/nonteaching hospitals, number of beds, and multihospital chains.

Length of Stay

Classifying hospitals by the average length of stay differentiates hospitals that provide acute care from those that provide long-term care. Acute care hospitals (also referred to as short-term hospitals) have an average length of stay of fewer than 30 days. Long-term hospitals have an average length of stay of 30 or more days (Health Forum, 2009). State and local government community hospitals have a higher average length of stay—6.3 days in 2008—than investor-owned community hospitals—5.3 days reported for 2008 (Health Forum, 2009).

Type of Service

Hospitals are also classified by the type of service provided. General hospitals provide a variety of services, including general medical and surgical services. Well-known general hospitals include the Massachusetts General Hospital and the San Francisco General Hospital Medical Center. Specialty hospitals, by contrast, concentrate on one disease process (e.g., psychiatric diseases or cancer) or on one segment of the population (e.g., children's hospitals or veterans' hospitals). Noted specialty hospitals include McLean Hospital, a psychiatric hospital in Massachusetts; Memorial Sloan-Kettering Cancer Center in New York; and Shriners Hospitals for Children, located in many cities throughout the country.

Ownership

Hospitals are further characterized by their ownership and control—federal government, nonfederal government (both also referred to as public hospitals), nongovernment and not-for-profit, and nongovernment and investor owned (for-profit) (Health Forum, 2009).

The federal government operates a number of hospitals for specific populations, including veterans, military personnel, and Native Americans. Examples of hospitals under the jurisdiction of the federal government include Veterans Affairs Medical Centers throughout the nation and the Walter Reed Army Medical Center in Washington, D.C.

Nonfederal government hospitals include hospitals owned and operated by city, county, or state governments. Most nonfederal government hospitals are general hospitals. State governments are primarily responsible for specialty care provided in psychiatric hospitals and caring for patients with mental disabilities.

Nongovernment-owned hospitals are divided into two groups: (1) not-for-profit (nonprofit) hospitals and (2) investor-owned (for-profit) hospitals. A number of differences exist between a nonprofit and a for-profit hospital, but the primary difference concerns what the organization does with any excess revenues at the end of the fiscal year. A nonprofit organization reinvests its excess revenues in the organization, usually in the form of capital, new equipment, remodeling, or new buildings. A for-profit organization uses its excess revenues in a similar manner; however, a portion of the excess is paid to the organization's investors in the form of a dividend. Nonprofit hospitals include those operated by the government, religious organizations, and other community hospitals.

Community Hospitals

Hospitals are described as either community or noncommunity hospitals. Community hospitals, such as the one to which Frank was admitted, include all nonfederal hospitals, short-term general, and specialty hospitals that are available to the public (Health Forum, 2009). Noncommunity hospitals are not open to the general public; they include federal hospitals for military personnel and the Veterans Affairs (VA) medical centers. Because Frank was a veteran of the armed services, he would have been eligible to go to a Veterans Affairs medical center if one was available in his area.

Teaching Hospitals

Hospitals are also classified as teaching or nonteaching hospitals. The designation of teaching hospital refers to the teaching and practice of medicine (Raffel & Raffel, 1989). Although a hospital may serve as a clinical training site for students in pharmacy, nursing, clinical laboratory, and any of the other allied health professions, it is not considered a teaching hospital unless it serves as a clinical training site for physicians. A teaching hospital may be expressly associated with a medical school, or it may have an affiliation with a medical school, serving as a site for physicians' residencies.

A teaching hospital can also be classified in another way, such as a community hospital—Frank received his medical care in this type of hospital. A teaching hospital can be a nonprofit, general, community hospital, such as Massachusetts General Hospital, or it can be a federal, general, teaching hospital, such as the many Veterans Affairs medical centers.

Number of Beds

American hospitals typically have fewer than 200 beds; indeed, 72.0% of U.S. hospitals fit this criterion (Health Forum, 2009). Larger hospitals are found in major urban areas, whereas smaller hospitals are found in the rural sections of the country.

Multihospital Chains

Multihospital systems emerged as a response to the changes in the healthcare environment in the 1990s, and their growth continues today. Systems of hospitals are created through mergers, acquisitions, or other legal arrangements. Multihospital systems are frequently national in scope, with hospitals being located in one or more geographic areas of the country. Not only do these national multihospital systems gain purchasing power with vendors, but they also have an advantage when competing for managed care contracts for businesses located in more than one state. Hospital Corporation of America is an example of a large multihospital system.

HOSPITAL MANAGEMENT

The following three sources of managerial authority and power exist in the hospital: the board of trustees, the hospital administration, and the medical staff.

The primary source of authority is the board of directors (in for-profit hospitals) or trustees (in nonprofit hospitals). The board is composed of members of the community who often have knowledge and skills specific to healthcare delivery. Its purpose is to determine the mission and goals of the hospital and to develop policies. It delegates more specific duties to the other two sources of managerial authority—the hospital administration and the medical staff (Raffel & Raffel, 1989).

Daily operations are the responsibility of hospital administration. The hospital administrator or chief executive officer is either a physician or an individual with an advanced degree in health administration or business. The hospital administration is responsible for implementing the policies developed by the board of trustees. The hospital management structure is usually a pyramid-like structure in which managers of departments report to assistants to the hospital administrator, who then report to the hospital administrator.

The medical staff is composed of staff physicians and community-based physicians who have staff privileges to admit and treat patients in the hospital. The medical staff is a self-governing body responsible for the quality of the medical services provided to hospitalized patients.

The organizational structure of hospitals follows the function or service provided. Direct patient care services include nursing, emergency department, urgent care, ambulatory care, surgery, and labor and delivery. Ancillary services include pharmacy, laboratory, and diagnostic imaging. Support services include housekeeping, dietary, laundry, purchasing, materials management, and security.

AMERICAN HOSPITAL ASSOCIATION

The American Hospital Association, founded in 1898, is composed of hospitals, healthcare systems and networks, and individuals. Its purpose is to provide education and resource material, collect statistics regarding its members, conduct research, and represent the point of view of hospitals in the legislative process (AHA, 2010).

HOSPITAL ACCREDITATION

The American College of Surgeons developed the first hospital standards in 1918. Those standards required hospitals to offer laboratory and radiology services for diagnostic purposes, to hold medical staff meetings to review clinical practices, and to maintain medical records (Roberts, Coale, & Redman, 1987).

The Joint Commission is a national organization founded in 1951 by the American Medical Association, American Hospital Association, American College of Physicians, and American College of Surgeons. Its purpose is to set standards and to subsequently accredit hospitals based on those standards. It accredits approximately 17,000 healthcare organizations and programs internationally and in the United States (Joint Commission, 2011b). In addition to the four founding organizations, the American Dental Association is represented on its board of commissioners. The Joint Commission accredits more than hospitals; it also accredits behavioral health facilities, long-term care facilities, office-based surgery organizations, home care organizations, ambulatory care facilities, and laboratory services (Joint Commission, 2011b).

Joint Commission accreditation is based on voluntary compliance with the standards. However, that accreditation has become critical for fulfilling state licensure requirements and is essential for receiving reimbursement in the Medicare and Medicaid programs.

The Joint Commission's mission is to improve the quality of health care in the United States. Its initial standards focused on the structure and the processes of healthcare delivery. However, as the environment of the healthcare delivery system changed, the Joint Commission changed the focus of its standards to include clinical processes and outcomes of care. Accreditation is earned after an evaluation of the organization's compliance with appropriate standards based upon an unannounced on-site inspection that traces care delivered to patients, as well as specific documents supporting compliance with standards (Joint Commission, 2011a).

THE FUTURE OF HOSPITALS

Predicting the future of hospitals is difficult and perhaps foolish. However, considering the continuing trend of healthcare cost containment, the focus on outcomes of services delivered, and the results of the Patient Protection and Affordable Care Act of 2010, some directions for change can be anticipated. Hospitals will continue to try to provide state-of-the-art services and technology while operating within limited budgets. This balancing act will be coupled with greater use of healthcare services resulting from the aging of the American population. Limited hospital budgets will likely be exacerbated by changes in the reimbursement policies of Medicare, Medicaid, and managed care organizations (Institute for the Future, 2003).

As more individuals seek health care, an increasing percentage of that care will be delivered in an outpatient setting. To contend with this trend, hospitals will continue to diversify their services, to operate clinics, and to offer other diagnostic and therapeutic services on an outpatient basis.

The change in the pattern of the delivery of care and budgets limited by capitated reimbursement policies will probably precipitate more hospital closures and mergers. To remain viable, hospitals will compete for managed care contracts, physicians, and patients.

One can expect that the trends that affected hospitals in the 1990s will become even more significant in the 21st century, as the U.S. population continues to age. Hospitals, along with the entire healthcare delivery system, must continue to adapt and evolve.

THE PHARMACIST'S ROLE IN A HOSPITAL-BASED PRACTICE

Most hospital pharmacies have an organizational structure that consists of a director of pharmacy, an associate or assistant director, pharmacy managers or supervisors, and pharmacists with clinical and/or distributive responsibilities. Depending on the size of the department, some pharmacists may be solely dedicated to providing clinical services in a specialized area such as infectious diseases or critical care. In addition to professional personnel, the pharmacy department includes technical and support staff who may assist with product preparation, distribution, and purchasing.

Director of Pharmacy

Based on what is expected of this position, the director of pharmacy has one of the most complex jobs within the hospital (Nold & Sander, 2004). The director of pharmacy must satisfy a variety of leadership and management responsibilities, including overseeing both personnel and department budget issues. The director justifies and develops job descriptions for new pharmacy positions and generally manages the recruitment and interview process.

A major challenge facing hospital pharmacy directors today is managing the drug budget in the face of escalating medication costs. While a formulary system (as described later in the chapter) may help control costs, it is often difficult to anticipate how the cost of a new drug will affect the overall drug budget. The inability to contain drug budget costs may have a negative impact on the personnel budget and result in the loss of existing positions or failure to get approval for new ones.

In addition to leadership and fiscal responsibilities, the director often serves as the department representative on a number of multidisciplinary hospital committees. The director is also responsible for setting quality standards for the department, especially those concerning medication safety, evaluating policies and procedures, implementing new programs, and ensuring compliance with regulating agencies such as the Joint Commission, Department of Public Health, and Board of Registration in Pharmacy.

In hospitals with larger pharmacy departments, an associate or assistant director may assist the director with these responsibilities. In addition, managers or supervisors may be responsible for specific areas of the department such as sterile product formulation, outpatient services, or clinical services (Abramowitz & Mork, 1992). By comparison, in smaller hospitals, the pharmacy director may have to provide some staffing as well. Such directors are often referred to as working directors. In some very small institutions (fewer than 50 beds), the director may be the only full-time pharmacist and would be generally supported by part-time or per-diem personnel.

Staff and Clinical Pharmacists

The staff and clinical pharmacists provide the daily distributive and clinical services for the department of pharmacy. Since many hospital pharmacists provide a combination of both distributive and clinical services, they may not be characterized as either a staff pharmacist or a clinical pharmacist. However, some institutions may still use these terms to distinguish pharmacists whose primary responsibility may be in one area or the other. Staff pharmacists are generally more involved with routine pharmacy operations (e.g., order entry/verification, checking medication carts, sterile product preparation), and they supervise the activities of the technicians and other support staff who help with these activities. Clinical pharmacists are generally more involved with patient-care-related activities, including rounding with medical teams, obtaining medication histories, providing discharge counseling, managing adverse drug reaction programs, and responding to drug information inquiries. Job satisfaction among hospital pharmacists has been shown to be directly correlated with the number of clinical activities that one performs. Both clinical pharmacists and those with more integrated functions report being more satisfied than staff pharmacists do (Kerschen, Armstrong, & Hillman, 2006).

Because hospitals operate 24 hours a day, 7 days a week, an appropriate number of professional staff must be available to provide continuous pharmaceutical services when the pharmacy is not open. Joint Commission standards require that a qualified pharmacist be on call or available at another institution to answer questions or provide any medications that are not readily accessible to nonpharmacist personnel (Joint Commission on Accreditation of Healthcare Organizations, 2011). The Joint Commission also mandates that only pharmacists should be allowed into a pharmacy after it is closed; nurses or other nonpharmacist personnel should not be able to gain access to the pharmacy to secure medications after hours.

Joint Commission standards also require that a pharmacist review all medication orders before they are dispensed unless a licensed independent practitioner (e.g., a physician) controls the ordering, preparation, and administration of the order, or if a delay would result in patient harm. If a pharmacist is not available 24 hours a day, then a qualified healthcare professional (e.g., a nurse) must review the order and a pharmacist must conduct a retrospective review as soon as he or she is available (Joint Commission on Accreditation of Healthcare Organizations, 2011).

Technical and Support Staff

The technical personnel of a hospital pharmacy department comprise pharmacy technicians. These personnel have received special training in drug distribution, either from the hospital or from a school, such as a community college, that offers technician training programs. Pharmacy students who are fulfilling internship requirements may perform some of the tasks of a technician. Under the supervision of the pharmacist, technicians perform many of the distribution functions within the pharmacy department such as filling unit-dose cassettes, preparing intravenous admixtures, and monitoring and restocking inventory within the pharmacy and on the nursing stations.

Two national voluntary technician certification programs have been established. These include the Exam for the Certification of Pharmacy Technicians, sponsored by the Institute for the Certification of Pharmacy Technicians, and the Pharmacy Technician Certification Exam, sponsored by the Pharmacy Technician Certification Board. Certification encourages technicians to expand their knowledge and skill base, and it provides technicians with formal national recognition of their training (Murer, 1996). The expanding role of the technician allows the pharmacist to concentrate on more direct patient care or clinical activities (see Chapter 3). In the case scenario, a technician was most likely responsible for initially preparing Frank's medications, which were then checked by the pharmacist.

In addition to technicians, the support staff of the pharmacy department may include clerical personnel and individuals responsible for inventory management.

RESPONSIBILITIES OF THE HOSPITAL PHARMACY

The hospital pharmacy is responsible for the safe and effective use of drug therapy for the entire institution. Its duties include drug product selection, procurement, and distribution. The pharmacy is also responsible for ensuring that medications are prescribed appropriately and that guidelines for proper drug administration are followed (Black & Nelson, 1992).

DRUG DISTRIBUTION SYSTEMS

Floor-Stock Distribution

Floor-stock distribution was the method of drug distribution for many years. This system involved supplying the nursing staff units with a predetermined number of dosage forms, which were stored in a separate drug room in each patient care area. Nurses dispensed the medications to any number of patients from this supply, and then they reordered from the pharmacy as needed.

Two major problems have been identified with floor-stock distribution. First, the pharmacist did not have the opportunity to review the physician's order for accuracy or potential drug interactions before the medication was administered to the patient. Second, the pharmacist did not have the chance to review the patient's profile to monitor drug therapy for safety and efficacy.

Although floor-stock distribution may sometimes still be used to provide bulk supplies such as powders, some basic intravenous solutions (e.g., D5W and normal saline), and selected emergency medications, the unit-dose distribution system is now the standard distribution system in hospitals.

Unit-Dose Distribution

The unit-dose distribution system was developed in the mid-1960s to encourage the pharmacist to become more actively involved in the patient's drug therapy (Barker & Heller, 1963). A recent survey of 1,310 hospital pharmacy directors at general and children's medical-surgical hospitals in the United States indicated that in noncritical care patients, 87% of the hospitals dispensed a majority of oral doses as unit doses and 70% of hospitals dispensed a majority of parenteral doses as unit doses (Pederson, Schneider, & Scheckelhoff, 2009).

The unit-dose distribution system consists of two key elements. First, a pharmacist reviews all physicians' orders for appropriateness and potential drug interactions before medications are dispensed. Second, medications are dispensed in unit doses, where each dose of medication is separately packaged and labeled with the drug name, strength, lot number, and expiration date in a ready-to-administer form (like the one that Frank received). Products may be purchased in unit-dose forms or repackaged from bulk dosage forms. While most hospitals report purchasing unit-dose products when commercially available, approximately 30% repackage oral medications and around 7% repackage parenteral medication, mainly for cost savings (Pederson et al., 2009). To increase patient safety, the practice of sending a medication to a patient care area that requires manipulation on the part of nurses (e.g., preparing intravenous doses from vials, splitting tablets) has declined over recent years and is reported more commonly in hospitals with fewer than 50 beds (Pederson et al., 2009).

With the unit-dose distribution system, each patient has an assigned drawer that is typically filled with a 24-hour supply of medication. For instance, if a patient is getting a medication every 8 hours, three doses of the drug would be supplied in that person's drawer. Patients' drawers are part of a medication cart for a specific patient care area; the drawers are exchanged at a predetermined time every day so they can be replenished by the pharmacy. In manual unit-dose distribution systems, the medication fill process is generally performed by a technician and verified by a pharmacist, although some hospitals use technicians to check other technicians (Woller, Stuart, Vrabel & Senst, 1991). Approximately 10% of hospitals have a robotic distribution system that automates the cart fill process, with larger hospitals being more likely to rely on such technology than smaller hospitals. Use of this technology has steadily increased over the past few years, indicating that the benefits are considered worth its relatively high cost (Pederson et al., 2009).

For new orders or medication changes, an alternative delivery system must be used to ensure that patients get their medication in a timely fashion. Either the pharmacy or another department is responsible for regular medication delivery to patient care areas.

A majority of hospitals (83%) surveyed reported using automated dispensing systems (Pederson et al., 2009). Automated dispensing systems are drug storage devices that can be used to electronically dispense stat. doses of medications or doses in the absence of routine unit dose deliveries. Those automated dispensing systems devices, such as those manufactured by Pyxis Technologies, which are available in patient care areas, interface with the pharmacy computer and dispense medications after the pharmacist reviews the order. Most of these devices require user identifiers and passwords and track usage information for billing purposes. These systems offer some potential advantages over traditional, manually processed cart exchange methods and stat. deliveries, including reduced drug delivery time and better inventory control. These devices also provide emergency doses of medications in the absence of 24-hour pharmacy services. If Frank had required an emergency medication for his heart condition, that drug would have been readily available in the cardiac care unit. Automated dispensing systems may also free up the pharmacist to engage in more patient-care–related activities.

The advantages of the unit-dose system include fewer medication errors, because the pharmacist reviews the medication order before dispensing. In addition, inventory costs are reduced by significantly cutting back on floor-stock supplies. However, labor costs are higher because more personnel are required to fill unit-dose drawers. In addition, sometimes it is necessary to prepare medication in unit doses that are not commercially available. Another drawback to the unit-dose system is the potential for delays in getting the medication to patients, although the increased use of automated dispensing systems makes some drugs now more readily available. In addition, certain drugs used in emergency situations, such as cardiac arrest, are available for immediate access at the patient's bedside as part of an emergency kit or crash cart, which is located on the nursing unit. Despite minor limitations, the unit-dose system remains the preferred drug distribution system owing to its potential for enhancing patient care and controlling drug costs by reducing waste.

CENTRALIZED VERSUS DECENTRALIZED PHARMACY SERVICES

Hospital pharmacy services may be provided either from a centralized area or from two or more satellite locations. These are not mutually exclusive and some hospitals incorporate a combination of both types of services.

Centralized pharmacy services originate from a single location within the hospital. This scheme is the distribution system most commonly utilized by hospital pharmacies, although the percentage of hospitals using a more decentralized system has increased from 19% in 2002 to 33% in 2008 (Pederson et al., 2009). Because all pharmacy services are provided from a single location, fewer professional and technical resources are required than with decentralized services (John, Burkhart, & Lamy, 1976). In addition, inventory remains more consolidated, which reduces overall drug and supply costs. Survey data indicate that the use of a particular type of distribution system is dependent on the number of beds in the facility, with centralized drug distribution systems being more common in smaller hospitals than in larger ones (Pederson et al., 2009).

Some hospital pharmacies provide pharmacy services from satellite locations in patient care areas or specialized areas, such as the operating room or emergency department. At a minimum, these decentralized services perform first-dose dispensing and pharmacist order review. Most satellites are supported by a centralized pharmacy that generally fills medication carts and performs other distributive functions. For example, Frank's first doses were provided from a satellite pharmacy in the cardiology unit to which he was admitted, but all subsequent doses were prepared in the central pharmacy. Decentralized services offer the primary advantage of having a pharmacist's presence in a patient care area, such as the pharmacist Frank encountered who specialized in cardiology. The major drawbacks of decentralization are the duplication of inventory and the additional professional and technical personnel needed to staff satellites, which increase the overall costs. However, despite some limitations, a recent survey found that more pharmacy directors are now more likely to consider decentralized systems than they were in the past (Pederson et al., 2009).

Whether centralized or decentralized, some initiatives related to drug distribution systems are used to increase medication safety in hospitals. One method that has been shown to reduce adverse reactions due to medication errors is the use of computerized prescriber order entry (Wietholter, Sitterson, & Allison, 2009). However, according to a recent survey by the Leapfrog Group, an initiative to improve the quality of health care in the United States, only 7% of hospitals met the standard for this criterion, which includes having at least 75% of orders entered through a computerized prescriber order entry system (Leapfrog Group, 2008). Most hospitals' pharmacies still receive copies of handwritten medication orders or orders via digital image capture or fax. Larger hospitals are far more likely to have computerized prescriber order entry than smaller hospitals (Pederson, Schneider, & Scheckelhoff, 2008). Although computerized prescriber order entry may enhance patient care by reducing medication errors, the cost of development, implementation, and operation of such a system may be cost prohibitive for many institutions (Wietholter et al., 2009).

Bar coding is another technology that can be used to scan and verify the correct patient and medication before the patient receives it in order to prevent serious administration errors. Although survey data report that this technology is currently utilized by only about 25% of hospitals, most hospitals report they planned to implement bar code–assisted medication administration in the near future (Pederson et al., 2009).

INTRAVENOUS ADMIXTURE SERVICES

Pharmacy personnel often prepare sterile dosage forms of medications. This requires special training in aseptic technique to ensure product integrity and to reduce infectious complications. Hospitals and other organizations that compound sterile products must be in compliance with more rigorous standards set by the *U.S. Pharmacopeia* (USP Chapter <797>). These FDA and Joint Commission–enforceable standards hold pharmacies more accountable for sterile products they compound and define how all these products should be prepared based on risk level. The risk level—low, medium, or high—is determined by factors such as how many manipulations are involved in compounding the final product and whether it is prepared from sterile or nonsterile ingredients (United States Pharmacopeial Convention, 2004).

Intravenous admixture services include the preparation of large-volume parenteral medications such as parenteral nutrition solutions and electrolyte replacement preparations (e.g., potassium chloride infusions), as well as small-volume parenteral medications such as antibiotics. Hospital pharmacies generally maintain special, environmentally controlled facilities, such as a clean room or laminar flow workbenches, in which to prepare sterile products. Such facilities are designed not only to protect the product from contamination, but also to protect the person preparing the product from potential exposure to hazardous or toxic products (e.g., chemotherapy). Some hospital pharmacies outsource bulk compounding of parenteral solutions (e.g., parenteral nutrition solutions) to an agency that specializes in sterile product preparations if this approach is more cost effective (Gates, Smolarek, & Stevenson, 1996). During his hospitalization, Frank required several large-volume intravenous solutions that were prepared by the pharmacy department in compliance with USP Chapter <797>.

NONDISTRIBUTIVE PHARMACY SERVICES

Drug Therapy Monitoring

In addition to being responsible for drug distribution, hospital pharmacists provide a wide variety of direct patient care services. The focus of most clinical pharmacy practice is drug therapy monitoring, to promote the safe and effective use of medications within the institution. Drug therapy monitoring involves verifying drug, dose, and route of administration and monitoring for medication-related problems to optimize drug therapy. By conducting admission and discharge drug histories, pharmacists also help resolve any discrepancies in what a patient may have been receiving before admission as compared to the admitting orders and any differences in the discharge orders as compared to what the patient may have been receiving while hospitalized. This is known as medication reconciliation and is now mandated by the Joint Commission. Some pharmacists, like Frank's cardiology specialist, routinely participate in patient care rounds with the medical staff to assess the patients' status and provide point-of-care input into the patients' therapy. During these rounds, the pharmacist has the opportunity to provide input on drug therapy before an order is written. A multidisciplinary approach for myocardial infarction patients such as Frank has been shown to improve patient care (Coons & Fera, 2007).

Given the cost constraints so prevalent in health care, pharmacists must consider both the fiscal implications and the clinical impact of each drug order. For example, can a less expensive therapeutic alternative be prescribed, or can the patient receive the medication orally rather than intravenously? During his hospitalization, Frank's cardiology pharmacist was able to suggest a more cost-effective oral antiplatelet therapy for him.

In-Service Education

Pharmacists serve as a valuable drug therapy resource to physicians, nurses, and other healthcare personnel within the hospital. They may also counsel patients on their medications before discharge or in the ambulatory clinics of the institution. Pharmacists often provide in-service education programs on issues related to drug therapy to physicians, nurses, and other interested parties. To support these educational endeavors, hospital pharmacies may publish a newsletter to help update the hospital community on a new drug, pharmacy service, or other related topic.

Medication-Utilization Evaluation

Medication-utilization evaluation (MUE) is a multidisciplinary quality assurance program that was incorporated into the Joint Commission's standards in 1992. Current standards do not require a specific method be used, but rather focus on the quality improvement aspect of MUE (Joint Commission on Accreditation of Healthcare Organizations, 2011).

MUE programs objectively evaluate the use of selected drugs in the hospital by comparing them to specific criteria established for these medications, including medication-related activities such as dispensing and administration. MUE criteria typically include justification for use, monitoring parameters that should be followed, and outcome measures to determine efficacy. Results of the MUE are reviewed, opportunities for improvement are noted, and corrective actions are taken to improve drug use.

MUE programs may focus on a specific medication, a particular class of medications, or an outcome or a component of the medication use process. Drugs may be selected for MUE because of their potential risk if used inappropriately or because of their high cost compared to alternative therapies. For example, inappropriate use of an expensive antibiotic may not only increase overall drug costs to the institution but also could result in the development of drug-resistant pathogens. The pharmacy department may dictate which medications should undergo MUE (e.g., expensive medications or potentially toxic drugs) and work in collaboration with other healthcare disciplines to establish the criteria for their use.

In addition to performing data collection and analysis, the pharmacy may direct the efforts to correct any deficiencies in drug use found during the MUE process. Such efforts may include in-service educational programs and pharmacy newsletters.

ADVERSE-DRUG-REACTION MONITORING

Adverse-drug-reaction monitoring is another quality assurance activity in which the pharmacy department participates. The major focus of adverse-drug-reaction monitoring is the reduction of preventable adverse drug reactions within the hospital. Suspected adverse drug reactions are reviewed by the pharmacy to determine the likelihood of an untoward event from a medication. In addition, the pharmacy can alert the medical staff to adverse drug reactions that may be associated with drugs that have recently been made available within the hospital.

Specialized Clinical Pharmacy Services

Pharmacists may specialize in an area of practice such as infectious diseases, nutrition support, critical care, or cardiology, such as the pharmacist on Frank's medical team. These specialists are responsible for monitoring drug therapy in a more selective patient population. For example, the infectious disease specialist may focus his or her efforts on appropriate antibiotic selection; the critical care pharmacist may be responsible for patients in the medical or surgical intensive care units of the hospital; the nutrition support specialist may monitor patients receiving parenteral nutrition; and the cardiology specialist may be responsible for monitoring anticoagulation therapy.

Certification or credentialing in the area of specialization may be strongly encouraged or required for pharmacists in these positions (see Chapter 3).

Some specialized clinical pharmacy services are provided as part of a formal consultation service, and the clinical activity is performed following the written order of a physician. Pharmacokinetic consultation services are provided by many hospital pharmacies to optimize therapy using serum drug concentrations. In some cases, pharmacies may be reimbursed by third parties for such consultation services.

Although all pharmacists are responsible for providing basic drug information, some hospitals have established formal drug information services. However, the number of formal hospital and university drug information centers has decreased over the past several years. This may be due to the fact that the entry-level PharmD degree has better prepared pharmacists to answer drug information questions, and the availability of electronic databases and the Internet has made drug information easier to obtain for both healthcare professionals and the lay public (Rosenberg, Schilit, Nathan, Zerilli, & McGuire, 2009).

HOSPITAL FORMULARY SYSTEM

The purpose of a hospital formulary system is to help ensure appropriate drug therapy and control drug costs. The drug budget can represent a significant amount of a hospital's budget, with recent estimates of pharmaceuticals accounting for more than $27 billion of the total nonfederal hospital spending of nearly $650 billion (Hoffman et al., 2009). The formulary itself is only one component of the overall system. The formulary is a "continually revised compilation of pharmaceuticals that reflects the current clinical judgment of the medical staff" (American Society of Hospital Pharmacists [ASHP], 1983, p. 1384). Whereas the formulary is essentially a list of medications and related products or devices routinely stocked in the pharmacy, the formulary system involves the overall process of evaluating and selecting medications to be included in the formulary. Consequently, only certain representatives of a class of drugs may be available. The decision to add or delete a drug from the formulary is based on the relative clinical benefit and cost of the medication as compared to other agents within a similar therapeutic class, or to nonpharmacotherapeutic options such as surgery.

In a hospital with a closed formulary system, physicians are directed to prescribe only those agents that are on the formulary unless the patient's medical condition dictates that a nonformulary drug is necessary. The prescriber typically has to document the reason why the alternative drug is required before the pharmacy will obtain it. As was the situation with Frank, nonformulary drugs are not routinely available within such a system and a therapeutically equivalent agent may need to be substituted for it. Therapeutic interchange is generally authorized based on previously established guidelines and allows the pharmacist to substitute an appropriate formulary equivalent without having to contact the prescriber (Tyler et al., 2008). Under an open formulary system, although physicians are encouraged to prescribe formulary drugs, nonformulary medications are generally more readily available.

The advisory group that manages the formulary system is commonly called the pharmacy and therapeutics committee. The pharmacy and therapeutics committee is a multidisciplinary committee made up of members of the medical, pharmacy, and nursing departments, as well as administrators and other individuals who are involved with medication use within the hospital. Pharmacy members generally include the director of pharmacy, who often is responsible for setting the committee agenda, and a drug information or other clinical pharmacist, who prepares an evidence-based, objective review of each agent requested for addition to the formulary. This review is presented to pharmacy and therapeutics committee members along with background material provided by the individual requesting the drug for formulary addition. The pharmacist's review provides an impartial perspective of the requested drug's potential benefits as compared to similar medications.

Some agents may be added to the formulary on a conditional basis; these drugs are reevaluated after a period of time to determine whether they should remain on the formulary based on clinical experience with the drug. In some cases, a drug may be added with restriction, meaning that the agent may be prescribed only by selected individuals. For example, an infectious disease specialist may have to approve an order for certain antibiotics before the pharmacy can distribute these drugs. Such restrictions usually apply to drugs that are very expensive or whose potential risks warrant that they be prescribed only by physicians who are very familiar with their appropriate use.

PURCHASING AND INVENTORY CONTROL

The pharmacy department is primarily responsible for drug management in the hospital, including purchasing and inventory control. Once the formulary status of a drug is determined, the decision regarding the brand of product acquired is ultimately made by the pharmacy; factors such as quality of manufacturer, cost, and dosage forms available all play a role in this decision.

Group Purchasing Agreements

Many hospitals participate in group purchasing agreements. Under such agreements, hospitals can collaborate with other institutions to negotiate more favorable pricing with pharmaceutical manufacturers.

Investigational Drugs

The pharmacy is also responsible for controlling the use of investigational drugs within the hospital. The pharmacist must be knowledgeable about investigational protocols being used within the hospital, including drug information, pharmaceutical data, record-keeping procedures, and proper administration techniques. In institutions that conduct a great deal of drug-related research, a specific investigational drug pharmacist is often responsible for coordinating these activities.

RESIDENCY PROGRAMS

A pharmacy residency is an organized, directed, postgraduate training program designed to develop competencies in a defined area of pharmacy practice (Lazarus & Letendre, 1992). Most residency programs last 12 months and are referred to as PGY1 (postgraduate year 1) residency training. Unlike undergraduate training programs such as internships, a residency is designed to develop skills beyond those required by the state board of pharmacy for licensure. A residency is distinguished from a fellowship, another type of postgraduate program, by its preparation of the pharmacist for practice rather than independent research (see Chapter 3). Pharmacy residents typically engage in patient-care–related activities, such as counseling Frank from the chapter-opening case scenario on his discharge medications.

Some residency programs may offer training at an advanced level or specialized level (e.g., infectious diseases, cardiology) and are referred to as PGY2 programs. These programs require that the trainee complete a PGY1 program first.

In response to an increased need for qualified hospital pharmacy practitioners, the American Society of Hospital Pharmacists (ASHP) established the first accredited postgraduate training program in 1962 (Lazarus & Letendre, 1992). The ASHP (now the American Society of Health-System Pharmacists) program was the first to assess compliance with minimal standards for postgraduate training by an external review process. Programs that are ASHP accredited have been reviewed by a team of individuals from outside the hospital who determine whether the institution complies with the minimal training standards established by the ASHP.

If someone is interested in pursuing a career in hospital pharmacy, doing a residency is strongly suggested. In fact, both ASHP and the American College of Clinical Pharmacy have recommended that by 2020, all pharmacy graduates complete PGY1 residency training before they can practice in an area involving direct patient care. Whether there will be sufficient residency programs available by that date to meet this goal has yet to be determined (Knapp, Shah, Kim, & Tran, 2009).

CONCLUSION

The changing healthcare environment presents significant challenges as well as opportunities for hospitals. Those institutions that adapt most quickly to these changes will position themselves more favorably to succeed in the future. Pharmacists play a significant role in the delivery of health care within the institutional setting. Individuals who wish to practice in the hospital may be advised to pursue postgraduate training experience.

QUESTIONS FOR FURTHER DISCUSSION

1. Describe the hospital of the future. Will hospitals exist as they are currently configured?
2. What role should hospitals play in the continuum of care?
3. What opportunities will be available in the future for hospital pharmacists? Will their roles expand?
4. How will automation affect drug delivery and the pharmacist's role in the hospital?

KEY TOPICS AND TERMS

Adverse drug reaction
American Hospital Association
Centralized pharmacy services
Decentralized pharmacy services
Diagnosis-related group (DRG)
Drug therapy monitoring
Floor-stock distribution
Formulary
Horizontal integration
Joint Commission
Length of stay
Medication use evaluation (MUE)
Residency program
Unit-dose distribution
Vertical integration

REFERENCES

Abramowitz, P. W., & Mork, L. A. (1992). The hospital and the department of pharmaceutical services. In T. R. Brown (Ed.), *Handbook of institutional pharmacy practice* (3rd ed., pp. 19–29). Bethesda, MD: American Society of Hospital Pharmacists.

American Hospital Association (AHA). (2010). *About the AHA.* Retrieved from http://www.aha.org/aha/about/index.html

American Society of Hospital Pharmacists (ASHP). (1983). American Society of Hospital Pharmacists statement on the operation of the formulary system. *American Journal of Hospital Pharmacy, 40,* 1384–1385.

Barker, K. N., & Heller, W. M. (1963). The development of a centralized unit dose dispensing system. Part one: Description of the UAMC experimental system. *American Journal of Hospital Pharmacy, 20,* 568–579.

Black, H. J., & Nelson, S. P. (1992). Medication distribution systems. In T. R. Brown (Ed.), *Handbook of institutional pharmacy practice* (3rd ed.) (pp. 165–174). Bethesda, MD: American Society of Hospital Pharmacists

Coons, J. C., & Fera, T. (2007) Multidisciplinary team for enhancing care for patients with acute myocardial infarction or heart failure. *American Journal of Health-System Pharmacy, 64,* 1274–1278.

Gates, D. M., Smolarek, R. T., & Stevenson, J. G. (1996). Outsourcing the preparation of parenteral nutrient solutions. *American Journal of Health-System Pharmacy, 53,* 2176–2178.

Health Forum. (2009). *AHA hospital statistics* (2010 ed.). Chicago, IL: Health Forum (American Hospital Association).

Hoffman, J. M., Shah, N. D., Vermeulen, L. C., Doloresco F, Martin P.K., Blake S, ... Schumock G.T. (2009). Projecting future drug expenditures—2009. *American Journal of Health-System Pharmacy, 66,* 237–257.

Institute for the Future. (2003). *Health and health care 2010: The forecase, the challenge* (2nd ed.). San Francisco, CA: Jossey-Bass.

John, G. W., Burkhart, V. D., & Lamy, P. P. (1976). Pharmacy personnel activities and costs in decentralized and centralized unit dose distribution systems. *American Journal of Hospital Pharmacy, 33,* 38–43.

Joint Commission on Accreditation of Healthcare Organizations. (2011). *Comprehensive accreditation manual for hospitals.* Oakbrook Terrace, IL: Joint Commission on Accreditation of Healthcare Organizations.

The Joint Commission. (2011a). *Accreditation process overview.* Retrieved from http://www. jointcommission.org/assets/1/6/Accreditation%20Process%20Overview%2012%20091.pdf

The Joint Commission. (2011b). *Facts about Joint Commission accreditation standards.* Retrieved from http://www.jointcommission.org/assets/1/18/Standards.pdf

Kerschen, A. M., Armstrong, E. P., & Hillman, T. N. (2006). Job satisfaction among staff, clinical, and integrated hospital pharmacists. *Journal of Pharmacy Practice, 9,* 306–312.

Knapp, K. K., Shah, B. M., Kim, H. B., & Tran, H. (2009). Visions for required postgraduate year I residency training by 2020: A comparison of actual versus projected expansion. *Pharmacotherapy, 29,* 1030–1038.

Lazarus, H. L., & Letendre, D. E. (1992). Residency programs in pharmacy practice. In T. R. Brown (Ed.), *Handbook of institutional pharmacy practice* (3rd ed., pp. 39–43). Bethesda, MD: American Society of Hospital Pharmacists.

The Leapfrog Group. *Leapfrog hospital survey results.* Retrieved from http://www.leapfroggroup. org/media/file/leapfrogreportfinal.pdf

Massachusetts Hospital Association. (1995). *Vision 2000: Caring for people into the 21st century.* Burlington, MA: Massachusetts Hospital Association.

Meites, S. (1995). Abraham Flexner's legacy: A magnificent beneficence to American medical education and clinical chemistry. *Clinical Chemistry, 41*(4), 627–632.

Murer, M. M. (1996). Technician certification leads to recognition, better patient care. *Journal of the American Pharmaceutical Association, 36*(8), 514, 519–520.

Nold E. G., & Sander, W. T. (2004). Role of the director of pharmacy: The first six months. *American Journal of Health-System Pharmacy, 61,* 2297–2310.

Pedersen, C. A., Schneider, P. J., & Scheckelhoff, D. J. (2008). ASHP national survey of pharmacy practice in hospital settings: Prescribing and transcribing—2007. *American Journal of Health-System Pharmacy, 65,* 827–843.

Pedersen, C. A., Schneider, P. J., & Scheckelhoff, D. J. (2009). ASHP national survey of pharmacy practice in hospital settings: Dispensing and administration—2008. *American Journal of Health-System Pharmacy, 66,* 926–946.

Raffel, M. W., & Raffel, N. K. (1989). *The U.S. health system: Origins and functions* (3rd ed.). Albany, New York: Delmar.

Roberts, J. S., Coale, J. G., & Redman, R. R. (1987). A history of the Joint Commission on Accreditation of Hospitals. *Journal of the American Medical Association, 258*(7), 936–940.

Rosenberg, J. M., Schilit, S., Nathan, J. P., Zerilli T, & McGuire, H. (2009). Update on the status of 89 drug information centers in the United States. *American Journal of Health-System Pharmacy, 66,* 1718–1722.

Tyler, L. S., Cole, S. W., May, J. R., Millares, M., Valentino, M. A., Lee, C., . . . Wison, A. L. (2008). ASHP guidelines on the pharmacy and therapeutics committee and the formulary system. *American Journal of Health-System Pharmacy, 65,* 1272–1283.

United States Pharmacopeial Convention. (2004). Pharmaceutical considerations—sterile preparations (general information chapter 797). In *The United States pharmacopeia* (26th rev.)/ *National formulary* (22nd ed.) (pp. 2350–2370). Rockville, MD: United States Pharmacopeial Convention, Inc.

Wietholter, J., Sitterson, S., & Allison, S. (2009). Effects of computerized prescriber order entry on pharmacy order-processing time. *American Journal of Health-System Pharmacy, 66,* 1394–1398.

Woller, T. W., Stuart, J. S., Vrabel, R., & Senst, B. (1991). Checking of unit dose cassettes by pharmacy technicians at three Minnesota hospitals. *American Journal of Hospital Pharmacy, 48,* 1952–1956.

CHAPTER

8

Ambulatory Care

David M. Scott

Case Scenario

As a consultant to George, a 45-year-old pharmacist, you have been asked to provide him with some advice about whether he should integrate pharmaceutical care into his community pharmacy practice. Over the past 20 years, George has developed a thriving independent community pharmacy practice in a rural community of 2,000 persons in a Midwestern state. However, the trend toward third-party prescription payment, greater managed care penetration (which is expected to continue in the next 5 years), and an increasing number of prescriptions being transferred to web-based (mail order) pharmacies has created financial difficulties for George's business.

To counter this economic pressure, George is considering developing a pharmaceutical care practice. If he decides to pursue this route, George plans to market the pharmaceutical care program initially to his private-pay patients, and by the 2nd year, to managed care organizations. Common disease states that are most prevalent in George's rural community are diabetes and asthma. George has maintained an adequate level of prescription care, but he realizes that a high-level pharmaceutical care practice does require a major shift in his practice.

What would you advise him to do? When formulating your answer, consider the trends in ambulatory care, the impact that pharmaceutical care has made on community pharmacy practice, and the training and workforce changes that George must incorporate to implement this change in his practice.

LEARNING OBJECTIVES

Upon completion of this chapter, the student shall be able to:

- Explain what is meant by the term ambulatory care
- Describe what settings provide ambulatory care
- Describe the concept of primary care
- Explain how managed care is affecting ambulatory care
- Describe the contributions the Indian Health Service has made in pharmaceutical care
- Describe the use of complementary and alternative medicine in an ambulatory care setting
- Depict the pharmacist's role in ambulatory care

INTRODUCTION

Ambulatory care services have rapidly evolved and expanded since 1980. Managed care has spirited the change away from the inpatient side of hospitals to less costly forms of services provided in the outpatient settings. As costs of health care continue to rise, employers, insurance companies, and policy makers are continually searching for new ways to provide care that maintain quality, yet are accessible and cost effective. This chapter will examine the settings that provide ambulatory care, depict how managed care is affecting ambulatory care, and describe the pharmacist's role in ambulatory care.

GROWTH OF AMBULATORY CARE

Ambulatory care comprises healthcare services that can be delivered on an outpatient basis and do not require overnight hospitalization. Ambulatory care services have greatly expanded in recent years because of the rapid growth of managed care and the greater emphasis placed on outpatient hospital care. One significant event underlying this change in focus was the 1983 introduction of the Medicare Prospective Payment System for inpatient hospitalizations. The prospective payment system stimulated hospitals to change from rendering more services to providing shorter lengths of stay and getting patients out of the hospital faster and sicker. These changes encouraged the development of ambulatory care programs and are referred to in the case scenario.

Common Problems

What types of problems are seen in ambulatory care settings? The National Ambulatory Medical Care Survey is an ongoing survey of ambulatory care. **Table 8-1** lists the distribution of office visits in the United States by the top 20 primary diagnosis groups. Three of the top five are chronic illnesses (i.e., hypertension, joint problems, and diabetes). **Table 8-2** summarizes the distribution of office visits by the major disease categories. The most common category is diseases of the respiratory system, followed by diseases of the circulatory system, nervous system, and musculoskeletal system. **Table 8-3** lists the distribution of office visits by physician specialty area and type; nearly 60% of visits comprise primary care (i.e., family practice, internal medicine, pediatrics, obstetrics, and gynecology).

Table 8-4 lists the distribution of office visits by medication therapy. Nearly two thirds of physician visits result in one or more medications prescribed by the physician. Of those visits where a medication was prescribed, about one fourth had one medication prescribed with almost an even distribution between males and females. As reported in

Table 8-1 Distribution of Office Visits in the United States by Top 20 Primary Diagnoses, 2006

Primary diagnosis group	Total visits N (1,000)	Total	% distribution Female	Male
All visits	901,954	100.0	100.0	100.0
Routine infant or child health check	39,298	4.4	3.5	5.5
Essential hypertension	35,784	4.0	3.7	4.3
Acute upper respiratory infections, excluding pharyngitis	30,916	3.4	3.6	3.2
Arthropathies and related disorders	27,736	3.1	3.2	2.9
Diabetes mellitus	23,779	2.6	2.4	2.9
Spinal disorders	23,760	2.6	2.6	2.7
Specific procedures and aftercare	22,875	2.5	2.4	2.8
Malignant neoplasms	20,923	2.3	2.0	2.8
Normal pregnancy	19,730	2.2	3.7	. . .
Rheumatism	16,221	1.8	1.6	2.1
Gynecologic examination	15,630	1.7	2.9	. . .
Otitis media and eustachian tube Disorders	13,784	1.5	1.2	2.0
Follow-up examination	13,676	1.5	1.4	1.6
General medical examination	13,594	1.5	1.1	2.1
Heart disease	13,323	1.5	1.4	1.6
Chronic sinusitis	12,971	1.4	1.7	1.1
Allergic rhinitis	12,150	1.3	1.3	1.5
Ischemic heart disease	10,859	1.2	0.8	1.8
Asthma	10,590	1.2	1.2	1.1
Cataract	10,239	1.1	1.1	1.1
All other diagnoses	514,117	57.0	57.1	56.9

Note: Numbers may not add to totals because of rounding.
Source: National Ambulatory Medical Care Survey. (2006). Advance Data No. 3, August 6, 2008, Table 12, p. 24. Hyattsville, Maryland: National Center for Health Statistics.

physician office visits (**Table 8-5**), the top ranked therapeutic drug category was analgesics, followed by antihyperlipidemic agents, antidepressants, antidiabetic agents, and anxiolytics, sedatives, and hypnotics. Upon review of the tables, one can see that most of the diagnoses and prescribed drugs in ambulatory care settings come from a few common disease states. For this reason, primary care providers and pharmacists should receive extensive training in the management of these common diseases.

Table 8-2 Distribution of Office Visits in the United States by Primary Diagnosis Classified by Major Disease Category, 2006

Major disease category[1]	Total visits N (1,000)	% distribution total
All visits	901,954	100.0
Infectious and parasitic diseases	22,214	2.5
Neoplasms	29,021	3.2
Endocrine, nutritional, metabolic, and immunity disorders	45,914	5.1
Mental disorders	41,573	4.6
Diseases of the nervous system and sense organs	85,182	9.4
Diseases of the circulatory system	72,151	8.0
Diseases of the respiratory system	103,969	11.5
Diseases of the digestive system	35,887	4.0
Diseases of the genitourinary system	38,404	4.3
Diseases of the skin	37,434	4.2
Diseases of the musculoskeletal and connective tissue	72,528	8.0
Symptoms, signs, and ill-defined conditions	54,999	6.1
Injury and poisoning	48,343	5.4
Supplementary classification[2]	181,679	20.1
All other diagnoses[3]	23,808	2.6
Unknown[4]	8,850	1.0

[1]Based on the *International Classification of Diseases, Ninth Revision, Clinical Modification* (ICD–9–CM).
[2]Includes general medical examination, routine prenatal examination, and health supervision of an infant or child, and other diagnoses not classifiable to injury or illness.
[3]Includes diseases of the blood and blood-forming organs; complications of pregnancy, childbirth, and congenital anomalies; certain conditions originating in the perinatal period; and entries not codable to the ICD–9–CM (e.g., left against medical advice, transferred).
[4]Includes blank diagnoses.
Note: Numbers may not add to totals because of rounding.
Source: National Ambulatory Medical Care Survey. (2006). Advance Data No. 3, August 6, 2008, Table 11, p. 23. Hyattsville, Maryland: National Center for Health Statistics.

Table 8-3 Distribution of Office Visits in the United States by Specialty Area and Type, 2006

Physician specialty	Total visits N (1,000)	% of total
All visits[1]	901,954	100.0
Specialty area		
General and family practice	208,475	23.1
Internal medicine	125,398	13.9
Pediatrics	122,344	13.6
Obstetrics and gynecology	69,436	7.7
Ophthalmology	57,815	6.4
Orthopedic surgery	48,066	5.3
Cardiovascular diseases	25,790	2.9

(continues)

Table 8-3 Distribution of Office Visits in the United States by Specialty Area and Type, 2006 *(continued)*

Physician specialty	Total visits N (1,000)	% of total
Dermatology	25,256	2.8
Psychiatry	25,150	2.8
Urology	18,307	2.0
Otolaryngology	17,508	1.9
Oncology	14,871	1.6
General surgery	14,048	1.6
Neurology	12,532	1.4
All other specialties	116,958	13.0
Specialty type		
Primary care	525,607	58.3
Medical specialty	198,654	22.0
Surgical specialty	177,693	19.7

[1]Visits provided by the physician specialty area and type.
Note: Numbers may not add to totals because of rounding.
Source: National Ambulatory Medical Care Survey. (2006). Advance Data No. 3, August 6, 2008, Table 1, p. 13. Hyattsville, Maryland: National Center for Health Statistics.

Table 8-4 Distribution of Office Visits in the United States by Medication Therapy, 2006

Visit characteristic	Total visits N (1,000)	% distribution Total	Female	Male
Medication therapy[1]				
All visits	901,954	100.0	100.0	100.0
Visits with mention of medication[2]	636,708	70.6	70.9	70.1
Visits without mention of medication	265,247	29.4	29.1	29.9
Number of medications provided or prescribed by a physician				
All visits	901,954	100.0	100.0	100.0
0	265,247	29.4	29.1	29.9
1	214,094	23.7	24.2	23.0
2	142,214	15.8	15.8	15.8
3	87,077	9.7	9.3	10.1
4	54,442	6.0	6.0	6.0
5	37,581	4.2	4.1	4.2
6	28,692	3.2	3.2	3.2
7	21,423	2.4	2.4	2.4
8	51,184	5.7	5.9	5.4

Note: Numbers may not add to totals because of rounding.
[1]Medications include prescription drugs, over-the-counter preparations, immunizations, and desensitizing agents.
[2]Drug visits are visits at which one or more medications are prescribed or provided by the physician.
Source: National Ambulatory Medical Care Survey. (2006). Advance Data No. 3, August 6, 2008, Table 21, p. 31. Hyattsville, Maryland: National Center for Health Statistics.

Table 8-5 Distribution of Office Visits in the United States for the Top 20 Therapeutic Drug Categories, 2006

Therapeutic drug category	N (1,000)	% of total[1]
Analgesics[2]	209,936	11.1
Antihyperlipidemic agents	101,640	5.4
Antidepressants	85,331	4.5
Antidiabetic agents	68,742	3.6
Anxiolytics, sedatives, and hypnotics	66,968	3.5
Beta-adrenergic blocking agents	63,428	3.3
Antiplatelet agents	62,430	3.3
Bronchodilators	60,170	3.2
Proton pump inhibitors	59,313	3.1
Diuretics	54,571	2.9
Dermatological agents	53,135	2.8
Anticonvulsants	49,800	2.6
Angiotensin converting enzyme inhibitors	49,301	2.6
Antihistamines	45,181	2.4
Ophthalmic preparations	40,197	2.1
Sex hormones	36,777	1.9
Calcium channel blocking agents	36,529	1.9
Adrenal cortical steroids	36,276	1.9
Vitamin and mineral combinations	33,634	1.8
Thyroid drugs	33,340	1.8

[1]Based on an estimated 1.90 billion drug mentions at office visits in 2006.
[2]Includes narcotic and non-narcotic analgesics and nonsteroidal anti-inflammatory drugs.
Source: National Ambulatory Medical Care Survey. (2006). Advance Data No. 3, August 6, 2008, Table 23, p. 33. Hyattsville, Maryland: National Center for Health Statistics.

Primary Care Providers

Primary care providers include physicians, midwives, nurse practitioners, and physician assistants. Although training programs and practice responsibilities vary among states, the primary care capabilities are similar. Scheffler and colleagues have estimated that nurse practitioners and physician assistants can perform about three fourths of services that physicians perform in adult practices and about 90% of services in pediatric practices (Scheffler, Waitzman, & Hillman, 1998). At both the federal and state levels, there is interest in increasing the number of these practitioners, especially in underserved areas (Mezey, 1999; see Chapter 2).

TYPES OF MEDICAL PRACTICES

Two major types of medical practices exist. The predominant form is care provided by private-practice physicians in solo, partnership, and private group practice settings on a fee-for-service basis. The second form, which has experienced dramatic growth in recent decades, is ambulatory care provided in organized settings that have an identity independent of that of the physicians practicing in it. This second category includes managed care programs such as health maintenance organizations and preferred provider organizations.

Solo Practice

Traditionally, solo medical practice has attracted the largest number of physicians. In recent years, however, the number of solo practitioners has been rapidly decreasing, largely because of managed care pressures. From a physician's perspective, solo practice offers an opportunity to avoid organizational dependence and to be self-employed. Primary care services provided by solo practitioners include family practice, internal medicine, pediatrics, and obstetrics and gynecology. These solo practitioners care for patients in office space owned or leased by the physician or in the physician's home. When patients are hospitalized, the physician sees them and provides care for them in the hospital.

Group Practice

Besides solo practice, office-based practice includes group practice. Group practice is an affiliation of three or more providers, usually physicians who share income, expenses, facilities, equipment, medical records, and support personnel, and who provide services through a formal organization (Roemer, 1981). Although other definitions exist, the essential elements are formal sharing of resources and distribution of income. The first successful nonindustrial group practice was the Mayo Clinic in Rochester, Minnesota. The Mayo Clinic was organized as a single-specialty group practice in 1887; later it was broadened into a multiple-specialty group that showed that group practice was feasible in the private sector.

Advantages of group practice from a physician's perspective include shared operation, joint ownership, centralized administrative functions, and availability of a professional business manager. From a financial viewpoint, the group practice relieves the provider of having to provide the large initial investment often required to establish a practice. Disadvantages of group practice from a provider's perspective include less individual freedom, less income, weak provider–patient relationships, and greater restrictions on referral practices (Williams, 1993).

MANAGED CARE

Managed care is the use of a planned and coordinated approach to providing health care, with the goal being delivery of quality care at the lowest cost, including emphasis on preventive care. The defining feature of managed care is the use of provider networks through a contractual arrangement specifying the types of services to be provided and the reimbursement to be received in return. With health maintenance organizations, the provider usually receives prepayment for services on a per-member, per-month basis. Thus a provider is paid the same amount of money every month for a member regardless of whether that member receives services and how much those services cost (a service contract). A health maintenance organization is a prepaid (capitation) health plan in which enrollees pay a fixed fee (often with a copayment) for designated health services.

A preferred provider organization is an insurance plan in which the managed care organization contracts with health providers to provide health services under a discounted-fee schedule. Such a healthcare plan is prepaid, and the member or family is enrolled usually for one year and is entitled to certain agreed-upon services. Healthcare services usually include physician visits, hospital services, prescription drugs, mental health services, and home healthcare services.

Typically, a primary care physician (gatekeeper) is chosen or assigned to coordinate an individual or family's healthcare services. When a specialist referral or hospital service is required, the gatekeeper physician must approve these services. If an individual or family goes outside the plan for these services, these services are usually not fully reimbursed or may not be reimbursable at all. Strong incentives are built in to encourage members to stay within the system (see Chapter 17).

HOSPITAL-RELATED AMBULATORY SERVICES

Hospital Clinics

Hospital clinics developed as American dispensaries in the 1700s and were intended to serve the urban poor and individuals who did not require inpatient care. Dispensaries were often freestanding buildings, so indigent patients did not mix with the paid hospital patients. The first U.S. dispensary was established in Philadelphia in 1786, followed by facilities in New York City, Boston, and Baltimore. A physician and/or apothecary who provided minor surgery, extracted teeth, and prescribed medications generally staffed the dispensary. By the mid-1850s, larger dispensaries had both a physician and a pharmacist. Financial support was meager and reliant on private donations. Most physicians volunteered their services without compensation. Freestanding dispensaries grew to about 100 by 1900 (Roemer, 1981).

By 1916, public health dispensaries' clinics experienced rapid expansion and numbered 1,300 sites, including about 500 for tuberculosis, 400 for baby hygiene, 250 for schoolchildren, and 150 for other purposes. Clinics maintained their preventive orientation, and clientele were usually limited to low-income groups. Private medical practitioners increasingly saw dispensaries as competitive and spoke of the abuse of the dispensary by patients who could properly afford private medical care. Since the end of World War I, private medical practice and hospitals have continued to flourish, causing the steady decline and closure of charitable dispensaries (Roemer, 1981). Hospital clinics have continued to provide health care for poor persons, although very little free care remains. Those patients not covered by Medicare, Medicaid, or commercial insurance usually pay according to a means-tested sliding fee scale. In some states, a free-care pool exists to offset the costs of providing unreimbursed care.

Teaching Hospital Clinics

In response to the managed care movement, teaching hospitals have reorganized their clinics to function as group practices. Many teaching hospitals now have three groups of clinics—(1) medical, (2) surgical, and (3) other. General medical clinics approximate a family practice or general internal medicine clinic but may also include other medicine areas, such as dermatology and cardiology. Surgical clinics generally include general surgery, urology, orthopedics, and plastic surgery, and they provide follow-up care for these patients. The other category of clinics includes pediatrics, obstetrics and gynecology, and other specialties, such as rehabilitation medicine (Mezey & Lawrence, 1995).

As the managed care movement casts its net even further, hospitals will become more responsive to community needs and move toward organizing medical care in a model that Madison (1983) has described as community-oriented primary care. Within this model, greater attention will be paid to common disease states, and the primary care practitioner will play an even more important role (Mezey & Lawrence, 1995). Academic health centers, for example, have been aggressively developing primary care networks to maintain their missions of clinical research, resident and student training, and patient care. Academic health centers have constructed new facilities, bought existing practices, or created partnerships with other hospitals to increase their primary care clinic base. For instance, the University of Nebraska Medical Center (a public, state-owned teaching hospital) merged with Clarkson Hospital (private, nonprofit) in Omaha, Nebraska, to expand its network of primary care clinics.

Veterans Affairs medical centers have been among the leaders in the expansion of pharmacists' roles in ambulatory care. Pharmacists have participated in Veterans Affairs primary care clinics' initiatives to improve blood pressure and increase medication compliance. Pharmacists have also become involved in pharmacist-managed anticoagulation clinics, where they have provided benefits over usual care in the form of desired therapeutic control with fewer adverse effects (Alsuwaidan, Malone, Billups, & Carter, 1998). Foss reported that two thirds of clinic patients were within the therapeutic range following such interventions, and the percentage of thromboembolic complications was one third that of usual-care patients (Foss, Shoch, & Sintek, 1999).

The Impact of Managed Pharmaceutical Care on Resource Utilization and Outcomes in Veterans Affairs Medical Centers study has been one of the largest studies to date to examine the outcomes with pharmaceutical care. Nine Veterans Affairs medical centers participated in this study, in which a total of 1,054 patients were randomized to either an intervention group (n = 523) or a control group (n = 531). After identifying patients at high risk for developing drug-related problems, pharmacists documented a total of 1,855 contacts in the intervention group and implemented 3,048 therapy-specific interventions over the 12-month study period. Following these interventions, both hemoglobin A1C and low-density-lipoprotein cholesterol levels measurements were more improved in the intervention group compared with the control group. Total healthcare costs increased in both groups over the 12-month period; however, this increase was lower in the intervention group ($1,020) compared to the control group ($1,313) (Carter et al., 2001).

The Impact of Managed Pharmaceutical Care on Resource Utilization and Outcomes in Veterans Affairs Medical Centers study also examined the impact of ambulatory pharmacist interventions in the management of drug-related problems addressed and resolved during each contact. More drug-related problems were addressed and resolved when visits were 15 minutes or longer and when the contact was in person compared to being a telephone contact. This amount of time and type of contact is vital information for pharmacists who are developing managed clinics for patients at high risk for drug-related problems (Ellis, Carter, Billups, Malone, Carter, Covey, et al., 2000).

With the growth of pharmacist roles in ambulatory care, guidelines have been developed outlining the minimum requirements for the operation and management of pharmaceutical services for patients in the ambulatory care setting. Clinical practice guidelines are being developed and increasingly incorporated into health information systems. Murray and colleagues, for example, reported on a study to measure the effects of the electronic display of guideline-based, patient-specific treatment suggestions on pharmacist work patterns (Murray, Loos, Eckert, Zhou, & Tierney, 1999). The results showed that a dramatic change in work patterns occurred when pharmacists were provided with an electronic display of guidelines. In comparison with the control group, pharmacists with access to treatment suggestions spent less of their time preparing and filling prescriptions and more of their time functioning in an advisory role with patients, physicians, and nurses. Pharmacists in the intervention group also spent more of their time solving problems (Murray et al., 1999).

Ambulatory Surgery Centers

Response to the prospective payment system and managed care pressures on hospitals has led to the establishment of ambulatory surgery centers. Ambulatory surgery centers can be housed in hospital-based settings or in a freestanding ambulatory surgical center. Numerous surgeries that in the past required lengthy hospital stays can now be done in outpatient surgery centers in less time and at a lower cost. Patients having surgeries such as hernia repair are often admitted by 8:00 a.m. and discharged before noon. In fact, many third-party payers require surgical procedures to be done on an ambulatory basis unless evidence suggests that the procedure would be unsafe for the patient. As a consequence, the majority of surgical procedures are now done on an outpatient basis. Generally, surgery centers report a high level of patient satisfaction, and patients think that the quality of care is good.

Other Outpatient Services

Other outpatient services include freestanding diagnostic imaging centers, home intravenous services, home care services, and women's health centers. Additional ambulatory services will undoubtedly emerge as government and managed care organizations continue to seek delivery of care at a reduced cost (see Chapter 17).

EMERGENCY SERVICES

Hospital Emergency Services

Approximately 93% of community hospitals in the United States have emergency departments. Misuse of the emergency department has drawn intense scrutiny because it leads to routine care being delivered in expensive facilities at high costs.

Weinerman, Ratner, Robbins, and Lavenhar (1966) defined the following three categories of cases presenting to the emergency departments: (1) nonurgent, (2) urgent, and (3) emergent cases. An emergent case is a condition requiring immediate medical attention where any time delay would be potentially threatening to life or function. An urgent case involves a condition that requires attention within a few hours, but is not necessarily life-threatening. A nonurgent condition is nonacute or minor in severity, and emergency service is not required. A review of cases entering emergency departments found that of all patients using emergency services, 5% are emergent, 45% are urgent, and 50% are nonurgent (Weinerman, Ratner, Robbins, & Lavenhar, 1966). Consequently, most of the nonurgent conditions presenting at emergency departments involve delivery of costly services that could be provided at a less expensive venue, such as a clinic, emergicenter, or physician's office. For this reason, some managed care systems require enrollees to get prior approval before authorizing emergency services.

Medicaid patients often seek care from an emergency department because it is the only option available when they believe they need immediate attention. After some states implemented Medicaid managed care programs, they showed substantial declines in emergency department use (American College of Healthcare Executives, 1993).

Emergency Medical Services

Federal legislation has stipulated the creation of greatly improved emergency medical services throughout the United States. The National Highway Safety Act of 1966, for example, established performance criteria that required states to submit their emergency medical services plans for federal approval. The Emergency Medical Services System Act of 1973 authorized funding over 3 years to states, counties, and nonprofit agencies in an effort to expand and modernize their emergency medical services. Components of these services were expected to include a uniform emergency telephone number (911) and modernization of ambulance design from a hearse-type vehicle to a light van with equipment to provide cardiopulmonary resuscitation. Ambulance attendants were given emergency medical training so they could provide life-support services and trauma treatment en route to the hospital. Thanks to the improved training and equipment, emergency medical services have increased survival rates for victims of both traumatic injuries and myocardial infarction (Hoffer, 1979; Roth, Stewart, Rogers, & Cannon, 1984; Sherman, 1979).

The same legislative acts that set the emergency medical services standards also established community trauma centers and developed trauma teams to handle emergencies. Level I trauma centers offer around-the-clock care, including medical and surgical specialists, diagnostic imaging, and operating rooms staffed by well-trained personnel in well-equipped, intensive care units (Mezey, 1999).

Emergi-Centers

Emergency centers (emergi-centers) are designed to provide medical care 24 hours a day, 7 days a week. Another type of facility called an urgi-center, provides emergency services but is open approximately 12 hours a day, 7 days a week. Both centers are designed to provide care for urgent and nonurgent problems. Most do not receive ambulance cases or serve emergent cases, however.

In comparison to services provided at the emergency department, costs are generally lower at emergi-centers. Advantages of these centers include the convenience of and access to services without appointments and long delays, and that health insurance carriers generally prefer them to emergency department treatment (Mezey, 1999).

GOVERNMENT PROGRAMS

Health Department Services

In large European cities, boards of health were established in the 1800s and 1900s to halt the spread of communicable diseases such as plague, cholera, and typhus. Generally, these bodies were temporary boards—once the disease was eradicated, they were dissolved.

In the United States, Massachusetts set up the first state department of health in 1869. In the early days, U.S. health departments dealt largely with the prevention of tuberculosis. Another health department initiative dealt with the reduction of infant mortality by establishing milk stations where mothers who could not breastfeed could obtain clean cow's milk to feed their babies. Later, this initiative was expanded to provide advice to low-income mothers on the care of infants; it also established child health clinics and the Visiting Nurse Association.

As an outgrowth of two federal acts passed in the 1920s, maternal and child health grants were provided to states for the development of well-baby clinics. In the late 1920s, however, a conservative antigovernment wave swept over the country, led by the American Medical Association, which attacked these maternal and child health grants as socialistic programs. As a result, the U.S. Congress ended this program in 1929. It was reactivated during the Great Depression as part of Title V of the 1935 Social Security Act (Roemer, 1981).

Most public health agencies in the early 1900s were devoted to environmental problems, sanitation, and collection of statistics on communicable diseases. The 1929 stock market crash and the massive poverty during the 1930s led to a resurgent American public health movement. Currently, the following four major categories of public health services exist: (1) communicable disease control, (2) maternal and child health services, (3) chronic diseases, and (4) general ambulatory care.

Communicable disease control, the first major category, involves the control of contagious diseases and sexually transmitted diseases such as AIDS. Immunizations against diseases such as diphtheria, pertussis (whooping cough), tetanus, polio, and measles are given to infants as part of well-baby clinics and other health department–sponsored activities.

The second major category encompasses the maternal and child health clinics that have risen and fallen based on funding provided at federal, state, and local levels. Federal funding for maternal and child health services has generally come from Title V of the Social Security Act and supports local health department services for babies and pregnant women. Maternal and child health services are provided to low-income families, while families with moderate to high income are referred to private physicians. As part of President Lyndon Johnson's Great Society program, comprehensive health care (treatment and prevention) was also established under Social Security Act amendments that authorized grants for maternal and infant care clinics and children and youth clinics.

In 1976, the author of this chapter established clinical and distributive pharmaceutical services in an ambulatory children and youth clinic serving low-income families in south Minneapolis (Scott & Nordin, 1980). Instead of filling prescriptions from a prescription blank, the prescriptions were filled from the patient's chart. The pharmacy was located inside the primary patient care area, so the pharmacist could consult with the appropriate health professional or refer the patient for more extensive evaluation. As part of the patient counseling program, the pharmacy staff also administered the first dose of medication prescribed for pediatric patients, including liquid preparations (e.g., antibiotics), ophthalmic drops, and ointments and otic preparations. As part of the clinic's interdisciplinary team, pharmacists provided therapeutic and pharmacokinetic consultations, drug monitoring, drug information, educational programs for the community, and poison prevention services. The pharmacy closed in 1984 because of federal and state funding cutbacks. However, such pharmaceutical care services are possible in clinic settings, community health centers, staff model health maintenance organizations, and other ambulatory care settings.

The third major category of public health services focuses on chronic (noncommunicable) diseases—for example, the cancer detection clinic. Other efforts have targeted smoking reduction, Pap smears for cervical cancer detection, breast examinations, and hypertension screening.

The fourth major category of public health services consists of generalized ambulatory care clinics. In the mid-1960s, health departments influenced by the War on Poverty movement expanded the scope of these clinics from preventive functions to the provision of general ambulatory care. These clinics were predominantly found in low-income neighborhoods, but the prevailing policy was to turn no one away on grounds of inability to pay. Patients with complex problems were typically referred to a contracted hospital outpatient department. Today, public health clinics are vulnerable to governmental funding priorities and organized medicine pressures to eliminate or reduce the services offered there. Accordingly, health departments generally provide services in areas where most physicians are not interested in working (Roemer, 1981).

Community Health Centers

In 1965, Congress funded the Neighborhood Health Center Act to provide comprehensive health care to low-income populations in urban and rural areas of the United States in an attempt to stimulate societal growth and decrease poverty (Mezey & Lawrence, 1995). The first Neighborhood Health Center, established in 1965, was the Gouverneur Health Center, which served poor persons from New York's lower east side. Other early health center projects were developed in Boston, Chicago, and south-central Los Angeles. Evaluations of these initiatives concluded that Neighborhood Health Center program performance was generally equal, and sometimes superior, to that of other established providers of health care (Morehead, Donaldson, & Servavelli, 1971; Sparer & Anderson, 1975). In 1973, the entire Neighborhood Health Center program under the Office of Economic Opportunity was ended, and the Neighborhood Health Center facilities were transferred to the U.S. Public Health Service (PHS) and were designated as community health centers (CHCs) (Roemer, 1981).

In 1974, Congress passed the Community Health Centers Act, which defined the scope of CHC services that must be offered to warrant receipt of federal grants. The criteria defining underserved areas were quantified and included poverty level as defined by local per-capita income, an excessive infant mortality rate, and a shortage of primary care physicians. Mandated services in these federally supported CHCs were diagnostic treatment, consultation, and other services by a physician or physician extender; laboratory and X-ray services; dental services; social services; and pharmaceutical services (Roemer, 1981). Approximately 1,250 CHCs in the United States serve more than 20 million with limited financial resources. The 1978 amendments to Sections 329 and 330 of the Public Health Services Act changed the supplemental services designation and made pharmacy a primary service in CHCs. All CHCs are required to provide prescription drugs for their patients either through on-site licensed pharmacies or through a contracted arrangement with an off-site pharmacy.

The Siouxland Community Health Center (SCHC) is an example of a CHC that provides in-house pharmacy services. SCHC is located in Sioux City, Iowa. The city has become more racially mixed and culturally diverse over the past 20 years, in part because of the changing demographics of the meat packing industry workforce. Hispanics account for more than one half of the minority population, followed by a significant number of Asian Americans, African Americans, and Native Americans. SCHC manages more than 50,000 patient visits per year, and the majority of clients are at or below 100% of the federal poverty level. SCHC facilities include 18 exam rooms, 2 minor procedure rooms, 8 dental operatories (dental chairs), a basic lab, and a pharmacy. The major health concerns encountered by the center's practitioners are diabetes and hypertension. The on-site pharmacy fills more than 300 prescriptions per day.

A number of colleges/schools of pharmacy are developing partnerships with CHCs to integrate clinical pharmacy services in CHCs and to provide training sites for pharmacy students. SCHC, in conjunction with the University of Nebraska's College of Pharmacy, was one of the first seven CHCs to receive funding from the U.S. Health Resources and Services Administration's clinical pharmacy demonstration project to develop and deliver clinical pharmacy services. The project objective was to determine whether provision of education services by the clinical pharmacist working with the SCHC team would improve glycosylated hemoglobin (A1C) levels and quality of life for patients with diabetes in an intervention group more than improvement shown by members of the control group (who received standard care) (Scott, Boyd, Stephans, Augustine, & Reardon, 2006). Based on a national evaluation, the SCHC project was deemed a successful clinical pharmacy demonstration project; it was one of only two clinical pharmacy demonstration projects in which the regression analysis showed significantly better health outcomes than the average project. It reached and retained patients in its diabetes disease management program better than most, and it has been sustained since the end of the grant period in August 2003. The Siouxland project used an intensive program of mostly individual diabetes counseling, along with incentives, as a means to encourage patient retention (Mathematic Policy Research, 2004).

In another study, Leal and colleagues assessed the improvement that a clinical pharmacist at a CHC can make as a provider for patients with diabetes and comorbid conditions (hypertension and hyperlipidemia) by using a medical staff–approved collaborative practice agreement. Although this study did not include a comparison group, the intervention at the El Rio Health Center in Tucson, Arizona, produced a statistically significant 2% drop in mean A1C in 199 patients compared to baseline. Regarding attainment of treatment goals, the pharmacist-managed service showed an almost sevenfold increase in the number of patients at target A1C levels (Leal, Glover, Herrier, & Felix, 2004).

Indian Health Service

Treaties signed between Native American tribes and the U.S. government stipulated that Native Americans would be provided certain medical and hospital services, and this obligation continues to the present day. Management of the Indian Health Service (IHS) is provided by the U.S. Department of Health and Human Services' PHS. Currently, the majority of IHS pharmacists are members of the PHS Commissioned Corps. Healthcare and pharmacy services are provided to 1.5 million Native Americans and Alaska Natives living on or near reservations in 35 states. IHS programs are carried out through 49 hospitals (7–150 beds) and 180 ambulatory clinics. Although they are distributed throughout the country, most of these facilities are concentrated in the western half of the continental United States and Alaska (Flowers, Wick, Figg, McClelland, Shiber, Britton, et al., 2009; Paavola, Kermanoski, & Pittman, 1997).

Pharmacists were first assigned as PHS officers to hospitals in 1953 to establish dispensing policies and practices. During the 1960s, several IHS innovations set the stage for a more active clinical role for pharmacists. The first innovation was that the patient's medical record replaced the traditional prescription blank as the primary document used to fill all prescriptions. By accessing the patient's chart, the pharmacist could provide a concurrent review of prescribed drug therapy for appropriateness before dispensing. The second innovation was that IHS pharmacists were the first to use private consultation rooms and provide patient counseling to every patient receiving a prescription.

The third major innovation was the provision of primary care to ambulatory patients with both acute and chronic health problems. This program began as pharmacists independently initiated and extended drug therapy. The primary care program has now progressed to pharmacists taking histories, doing physical assessments, and prescribing treatment including prescription medication. These programs were developed under the leadership of Dr. Allen J. Brands, an IHS pharmacist from 1955 through 1981, and they remain an important part of pharmacy practice today.

Since 1972, IHS pharmacists have obtained didactic and clinical training that enables them to become certified as pharmacist practitioners (Copeland & Apgar, 1980). These trained pharmacists perform physical assessments and manage both acute and chronic disease states using protocols. The protocols provide guidelines for pharmacists, including the requirement that complex and severe cases be referred to physicians. The notion of the pharmacist as a primary care provider similar to a PA or nurse practitioner is more comprehensive in the IHS than the roles found in most ambulatory care settings. This unique conception of the pharmacist's primary care role was originally evolved to counteract a physician undersupply and the unmet needs of the underserved Native American population, but it is also well suited for many other rural areas.

IHS encourages pharmacists to broaden their scope of practice. Advantages include full access to patient records, collegial relationships with health professionals, opportunities to participate in pharmacy specialized clinics, and direct patient care and emergency life support. IHS pharmacists also have opportunities to become disease state experts, often managing and participating in chronic care specialty clinics (e.g., anticoagulation, asthma, congestive heart failure, diabetes, dyslipidemia, HIV/AIDS, hypertension, immunization, pain management, and smoking cessation) (Flowers, Wick, Figg, McClelland, Shiber, Britton, et al., 2009). Although the pharmaceutical care role has recently been advocated in the ambulatory setting, most of these innovations were first developed in the IHS (see Chapter 16).

MISCELLANEOUS PROGRAMS

School Health Clinics

The vast majority of children older than age 5 attend school in the United States; when first aid is needed or acute illness occurs, schools must provide at least limited services for these children. School health services in the United States can be traced back to 1840, when William Alcott, a distinguished educator, called for periodic visits to schools by physicians who would see children referred by teachers (Roemer, 1981). The first permanent school medical officer was appointed in New York City in

1892, followed by one in Boston, to ensure that school children with contagious diseases were identified, removed from school, and treated. School nursing services were brought into schools in New York City in 1902 and later adopted in other U.S. cities.

A wide disparity of nursing services exists in U.S. schools because communities have different socioeconomic levels, and local property taxes are usually the schools' major financial support. Ambulatory services vary between education levels because health needs change from childhood to young adult years (Roemer, 1981).

At the elementary school level, the following three components are ideally addressed: (1) health education of the child, (2) maintenance of a safe and healthy school environment, and (3) personal health services. To control communicable diseases, immunizations are required for entrance into school. Personal health services include health status appraisals (examinations), first aid to trauma cases, referral for needed medical care, psychologic services, and dental care. School nurses are the most commonly employed school health personnel, although the number working in full-time and part-time positions is unavailable.

Secondary schools require a different pattern of health services than in elementary schools to serve adolescent needs. Passage through puberty requires programs for sexuality, sexually transmitted diseases, premarital pregnancy, substance abuse prevention and treatment, violence prevention, and sports medicine. The pharmacist as a health educator is well trained to provide accurate and appropriate information on alcohol, tobacco, and other drug usage. Some colleges of pharmacy have speakers' bureaus that give presentations on a variety of substance abuse topics (e.g., smoking prevention and cessation, alcohol use, anabolic steroid use, amphetamines, marijuana, and diet pills). Health education programs on sexually transmitted diseases and birth control can be given at the school and then augmented at the community pharmacy level.

The first school health clinic was developed at a high school in St. Paul, Minnesota. Since then, clinics have been established in other schools throughout the country. Students can receive personal health services at school health clinics, which are especially important in underserved population areas.

Prison Health Services

The U.S. Department of Justice operates a system of federal prisons or penitentiaries through its Federal Bureau of Prisons. Federal prisons' capacities range from 200 to more than 2,200 inmates, and prisons are linked to more than 28 hospitals, each with a clinic for ambulatory care. Larger prisons are staffed by the PHS with full-time salaried physicians, and smaller prisons are staffed by part-time private physicians working under contract (Roemer, 1981). As part of the PHS, more than 150 pharmacists work in the Bureau of Prisons. Practice settings range from ambulatory care sites to 500-bed hospitals. Responsibilities of the pharmacist include distributing drugs from a national drug formulary, counseling patients, providing drug use reviews, monitoring labs, working in chronic care clinics, immunizing patients, administering medications, and assisting in the daily duties of the correctional facility (Flowers, Wick, Figg, McClelland, Shiber, Britton, et al., 2009).

Since 2004, selected PHS pharmacists were trained in HIV disease and pharmacotherapy, and they manage care for Bureau of Prisons patients with HIV/AIDS under collaborative practice agreements. Here they initiate treatment, order laboratory tests to stage the severity of the infection, and modify existing antiretroviral therapy (Flowers, Wick, Figg, McClelland, Shiber, Britton, et al., 2009).

Voluntary Agencies and Free Health Clinics

Many voluntary health agencies exist in the United States, including those run by the American Red Cross, the Salvation Army, and some overseas church missions that provide ambulatory care services in developing countries.

Another voluntary health service was the free clinic movement, a dramatic innovation in ambulatory care. Its first facility was the Haight-Ashbury Free Medical Clinic, which opened in a bohemian section of San Francisco, California, in the summer of 1967. These clinics opened without substantial grants from the federal government and were planned and supported by consumers, who were usually groups of young adults. Other free clinics opened in Cincinnati, Ohio; Detroit, Michigan; Seattle, Washington; and Minneapolis, Minnesota. By 1971, about 175 free clinics had been established throughout the country, with the greatest concentration in California. Roemer (1981) suggested that the rationale for these clinics was the feeling of distrust by socially alienated youths (such as hippies) of the establishment in the American healthcare system.

These alienated youths generally did not want to go to hospital outpatient departments and public health clinics. Free clinics were often located in vacant stores, old houses, and church basements, and they were open to everyone who came—at no charge—although donations were welcomed.

Jerome Schwartz (1971) defined free clinics as having the following seven characteristics: (1) a physical facility; (2) trained health personnel; (3) other health staff or volunteers; (4) direct provision of medical, dental, or psychologic service, including treatment of drug abuse; (5) availability to everyone without eligibility tests; (6) specified hours of service; and (7) no set payment required, although small fees might be charged for specified services and donations might be requested (Schwartz, 1971). Services are provided predominantly by volunteer physicians, nurses, pharmacists, and paraprofessionals.

Free clinics provide professional and community service opportunities to pharmacy, medical, dental, and nursing students. The author of this chapter participated as a pharmacy student at the Union Gospel Mission Free Clinic in St. Paul, Minnesota, from 1970 through 1973. Services provided at this free clinic included medical care, dental care, nursing care, and pharmaceutical care. Clientele included homeless men, women, and children, and runaway youth. Many homeless men had a variety of medical problems, including alcoholism. A pharmacist oversaw distribution of medications when possible, although a volunteer pharmacist was not always at the site. Consequently, a pharmacy student dispensed medication and provided counseling under the supervision of a volunteer physician. Medical students diagnosed and prescribed following consultation with the pharmacist and physician. Medications were generally donated to this free clinic by community hospitals and by some drug companies. Opportunities to provide pharmaceutical care increased as pharmacists and pharmacy students gained further insight and skills.

Free clinics' major obstacles are continual financial crises and staffing by voluntary health professionals. Since the 1971 Schwartz study, no general survey has been conducted of the free clinic movement (Roemer, 1981). Many free clinics remain, under the name of free health clinic, free medical clinic, or the local health department. The National Association of Free Clinics is the nonprofit organization whose mission is focused on the issues and needs of the more than 1,200 free clinics and the people they serve in the United States (http://freeclinics.us/resources.php). Many of the free clinics have changed their names to community clinics, and some have evolved into community health centers or migrant health centers as described earlier.

Complementary and Alternative Medicine

The use of complementary and alternative medicine (CAM) continues to grow in the United States and is used for many conditions and diseases. According to the 2007 National Health Interview Survey, which is an annual in-person survey of Americans, about 38% of adults and 12% of children were using some form of CAM. CAM is a set of diverse medical and healthcare systems, practices, and products that are not typically considered part of traditional conventional medicine. Alternative medicine is regarded as nontraditional and includes a broad range of treatments, including acupuncture, biofeedback, colonics, homeopathy, hot/cold therapy, and prayer or spiritual guidance. Chiropractic is often regarded as a complementary medicine, which is used together with conventional medicine. However, some chiropractors may also use alternative medicine (e.g., herbal supplements) in their practice.

Integrative medicine combines CAM treatments with conventional medicine where there is evidence of safety and effectiveness. However, this is a major area of controversy, since there is little scientific evidence that exists for most CAM therapies. Some key questions remain to be answered through well-designed scientific studies. For instance, are these therapies safe and effective for the purposes for which they are used? Presently, alternative medicine is not a system of healing widely endorsed by conventional Western medicine. However, Western medicine has shown a growing interest in determining the efficacy of alternative therapies (Shi & Singh, 2008).

As reported in the National Health Interview Survey, the most commonly used CAM therapies among adults were natural products, deep breathing exercises, meditation, chiropractic, massage therapy, and yoga (**Table 8-6**). CAM is used frequently for musculoskeletal problems (i.e., back, neck, joint pain, and arthritis), anxiety, cholesterol, colds, headaches, and insomnia (Barnes & Bloom, 2008). Pharmacists should ask patients about any CAM therapies they may be using when they counsel patients about their medications.

Most commonly used dietary supplements in adults are multivitamins, multiminerals, vitamins E and C, calcium, and B-complex vitamins (Barnes & Bloom, 2008). Herbal supplements (botanicals) are a type of dietary supplement containing a plant or plant part (e.g., leaves, flowers, or seeds) that is used as a flavor or scent and/or for its therapeutic properties. The most popular natural products are fish oil/omega 3, glucosamine, *Echinacea*, flaxseed oil or pills, ginseng, combination herb pills, ginkgo, chondroitin, and garlic supplements (Barnes & Bloom, 2008).

As demonstrated by recent Gallup polls, the pharmacist has been ranked among the top two professions for honesty and integrity. With this public trust, patients are likely to tell their pharmacist about CAM treatments they are using and that the pharmacist's advice is valued by his or her patients. The following case scenario demonstrates the need for a trusting relationship with the pharmacist (and provider) working in ambulatory care settings, so patients will be more likely to share this important information.

> This case occurred when the author was practicing at a community health center (CHC). A patient came in to pick up a prescription for an increased dose of levothyroxine (Synthroid). During patient counseling, the patient asked my advice about an

Table 8-6 Selected CAM Therapies

Acupuncture	Movement therapies
Antioxidants	Natural products (nonvitamin and
Behavioral approaches	nonmineral, such as herbs and other
Biofeedback	products from plants, enzymes, etc.)
Chelation therapy	Naturopathy
Chiropractic manipulation	Prayer (spirituality)
Deep breathing exercises	Progressive relaxation
Diet-based therapies	Sexual enhancement
Energy-healing therapy/Reiki	Tai chi
Guided imagery	Traditional Chinese medicine
Homeopathic treatment	Traditional healers
Hypnosis	Vitamins and minerals
Massage	Yoga
Meditation	

Source: Adapted from *Health topics A–Z* on the NCCAM website, http://nccam.nih.gov/health/atoz.htm.

herbal supplement he was taking instead of his previously prescribed levothyroxine. The herbal supplement was recommended by a naturopathic doctor (non-CHC), whom the patient was seeing. The herbal product's label stated, "no T4 present." The lab value on the patient chart showed there was a decrease in the T4 level, and this lower level was the reason the CHC physician had increased the levothyroxine dose. I consulted with the CHC physician, who was unaware that the patient was taking the herbal supplement instead of the levothyroxine that he had prescribed. Consequently, I explained the importance of the prescription drug levothyroxine with the patient and why the patient should avoid this herbal supplement.

Pharmacists and physicians working in ambulatory care and institutional settings have similar stories (cases) to tell about herbal supplements. While herbal supplements are popularly used and promoted as safe because they are natural, the inappropriate use of any herbal supplement may have a harmful effect. This stresses the importance of transparent communications between the patient, physician, and pharmacist to achieve the best therapy outcome for the patient.

While many dietary sources come from natural sources, natural should not be interpreted as safe. A good source of nonbiased information is at (http://nccam.nih.gov/health/supplements/wiseuse.htm). Safety considerations when using a dietary supplement include telling the provider (and the pharmacist) when an individual is (1) thinking about replacing his or her regular medication with one or more dietary supplements; (2) taking any supplement that may have an interaction with a prescription or nonprescription drug; (3) pregnant, nursing, or a child, since most dietary supplements have not been tested in these populations and should be avoided; or (4) planning to have surgery that may increase bleeding risk or affect response to anesthesia (NCCAM, 2010a).

The CAM area has grown considerably for several reasons. One reason is that some patients who seek alternative therapies are frustrated with their relationship with a traditional provider, who typically deals with patients from a biologic disease model perspective, featuring a diagnostic focus (see Chapter 4). Instead, some patients prefer a holistic (sociobehavioral) perspective and an empathetic, caring relationship with their provider, who spends time listening to their psychologic needs as well as their physiologic needs (Gordon, 1996). Today, the holistic concept of health has widespread appeal among Americans. Some providers (including pharmacists) working in various ambulatory care settings prefer spending more time practicing holistic medicine, since it is more conducive to their own health beliefs and value systems.

A second reason that CAM use has grown is that patients often believe that CAM is harmless, since it is natural, so there is no harm in trying one of these treatments (Gordon, 1996). However, these same individuals may fear prescription medications (conventional medicine) and believe that if it comes from a synthetic source, it may pose harm to them.

More evidence-based resources are available on the efficacy and safety of natural products. For pharmacists, one of the best sources is the National Institutes of Health, National Center for Complementary and Alternative Medicine, which is one of 27 institutes and centers of the National Institutes of Health. Its mission is to support rigorous CAM research on natural products, to train researchers to provide education and outreach to consumers and health professionals, and to encourage integration of scientifically proven CAM approaches into conventional medical practice (U.S. Department of Health and Human Services, 2010).

A second evidence-based resource is the Natural Medicines Comprehensive Database, which is a comprehensive database of botanic and nonbotanic products. A third source is an electronic database called the Natural Standard, which produces professional level monographs that are descriptive of available evidence. A fourth source is the *Handbook of Nonprescription Drugs*, which has several chapters devoted to botanic and nonbotanic natural medicines (McQueen & Hume, 2006).

There has also been an explosion of information that is available on the Internet, television, and other forms of mass media. Some of this information is good, yet most sources are very poor quality. This is demonstrated by the proliferation of paid advertisements and infomercials that are featured on television and other forms of mass media. One important point to remember when consulting any source on natural medicine is that all resources have errors, omissions, and inconsistencies.

AMBULATORY PHARMACY SERVICES

Hospital Outpatient Clinics

Since 1983, community hospitals in the United States have experienced a significant reduction on the inpatient side and a significant increase in outpatient visits. To compensate for the loss of inpatient revenue, most community hospitals have moved toward expansion and modernization of ambulatory care clinics (Iglehart, 1993).

Clinical pharmacy is evolving from primarily an inpatient hospital focus to a greater concentration on ambulatory care. To meet the mandatory counseling requirements of OBRA 1990 (covering Medicaid) and state-passed legislation (extension to non-Medicaid patients), outpatient hospital pharmacies are undergoing layout redesign by incorporating semiprivate consultation areas and patient consultation rooms. Pharmacist participation in the management of specific disease states (e.g., anticoagulant therapy, hypertension, asthma, and diabetes) has already been described. Pharmacists and physicians working together have developed practice guidelines for pharmacists' management of patients with these chronic disease states (Reinders, 1986). Thanks to the pharmacist's contribution in these clinics, patient compliance with both medication therapy and future clinic appointments has improved.

Primary Care and Family Practice Clinics

Carter and Helling (1992) have described pharmacy services in primary care clinics and family practice clinics, and some of the following review is based on their description. Pharmaceutical care services have been reported in clinics associated with Appalachian Regional Hospitals, especially clinics for patients with specific diseases. As members of an interdisciplinary team, pharmacists lend their expertise to physicians and other healthcare professionals who are caring for their patients. Typically, the pharmacist performs physical assessments, orders laboratory tests, and changes medication regimens (Carter & Helling, 1992). Clinical pharmacists' participation in physician group practices in area health education centers and in North Carolina and South Carolina have also been documented (Eichelberger, 1980; Johnston & Heffron, 1981; Robertson & Groh, 1982).

Pharmacists' interventions have been shown to improve care. Morse and colleagues showed that blood pressure control could be improved and its cost reduced by pharmacy interventions (Morse, Douglas, Upton, Rodgers, & Gal, 1986). In a clinic for diabetic patients, intensive monitoring and follow-up by the pharmacist resulted in improved compliance, improved control, and reduced hospitalizations (Sczupak & Conrad, 1977).

After passage of California Assembly Bill 717 in 1977, some California pharmacists were allowed to prescribe medications after participating in a specific training program (Stimmel & McGhan, 1981). Pharmacists who completed the training program came from ambulatory care settings such as mental health centers, anticoagulation clinics, county clinics, and offices of private practice physicians. McGhan and colleagues (1983) compared the quality of pharmacists' ($n = 2$) and physicians' ($n = 3$) drug prescribing for ambulatory hypertensive patients in a California health maintenance organization. They found that more of the patients had controlled blood pressure in the pharmacists group than the physicians group (96.8% versus 78.1%) (McGhan, Stimmel, Hall, & Gilman, 1983).

Pharmacist-managed anticoagulation clinics have shown that better anticoagulation control results in fewer hospitalizations and improved management of patients (Garabedian-Ruffalo, Gray, Sax, & Ruffalo, 1985). In an economic evaluation, Garabedian-Ruffalo and colleagues found that the hospitalization rate was 3.2 days per patient treatment year in the control group and only 0.05 day in the pharmacist study group. The net savings in hospitalizations was estimated to be $11,776 per year in the pharmacist-managed group (Gray, Garabedian-Ruffalo, & Chretien, 1985).

Chrischilles and colleagues' cost-effectiveness analysis of pharmacy services' effects on family practice identified pharmacy services as improving physician efficacy, reducing adverse reactions, improving compliance, and improving the quality of care (Chrischilles, Helling, & Rowland, 1984a, 1984b). Given their expanding role in ambulatory care settings, pharmacists should aggressively pursue these practice opportunities, document their effectiveness, and publish these findings after developing good research designs (Carter & Helling, 1992).

Another study compared newly anticoagulated patients who were treated with usual medical care with those treated at an anticoagulation clinic. The anticoagulation clinic group had lower rates of significant bleeding (8.1% vs. 35.0%) and thromboembolic events (3.3% vs. 11.8%), significantly lower annual rates of warfarin-related hospitalizations (5% vs. 19%) and emergency department visits (6% vs. 22%), and reduced annual healthcare costs by $132,086 per 100 patients. Hence, a pharmacist-run anticoagulation clinic improved anticoagulation control, reduced bleeding and thromboembolic event rates, and was cost effective (Chiquette, Amato, & Bussey, 1998).

Community Pharmacy

Pharmacists are in a unique position in the healthcare system: They are the most accessible of healthcare professionals, and they are highly regarded by their patients. Pharmacists know that their everyday activities benefit patients. They are responsible for saving money for patients and third-party payers, improving therapeutic regimens, and averting therapeutic failures. Recent Gallup Public Opinion polls shows that pharmacists are listed among the most trusted professionals in society. This trust, along with the fact that most people visit their pharmacist several times for every visit they make to their physician, means that the pharmacist plays a crucial role in providing pharmaceutical care and improving patient outcomes.

Many independent pharmacies have survived by diversifying their revenue bases, including consulting with skilled nursing facilities, selling durable medical equipment, and building home healthcare businesses. Chain pharmacies have also been faced with declining revenues as they compete with mail-order pharmacies, web-based pharmacies, supermarket pharmacies, and super drugstores (big box stores, mass merchants). Part of chain pharmacies' acceptance of lower margins on prescriptions reflects the thought that pharmacy departments generate more foot traffic through their stores; thus the lower margins on prescriptions are thought to be more than offset by increases in nonprescription and sundry sales and/or increased prescription volume (Tootelian & Gaddeke, 1993).

One way that community pharmacies have diversified is through the development of miniclinics or "minute clinics." The miniclinic is located in retail stores, such as grocery stores and drugstores (e.g., CVS, Target, Walgreens), and offers relatively inexpensive healthcare services, including camp and school physicals, care for minor ailments (e.g., colds, earaches, bronchitis, flu, strep throat, minor rashes, and minor wounds) and common vaccinations.

Miniclinics are usually staffed by nurse practitioners, who (in most states) can write prescriptions and conduct basic medical exams and procedures. Not surprisingly, such clinics have met with some resistance from competing health providers (family practitioners and emergi-centers) and are seen as providing limited service competition. Critics suggest that they present problems in areas of continuity of care, quality of care, referral, and insurance issues. Nevertheless, the cost of a miniclinic visit is typically about one half the cost of a physician visit, so miniclinics are drawing interest from both health insurance companies and employers, which are constantly seeking innovative ways to reduce healthcare costs (Kher, 2006).

Another way that community pharmacists have diversified is through the provision of pharmaceutical care. Hepler and Strand (1990) define pharmaceutical care as "the responsible provision of drug therapy for the purpose of achieving definite outcomes that improves a patient's quality of life" (p.539). The four possible outcomes include (1) cure of a disease, (2) elimination and reduction of a patient's symptomatology, (3) arresting or slowing of the disease process, and (4) preventing a disease or symptomatology. Traditionally, pharmacists have been primarily concerned with the process of care—that is, what they do when the patient receives care (determining whether the correct drug and the right dose at the right time are provided). With the focus on outcomes, the pharmacist also takes responsibility for what happens to the patient when the drug is given (the outcome of care). Examples of outcome criteria include increased patient knowledge of the specific disease, improved medication compliance, improved medication therapy, decreased adverse reactions, decreased misuse and abuse, and higher patient satisfaction levels (see Chapter 4).

Given that more independent community pharmacies are facing the threat of closure because of steadily declining gross margins and increasing competition by high-volume pharmacies and mail-order centers, an increasing impetus exists for pharmacists to adopt the pharmaceutical care role. As managed care programs continue to lower prescription drug reimbursements, pharmacists should investigate other revenue sources, such as providing cognitive services.

To assume this role, community pharmacists must be trained to provide pharmaceutical care. The emphasis in such training programs is to encourage the community pharmacist to assume the role of the drug therapy expert and to be responsible for the reduction of drug-related problems. This training should include documenting clinical and financial successes rather than assuming savings. These programs also strive to get the pharmacist more involved in patient care in the hope that it will result in improved treatment outcomes and reduce utilization of more expensive services, such as hospitalization and unnecessary physician visits, thereby reducing the overall cost of health care.

The University of Minnesota's College of Pharmacy was one of the pioneers in development, training, and support of community pharmacists in the pharmaceutical care role. Another early developer of pharmaceutical care training programs can be found in Iowa, where the two colleges of pharmacy (University of Iowa and Drake University) and the Iowa Pharmacists Association came together to promote pharmaceutical care training and development in community pharmacy practice settings. Presently, some national pharmacy organizations (e.g., American Pharmacists Association, American Society of Health-Systems Pharmacists) and a number of state organizations offer pharmaceutical care training programs. For example, training programs have been developed in the areas of anticoagulation, asthma, diabetes, dyslipidemias, and hypertension.

Although the pharmacist's role in pharmaceutical care is promoted by pharmacy academia and organizational leaders, the concept of pharmaceutical care is not yet widely accepted by consumers, physicians, and health insurance carriers. Before insurance carriers begin reimbursing pharmacists for pharmaceutical care services, they are requesting evidence that the programs are cost effective (Scott & Miller, 1997). Some of the research supporting their effectiveness is presented next.

Pharmacist responsibilities have evolved from the traditional dispensing of medications to an expanded patient-oriented profession known as pharmaceutical care.

Studies conducted in the 1990s and early in the 2000s have confirmed the effectiveness of pharmacists' clinical services in helping to assure the safe, effective, and cost-conscious use of medications. One of these studies suggests that for every $1 invested in clinical pharmacy services, nearly $17 is saved in the form of reduced medication expenditures associated with a reduction in drug-related morbidity (Schumock, 2008).

Pharmacists in the Asheville project in North Carolina have been providing services to patients with diabetes since 1997. Pharmacists received reimbursement from two local employers for providing cognitive services (e.g., education, assessment, monitoring, follow-up, and referral). The pharmaceutical care group's A1C concentrations and satisfaction with services improved more significantly than a comparison group. The Asheville project showed that face-to-face meetings between diabetic patients and trained pharmacists resulted in significant improvements in clinical, humanistic, and economic outcomes (Cranor & Christensen, 2003; Cranor, Bunting, & Christensen, 2003a, 2003b).

In the Diabetes Ten City Challenge conducted by the American Pharmaceutical Association, 30 employers in 10 U.S. cities established a voluntary health benefit for employees, dependents, and retirees with diabetes. Employers used incentives, such as waiving copayments for diabetes medications and supplies, to encourage people to manage their diabetes. Local pharmacists were trained as coaches, who helped patients track their blood sugar levels and cholesterol and to control their disease through exercise, nutrition, and lifestyle changes. Data on 573 diabetic patients enrolled in the program for at least 1 year reported that average total healthcare costs per patient were reduced by $1,079 (7.2%), compared to projected costs. Each patient also saved an average of $593 per year on diabetes medications and supplies. Statistically significant improvements were observed for clinical measures including a decreased mean glycosylated hemoglobin level (from 7.5% to 7.1%), a decreased mean low-density lipoprotein cholesterol level, and a decreased mean systolic blood pressure. So compared with baseline data, more positive clinical and economic outcomes were achieved for patients who participated in the Diabetes Ten City Challenge program for 1 year (Fera, Blumi, & Ellis, 2009). Both the Asheville study and the Diabetes Ten City Challenge study demonstrate the value of pharmaceutical care provided by the community pharmacist.

In a randomized trial, Tsuyuki and colleagues reported on the impact of community pharmacists' ($n = 54$ pharmacies) intervention in the process of cholesterol risk management in patients at high risk for cardiovascular events. The pharmacist intervention group received education and a brochure on risk factors, point-of-care cholesterol measurement, physician referral, and follow-up for 16 weeks. In the intervention group, pharmacists faxed a form to the primary care physician listing risk factors and suggestions. Usual-care patients received the same brochure and general advice with only minimal follow-up. Among the 675 patients enrolled in this study, the primary end point was reached in 57% of intervention patients versus 31% of usual-care patients, and the results were statistically significant. The cholesterol risk management program demonstrates the value of community pharmacists working in collaboration with physicians (Tsuyuki et al., 2002).

During a 3-year cholesterol management program, Project ImPACT (Improve Persistence and Compliance with Therapy) included 26 ambulatory care pharmacists who managed patients with lipid disorders. The rate for compliance with lipid-lowering drug therapy improved to about 90%, and nearly two thirds of participants maintained accepted treatment goals (Blumi, McKenney, & Cziraky, 2000).

However, not all studies have demonstrated the value of pharmaceutical care programs. For instance, Weinberger and colleagues (2002) assessed the effectiveness of a pharmaceutical care program for patients with asthma or chronic obstructive pulmonary disease in a randomized trial involving 898 patients who were monitored over 12 months at 36 community drug stores in Indianapolis, Indiana. The pharmaceutical care program ($n = 447$) provided pharmacists with clinical data (peak expiratory flow rates, emergency department visits, hospitalizations, and medication compliance), training, and patient education materials. The peak expiratory flow rates monitoring group ($n = 363$) received a peak flow meter, instructions about its use, and monthly calls to elicit peak expiratory flow rates. The usual-care group ($n = 303$) did not receive the same items as the monitoring group. At 12 months, patients receiving pharmaceutical care had significantly higher peak flow rates than the usual-care group, but not higher than the rates seen in the peak expiratory flow rate monitoring control group. Asthma patients receiving pharmaceutical care had significantly more breathing-related emergency department or hospital visits than the usual-care group. The researchers concluded that this program increased patients' peak expiratory flow rates compared with usual care, but provided little benefit compared with peak flow monitoring alone. While pharmaceutical care increased patient satisfaction, the investigators also found that it increased the amount of breathing-related medical care sought (Weinberger et al., 2002).

In another project, an asthma project was incorporated into the Asheville project and the objective was to assess the clinical, humanistic, and economic outcomes of a community-based medication therapy management (MTM) program for 207 adult patients with asthma over 5 years in 12 pharmacies in Asheville, North Carolina. The intervention was done by 18 certificate-trained community and hospital pharmacists who were trained by a certified asthma educator; follow-up was conducted using scheduled consultations, monitoring, and recommendations to physicians. The main outcomes measured were changes in forced expiratory volume in 1 second, asthma severity, related emergency department/hospital events, and changes in costs over time. The results reported significantly improved measures of asthma control (forced expiratory volume in 1 second and severity classification) that were sustained for as long as 5 years. The percentage of patients with asthma action plans increased from 63% to 99%, emergency department visits decreased from 9.9% to 1.3%, and hospitalizations from 4.0% to 1.9%. Spending on asthma medications increased; however, total asthma-related costs were significantly lower than the projections, based on the study population's historical trends. Direct cost savings averaged $725/patient/year, and indirect cost savings were estimated to be $1,230/patient/year. Despite the increased medication costs that resulted from increased use, the authors concluded that patients with asthma who received education and long-term medication therapy management services had maintained significant improvements and had significantly decreased overall asthma-related costs (Bunting & Cranor, 2006).

In 2006, the Centers for Medicare and Medicaid Services implemented the Medicare Prescription Drug Benefit (Part D) for seniors. As part of this program, some Medicare beneficiaries will receive MTM services. The intention of this program is to ensure that seniors who have annual prescription costs of $4,000 or more, have multiple chronic disease states, and are taking multiple chronic prescription medications receive management assistance with their medication regimens, thereby ensuring that their drugs are used safely, effectively, and within a reasonable cost range. While pharmacists continue to be the leading provider of MTM services, it is also performed by other providers (e.g., nurse or physician). Sponsors can use internal and/or outside personnel (e.g., pharmacy benefit manager, MTM vendor, disease management vendor, community pharmacists, long-term care pharmacists, etc.) to provide the MTM services. Some of the research supporting the pharmacist's role in providing MTM is presented next.

In the first study, pharmacist-based MTM service for the North Carolina State Health Plan enrollees was assessed. Pharmacists identified 3.6 potential drug therapy problems per resident at the initial visit and recommended a drug therapy change in about 50% of residents and contacted the prescriber about 85% of the time, and about 50% of residents with a potential drug therapy problem had a change in drug therapy (Christensen, Roth, Trystad, & Byrd, 2007).

In a second study, MTM services were assessed for hypertension and dyslipidemia provided by pharmacists for six Minnesota ambulatory clinics. Since total health expenditures decreased significantly from $11,965 to $8,197, they reported that every $1 invested in MTM services saved $12 in other healthcare expenses (Isetts, Schondelmeyer, Artz, Lenartz, Heaton, Wadd, et al., 2008).

Multiple studies have been done to assess the clinical, humanistic, and economic impact of pharmaceutical care. Despite the evidence presented and the valuable inroads that community pharmacists have made into patient care, pharmaceutical care to the average patient remains an enigma, primarily because it is not provided on a broad scale and in an identifiable manner in the community pharmacies, where most people encounter pharmacists. National and state pharmaceutical organizations, community pharmacists, and researchers need to work together to demonstrate the impact of pharmaceutical care programs before the concept will be broadly accepted. For example, in the case study, George is considering whether he should integrate pharmaceutical care into his community pharmacy practice.

CONCLUSION

Ambulatory care services have undergone rapid development and expansion since 1990. With managed care being established as the pinnacle of healthcare reform, continued emphasis will be placed on developing innovative and cost-effective services.

QUESTIONS FOR FURTHER DISCUSSION

1. What pharmaceutical care innovations from the Indian Health Service can be adapted for use in community pharmacy practice?
2. Several ambulatory care services have developed in the past decade. What new services do you envision in the next decade?
3. Contrast ambulatory medical practice in rural and urban areas in your state.
4. Contrast ambulatory pharmacy practice in rural and urban areas in your state.

KEY TOPICS AND TERMS

Community health centers
Community pharmacy
Emergency services
Health department
Hospital clinics
Indian Health Service
Managed care
Pharmaceutical care
Primary care
Public health

REFERENCES

Alsuwaidan, S., Malone, D. C., Billups, S. J., & Carter, B. L. (1998). Characteristics of ambulatory care clinics and pharmacists in Veterans Affairs medical centers. *American Journal of Health-Systems Pharmacy, 55,* 68–72.

American College of Healthcare Executives. (1993). *Managed care in Medicaid: Lessons for policy and program design.* Melrose Park, IL: Health Administration Press.

Barnes, P.M., Bloom B. (2008). Complementary and alternative medicine use among adults and children: United States, National Health Statistics Reports. Number 12, December 10, 2008.

Blumi, B. M., McKenney, J. M., & Cziraky, M. J. (2000). Pharmaceutical care services and results in Project ImPACT: Hyperlipidemia. *Journal of the American Pharmacists Association, 40,* 157–165.

Bunting, B. A., & Cranor, C.W. (2006). The Asheville project: Long-term clinical, humanistic, and economic outcomes of a community-based medication therapy management program for asthma, *Journal of the American Pharmacists Association, 46,* 133–147.

Carter, B. L., & Helling, D. K. (1992). Ambulatory care pharmacy services: The incomplete agenda. *Annals of Pharmacotherapy, 26,* 701–708.

Carter, B. L., Malone, D. C., Billups, S. J., Valuck R. J., Barnette, D.J., Sintek, C.D., … Amato, M. (2001). Interpreting the findings of the IMPROVE study. *American Journal of Health-Systems Pharmacy, 58,* 1330–1337.

Chiquette, E., Amato, M. G., & Bussey, H. I. (1998). Comparison of an anticoagulation clinic with usual medical care. *Archives of Internal Medicine, 158,* 1641–1647.

Chrischilles, E. A., Helling, D. K., & Rowland, C. R. (1984a). Clinical pharmacy services in family practice: Cost-benefit analysis. I: Physician time and quality of care. *Drug Intelligence in Clinical Pharmacy, 18,* 333–341.

Chrischilles, E. A., Helling, D. K., & Rowland, C. R. (1984b). Clinical pharmacy services in family practice: Cost-benefit analysis. II: Referrals, appointment, compliance and cost. *Drug Intelligence in Clinical Pharmacy, 18,* 436–441.

Christensen, D. B., Roth, M., Trystad T., & Byrd, J. (2007). Evaluation of a pilot medication therapy management project within the North Carolina state health plan. *Journal of the American Pharmacists Association, 47,* 471–483.

Copeland, G. P., & Apgar, D. A. (1980). The pharmacist–practitioner training program. *Drug Intelligence in Clinical Pharmacy, 14,* 114–119.

Cranor, C. W., & Christensen, D. B. (2003). The Asheville project: Short-term outcomes of a community pharmacy diabetes care program. *Journal of the American Pharmacists Association, 43,* 149–159.

Cranor, C. W., Bunting, B. A., & Christensen, D. B. (2003a). The Asheville project: Factors associated with outcomes of a community pharmacy diabetes care program. *Journal of the American Pharmacists Association, 43,* 160–172.

Cranor, C. W., Bunting, B. A., & Christensen, D. B. (2003b). The Asheville project: Long-term outcomes of a community pharmacy diabetes care program, *Journal of the American Pharmacists Association, 43,* 173–184.

Eichelberger, B. N. (1980). Family practice clinical pharmacy opportunities in the community setting. *American Journal of Hospital Pharmacy, 37,* 740–742.

Ellis, S. L., Carter, B. L., Billups, S. J., Malone, D.C., Carter, B.L., Covey, D., ... Amato, M. (2000). Types of interventions made by clinical pharmacists in the IMPROVE study. *Pharmacotherapy, 20,* 429–435.

Fera, T., Blumi, B. M., & Ellis, W. M. (2009). Diabetes Ten City Challenge: Final economic and clinical results. *Journal of American Pharmacists Association, 49,* e52–e60.

Flowers, L., Wick, J., Figg, W. D., McClelland, R. H., Shiber, M. Britton, J.E., ... Huntzinger, P. (2009). U.S. public health service commissioned corps pharmacists: Making a difference in advancing the nation's health. *Journal of the American Pharmacists Association, 49,* 446–452.

Foss, M. T., Shock, P. H., & Sintek, C. D. (1999). Efficient operation of a high-volume anticoagulation clinic. *American Journal of Health-Systems Pharmacy, 56,* 43–48.

Garabedian-Ruffalo, S. M., Gray, D. R., Sax, M. J., & Ruffalo, R. L. (1985). Retrospective evaluation of a pharmacist-managed warfarin anticoagulation clinic. *American Journal of Hospital Pharmacy, 42,* 304–308.

Gordon, J. S. (1996). Alternative medicine and the family practitioner. *American Family Physician, 54,* 2205–2212.

Gray, D. R., Garabedian-Ruffalo, S. M., & Chretien, S. D. (1985). Cost justification of a clinical pharmacist-managed anti-coagulation clinic. *Drug Intelligence in Clinical Pharmacy, 19,* 575–580.

Hepler, C. D., & Strand, L. M. (1990). Opportunities and responsibilities in pharmaceutical care. *American Journal of Hospital Pharmacy, 47,* 533–542.

Hoffer, E. (1979). Emergency medical services. *New England Journal of Medicine, 301,* 1118.

Iglehart, J. K. (1993). The American health care system: Community hospitals. *New England Journal of Medicine, 329,* 372–376.

Isetts, B. J., Schondelmeyer, S. W., Artz, M. B., Lenartz, L.A., Heaton, A.H., Wadd, W.B, Brown, L.M., & Cipolle, R.J. (2008). Clinical and economic outcomes of medication therapy management services: The Minnesota experience. *Journal of the American Pharmacists Association, 48,* 203–211.

Johnston, T. S., & Heffron, W. A. (1981). Clinical pharmacy in family practice residency programs. *Journal of Family Practice, 13,* 91–94.

Kher, U. (2006, March 20). Get a check-up in Aisle 3. *Time,* pp. 52–53.

Leal, S., Glover, J. J., Herrier, R. N., & Felix, A. (2004). Improving quality of care in diabetes through a comprehensive pharmacist-based disease management program. *Diabetes Care, 27,* 2983–2984.

Madison, D. L. (1983). The case for community oriented primary care. *Journal of the American Medical Association, 249,* 1279–1282.

Mathematic Policy Research, Inc. (2004, November 30). Evaluation of HRSA's clinical pharmacy demonstration projects. Final report, volume II: Case studies, chapter II. *Siouxland Community Health Center Network,* pp. 11–20.

McGhan, W. F., Stimmel, G. L., Hall, T. G., & Gilman, P. M. (1983). A comparison of pharmacists and physicians on the quality of prescribing for ambulatory hypertensive patients. *Medical Care, 21,* 435–444.

McQueen, C. E., & Hume, A. L. (2006). Introduction to botanical and nonbotanical natural medicines. In R. R. Berardi, L. A. Kroon, & J. H. McDermott, et.al. (Eds.), *Handbook of nonprescription drugs: An integrative approach to self-care* (pp.1096–1101). Washington, DC: APhA.

Mezey, A. P. (1999). Ambulatory care. In S. Jonas & A. R. Kovner (Eds.), *Health care delivery in the United States* (pp. 183–205). New York, NY: Springer.

Mezey, A. P., & Lawrence, R. S. (1995). Ambulatory care. In A. R. Kovner (Ed.), *Jonas's health care delivery in the United States* (pp. 122–161). New York, NY: Springer.

Morehead, M. A., Donaldson, R. S., & Servavelli, M. R. (1971). Comparisons between OEO neighborhood health centers and other health care providers of ratings of the quality of health care. *American Journal of Public Health, 61,* 1294–1306.

Morse, G. D., Douglas, J. V., Upton, J. H., Rodgers, S., & Gal, P. (1986). Effect of pharmacist intervention and control of resistant hypertension. *American Journal of Hospital Pharmacy, 43,* 905–909.

Murray, M. D., Loos, B., Eckert, G. J., Zhou, X., & Tierney, W. M. (1999). Work patterns of ambulatory care pharmacists with access to electronic guideline-based treatment suggestions. *American Journal of Health-Systems Pharmacy, 56,* 225–232.

Paavola, F. G., Kermanoski, K. R., & Pittman, R. E. (1997). Pharmaceutical services in the United States Public Health Service. *American Journal of Health-Systems Pharmacy, 54,* 766–772.

Reinders, T. P. (1986). Clinical services and ambulatory care. In T. R. Brown, & M. C. Smith (Eds.), *Handbook of institutional pharmacy practice* (pp. 509–515). Baltimore, MD: Williams and Wilkins.

Robertson, D. L., & Groh, M. (1982). Activities of the clinical pharmacist in a private family practice. *Journal of Family Practice Research, 1,* 188–194.

Roemer, M. (1981). *Ambulatory health services in America.* Rockville, MD: Aspen Systems.

Roth, R., Stewart, R. D., Rogers, K., & Cannon, G. M. (1984). Out of hospital cardiac arrest: Factors associated with survival. *Annals of Emergency Medicine, 13,* 237–243.

Scheffler, R. M., Waitzman, N. J., & Hillman, J. M. (1998). The productivity of physician assistants and nurse practitioners and health force policy in the era of managed care. *Journal of Allied Health, 25,* 207–217.

Schumock, G. T., Meek, P. D., Ploetz, P. A., & Vermeulen, L. C. (1996). Economic evaluations of clinical pharmacy services—1988–1995. *Pharmacotherapy, 16,* 1188–2008.

Schwartz, J. L. (1971). Preliminary observations of free clinics. In D. E. Smith, D. J. Bentel, & J. L. Schwartz (Eds.), *The free clinic: A community approach to health care and drug abuse* (pp. 144–206). Beloit, WI: Stash Press.

Scott, D. M., Boyd, S. T., Stephans, M., Augustine, S. C., & Reardon, T. P. (2006). Outcomes of pharmacist-managed diabetes care services in a community health center. *American Journal of Health-Systems Pharmacy, 63(21),* 116–122.

Scott, D. M., & Miller, L. G. (1997). Reimbursement for pharmacy cognitive services: Insurance company assessment. *Journal of Managed Care Pharmacy, 2,* 699–714.

Scott, D. M., & Nordin, J. D. (1980). Pharmacist role in projects for children and youth. *American Journal of Hospital Pharmacy, 37,* 1339–1342.

Sczupak, C. A., & Conrad, W. F. (1977). Relationship between patient-oriented pharmaceutical services and therapeutic outcomes of ambulatory patients with diabetes mellitus. *American Journal of Hospital Pharmacy, 34,* 1238–1242.

Sherman, M. A. (1979). Mobile intensive care units: An evaluation of effectiveness. *Journal of the American Medical Association, 241,* 1899–1901.

Shi, L., Singh, D. A. (2008). Outpatient and primary care services. In L. Shi, & D. A. Singh (Eds.). *Delivering health care in America: A systems approach* (4th ed., pp. 243–287). Sudbury, MA: Jones and Bartlett.

Sparer, G., & Anderson, A. (1975). *Cost of services at neighborhood health centers: A comparative analysis.* Washington, DC: Office of Economic Opportunity.

Stimmel, G. L., & McGhan, W. F. (1981). The pharmacist as prescriber of drug therapy: The USC pilot project. *Drug Intelligence of Clinical Pharmacy, 15,* 665–772.

Tootelian, D. H., & Gaddeke, R. M. (1993). *Essentials of pharmacy management.* St. Louis, MO: Mosby-Yearbook.

Tsuyuki, R. T., Johnson, J. A., Teo, K. K., Simpson, S. H., Ackman, M.L., Biggs, R.S., . . . Taylor, J. G. (2002). A randomized trial of the effect of community pharmacist intervention on cholesterol risk management: The study of cardiovascular risk intervention by pharmacists (SCRIP). *Archives of Internal Medicine, 162,* 1149–1155.

U.S. Department of Health and Human Services, National Institutes of Health, National Center for Complementary and Alternative Medicine (NCCAM). (2010, February 24). *The Use of*

Complementary and Alternative Medicine in the United States. Retrieved February 4, 2011 from http://nccam.nih.gov/news/camstats/2007/camsurvey_fs1.htm

Weinberger, M., Murray, M. D., Marrero, D. G., Brewer, N. Lykens, M. Harris, L.E., … Tierney, W. M. (2002). Effectiveness of pharmacist care for patients with reactive airways disease: A randomized controlled trial. *Journal of the American Medical Association, 288,* 1594–1602.

Weinerman, E. R., Ratner R. S., Robbins, A., & Lavenhar, M. A. (1966). Yale studies in ambulatory medical care: Determinants of use of hospital emergency services. *American Journal of Public Health, 56,* 1037–1056.

Williams, S. J. (1993). Ambulatory health care services. In S. J. Williams & P. R. Torrens (Eds.), *Introduction to health services* (4th ed., vol. 1, pp. 108–113). Albany, NY: Delmar.

CHAPTER 9

Long-Term Care

Aleda M. H. Chen and Kimberly S. Plake*

Case Scenario

In the past year, Betty, a 76-year-old widow, has experienced a decline in her health. Until recently, she was an active and reasonably healthy woman. One morning in January, she slipped on some ice in her driveway, fell, and broke her hip. During her recovery, Betty received rehabilitative care while residing at a local nursing home, which was covered by Medicare. After she completed her rehabilitation, Betty was discharged and moved in with her daughter for a short time until she was able to return home.

Tracy, her 44-year-old daughter, works full-time as a real estate agent. In addition, she has a son in high school and a daughter in college. Initially, Tracy did not have much difficulty in caring for her mother. Although her mother had experienced a serious injury, she was recovering well and, for the most part, was still able to care for herself. Unfortunately, Betty experienced a setback when she had a heart attack later in the year and needed significant help from her daughter. It became more challenging for Tracy to balance her work and family responsibilities, and she needed to continue to work full-time to support her family. Tracy's siblings lived out of state, so they were unable to help provide care for their mother.

When her mother continued to need assistance with caring for herself—dressing, bathing, and toileting—Tracy talked to her mother about care alternatives, such as visiting nursing services, assisted living facilities, and nursing homes. Costs associated with these alternative care options were a concern. Because of her age, Betty is covered by Medicare. She also has a Medigap insurance policy and a Medicare Part D prescription drug plan. However, neither of these plans covers the type of care that Betty needs—that is, custodial care rather than skilled nursing care. As a consequence, most of the bills would be paid for by Betty's limited financial resources.

Ultimately, Tracy and Betty decided on a nursing home nearby. Betty sold her home and paid out of pocket until her financial resources were depleted. At that time, she qualified for Medicaid, which paid for her nursing home stay.

*With acknowledgment to Kristin B. Meyer and Ernest J. Dole.

LEARNING OBJECTIVES _____

Upon completion of this chapter, the student shall be able to:

• Define *long-term care*
• Compare and contrast Medicare and Medicaid regarding their coverage of long-term care services
• Explain the reasons patients face financial difficulties in paying for long-term care services
• Identify and explain the types of institutional and community-based long-term care services available to patients and their families
• Describe the types of patients who use long-term care services
• Explain why there is a need for extended-care services
• Distinguish between the philosophies of institutional and community-based long-term care
• Define *aging in place*
• Compare and contrast medication regimen review (MRR), drug utilization evaluation (DUE), and drug utilization review (DUR)
• List the opportunities for pharmacist involvement in the care of residents in long-term care facilities
• Describe the benefits of pharmacist involvement in the care of residents in long-term care facilities
• Identify resources available to consultant pharmacists who wish to further develop their patient care skills

CHAPTER QUESTIONS

1. What factors have led to the increasing need for long-term care (LTC) facilities?
2. What opportunities are available for pharmacists in the LTC setting?
3. What are the financing mechanisms available to persons who use LTC services?
4. What types of patients use LTC services?

INTRODUCTION

In the United States, many types of healthcare services are available. One type of care for which use is increasing is called extended-care or long-term care (LTC). LTC is defined as a "set of health, personal care, and social services delivered over a sustained period of time to persons who have lost or never acquired some degree of functional capacity" (Kane & Kane, 1987, p. 4). In addition, it is defined as "health, social, and residential services provided to chronically disabled persons with functional or cognitive impairments" (Liu, 1994, p. 476). Primarily, LTC assists people who have disabilities due to limitations in performing activities of daily living (ADLs) such as bathing, dressing, and toileting, or instrumental activities of daily living (IADLs) such as shopping and food preparation (Katz, Ford, Moskowitz, Jackson, & Jaffe, 1963; Lawton & Brody, 1969). For example, Betty, in our case scenario, had problems with the ADLs of dressing, bathing, and toileting and needed additional care beyond the capabilities of her family. It was at this time that she entered the nursing home, which could provide assistance with those activities.

Many people assume that LTC refers only to nursing home care, but LTC can occur in both community and institutional settings. Estimates indicate that 10.9 million individuals in the community setting receive LTC, and 1.8 million individuals receive institution-based care (Kaye, Harrington, & LaPlante, 2010). The determination of the type of care received is based on the individual patient's needs and circumstances. The factors determining the type of LTC needed include the level of disability, availability of informal caregivers, financial circumstances, availability of public programs, and other personal circumstances (Andel, Hyer, & Slack, 2007; Liu, 1994). The main risk factors for institutionalization include advanced age, number and types of chronic conditions, difficulties with ADLs, and living alone (Andel et al., 2007; Gaugler, Duval, Anderson, & Kane, 2007; Nihtila et al., 2008). Other risk factors include cognitive impairment, ethnicity (minorities are generally at a lower risk), low social support, poverty, difficulties with IADLs, outpatient admission, and hospital admission (Andel et al., 2007; Banaszak-Holl et al., 2004; Bharucha, Pandav, Shen, Dodge, & Ganguli, 2004; Gaugler et al., 2007).

This chapter addresses many of the LTC options available to individuals in the United States, including institutional services (such as nursing homes, continuing care retirement communities, and psychiatric institutions), community-based services (such as home health care and hospice), and community facility services (such as adult day care). In addition, it examines the changing role of pharmacy and pharmacists in these healthcare environments.

PATIENTS WHO MAY REQUIRE LONG-TERM CARE SERVICES

Older Adults

Although the majority of older adults are not seriously impaired and do not need LTC services, the primary users of these services are individuals older than age 65 (Jones, Dwyer, Bercovitz, & Strahan, 2009). In general, the need for LTC services increases with age (Andel et al., 2007). As people age, they are more likely to develop chronic diseases and incur disabilities similar to Betty's. Approximately 80% of people older than age 65 have at least one chronic disease, and 50% have two such conditions (He, Sengupta, Velkoff, & DeBarros, 2005). In addition, 19% of adults over the age of 65 experience disability or physical limitations, which leads to difficulty in performing IADLs or ADLs (Manton, 2008).

For people with a disability, LTC services may be provided by family and friends—often called informal caregiving—as was the case initially with Betty (Wolff & Kasper, 2006). Although friends may contribute to care, the primary providers of informal caregiving are spouses and adult children, with spouses and children collectively providing 79.7 percent of care (Wolff & Kasper, 2006) (**Exhibits 9-1** and **9-2**).

In the case of informal caregiving, the typical caregiver is a woman who is 48 years old, has some college education, lives within 20 or 30 minutes of the care recipient, and provides care for her mother approximately 20 hours per week (National Alliance for Caregiving & American Association of Retired Persons, 2009; Wolff & Kasper, 2006). Males are increasingly providing care, as 34% of caregivers were men in 2009 (National Alliance for Caregiving & American Association of Retired Persons, 2009; Wolff & Kasper, 2006). However, female caregivers often spend more time providing

Exhibit 9-1   The Spectrum of the Long-Term Care Environment

Hospital-based nursing facility   Community-based care
Subacute care   Adult congregate living
Nursing facility   Adult day care
Psychiatric hospital   Home health care
Intermediate care facility for the   Community mental health center
   mentally retarded   Hospice
                                         Senior center
                                         Retirement housing
                                         Correctional facility
                                         Home care
                                         Independent community living

Source: From Pharmacy Practice in the Long-Term Care Environment by W. Simonson. This figure is reprinted with permission from the *Journal of Managed Care Pharmacy*, 1997;3(2):190.

care compared to their male counterparts. In addition, females are more likely to provide direct personal care, such as bathing, toileting, and dressing. Men are more likely to provide indirect caregiving by arranging services or outside care (National Alliance for Caregiving & American Association of Retired Persons, 2009).

Approximately 70% of older adults will require long-term care at some point during their lifetime and at least 40% will spend time in a nursing home (U.S. Department of Health and Human Services, 2009). Only 4.5% reside in a nursing home (Hetzel &

Exhibit 9-2   Terminology Describing Community-Based Care Environments

Residential care facility   Leisure care facility
Assisted living home   Retirement home
Board and care home   Adult care facility
Chronic custodial care   Life care–continuing care
Congregate care   retirement community
Domiciliary care   Catered housing
Home for adults   Personal board and care
Residential home   Sheltered care
Rest home   Subsidized apartment building
Sheltered home   Residential board and lodging
Group home for mentally   facility
   retarded persons   Senior apartment building
Adult foster home   Personal care home
Community-based care facility

Source: Reprinted with permission from W. Simonson, *Consultant Pharmacy Practice,* (2nd ed.), 1996, p. 49.

Smith, 2001). In 2004, nearly 88.3% of the 1.5 million U.S. nursing home residents were older than age 65, and 45.2% were 85 years or older. The majority of these residents were female (71.2%) and white (85.5%) (Jones et al., 2009). Approximately 84.9% of older adults in nursing homes received assistance with three or more ADLs, and 75% received assistance with at least five ADLs. Only 1.6% did not need assistance in performing any ADLs. The majority of residents needed some assistance with bathing (96.5%), dressing (88.5%), and toileting (82.6%). In addition, 57.5% needed help with eating (Jones et al., 2009). Conditions that are commonly found in older adults who reside in nursing homes include diseases of the circulatory system (e.g., hypertension, heart disease, and cerebrovascular disease), mental disorders (e.g., dementia, mental retardation), diseases of the nervous system and sensory organs (e.g., Parkinson's disease), and bowel and bladder incontinence (Jones et al., 2009).

The use of long-term care services is expected to increase in coming years, primarily because of the aging of the baby boomer population (born from 1946 to 1964). In 2011, the first of the baby boomers began reaching age 65. Although the current population of older adults have decreasing rates of disability due to advances in health care (Manton, 2008), the baby boomer generation is expected to have greater rates of disability, which may be attributed to rising rates of obesity (Martin, Schoeni, Freedman, & Andreski, 2007; Seeman, Merkin, Crimmins, & Karlamangla, 2010). According to current predictions, disabilities among older adults will increase, which will increase healthcare utilization (Seeman et al., 2010). Given that LTC use is more predominant in persons 65 years of age and older, demand for LTC is expected to grow even more from 2011 to 2020, as 12 million older adults are expected to need LTC services in 2020 (U.S. Department of Health and Human Services, 2009).

Patients With Chronic Diseases

Although the elderly are the primary users of LTC, other individuals also use these services. Some patients younger than age 65 who live with chronic diseases and terminal illnesses require assistance beyond the informal caregiving provided by family and friends (Jones et al., 2009; Kaye et al., 2010). For example, a younger adult with end-stage renal failure may need nursing home care as the disease progresses. Besides nursing home care, these patients often receive services from hospice, home health care, and other community-based care providers. Because of the progressive nature of chronic disease, these patients may require assistance in performing daily activities and complying with their healthcare regimens. Diagnoses commonly associated with LTC services include dementia, Parkinson's disease, stroke, depression, hip fractures, and diabetes (Nihtila et al., 2008).

Alzheimer's disease is an example of a chronic disease that often requires LTC services. Approximately 10.5% of older adults in nursing homes have Alzheimer's disease (Jones et al., 2009). Individuals with Alzheimer's begin to experience memory impairment and have difficulty remembering new things. Over time, these individuals lose the ability to manage their finances, perform IADLs or ADLs, and may forget family and friends. These patients typically require assistance with ADLs and with maintaining health (such as taking medications), regardless of whether they reside in the home or in an institution. In addition, individuals with Alzheimer's disease have a tendency to wander from their homes or rooms and may not be able to return. They become disoriented and often cannot provide information, such as their name or the address where they live (National Institute on Aging, 2010).

While Alzheimer's disease generally strikes individuals 60 years or older, other illnesses requiring LTC services can occur in individuals much younger. Any disease that can limit physical functioning to a significant extent can increase the likelihood that the affected individual will need some type of LTC services, regardless of his or her age. For example, individuals who have severe head or spinal injuries as the result of an accident often require LTC as they often cannot perform ADLs.

Patients With Rehabilitative Needs

Like Betty with her broken hip, some patients may need LTC services for a short time. These patients generally require additional time to recover before returning home after discharge from a hospital or some type of rehabilitative services. Because of the emphasis on cost containment, patients frequently are released from the hospital earlier—and sicker—than in past years. If they are not ready to return to their homes, they may be discharged for additional care in a nursing home setting or to a rehabilitation center, similarly to Betty. Other patients may be ready to return home but need assistance there (such as patients recovering from a broken hip, other broken bones, or major surgery). In such cases, home health care may be provided. As stated earlier, the type of service used depends on the level of care required, the availability of informal caregivers (such as family and friends), and the patient's insurance coverage and other financial resources (Andel et al., 2007; Liu, 1994). The patient's physical and mental health also play a role in the decision-making process (Marengoni, Aguero-Torres, Timpini, Cossi, & Fratiglioni, 2008).

Patients With Terminal Illness

Patients who are terminally ill include individuals whose prognosis is poor and are thought to be close to death (typically within 6 months). For these patients, hospice care is often used to help with physical, social, and spiritual aspects of their illnesses. Although there are increasing numbers of institutional hospice facilities available, hospice services do not necessarily require institutionalization of the patient. Instead, they may allow patients to remain at home with family and friends while receiving palliative (comfort) care (Grant, Elk, Ferrell, Morrison, & von Gunten, 2009). Hospice or palliative care services can also provide informal caregivers with relief and support systems (Stevens, Lynm, & Glass, 2006).

FINANCING LONG-TERM CARE

This section provides a brief description of the types of financing available to individuals to pay for LTC services. Extended care services are financed in four major ways: (1) Medicare, (2) Medicaid, (3) private insurance, and (4) out-of-pocket resources.

Medicare is a federally operated insurance program primarily intended for individuals older than age 65. In addition, younger persons with disabilities or with end-stage renal disease may have coverage through Medicare. Eligibility for these individuals depends on the length of the person's disability, the type of disability, and the severity of the kidney damage. For instance, renal dialysis patients automatically qualify for Medicare coverage (Centers for Medicare and Medicaid Services, 2010).

Medicare has several components. Medicare Part A provides limited benefits for LTC institutional services such as skilled nursing care in residential homes. It also covers in-home or institutional-based hospice services for individuals who are expected to live 6 months or fewer (Centers for Medicare and Medicaid Services, 2010). In 2007, approximately 25% of nursing home care was paid for by Medicare (Ng, Harrington, & Kitchener, 2010). For Medicare to reimburse these services, the patient must be hospitalized at least 3 consecutive days and admitted to a skilled nursing facility within 30 days of discharge, and a doctor must certify that the patient requires rehabilitation or skilled nursing care on a daily basis for a hospital-treated condition (Centers for Medicare and Medicaid Services, 2010; U.S. Department of Health and Human Services, 2009). Medicare will pay for covered services for the first 20 days of care. For days 21 through 100, the patient must pay a co-payment for each day the service is used. For example, patients paid $137.50 per day in 2010. After 100 days, patients are expected to pay the full costs associated with their care in a skilled nursing facility. In addition, Medicare reimburses home healthcare services through Part A. Home healthcare services also are reimbursed by Part B (Centers for Medicare and Medicaid Services, 2010). Although Medicare pays for skilled nursing care, it usually does not pay for those who need only custodial care (e.g., help with bathing, dressing, using the bathroom, or eating) or other residential care services that older adults like Betty need (see Chapter 18). These services are primarily financed by Medicaid, private insurance, or out-of-pocket resources (Centers for Medicare and Medicaid Services, 2010; U.S. Department of Health and Human Services, 2009).

With the advent of Medicare Part D in 2006 (i.e., the prescription drug benefit for Medicare beneficiaries), there is now an added level of payment complexity for those receiving LTC services. For Medicare beneficiaries receiving LTC services, the type of service or the setting in which the services are delivered determines who pays for the prescription medications. For example, if a patient receives skilled nursing care in a nursing home within his or her benefit period, then Medicare Part A pays for the patient's prescription medications. Once the benefit period offered through Medicare Part A ends, the patient's prescriptions are paid for by Medicare Part D (if the patient is enrolled in the program) (Centers for Medicare and Medicaid Services, 2007). Since Betty, in our example, had Medicare Part D, her medications in the nursing home would be paid for by Medicare Part D. For hospice patients, symptom management and pain medications are covered by Part A, and Part D covers nonhospice medications (such as cardiac medications) (Centers for Medicare and Medicaid Services, 2010). Chapter 18 describes the Medicare program in detail.

Medicaid is a federally regulated, public welfare program for the poor. Although the program is regulated by the federal government, it is financed by both the federal and state governments and administered by the state. As a consequence, Medicaid programs vary from state to state with different qualifications for eligibility (usually based on income and assets) and services. In the example, Betty became eligible for Medicaid once she used up the majority of her personal financial resources. Currently, all 50 states include some type of benefits for LTC services for participants in the program (U.S. Department of Health and Human Services, 2009). Because custodial care is not reimbursed by Medicare, Medicaid often is the primary payer for nursing home care in many, if not all, states. In 2007, 42% of nursing home care was paid by Medicaid and 25% was paid by Medicare (Ng et al., 2010).

In the past, much of the LTC paid for by Medicaid was institutional care or nursing home care. Today, however, there is increasing interest in community-based health care services, such as assistance with ADLs in the home setting. In fact, Medicaid expenditures for home and community care have been growing over the last several years, with $41.8 billion going to this type of care in 2007, a 95% increase since 1999 (Ng et al., 2010). These care services often provide help with ADLs, such as bathing, toileting, and dressing. Community-based health care is likely to become even more popular in the future, given the desire of individuals to remain in the community and the lower costs associated with this type of care as compared to nursing home care (Ng et al., 2010).

Patients also use private insurance to finance their care. Many older individuals, like Betty, have policies that pay for those charges not covered by traditional Medicare. These health insurance policies are called Medigap insurance policies because they fill in the gaps in Medicare reimbursement. Depending on the policy, benefits may include payment of Medicare deductibles, Medicare co-payments, and extended home healthcare services. For example, many Medigap policies pay for the $137.50 co-payment during days 21 to 100 of eligible nursing home stays. Like Medicare itself, these policies do not include custodial or residential care benefits (U.S. Department of Health and Human Services, 2009). Older adults who chose to participate in Medigap plans must pay monthly insurance premiums in addition to co-payments (Centers for Medicare and Medicaid Services, 2010).

Many older adults purchase LTC insurance for the following two primary reasons: (1) Medicare and Medigap do not cover custodial care and skilled care beyond 100 days and (2) to avoid the spend-down of their assets before meeting financial eligibility requirements for Medicaid. This private insurance provides financial assistance in the event that a person needs to enter an assisted living or LTC facility. Some policies also assist individuals in paying for home healthcare services, hospice care, and adult day centers. Other popular benefits include case management services, homemaker services, transportation to medical appointments, and some medical equipment. Limits to these LTC policies are based on the expense, scope, duration of benefits, and exclusion of high-risk applicants. Individuals who already receive LTC services are not eligible for LTC insurance. These policies also can be expensive, with the average yearly premium cost in 2007 being $2,207 (U.S. Department of Health and Human Services, 2009).

In addition, some policies do not provide inflation protection, which would allow the benefit paid to increase as inflation increases. If a policy does not have such a clause, the benefit paid is the one stated at the time of purchase (U.S. Department of Health and Human Services, 2009). At first, this may not seem like a problem; however, if a person buys a policy at age 50 and does not need to use the policy until he or she is 70, there will be a significant difference in the benefit paid and the actual cost of care. Of course, inflation protection can greatly increase the premium, rendering some policies unaffordable. In addition, it is not certain that everyone will need LTC services, which makes it difficult for consumers to decide whether to purchase a policy. Also, policies are generally less expensive when purchased at a younger age. For example, the premium for individuals under 40 is, on average, $881 per year. The premium continues to rise until age 70, where it averages $3,206 per year (U.S. Department of Health and Human Services, 2009). This purchase decision is more difficult for younger consumers, however, because they do not know whether they will need LTC or LTC insurance benefits.

LTC insurance policies have been improving over the past several years, and some now include lifetime benefits, coverage for home health care, short deductible periods, and inflation protection. Nevertheless, this type of insurance is not as tightly regulated as Medigap policies are, and it may be confusing to some consumers. Consumers should compare policies and identify the benefits of these policies before purchasing. Buying policies at a younger age is cheaper, and individuals considering buying a policy should consult a professional if they have questions (U.S. Department of Health and Human Services, 2009).

If a patient does not have private insurance that covers LTC or if he does not qualify for Medicaid, the costs of care must be paid from the patient's financial resources. Family resources may be quickly depleted, depending on the location and type of nursing home selected. For example, in 2009, the national average cost for a yearlong stay in a semiprivate nursing home room was $72,270. Assisted living one-bedroom apartments cost approximately $37,572 per year (U.S. Department of Health and Human Services, 2009). Indeed, nursing home care for a sustained period of time can prove catastrophic to a patient's financial stability. In such cases, patients may have to spend down their assets to qualify for Medicaid. Betty paid for her own nursing home bills until her assets were exhausted.

Since paying for LTC services often can exhaust some families' financial resources, some older adults are seeking the advice of estate planners to set up trusts, long-term care annuities, and other financing options. An example of a financing option for older adults needing additional healthcare services is the reverse mortgage. Many older adults are homeowners, and a reverse mortgage allows them to receive a lump-sum payment, monthly payments, or a line of credit, thereby enabling them to remain in their own home despite a cash flow crunch. The borrower never owes more than the value of the home, and the loan comes due when the borrower moves, sells the home, or dies (U.S. Department of Health and Human Services, 2009).

INCREASING NEED FOR FACILITIES

In 1935, when the Social Security Act was adopted, the United States used the age of 65 or older as one of the criteria for eligibility (Social Security Administration, 2010). Thus the older adult population was defined as 65 years or older from then forward. Today's older adults can be divided into three categories: (1) the young old—aged 65 to 74; (2) the middle old—aged 75 to 84; and (3) the old old—85 years old and older (Rosenwaike, 1985). In 2008, 12.8% of the U.S. population was 65 years of age and older (U.S. Census Bureau, 2009a). A rapid increase in the number of older adults is expected between 2010 and 2030, when the baby boomers will reach age 65. By 2030, approximately 21.7% of Americans will be age 65 years or older. The fastest growing segment of the elderly population consists of those 85 years and older. By 2040, the number of people 85 years and older will more than triple to over 14.2 million (U.S. Census Bureau, 2009c). In addition, life expectancy has been increasing, such that the average life expectancy was 80.4 years for women and 75.3 years for men in 2007 (Minino, Xu, Kochanek, & Tejada-Vera, 2009). For babies born today, 82% will likely live to 65 years of age, with 35% surviving to 85 years (He et al., 2005).

Not only is America aging, but the demographics of the population also are changing. In 2008, 65.9% of the population was recognized as non-Hispanic white, 12.3% as African American, 15.1% as Hispanic, 4.4% as Asian American, and 0.8% as American Indian (some people identified themselves as belonging to more than one ethnic group) (U.S. Census Bureau, 2009b). The U.S. Census Bureau estimates that by 2020, nearly 40% of the U.S. population will be nonwhite, with Hispanics constituting the largest ethnic group. By 2050, non-Hispanic white Americans will account for approximately 46% of the country's population, becoming minorities (U.S. Census Bureau, 2009d).

The older population is currently less diverse than the population of the United States as a whole. In 2008, it was estimated that 14.8% of people 65 years and older were minorities, with African Americans representing the largest minority group at 8.4% (U.S. Census Bureau, 2009b). Over time, however, the trend seen in the national population of increasing diversity is expected to occur in the older population as well, with minorities predicted to account for 39% of the elderly population in 2050 (Federal Interagency Forum on Aging-Related Statistics, 2008). The changing demographics of the older population, along with the cultural expectations within various minority groups, will undoubtedly influence the provision of LTC services.

In addition, the roles of women are changing. This trend is of prime importance to the delivery of LTC services because wives, daughters, daughters-in-law, and even granddaughters provide two thirds of all informal caregiving services. One of a woman's primary societal roles is as a mother. The nature of the life cycle does provide some insulation against a woman's shouldering the responsibilities for aging parents and child care responsibilities at the same time. In recent decades, however, some women have postponed childbearing until their late 20s and 30s. Because of this delay in starting their own families, they may have to balance the dual responsibilities of caring for parents and children as Tracy did in the case scenario. Some women also have assumed responsibility for raising their grandchildren. The average age of an informal caregiver was 50 in 2009, so these women could be assuming several family roles (National Alliance for Caregiving & American Association of Retired Persons, 2009). In addition to their familial responsibilities, many women, like Tracy, work outside the home; which can make it difficult to care for an elderly parent. Approximately 75% of informal caregivers continue to work outside the home while caring for an aging family member (National Alliance for Caregiving & American Association of Retired Persons, 2009). The average family caregiver spends 19 hours per week in care-related activities, and women who must bear the double burden of performing paid work and caregiving for a parent deal with the situation in a variety of ways, such as transitioning to working part-time, taking a less demanding job, or leaving the workforce. In addition, they may consider using LTC services to care for their family members (National Alliance for Caregiving & American Association of Retired Persons, 2009).

The growth and increased interest in extended care have been primarily driven by the changing economics of health care. Between 1976 and 1987, U.S. spending for medical care exceeded inflation by approximately 80%. In 1987, national health expenditures were 11.1% of the gross national product and totaled $500 billion. Spending for federal Medicaid and Medicare programs grew from $70 billion in 1982 to $111 billion in 1987 (Schneider & Guralnik, 1990). In 1993, the average daily private room rates for skilled nursing care and unskilled nursing care in extended care facilities were $111 and $96, respectively (Marion Merrell Dow Inc., 1994). In the same year, the average charge for one day of hospitalization ranged from $700 to $1,000 (Brooks, 1994).

Costs have continued to spiral upward. In 2007, U.S. national health expenditures were 16.2% of the country's gross domestic product, amounting to more than $2.2 trillion. Spending by the federal government for health care totaled $754.4 billion, and state and local expenditures for health care amounted to $281.3 billion. With the first of the baby boomers turning 65 in 2011, health expenditures are expected to increase to 20.3% of the gross domestic product in 2019, equaling $4.4 trillion (Sisko et al., 2009). In 2009, the average rate for a semiprivate room in a nursing home was $198 a day and $3,131 per month for a one-bedroom assisted living unit (U.S. Department of Health and Human Services, 2009). Hospitalization rates have also increased since 1994, as the average Medicare payment for rehospitalization from a LTC facility was $10,352 in 2006 (Mor, Intrator, Feng, & Grabowski, 2010). The average length of stay in 2006 was 5.5 days for adults over 65 (DeFrances, Lucas, Buie, & Golosinskiy, 2008), making the average cost an estimated $1,882.18 per day.

Although extended care facilities are less costly than hospitals, their cost is still a major concern. National health expenditures for nursing home care totaled $190.4 billion in 2007 (Sisko et al., 2009). Approximately 70% of these services were paid by Medicare and Medicaid, with Medicaid paying for 49% of these costs (U.S. Department of Health and Human Services, 2009). LTC expenditures are predicted to increase by 6.4% a year between 2007 and 2018, costing $375.8 billion in 2018 (Sisko et al., 2009). If these forecasts prove correct, LTC expenditures will nearly double by 2018. The aging of America coupled with a stressful economic climate makes it necessary to construct creative solutions to funding extended care.

INSTITUTIONAL SERVICES

As defined earlier, LTC or extended care is care that is delivered over extended time. LTC is not environment specific; it encompasses a spectrum of care levels ranging from acute hospitalization to ambulatory, home-based health care. LTC facilities offer continuity of care and services to optimize a patient's recovery. In addition, LTC facilities are based on an interdisciplinary philosophy of care (Voisine, Walke, & Jeffery, 2009).

Nursing Facilities

Nursing facilities (NFs) encompass a wide spectrum of care, with nursing homes being the most recognizable form. Since the passage of the Omnibus Budget Reconciliation Act of 1987 (OBRA, 1987), it is preferable to refer to nursing homes as nursing facilities.

Although the average length of stay in a nursing facility was 835 days as of 2004, the length of stay in an NF can vary greatly. Approximately 19.4% of the admissions into NFs are short stayers who remain in the facility fewer than 3 months (Jones et al., 2009). Short stayers can be further classified as residents who enter the NF extremely ill and with a short life expectancy or as residents who enter the NF for short-term rehabilitation (U.S. Department of Health and Human Services, 2009). Approximately 24.2% of residents will stay more than 3 months, with 56.4% staying longer than 1 year (Jones et al., 2009). These long-stayers can be further classified as residents with impairments primarily of cognitive function (such as ambulatory patients with dementia) or impairments of physical function (such as residents with severe degenerative joint disease or end-stage heart failure) or as residents with both impairments (U.S. Department of Health and Human Services, 2009).

The most medically and therapeutically intensive of the NFs are the skilled nursing facilities, which must comply with Medicare and Medicaid regulations in order to receive reimbursement. Skilled nursing facilities provide medical and nursing care in addition to restorative therapy, physical therapy, and occupational therapy (Center for Medicare and Medicaid Services, 2007). Pharmacists' roles in these facilities are typically related to dispensing or consultant activities, which are discussed in greater detail later. Skilled nursing facilities that are associated with a hospital are referred to as long-term acute care hospitals or long-term acute care facilities (Munoz-Price, 2009).

Long-term acute care hospitals are designed for patients who need clinical and rehabilitative services and for patients who need continuous care that may not be available in all NFs. They were originally started to decrease the costs associated with hospitalization for patients who were not ready to be discharged to a nursing facility. Patients with clinical conditions, such as postcerebrovascular accident or chronic obstructive pulmonary disease, and those who require parenteral nutrition, intravenous antibiotics, postsurgical wound care, and mechanical ventilator weaning may use long-term acute care hospitals. The average stay in these facilities is 25 days (Eskildsen, 2007; Munoz-Price, 2009). Pharmacists have a variety of roles in a long-term acute care hospital, as these facilities must have an inpatient pharmacy. Besides dispensing activities, pharmacists can participate in interdisciplinary team rounds and educational services. In these settings, pharmacists often have clinical backgrounds, specializing in acute care (Chander & Kirkwood, 2006).

Psychiatric Facilities

Psychiatric facilities provide a distinctive environment for a pharmacist's practice. Although little of the literature has focused on this practice site, pharmacists in these settings can provide treatment recommendations, patient education, medication reviews, and group patient medication clinics. Pharmacists also can participate in interdisciplinary team conferences regarding the therapy of patients and contribute to pharmacy and therapeutics committees, quality assurance activities, and activities to ensure that the facility meets the standards set by the Joint Commission. Studies have demonstrated that pharmacists in mental health facilities improve patient outcomes (Finley, Crismon, & Rush, 2003). For more information on this subject, see Chapter 10.

Correctional Facilities

Correctional facilities often provide long-term health care to their residents. As the general population ages, so does the inmate population. Approximately 5.3% of inmates are age 55 and older, and older adults are the fastest growing segment of the prison population. Projections estimate that by 2030, one third of the prisoners will be older adults. Older adult inmates have chronic diseases and medical problems, just like the general population, and they typically experience them sooner than their cohort due to lifestyle differences and lack of routine medical care. However, many prisons were built decades ago and are not currently equipped to care for prisoners with ADL impairments. The need for pharmaceutical care in this population offers a unique practice opportunity for pharmacists, such as providing medication information, monitoring HIV therapy, monitoring adverse drug events, and helping with the newly evolving geriatric wards in prisons (Wick & Zanni, 2009b).

Specialized Institutional Care

Patients with cognitive deficits are a distinct population that is often overlooked in the LTC setting. However, there are a growing number of LTC facilities that specialize in care of patients with cognitive decline, such as Alzheimer's disease or other forms of dementia. Depending on their specialized needs, these patients may reside in intermediate care facilities (which provide 24-hour care on a temporary basis) for patients with cognitive deficits, foster homes, group homes, assisted living facilities, and state homes. Adult day centers also have services for patients with cognitive decline (National Institute on Aging, 2010). Pharmacists working with these patients can offer many of the same services found in psychiatric hospitals and in LTC facilities, such as dispensing and consultant work.

Hospice and Palliative Care

The word *hospice* comes from the Latin root for hospitality and hospitable (Storey, 1996). The focus of hospice, or palliative care, is the humane and compassionate management of patients with terminal diseases. The goal of therapy is to maintain the quality of the patient's life rather than to cure the patient's disease. Growth in hospice care has been spurred on by its transformation from an alternative healthcare choice to a Medicare-reimbursable benefit with the 1982 enactment of the Medicare Hospice Benefit program (National Hospice and Palliative Care Organization, 2009). For a patient to be eligible for hospice under Medicare, a physician must certify that death is imminent (expected within 6 months). Medicare will reimburse services related to palliative care, or comfort care (Center for Medicare and Medicaid Services, 2010). Although services provided to patients may vary from organization to organization, services include physician services, regular home visits by registered and licensed practical nurses, home health aide and homemaker services to help patients with ADLs, social work and counseling services, medical equipment (e.g., hospital beds), medical supplies, medications for symptom control and pain relief, volunteer support for the patient and family, physical therapy, speech therapy, occupational therapy, and dietary counseling (Centers for Medicare and Medicaid Services, 2010; National Hospice and Palliative Care Organization, 2009).

The National Hospice and Palliative Care Organization (NHPCO) estimates that there were more than 4,850 hospice programs in the United States in 2008 serving 1.45 million patients. Although the majority of hospice patients are 65 years and older, approximately 16.8% are younger than 65. Approximately 38% of patients are admitted with a cancer diagnosis. The rest are admitted with noncancer diagnoses such as end-stage heart disease, dementia, debility, lung disease, stroke, and end-stage renal disease. In 2008, the average length of stay in hospice care was 69.5 days, with a median of 21.3 days (National Hospice and Palliative Care Organization, 2009).

In 2008, 57.5% of hospices were independent, freestanding agencies; 21.8% were hospital based; 19.4% were home-health agency based; and 1.4% were based in LTC facilities. Hospice services are primarily covered by Medicare (84.3%), with 7.8% of care covered by private insurance and 5.1% covered by Medicaid. Approximately 95.9% of hospice care days are provided in patients' homes, thereby avoiding more expensive hospitalizations. It is estimated that hospice care reduces Medicare costs by $2,309 per patient (National Hospice and Palliative Care Organization, 2009).

Hospice care teams are highly interdisciplinary, as doctors, nurses, pharmacists, social workers, counselors, and many other healthcare professionals work together to provide palliative care (Martin, 2006). Furthermore, these teams include over 550,000 hospice volunteers who provide patient care through spending time with patients and families, providing support services for hospice staff, and assisting with fund-raising efforts (National Hospice and Palliative Care Organization, 2009). Within the hospice interdisciplinary care team, there is a broadening role for pharmacists. Medicare is the primary payer for hospice services, and in order to continue to receive funding, hospice facilities must comply with Medicare's conditions of participation. New rules went into effect in 2008 that require that the hospice team work with an individual who is educated and trained in drug management. Comprehensive medication therapy assessments must be done within a few days of entering hospice care and updated every 15 days. Patients and family members must also be educated in medication disposal (Martin, 2009).

While the rule does not specifically require a pharmacist to provide these services, pharmacists are uniquely qualified through their training and experience to provide drug management services. Working with hospice programs offers the pharmacist the opportunity to show their drug expertise, especially in the management of patients' pain and other palliative care. Pharmacists also can participate in patient and family education about medications, review and manage patients' medication therapy, and ensure compliance with state, local, and federal regulations (Martin, 2009).

HOME AND COMMUNITY-BASED SERVICES

Home and community-based services is care that falls between institutional LTC and care for the ambulatory patient. In other words, the patient does not need nursing home care, yet he or she cannot live completely independently. To help these individuals, home and community-based services often include a combination of housing, health care, and social support. In addition, home and community-based services can provide help to patients with their ADLs, such as eating, dressing, bathing, and transferring (Voisine et al., 2009).

Adult Day Care Services

Adult day care services are community-based group programs for adults with functional or cognitive impairments, giving families relief from care for several hours. Adult day care services are typically available during normal business hours, Monday through Friday, but some adult day care centers now offer evening hours and weekend care. However, none offer 24-hour care. A wide variety of services is offered, including therapy (physical and mental), health monitoring, personal care, caregiver support, social activities, transportation, and provision of meals/snacks (National Adult Day Services Association, 2010; Voisine et al., 2009).

Often patients enrolled in adult day care are functionally impaired and need to be cared for in a supervised environment. The care focuses primarily on maintenance and rehabilitation. Patients reside in their own or their families' homes and travel to a central location for services. The individual's family can continue their daily activities, such as work, because their loved one can be cared for in a supervised setting. There are three different models for adult day care services, which include the medical model, the social model, and the specialized model. In the medical model, the most intensive health-related services, such as therapy and nursing care, are provided in addition to social activities. The social model provides social activities, meals, and recreation. Some health services are provided in the social model, such as medication administration. The specialized model focuses on specific groups of patients, such as those with cognitive impairment or developmental disabilities (e.g., dementia, Alzheimer's disease, or mental retardation) (National Adult Day Services Association, 2010; U.S. Department of Health and Human Services, 2009; Voisine et al., 2009).

In 2010, there were 4,601 adult day care centers in the United States. Adult day care centers can be stand alone or can be affiliated with or part of larger organizations, such as home healthcare agencies, skilled nursing facilities, medical centers, or senior citizen centers. No federal regulations exist yet for these centers, but the National Adult Day Services Association has developed standards of care (National Adult Day Services Association, 2010). Medicare does not cover adult day services, and the average cost per day for adult day care services is $61, with a range of $21 to $130. The cost depends on the type of services offered. Medicaid in some states will cover adult day care services, and private medical or LTC insurance companies also may include coverage in their plans (Voisine et al., 2009). For example, Pennsylvania Medicaid covers adult day care services at Medicaid-licensed facilities (U.S. Department of Health and Human Services, 2009). There are many potential opportunities for pharmacist involvement, as consultant pharmacists providing staff, patient, and family education; advice on medication use and storage; maintenance of medication profiles; and drug-utilization review (DUR).

Assisted Living Facilities

Group residential settings are available in the community. Assisted living communities provide supportive, individualized, and personal services in a residential setting. The amount of care needed typically depends on the individual's ability to perform ADLs. In general, the level of care is not as extensive or as skilled as that found in a nursing home setting, even though assisted living facilities may house people who are disabled enough to qualify for nursing home care. Individuals in assisted living facilities have their own room or apartment and receive support services, such as meals, personal care assistance, nursing assistance (e.g., help with medications), and housekeeping. The services offered can vary, however, depending on the assisted living facility and the needs of the residents (U.S. Department of Health and Human Services, 2009; Voisine et al., 2009). Assisted living facilities promote independence, privacy, and choices, along with providing care services (Cameron & Pinkowitz, 2009).

As of 2009, there were over 36,000 licensed assisted living residencies with over 1 million residents (Assisted Living Federation of America, 2009). The average cost per month was $3,131 in 2009, but these costs varied by services offered. Costs associated with assisted living facilities are not covered by Medicare or Medigap insurance policies. Some state-run Medicaid programs pay for components of assisted living facility care, but do not pay for room and board. Private health insurance or LTC insurance may cover assisted living facility costs (U.S. Department of Health and Human Services, 2009).

There are opportunities for pharmacists within assisted living facilities, since approximately 85% of the residents need help with their medications. Residents are free to obtain medications from their pharmacy of choice, but some assisted living facilities now contract with LTC pharmacies and consultant pharmacists to provide medication management services. These services can include medication reviews, special packaging of medications, and medication education for patients, families, and assisted living staff (Cameron & Pinkowitz, 2009; Voisine et al., 2009).

FUTURE OF LONG-TERM CARE

Because the accessibility and affordability of long-term care are major concerns, the federal government and state governments are beginning to explore alternative financing and care options. Such alternatives include expanding home and community-based services, encouraging the purchase of long-term care insurance, waiving Medicaid requirements for certain groups, and implementing personal care service programs (Doty, Mahoney, & Sciegaj, 2010; Ng et al., 2010; U.S. Department of Health and Human Services, 2009).

In looking for alternatives, the idea of aging in place has gained momentum. Aging in place refers to staying in the same home and community as care needs change. The definition has broadened to include moving to a new community and staying there as care needs change. This approach seeks to support independent living, social activity, and community ties. Many older adults prefer to age in place, and court rulings have upheld this idea (Wick & Zanni, 2009a). In 1999, the Supreme Court ruled in the *Olmstead* case that older adults have the right to remain in their homes if able (as determined by a healthcare professional) and willing, as moving older adults to facilities before necessary would isolate and limit them from community-based interactions. This and subsequent rulings prompted states to increase the number of home and community-based services available. For example, home and community-based waivers through Medicaid allow states greater flexibility in providing extended care services to older adults (Ng et al., 2010).

One of the fastest-growing types of senior housing is the continuing care retirement community (CCRC). CCRCs are based on the aging-in-place philosophy and provide a continuum of independent living, assisted living, and skilled nursing care on a single campus. As an older adult's health status changes, he or she can move among the different levels of care without having to relocate from the campus. In 2007, there were 2,240 CCRCs with 745,000 residents (Shippee, 2009). Most CCRCs require an entry fee, which can be as high as $500,000, in addition to monthly fees of up to $4,800. None of these fees are covered by Medicare, Medicaid, or insurance. Depending on the CCRC, a variety of services and amenities may be offered to residents, such as golf courses, swimming pools, specialized facilities, concierge services, and restaurants (Voisine et al., 2009; Wick & Zanni, 2009a). Some CCRCs are even affiliated with universities and offer college classes (Larkin, 2007). Individuals in CCRCs typically have Medicare Part D insurance, so pharmacists can implement medication therapy management (MTM) services in these settings and help provide continuity of care (Voisine et al., 2009).

Another example of an aging-in-place approach is the Medicare Program of All-Inclusive Care for the Elderly. This program integrates all aspects of care covered by Medicare and Medicaid, including medical, social, and LTC services, in addition to services not traditionally covered, such as meals, transportation, and adult day care. Older adults who are frail and individuals who are disabled are eligible for the program, but they must meet the following criteria to qualify: (1) age 55 or older, (2) live in an area with a Program of All-Inclusive Care for the Elderly, (3) certified eligible for care, and (4) can live safely in the community with program services. If they do not qualify for Medicaid, individuals enrolled in the Program of All-Inclusive Care for the Elderly pay only small fees (Center for Medicare and Medicaid Services, 2008).

PHARMACY SERVICES IN LONG-TERM CARE

Pharmacy services in long-term care can be divided into two categories—distribution and consulting. Medications can be provided to residents in a facility from a pharmacy in a variety of unit-dose packaging systems, according to the needs of the facility. Distribution-related services also can address problems on an individual level. Many older adults have problems with packaging of medications, dosage forms, and picking up prescription medications. Pharmacies that service LTC facilities can help provide specialized packaging, discuss dosage form alternatives with the healthcare team, and provide delivery services and on-site counseling services (Mort, 2009). For example, pharmacies can provide patients with individual packets of medications with pre-sorted packets containing the date and time to be taken (for further information, go to http://www.DailyMedRx.com). In addition to medications, the pharmacy may provide other distribution-related services, forms, and reports and be involved in the development of policies and procedures (see **Exhibit 9-3**).

In the case of consultant services, a consultant pharmacist may be employed by the distribution pharmacy, employed by a network of LTC facilities, or self-employed as an independent consultant who contracts individually with a facility. Pharmacy consulting offers the practitioner a number of special opportunities (**Exhibit 9-4**), and

Exhibit 9-3   Distribution Pharmacy Functions

Drug Distribution
Initial screening of medication orders
Drug packaging and labeling
Drug delivery (routine and emergency)
Medication reordering
Audit system for controlled medications
Emergency medication supply
Monitoring of proper storage of medication

Other
Policy and procedure development
Drug information
Durable medical equipment
Medical/surgical supplies
Enteral products
Intravenous services

Provision of Forms and Reports
Computer-generated patient medication
   profile
Medication administration record
Treatment records
Patient cardex
Physician order forms
Automatic stop orders
Treatment records
Patient care plans
Drug utilization reports
Billing statements

Source: Reprinted with permission from W. Simonson, *Consultant Pharmacy Practice,* (2nd ed.), 1996, p. 71.

Exhibit 9-4   Selected Pharmacist Activities in the Long-Term Care Environment

Drug regimen review (DRR)	Drug information
Nutrition assessment and support services	In-service education programs
	Enteral feeding products
Durable medical equipment (DME)	Outpatient compliance packaging
Surgical appliance fitting	Home diagnostic services
Clinical research programs	Laboratory test ordering and interpretation
Pharmacokinetic dosing services	
Pain management counseling	Specialized medication delivery systems
Patient counseling	
Intravenous therapy services	Medical and surgical supplies
Therapeutic drug monitoring	Quality assurance programs
Formulary development	Computer generated forms and reports
Medication pass observation	
Committee participation	Infection control
Resident assessment and care planning	Participation in state survey process
	Specialized clinical activities
Drug use evaluation (DUE)	Drug utilization or use review (DUR)

many pharmacists have found a rewarding practice niche in this area. In this setting, pharmacists are hampered only by their imagination. Pharmacists provide special pharmaceutical care services such as medication regimen review (MRR) as well as monitoring for patient outcomes, identifying and resolving drug interactions, selecting cost-effective medications, using pharmacokinetic dosing principles to ensure proper dosing, following good formulary management practice, conducting drug utilization reviews (DURs), educating healthcare providers, and providing case management to coordinate medication use as a patient moves through various case settings (Levenson & Saffel, 2007; Voisine et al., 2009). Additional opportunities may exist in some settings for creating collaborative practice agreements with physicians for disease state management services in areas such as anticoagulation, asthma, diabetes, hypertension, lipid management, pain management, and smoking cessation.

Both skilled nursing facilities and intermediate care facilities are governed at the federal level by the Centers for Medicare and Medicaid Services. The Centers for Medicare and Medicaid Services develops and periodically updates guidelines to help nursing facility staff and consultant pharmacists provide the best care possible to the residents of the facilities they serve. These regulations and interpretive guidelines can be found in the *State Operations Manual* (see http://www.cms.hhs.gov/Manuals/IOM/item detail.asp?filterType=none&filterByDID=-99&sortByDID=1&sortOrder=ascending&item ID=CMS1201984&intNumPerPage=10). Historically, as part of OBRA 87, federal legislation was enacted to address quality and care issues of nursing home residents. An important concept in the OBRA 87 requirements was that outcome indicators should be measurable and objective. In particular, this law mandated the use of a resident assessment instrument, which is a standardized review instrument to provide comprehensive, accurate, standardized, and reproducible assessments of each resident's functional capacity. It is also required to be completed in order for a long-term care facility to be Medicare and Medicaid certified.

Assessment of the resident is the essential first step in the care planning process. This process includes the utilization of the resident assessment instrument upon patient admission to collect information regarding the patient's functional capabilities and health problems. The resident assessment instrument is used to promote an outcome-oriented resident care plan so as to ensure the quality of care and the resident's quality of life through the early identification of problems and risk factors that can be avoided, managed, or reversed (American Society of Consultant Pharmacists, 2010). This instrument includes three sections: (1) the minimum data set, a tool used to collect the information needed to evaluate a resident; (2) the resident assessment protocols, which address and assess the issues identified from the information on the resident's minimum data set; and (3) the utilization guidelines.

The minimum data set helps to identify issues that place a resident at risk for an adverse outcome. These issues or triggers are addressed by using the resident assessment protocol, a protocol that helps to mitigate the trigger. The resident assessment protocols are structured, problem-oriented frameworks developed by clinical experts to address the 18 areas that represent the most common problem areas or risks for nursing home residents. Through this process, the resident assessment protocols provide a systematic linkage to the resident's care plan (Rahman & Applebaum, 2009). As part of these requirements, the medication regimen for each resident must be reviewed monthly by a pharmacist (Levenson & Saffel, 2007).

Another part of OBRA 87 dealt with the use of unnecessary drugs. Under this section of the legislation (F329), patients' medication regimens must be free from unneeded medications—defined as any medications used in excessive doses (including duplicate therapy), for excessive durations, without adequate monitoring, without indications for use, in the presence of adverse drug reactions that indicate that the dose should be reduced or discontinued, or any combination of these reasons (Gooen, 1990). The Centers for Medicare and Medicaid Services *State Operations Manual* guidelines were updated in 2006 to promote appropriate drug and dosage selection and monitoring of medication therapeutic efficacy. It also emphasizes monitoring of adverse drug events. This can directly affect the consultant pharmacist's practice in long-term care (Levenson & Saffel, 2007). For additional information, please consult appendix PP of the *State Operations Manual* (Center for Medicare and Medicaid Services, 2009).

Pharmacy services (F425) and MRR (F428) also were updated in the 2006 revision. Interdisciplinary collaboration between pharmacists and other LTC providers is encouraged, with emphasis placed on identifying and solving medication-related issues. Much of the previous guidance in the pharmacy services section has been moved to F329 (unnecessary drugs). MRR continues to be, at minimum, a monthly requirement, and the MRR has expanded to include a more comprehensive review (Levenson & Saffel, 2007). Included in Appendix PP of the *State Operations Manual* are general guidelines for the MRR process performed by the consultant pharmacist and guidance for the use of medications in the elderly (Center for Medicare and Medicaid Services, 2009). Identification of use of inappropriate medication in this population is primarily based on the Beers criteria, which specifically outlines inappropriate medications for older adults. Many of the medications are included in the Beers criteria because of age-associated changes in physiology leading to increased prevalence of adverse effects.

Examples of medications included in the Beers criteria are amitriptyline, lorazepam, diazepam, and cyclobenzaprine (Beers, 1997; Beers et al., 1991; Fick et al., 2003).

Medication Regimen Review

The role of pharmacists has evolved since MRR first emerged in 1974 as part of a quality assurance program for the care of Medicare recipients in skilled nursing facilities (Levenson & Saffel, 2007). The term MRR was previously known as drug regimen review, and these abbreviations can be used interchangeably in LTC and the literature. However, according to the Medicare *State Operations Manual*, MRR is a

> thorough evaluation of the medication regimen of a resident, with the goal of promoting positive outcomes and minimizing adverse consequences associated with medication. The review includes preventing, identifying, reporting, and resolving medication-related problems, medication errors, or other irregularities, and collaborating with other members of the interdisciplinary team. (Center for Medicare and Medicaid Services, 2009, p. 348)

As directed by federal mandate, the guidelines for MRR can be divided into several categories—for example, unnecessary medications/excessive doses, excessive duration of drug therapy, inadequate drug monitoring, and absence of documented diagnosis or clinical symptoms (Center for Medicare and Medicaid Services, 2009). To be efficient in the process of MRR, a pharmacist must develop a systematic approach of identifying actual and potential drug therapy problems. **Exhibit 9-5** provides an organized framework for the pharmacist to utilize when conducting MRR, along with examples for each category.

MRR has been shown to be an effective mechanism to reduce medication use and costs. The North Carolina Polypharmacy initiative (for more information see the "Examples of Consultant Pharmacy Services" section) had pharmacists perform MRRs for nursing home Medicaid patients. Researchers found that MRRs and subsequent therapy recommendations decreased polypharmacy and cut medication costs by $30.33 per patient each month. The savings in 1 month compensated for pharmacist services (Christensen, Trygstad, Sullivan, Garmise, & Wegner, 2004). Other studies have shown MRRs to reduce unnecessary medication use (Suhrie et al., 2009) and to reduce antipsychotic drug prescribing (Nishtala, McLachlan, Bell, & Chen, 2008).

Drug Utilization Evaluation

Drug utilization evaluation (DUE) entails a sophisticated analysis of medications, their uses, and their contributions to various patient outcomes. Institutions accredited by the Joint Commission regularly perform DUEs. A DUE may focus on a particular medication, evaluate the use of an entire class of medications, or monitor the therapy of a medical condition (The Joint Commission, 2010).

DUE is a criteria-based, ongoing, planned, and systematic review of medication. It is often prospective, in that the criteria to be applied are determined first, and then the medication for review is evaluated. Patient data and laboratory data are often included and available for review. DUEs are frequently population based in a specific institution and often part of an institution's quality assessment program. The Joint Commission recommends that a medication's inclusion be based on the following criteria: frequently prescribed, known or suspected to present significant risk, known or sus-

Exhibit 9-5 Drug Regimen Review Framework

1. Drug use without indication. The resident is taking a medication for no medically valid indication.
2. Untreated indication. The resident has a medical problem that requires drug therapy but is not receiving a drug for that indication.
3. Improper drug selection. The resident has a drug indication but is taking the wrong drug or is taking a drug that is not the most appropriate for the special needs of the resident.
4. Subtherapeutic dosage. The resident has a medical problem that is being treated with too little of the correct medication.
5. Overdosage. The resident has a medical problem that is being treated with too much of the correct medication.
6. Adverse drug reaction. The resident has a medical problem that is the result of an adverse drug reaction or adverse effect.
7. Drug interaction. The resident has a medical problem that is the result of a drug-drug, drug-food, or drug-laboratory test interaction.
8. Medication errors. A deficiency or weakness of the medication use process of the facility has resulted in an actual or potential medication error.
9. Medication monitoring. Evaluation of medications for effectiveness and toxicity or adverse effects.
10. Medication costs. Intervention is needed to assist the resident with obtaining access to a lower-cost medication or overcoming a barrier to medication access, such as formulary restriction or prior authorization.

Source: From "Revisiting drug regimen review, part III: A systematic approach," *The Consultant Pharmacist,* 18, pp. 656–666, 2003. Reprinted with permission of The American Society of Consultant Pharmacists, Alexandria, VA. All rights reserved.

pected to be problem prone, or a critical component of the care provided for a specific diagnosis, condition, or procedure.

As of 1995, the Joint Commission encouraged the use of an interdisciplinary approach to DUEs and development of collaborative medication use review. Standards continue to support an interdisciplinary approach and focus on how patient care can be improved in LTC facilities as a result of problems identified through the review process (Kubacka, 1996).

Drug Utilization Review

Drug utilization reviews (DURs) were established by the 1990 Omnibus Budget Reconciliation Act (OBRA, 1990). Pharmacists performing DURs are required to review past patterns of medication misuse, monitor current medication therapy, and offer patient counseling. By some practitioners' definition, DUR is a subset of DUE. Whereas DUE is prospective, DUR is frequently retrospective. DURs may use large databases and become part of a system's quality assurance program. In the past, use of such reviews has decreased medication costs and the use of inappropriate medications in LTC facilities (Kubacka, 1996).

MRR, DUE, and DUR have comparable functions, and the outcomes they measure can be classified into the following four categories: (1) therapeutic, (2) functional, (3) quality of life, and (4) economic (Gore, 1994; Kubacka, 1996). Documenting the patient outcomes of pharmacists' recommendations allows the practitioner to chronicle internal quality assurance. Documentation of patient outcomes also provides evidence that the pharmacists themselves are delivering quality patient care (Gore, 1994).

Medication Reconciliation

LTC facilities accredited by the Joint Commission have also performed medication reconciliation since 2005. Medication reconciliation is a process by which medications are accurately and completely accounted for throughout the care process. At admission, a complete list of medications is obtained, including dosage, route of administration, and dosing frequency. The indication for each medication also is obtained. As medications are added during the care process, they are compared to the list generated at admission and any discrepancies are reconciled. Upon discharge to another facility or home, the new facility or the patient and his family are informed about the current medication list. The goal of medication reconciliation is to avoid adverse drug events due to inadequate communication between and among healthcare providers, especially during the transfer process (The Joint Commission, 2010).

Examples of Consultant Pharmacy Services

Fleetwood Project

In an effort to demonstrate how consultant pharmacists can influence patient care in the nursing home environment, the American Society of Consultant Pharmacists initiated the Fleetwood Project. This project includes the following three phases: (1) assessment of the baseline costs of medication-related problems in the nursing home setting and the impact pharmacist MRR has on patient outcomes and costs; (2) assessment of prospective interventions utilizing a formal pharmaceutical care planning model for nursing home patients at high risk for medication-related problems (the Fleetwood model); and (3) assessment of the effectiveness of the Fleetwood model in assisted living facilities and nursing homes (Lombardi & Kennicutt, 2001).

In the first phase of the model, researchers conducted a cost-of-illness study to assess medication therapy in nursing homes. This study estimated that consultant pharmacists reduce medication-related morbidity and mortality costs by $3.6 billion annually in the United States (Bootman, Harrison, & Cox, 1997).

The second phase of the project focused on the feasibility of implementing formal pharmaceutical care planning in the nursing home setting. A 6-month pilot program was implemented in six nursing homes in Wisconsin. From the pilot study, it appeared that this approach to care was feasible (Moskowitz, 2003).

The third phase of the Fleetwood Project tested the effectiveness of the Fleetwood model and was conducted in 26 nursing facilities in North Carolina (Cameron, Feinberg, & Lapane, 2002). The investigators developed screening tools to help pharmacists identify patients at high risk for adverse events and treatment algorithms for alternatives to potentially inappropriate medications (Christian, vanHaaren, Cameron, & Lapane, 2004; Lapane & Hughes, 2004a). In addition, Fleetwood phase III reported high job satisfaction among pharmacists participating in the project (Lapane & Hughes, 2004b).

North Carolina Nursing Home Polypharmacy Initiative

After determining that many nursing home patients covered by Medicaid were taking six or more prescription medications daily, the state of North Carolina initiated a pharmacy case management program. Thirteen nursing homes were selected to participate in this program. The goal was to reduce the total number of prescription medications taken by addressing problems such as therapeutic duplication, inappropriate drug utilization, multiple prescriber issues, and higher-than-normal drug use. In addition, there was an effort to switch brand prescription medications to generics or other therapeutic alternatives. After analysis by pharmacist–physician teams, 37% of patients were identified as needing medication changes. Results from the analysis indicated that the economic benefits outweighed the costs of implementing the program by a ratio of 13 to 1 (Henry, Mendelson, & Fallieras, 2003).

Medication Therapy Management (MTM)

With the advent of Medicare Part D and the ability to be compensated for managing medications, many pharmacies and pharmacists are providing MTM services to the community. These services can improve patient outcomes and reduce healthcare costs in older adults. A pharmacy practice resident (postgraduate year 1) evaluated the medication therapies of older adults in an assisted living facility and provided drug-therapy recommendations to their primary care physicians. The goal of the project was to examine the economic impact of the intervention. The analysis identified problems such as missed drug therapy, inappropriate dosing, adverse drug reactions, and high costs; these problems were then addressed with the primary care physician. A total of 125 recommendations were made, and 72 were acted upon. The recommendations that were accepted resulted in a cost savings greater than the cost of the pharmacy services provided (Maack, Miller, Johnson, & Dewey, 2008).

Opportunities for Pharmacists in Long-Term Care

Participation in other quality assurance activities and on the pharmacy and therapeutics committees of LTC institutions offers the pharmacist more chances to expand beyond the traditional dispensing role (Levenson & Saffel, 2007). The areas of palliative care, prison inmate care, and managing patients with substance abuse problems also offer distinctive practice opportunities (Martin, 2006, 2009; Wick & Zanni, 2009b). At present, these areas have little pharmacist involvement. In addition, pharmacists are teaming up with primary care providers in providing disease state management. Collaborative efforts include patient-specific medication recommendations, identification of inappropriate medication prescribing, and working with the interdisciplinary team to gather information to provide optimum care (Levenson & Saffel, 2007).

The Medicare Prescription Drug, Improvement, and Modernization Act of 2003 also provided an opportunity for pharmacists to offer medication therapy management services to Medicare beneficiaries since 2006. The eligible providers, covered services, and reimbursement structures vary among the prescription drug plans, but pharmacists can offer services related to medication therapy review, personal medication records, and medication-related action plans, as well as provide interventions and/or referrals, medication documentation, and follow-up (Truong, Layson-Wolf, Rodriguez de Bittner, Owen, & Haupt, 2009). Community and consultant pharmacists can provide MTM services in adult day care centers, CCRCs, and assisted living facilities, in addition to offering them in community pharmacies (Cameron & Pinkowitz, 2009; Voisine et al., 2009).

Many training programs are offered for pharmacists who are interested in working with the elderly population. The American Society of Consultant Pharmacists (ASCP) Research and Education Foundation is just one organization that has partnered with industry sponsors to offer advanced training in this area.[1] Programs available from the American Society of Consultant Pharmacists Foundation and its partners include those that focus on Alzheimer's disease/dementia, geriatric psychiatric/behavioral disorders, pain management, and Parkinson's disease. In addition, there are specific disease-related pharmacotherapy programs, such as prescription labeling for those dealing with vision loss.

Some pharmacists may choose to enhance their practices by obtaining certification in geriatric pharmacy. This is an optional process beyond required pharmacy licensure. A certified geriatric pharmacist has met certain educational and experiential require- ments and passed an examination designed to test his or her knowledge and skills in geriatric pharmaceutical care. Continuing education guidelines must be met to main- tain this certification.[2]

Rotations, residencies, and fellowships also are available for those interested in work- ing with older adults. Many pharmacy schools offer introductory and advanced phar- macy practice experiences in geriatrics, which can introduce pharmacy students to pharmaceutical care of older adults (Odegard, Breslow, Koronkowski, Williams, & Hudgins, 2007). There are several American Society of Health-System Pharmacists– accredited postgraduate year 2 residencies available in geriatric pharmacy.[3] Typical postgraduate year 2 residencies in geriatric pharmacy give experience in ambulatory, acute, intermediate, and long-term care, as well as in therapeutic monitoring of chronic diseases such as anticoagulation and diabetes. Fellowships can offer opportunities for research regarding older adults in addition to providing clinical training.

CONCLUSION

Long-term care encompasses a variety of services that are provided to individuals who have lost some aspect of functioning. Like Betty in the case scenario, many individuals need help with normal daily activities, such as bathing, toileting, or dressing, which family or friends may be unable to provide. As the number of older adults continues to rise, there will be increasing demands for long-term care services. Costs associated with long-term care services also continue to rise with the demand for services. Many individuals purchase long-term care health insurance to defray some of the costs. How- ever, the majority of long-term care costs are covered by Medicare and Medicaid, and creative solutions are needed to address the high costs of long-term care for the future.

---

[1]For more information on these training programs, contact the foundation at: 1321 Duke Street, Alexan- dria, VA 22314-3563; phone: (703) 739-1300, fax: (703) 739-1500, email: info@ascpfoundation.org, website: http://www.ascpfoundation.org/index.cfm.

[2]For more information on becoming a certified geriatric pharmacist, contact the Commission for the Certifica- tion of Geriatric Pharmacy, 1321 Duke Street, Suite 400, Alexandria, VA 22314-3563; phone: (703) 535-3036, fax: (703) 739-1500, email: info@ccgp.org, website: http://www.ccgp.org/.

[3]For more information, see: http://accred.ashp.org/aps/pages/directory/residencyProgramSearch.aspx.

The roles for pharmacists in long-term care are expanding and evolving to meet patient needs. Pharmacists provide many different services, including dispensing medications, consulting with long-term care facilities and healthcare providers, and managing complex medication regimens. Training for pharmacists interested in working in long-term care is available through numerous outlets, including advanced pharmacy practice experiences, residencies, fellowships, and geriatric pharmacy certification programs. Through efforts such as the Fleetwood Project and MTM services, pharmacists have demonstrated that they are well-prepared to provide long-term care services and address patient care needs.

QUESTIONS FOR FURTHER DISCUSSION

1. Given that the population of older adults is growing and that healthcare dollars are finite, how would you guarantee access to LTC facilities for all patients who need that access?
2. The role of the pharmacist in the LTC setting is evolving. How would you ensure this role's continued progress? (Suggest curricular, research, and legislative solutions.)
3. Given the current financing mechanisms of LTC, how would you recommend that your parents or grandparents prepare for their potential future LTC needs?
4. Because the baby boomer population will significantly affect the need for health services, how should the healthcare community and country prepare for 2030?

KEY TOPICS AND TERMS

Activities of daily living
Adverse drug reaction
Aging-in-place
Community-based health care
Consultant pharmacist
Continuing care retirement community
Drug utilization evaluation (DUE)
Drug utilization review (DUR)
Health insurance
Hospice
Informal care or caregiving
Instrumental activities of daily living
Interdisciplinary
Long-term care services
Medication regimen review (MRR)
Older adults
Skilled nursing facility

REFERENCES

American Society of Consultant Pharmacists. (2010). Minimum data set resources. Retrieved from http://www.ascp.com/articles/minimum-data-set-mds-resources

Andel, R., Hyer, K., & Slack, A. (2007). Risk factors for nursing home placement in older adults with and without dementia. *Journal of Aging and Health, 19*(2), 213–228.

Assisted Living Federation of America. (2009). *Assisted living.* Retrieved from http://www.alfa. org/alfa/Assisted_Living_Information.asp?SnID=1730245619

Banaszak-Holl, J., Fendrick, A. M., Foster, N. L., Herzog, A. R., Kabeta, M. U., Kent, D. M., ... Langa, K. M. (2004). Predicting nursing home admission: Estimates from a 7-year follow-up of a nationally representative sample of older Americans. *Alzheimer's Disease and Associated Disorders, 18*(2), 83–89.

Beers, M. H. (1997). Explicit criteria for determining potentially inappropriate medication use by the elderly: An update. *Archives of Internal Medicine, 157*(14), 1531–1536.

Beers, M. H., Ouslander, J. G., Rollingher, I., Reuben, D. B., Brooks, J., & Beck, J. C. (1991). Explicit criteria for determining inappropriate medication use in nursing home residents. *Archives of Internal Medicine, 151*(9), 1825–1832.

Bharucha, A. J., Pandav, R., Shen, C., Dodge, H. H., & Ganguli, M. (2004). Predictors of nursing facility admission: A 12-year epidemiological study in the United States. *Journal of the American Geriatrics Society, 52*(3), 434–439.

Bootman, J. L., Harrison, D. L., & Cox, E. (1997). The health care cost of drug-related morbidity and mortality in nursing facilities. *Archives of Internal Medicine, 157*(18), 2089–2096.

Brooks, S. (1994). Subacute care. *Contemporary longterm care, 17,* 42–50.

Cameron, K., Feinberg, J. L., & Lapane, K. (2002). Fleetwood Project phase III moves forward. *The Consultant Pharmacist, 17,* 181–198.

Cameron, K., & Pinkowitz, J. (2009). Connecting with assisted living consumers. *The Consultant Pharmacist, 24*(1), 16–28.

Centers for Medicare and Medicaid Services. (2007). *Medicare coverage of skilled nursing facility care.* Retrieved from www.medicare.gov/Publications/Pubs/pdf/10153.pdf

Centers for Medicare and Medicaid Services. (2008). *Quick facts about Programs of All-inclusive Care for the Elderly (PACE).* Retrieved from http://www.medicare.gov/Publications/Pubs/pdf/11341.pdf

Centers for Medicare and Medicaid Services. (2009). *State Operations Manual Appendix PP: Guidance to surveyors for long term care facilities (Rev. 52, 09-25-09).* Retrieved November 10, 2009, from http://www.cms.hhs.gov/manuals/Downloads/som107ap_pp_guidelines_ltcf.pdf

Centers for Medicare and Medicaid Services. (2010). *Medicare & you.* Retrieved from http://www.medicare.gov/Publications/Pubs/pdf/10050.pdf

Chander, M., & Kirkwood, K. L. (2006). Pharmacist's role in long-term acute care hospitals. *Drug Topics, 150*(4), 56.

Christensen, D., Trygstad, T., Sullivan, R., Garmise, J., & Wegner, S. E. (2004). A pharmacy management intervention for optimizing drug therapy for nursing home patients. *The American Journal of Geriatric Pharmacotherapy, 2*(4), 248–256.

Christian, J. B., vanHaaren, A., Cameron, K. A., & Lapane, K. L. (2004). Alternatives for potentially inappropriate medications in the elderly population: Treatment algorithms for use in the Fleetwood phase III study. *The Consultant Pharmacist, 19,* 1011–1028.

DeFrances, C. J., Lucas, C. A., Buie, V. C., & Golosinskiy, A. (2008). 2006 national hospital discharge survey. *U.S. Department of Health and Human Services: National Health Statistics Reports, 5,* 1–20.

Doty, P., Mahoney, K. J., & Sciegaj, M. (2010). New state strategies to meet long-term care needs. *Health Affairs, 29*(1), 49–56.

Eskildsen, M. A. (2007). Long-term acute care: A review of the literature. *Journal of the American Geriatrics Society, 55*(5), 775–779.

Federal Interagency Forum on Aging-Related Statistics. (2008). *Older Americans 2008: Key indicators of well-being.* Federal Interagency Forum on Aging-Related Statistics. Washington, DC: U.S. Government Printing Office.

Fick, D. M., Cooper, J. W., Wade, W. E., Waller, J. L., Maclean, J. R., & Beers, M. H. (2003). Updating the Beers criteria for potentially inappropriate medication use in older adults: Results of a U.S. consensus panel of experts. *Archives of Internal Medicine, 163*(22), 2716–2724.

Finley, P. R., Crismon, M. L., & Rush, A. J. (2003). Evaluating the impact of pharmacists in mental health: A systematic review. *Pharmacotherapy, 23*(12), 1634–1644.

Gaugler, J., Duval, S., Anderson, K., & Kane, R. (2007). Predicting nursing home admission in the U.S: A meta-analysis. *BMC Geriatrics, 7*(1), 13.

Gooen, L. C. (1990). Consultant pharmacy: An evolving practice. *Pharmacy Times, 56,* 47–53.

Gore, M. J. (1994). Embracing pharmaceutical care: Consultant pharmacists lead the way. *The Consultant Pharmacist, 9*(2), 143–156.

Grant, M., Elk, R., Ferrell, B., Morrison, R. S., & von Gunten, C. F. (2009). Current status of palliative care: Clinical implementation, education, and research. *CA: A Cancer Journal for Clinicians, 59*(5), 327–335.

He, W., Sengupta, M., Velkoff, V. A., & DeBarros, K. A. (2005). *U.S. Census Bureau: Current population reports, 65+ in the United States.* Washington, DC: Government Printing Office.

Henry, D., Mendelson, D., & Fallieras, A. (2003). *Clinical pharmacy management initiative: Integrating quality into Medicaid cost containment.* Lawrenceville, NJ: Center for Health Care Strategies.

Hetzel, L., & Smith, A. (2001). *The 65 years and over population: 2000.* Washington, DC: U.S. Census Bureau.

The Joint Commission. (2010). *The Joint Commission requirements for hospitals.* Retrieved from http://www.jcrinc.com/Joint-Commission-Requirements/Hospitals/

Jones, A. L., Dwyer, L. L., Bercovitz, A. R., & Strahan, G. W. (2009). The National Nursing Home survey: 2009 overview. *Vital Health Statistics, 13*(167), 1–164.

Kane, R. A., & Kane, R. L. (1987). *Long-term care: Principles, programs, and policies.* New York: Springer.

Katz, S., Ford, A. B., Moskowitz, R. W., Jackson, B. A., & Jaffe, M. W. (1963). Studies of illness in the aged: The index of ADL: A standardized measure of biological and psychosocial function. *JAMA: Journal of the American Medical Association, 185*(12), 914–919.

Kaye, H. S., Harrington, C., & LaPlante, M. P. (2010). Long-term care: Who gets it, who provides it, who pays, and how much? *Health Affairs, 29*(1), 11–21.

Kubacka, R. T. (1996). A primer on drug utilization review. *Journal of the American Pharmaceutical Association, 36*(4), 257–262, 279.

Lapane, K. L., & Hughes, C. M. (2004a). Identifying nursing home residents at high-risk for preventable adverse drug events: Modifying a tool for use in the Fleetwood phase III study. *The Consultant Pharmacist, 19,* 533–537.

Lapane, K. L., & Hughes, C. M. (2004b). Job satisfaction and stress among workers providing long-term care pharmacy services. *The Consultant Pharmacist, 19,* 1029–1037.

Larkin, M. (2007). University-based retirement communities on the rise. *The Journal of Active Aging, 6*(2), 52–59.

Lawton, M. P., & Brody, E. M. (1969). Assessment of older people: Self-maintaining and instrumental activities of daily living. *The Gerontologist, 9*(3 Part 1), 179–186.

Levenson, S. A., & Saffel, D. A. (2007). The consultant pharmacist and the physician in the nursing home: Roles, relationships, and a recipe for success. *The Consultant Pharmacist, 22*(1), 71–82.

Liu, K. (1994). A data perspective on long-term care. *The Gerontologist, 34*(4), 476–480.

Lombardi, T. P., & Kennicutt, J. D. (2001). Promotion of a safe medication environment: Focus on the elderly and residents of long-term care facilities. *Medscape Pharmacists, 2*(1). Retrieved from http://www.medscape.com/viewarticle/421217

Maack, B., Miller, D. R., Johnson, T., & Dewey, M. (2008). Economic impact of a pharmacy resident in an assisted living facility-based medication therapy management program. *Annals of Pharmacotherapy, 42*(11), 1613–1620.

Manton, K. G. (2008). Recent declines in chronic disability in the elderly U.S. population: Risk factors and future dynamics. *Annual Review of Public Health, 29*(1), 91–113.

Marengoni, A., Aguero-Torres, H., Timpini, A., Cossi, S., & Fratiglioni, L. (2008). Rehabilitation and nursing home admission after hospitalization in acute geriatric patients. *Journal of the American Medical Directors Association, 9*(4), 265–270.

Marion Merrell Dow Inc. (1994). *Managed care digest: Long term care edition.* Kansas City, MO: Marion Merrell Dow, Inc.

Martin, C. M. (2006). Understanding palliative care. *The Consultant Pharmacist, 21*(9), 698–713.

Martin, C. M. (2009). Exploring new opportunities in hospice pharmacy. *The Consultant Pharmacist, 24*(2), 114–119.

Martin, L. G., Schoeni, R. F., Freedman, V. A., & Andreski, P. (2007). Feeling better? Trends in general health status. *The Journals of Gerontology: Series B: Psychological Sciences and Social Sciences, 62B*(1), S11–S21.

Minino, A. M., Xu, J., Kochanek, K. D., & Tejada-Vera, B. (2009, December). Death in the United States, 2007. *National Center for Health Statistics Data Brief, 26,*1–8.

Mor, V., Intrator, O., Feng, Z., & Grabowski, D. C. (2010). The revolving door of rehospitalization from skilled nursing facilities. *Health Affairs, 29*(1), 57–64.

Mort, J. (2009). Implications and management of decline for the elderly patient. *The Consultant Pharmacist, 24*(8), 611–625.

Moskowitz, D. B. (2003). The pharmacist as care provider: Three projects support role. *Drug Benefit Trends, 15*(7), 43–46.

Munoz-Price, L. S. (2009). Healthcare epidemiology: Long-term acute care hospitals. *Clinical Infectious Diseases, 49*(3), 438–443.

National Adult Day Services Association. (2010). *Adult day services: Overview and facts.* Retrieved from http://www.nadsa.org/knowledgebase/col.php?pid=29&tpid=15

National Alliance for Caregiving & American Association of Retired Persons. (2009). *Caregiving in the U.S.: A focused look at those caring for the 50 +.* Retrieved from http://www.caregiving.org/data/2009CaregivingAARP_Full_Report.pdf

National Hospice and Palliative Care Organization. (2009). NHPCO facts and figures: Hospice care in America. Retrieved from http://www.nhpco.org/files/public/Statistics_Research/NHPCO_facts_and_figures.pdf

National Institute on Aging. (2010). *Alzheimer's information.* Retrieved from http://www.nia.nih.gov/Alzheimers/

Ng, T., Harrington, C., & Kitchener, M. (2010). Medicare and Medicaid in long-term care. *Health Affairs, 29*(1), 22–28.

Nihtila, E. K., Martikainen, P. T., Koskinen, S. V. P., Reunanen, A. R., Noro, A. M., & Hakkinen, U. T. (2008). Chronic conditions and the risk of long-term institutionalization among older people. *European Journal of Public Health, 18*(1), 77–84.

Nishtala, P. S., McLachlan, A. J., Bell, J. S., & Chen, T. F. (2008). Psychotropic prescribing in long-term care facilities: Impact of medication reviews and educational interventions. *American Journal of Geriatric Psychiatry, 16*(8), 621–632.

OBRA. (1987). *Omnibus Reconciliation Act (1987). Public Law 100–203.*

OBRA. (1990). *Omnibus Reconciliation Act (1990). Public Law 101–108.*

Odegard, P. S., Breslow, R. M., Koronkowski, M. J., Williams, B. R., & Hudgins, G. A. (2007). Geriatric pharmacy education: A strategic plan for the future. *American Journal of Pharmaceutical Education, 71*(3), article 47.

Rahman, A. N., & Applebaum, R. A. (2009). The nursing home minimum data set assessment instrument: Manifest functions and unintended consequences—past, present, and future. *The Gerontologist, 49*(6), 727–735.

Rosenwaike, I. (1985). A demographic portrait of the oldest old. *The Milbank Memorial Fund Quarterly. Health and Society, 63*(2), 187–205.

Schneider, E. L., & Guralnik, J. M. (1990). The aging of America: Impact on health care costs. *JAMA: Journal of the American Medical Association, 263*(17), 2335–2340.

Seeman, T. E., Merkin, S. S., Crimmins, E. M., & Karlamangla, A. S. (2010). Disability trends among older Americans: National Health and Nutrition Examination surveys, 1988–1994 and 1999–2004. *American Journal of Public Health, 100*(1), 100–107.

Shippee, T. P. (2009). "But I am not moving": Residents' perspectives on transitions within a continuing care retirement community. *The Gerontologist, 49*(3), 418–427.

Sisko, A., Truffer, C., Smith, S., Keehan, S., Cylus, J., Poisal, J. A., ... Lizonitz, J. (2009). Health spending projections through 2018: Recession effects add uncertainty to the outlook. *Health Affairs, 28*(2), w346–w357.

Social Security Administration. (2010). *Historical background and development of Social Security*. Retrieved from http://www.socialsecurity.gov/history/briefhistory3.html

Stevens, L. M., Lynm, C., & Glass, R. M. (2006). Palliative care. *JAMA: Journal of the American Medical Association, 296*(11), 1428.

Storey, P. (1996). *Primer on palliative care*. Gainesville, FL: American Academy of Hospice and Palliative Care.

Suhrie, E. M., Hanlon, J. T., Jaffe, E. J., Sevick, M. A., Ruby, C. M., & Aspinall, S. L. (2009). Impact of a geriatric nursing home palliative care service on unnecessary medication prescribing. *The American Journal of Geriatric Pharmacotherapy, 7*(1), 20–25.

Truong, H.-A., Layson-Wolf, C., Rodriguez de Bittner, M., Owen, J. A., & Haupt, S. (2009). Perceptions of patients on Medicare Part D medication therapy management services. *Journal of the American Pharmacists Association, 49*(3), 392–398.

U.S. Census Bureau. (2009a). *Annual estimates of the resident population by sex and five-year age groups for the United States: April 1, 2000 to July 1, 2008 (NC-EST2008-01)*. Retrieved November 10, 2009, from http://www.census.gov/popest/national/asrh/NC-EST2008-sa.html

U.S. Census Bureau. (2009b). *Annual estimates of the resident population by sex, race, and Hispanic origin for the United States: April 1, 2000 to July 1, 2008 (NC-EST2008-03)*. Retrieved from http://www.census.gov/popest/national/asrh/NC-EST2008-srh.html

U.S. Census Bureau. (2009c). *Projections of the population by selected age groups and sex for the United States: 2010 to 2050*. Retrieved from http://www.census.gov/population/www/projections/summarytables.html

U.S. Census Bureau. (2009d). *Projections of the population by sex, race, and Hispanic origin for the United States: 2010 to 2050*. Retrieved from http://www.census.gov/population/www/projections/summarytables.html

U.S. Department of Health and Human Services. (2009). *Understanding long-term care*. Available at www.longtermcare.gov

Voisine, J., Walke, L., & Jeffery, S. (2009). Home is where the heart is: Living arrangements for older adults. *The Consultant Pharmacist, 24*(2), 134–145.

Wick, J., & Zanni, G. (2009a). Aging in place: Multiple options, multiple choices. *The Consultant Pharmacist, 24*(11), 804–812.

Wick, J., & Zanni, G. (2009b). Challenges in caring for aging inmates. *The Consultant Pharmacist, 24*(6), 424–436.

Wolff, J. L., & Kasper, J. D. (2006). Caregivers of frail elders: Updating a national profile. *The Gerontologist, 46*(3), 344–356.

Mental Health Services

Ardis Hanson, Bruce Lubotsky Levin, Carol A. Ott, and Helen Meldrum

Case Scenario

You are newly graduated from pharmacy school and have taken a position in a community pharmacy setting that is near a community mental health center. Many of the clients of the center come to your pharmacy to have their prescriptions filled. In pharmacy school, you learned about the treatment of mental illness, but were never taught how to interact with people with mental illness. You understand that empathy is a part of your professional demeanor, but you find you have beliefs about people with mental illnesses and their ability to understand your patient counseling efforts. Occasionally, pharmacy technicians interact with these patients and you feel uncomfortable with the jokes and laughter that sometimes follows these patient visits.

On one occasion, DL, a 42-year-old man with chronic paranoid schizophrenia, comes to the pharmacy to pick up his antipsychotic prescription. It is apparent that he hasn't been taking care of himself and is becoming more ill. On previous visits, the pharmacy staff has simply handed him his prescription without offering to discuss it with him. When DL approaches the counter, you move to the window to dispense his prescription to him. You ask him how his medicine is working for him, if he has any problems, and if he recognizes the pills as ones he has taken previously. He doesn't look at you and seems surprised that you would take the time to speak with him. Upon further questioning, you realize that DL has tremors in his hands and has difficulty finding the words to express himself, although he tries. You review his medications with him, including the fact that his tremors may be due to his medicine and that he should talk to his physician about this, as there are treatments available. He thanks you and leaves the store. Several days later, DL returns to the pharmacy to pick up a prescription for a medication to treat his tremors and again thanks you for the time you took to explain this problem to him. You realize that taking the step of engaging DL and providing him encouragement has caused him to make an effort to take care of himself. You have also provided your technicians and coworkers with a model for your expectations in working with people with mental illnesses.

LEARNING OBJECTIVES _____

Upon completion of this chapter, the student shall be able to:

- Provide a brief overview of current mental health services in the United States
- Understand the role of epidemiology, service delivery systems, and healthcare professionals, such as clinical psychiatric pharmacists, in caring for individuals with mental disorders
- Understand evidence-based practice/treatment guidelines for the clinical and community psychiatric pharmacist
- Better assess the potential role for pharmacists as members of mental health teams
- Identify emerging issues, including medical homes, the Employee Retirement Income Security Act (ERISA), and rural health

---

CHAPTER QUESTIONS

1. Which two national laws had the most significant impact on the organization, financing, and delivery of mental health services in the United States?
2. Explain the importance of measuring the burden of disease.
3. What are some of the implications of disparities in access and utilization of mental health services?
4. Discuss the difference between evidence-based practice and expert consensus.
5. Describe the use of preferred drugs lists (PDLs) as a means to control drug costs. Give an example of a statewide implementation.

INTRODUCTION

This chapter presents a brief overview of mental health services in the United States, including epidemiologic evidence from national studies on the prevalence of mental disorders in noninstitutionalized populations. It reviews the critical issues involved in mental health services delivery, disease prevention and health promotion, the treatment of mental disorders, and ethical and legal issues in mental health services. In addition, the chapter identifies emerging issues critical to pharmacists who must understand the increasingly complex nature of health and mental healthcare delivery in the United States. The chapter is also designed to help pharmacy students develop a better understanding of the needs of individuals with mental disorders, illustrated in the chapter scenario.

Global Burden of Disease

Mental illness is a significant global public health issue. Mental, neurologic, and behavioral disorders cause considerable suffering and are common to individuals living in countries throughout the world. People with mental disorders endure social isolation, poor quality of life, and increased mortality (World Health Organization, 2005). Furthermore, these disorders are the cause of significant economic and social costs (World Health Organization, 2001). The incidence of mental illnesses has grown exponentially, creating large at-risk and vulnerable populations throughout the world. The

World Health Organization (World Health Organization, 2002; World Health Organization, 2005) estimates that 14% of the global disease burden is due to mental disorders.

Both the United Nations and the World Health Organization (WHO) stress the importance of treating mental disorders to improve population health by focusing on vulnerable and at-risk populations (Miranda & Patel, 2005). In addition, mental disorders also increase the risk for developing many physical illnesses and are major risk factors for communicable and noncommunicable diseases and unintentional and intentional injury (World Health Organization, 2001). At the same time, many health conditions increase the risk for mental disorders and complicate diagnosis and treatment. The aggregate social costs of these adverse consequences are enormous.

Costs of Treatment for Mental and Substance Use Disorders Globally and in the United States

It is difficult to estimate the costs associated with mental disorders since cost estimates are not available globally for all mental disorders. In 2006, U.S. healthcare costs reached 16% of the nation's gross domestic product (Poisal et al., 2007), with mental disorders accounting for an estimated 6.2% of the nation's spending (Mark et al., 2007). However, this does not reflect the total (direct and indirect) costs of care. Although it is possible to note the direct costs of medications, treatment visits, and hospitalizations, these costs likely would exclude the indirect costs of incarceration, homelessness, public benefits, supported programs and services, reduced labor supply, reduced educational attainment, and the medical complications associated with mental disorders (Insel, 2008). From 2008 to 2014, there is a projected 6.6% annual increase in spending for mental health and substance use services in the United States (Levit et al., 2008).

Complexity Exacerbated by Co-Occurring Disorders

Providing high-quality health care for persons with co-occurring disorders is exacerbated by a number of factors, such as lifestyle issues, at-risk behaviors, service utilization, and barriers to care. Persons with co-occurring disorders often have more instances of premature death and higher rates of disability than those who don't have co-occurring disorders.

Gender also plays a role in the incidence and treatment of co-occurring disorders. In the United States, depression is the 2nd leading cause of disability-adjusted life years in women but the 10th leading cause in men (Egede, 2004). Although the interaction between co-occurring disorders with regard to prevalence, disease severity, and causative factors (Welch, Czerwinski, Ghimire, & Bertsimas, 2009) is not completely understood, it is estimated that for every dollar invested in drug treatment, seven dollars are saved in health and social costs (World Health Organization & Noncommunicable Disease and Mental Health Cluster, 2003).

Criminal Justice Settings as de Facto Mental Health Treatment Facilities

In the United States, there are over 12 million adults held every year in jails, in excess of 760,000 persons on any given day (Veysey, 2010). More than half of all prison and jail inmates have a mental health problem. This includes 479,900 in local jails, 705,600 inmates in state prisons, and 78,800 in federal prisons (James & Glaze, 2006). Seventy-five percent of women in jail exhibit symptoms of mental disorders compared to 63% of men (James & Glaze, 2006). Furthermore, men and women are both at risk of dependence to alcohol (approximately 29% and 41%, respectively) and other drugs (approximately 24% and 41%, respectively) (Zhang, 2003).

In the community, law enforcement officials are increasingly concerned with calls to apprehend individuals with mental disorders. At the same time, there have been reports of "mercy arrests"—in essence, taking an individual with a mental disorder into custody because he or she was involved in a minor scuffle on the street or similar incident (Earley, 2006). Law enforcement officials report that this is often their only solution to ensuring a person receives food, shelter, and medical care, since psychiatric beds in community hospitals are often unavailable and many state residential treatment facilities have been closed.

It is obvious that the majority of individuals with behavioral disorders are not treated within mental-healthcare delivery systems. Prisons, much like nursing homes, have become the nation's de facto mental healthcare provider. With the closing of state and residential treatment facilities, the transinstitutionalization of persons with mental disorders has shifted to alternative public settings. James and Glaze (2006) conclude that only one in three state prisoners, one in four federal prisoners, and one in six jail inmates who have mental health problems received treatment while incarcerated. Further, while a patient leaving a psychiatric facility may have a discharge plan, a drug regimen, and a referral for medical assistance or an aftercare program, jails and prisons have no obligation to help the released person reentering society cope with his or her problems.

EPIDEMIOLOGY OF MENTAL DISORDERS

A Global Epidemiologic Perspective

Fundamental to a discussion of mental health services is an understanding of the epidemiology of mental disorders—the study of the factors that determine the frequency and distribution of mental disorders in human populations. Global estimates by the WHO indicate that 154 million people suffer from depression, 25 million people suffer from schizophrenia, 91 million people are affected by alcohol use disorders, and 15 million people are affected by drug use disorders (World Health Organization, 2002). If one adds traumatic brain injuries, dementia, and other neuropsychiatric disorders, the estimated population suffering from mental and behavioral disorders totals approximately 450 million people (World Health Organization, 2002).

Disability-adjusted life years is a measure developed by the WHO that represents the loss of 1 year of full health. Using disability-adjusted life years, one is able to compare the burden of diseases that cause premature mortality (but little or no disability) to diseases that do not cause death (but do cause disability). In 2004, the global average burden of disease was estimated to be 237 disability-adjusted life years per 1,000 population, of which about 60% was due to premature death and 40% to nonfatal health outcomes (Mathers, Fat, & Boerma, 2008). Depression is the third leading cause of disease burden in the world. Alcohol use disorders (7th), bipolar disorders (12th), schizophrenia (14th), and substance abuse disorders (20th) are among the top 20 leading causes of disability (Mathers et al., 2008).

National Epidemiologic Studies

The most comprehensive mental health epidemiologic study conducted in the United States was the Epidemiologic Catchment Area study in 1978 (Robins & Regier, 1991). The Epidemiologic Catchment Area study included more than 20,000 respondents from five catchment areas (New Haven, Connecticut; Durham, North Carolina; Baltimore, Maryland; Los Angeles, California; and St. Louis, Missouri).

The major objective of the Epidemiologic Catchment Area study was to obtain prevalence rates of specific mental disorders rather than overall prevalence rates of all mental disorders. In summary, 20% of the people interviewed had a diagnosable mental disorder during a given year, with a lifetime prevalence of 32% for a mental illness or substance disorder. Annually, more than 5% of adults in the United States have a severe mental disorder, e.g. schizophrenia, major depression, panic disorder, or manic-depressive disorder (Kessler et al., 1996). In addition, nearly 6% of adults in the United States have addictive disorders (alcohol and drug problems). Approximately 75% of individuals in need of services for alcohol and drug abuse do not receive treatment, which potentially has an enormous impact upon the health and stability of individuals, families, and communities.

Another important national study on serious mental illness and co-occurring disorders was the National Comorbidity Survey (NCS) (Kessler et al., 1994). The NCS incorporated revised nomenclature from the *Diagnostic and Statistical Manual of Mental Disorders* (DSM), *Third Edition* (American Psychiatric Association, 1987), examined risk factors that affect particular mental disorders; and estimated the comorbidity of mental disorders (Blazer, Kessler, McGonagle, & Swartz, 1994). The NCS study found that only 21% of patients had a single mental disorder. Seventy-nine percent of the respondents had a comorbid disorder, i.e., a combination of one or more mental, physical, or alcohol/substance abuse disorders occurring simultaneously. In addition, more than half of all lifetime mental disorders occurred in 14% of the population.

In 2003, in the National Comorbidity Survey Replication Study (NCS-R), Kessler and associates (Kessler et al., 2003) found that the prevalence of mental disorders did not change significantly from the earlier NCS. However, what did change was an increase in the rate of treating individuals with mental disorders, from approximately 20% in the NCS to nearly 33% in the NCS-R. Nevertheless, despite an increase in treating individuals with mental disorders from the NCS to the NCS replication, the majority of individuals with mental disorders did not receive treatment. While space does not permit a more extensive review of the results of epidemiologic studies of mental disorders in the United States, Levin, Hennessey, and Petrila (2010) present additional information about the epidemiology of mental disorders in selected at-risk populations.

In addition, disparities in mental health care result in at-risk populations, such as cultural and linguistic minorities, rural populations, and women and children who have a lower socio-economic status, being more likely to delay or not seek mental health care, receive inadequate care, terminate care early, and have a higher rate of prescriptions for psychotropic drug use (Garland et al., 2005; Han & Liu, 2005; Miranda, McGuire, Williams, & Wang, 2008; Zimmerman, 2005). For example, although rates for most mental disorders are lower in Hispanics and African Americans than in whites, Hispanics and African Americans have poorer prognoses and more chronic disorders (Breslau et al., 2006; Williams & Earl, 2007).

According to a 2009 Department of Housing and Urban Development report, 42% of persons who are homeless are African American/black; 38% are white, non-Hispanic, and 11.6% are Hispanic. Further, 51% of African American/black individuals who are homeless are persons in families, 24.4% of white, non-Hispanic individuals who are homeless are persons in families, and 13.1% of Hispanic individuals who are homeless are persons in families (U.S. Department of Housing and Urban Development, 2009).

Furthermore, an estimated 3.5 million people in the United States are homeless during a given year and between 700,000 and 800,000 people are homeless on a given night (National Law Center on Homelessness & Poverty, 2004). Approximately 58% of persons who are homeless are living in shelters and transitional housing and 42% were unsheltered (U.S. Department of Housing and Urban Development, 2009). In addition, more than two fifths of sheltered homeless persons are disabled. Approximately 26% of individuals who are homeless have a serious mental disorder (Nickels, Kautz, Villaraigosa, Newsom, Stultz, & Cochran, 2009). In addition, 38% of individuals who are homeless report an alcohol dependency problem (U.S. Department of Housing and Urban Development, 1999), 26% of individuals who are homeless abuse other drugs, and an estimated 37% of individuals who are homeless have chronic substance abuse issues (U.S. Department of Housing and Urban Development, 2009).

Although common demographic features of homelessness are being male, a member of a minority group, older than age 31, and alone, other sizable segments of the homeless population are white, non-Hispanic (38%), children (20%), homeless together with at least one other person (33%), or veterans (12%); 13% of individuals who are homeless are victims of domestic violence, and approximately 2% are unaccompanied youth (U.S. Department of Housing and Urban Development, 2009).

Finally, persons who are the most vulnerable are the elderly who receive both Medicaid and Medicare. These persons (dually eligible) are among the oldest, poorest, sickest, and most disabled individuals in the United States. Their services utilization makes them the most expensive population served by publicly funded healthcare programs. They account for a disproportionate share of Medicaid utilization and payments. The Medicare Payment Advisory Commission (MedPac, 2004) provides the following demographics. Over one third of persons who are dually eligible are under the age of 65. Approximately 38% have cognitive or mental impairments; 22% have multiple physical impairments; and 23% are institutionalized (MedPac, 2004, p. 72). Approximately 15% of the Medicaid population, persons who are dually eligible, account for approximately 41% of Medicaid payments (Lied, 2006). In addition, approximately 75% of persons who live in nursing homes are dually eligible (Liu, Wissoker, & Swett, 2010).

LANDMARK REPORTS AND LEGISLATION IN MENTAL HEALTH

Historically, the organization, financing, and provision of alcohol, drug abuse, and mental health (also collectively referred to as behavioral health) services in the United States have been complicated by a confusing assortment of uncoordinated public and private delivery systems and multiple funding mechanisms that have been parallel to, rather than integrated with, general (somatic) health services (Levin, Hennessey, & Petrila, 2010).

The post–World War II era fostered optimism that mental disorders were treatable as well as preventable. Based upon the findings of the Joint Commission on Mental Health and Illness in 1961, the U.S. Congress initiated the largest commitment to prevention and treatment of mental disorders in the history of the United States with passage of the Community Mental Health Centers Act of 1963. At the height of the CMHC movement in 1981, 52% of the U.S. population was living in areas served by a community mental health center (U.S. Department of Health and Human Services, 1999). For a more comprehensive review of the history of mental health in America, see Deutsch, 1949.

Other than the Community Medical Health Center legislation in 1963, no other federal legislation has affected the financing and delivery of mental health services more than the 1965 passage of Titles XVIII and XIX of the Social Security Act, which established the Medicare and Medicaid programs (U.S. Congress, 1965). These programs pay for health services provided to the elderly and the poor, two populations who historically have not been covered by private health insurance. While care for the elderly and medically disabled (Medicare) is administered by the federal government, Medicaid is a jointly administered federal/state program that finances long-term care and acute care.

Two seminal federal reports on mental health include *Mental Health: A Report of the Surgeon General* (United States Department of Health and Human Services, 1999) and *Achieving the Promise* (President's New Freedom Commission on Mental Health, 2003). Both reports examined the multiple, disjointed, and dysfunctional behavioral healthcare delivery systems in America, the insurance and financial limitations placed upon individuals with mental disorders, and the long-term consequences of the stigma of mental illnesses. The goals of the two reports are remarkably similar.

The President's New Freedom Commission on Mental Health report (2003) identified six goals. First, it framed mental health as an essential component of overall (somatic) health and well-being. Second, it located the focus on outcomes of care to be consumer and family focused. The next three goals addressed disparities of services, urged implementation of early screening, assessment, and referral to mental health services, and prioritized mental health services delivery and mental health services research initiatives. Finally, it urged increased utilization of emergent information technology in mental health.

The Paul Wellstone and Pete Domenici Mental Health Parity and Addiction Equity Act of 2008 (U.S. Congress, 2008) was part of the Emergency Economic Stabilization Act of 2008. The Paul Wellstone and Pete Domenici Mental Health Parity and Addiction Equity Act requires a group health plan of 50 persons or more (that provides both medical/surgical and mental health/substance use disorder benefits) to ensure that mental health or substance use disorder benefits are equal in benefits and treatment offered for medical/surgical services. Therefore, there are no separate cost sharing requirements or treatment limitations placed upon mental health and substance use disorder benefits that are different than the requirements or limitations placed upon medical/surgical benefits.

MENTAL HEALTH SERVICES DELIVERY AND THE COMMUNITY PHARMACIST

Medication adherence is a significant difficulty for many people who suffer from a chronic medical illness. While it is often assumed that people with chronic mental illnesses have greater medication nonadherence than those with long-term medical or physical illnesses, in reality, studies evaluating adherence maintain that those with chronic conditions do not take approximately one half of the doses they are prescribed, regardless of the condition (Haynes, Ackloo, Sahota, McDonald, & Yao, 2008). The reasons for nonadherence in persons with mental illnesses are similar to those for chronic medical conditions, with a few additions. Lack of insight into the severity, or even the presence, of a serious mental illness is a common factor in medication adherence in mental illness. Other factors include difficulty paying for medications, unstable housing and support systems, and the lack of access to care. It has been documented that improving medication adherence may decrease rates of hospitalization and utilization of acute care medical services in persons with schizophrenia (Ascher-Svanum, Zhu, Farias, Furiak, & Montgomery, 2009).

The role of the pharmacist in medication adherence is expanding. Several studies have assessed the roles of both clinical and community pharmacists in interventions to improve the use of medications in individuals with mental illness. Crockett, Taylor, Grabham, and Stanford (2006) studied patient outcomes related to the involvement of rural community pharmacists who provided greater patient counseling and support upon dispensing antidepressant medications. The patients who received extra support had improvement in their symptoms in a shorter period of time than those patients who received care as usual (Crockett et al., 2006). The majority of studies of pharmacist intervention have focused on depression. There is a lack of published evidence of pharmacist impact on other serious mental disorders, although clinical pharmacists working in psychiatry commonly provide extended counseling to and interventions for individuals with mental disorders.

To assess adherence problems, practitioners must recognize both behaviors and attitudes associated with medication use (Velligan et al., 2010). Providers commonly assume that patients take all of their doses. However, in the face of seemingly noneffective treatment, providers increase medication doses. This decision results in adverse consequences to the patient, including receiving an excessive dose, increased nonadherence, and/or development of side effects. It is important to question the patients closely about their medication use, in a nonjudgmental way, to ascertain adherence.

There are a variety of reasons for nonadherence, such as patient beliefs about taking medication, an unwillingness to take medications, finances, living conditions, or forgetfulness. Hence, it is critical for the pharmacist to build an alliance in which the individual feels in control of his or her treatment options as well as to provide complete patient counseling related to medications. Both of these strategies will promote adherence to the treatment plan.

EVIDENCE-BASED PRACTICE/TREATMENT GUIDELINES

Evidence-based practice is considered to be a practice or treatment that is supported by research that is published in the clinical literature. This type of practice is the basis of the curriculum now offered by healthcare professions' schools and colleges. Treatment guidelines that are developed for medical conditions can be evidence based in nature—that is, clinical literature that is reviewed and summarized by professionals with expertise in the specific area—or they can be expert consensus guidelines. There is an important difference between evidence-based guidelines and expert consensus guidelines. Expert consensus guidelines often consist of surveys that are completed by experts in a particular area, based upon their current practice, not simply the clinical literature. These surveys are then collated, and the treatment most often preferred is listed first. It is essential to understand that expert consensus guidelines are prone to individual provider bias, whereas evidence-based treatment guidelines are expected to provide treatment recommendations that are established by the clinical literature. Many guidelines in psychiatry are a combination of clinical consensus and published research studies.

The American Psychiatric Association practice guidelines and the Texas Medication Algorithm Project are frequently utilized in psychiatric practice in the United States. The Texas Medication Algorithm Project has been in existence since its 1996 development by the Texas Department of State Health Services and uses a combination of clinical expertise and evidence-based practice to form algorithms for treatment with a goal of improving quality of care and patient outcomes (Gilbert et al., 1998; Miller et al., 2004; Moore et al., 2007; Trivedi et al., 2004). Algorithms for the treatment of major depressive disorder, schizophrenia, and bipolar disorder in adults have been developed. The Children's Medication Algorithm Project focuses on attention deficit/ hyperactivity disorder and major depressive disorder treatment in children (Emslie et al., 2004; Pliszka et al., 2003). These sets of guidelines are revised and updated on the Texas Medication Algorithm Project website on a routine basis. The American Psychiatric Association guidelines are more extensive in scope and cover a wider range of psychiatric disease states, including assessment of the person with mental illness.[1] The American Psychiatric Association guidelines are revised routinely and serve to provide consistent and informed clinical treatment of psychiatric disorders. The Schizophrenia Patient Outcomes Research Team recently published evidence-based guidelines for the treatment of schizophrenia (Kreyenbuhl, Buchanan, Dickerson, & Dixon, 2010).

The authors recommend pharmacologic and nonpharmacologic treatment of schizophrenia based upon literature review and rate the strength of their recommendations. While levels of algorithms used to treat psychiatric disorders may name specific drugs, most often, the clinician using the guidelines finds a class of drugs or several drugs listed in each level. There is broad interpretation of treatment guidelines, which often requires a further knowledge of the clinical literature to provide individualized patient treatment. Even as there is increasing interest among psychiatric providers in treatment guidelines, there is also concern that the use of treatment guidelines will decrease the control that the clinician has over individual practice, as well as skepticism related to the financial motivation for guideline implementation (Forsner, Hansson, Brommels, Wistedt, & Forsell, 2010).

It is clear that the practice of psychiatry is becoming ever more complex. New drug therapies that increase the pharmaceutical armamentarium are marketed annually, adding to the necessity of knowledge relative to drug mechanism of action, pharmacology, drug interactions, and adverse events. Various medications that are FDA approved for a particular use in psychiatry are regularly used off-label for other psychiatric indications. The role of the pharmacist in managing the drug therapy regimens of persons with mental illness is expanding beyond simply dispensing and counseling. The community pharmacist is in a unique position to offer specialized medication therapy

---

[1]To review the American Psychiatric Association practice guidelines, see http://www.psychiatryonline.com/pracGuide/pracGuideHome.aspx

management (MTM) services to this vulnerable population to improve adherence and patient understanding.

Open Access to Behavioral Health Drugs—The Indiana Example

Medicaid programs in the United States frequently utilize preferred drugs lists (PDLs) as a means to control drug costs. The PDL process requires that the physician prescribes and the patient takes certain medications in a therapeutic class prior to employing other options. Concern exists related to the overall cost-effectiveness of PDLs, the criteria that is used to develop PDLs, and the impact of the use of PDLs on quality of care (West et al., 2009). Medication access problems related to PDLs can result in a delay in treatment, increased adverse events, diminished continuity of care, and increased rate of acute medical care services (Lieberman et al., 2005). The argument for preferred drug lists and limiting access to medications often centers on the increasing costs of mental health drug therapy, as well as recent clinical trial publications that show similar effectiveness of older, generic drug therapies relative to newer, more expensive treatments (Caballero, Souffrant, & Heffernan, 2008).

In 2005, the State of Indiana enacted legislation known as House Bill 1325 that prohibited prior authorization for mental health drugs except under very specific circumstances and created the Mental Health Quality Advisory Committee (IC 12, 2004; HB 1325, 2005). The Mental Health Quality Advisory Committee is comprised of seven members who represent managed care, psychiatry, community pharmacy, and Indiana Medicaid and is a subcommittee of the Indiana Drug Utilization review board. The Mental Health Quality Advisory Committee is charged with applying HB 1325 to maintain open access to behavioral health drugs without PDLs, while utilizing efforts directed at cost-effective care of those with mental illness. In Indiana Medicaid, there are what is termed *quality of use* edits, which require that drug therapy be adherent to principles of quality of care. These edits are developed to reduce polytherapy and inappropriate medication use.[2]

Currently, data is in development to determine the impact of these edits on patient outcomes, including rate of hospitalization, refill utilization, and rate of prior authorization.

MENTAL HEALTH TEAMS AND THE ROLE OF THE PHARMACIST

The mental health treatment team consists of a psychiatrist, clinical nurse specialist, psychiatric nurse, social worker, therapist, psychologist, and care manager. In many treatment settings, including Veterans Administration hospitals and clinics and university teaching hospitals and clinics, a clinical psychiatric pharmacist plays a pivotal role. The clinical psychiatric pharmacist may function as a part of the team or see patients on an individual basis under a scope of practice in collaboration with a psychiatrist. Potential responsibilities of the clinical pharmacist include medication management, including initiation and adjustment of therapy, laboratory monitoring, authorization/monitoring of prescription refills, and interaction with the treatment team. In some states, clinical pharmacists are able to bill insurance plans for their services.

---

[2]For more information on the Mental Health Quality Advisory Committee, see http://provider.indiana medicaid.com/provider-specific-information/pharmacy-services/boards-and-committees/mental-health-quality-advisory-committee-%28mhqac%29.aspx

The role of the clinical psychiatric pharmacist expanded from 2000 to 2010. In 1996, the Board of Pharmaceutical Specialties authorized and began to administer a board certification examination in psychiatric pharmacy. To be eligible to sit for this exam, the pharmacist needs to graduate from an accredited school or college of pharmacy and have at least 4 years of primary practice (at least 40% of that time) in psychiatric pharmacy. The pharmacist may also complete a postgraduate year 2 residency specializing in psychiatric pharmacy, which reduces the number of years required to sit for the exam to 1 year postresidency. Completion of a postgraduate year 2 psychiatric pharmacy residency and the board-certified psychiatric pharmacist designation provides the pharmacist with the training and certification necessary to be an active and productive provider of psychiatric pharmacy services. To date, more than 500 clinical pharmacists have received the board-certified psychiatric pharmacist designation.[3]

Because of the lack of psychiatric providers in many settings, the role of the clinical psychiatric pharmacist is expanding into underserved areas of the population. In rural areas, clinical psychiatric pharmacists are working with primary care physicians as physician extenders to improve mental health services, often functioning as the psychiatric provider for an outpatient clinic (Knight, Draeger, Heaton, & Patel, 2008). Depression screening is provided by pharmacists in primary care settings (Finley, Crismon, & Rush, 2003). Simple screening tools are available that are easy for the patient to complete while in the waiting room prior to an appointment. The pharmacist evaluates the screening responses and provides feedback to the physician to improve patient care. If a screen is positive, the pharmacist can utilize the patient medical record to make appropriate treatment recommendations prior to the patient leaving the clinic. Psychiatric pharmacists also work in state hospitals, prison and jail systems, and nonteaching hospital settings.

The community pharmacist is in a unique position to provide mental health services. As the professional who sees the patient on a routine basis for medication refills, the pharmacist is often the first person to understand if a patient is missing refills, suffering from side effects, or beginning to have symptoms of their mental illness. It is very important in mental health treatment that new symptoms are identified early in order to prevent a relapse or decrease the severity of a mood or psychotic episode. The community pharmacist can form alliances with both the patient and area psychiatric providers to build a network of support for the individual suffering from mental illness. Because he is an integral part of the mental health treatment and support team, the community pharmacist should work to improve his understanding of mental illnesses and his comfort level in working with these patients. Community pharmacists should take advantage of additional professional development opportunities to become familiar with basic psychiatric screening tools and become certified to administer and interpret them, especially if they are part of a medical home or other treatment team.

PREVENTION AND PROMOTION

The field of public health has long utilized the concept of prevention in order to prevent disease occurrence of major public health problems (primary prevention), to prevent recurrences or exacerbations of diseases already diagnosed (secondary

---

[3]For more information on this program, see http://www.bpsweb.org/specialties/psychiatric.cfm

prevention), and to reduce the amount of disability caused by diseases in order for at-risk populations to reach the highest possible level of functioning (tertiary prevention).

Mental health promotion activities are developed for individuals, groups, or communities to enhance competence, self-esteem, and a sense of well-being rather than to intervene in the prevention of emotional problems, social problems, or mental disorders. Mental health promotion initiatives (including the enhancement of mental health, positive mental health, mental well-being, and self-esteem maintenance and enhancement) have been introduced by a variety of organizations, including schools, health organizations, industry, and government organizations, as well as religious institutions. In addition, societies and their multiple cultures vary in their ability to provide mental health promotion activities.

Starting in 1979, *Healthy People* provided 10-year national objectives for promoting health and preventing disease. It sets and monitors national health objectives and measures impacts of prevention activity. *Healthy People 2010* established 14 mental health objectives for the United States, grouped under the following three categories: mental health status improvement; treatment expansion; and state activities (U.S. Department of Health and Human Services, 2000).

Healthy People 2020 (U.S. Department of Health and Human Services, 2009) continues in that same vein; however, a new focal area is on the reduction of depression through screening and treatment. Objectives retained from 2010 include those relating to eating disorders, children with mental disorders, and specialized services for the elderly. A modified objective focuses on increasing treatment for persons with co-occurring mental and substance abuse disorders.

In *Informing the Future: Critical Issues in Health* (2009), the Institute of Medicine recommended a framework that integrates health, mental health, and public health, with a focus on improving the mental, emotional, and behavioral health among young people. Additional recommendations to ensure healthy communities addressed improving vaccines, educating the public regarding immunizations, helping to improve medication safety, and improving emergency preparedness (e.g., pandemics) (Institute of Medicine, 2009).

IMPLICATIONS FOR PHARMACISTS AND PHARMACY PRACTICE

As we consider emergent areas of behavioral health, the following two issues seem most relevant for pharmacists and pharmacy students: the passage of the health reform bill signed into law in 2010 and its subsequent amendments, and the continued movement toward integrating primary and behavioral healthcare systems. While there are many topics critical to the implementation of the healthcare reform bill and integrated services, we have chosen the following four topics as the most important for consideration in this chapter: medical home, the Employee Retirement Income Security Act (ERISA), rural behavioral health, and legal and ethical issues.

Medical Home

Developed over forty years ago, the concept of a medical home originally focused on children with special healthcare needs (Sia, Tonniges, Osterhus, & Taba, 2004; American Academy of Pediatrics Ad Hoc Task Force on Definition of the Medical Home, 1992). Today, the concept of a medical home "is a patient-centered, multifaceted source of personal primary health care." (Rosenthal, 2008, p.427). Extending that concept, the patient-centered medical home, is defined as "an approach to providing comprehensive primary care ... that facilitates partnerships between individual patients, and their personal providers, and when appropriate, the patient's family" (American Academy of Family Physicians, American Academy of Pediatrics, American College of Physicians, & American Osteopathic Association, 2007, p. 1).

There are many implications of the medical home concept for pharmacists and pharmacy students. First, the healthcare reform bill emphasizes new patient care models, such as the patient-centered medical home, which includes pharmacists as part of any standard healthcare benefit package, in the creation of accountable care organizations, and a medical home demonstration program. This will increase the role of the pharmacist in MTM services, patient outcomes, and symptom tracking. Smith and Sederer (2009) argue the rewards of creating mental health homes will be that patients with serious mental illnesses will have a better quality of life both physically and psychically and, at the same time, unnecessary social costs will be reduced.

The Employee Retirement Income Security Act

The Employee Retirement Income Security Act of 1974 (ERISA) was originally designed to regulate employee pension plans. It also covers employee welfare plans, which includes programs established by an employer or union that provides a variety of benefits. These benefits may include coverage for health conditions, accidents, unemployment, and disability. Approximately 47% of employees in firms with 200 to 999 workers are self-funded (Claxton et al., 2009). Companies and employers may operate their pension and healthcare benefit plans across and within state and municipal borders under the protection of ERISA. This type of self-funding has grown increasingly popular as a means to control costs, promote wellness initiatives, and provide improved access to claims utilization data.

ERISA defines a person (or organization) who provides services to an employee health plan as a party-in-interest. Any party-in-interest (person or organization) who, with respect to an employee benefit plan, exercises any discretionary authority or control with regard to managing a plan or its assets is considered a fiduciary. A *fiduciary* is any individual or entity that enters into a legal or ethical relationship of confidence or trust between two or more parties, with the intent of acting on the behalf of another individual, group, or system. For example, a fiduciary may administer or manage a health plan package (or a part of a package) for state employees.

A pharmacy benefit manager (PBM) may fall under ERISA as a fiduciary. PBMs administer outpatient prescription drug benefits for most Americans who have employer-based healthcare coverage. Contracted by health plans, PBMs provide drugs at set prices to plan participants, negotiate volume discounts and rebates with pharmaceutical manufacturers, and provide drug utilization reviews. Therefore, as a fiduciary, a PBM must operate in a manner that ensures full transparency and full disclosure and acts in the best interest of its health plan beneficiaries (Slade, 2009).

In recent state and federal court cases, PBMs have been accused of alleged breaches of their fiduciary duties to self-funded employee benefit plans. Class action and other lawsuits against PBMs have alleged violations of ERISA's fiduciary duty requirements, breach of contract, and have launched federal fraud investigations into price manipulations and financial rebates surrounding pharmaceutical care and formularies. This has led to organizations, such as the National Community Pharmacists Association, to create guides for company benefit managers on questions they should ask their PBMs (e.g., http://www.ncpanet.org/pdf/leg/leg_pbm_ten_questions.pdf).

Because ERISA was originally designed to regulate employee pension plans, it contains few codes pertaining to health care. Further, ERISA preempts state laws that attempt to regulate private-sector health plans, but it allows states to regulate the business of insurance. Since ERISA does not allow states to consider self-funding employee plans to be insurers, state insurance commissioners cannot regulate self-funding employee plans. In addition, ERISA does not establish standard employee health plan protections. Therefore, the federal government created a regulatory gap that has frustrated states' efforts to successfully bring an individual or class action lawsuit against companies protected under the ERISA law, especially since negligence or breach of contract cannot be litigated if it relates to employee benefits plans. However, recent legal cases may change ERISA's oversight role regarding the provision of healthcare benefits. For a more detailed review of ERISA, see the *ERISA Preemption Manual for State Health Policymakers*, published by the National Academy for State Health Policy.

Rural Populations

The need for pharmacists and changing pharmacy practice to address the needs of persons with mental illnesses and substance abuse disorders in rural areas continues. To do so will require continuous professional development and increased competencies. In a recent survey of pharmacists, training recommendations were made to increase the knowledge base and competencies of rural pharmacists who reported less preparation on patient care–related issues (Scott, 2010).

Health promotion is a growing service area for rural pharmacy practice. Although studies report that 65% of patients never discuss health issues with their pharmacists (Black, Murphy, & Gardner, 2009) or that traditional pharmacy services are more important than more clinically oriented services (Laubscher, Evans, Blackburn, Taylor, & McKay, 2009), rural pharmacists reported increased provision of disease state management programs and MTM services (Gadkari, Mott, Kreling, & Bonnarens, 2009). Concerns about privacy and pharmacists' time did not outweigh patients' perceptions that MTM services can improve medication use. A Texas study indicated that pharmacists want to expand their roles as patient care providers (Moczygemba, Barner, & Roberson, 2008).

Pharmacists working in the U.S. Public Health Service Commissioned Corps have expanded their practice outside of the traditional role of the pharmacist (Flowers Wick, Figg, McClelland, Shiber, Britton, ... Huntzinger, 2009). The Indian Health Service employs pharmacists to work in multidisciplinary teams in isolated areas of the western part of the United States and Alaska to reach approximately 1.5 million American Indians and Alaska Natives. These pharmacists not only dispense prescriptions, but are also charged with duties including laboratory monitoring, physical assessment, and MTM under physician-approved treatment guidelines.

Legal and Ethical Issues

There remain a number of legal and ethical issues in behavioral health services delivery systems, including the capacity of individuals with mental disorders to decline health care and mental health care (the right to refuse treatment and informed consent), coercion, the sexual or financial exploitation of patients by clinicians (i.e., regulation of the patient–therapist relationship), confidentiality, professional licensing laws (particularly in this era of continuous emerging technology), and the protection of patients from decisions made by clinical self-interest. For a more complete discussion on these issues, see Levin & Petrila, 2010.

Two issues pertinent to pharmacists are (1) resource limitations or rationing of health and mental health services and (2) denial of service. This, of course, has practice implications for pharmacists. Not only will pharmacists require more time- and labor-intensive interactions with their patients, but they will also need to spend more time with other members of the patient or healthcare team's medical home. The second issue, denial of service, was at the very heart of the debates in Congress during 2009–2010. The chapter on managed care in this text will provide more background on this phenomenon.

Still, it would be remiss if we did not point out that the denial of coverage issue becomes more complicated under the mental health parity laws. Rosenbach, Lake, Williams, and Buck (2009) found mental health providers often selected a parity diagnosis for patients in order to ensure insurance coverage for diagnosis and treatment. A parity diagnosis is a diagnosis selected from a subset of psychiatric conditions eligible for coverage under the parity law, instead of covering all mental disorders in the *Diagnostic and Statistical Manual of Mental Disorders*. States, for example, may provide parity for a limited number of mental disorders but not include any substance use disorders. If a provider changes the patient's diagnosis to a nonparity diagnosis, then there would be no insurance coverage. This will remain as a potential ethical problem despite parity law implementation by 2012.

In addition to a basic right to privacy, all patients with mental or emotional disorders have a right to know about their therapists' credentials, procedures, services, and policies regarding access to patient records. In the past, patients could be assured that confidentiality would be maintained unless they specifically requested sharing of information, they brought charges against the mental health therapist, or the mental health professional believed the patient posed a clear danger to self or others. Questions are now being raised about whether patient privacy is violated when mental health providers conduct an Internet search for their own patients (Clinton, Silverman, & Brendel, 2010). Further, the Health Insurance Portability and Accountability Act provides protection for psychotherapy notes (for example, records must now be kept separate from medical profiles and may not be transferred without consent). Although this is considered an improvement in safeguarding confidentiality, further protection is needed for people being treated for stigmatizing disorders (DeLettre & Sobell, 2010).

CONCLUSION

Growing collaboration among healthcare providers, with the passage of the health reform bill, creates a more integral role in the public and the private health and mental health sectors for the community pharmacist and the psychiatric clinical pharmacist. MTM and the medical home become increasingly important with the move toward the integration between primary care services and behavioral healthcare services. The increased collaboration also will affect pharmacy education.

Skills needed for working on an integrated team are not generally part of the academic preparation for healthcare professionals. For pharmacy education, this may require a retooling of curriculum and internships to provide more in-depth knowledge and practice for pharmacy students as well as returning professionals, especially for community pharmacists. It also may require foci on community-centered approaches to pharmacy practice. These include increased awareness of current epidemiologic and disease surveillance information as well as an increased emphasis on health information technologies, such as electronic health record systems and use of additional public health information systems.

Federal and state policies are not structured to promote collaborative practice. State regulations for collaborative practice, including the definition of collaborative practice, differ significantly. For example, in one Midwest state, a clinical psychiatric pharmacist provides medication management services, including drug initiation and discontinuation, dose changes, refill authorizations, laboratory monitoring, and assessment for an outpatient mental health practice that includes more than 50 patients with early psychosis. The pharmacist practices under a scope of practice that is approved by the institution and signed by the clinic psychiatrists, which allows patients to be scheduled for individual clinic appointments with the pharmacist for medication management. Pharmacists should take advantage of opportunities to engage in policy work groups. This allows them to keep abreast of critical public health issues and to bring their concerns on quality of care, care coordination, and patient-centered outcomes to policy makers and legislators. Education of physicians about the training and ability of pharmacists to manage and monitor complex drug therapy regimens is paramount in gaining strong advocates for the expanded role of pharmacists in patient care. These are important considerations as community pharmacists and psychiatric clinical pharmacists continue to be a more integral part of mental health services and treatment teams.

QUESTIONS FOR FURTHER DISCUSSION

1. Should mental health services be integrated into healthcare delivery systems?
2. What are some of the ethical issues in mental health services delivery?
3. What can be done to address the needs of homeless individuals with mental disorders?
4. How involved should pharmacists become in caring for individuals with mental illness?

KEY TOPICS AND TERMS

Disability-adjusted life years
Disease state management
Medication adherence
Medication therapy management (MTM)
Mental health
Pharmacy benefit manager (PBM)
Substance abuse disorders

REFERENCES

American Academy of Family Physicians, American Academy of Pediatrics, American College of Physicians, and American Osteopathic Association. (2007). *Joint principles of the patient-centered medical home.* Retrieved from http://www.acponline.org/hpp/approve_jp.pdf.

American Academy of Pediatrics Ad Hoc Task Force on Definition of the Medical Home. (1992). American Academy of Pediatrics Ad Hoc Task Force on Definition of the Medical Home: The medical home. *Pediatrics, 90*(5), 774.

Ascher-Svanum, H., Zhu, B., Farias, D. E., Furiak, N. M., & Montgomery, W. (2009). Medication adherence levels and differential use of mental-health services in the treatment of schizophrenia. *BMC Research Notes, 12*, 2–6. doi:10.1186/1756-0500-2-6

Black, E., Murphy, A. L., & Gardner, D. M. (2009). Community pharmacist services for people with mental illnesses: Preferences, satisfaction, and stigma. *Psychiatric Services, 60*(8), 1123–1237. doi: 10.1176/appi.ps.60.8.1123

Blazer, D. G, Kessler, R. C, McGonagle, K. A, & Swartz, M. S. (1994). The prevalence and distribution of major depression in a national community sample: the National Comorbidity Survey. *American Journal of Psychiatry, 151*(7), 978–986.

Breslau, J., Aguilar-Gaxiola, S., Kendler, K. S., Su, M., Williams, D., & Kessler, R. C. (2006). Specifying race-ethnic differences in risk for psychiatric disorder in a USA national sample. *Psychological Medicine, 36*(1), 57–68. doi:10.1017/S0033291705006161

Caballero, J., Souffrant, G., & Heffernan, E. (2008). Development and outcomes of a psychiatric pharmacy clinic for indigent patients. *American Journal of Health-System Pharmacy, 65*(3), 229–233. doi: 1079-2082/04/0602-1242$06.00

Claxton, G., DiJulio, B., Finder, B., Lundy, J., McHugh, M., Osei-Anto, A., … Gabel, J. (2009). *Employer health benefits, 2009 annual survey.* Chicago, IL: Kaiser Family Foundation, Health Research and Educational Trust, & National Opinion Research Center. Retrieved from http://ehbs.kff.org/pdf/2009/7936.pdf

Clinton, B. K., Silverman, B. C., & Brendel, D. H. (2010). Patient-targeted googling: The ethics of searching online for patient information. *Harvard Review of Psychiatry, 18*(2), 103–112.

Crockett, J., Taylor, S., Grabham, A., & Stanford, P. (2006). Patient outcomes following an intervention involving community pharmacists in the management of depression. *Australian Journal of Rural Health, 14*, 263–269. doi:10.1111/j.1440-1584.2006.00827.x

DeLettre, J. L., & Sobell, L. C. (2010). Keeping psychotherapy notes separate from the patient record. *Clinical Psychology & Psychotherapy, 17*(2), 160–163.

Deutsch, A. (1949). *The mentally ill in America: A history of their care and treatment from colonial times* (2nd ed.). New York, NY: Columbia University Press.

Earley, P. (2006). *Crazy: A father's search through America's mental health madness.* New York, NY: G. P. Putnam and Sons.

Egede, L. E. (2004). Diabetes, major depression, and functional disability among U.S. adults. *Diabetes Care, 27*(2), 421–428. doi: 10.1016/j.genhosppsych.2007.06.002

Emslie, G. J., Hughes, C. W., Crismon, M. L., Lopez, M., Pliszka, S., Toprac, M. G., … Texas Children's Medication Algorithm Project. (2004). A feasibility study of the childhood depression medication algorithm: the Texas Children's Medication Algorithm Project (CMAP). *Journal of the American Academy of Child and Adolescent Psychiatry, 43*(5), 519–527. doi:10.1097/00004583-200405000-00005

Finley, P. R., Crismon, M. L., & Rush, A. J. (2003). Evaluating the impact of pharmacists in mental health: A systematic review. *Pharmacotherapy, 23*(12), 1634–44.

Flowers, L., Wick, J., Figg Sr., W. D., McClelland, R. H., Shiber, M., Britton, J. E., … Huntzinger, P. (2009). U.S. Public Health Service Commissioned Corps pharmacists: Making a difference in advancing the nation's health. *Journal of the American Pharmaceutical Association, 49*(3), 446–452.

Forsner, T., Hansson, J., Brommels, M., Wistedt, A. A., & Forsell, Y. (2010). Implementing clinical guidelines in psychiatry: A qualitative study of perceived facilitators and barriers. *BMC Psychiatry, 10*, 10–18. doi: 10.1186/1471-244X-10-8

Gadkari, A. S., Mott, D. A., Kreling, D. H., & Bonnarens, J. K. (2009). Pharmacy characteristics associated with the provision of drug therapy services in nonmetropolitan community pharmacies. *The Journal of Rural Health, 25*(3), 290–295. doi: 10.1111/j.1748-0361.2009.00232.x

Garland, A. F., Lau, A. S., Yeh, M., McCabe, K. M., Hough, R. L., & Landsverk, J. A. (2005). Racial and ethnic differences in utilization of mental health services among high-risk youths. *American Journal of Psychiatry, 162*(7), 1336–1343. doi:10.1016/j.childyouth.2007.01.003

Gilbert, D. A., Altshuler, K. Z., Rago, W. V., Shon, S. P., Crismon, M. L., Toprac, M. G., ... Rush, A. J. (1998). Texas Medication Algorithm Project: Definitions, rationale, and methods to develop medication algorithms. *The Journal of Clinical Psychiatry, 59*(7), 345–351.

Han, E., & Liu, G. G. (2005). Racial disparities in prescription drug use for mental illness among population in U.S. *Journal of Mental Health Policy & Economics, 8*(3), 131–143.

Haynes, R. B., Ackloo, E., Sahota, N., McDonald, H. P., & Yao, X. (2008). Interventions for enhancing medication adherence. *Cochrane Database of Systematic Reviews (Online), (2)*, CD000011.

HB 1325. (2005). *A bill for an act to amend the Indiana code concerning human services.* Retrieved from www.in.gov/legislative/bills/2005/SCRP/CR132502.001.html

IC 12. (2004). Vol. 15-35.5-3. *Prohibits prior authorization of mental health drugs.* Retrieved from http://www.in.gov/legislative/ic/2004/title12/ar15/ch35.5.html

Insel, T. R. (2008). Assessing the economic costs of serious mental illness. *American Journal of Psychiatry, 165*(6), 663–665. doi: 10.1176/appi.ajp.2008.08030366

Institute of Medicine. (2009). *Informing the future: Critical issues in health* (5th ed.). Washington, DC: National Academies Press. Retrieved from http://books.nap.edu/openbook.php?record_id=12709

James, D. J., & Glaze, L. E. (2006). *Mental health problems of prison and jail inmates* (Bureau of Justice Statistics Bulletin No. NCJ-213600). Washington, DC: U.S. Department of Justice. Retrieved from http://bjs.ojp.usdoj.gov/content/pub/pdf/mhppji.pdf

Kessler, R. C., Berglund, P., Demler, O., Jin, R., Koretz, D., Merikangas, K. R., ... Wang, P. S. (2003). The epidemiology of major depressive disorder: Results from the National Comorbidity Survey Replication (NCS-R). *JAMA, 289*(23), 3095–3105.

Kessler, R. C., Berglund, P. A., Zhao, S., Leaf, P. J., Kouzis, A. C., & Bruce, M. L. (1996). The 12-month prevalence and correlates of serious mental illness (SMI). In R. W. Mandersheid, & M. A. Sonnenschein (Eds.), *Mental health, United States 1996* (pp. 59–70). Washington, DC: Government Printing Office.

Kessler, R. C., McGonagle, K. A., Zhao, S., Nelson, C. B., Hughes, M., Eshleman, S., ... Kendler, K. S. (1994). Lifetime and 12-month prevalence of DSM-III-R psychiatric disorders in the United States. Results from the National Comorbidity Survey. *Archives of General Psychiatry, 51*(1), 8–19.

Knight, D. E., Draeger, R. W., Heaton, P. C., & Patel, N. C. (2008). Pharmacist screening for depression among patients with diabetes in an urban primary care setting. *Journal of the American Pharmacists Association, 48*(4), 518–521. doi: 10.1331/JAPhA.2008.07048

Kreyenbuhl, J., Buchanan, R. W., Dickerson, F. B., & Dixon, L. B. (2010). The schizophrenia patient outcomes research team (PORT): Updated treatment recommendations 2009. *Schizophrenia Bulletin, 36*(1), 94–103. doi: 10.1093/schbul/sbp130

Laubscher, T., Evans, C., Blackburn, D., Taylor, J., & McKay, S. (2009). Collaboration between family physicians and community pharmacists to enhance adherence to chronic medications: Opinions of Saskatchewan family physicians. *Canadian Family Physician: Medecin De Famille Canadien, 55*(12), e69–e75. Retrieved from http://www.ncbi.nlm.nih.gov/pmc/articles/PMC2793205/?tool=pubmed

Levin, B. L., Hennessey, K. D., & Petrila, J. (2010). *Mental health services: A public health perspective* (3rd ed.). New York, NY: Oxford University Press.

Levin, B. L., & Petrila, J. (2010). Law, services delivery, & policy. In B. L. Levin, K. D. Hennessey, & J. Petrila (Eds.), *Mental health services: A public health perspective* 3rd ed., pp. 43–66. New York, NY: Oxford University Press.

Levit, K. R., Kassed, C. A., Coffey, R. M., Mark, T. L., McKusick, D. R., King, E. C., . . . Ryan, K. (2008). *Projections of national expenditures for mental health services and substance abuse treatment, 2004–2014.* Rockville, MD: U.S. Dept. of Health and Human Services, Substance Abuse and Mental Health Services Administration. Retrieved from http://store.samhsa.gov/product/SMA08-4326

Lieberman, J. A., Stroup, T. S., McEvoy, J. P., Swartz, M. S., Rosenheck, R. A., Perkins, D. O., . . . Hsiao, J. K. (2005). Effectiveness of antipsychotic drugs in patients with chronic schizophrenia. *The New England Journal of Medicine, 353*(12), 1209–1223. doi10.1056/NEJMoa051688

Lied, T. R. (2006). Dually eligible enrollees: 2002. *Health Care Financing Review, 27*(4), 137–144.

Liu, K., Wissoker, D., & Swett, A. (2010). Nursing home use by dual-eligible beneficiaries in the last year of life. *Inquiry, 44*(1), 88–103.

Mark, T. L., Levit, K. R., Coffey, R. M., McKusick, D. R., Harwood, H. J.,King, E. C., . . . Ryan, K. (2007). *National expenditures for mental health services and substance abuse treatment, 1993–2003* (SAMHSA Publication SMA No. 07-4227). Rockville, MD: Substance Abuse and Mental Health Services Administration.

Mathers, C., Fat, D. M., & Boerma, J. T. (2008). *The global burden of disease: 2004 update.* Geneva, Switzerland: World Health Organization.

MedPac. (2004). *Report to the Congress: New approaches in Medicare.* Washington, DC: Medicare Payment Advisory Commission. Retrieved from http://www.medpac.gov/documents/June04_Entire_Report.pdf

Miller, A. L., Crismon, M. L., Rush, A. J., Chiles, J., Kashner, T. M., Toprac, M., . . . Shon, S. (2004). The Texas medication algorithm project: Clinical results for schizophrenia. *Schizophrenia Bulletin, 30*(3), 627–647.

Miranda, J., McGuire, T. G., Williams, D. R., & Wang, P. (2008). Mental health in the context of health disparities. *American Journal of Psychiatry, 165*(9), 1102–1108. doi: 10.1176/appi.ajp.2008.08030333

Miranda, J. J., & Patel, V. (2005). Achieving the millennium development goals: Does mental health play a role? *PLoS Medicine, 2*(10), e291. doi: 10.1371/journal.pmed.0020291

Moczygemba, L. R., Barner, J. C., & Roberson, K. (2008). Texas pharmacists' opinions about and plans for provision of medication therapy management services. *Journal of the American Pharmacists Association, 48*(1), 38–45. doi: 10.1331/JAPhA.2008.07015

Moore, T. A., Buchanan, R. W., Buckley, P. F., Chiles, J. A., Conley, R. R., Crismon, M. L., & Miller, A. L. (2007). The Texas Medication Algorithm Project antipsychotic algorithm for schizophrenia: 2006 update. *The Journal of Clinical Psychiatry, 68*(11), 1751–1762.

National Law Center on Homelessness & Poverty. (2004). *Homelessness in the United States and the human right to housing.* Washington, DC: The Center. Retrieved from http://www.nlchp.org/content/pubs/HomelessnessintheUSandRightstoHousing.pdf

Nickels, G., Kautz, E. B., Villaraigosa, A. R., Newsom, G., Stultz, J. T., & Cochran, T. (2009). *Hunger and homelessness survey: a status report on hunger and homelessness in America's cities a 27-city survey.* Washington, DC: United States Conference of Mayors. Retrieved from http://www.usmayors.org/pressreleases/uploads/USCMHungercompleteWEB2009.pdf

Pliszka, S. R., Lopez, M., Crismon, M. L., Toprac, M. G., Hughes, C. W., Emslie, G. J., . . . Boemer, C. (2003). A feasibility study of the children's medication algorithm project (CMAP) algorithm for the treatment of ADHD. *Journal of the American Academy of Child and Adolescent Psychiatry, 42*(3), 279–287.

Poisal, J. A., Truffer, C., Smith, S., Sisko, A., Cowan, C., Keehan, S., . . . Dickensheets, B. (2007). Health spending projections through 2016: Modest changes obscure Part D's impact. *Health Affairs, 26*, w242–253. [Web exclusive]. doi: 10.1377/hlthaff.26.2.w242.

President's New Freedom Commission on Mental Health. (2003). *Achieving the promise: Transforming mental health care in America: Final report* (DHHS publication No. SMA-03-3832). Rockville, MD: President's New Freedom Commission on Mental Health. Retrieved from http://purl.access.gpo.gov/GPO/LPS36928

Robins, L. N., & Regier, D. A. (1991). *Psychiatric disorders in America: The epidemiologic catchment area study.* New York, NY: Free Press.

Rosenbach, M., Lake, T., Williams, S., & Buck, J. (2009). Implementation of mental health parity: Lessons from California. *Psychiatric Services, 60*(12), 1589–1594.

Rosenthal, T. (2008). The medical home: Growing evidence to support a new approach to primary care. *Journal of the Board of Family Medicine, 21*(5), 427–440.

Scott, D. M. (2010). Assessment of pharmacists' perception of patient care competence and need for training in rural and urban areas in North Dakota. *The Journal of Rural Health, 26*(1), 90–96.

Sia, C., Tonniges, T. F., Osterhus, E., & Taba, S. (2004). History of the medical home concept. *Pediatrics, 113*(5 Suppl):1473–1478.

Slade, D. H. (2009). ERISA preemption and the question of pharmacy benefit managers' fiduciary duty. *The Journal of Legal Medicine, 30*(3), 409–425.

Smith, T. E. & Sederer, L. I. (2009). A new kind of homelessness for individuals with serious mental illness? The need for a "mental health home." *Psychiatric Times, 60*(4), 528–533.

Trivedi, M. H., Rush, A. J., Crismon, M. L., Kashner, T. M., Toprac, M. G., Carmody, T. J., ... Shon, S. P. (2004). Clinical results for patients with major depressive disorder in the Texas Medication Algorithm Project. *Archives of General Psychiatry, 61*(7), 669–680.

U.S. Congress. (1965). The Social Security Act Amendment. Public Law 89–97.

U.S. Congress. (2008). Paul Wellstone and Pete Domenici Mental Health Parity and Addiction Equity Act of 2008. Public Law 110–343.

U.S. Department of Health and Human Services. (1999). *Mental health: A report of the surgeon general.* Rockville, MD: Dept. of Health and Human Services, U.S. Public Health Service. Retrieved from http://purl.access.gpo.gov/GPO/LPS3863

U.S. Department of Health and Human Services. (2000). *Healthy people 2010: Understanding and improving health* (2nd ed.). Washington, DC: U.S. Government Printing Office. Retrieved from http://www.healthypeople.gov/2010/Publications/

U.S. Department of Health and Human Services. (2009). *Healthy people 2020: Public meetings for the 2009 draft objectives.* Washington, DC: U.S. Government Printing Office. Retrieved from http://www.healthypeople.gov/hp2020/Objectives/files/Draft2009Objectives.pdf

U.S. Department of Housing and Urban Development. (1999). *Homelessness: Programs and the people they serve.* Washington, DC: Retrieved from http://www.huduser.org/publications/homeless/homelessness/ch_2c.html

U.S. Department of Housing and Urban Development. (2009). *The 2008 annual homeless assessment report to Congress.* Washington, DC: The Department. Retrieved from http://www.huduser.org/portal/publications/pdf/4thHOmelessAssessmentReport.pdf

Velligan, D. I., Weiden, P. J., Sajatovic, M., Scott, J., Carpenter, D., Ross, R., ... Docherty, J. P. (2010). Assessment of adherence problems in patients with serious and persistent mental illness: recommendations from the expert consensus guidelines. *Journal of Psychiatric Practice, 16*(1), 34–45.

Veysey, B. M. (2010). Mental health issues for incarcerated women. In B. L. Levin & M. A. Becker (Eds.), *A public health perspective on women's mental health.* New York, NY: Springer.

Welch, C. A., Czerwinski, D., Ghimire, B., & Bertsimas, D. (2009). Depression and costs of health care. *Psychosomatics, 50*(4), 392–401.

West, J. C., Wilk, J. E., Rae, D. S., Muszynski, I. S., Stipec, M. R., Alter, C. L., ... Regier, D. A. (2009). Medicaid prescription drug policies and medication access and continuity: Findings from ten states. *Psychiatric Services, 60*(5), 601–610.

Williams, D. R., & Earl, T. R. (2007). Commentary: Race and mental health; More questions than answers. *International Journal of Epidemiology, 36*(4), 751–758.

World Health Organization. (2001). *The world health report 2001 mental health: New understanding, new hope.* Geneva, Switzerland: World Health Organization.

World Health Organization. (2002). *The world health report 2002: Reducing risks, promoting healthy life.* Geneva, Switzerland: World Health Organization.

World Health Organization. (2005). *Preventing chronic diseases: A vital investment: WHO global report.* Geneva, Switzerland: WHO.

World Health Organization & Noncommunicable Disease and Mental Health Cluster. (2003). *Investing in mental health.* Geneva, Switzerland: World Health Organization. Retrieved from http://www.who.int/mental_health/en/investing_in_mnh_final.pdf

Zhang, Z. (2003). *Drug and alcohol use and related matters among arrestees.* Chicago, IL: University of Chicago National Opinion Research Center. Retrieved from http://www.ncjrs.gov/nij/adam/ADAM2003.pdf

Zimmerman, F. J. (2005). Social and economic determinants of disparities in professional help-seeking for child mental health problems: Evidence from a national sample. *Health Services Research, 40*(5, Pt. 5), 1514–1533.

CHAPTER

11

Home Care

William W. McCloskey, Frank Marr, and Maureen A. McCarthy*

Case Scenario

Mary is a 70-year-old woman with osteomyelitis of the left foot who is referred to your home care service for continuation of intravenous (IV) antibiotic therapy upon discharge from a local hospital. Her physician has prescribed cefazolin 2 g every 8 hours for 4 weeks. Mary received her first three doses of cefazolin before leaving the hospital, although the nurse had a difficult time establishing a peripheral IV line. In addition to her infection, Mary has a history of hypertension, insulin-dependent diabetes, osteoarthritis, and an allergy to oxycodone.

The case manager states that Mary is scheduled to leave the hospital today. She lives alone, but her daughter is willing to help, and she can visit her mother each day after work. Mary's insurance is provided by a health maintenance organization (HMO) that has contracted with the home care service in the past. This HMO expects the home care provider to service Mary in the least expensive way. The company sales representative is excited because he has been trying to get business from this case manager for the past month.

LEARNING OBJECTIVES

Upon completion of this chapter, the student shall be able to:

- Explain what home care is
- Describe the various types of home care industries
- Describe the various types of therapies provided by home infusion therapy providers
- Explain the major factors influencing the home care industry
- Explain the role of the pharmacist in providing home care services

*The authors wish to acknowledge the contributions of Robert L. McCarthy who coauthored this chapter for the previous four editions of this text.

INTRODUCTION

The home healthcare industry is very broad in scope, encompassing a variety of products and services. Three home care industries—home health services, home infusion therapy, and home medical equipment—provide the majority of these products and services. Each of these industries is influenced by government legislation, regulatory agencies, reimbursement policies, and technological developments. Home care services are generally initiated when a patient is unable to provide for self-care due to illness, and they are intended to restore and maintain the patient's optimal level of well-being in a familiar environment (Council on Scientific Affairs, 1990).

The growth of home care has been made possible by advances in clinical practice, medicine, and technology. The first home care agencies were established in the 1880s, and today around 17,000 home care providers deliver care to nearly 8 million people in the United States (National Association of Home Care & Hospice, 2008). In 2009, U.S. expenditures for home healthcare services were estimated to be nearly $58 billion; this amount is projected to grow at an annual rate of 8.0% for 2011 through 2019. This is due in part to Medicaid focusing on home care rather than institutional settings for providing long-term care services (Centers for Medicare and Medicaid Services, 2009). In contrast, private insurance payers generally limit home care coverage to only a small percentage of their overall budgets (Levine, Boal, & Boling, 2003).

Because of the large role that home care plays in today's healthcare system, pharmacists must understand the diverse nature of the products and services offered by the home care industry and the factors that influence their provision. Armed with this knowledge, the pharmacist can more effectively work with other healthcare professionals to manage the clinical and financial needs of a home care patient.

This chapter presents an overview of home care by describing the products and services offered by members of each industry, the factors that affect the delivery of those products and services, and the role of the home care pharmacist.

HOME CARE INDUSTRIES

Home Health Services

Home health services are usually associated with nursing care that is provided through a home health agency. Nursing care, however, is only one type of service offered by these agencies. Additional services may include speech therapy, physical therapy, or other types of rehabilitation therapies; homemaker services; social services; and hospice care. Home health agencies employ specially trained staff who provide a variety of services with multiple levels of complexity. These professionals work with other home care providers to obtain additional products, such as medical equipment, medication, and surgical supplies, needed to care for the patient. Home health providers perform a vital role in home care by coordinating the patient's care with family caregivers and other healthcare professionals. Effective communication between the home health provider and everyone involved with the patient's care is essential to the success of a patient's therapy. The following are some examples of home health services.

Nursing Services

Nursing services are also referred to as "skilled nursing services." Patients in the home may require the insertion and maintenance of an intravenous (IV) line, the application of dressings for wound care, assistance with disease management, or self-care education. Skilled services need to be performed by a licensed nurse to ensure patient safety and therapy effectiveness. Based on the information in the chapter-opening case scenario, Mary would most likely require a nurse to help maintain and reestablish her IV site as necessary.

With the advent of high-tech home IV therapy, the role of the home care nurse has become more diverse and sophisticated. Consequently, it is desirable for nurses to have experience in critical care nursing, IV therapy, and the administration of blood products. The introduction of new therapies often requires that the nurse undergo training in the use of complex infusion devices and access methods.

Home care nurses may be employed by a variety of organizations, including the Visiting Nurse Association of America. The Visiting Nurse Association of America is a nonprofit entity that coordinates and provides a variety of nursing services in the home. In addition, nursing services may be available through home care companies and pharmacies that provide home care products and services. Some nurses may even practice as independent contractors.

Hospice Services

Hospice services help manage the end-of-life process for terminally ill patients and their families. These services address the clinical, emotional, and spiritual needs of the patient. Support is extended to family members to help them cope with the end-of-life and bereavement processes. The number of hospices participating in Medicare rose from 31 in 1984 to 3,346 in 2009, with over 600 being home-care–based organizations. Based on the most recent Medicare data, more than 1 million people were serviced by hospice in 2007 (Hospice Association of America, 2009).The focus of hospice is on maintaining quality of life for terminally ill patients. Hospice care aims to make patients as comfortable as possible. Hospice organizations care for patients using a team approach, which usually includes healthcare professionals, clergy, homemakers, and volunteers who work together to manage the many different aspects of patient care.

Pharmacists are important members of the hospice team. As therapeutic drug experts, they recommend appropriate medications and dosage regimens, especially concerning pain control, while monitoring for side effects and drug–drug interactions.

Speech and Physical Therapy

Rehabilitative services such as speech therapy and physical therapy are commonly offered by home healthcare agencies. Speech therapy, for example, may be provided to stroke patients who are suffering from aphasia, a condition resulting in the loss of ability to speak or to understand spoken or written communication. Physical therapy may be provided to postoperative orthopedic patients or accident victims. Given Mary's foot infection and history of osteoarthritis, she may require the services of a physical therapist. The opportunity to have these traditionally hospital-based services provided at home is particularly convenient for patients who have difficulty with transportation.

Social Services

Social workers have an important role in facilitating the transition of a patient from a hospital or long-term care facility to home and coordinating the provision of required home care services. Social services include support with both economic issues (e.g., dealing with the insurance company and assisting with paperwork) and social issues (e.g., coordinating activities with a senior center) (Gill, 1991). Although Mary's daughter may be willing to be a caregiver, she may need the support of a social worker to deal with the complexities that home care entails, especially for older people.

Homemaker Services

With the growing elderly population in the United States, the need for homemaker services has increased rapidly since 2000. Employment of home health aides is expected to grow much more rapidly than the average for all occupations through 2019 (U.S. Department of Labor, 2009). Many elderly individuals require assistance with at least one of their activities of daily living or instrumental activities of daily living. Activities of daily living include personal care activities such as the provision of meals and bathing. Instrumental activities of daily living include house cleaning and grocery shopping. Agencies exist that provide support for elders like Mary who may be unable to complete one or more of these activities.

One of the most well-known homemaker services is the Meals on Wheels program. Meals on Wheels ensures that low-income elderly individuals receive at least one well-balanced meal a day at minimal or no cost. These meals may be served in a congregate setting (e.g., an adult day care center or senior center) or in the senior's home.

Home Infusion Therapy

The home infusion therapy market in the United States is currently estimated to be $11 billion and is expected to grow to $16 billion by 2012 (McClinton, 2009). Home infusion therapy refers to the parenteral and enteral administration of drugs, solutions, and nutrition to patients in their homes. In the past, infusion therapies required hospitalization because of their complexity. As healthcare providers gained more clinical knowledge about infusion therapies, however, they were able to develop clinical policies and procedures to ensure their safe administration in the home setting. Home infusion therapy is generally a more cost-effective alternative to hospitalization and is preferred by most patients. In many cases, caregivers or patients may be taught to administer infusion therapies at home. For example, Mary's daughter could be trained to administer her antibiotic therapy. The acceptance of home infusion therapy has reduced the length of hospitalizations and allowed patients to continue active lives.

The following are the primary types of infusion therapies that are administered in the home: nutrition, anti-infective therapy, pain management therapy, chemotherapy, biologics and related plasma-derived therapies, and miscellaneous therapies.

Nutrition

Parenteral nutrition refers to the IV administration of either all (total parenteral nutrition) or some (partial parenteral nutrition) of a patient's daily nutritional requirements. Parenteral nutrition may be considered the grandfather of home infusion therapies. Home parenteral nutrition has been used for more than 2 decades (Howard et al., 1993) because healthcare providers quickly recognized that most patients requiring chronic therapy did not need to be hospitalized to receive IV feedings.

Home parenteral nutrition is usually administered to home care patients via a central venous catheter or a peripherally inserted central catheter. The choice of venous access is primarily dictated by the concentration of dextrose in the solution to be administered. High concentrations of dextrose (generally greater than 10%) must be administered centrally through a large vein, such as the superior vena cava, to allow for rapid dilution by the blood so as to avoid vascular irritation. In addition to dextrose (as a source of carbohydrates), parenteral nutrition solutions contain amino acids (a source of protein), electrolytes, vitamins, and trace elements. They may also contain fat emulsion (a source of lipids), heparin, insulin, or other compatible medications.

Although enteral nutrition is not a parenteral therapy, patients requiring long-term enteral feedings are often serviced by home infusion providers. Many of these patients have special feeding tubes through which enteral feedings are delivered directly into the stomach (G-tube) or jejunum (J-tube). Consequently, home care therapy providers need to have the expertise to maintain these devices.

Anti-Infective Therapy

Anti-infective therapy was one of the earliest nonnutritive therapies offered at home (Bennett & Allen, 1990), and it remains the most common home infusion therapy. Anti-infective therapy is generally used to manage infections that require relatively long-term IV administration (2 weeks or longer), such as osteomyelitis, cellulitis, Lyme disease, and respiratory infections in cystic fibrosis patients. Even some serious infections, including endocarditis, can be treated in the home setting.

Pain Management Therapy

The hospice movement and the desire of many patients with a terminal illness (and their families) not to be hospitalized in the final days of life have led to the need for the home infusion of narcotic analgesics. Morphine, hydromorphone, fentanyl, and (less commonly) other opiates are administered via continuous infusion to provide chronic pain relief while allowing the patient to remain alert. Ambulatory infusion devices can be programmed to enable patients to self-administer bolus doses of medication on demand for breakthrough pain. Pharmacists are often consulted to convert an oral or transdermal dose of analgesic medication to an appropriate infusion dose.

Chemotherapy

The administration of potent antineoplastic medications in the home setting may be considered for certain patients. Clinician acceptance of this type of home care has increased as the understanding of how to manage the complications of chemotherapy has improved (Bennett & Allen, 1990). Moreover, physicians may not have facilities adequate for the safe preparation (e.g., vertical laminar flow containment hood) of cytotoxic agents or lack USP 797 compliance, so they may utilize the services of a home infusion therapy provider. In addition, changes in the reimbursement structure for administering chemotherapy in the outpatient setting have changed the demand for treatment in the home care setting. Agents that are administered over several days (e.g., 5-fluorouracil) are the antineoplastic medications most commonly administered at home.

Biologics and Related Plasma-Derived Therapies

With the advances that we have seen in biotechnology, a number of drugs have been utilized in home infusion for treatment of diseases that would otherwise be treated in a more controlled setting. Some examples include growth hormone (for treatment of growth hormone deficiency in children), and rare enzyme deficiency diseases such as Gaucher's disease (manifested by mental effects and musculoskeletal effects and treated with alglucerase). Rheumatoid arthritis is another disease that is commonly treated in the home setting with infliximab, adalimumab and etanercept. Patients with multiple sclerosis may receive injections of interferon beta-1A (Avonex and Rebif), interferon beta 1-B (Betaseron) and etanercept (Enbrel) in their home. Moving forward, surely the home infusion setting will be seeing the use of additional biotechnology-derived agents that will be suitable for administration in the home environment. Biologic agents have additional complications that may be somewhat unique to the group. Some of these agents require extensive infusion periods of up to 6 hours, which must be monitored throughout by nursing staff. Other problems are incurred if any of the drugs are utilized for a non-FDA approved indication. This off-label use is impacted by medico-legal and reimbursement risk.

Miscellaneous Therapies

Several other infusion therapies have also been delivered in the home, including hydration for such conditions as hyperemesis and inflammatory bowel disease; inotropic therapy for the treatment of refractory congestive heart failure; and blood products for hemotherapy. As more of these products emerge, it is anticipated that they will find roles in the management of patients in their homes.

Home Medical Equipment

The home medical equipment (HME) industry provides medical equipment and disposable supplies to treat patients at home. For example, medical equipment is used to facilitate patients' breathing, improve their mobility, and perform diagnostic testing. Such equipment often requires the use of disposable supplies by the patient. Home health providers also use surgical supplies for wound care dressings and diagnostic strips to check sugar levels in blood.

The following are examples of products and services that are provided by the HME industry.

Durable Medical Equipment

Durable medical equipment is reusable medical equipment that patients have an option to lease or purchase. Examples include wheelchairs, bathroom safety supplies, hospital beds, and ambulatory aids such as canes, crutches, and walkers. Providing durable medical equipment was one of the original home care services delivered by pharmacists.

One of the specialized categories of durable medical equipment is infusion pumps. Mary, in our case example, is to receive cefazolin every 8 hours. The drug must be administered at an equal interval of 8 hours, not 3 times per day. This type of administration may become problematic in the home and require a programmable pump. The pump is attached to the patient for the entire 24 hours and administers the dose at the programmed 8-hour interval. Thus, the patient does not have to be concerned about being awake for the dose at the time of administration. Infusion may be particularly important if the patient is to receive a drug at a frequency of every 4 or 6 hours. The pumps may also be used for pain management medication administration. The unique characteristic of this type of therapy is that the patient, in addition to receiving a baseline infusion, may also be allowed bolus dosing on a limited basis. The programmable pumps accommodate this type of administration quite well, by allowing for the bolus dosing and providing a limit on the total number of bolus doses a patient may self-administer within a prescribed time period. The programming feature also limits the frequency of self-administered bolus doses. Two typical pumps with these characteristics are shown in **Figure 11-1** and **Figure 11-2.**

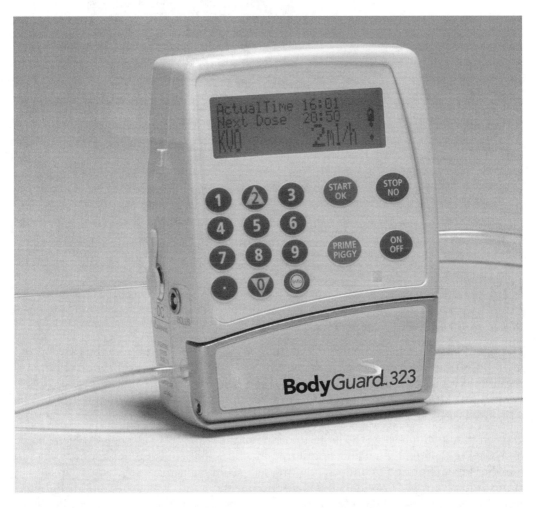

Figure 11-1 CME BodyGuard® 323 infusion pump.
Source: Courtesy of CME America, LLC.

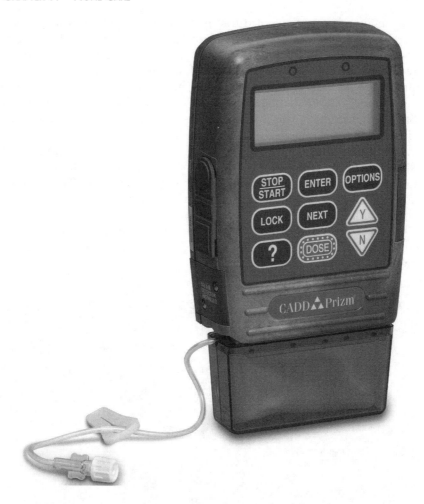

Figure 11-2 CADD Prizm VIP infusion pump by Sims Deltec.
Source: Courtesy of Smiths Medical ASD, Inc., St. Paul, Minnesota.

Respiratory Therapy and Supplies

Many patients suffering from chronic pulmonary conditions, who previously required hospitalization, may now receive respiratory therapy at home. Respiratory therapies include oxygen, aerosolized medications, continuous positive airway pressure, and ventilators. All of these therapies require special monitoring and patient education by a licensed respiratory therapist.

Oxygen therapy represents the largest portion of the respiratory market. Oxygen can be delivered to a patient via a concentrator, a machine that concentrates room oxygen to a higher level of purity; cylinders; compressed gas in tanks; or a liberator, a vessel that stores liquid oxygen. Providers evaluate the individual needs of the patient to determine the best method of delivery. Providing oxygen therapy is extremely profitable for HME providers.

Many patients are able to treat their respiratory conditions by administering medications via nebulization at home. In addition, some providers have developed specialty programs to treat conditions such as asthma. Once a patient is enrolled in such a program, the provider will deliver bronchodilators on a recurring basis and monitor patient compliance. The outcome of the patient's therapy is then reported to the patient's insurance carrier for review.

Miscellaneous Supplies

Miscellaneous products provided by HME dealers and pharmacies allow patients to care for themselves at home. Patients with diabetes (such as Mary) can monitor their blood glucose levels using portable monitors. A wide variety of appliances and skin care products are readily available to ostomy patients to care for their condition. The urinary incontinence market has expanded rapidly and provides home care patients, particularly the elderly, with many options. Wound care and surgical supplies are available to treat bedridden and postsurgical patients.

FACTORS THAT INFLUENCE THE HOME CARE INDUSTRY

Financial and regulatory issues present difficult challenges to the home care industry. One of the toughest challenges facing home care providers is the ability to provide patients with high-quality care given payers' reimbursement rates. The cost of caring for patients at home is increasing because home care providers are increasingly treating sicker patients with more complex therapies. Home care providers must also satisfy the requirements of statutory laws, regulations, and professional standards. These requirements improve patient care, but they also increase the cost of providing therapy.

Whereas the cost of providing therapy is on the rise, many insurance carriers are reducing reimbursement rates. To do more for less, home care providers will need to take advantage of advances in technology and changes in business practices to survive. The following sections explain some of the significant factors affecting the home care industry.

Reimbursement Issues

Insurance carriers or third-party payers exert a strong influence on the home care industry because they reimburse providers for home care products and services that are provided to patients. Many types of third-party payers exist, including government, managed care organizations (MCOs), and private insurance. Each payer determines its own levels of coverage, billing rules, and reimbursement rates. This inconsistency makes it difficult for home care providers to be reimbursed quickly and easily for the services they provide.

Government Insurance

The Centers for Medicare and Medicaid Services is the federal agency that oversees the Medicare and Medicaid programs in the United States. This agency was formerly called the Health Care Financing Administration. The Medicare program provides coverage to nearly 60 million people (Kaiser Family Foundation, 2010b), and Medicaid provides coverage to approximately 47 million (Kaiser Family Foundation, 2010a). See Chapters 16 and 18.

Medicare

Medicare is a national health insurance program for patients with end-stage kidney disease, elderly patients, and selected patients with disabilities. It is divided into four components known as Parts A, B, C, and D. Part A refers to hospital insurance, and Part B provides medical (physician) insurance. Medicare Part A covers inpatient hospital services, skilled nursing facilities, home health services, and hospice care; Medicare Part B helps pay for the cost of physician services, outpatient hospital services, medical equipment, and supplies (Centers for Medicare and Medicaid Services, 2010). Beneficiaries were given another option in 1997 under Medicare Part C, called Medicare Advantage (originally called Medicare + Choice). This program allows the patient to choose benefits through risk-based plans such as an HMO or other managed care plan or a private fee-for-service plan. Under Part C, beneficiaries must pay monthly Part B premiums in addition to those for the private insurance. In January 2006, Medicare Part D was implemented. This program expanded coverage to include prescription drugs.

Mary was eligible for Medicare once she reached the age of 65. She chose a Medicare Advantage HMO option.

Unfortunately, Medicare does not generally cover home infusion therapies. Only a small number of therapies that are administered using an electronic infusion device are covered, such as antiviral therapies, some chemotherapies, and dobutamine. For most other therapies, patients need to have alternative insurance coverage.

Medicaid

Medicaid is a health insurance program for low-income and needy people. Unlike Medicare, which is entirely a federal program, Medicaid is actually administered by the states within federal guidelines. Medicaid is more comprehensive than Medicare, and it provides home care coverage as part of its required benefits. Many Medicaid programs also offer outpatient prescription drug coverage, although they are not required to do so. Even when prescription drugs are covered, however, infusion medications may not be. Managed Medicaid plans that provide for shared risk on the part of the Medicaid plan and the private insurer that contracts with the state to provide coverage for the patient have emerged. The private contracted insurer would offer a plan that is specifically designed to control costs by limiting the drug formulary and the services covered.

Managed Care Organizations

The goal of MCOs is to balance the delivery of high-quality health care with cost controls. MCOs control their expenditures by limiting coverage for healthcare products and services based on the needs of their patients. An HMO (like the one that covers Mary) is an example of an MCO. HMOs contract with multiple healthcare providers to meet the needs of individual groups. Employers and patients pay an HMO a set fee to manage their healthcare needs.

As large numbers of patients joined MCOs, these payers were able to negotiate sharp reductions in reimbursement rates from home care providers. Managed care principles decreased the costs of health care, but made many providers unprofitable. In response, a number of providers closed or merged with other providers. Home care providers now try to negotiate prices with MCOs. If the reimbursement levels are not favorable, providers may choose not to work with the organization. Managed care contracts can be successful only if they are beneficial to both provider and payer (see Chapter 17).

The process that a home infusion provider must go through in order to get paid for services, as provided to Mary in our case, generates risk for the provider. During the intake process, the provider may be required to obtain prior authorization for services. Once this is obtained, the provider must realize that it is not a guarantee of payment. The payer may decide that the therapy is not medically indicated or that the use of the drug is off label (a non-FDA approved indication). When this occurs, the provider is not paid, even though it may have a confirmed prior authorization.

Private Sector

Many private third-party payers exist, and some large corporations may be self-insured. These payers reimburse for many home care services in an effort to reduce their costs. The rationale for this coverage is simple: by eliminating the cost of a hospitalization, the care is less expensive. As with many other payers, the private sector may use managed care principles to contain the rising costs of health care.

Legal, Regulatory, and Professional Standards

The Balanced Budget Act of 1997

The Balanced Budget Act of 1997 introduced legislation that significantly affected the home care industry. Congress passed this act to control healthcare spending and reduce fraud within the Medicare system. The act required the institution of a prospective payment system for home health services, reductions in reimbursement rates for HME, and implementation of competitive bidding processes. Under a prospective payer system, the home health agency is paid a flat rate to care for a Medicare recipient. This rate reimburses the home health agency for all labor and medical supplies needed to care for the patient during a 60-day episode. Even though it has been in effect for some time, the overall impact of this legislation on the home care industry remains unclear, but it is expected that there will be changes in how home care providers conduct business so that they can remain profitable (see Chapter 17).

The Health Insurance Portability and Accountability Act of 1996

The Health Insurance Portability and Accountability Act (HIPAA) was enacted as a direct result of consumer demand. HIPAA is best known for its mandating confidentiality of protected health information, which affects how pharmacies and other providers handle a patient's healthcare information. However, HIPAA regulations are complex, and two other provisions of this act affect the home care industry, including (1) insurance reform and (2) administrative simplification.

The insurance reform provision of HIPAA improves insurance coverage when an individual changes employment or health plans. Exclusion from a health plan for preexisting conditions is now subject to strict limitations, which should expand the number of patients who are eligible for home care services.

The administrative simplification provision of HIPAA requires standardization of electronic claims submission. Such standardization will improve operational efficiency and payment cycles for home care providers.

Regulatory Agencies

Many federal and state agencies regulate the home care industry. It is the responsibility of home care providers to understand the legal and regulatory processes that must be followed where they practice. Home health services may be monitored by the state's department of public health. Pharmacies are monitored by the Drug Enforcement Administration and the Food and Drug Administration (FDA). HME providers may be monitored by the Department of Transportation. Providers may also be accountable to their state board of professional registration. These boards may license the facility as well as the pharmacists, nurses, respiratory therapists, and other healthcare professionals who work there.

Accrediting Organizations

Accrediting organizations are not federal or state agencies, but rather independent organizations that develop standards of practice for home care providers. Standards address issues such as clinical care, business management, and staff competency. By winning a seal of approval from these organizations, home care providers prove the quality of care that they provide to insurance carriers and patients. Providers are required to achieve accreditation by most third-party payers to be eligible for reimbursement.

The Joint Commission is perhaps the best recognized accrediting agency. Other home care accrediting agencies include the Accreditation Commission for Health Care and the Community Health and Preventative Services Organization.

Advances in Technology

The delivery of many parenteral medications to patients in their homes has been greatly improved by advances in technology. Infusion pumps are a good example of advanced technology that has improved the care delivered by the home care industry. Once heavy and bulky, infusion pumps have evolved to be ambulatory, lightweight, and inconspicuous. The latest ambulatory models have the ability to infuse multiple therapies. Taken collectively, these advances provide both clinical advantages and cost savings.

Advances in Internet and wireless communications have enabled home care providers to readily share patient data with other healthcare professionals. Using point-of-care devices, palm-sized computers, and voice recognition software, pharmacists, nurses, physicians, and other healthcare professionals can transfer patient data quickly and securely. For more than a decade, telemedicine (i.e., transmission of medical data from a remote site to a central location) has been employed to help monitor patients with chronic conditions such as congestive heart failure, diabetes, and chronic obstructive lung disease as well as patients with acute infections (Eron, King, Marineau, & Yonehara, 2004). Home care providers can also communicate with insurance carriers to approve benefits and submit claims. The latest drug and healthcare information is also available online. Important sites include those operated by the Centers for Medicare and Medicaid Services (www.cms.hhs.gov) and the Food and Drug Administration (www.fda.gov). Easy access to information and increased communication can reduce costs and improve patient care. In addition, there are numerous subscription services that provide both drug and disease information.

Information technology systems have developed more slowly in the home infusion industry due to the small size of the industry. The market that software vendors are selling to is limited, and thus it limits the total profits available to invest in the further evolution of the software. As a result, the rate of sophistication development of the software is behind the overall medical software industry.

THE ROLE OF THE HOME CARE PHARMACIST

Pharmacists working in home care may do so through a community pharmacy, home care company, or hospital outpatient setting. In all home care organizations, the pharmacist must act as a vital member of a healthcare team that cares for the patient. This team may include nurses, physicians, caregivers, and the patient. The team members work together to develop a plan of care that will achieve the desired outcome for the patient's therapy.

Pharmacists are relied on for their pharmaceutical expertise, but they must also be competent in other areas to fulfill their role as a member of a healthcare team. A home care pharmacist may be responsible for the following roles when providing home care services.

Selection of Home Care Patients: Criteria Evaluation

Although Mary was discharged home to finish her course of IV antibiotic therapy, not all patients are appropriate candidates for home care. The decision to treat a patient at home is generally made jointly by nursing and pharmacy staff, in conjunction with the patient's physician. Patients must be clinically stable, have adequate support systems (e.g., telephone, family), and must be willing to accept responsibility for their own care. Given the current financial climate, patients must also have the ability to pay for home care either independently or through a third party.

Insurance

With the exception of IV medications, the major public-sector insurance programs (Medicare and Medicaid) provide good coverage for general home care services. The advent of Medicare Part D coverage in 2008 provided partial or full coverage of home care medications. Likewise, most private third-party payers provide reasonable coverage for home care. As discussed previously, the incentive to cover home care services is linked to the notion that it is less expensive than hospitalization.

Nevertheless, the patient's ability to pay is a component of the assessment process conducted before his or her discharge. Patients who meet medical and social criteria for home care may not qualify financially. Unlike many nonprofit hospitals, for-profit home care companies are not required to provide free care. Some home care companies accept a percentage of no-pay patients if they believe that this action will generate additional business with a specific physician, group practice, or hospital. It is the responsibility of the patient care coordinator or reimbursement specialist to verify a patient's insurance coverage before a patient such as Mary is considered eligible for home care.

Social Factors

Social factors play a crucial role in the decision to treat a patient at home. Patients should have family members who are willing and able to support or administer care, because 24-hour nursing care is not cost effective. Generally, patients and family members are taught to administer therapy without the assistance of a nurse or another healthcare professional. Further, patients must be positive about receiving their therapy at home for it to be successful. Some patients are reluctant to be discharged from a hospital for fear that they will lose the support a hospital offers (Bennett & Allen, 1990). Fortunately, the support that Mary's daughter provides and Mary's own willingness to be discharged will help with her transition to home care.

Other social factors are also important. For example, the physical condition of the home, its cleanliness, and the availability of refrigeration, running water, and electricity must be considered before providing complex therapies at home. Less invasive treatments such as rehabilitation services are possible without the presence of these conditions.

Another potential hazard is the presence in the home of a family member or others who may be abusing illicit substances. Home infusion therapy patients are supplied with needles and syringes to administer their treatment. Some may receive narcotic analgesics. A careful evaluation and monitoring of the home environment for substance abuse is therefore important.

Development of a Patient Plan of Care

Once a patient is discharged to the home, clear objectives must be developed as part of the patient's plan of care. These objectives include the selection of therapy, nature and frequency of monitoring parameters, including laboratory results, and desired therapeutic outcomes. The development of a care plan that outlines the individual care for a given patient will help reduce the possibility of a drug-related misadventure, including the situation in which the patient does not respond to therapy. Specific patient problems should be identified and associated with goals. Detailed interventions should then be designed to ensure the resolution of the problems. The patient care plan should include all of the patient's medical problems, not just the one requiring immediate attention. For example, in addition to her osteomyelitis, Mary's care plan should address her hypertension, diabetes, arthritis, drug allergy, and current medications. Home care accrediting bodies require the development of such a care plan.

Selection of Therapy

The choice of drug therapy is even more critical in the home than in an institutional setting. The usual safeguards (24-hour nursing and physician availability and emergency equipment) that are standard procedure in institutions may be absent in the home. As a result, several safety and convenience factors should be considered when selecting a therapy for the home care patient.

For example, because of the potential risks of allergy associated with some medications (such as antibiotics), the first dose should be administered in a controlled setting such as a hospital or clinic. If the first dose is administered at home, it should be done under medical supervision with careful screening of associated allergy history and with the presence of anaphylaxis medications. Other considerations include frequency and ease of administration. Drugs that can be administered once daily are more suitable for home care. In Mary's case, the pharmacist might recommend an alternative antibiotic that could be dosed less frequently than every 8 hours. Medications that are less likely to cause phlebitis (inflammation of the vein) and that do not require administration of large volumes of fluid are also more appropriate for home delivery.

Compounding Issues

A number of pharmaceutical compounding issues are unique to home care. These include drug/solution stability, packaging, infusion devices, and delivery schedules.

Drug/Solution Stability

In the past, most manufacturer-generated stability data were predicated on patients receiving medications in a hospital setting. As a result, expiration dating has traditionally been limited to 24 hours after product preparation. To deliver medications in a cost-effective manner at home, pharmacists need to extend stability data often for more than a week, depending on the product. Manufacturers realize that if they can demonstrate that their product is stable for more than 24 hours, it is feasible to use in the home setting; thus longer range stability data are now available.

It is important to distinguish between sterility and stability. Unless strict aseptic technique is adhered to, microbial contamination may potentially compromise the integrity of the product—regardless of its chemical stability. Consequently, all home infusion providers should have specially designed, environmentally controlled areas (such as clean rooms and laminar flow hoods) for preparation of sterile products. Home infusion companies and any organization that compounds sterile products must now be in compliance with new standards described in USP Chapter <797>. These standards define how sterile products should be prepared based on three risk levels: low, medium, and high. Risk level is determined by factors such as how many manipulations are involved in preparing the product and whether the final product is prepared from sterile or nonsterile ingredients (United States Pharmacopeial Convention, 2004).

Packaging

In institutional settings, both glass and plastic IV containers are used. However, because of the risk of breakage and potential for patient injury, plastic is generally used at home. Some products may be available or stable only in glass. In such instances, glass containers are used but with appropriate cautions to patients and caregivers.

Infusion Devices

Two major changes have occurred in IV infusion devices as a result of the growth of home care. First, the size and weight of infusion devices have decreased dramatically. These changes have allowed some patients to receive their medication while going to work or school. The devices are simply placed in a pouch, which may be concealed under the patient's clothing. Second, manufacturers have introduced disposable infusion devices, which are designed to deliver one or more doses of medication and be discarded after use. Pharmacists must be able to choose the appropriate device based on the drug therapy and the patient's needs. The selection and use of the device should be incorporated into the patient's plan of care.

Delivery Schedules

Frequency of drug administration is an important consideration when selecting parenteral medications to be used in the home. Drugs that may be administered once or twice per day are more suitable than those that must be administered four to six times per day. Pharmacists should advise prescribers who are discharging patients to the home about alternative medications that may be more suitable for home use.

Monitoring Drug Therapy

Because home care patients lack the support systems available to hospital patients, monitoring drug therapy for efficacy and for adverse drug events is critical to successful patient management. The pharmacist plays an important role in establishing and coordinating monitoring parameters such as serum drug levels and blood chemistries. The pharmacist needs to ensure that the proper tests are ordered from the time the patient is accepted for care at home until the time the therapy is completed. The pharmacist also communicates the results of these tests to the prescriber and recommends changes as appropriate.

Communication With Physicians, Nurses, Patients, and Others

Good communication among members of the healthcare team is essential for the successful care of home patients. Because the home lacks institutional safeguards, poor communication can quickly result in an adverse event for the patient. Adverse events may result in rehospitalization, which negates any benefits afforded by an early discharge.

The pharmacist has an even greater opportunity to affect patient care in the home than in an institutional setting. This impact, however, is predicated on the pharmacist's ability to communicate effectively with all members of the patient's healthcare team. For example, a pharmacist might receive lab data regarding Mary that may require a dosage adjustment in her antibiotic. The pharmacist must first communicate with the prescriber to effect a dosage change and then ensure that Mary's nurse is aware of the modification in therapy and the reasons for it.

Drug Information

Home care pharmacists must have adequate information resources to support the care of the patient. As a result, access to a drug information center—or, at the very least, to drug information services—is vital. The pharmacist must have the information necessary to determine whether a medication typically administered in an institutional setting can be safely delivered at home. Pharmacists should have ready access to stability and compatibility information, administration modalities, and potential complications.

American Society of Health-System Pharmacists Home Care Standards

The American Society of Health-System Pharmacists is a professional organization that has established standards for a number of activities pertaining to pharmacy practice, including home care. These standards establish a minimum level of pharmacy services within a component of pharmacy practice.

The home care standards for pharmacists focus on the following issues:

- Preadmission assessment
- Initial patient database and assessment
- Selection of products, devices, and ancillary supplies
- Development of care plans
- Patient education and counseling
- Clinical monitoring
- Effective communication with prescribers, nurses, and other healthcare providers
- Communication with the patient and the caregiver

- Coordination of drug preparation, delivery, storage, and administration
- Standard precautions for employee and patient safety
- Documentation in the home care record
- Adverse drug event reporting and performance improvement
- Participation in clinical drug research in the home
- Participation in performance improvement activities
- Policies and procedures
- Licensure
- Training, continuing education, and competence (American Society of Health-System Pharmacists, 2000)

Education/Training

Many pharmacists who practice in home care do not have additional training beyond their entry-level degree (BS or PharmD). Curricula in U.S. colleges of pharmacy typically provide either required or elective coursework in sterile product preparation or parapharmaceuticals such as ostomy supplies and durable medical equipment, which may help better prepare practitioners for a career in home care. Some colleges of pharmacy may offer a course or component of a course that addresses home care, issues of reimbursement, and business management. It is anticipated that as home care pharmacy practice grows, pharmacy programs will incorporate more home care–related courses into their curricula.

Practice Experiences

A number of colleges of pharmacy, in conjunction with home care companies, are offering experiential training in the form of introductory and advanced practice experiences in home care. Introductory practice experiences provide students with opportunities to gain initial exposure to home care as a career option early in the professional pharmacy curriculum. Advanced practice experiences are more extended, with a focus on patient care, and occur during the final year of the curriculum.

Residency Programs

At this time, only a very limited number of postgraduate, practice-based training programs—that is, residencies—exist in home care. These programs are available to pharmacists who wish to gain additional skills in home care practice. Expansion of such programs may remain somewhat restricted given the proprietary nature of home care businesses. In particular, concerns exist about training pharmacists who will eventually work for the competition.

CONCLUSION

Home care encompasses the provision of many healthcare products and services to patients. To care for themselves, home care patients like Mary rely on home health agencies, home infusion providers, and home medical equipment dealers to provide products, service, and training.

The provision of home care is influenced by factors such as reimbursement issues, regulatory requirements, and advances in technology. To ensure proper care, each provider must account for these factors when developing a patient's plan of care.

Pharmacists must maintain their competency to fulfill their roles as home care providers. As advances in technology result in new therapies and methods of delivery, the importance of the pharmacist's role in home care will continue to grow.

QUESTIONS FOR FURTHER DISCUSSION

1. Will the expansion of managed care affect the growth and development of home care? How?
2. What opportunities are available for other players (e.g., hospitals) in the healthcare delivery system in home care?
3. How do you believe the role of the home care pharmacist will change in the future?

KEY TOPICS AND TERMS

Accrediting agency
Balanced Budget Act
Health Insurance Portability and Accountability Act (HIPAA)
Home care
Home care standards for pharmacists
Home health services
Home infusion therapy
Managed care
Medicaid
Medicare
Regulatory agency
Technology

REFERENCES

American Society of Health-System Pharmacists. (2000, July). ASHP guidelines on the pharmacist's role in home care. *American Journal of Health-System Pharmacy, 57,* 1252–1257.

Bennett, M. A., & Allen, R. D. (1990). High-technology home pharmacotherapy. I: An overview of antiinfective and antineoplastic therapies. *Journal of Pharmacy Practices, 3*(1), 34–39.

Centers for Medicare and Medicaid Services. (2009). *National health care expenditures projections 2009–2019.* Retrieved from www.cms.hhs.gov/NationalHealthExpendData

Centers for Medicare and Medicaid Services. (2010). Medicare and you. Retrieved from http://www.medicare.gov/Publications/Pubs/pdf/10050.pdf

Council on Scientific Affairs, American Medical Association. (1990). Home care in the 1990s. *Journal of the American Medical Association, 263*(9), 1241–1244.

Eron, L., King, P., Marineau, M., & Yonehara, C. (2004). Treating acute infections by telemedicine in the home. *Clinical Infectious Diseases, 39,* 1175–1181.

Gill, G. M. (1991). Social work intervention with stroke patients and their families. *Journal of Home Health Care Practice, 4*(1), 57–62.

Hospice Association of America. (2009). *Hospice facts and statistics.* Retrieved from http://www.nahc.org/facts/HospiceStats09.pdf

Howard, L., Alger, S., Michalek, A., Heaphey, L., Aftahi, S., & Johnston, K. R. (1993). Home parenteral nutrition in adults. In J. L. Rombeau & M. D. Caldwell (Eds.), *Clinical nutrition: Parenteral nutrition* (2nd ed., pp. 814–839). Philadelphia, PA: W. B. Saunders.

Kaiser Family Foundation. (2010a). *Medicaid financial eligibility: Primary pathways for the elderly and people with disabilities.* Retrieved from http://www.kff.org/medicaid/upload/8048.pdf

Kaiser Family Foundation. (2010b). *Medicare: A primer.* Retrieved from http://www.kff.org/medicare/upload/7615-03.pdf

Levine, S. A., Boal, J. B., & Boling, P. A. (2003). Home care. *Journal of the American Medical Association, 290*(9), 1203–1207.

McClinton, D. H. (2009, October 1). The right dose. *Home Care Magazine.* Retrieved from http://homecaremag.com/mag/home-infusion-therapy-market-200910/

National Association for Home Care and Hospice. (2008). *Basic statistics about home care.* Retrieved from http://www.nahc.org/facts/08HC_Stats.pdf

United States Pharmacopeial Convention. (2004). Pharmaceutical considerations—sterile preparations (general information chapter 797). In *The United States Pharmacopeia/National Formulary* (22nd ed., 26th rev., pp. 2350–2370). Rockville, MD: U.S. Pharmacopeial Convention, Inc.

U.S. Department of Labor, Bureau of Labor Statistics. (2009). *Personal and home care aides.* Retrieved from http://www.bls.gov/oco/ocos326.htm#outlook

Informatics in Health Care

Ardis Hanson, Bruce Lubotsky Levin, and David M. Scott

Case Scenario

As a consultant to a 40-year-old pharmacist, you have been asked to provide Darcy with some advice on whether she should integrate an automated dispensing machine and web-based patient safety program into her community pharmacy practice. For the past 10 years, Darcy has developed a thriving independent community pharmacy practice in a rural community of 3,000 people in a Midwest state. While the trend toward an increasing number of prescriptions being transferred to web-based and mail order pharmacies is a competitive pressure for most community pharmacies, Darcy's pharmacy has been affected at a relatively low level (< 10%), due to her loyal customer base combined with her ability to offer competitive prescription pricing. In the last few years, Darcy's pharmacy has experienced a large increase in prescription workload and she has difficulty maintaining adequate staffing levels. She is also concerned about a recent increase in medication dispensing errors. Darcy has difficulty recruiting a pharmacy technician and she is considering buying an automated dispensing machine to assume part of the increased dispensing load. Darcy is also considering a web-based patient safety program to reduce medication dispensing errors. Darcy wants to discuss with you her plans to purchase an automated dispensing machine and implement a web-based patient safety program in the next 6 months. She would also like to make sure there are no other issues to resolve before she proceeds with these two projects. What should you advise her to do? In your answer, consider a discussion of the impact that automation and patient safety have had on pharmacy practice.

LEARNING OBJECTIVES

Upon completion of this chapter, the student shall be able to:

- Describe the application of information technology in healthcare delivery and pharmacy practice
- Describe how automation in distribution is affecting pharmacy practice
- Describe major information technology trends in pharmacy practice today
- Describe the redesign of pharmacy practice with regard to information technology, with a focus on federal policy and public safety
- Describe the challenges and innovations in rural telepharmacy

CHAPTER QUESTIONS

1. Describe the benefits of telepharmacy programs.
2. Describe meaningful use criteria for electronic health records.
3. Describe components of e-prescribing software.
4. With the continued development of databases for pharmaceutical research, what are possible scenarios for computer-based research?

INTRODUCTION

Although telecommunication plays an increasingly important and prominent role in society in knowledge exchange and in commerce, it is in the fields of public health, medical care, and pharmacy practice where the most remarkable opportunities and challenges have emerged. Telecommunication or "telehealth" strategies, particularly with the growth of broadband services, continue to broaden access to medical care, health education, and health and mental health services delivery for at-risk populations in America (Hanson & Levin, 2004; Hanson, Levin, Heron, & Burke, 2003; National Telecommunications and Information Administration, 2004). Computer-based patient records, health information systems, and unified electronic claims systems use various technologies to streamline and centralize databases. Recent initiatives, such as the President's New Freedom Commission (2003) and the national electronic health record, encourage policy makers and health professionals to transform existing health services into more efficient and effective healthcare delivery systems (Levin & Hanson, in press).

This chapter will examine some of the major issues related to health and pharmacoinformatics. It will include a general discussion of the history of informatics technology and the categories of healthcare information systems, with an emphasis on pharmacy applications.

Definitions

Telemedicine (or telehealth) has been described as the use of telecommunications technologies to provide health care in a cost-efficient manner and to improve health care, particularly when distance separates healthcare consumers and providers (Angaran, 1999). However, new terms continue to be added to enlarge the scope of telemedicine and telehealth.

Informatics is the field of information science concerned with the analysis and dissemination of data through the application of computers. Informatics had its origins in science, engineering, computer technology (hardware and software), and communications (Collen, 1994). Early work in the field of informatics focused on its role in information processing, such as the use of medical databases for clinical research and the possible use of computer-stored clinical practice records in the practice of medicine (Goldman, Mushlin, & Lee, 1986; Hasman, 1987; McDonald & Tierney, 1986). Informatics is now utilized in the medical, nursing, pharmacy, and other allied health disciplines.

Pharmacoinformatics, or *pharmacy informatics*, "... is the scientific field that focuses on medication-related data and knowledge within the continuum of healthcare systems—including its acquisition, storage, analysis, use, and dissemination—in the delivery of optimal medication-related patient care and health outcomes" (HIMSS, 2007, p. 1). By 1992, hospital pharmacists were using computers for information on drug interactions, monitoring therapy, drug distribution and dosing, and financial analysis and inventory control (Dasta, Greer, & Speedie, 1992). Today, pharmacoinformatics is a key part of the pharmaceutical industry for research, product development, quality assurance, business development, marketing, and sales, as well as community and hospital pharmacies.

Health information technology is the use of information and communication technology in health care. Health information technology may include electronic health records and personal health records, computerized decision support systems, and other technologies that play a role in the use and electronic transfer of clinical, administrative, and financial information within and among healthcare settings and providers.

At a symposium on computer applications in medical care (Orthner, 1987), integrating informatics into practice and education, decision making, artificial intelligence, modeling and simulation; and image processing, three-dimensional graphics, and computer networks were determined as critical issues in the field. In addition to these technology issues are administrative and policy concerns, such as reimbursement policy; legal, ethical, and regulatory issues; encoding and representation of medical meaning; ambulatory medical records systems; hospital information systems; and software for developing informatics and health information technology systems. These areas remain important issues in the coordination of health information technology programs and policies.

Electronic Health Records

The American Recovery and Reinvestment Act (P.L. 111-5) was enacted in 2009 by the U.S. Congress. Also referred to as the Stimulus Act, Section 3 of the act included a provision to continue investments needed to increase economic efficiency by encouraging technological advances in science and health. Nineteen billion dollars were set aside for health information technology.

As part of the American Recovery and Reinvestment Act, the Health Information Technology for Economic and Clinical Health Act amends Title XXX of the Public Health Service Act and promotes the widespread adoption of health information technology to support the electronic sharing of clinical data among healthcare stakeholders. This initiative is reflected in the objectives for health communication and health information technology in *Healthy People 2020*, including increasing the "proportion of providers who use health information technology to improve individual and population health" and to increase the "proportion of providers and governmental health agencies that use advanced connectivity to optimize electronic health information exchange to improve individual and population health" (U.S. Department of Health and Human Services, 2009, p. 1). A major component of the electronic sharing of clinical data is the electronic health record (EHR).

The EHR is a record of every healthcare encounter of an individual. It contains all types of data, ranging from patient demographics, provider notes, medications, medical histories, laboratory data, and other test reports. Since the EHR will generate a complete record of each patient encounter, it will be an important element in clinical decision making, outcomes assessment, and quality management. It should also increase the patient's participation in his or her individual health care (Staroselsky et al., 2006).

Between 2005 and 2020, EHR systems may result in a net savings of $371 billion for hospitals and $142 billion for physician practices (Hillestad et al., 2005). These savings are expected to result from increased safety and efficiencies in health care. In addition, it has been suggested that the EHR may more than double these savings due to more effective management of chronic diseases and increased opportunities for prevention. However, from a provider perspective, "... very little systematic evidence has been gathered on the usability of EHRs in practice and the implications of their design on cognitive task flow, continuity of care, and efficiency of workflows" (Armijo, McDonnell, & Werner, 2009, p. 1). This is an area under further study by several federal agencies, including the Agency for Healthcare Research and Quality.

EHRs are often part of patient portals, which link patients to their EHRs. Schnipper and colleagues (2008) suggest that medications modules in the EHR can improve patient medication lists, reduce adverse drug events, and improve patient–health care provider interactions. In the Partners HealthCare patient portal, patients can review and renew their medications, update contact information, schedule appointments, exchange emails with their providers, and access a licensed health information library (Schnipper et al., 2008). Patients are more satisfied with their involvement with their treatment and see improved communication and medical visit experiences as major benefits (Businger et al., 2007).

Meaningful Use Criteria and Standards

However, before the EHR can be implemented in all healthcare settings, there are two important issues to be resolved—meaningful use criteria and standards development. Defined by the Centers for Medicaid and Medicare Services, *meaningful use* describes how health information technology will be implemented to expand the use of information exchange among healthcare professionals and usage benchmarks for physicians and for hospitals (Centers for Medicare & Medicaid Services, 2010, p. 1850). The Centers for Medicaid and Medicare Services (2010) has established three criteria for meaningful use. The first criterion is to electronically capture health information, track key clinical conditions, use the information for care coordination, report clinical quality measures, and report relevant public health information. The second criterion is to expand the use of electronic health information to disease management, clinical decision support, medication management, patient access, transitioning care, quality measurement, and services research. An important component of this second criteria addresses the use of information as public health surveillance data (Centers for Medicare & Medicaid Services, 2010). The third criterion extends the use of health information to quality management, identifying and managing high priority health conditions (such as the objectives in *Healthy People 2020*), patient self-management tools, and improving population health outcomes (Centers for Medicare & Medicaid Services, 2010).

As part of its definition of meaningful use of health information technology, the Health IT Policy Committee recently recommended that providers be required to participate in seven types of electronic health information exchanges starting in 2011. The seven types of data to be exchanged are prescriptions, lab results, clinical data summaries, biosurveillance data, immunization registries, public health, and quality measurement.

EHR systems must also meet minimum technical standards to receive certification for meaningful use. These include standard formats for clinical summaries and prescriptions; standard terms to describe clinical problems, laboratory tests, medications, and procedures; and standards for secure transmission of online data. The Healthcare Information Technology Standards Panel was established to standardize and integrate standards to meet clinical and administrative needs for health information sharing. There are eight EHR standards areas, which include the following: interoperability specification; capability; service collaboration; transaction package; transaction; component; technical note; and requirements design and standards selection (Healthcare Information Technology Standards Panel, 2010). The National Institute of Standards and Technology will assist the Office of the National Coordinator for Health Information Technology in establishing the certification programs as called for under the Health Information Technology for Economic and Clinical Health Act.

In order to evaluate the effectiveness of an information system, use cases are created. A use case helps establish usability of a system, the information necessary for decision making and other user requirements specific to a health need (e.g., treatment for acute episodes or chronic diseases as well as disease prevention and health promotion). For example, an EHR would support and enhance the use of rules-based decision making for each of the health providers' disciplines and be grounded in the practice of that discipline. A display for a pharmacist may look very different than the display for a nurse or other clinical support staff, even if they are all looking at medications. Information would be prioritized to reduce cognitive load and increase the provider's ability to locate and synthesize relevant information.

Although all of the standards in the EHR are important in the delivery and use of health information, of particular interest for pharmacists are IS07, CAP 117 and 118, TP 46, and T 40, 42, 68, 79, 85. IS07, Medication Management Interoperability Specification, defines the access standards for medication and allergy information for clinicians and providers. CAP 117 and 118, Communicate Ambulatory and Long Term Care Prescription and Communicate Hospital Prescription, address ambulatory, long-term care, and hospital prescriptions. Both address data elements to handle electronic prescribing. TP 46, Medication Formulary and Benefits Information Transaction Package, performs an eligibility check on a patient's pharmacy benefits and provides the medication formulary and benefit information. T 40, 42, 68, 79, and 85 describe transaction types—health plan eligibility verification; medication dispensing; health plan authorization for pharmacy provision of products and services; and administrative transactions between health plan and healthcare provider, such as a clinician or pharmacist.

APPLICATIONS IN HEALTH CARE AND PHARMACY

Clinical Decision Support

Clinical decision support systems (CDSS) are "active knowledge systems which use two or more items of patient data to generate case-specific advice" (Wyatt & Spiegelhalter, 1991, p. 3). A more updated concept of a CDSS is that of a decision tool: "an active knowledge resource that uses patient data to generate case-specific advice which support decision making about individual patients by health professionals, the patients themselves or others concerned about them" (Liu, Wyatt, & Altman, 2006, paragraph 26).

However, the key functions of a CDSS or decision tool are the same—administrative; managing clinical complexity and details; cost control; and decision support (Perreault & Metzger, 1999). Administrative functions address clinical coding and documentation, authorization of procedures, and referrals. Managing clinical complexity and details focuses on the treatment process and workflow as patients move through the healthcare system and between providers. Cost control monitors treatment and medication orders, with a focus on avoiding duplicate or unnecessary tests or treatment. Decision support enhances clinical diagnoses and treatment plan processes (Perreault & Metzger, 1999). All of these functions work within the framework of best practices, condition-specific guidelines, population-based disease management, disease prevention, and health promotion.

A CDSS provides a number of tools for clinicians. A process map, derived from treatment and workflow processes, determines health and safety concerns in patient care (Colligan, Anderson, Potts, & Berman, 2010). Patient-reported outcome measures, captured in a paper record or in an EHR, can improve treatment, enhance disease management programs, and address long-term or chronic care concerns (Coons et al., 2009; Mailloux, Cummings, & Mugdh, 2010; Subramanian et al., 2007).

A CDSS is critical in quantitative pharmacology. Since early diagnosis and drug treatment for Alzheimer's patients reduces the progression of the disease, the sooner drugs are developed, the better the outcomes for the patients and their families. Lehr and colleagues (2010) describe a quantitative pharmacology approach in the treatment of Alzheimer's disease. Used in concert with model-based drug development, they were able to select the most promising compound and facilitate a "fast, efficient, and rational drug development process" (Lehr, Staab, Trommeshauser, Schaefer, & Kloft, 2010, p. 117).

Bioinformatics

According to the National Institutes of Health, bioinformatics is the "research, development, or application of computational tools and approaches for expanding the use of biological, medical, behavioral or health data, including those to acquire, store, organize, archive, analyze, or visualize such data" (Bioinformatics Definition Committee, 2000, p. 1). This definition complements a second definition by the National Institutes of Health on computational biology, which is the "development and application of data-analytical and theoretical methods, mathematical modeling and computational simulation techniques to the study of biological, behavioral, and social systems" (Bioinformatics Definition Committee, 2000, p. 1).

Bioinformatics databases were first constructed a few years after the first protein sequences became available (Abola, Bernstein, Bryant, Koetzle, & Weng, 1987; Bairoch & Boeckmann, 1991; Dayhoff, 1972; Holley et al., 1965). The unprecedented volume of data arising from the Human Genome Project and other projects of this magnitude will have a profound effect on the ways in which data are used and experiments performed in drug discovery, product development, clinical diagnosis, and treatment (Ioannidis et al., 2006; Kaiser, 2006).

To be successful, all pharmaceutical companies must invest in new technologies that provide a more scalable framework for handling information beyond the traditional informatics domain. These technologies, such as high-throughput computation, combinatorial chemistry, microarrays, and interactive visualization tools, reduce execution time of the specific steps required for a complete analysis using distributed processes and parallelized software (D'Agostino, Aversano, & Chiusano, 2005; Desiere et al., 2006; Kruglyak, 2005; Teufel, Krupp, Weinmann, & Galle, 2006). Newer technologies allow more specificity in mapping, classification, visualization, and clustering of data, based upon user-defined subsets, with user-editable features for enormous data sets (Shah et al., 2005; Zhu et al., 2006).

Genomics and related disciplines, engineered cell-based and microfluidics systems, and nanotechnologies are used in pharmaceutical research and development (Bhogal & Balls, 2008). However, building genomics and related disciplines into research, clinical practice, and policy raises several challenges, including lack of linked data; the need for relevant research frameworks and methodologies; and the clinical complexities of genomic-based diagnostics and treatment (Phillips, Liang, & Van Bebber, 2008).

Pharmacy Benefit Managers

Prescription Drugs Claims Adjudication

The high costs of prescription drugs remain a major concern in the United States. Over the years, insurance coverage for prescription drugs for Americans has improved steadily. As prescription medication insurance coverage has become more prevalent, this has led to the development of pharmacy benefit managers (PBMs) who administer components of prescription drug programs, including claims processing, formulary management, drug utilization review, online claims adjudication, eligibility verification, copayment verification, and contracting with pharmaceutical manufacturers. Some PBMs also offer mail-order pharmacy services and are developing disease-state management and other chronic care illness programs. Some of the largest pharmacy benefit managers are Medco and Express Scripts. Retail pharmacies, particularly chains, have started their own PBMs, including Walgreens Health Care Plus and CVS/Caremark. Of particular interest for informatics is how PBMs manage databases that require integration of patient histories, clinical information, and drug price files.

Prescription Drug Costs

Given the rapidly increasing costs of prescription drugs, employers and insurers have pressured PBMs to increase their vigilance of prescription costs and have integrated strategies to reduce drug costs. Multiple factors have led to the growth in drug spending (Lundy, 2008). The implementation of Medicare Part D, especially with formulary and required pharmacy benefit management, was a major factor. Other factors include changes in the therapeutic mix of drugs, new uses for existing drugs, and increased use of specialty drugs. Finally, new growth in several therapeutic classes and lower rebates from drug manufactures also contributed to the increase in drug spending (Lundy, 2008). Use of generic drugs, formularies, multitiered copayment programs, prior authorization, step therapy, and other management strategies have been used to control costs. However, not all of these strategies have been successful in controlling costs.

Potential issues of abuse and pharmacist concern with PBMs includes rebates from drug companies and spread pricing (Garis & Clark, 2004), limiting pharmacy choice to mail order pharmacies, lack of disclosure, and favoritism towards some pharmaceutical companies. While PBMs serve a vital claim adjudication function, there are areas of concern that may lead to higher costs for prescription drugs.

One of these concerns is the lack of transparency in contract negotiations between the PBMs and pharmacies, employers, and drug manufacturers. When contracts are negotiated, there are often undisclosed contractual terms between groups that result in one price that the PBM charges to the employer and a lower price they reimburse to the community pharmacy. Unfortunately, this price difference is not consistently passed along to the consumer and results in an unfair profit for the PBM. To discourage these unfair practices, some states, such as North Dakota, have passed transparency laws that require health insurance companies and PBMs that operate in the state to pass these savings (profits) along to consumers (http://www.legis.nd.gov/cencode/t261c271.pdf).

Mail Order and Web-Based Pharmacy

As an alternative to community pharmacies (e.g., independent, chain, grocery store, mass merchant), a patient can also have his prescriptions filled at a mail order or web-based pharmacy. Examples of mail order pharmacies include CVS/Caremark, Express Scripts, Medco, AARP Mail Order Pharmacy, and Walgreens Pharmacy. Insurance companies and managed care organizations also have mail order outlets (e.g., AETNA Rx Home Delivery, Cigna, Group Health Mail Order Pharmacy, and Health Partners). The federal government is also involved with mail order pharmacies through the Veterans Affairs Mail Pharmacy and TRICARE Mail Order Pharmacy.

Web-based pharmacies were developed in the late 1990s. A patient could contact a web-based pharmacy to obtain drug prices and have questions answered by pharmacy staff. The National Community Pharmacists Association launched CornerDrugstore.com in 1999 as one Internet solution for independent community pharmacies (America's Pharmacist, 2000). Many of the features that were innovative at the time are still available on today's community pharmacy websites. Each of its member pharmacies has its own website featuring a health information center with health news, drug information, and medical resources. The prescription center page provides patients a way to communicate with a pharmacist and to check drug interactions online. A store locator shows the patient the nationwide network of community pharmacies and the pharmacy nearest the visitor's home. Patients can create accounts to place orders or to maintain family health records. The sites also send patients refill reminders as well as notifications concerning new products or health information.

As the expansion of web-based pharmacies has increased, so has the possibility for fraud and misuse of prescription drugs. In late 2009, the FDA issued a warning on fraudulent online pharmacies (Kelly, 2009). Possible scams include the selling of counterfeit drugs (such as phony Viagra [sildenafil] or a miracle drug for arthritis) or obtaining patients' credit card details. The idea is to profit off vulnerable patients seeking help or relief for their health condition. Patients should be advised to use only trusted pharmacy sources and seek advice on health matters from their pharmacist and other healthcare providers.

In response to public concern for the safety of pharmacy practices on the Internet, the National Association of Boards of Pharmacy developed the Verified Internet Pharmacy Practice Sites (VIPPS) accreditation program. Pharmacies with this accreditation have demonstrated National Association of Boards of Pharmacy compliance with Verified Internet Pharmacy Practice Sites criteria, including protection of patient privacy, appropriate processing of prescription orders, ongoing quality assurance, and provision of suitable patient counseling. The National Association of Boards of Pharmacy website (www.nabp.net) can be used to search for a Verified Internet Pharmacy Practice Sites Internet pharmacy.

Warehouse and Distribution Systems

For all systems, it is important that accurate and appropriate information is entered into the computerized system so that the correct medications are matched to the appropriate patients. If an adverse drug event occurs, the bar code point of care system provides an audit path for follow-up (Forni, Chu, & Fanikos, 2010; Grotting, Yang, Kelly, Brown, & Trohimovich, 2002). Bar code point-of-care systems are used by most drug wholesalers, including Cardinal Health and McKesson. Computer processing systems allow for reporting of product shipments, and planning tools allow for scheduling of manufacturing and distribution capacity to allow pharmaceutical manufacturing companies to meet demand (Kager & Mozeson, 2000). Since most prescriptions are processed by third-party payers, pharmacies use health information technology systems to streamline the prescription filling process and to make the distribution process more effective and efficient.

McKesson's and Cardinal's distribution system address operational challenges in delivering pharmaceutical products to hospital and community pharmacies. Their nationwide distribution centers concentrate on quality of service, returns processing time, and location accuracy. McKesson serves over 30,000 pharmacies and more than 450 pharmaceutical manufacturers, in addition to hospital, long-term care, and home-care facilities through its 29 distribution centers, a master redistribution center, a strategic redistribution center, and two repackaging facilities (McKesson, 2009). Cardinal Health serves more than 30,000 hospital, community, and retail chain pharmacies (Cardinal Health, 2009). Its CORxE program helps its customers manage procurement, costs, inventory management, and logistics. More than 25% of all branded prescriptions in the United States are distributed by Cardinal Health through its 23 distribution centers and its national logistics center (Cardinal Health, 2009).

ELECTRONIC PRESCRIBING

A significant trend in pharmacy practice is increased electronic delivery of prescription orders (e-prescribing). Members of the National Community Pharmacists Association (NCPA) and the National Association of Chain Drug Stores (NACDS) formed SureScript Systems, Inc. to permit electronic prescribing between physicians and pharmacies. At the same time, the three largest PBMs in the United States, AdvancePCS (Texas), Express Scripts (Missouri), and Merck-Medco Managed Care (New Jersey) also formed their own e-prescribing company called RxHub (America's Pharmacist, 2003).

RxHub also played a major role in the development of e-prescribing standards for the Medicare electronic prescribing pilots, which are part of the Medicare Modernization and Prescription Drug Improvement Act (Staff, 2006). Its proprietary standards for formulary and benefit messages and medication history information received American National Standards Institute accreditation in 2005, which increased data portability and interoperability across health information technology systems. RxHub provided patient-specific prescription information for more than 200 million Americans. RxHub uses Initiate software (produced by IBM) for its nationwide electronic information exchange that links prescribers, pharmacies, PBMs, and benefit plans together. When major PBMs feed their large membership rosters to RxHub, the database searches and links records for matches in a quarter of a second per record. From initial request until information is provided to a physician or pharmacist using the network to access prescription benefit information, response time is less than four seconds (Initiate Systems, 2010). In 2008, SureScripts and RxHub merged, connecting SureScripts e-prescribing providers and pharmacies to RxHub's nationwide patient, formulary, and medication history information system.

Several companies are using handheld devices or other variations to permit physician point-of-care electronic prescribing capabilities. These handheld devices may capture a managed care formulary, drug information, patient medication profile, or a list of pharmacies. Allscripts was the first company to enter the electronic prescribing market, and its TouchScript prescribing software is accessible by Internet on computers, handheld devices, and cell phones (Bazzoli, 2000). TouchScript enabled the provider to access patients' medication history, to write e-prescriptions, and to electronically transmit prescriptions via SureScripts or by fax. In addition, its software had a built-in decision support feature that instantly runs a drug utilization review at the point of care to monitor drug interactions, adverse reactions, dosage, duplicate therapy, and drug-to-health-state verification. Other features allowed the provider to access drug monographs and instructions on medications (Bazzoli, 2000). Since this is a growing marketplace, more companies will provide additional services and resources, especially as we approach the implementation of a national EHR.

E-prescribing also holds promise for reduction of medication errors. An Institute of Medicine (IOM) report estimated that 7,000 people die annually from prescription errors made in hospitals and outpatient settings, such as physician offices and pharmacies (Kohn, Corrigan, & Donaldson, 2000). This translates to 1 in 131 outpatient deaths and 1 in 854 inpatient deaths annually (Kohn et al., 2000). E-prescribing, therefore, has the potential to reduce medication errors and deaths, since they address contributing problems such as illegible physician handwriting, real-time updates on medication interactions, and access to more complete patient records with pharmacy notes.

National interest in e-prescribing increased in 2003 with passage of the Medicare Modernization Act Part D, which addresses prescription benefit plans and supports adoption of an electronic prescription program. In 2008, the Medicare Improvements for Patients and Providers Act was passed, offering physicians financial incentives for electronic prescribing. Under this law, Medicare physicians who e-prescribe will receive a payment bonus. Conversely, payments to Medicare physicians who do not e-prescribe will be reduced by a similar amount.

Computer Provider Order Entry

Computer provider order entry (CPOE) refers to a variety of computer-based systems of ordering medications, which automates the medication ordering process. CPOE accepts typed orders in a standard format and usually has an interface with clinical decision support systems (CDSSs) of varying levels (Kaushal, Shojania, & Bates, 2003). A basic CDSS may include suggestions for drug doses, routes, and frequencies. A moderate-level CDSS can perform checks at the time of drug ordering for allergies and drug interactions. A higher level CDSS incorporates prescriber guidelines for patient care, such as recommendations for anticoagulation regimens or anti-infective regimens (Kaushal et al., 2003).

Adverse drug events (ADEs) and medication errors result in approximately 7,000 deaths a year (Kohn et al., 2000). Further, in that same year, 1.5 million people are harmed by adverse drug events, with the cost of ADEs estimated at $3.5 billion per year (Dunham & Makoul, 2008). A precise estimate of ADE incidence rates is impossible to obtain due to the variety of definitions and criteria used (General Accounting Office, 2000). Based on the limited number of published ADE studies, ADEs range from 2 to 7 per 100 admissions (Kaushal & Bates, 2001). In a large academic medical center, Bates and colleagues at the Brigham and Women's Hospital in Boston conducted a series of studies examining the impact of ADEs. In one ADE study of adult inpatients, 56% occurred at the stage of ordering, 6% at transcribing, 4% at dispensing, and 34% at administration (Bates et al., 1995). These results were supported by two other inpatient studies that found approximately half of medication errors occur at the drug ordering stage (Kelly & Rucker, 2006; King, Paice, Rangrej, Forestell, & Swartz, 2003) and about that many errors occur at the administration stage (Kaushal et al., 2003).

CPOE can reduce error rates by 55% (Kelly & Rucker, 2006). Another CPOE study at the same hospital reported a decrease of 88% in serious medication errors (van der Sijs, Aarts, Vulto, & Berg, 2006). Dunham and Makoul (2008) estimated that CPOE in hospital settings may decrease the number of medication errors by 55–80% (Dunham & Makoul, 2008).

Despite growing evidence and public mandates, implementation of CPOE has been limited. The Leapfrog Group, which is a consortium of business roundtable companies, selected CPOE as one of its safety standards in hospitals that would improve patient safety in America (Cutler, Feldman, & Horwitz, 2005). Leapfrog's CPOE standard is based on research and consultation with experts in medication errors and has incorporated input from the hospital and physician communities (Birkmeyer & Dimick, 2004). Implementing CPOE systems at all nonrural U.S. hospitals would result in a reduction of approximately 570,000 serious medication errors annually (Kuperman et al., 2007).

AUTOMATED DISPENSING SYSTEMS

Hospital inpatient pharmacies in the early 1970s largely adopted the unit-dose distribution system. With unit-dose systems, doses of medications are individually wrapped and labeled; therefore, from the time of dispensing to the time of administration to the patient, each dose is identified. Two automated approaches are typically used. One approach is the use of the point of use unit-dose system at the nursing unit; a second approach is the use of a centralized pharmacy system that automates the unit-dose cart-fill process.

Utilizing an automated system in a central inpatient pharmacy brings efficiency to the unit-dose cart-filling process. Robotic technology is used to automate the unit-dose cart filling of patient medication cassettes that are checked by the use of bar code technology. This technology decreases the need for pharmacists to check individual doses in the cassette trays. However, it is critical that complete and accurate information is entered into the computerized system to ensure that cassettes are filled with appropriate medications.

Bar Code Electronic Medication Administration Record System

In 2003, the FDA required bar codes on all medications (when dispensing and on prescription bottles) to ensure that patients receive the right drugs in hospitals (Food and Drug Administration, 2003). Physicians enter prescriptions for hospitalized patients into a computer and the prescriptions are sent to the pharmacy. Pharmacists then fill and check the prescriptions against the patient's age, weight, diagnosis, other drugs, allergies, and drug interactions. At the patient's bedside, a nurse scans the bar code on the patient's bracelet and the bar code on the medication, and the computer matches the dose ordered by the physician and sounds an alarm if a mismatch occurs.

A bar code electronic medication administration record (eMAR) system is a combination of technologies that ensures that the correct dose of medication is administered at the correct time to the correct patient. An eMAR system is a workflow management system that automates the paper medication administration record workflow process, which starts with the medication order, follows through the medication dispensing system, and finally ends at the medication administration at the patient bedside. Barcode medication administration software is the software that tracks the medication, dosage, and time of delivery to the patient.

A bar code eMAR requires creating a drug inventory and electronic order entry, defining order entry roles when pharmacy staff are not available, and establishing system security parameters for permissions for certain types and levels of activities within the eMAR system/bar code medication administration. An eMAR system must meet compliance with regulatory standards and industry best practices to minimize medication errors.

Studies show substantial error reductions in order transcription and medication administration (Aspden, Wolcott, Bootman, & Cronenwett, 2007). In two studies, computerized physician order entry and the eMAR system increased patient safety, improved the delivery of care, and resulted in a reduction in length of stay due to ADEs (Mekhjian et al., 2002; Franklin, O'Grady, Donyai, Jacklin, & Barber, 2007). Researchers at Brigham and Women's Hospital found that the rate of dispensing errors decreased by 85% and the rate of potential ADEs decreased by 63% (Poon et al., 2006). Another study revealed that nearly 4% of drug orders had errors. Although the hospital pharmacist caught most of these errors, some of the drug fills left the pharmacy as undetected errors. Approximately 24% resulted in ADEs, of which over a quarter were serious and approximately 1% were life threatening (Cina et al., 2006). The most frequent ADEs were incorrect medications, strength, and dosage. Hence, even a low rate of drug dispensing errors may result in a large number of ADEs, with the potential to significantly harm patients.

Most recently, Poon and colleagues (2010) examined over 14,000 medication administrations and reviewed approximately 3,100 order transcriptions. They found the bar code eMAR system substantially reduced the rate of errors in order transcription, medication administration, and potential adverse drug events. Although the bar code eMAR system did not eliminate all errors, this clinical trial showed that the bar code eMAR system does improve medication safety (Poon et al., 2010). Further, cost-benefit studies performed on a bar code–assisted medication dispensing system within a hospital pharmacy found the primary benefit was a decrease in ADEs from dispensing errors. Further, the break-even point for the hospital's investment occurred within a little more than 2 years after becoming operational (Maviglia et al., 2007).

Organizational culture changes, as well as workflow changes, may be problematic in the adoption of new technologies. Pharmacists were interviewed about their experiences during implementation of a bar-coding dispensing system. The following implementation barriers emerged from a review of the interview data: process; technology; and staff resistance (Nanji et al., 2009). The three issues were interrelated. Concerns about training on the new technology addressed changing staff roles and workflow processes as well as staff unease about the effectiveness of the technology to increase, not impede, communication among staff (Nanji et al., 2009). A study on nurse knowledge and use of the Pyxis MedStation found a decrease in medication errors on administration by the nursing unit (Straight, 2008). This study also recommended changes in staff training to increase patient safety.

The issues identified in these studies are similar to the implementation of any major technology change in a pharmacy. It is important to involve all levels of pharmacy staff in the planning, training, and group communication involved in incorporating a bar-coding system in the hospital pharmacy. When considering automation in pharmacy, the decision to automate is largely dependent upon the need and payback on the equipment. If the workload in any of these areas (e.g., unit-dose filling machines, syringe-filling machines, or IV admixtures) is relatively low, then the need for the automated machine may be difficult to justify. However, in a busy urban hospital pharmacy, the need for an automated machine is easier to justify.

Outpatient and Community Pharmacy Distribution Systems

Establishment of the Medicare prospective payment system, combined with managed care cost-control strategies, has resulted in shifting many patients from inpatient hospitals to ambulatory care facilities. Outpatient pharmacy workload is composed of prescriptions that are generated from a variety of primary care providers and specialists. Prescription dispensing turnaround time is important, and automation of this process will reduce patient waiting time.

Community pharmacies are also increasingly implementing automated dispensing systems. Tablet-weighing scales (e.g., Baker scale, Torbal Rx scales) are typically the first step in automation, followed by a more sophisticated and expensive system, which often is a fully automated system. The ScriptPro 200, for example, fills, labels, and dispenses at a rate of 150 prescriptions per hour (Perry, 2008). In addition to its rates of fill, the ScriptPro has a relatively small footprint (15 square feet of floor space) and contains up to 200 dispensing cells (www.automedrx.com). The system includes barcode controls for all dispensing functions, on-screen images for verification, managerial tools to monitor and control the dispensing process, standardized labeling, and an automated, paperless patient prescription collection (Tarnowski, 2006).

Since patient safety remains the foremost area of concern for both vendors and pharmacists, no other piece of pharmacy technology comes under the type of scrutiny that is given to automated drug dispensing machines. Further, given the increased volume of prescriptions, a tight labor market, and a shortage of pharmacists, one of the solutions that independents and chain stores are using is the central processing facility. Prescriptions from a community pharmacy are electronically transferred to a central processing facility where dispensing is completed; the drugs are then delivered to the pharmacy.

FUTURE CHALLENGES

There are numerous challenges for pharmacists and pharmacy students as we look to the future of pharmacy and pharmacoinformatics. In this section, we have chosen to concentrate on pharmacoepidemiology and rural telepharmacy.

Pharmacoepidemiology

Epidemiology is the study of the factors that determine the frequency and distribution of disease in populations (MacMahon & Pugh, 1970). Pharmacoepidemiology is defined as the study of the use and the effects of drugs in large groups of people (Strom, 1994, p. 3). Since the focus of pharmacoepidemiology is on estimating the efficacy, effectiveness, and safety of pharmaceutical products, epidemiologic (i.e., population-based) studies cover areas from prescribing patterns of antipsychotic drugs in a community (Verdoux, Tournier, & Begaud, 2010) to trends in drug withdrawals (Issa et al., 2007) to working with specific populations, such as children and adolescents (Zito, 2007).

Combining pharmacoinformatics and pharmacoepidemiology addresses operational research in drug procurement, medication adherence support, ADE interaction monitoring, and management of patients with chronic diseases. Pharmacoinformatics uses methods and theories in pharmacoepidemiologic and pharmacoeconomic analyses to provide additional ways of understanding issues in population health and to enhance patient outcomes.

From a public health perspective, pharmacoepidemiology can minimize the impact of ADEs at a population health level by early detection. In addition, pharmacoepidemiology can highlight medications that have value when used in an atypical fashion, through better assessments of the risk/benefit balance and through postmarketing drug surveillance. For a larger discussion on epidemiology and pharmacoepidemiology, see Chapter 6.

Remote and Community Telepharmacy

One trend in pharmaceutical services that deserves attention is the role of the rural pharmacist, since many pharmacists are the first health providers seen by patients, especially in rural settings (Scott, 2010; Scott, Miller, & Letcher, 1999). Although telepharmacy shares the same basic definition as telehealth, it primarily refers to provision of pharmaceutical services. Telepharmacy allows for the safe delivery of medications and pharmaceutical services including drug utilization review and patient counseling. Telepharmacy may be the only way rural communities can retain or restore pharmacy services without the actual presence of a licensed pharmacist. Telepharmacy also provides new clinical training sites for pharmacy students utilizing the latest advances in technology.

The delivery of pharmaceutical products by telepharmacy typically involves the use of automated dispensing machines for the delivery of medications in a rural setting. For example, a pharmacy technician in North Dakota might work in a remote pharmacy location with a full inventory of medications and be supervised by the pharmacist using technology at another pharmacy setting. While this is the primary telepharmacy model, there are also several hybrid models in North Dakota. Accordingly, telepharmacy is still evolving and there are several different practice models. Described next are applications of telepharmacy in community settings and then in rural critical hospital settings.

Rural Community Telepharmacy Partnerships

Since the lack of pharmaceutical services access is a rural healthcare crisis that is an increasing problem throughout the United States, development of academic and community partnerships can benefit rural practitioners and communities. The North Dakota Telepharmacy Project, with financial assistance from the U.S. Health Resources and Services Administration Office for the Advancement of Telehealth, is addressing the issue of rural community pharmacy closings. In 2001, the state of North Dakota passed legislation that allowed pharmacists at a central hub pharmacy to supervise a technician dispensing prescriptions by telepharmacy at a remote site (where a pharmacist is not physically present) (Peterson & Anderson, 2004). This legislation, and the subsequent regulations established by the North Dakota Board of Pharmacy, also allows each patient to receive counseling from the pharmacist through videoconferencing before the patient leaves the remote site. North Dakota State University College of Pharmacy, the North Dakota Board of Pharmacy, the North Dakota Pharmacists Association, rural community pharmacists, and targeted rural communities joined together as part of the North Dakota Telepharmacy Project (Peterson & Anderson, 2004).

The project's goals are to provide pharmacists with financial assistance to implement telepharmacy in rural locations and to assess the impact of these services on the targeted communities. Not only have studies demonstrated a high level of patient satisfaction (Friesner & Scott, 2009), but a business case study found the project model was fiscally sound. One community pharmacy that added two remote telepharmacy sites was profitable in the 3rd year of operation (Khan, Snyder, Rathke, Scott, & Peterson, 2008).

Rural Critical Access Hospitals Telepharmacy

Smaller critical access hospitals continue to be challenged in finding sufficient pharmacist staffing to deliver quality pharmacy services. Innovative solutions are being explored, including use of technology to address the problem of access to pharmacy services in remote, rural areas (Casey, Elias, Knudson, & Gregg, 2008; Peterson, Rathke, Skwiera, & Anderson, 2007). One telepharmacy model in North Dakota appears to be an effective and affordable means of delivering pharmacy services to remote rural hospitals. Nine remote rural hospitals are critical access hospitals, with 25 beds or fewer. Six of the nine remote rural hospitals are Catholic Health Initiatives affiliates and three are non-Catholic Health Initiatives hospitals. All nine hospitals receive telepharmacy services from the Catholic Health Initiatives central order entry (Peterson, Scott, Rathke, Killingsworth, & Hill, 2010).

One group of project partners are establishing a reporting system for rural hospitals participating in the hospital telepharmacy program (Peterson et al., 2010). The investigators are working with the National Alliance of State Pharmacy Associations (NASPA), Pharmacy Quality Commitment (http://www.pqc.net), and two consultant pharmacists from Catholic Health Initiatives, to develop two software components to detect ADEs and medication error reporting and to track quality indicators. The rates and types of ADEs and medication errors that occur over 36 months will be assessed and compared with national data.

For the quality component (also Pharmacy Quality Commitment), a number of quality indicators (standard measures) for each critical access hospital site will be monitored at baseline and monthly over 36 months. General quality indicators include number of medication orders processed, number of potential harmful ADEs caught, and number of minor ADEs caught. Disease-specific indicators include percentage of patients on aspirin with acute myocardial infarction on arrival, and percentage of pneumonia patients with influenza vaccination. The quality measures were adapted from those used in the Medicare Rural Hospital Flexibility Program (Flex Program) for Critical Access Hospitals (Casey, Burlew, & Moscovice, 2008; Casey, Burlew, & Moscovice, 2009).

CONCLUSION

Technology is increasingly being used to assess and reduce the level of dispensing errors in both community and hospital settings in urban and rural areas. While the informatics evolution continues at a rapid pace, pharmacists should carefully choose applications that will substantially improve patient care.

QUESTIONS FOR FURTHER DISCUSSION

1. What information technology innovations are adaptable for use in institutional and community pharmacy practice?
2. Several information technology applications to pharmacy practice in drug distribution and telepharmacy have developed since 2000. What innovations do you envision in the coming decade?
3. Contrast strengths and limitations of information technology applications in rural and urban areas in your state.
4. What aspects of technology are nice to have, yet are currently unnecessary for improving patient care?
5. What are important educational technology components in pharmacy school curriculum from a student's perspective? From a professor's perspective?

KEY TOPICS AND TERMS

Pharmacoinformatics
Pharmacy practice
Quality assurance
Technology
Telehealth
Telepharmacy

REFERENCES

Abola, E. E., Bernstein, F. C., Bryant, S. H., Koetzle, T. F., & Weng, J. (1987). Protein data bank. In F. H. Allen, G. Bergeroff, & R. Sievers (Eds.), *Crystallographic databases: Information content, software systems, scientific applications* (pp. 101–132). Bonn, Germany: Data Commission of the International Union of Crystallography.

America's Pharmacist. (2000). Pharmacy automation: Central fill possible solution to independents workload? *America's Pharmacist, 122*(6), 18–22.

America's Pharmacist. (2003). Community pharmacy stands at the dawn of the e-prescribing era. *America's Pharmacist, April,* 16–21.

Angaran, D. M. (1999). Telemedicine and telepharmacy: Current status and future implications. *American Journal of Health-System Pharmacy, 56*(14), 405–426.

Armijo, D., McDonnell, C., & Werner, K. (2009). *Electronic health record usability: Evaluation and use case framework* (AHRQ Publication No. 09(10)-0091-1-EF). Rockville, MD: Agency for Healthcare Research and Quality. Retrieved from http://healthit.ahrq.gov/portal/server. pt/gateway/PTARGS_0_1248_907504_0_0_18/09(10)-0091-1-EF.pdf

Aspden, P., Wolcott, J., Bootman, J. L., & Cronenwett, L. R. (2007). *Preventing medication errors: Quality chasm series.* Washington, DC: The National Academies Press.

Bairoch, A., & Boeckmann, B. (1991). The SWISS-PROT protein sequence data bank. *Nucleic Acids Research, 19*(Suppl), 2247–2249.

Bates, D. W., Cullen, D. J., Laird, N., Petersen, L. A., Small, S. D., Servi, D., ... Edmondson, A. (1995). Incidence of adverse drug events and potential adverse drug events. Implications for prevention. ADE Prevention Study Group. *Journal of the American Medical Association, 274*(1), 29–34.

Bazzoli, F. (2000). Offering a new script for prescribing drugs: Allscripts is hoping that its hand-held system and Internet capabilities will lure physicians to change their habits. *Internet Health Care Magazine, 72.*

Bhogal, N., & Balls, M. (2008). Translation of new technologies: From basic research to drug discovery and development. *Current Drug Discovery Technologies, 5*(3), 250–262.

Bioinformatics Definition Committee. (2000). *NIH working definition of bioinformatics and computational biology.* Rockville, MD: National Institute of Health. Retrieved from http://www. bisti.nih.gov/docs/CompuBioDef.pdf

Birkmeyer, J. D., & Dimick, J. B. (2004). *Leapfrog safety standards: Potential benefits of universal adoption.* Washington, DC: The Leapfrog Group.

Businger, A., Buckel, L., Gandhi, T., Grant, R., Poon, E., Schnipper, J., ... Middleton, B. (2007). Patient review of selected electronic health record data improves visit experience. *AMIA Annual Symposium Proceedings, 11,* 887.

Cardinal Health. (2009). *Essential focus: 2009 annual report.* Dublin, OH: Cardinal Health. Retrieved from http://phx.corporate-ir.net/External.File?item=UGFyZW50SUQ9MTYxMzN8 Q2hpbGRJRD0tMXxUeXBlPTM=&t=1

Casey, M., Burlew, M., & Moscovice, I. (2008). *Critical access hospital year 3: Hospital compare participation and quality measure results* (Flex Monitoring Team briefing paper No. 20). Minneapolis, MN: Flex Monitoring Team, University of Minnesota, University of North Carolina at Chapel Hill, & University of Southern Maine. Retrieved from http://www.flexmonitoring. org/documents/BriefingPaper20_HospitalCompare3.pdf

Casey, M., Burlew, M., & Moscovice, I. (2009). *Critical access hospital year 4: Hospital compare participation and quality measure results* (Flex Monitoring Team briefing paper No. 22). Minneapolis, MN: Flex Monitoring Team, University of Minnesota, University of North Carolina at Chapel Hill, & University of Southern Maine. Retrieved from http://www.flexmonitoring. org/documents/BriefingPaper22_HospitalCompare4.pdf

Casey, M., Elias, W., Knudson, A., & Gregg, W. (2008). *Implementation of telepharmacy in rural hospitals: Potential for improving medication safety.* Minneapolis, MN: Upper Midwest Rural Health Research Center. Retrieved from http://www.uppermidwestrhrc.org/pdf/report_ telepharmacy.pdf

Centers for Medicare & Medicaid Services. (2010). *Federal Register, 75*(8), 1850–1870. Retrieved from http://edocket.access.gpo.gov/2010/pdf/E9-31217.pdf

Cina, J. L., Gandhi, T. K., Churchill, W., Fanikos, J., McCrea, M., Mitton, P., ... Poon, E. G. (2006). How many hospital pharmacy medication dispensing errors go undetected? *Joint Commission Journal on Quality and Patient Safety/Joint Commission Resources, 32*(2), 73–80.

Collen, M. F. (1994). The origins of informatics. *Journal of the American Medical Informatics Association: JAMIA, 1*(2), 91–107.

Colligan, L., Anderson, J. E., Potts, H. W., & Berman, J. (2010). Does the process map influence the outcome of quality improvement work? A comparison of a sequential flow diagram and a hierarchical task analysis diagram. *BMC Health Services Research, 10*, 7.

Coons, S. J., Gwaltney, C. J., Hays, R. D., Lundy, J. J., Sloan, J. A., Revicki, D. A., ... Basch, E. (2009). Recommendations on evidence needed to support measurement equivalence between electronic and paper-based patient-reported outcome (PRO) measures: ISPOR ePRO Good Research Practices Task Force report. *Value in Health: the Journal of the International Society for Pharmacoeconomics and Outcomes Research, 12*(4), 419–29.

Cutler, D. M., Feldman, N. E., & Horwitz, J. R. (2005). U.S. adoption of computerized physician order entry systems. *Health Affairs (Project Hope), 24*(6), 1654–1663.

D'Agostino, N., Aversano, M., & Chiusano, M. L. (2005). ParPEST: A pipeline for EST data analysis based on parallel computing. *BMC Bioinformatics, 6 Suppl 4*, S9.

Dasta, J. F., Greer, M. L., & Speedie, S. M. (1992). Computers in healthcare: Overview and bibliography. *Annals of Pharmacotherapy, 26*(1), 109–117.

Dayhoff, M. (1972). *Atlas of protein sequences and structure, Vol 5* (pp. 89–99). Silver Spring, MD: National Biomedical Research Foundation.

Desiere, F., Deutsch, E. W., King, N. L., Nesvizhskii, A. I., Mallick, P., Eng, J., ... Aebersold, R. (2006). The PeptideAtlas project. *Nucleic Acids Research, 34* (Database issue), D655–D658.

Dunham, D. P., & Makoul, G. (2008). Improving medication reconciliation in the 21st century. *Current Drug Safety, 3*(3), 227–229.

Flynn, E. A., Barker, K. N., & Carnahan, B. J. (2003). National observational study of prescription dispensing accuracy and safety in 50 pharmacies. *Journal of the American Pharmaceutical Association, 43*(2), 191–200.

Food and Drug Administration. (2003, March 13,). *Secretary Thompson announces steps to reduce medication errors.* [Press release]. Retrieved from http://archive.hhs.gov/news/press/2003pres/20030313.html

Forni, A., Chu, H. T., & Fanikos, J. (2010). Technology utilization to prevent medication errors. *Current Drug Safety, 5*(1), 13–18.

Franklin, B. D., O'Grady, K., Donyai, P., Jacklin, A., & Barber, N. (2007). The impact of a closed-loop electronic prescribing and administration system on prescribing errors, administration errors and staff time: A before-and-after study. *Quality & Safety in Health Care, 16*(4), 279–284.

Friesner, D., & Scott, D. M. (2009). Exploring the formation of patient satisfaction in rural community telepharmacies. *Journal of the American Pharmacists Association, 49*(4), 509–518.

Garis, R. I., & Clark, B. E. (2004). The spread: Pilot study of an undocumented source of pharmacy benefit revenue. *Journal of the American Pharmacists Association, 44*(1), 15–21.

General Accounting Office. (2000). *Adverse drug events: The magnitude of health risk is uncertain because of limited incidence data.* Washington, DC: The Office.

Goldman, L., Mushlin, A. I., & Lee, K. L. (1986). Using medical databases for clinical research. *Journal of General Internal Medicine, 1*(4 Suppl), S25–S30.

Grotting, J. B., Yang, M., Kelly, J., Brown, M. M., & Trohimovich, B. (2002). *The effect of barcode-enabled point-of-care technology on patient safety.* Huntingdon Valley, PA: Bridge Medical, Inc. Available at http://www.bridgemedical.com/pdf/whitepaper_barcode.pdf

Hanson, A., & Levin, B. L. (2004). Mental health informatics. In B. L. Levin, J. Petrila, J., & K. D. Hennessy (Eds.), *Mental health services: A public health perspective* (2nd ed., pp. 397–418). New York, NY: Oxford University Press.

Hanson, A., Levin, B. L., Heron, S. J., & Burke, M. (2003). Introduction: Technology, organizational change and virtual libraries. In A. Hanson & B. L. Levin (Eds.), *Building a virtual library* (pp. 1–19). Hershey, PA: IDEA Group Publishing.

Hasman, A. (1987). Medical applications of computers: An overview. *International Journal of Bio-Medical Computing, 20*(4), 239–251.

Healthcare Information Technology Standards Panel. (2010). *Program of work.* New York, NY: Healthcare Information Technology Standards Panel. Retrieved from http://www.hitsp.org

Hillestad, R., Bigelow, J., Bower, A., Girosi, F., Meili, R., Scoville, R., ... Taylor, R. (2005). Can electronic medical record systems transform health care? Potential health benefits, savings, and costs. *Health Affairs, 24*(5), 1103–1117. doi: 10.1377/hlthaff.24.5.1103.

HIMSS Pharmacy Informatics Task Force develops definition. (2007). *HIMSS Weekly E-News.* Retrieved from http://www.himss.org/content/files/ENews/2007/indi_20070103.htm

Holley, R. W., Apgar, J., Everett, G. A., Madison, J. T., Marquisee, M., Merrill, S. H., ... Zamir, A. (1965). Structure of a ribonucleic acid. *Science, 147*(3664), 1462–1465.

Initiate Systems. (2010). *Initiate and RxHub build nationwide electronic information exchange.* Retrieved from http://www.initiate.com/customers/success_stories/Documents/Initiate-Systems-and-RxHub-Build-Nationwide-Electronic-Information-Exchange.pdf

Ioannidis, J. P., Gwinn, M., Little, J., Higgins, J. P., Bernstein, J. L., Boffetta, P., ... Khoury, M. J. (2006). A road map for efficient and reliable human genome epidemiology. *Nature Genetics, 38*(1), 3–5.

Issa, A. M., Phillips, K. A., Van Bebber, S., Nidamarthy, H. G., Lasser, K. E., Haas, J. S., ... Bates, D. W. (2007). Drug withdrawals in the United States: A systematic review of the evidence and analysis of trends. *Current Drug Safety, 2*(3), 177–185.

Kager, P., & Mozeson, M. (2000). Supply chain: The forgotten factor. *Pharmaceutical Executive, 20*(6), 84–90.

Kaiser, J. (2006). Genomic databases NIH goes after whole genome in search of disease genes. *Science, 311*(5763), 933.

Kaushal, R., & Bates, D. (2001). The clinical pharmacist's role in preventing adverse drug events. In In K. Shojania (Ed.), *Making health care safer: A critical analysis of patient safety practices* (pp. 71–77). Rockville, MD: AHRQ.

Kaushal, R., Shojania, K. G., & Bates, D. W. (2003). Effects of computerized physician order entry and clinical decision support systems on medication safety: A systematic review. *Archives of Internal Medicine, 163*(12), 1409–1416.

Kelly, C. (2009). *FDA warns of unapproved and illegal H1N1 drug products purchased over the internet. FDA News & Events.* Retrieved from http://www.fda.gov/NewsEvents/Newsroom/PressAnnouncements/ucm186861.htm

Kelly, W. N., & Rucker, T. D. (2006). Compelling features of a safe medication-use system. *American Journal of Health-System Pharmacy: Official Journal of the American Society of Health-System Pharmacists, 63*(15), 1461–1468.

Khan, S., Snyder, H. W., Rathke, A. M., Scott, D. M., & Peterson, C. D. (2008). Is there a successful business case for telepharmacy? *Telemedicine Journal and E-Health: The Official Journal of the American Telemedicine Association, 14*(3), 235–244.

King, W. J., Paice, N., Rangrej, J., Forestell, G. J., & Swartz, R. (2003). The effect of computerized physician order entry on medication errors and adverse drug events in pediatric inpatients. *Pediatrics, 112*(3 Pt 1), 506–509.

Kohn, L. T., Corrigan, J. M., & Donaldson, M. S. (2000). *To err is human: Building a safer health system.* Washington, DC: National Academy Press.

Kruglyak, L. (2005). Power tools for human genetics. *Nature Genetics, 37*(12), 1299–1300.

Kuperman, G. J., Bobb, A., Payne, T. H., Avery, A. J., Gandhi, T. K., Burns, G., ... Bates, D. W. (2007). Medication-related clinical decision support in computerized provider order entry systems: A review. *Journal of the American Medical Informatics Association, 14*(1), 29–40.

Lehr, T., Staab, A., Trommeshauser, D., Schaefer, H. G., & Kloft, C. (2010). Quantitative pharmacology approach in Alzheimer's disease: Efficacy modeling of early clinical data to predict clinical outcome of tesofensine. *The AAPS Journal, 12*(2), 117–129. Retrieved from http://www.ncbi.nlm.nih.gov/pmc/articles/PMC2844519/?tool=pubmed

Levin, B. L., & Hanson, A. (in press). Mental health informatics. In N. A. Cummings & W. T. O'Donohue (Eds.), *The promise of integrated healthcare.* New York, NY: Routledge, Taylor & Francis Group.

Liu, J., Wyatt, J. C., & Altman, D. G. (2006). Decision tools in health care: Focus on the problem, not the solution. *BMC Medical Informatics and Decision Making, 20*(6), 4.

Lundy, J. (2008). *Prescription drug trends*. Menlo Park, CA: Kaiser Family Foundation. Retrieved from http://www.kff.org/rxdrugs/upload/3057_07.pdf

MacMahon, B., & Pugh, T. F. (1970). *Epidemiology; principles and methods*. Boston, MA: Little, Brown.

Mailloux, A. T., Cummings, S. W., & Mugdh, M. (2010). A decision support tool for identifying abuse of controlled substances by ForwardHealth Medicaid members. *Journal of Hospital Marketing & Public Relations, 20*(1), 34–55.

Managed Care Business Week Staff. (2006, February 21). Medicare; RxHub participates in Medicare electronic prescribing pilots. *Managed Care Business Week*, p. 94.

Maviglia, S. M., Yoo, J. Y., Franz, C., Featherstone, E., Churchill, W., Bates, D. W., . . . Poon, E. G. (2007). Cost-benefit analysis of a hospital pharmacy bar code solution. *Archives of Internal Medicine, 167*(8), 788–794.

McDonald, C. J., & Tierney, W. M. (1986). Research uses of computer-stored practice records in general medicine. *Journal of General Internal Medicine, 1*(4 Suppl), S19–S24.

McKesson. (2009). *Annual report fiscal year ended March 31, 2009*. San Francisco, CA: McKesson. Retrieved from http://www.mckesson.com/en_us/McKesson.com/Investors/Financial%2BInformation/Annual%2BReports.html

Mekhjian, H. S., Kumar, R. R., Kuehn, L., Bentley, T. D., Teater, P., Thomas, A., . . . Ahmad, A. (2002). Immediate benefits realized following implementation of physician order entry at an academic medical center. *Journal of the American Medical Informatics Association, 9*(5), 529–539.

Nanji, K. C., Cina, J., Patel, N., Churchill, W., Gandhi, T. K., & Poon, E. G. (2009). Overcoming barriers to the implementation of a pharmacy bar code scanning system for medication dispensing: A case study. *Journal of the American Medical Informatics Association, 16*(5), 645–650.

National Telecommunications and Information Administration. (2004). *A nation online: Entering the broadband age*. Washington, DC: National Telecommunications and Information Administration. Retrieved from http://www.ntia.doc.gov/reports/anol/NationOnlineBroadband04.pdf

Orthner, H. F. (1987). Ten years of medical informatics. Introduction. *Computer Methods and Programs in Biomedicine, 25*(2), 73–85.

Perreault, L., & Metzger, J. (1999). A pragmatic framework for understanding clinical decision support. *Journal of Healthcare Information Management, 13*(2), 5–21.

Perry, L. (2008). Automated dispensing machines and robots are taking safety to new heights. *Drug Topics, 152*(8), 32–33.

Peterson, C. D., & Anderson, H. C. (2004). The North Dakota telepharmacy project: Restoring and retaining pharmacy services in rural communities. *Journal of Pharmacy Technology, 20* (Part 1), 28–39.

Peterson, C. D., Rathke, A., Skwiera, J., & Anderson, H. (2007). Hospital telepharmacy network: Delivering pharmacy services to rural hospitals. *Journal of Pharmacy Technology, 23*, 158–165.

Peterson, C. D., Scott, D. M., Rathke, A., Killingsworth, P., & Hill, G. (2010). Establishing a central order entry system for delivering telepharmacy services to remote rural hospitals. *Journal of Pharmacy Technology, 26*(4), 179–186.

Phillips, K. A., Liang, S. Y., & Van Bebber, S. (2008). Challenges to the translation of genomic information into clinical practice and health policy: Utilization, preferences and economic value. *Current Opinion in Molecular Therapeutics, 10*(3), 260–266.

Poon, E. G., Cina, J. L., Churchill, W., Patel, N., Featherstone, E., Rothschild, J. M., . . . Gandhi, T. K. (2006). Medication dispensing errors and potential adverse drug events before and after implementing bar code technology in the pharmacy. *Annals of Internal Medicine, 145*(6), 426–434.

Poon, E. G., Keohane, C. A., Yoon, C. S., Ditmore, M., Bane, A., Levtzion-Korach, O., . . . Gandhi, T. K. (2010). Effect of bar-code technology on the safety of medication administration. *The New England Journal of Medicine, 362*(18), 1698–1707.

Schnipper, J. L., Gandhi, T. K., Wald, J. S., Grant, R. W., Poon, E. G., Volk, L. A., . . . Middleton, B. (2008). Design and implementation of a web-based patient portal linked to an electronic health record designed to improve medication safety: The patient gateway medications module. *Informatics in Primary Care, 16*(2), 147–155.

Scott, D. M. (2010). Assessment of pharmacists' perception of patient care competence and need for training in rural and urban areas in North Dakota. *The Journal of Rural Health: Official Journal of the American Rural Health Association and the National Rural Health Care Association, 26*(1), 90–96.

Scott, D. M., Miller, L. G., & Letcher, A. L. (1999). Assessment of desirable pharmaceutical care practice skills by urban and rural Nebraska pharmacists. *American Journal of Pharmaceutical Education, 62*, 243–252.

Shah, N., Teplitsky, M. V., Minovitsky, S., Pennacchio, L. A., Hugenholtz, P., Hamann, B., . . . Dubchak, I. L. (2005). SNP-VISTA: An interactive SNP visualization tool. *BMC Bioinformatics, 6*, 292.

Staroselsky, M., Volk, L. A., Tsurikova, R., Pizziferri, L., Lippincott, M., Wald, J., Bates, D. W., . . . (2006). Improving electronic health record (EHR) accuracy and increasing compliance with health maintenance clinical guidelines through patient access and input. *International Journal of Medical Informatics, 75*(10–11), 693–700. doi:10.1016/j.ijmedinf.2005.10.004.

Straight, M. (2008). One strategy to reduce medication errors: The effect of an online continuing education module on nurses' use of the Lexi-Comp feature of the Pyxis MedStation 2000. *Computers, Informatics, Nursing, 26*(1), 23–30.

Strom, B. L. (1994). What is pharmacoepidemiology? In B. L. Strom (Ed.), *Pharmacoepidemiology* (2nd ed.). Chichester, England: John Wiley & Sons.

Subramanian, S., Hoover, S., Gilman, B., Field, T. S., Mutter, R., & Gurwitz, J. H. (2007). Computerized physician order entry with clinical decision support in long-term care facilities: Costs and benefits to stakeholders. *Journal of the American Geriatrics Society, 55*(9), 1451–1457.

Tarnowski, J. (2006). Smooth scripts. *Progressive Grocer, 85*(8), 56–58.

Teufel, A., Krupp, M., Weinmann, A., & Galle, P. R. (2006). Current bioinformatics tools in genomic biomedical research (Review). *International Journal of Molecular Medicine, 17*(6), 967–973.

U.S. Department of Health and Human Services. (2009). Health communication and health IT. In *Healthy People 2020.* Washington, DC: U.S. Department of Health and Human Services, Office of Disease Prevention & Health Promotion. Retrieved from http://www.healthypeople.gov/HP2020/Objectives/TopicArea.aspx?id=25&TopicArea=Health+Communication+and+Health+IT

van der Sijs, H., Aarts, J., Vulto, A., & Berg, M. (2006). Overriding of drug safety alerts in computerized physician order entry. *Journal of the American Medical Informatics Association, 13*(2), 138–147.

Verdoux, H., Tournier, M., & Begaud, B. (2010). Antipsychotic prescribing trends: A review of pharmaco-epidemiological studies. *Acta Psychiatrica Scandinavica, 121*(1), 4–10.

Wyatt, J., & Spiegelhalter, D. (1991). Field trials of medical decision-aids: Potential problems and solutions. *Proceedings of the Annual Symposium on Computer Applications in Medical Care, 1*, 3–7.

Zhu, T., Zhou, J., An, Y., Zhou, J., Li, H., Xu, G., . . . Ma, D. (2006). Construction and characterization of a rock-cluster-based EST analysis pipeline. *Computational Biology and Chemistry, 30*(1), 81–86.

Zito, J. M. (2007). Pharmacoepidemiology: Recent findings and challenges for child and adolescent psychopharmacology. *The Journal of Clinical Psychiatry, 68*(6), 966–967.

ECONOMIC ASPECTS OF HEALTHCARE DELIVERY

CHAPTER 13

Basic Economic Principles Affecting Health Care

Kenneth W. Schafermeyer

Case Scenario

Angie Plasty, a recent pharmacy graduate, is trying to determine the reasons for a 15% increase in prescription drug expenditures for a large managed care organization. Angie attributes some of the increased expenditures to manufacturers' price increases. While modest price increases for some commodities can result in large decreases in quantity demanded and, therefore, a decrease in total expenditures, Angie knows that this is not true for most healthcare services, including prescription drugs. Of even greater concern to Angie, however, is that the prescription drug program experienced a large increase in prescription utilization rates.

Before she can suggest any solutions, Angie must first know the factors that contributed to an increase in demand for prescription drugs. She also needs to know why the quantity of prescription drugs demanded continues to increase even while prices are increasing.

What recommendations could Angie make to try to control the increases in prescription drug expenditures? To answer these questions adequately, one needs to understand some of the basic economic principles affecting health care.

LEARNING OBJECTIVES

Upon completion of this chapter, the student shall be able to:

- Define the basic economic concepts of utility, demand, supply, equilibrium price, the price system, price discrimination, and elasticity of demand
- Explain the factors that cause a change in the demand or supply of a product or service
- Determine the impact that a change in demand or supply will have on the equilibrium price and equilibrium quantity of a product or service
- Explain how elasticity of demand influences the effect that a change in price will have on the total revenue earned by a firm

CHAPTER QUESTIONS

1. What factors cause changes in the supply or demand of a product or service?
2. How does a change in the supply or demand of a commodity affect its price and the quantity sold?
3. Under what circumstances will an increase in the price of a company's product result in either an increase or a decrease in the total revenue earned by the firm?
4. What factors cause consumers to be more sensitive to changes in price?

INTRODUCTION

Economics is involved in nearly all contemporary issues facing health care, such as the growing demand for healthcare services, prices for pharmaceuticals, competition among health care organizations, and remuneration for healthcare professionals. A lack of understanding of basic economic principles contributes to faulty decision making—people form opinions on issues based on emotions and feelings rather than on sound economic principles.

Using real-world examples, this chapter examines the fundamental economic principles that govern how the price system allocates resources in various industries, especially health care. It describes the concepts of utility, demand, supply, and equilibrium price; the causes of shortages and surpluses; the price system; price discrimination; and the effect of elasticity of demand on a firm's pricing decisions and total revenue. Knowledge of basic economic principles will help students and practitioners understand and respond to the economic forces shaping the healthcare market.

ECONOMIC CONCEPTS IN INDIVIDUAL CONSUMER DECISION MAKING

Consumers' wants may be considered limitless. Our society has never had enough resources to meet the demands of everyone. Because of this scarcity of resources, the science of economics has been developed. Economists have defined economics as "the study of how individuals and societies allocate their limited resources in attempts to satisfy their unlimited wants." The study of economics seeks to answer three important questions:

1. What shall we produce with society's limited resources?
2. How shall they (resources) be used in production?
3. Who shall receive the resulting goods and services?

Utility is the economic term for satisfaction obtained from purchasing a particular good or service. Utility is difficult to measure. For example, if a person eats a pizza, he or she would receive some satisfaction, but the amount of satisfaction could be described only in hypothetical terms. We may conclude with confidence, however, that the pizza provided some utility. The assumption is made in economics that people continually try to maximize their utility, usually within their budget constraints. Generally speaking, if the utility of a good is greater than its cost, people will buy more of that good. Conversely, when the cost exceeds a good's utility, they will not purchase it.

As stated previously, we have an economic system for only one reason: Resources are scarce relative to human wants. Our three basic resources are (1) land, including all natural resources; (2) labor; and (3) capital, including physical resources produced by labor. Economists refer to these resources as factors of production because they are used to produce those things that people desire, which are called commodities. Commodities may be divided into goods and services. Pharmacists provide both goods and services, although when a transaction involves both, they typically receive reimbursement only for the product. However, as pharmacists learn to market cognitive services separately from products, they are beginning to find ways to be reimbursed for these services.

Cost originates from constraints on our resources. With unlimited resources, every good would be free, like air. In reality, we live in a state of economic scarcity. Economic resources, therefore, are allocated according to the price system. Most goods and services are obtained only by those individuals who are willing and able to pay for them.

If no limits existed on resources, goods would have no value because we would use them until totally satisfied. Also, the marginal utility of any good would be zero because the value of any commodity is determined by its marginal utility. Value, then, originates from our personal desires.

Marginal is the economic term for "extra." Thus the value of a good is measured by its marginal utility. For example, the marginal utility of purchasing one pair of tennis shoes may be high if you currently do not have any tennis shoes, but the marginal utility of purchasing a second pair of tennis shoes at the same time would be lower.

When someone decides to make a purchase, he or she is, in a sense, deciding to forgo some other use of that money. This tradeoff is known as an opportunity cost, the value of the best forgone use of a given resource. For example, if a person has enough money for only one pair of shoes, the shoes he or she buys will not only cost the money he or she pays for them, but also the satisfaction (utility) that he or she gives up by not being able to spend that money on something else, such as a new pair of pants. An example that every college student understands is that the true economic cost of going to school full time is more than just the cost of tuition, books, and other direct expenditures; it also includes the loss of the income that could have been earned had the student decided to work rather than go to school. Although this lost income is not a direct expenditure, it certainly is an opportunity cost.

LAW OF DIMINISHING MARGINAL UTILITY

The *law of diminishing marginal utility* states that the value of any additional goods declines as one consumes more of it. In other words, the more we have of a good, the less we desire more of it. A person who likes pizza will receive some utility if he or she eats a piece of pizza for lunch. If the same person eats a second piece, it provides less utility than the first one. A third piece of pizza would provide still less utility. Eventually, the cost of a pizza would exceed its marginal utility, and the person would not purchase more (see **Table 13-1**).

Table 13-1 Illustration of the Law of Diminishing Marginal Utility

Quantity consumed	Total utility	Marginal utility
0	0	—
1	3	3
2	5	2
3	6	1
4	6	0

THE LAW OF DEMAND

The two most important economic concepts are demand and supply. The theories of supply and demand explain how millions of individual consumer and supplier decisions interact to determine market prices for available goods and services. Buyers exert a market force on prices by the amount of goods and services they demand, and suppliers exert a market force based on their ability and willingness to supply products for consumption.

A demand schedule shows the various amounts of a commodity consumers are willing and able to purchase at each specific price in a set of possible prices during some specified period of time. Note that demand is not synonymous with "need" or "want." As the term is used in economics, for a person to have a demand, he or she must have both the ability and willingness to pay. Merely wanting a given commodity that he or she cannot afford or is not willing to buy does not constitute a demand for that commodity.

Table 13-2 shows a hypothetical demand schedule for pizza. Two variables exist: (1) the price charged (independent variable) and (2) the quantity demanded at each given price (dependent variable). It is assumed, for the sake of simplicity, that all other variables are held constant. According to the table, as the price of pizza increases, less of it is purchased. This illustrates the *law of demand:* As price falls, the corresponding quantity demanded rises; alternatively, as price increases, the corresponding quantity demanded falls. In short, an inverse relationship exists between price and quantity demanded.

The Demand Curve

The law of demand can be illustrated by drawing a demand curve. **Figure 13-1** represents the demand curve for the demand schedule shown in Table 13-2. Readers who have not been exposed to economics before may notice two unusual things about Figure 13-1. First, the relationship between the two variables is often illustrated as a

Table 13-2 A Demand Schedule for Pizza

Price per pizza	Pizzas purchased per week
$ 6	80
$ 8	64
$10	48
$12	32
$14	16

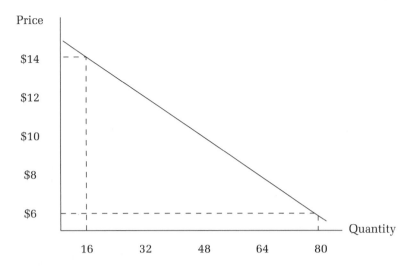

Figure 13-1 A Demand Curve for Pizza

straight line, even though we still call it a "curve." Second, the independent variable (the price charged for the commodity) is plotted on the *Y*-axis rather than the more conventional way of plotting it on the *X*-axis. Demand curves slope downward and to the right. This graphic illustration of the data in Table 13-2 shows the inverse relationship between the price of pizzas and the quantity demanded.

Changes in Demand

It is important to distinguish between the terms "change in quantity demanded" and "change in demand." A change in quantity demanded refers to movement along a given demand curve. In Figure 13-1, for example, a decrease in the price of a pizza from $10 to $8 results in an increase in the quantity demanded, from 48 to 64 pizzas. This increase is referred to as a change in the quantity demanded.

Some factors can result in an entire demand curve shifting; this movement is referred to as a change in demand. **Figure 13-2** shows that demand curve *D* has moved to the right toward demand curve D_1, representing what is meant by a change in demand. Since the demand curve has shifted to the right, the demand has increased. A movement from right to left would mean demand has decreased.

Changes in one or more of five factors can cause consumers to change their demand for a good:

- Prices of related goods
- Money income of the consumer
- Number of consumers in the market
- Attitudes, tastes, and preferences of the consumer
- Consumer expectations with respect to future prices and incomes

Prices of Related Goods

When the price of one good and the demand for another good are directly related, the pair are called substitute goods. An example is the relationship between beef and chicken. As the price of beef increases, the demand for chicken increases (assuming the

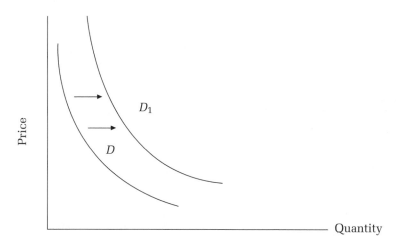

Figure 13-2 Illustration of a Change in Demand

chicken was reasonably priced), all else being equal. As another example, increases in coffee prices cause the demand for tea to increase. To some degree, many drugs or drug classes may be substitutes for each other (e.g., aspirin, acetaminophen, nonsteroidal anti-inflammatory drugs [NSAIDs], and now COX-2 inhibitors).

When the price of one good and the demand for another good are inversely related, the two products are referred to as complementary goods. In this case, an increase in the price of one good may cause a decrease in the demand for another good. An example would be the relationship between computer printers and printer cartridges. As the price of computer printers decreases, more people will purchase them, thus causing an increase in the demand for printer cartridges. In the prescription market, potassium supplements are often complements of potassium-depleting diuretics. For some patients taking NSAIDs, antacids, H_2 antagonists, or proton pump inhibitors may be complementary products.

Money Income of the Consumer

Commodities whose demand increases with an increase in consumer income are called superior or normal goods. Examples include sirloin steak, new sports cars, and summer homes. Because the demand for healthcare services increases as consumers' incomes rise, health care is a normal good. (Poor people may have as much need for health care, of course, but their demand—their ability and willingness to pay—is less than that of wealthier individuals. This helps to explain why a higher concentration of hospitals and physicians exists in high-income areas than in the inner city.)

If the demand for a good decreases as income increases, it is known as an inferior good. Examples include used cars and generic liquor or film. An example of an inferior good related to pharmacy could be an over-the-counter (OTC) antacid product that is purchased by a patient who cannot afford to see a physician or purchase a more expensive product such as Pepcid AC.

Number of Consumers in the Market

If a manufacturer is able to attract new customers to a market, demand naturally increases (the demand curve shifts to the right). For example, the U.S. Postal Service discovered that it could increase the number of stamp collectors (and increase its revenue) by creating stamps that are more appealing to children (e.g., cartoon characters rather than historical events or "old dead guys"). Likewise, breweries and cigarette companies have allegedly increased demand for their products by attracting newer, younger customers with advertising featuring cartoon characters.

Manufacturers also use a variety of strategies to increase the number of consumers who are willing to purchase a particular type of pharmaceutical product. That explains why aspirin products are promoted as treatments for minor arthritis, and arthritis products are promoted as treatments for headaches and assorted pains. By finding new indications for prescription drugs, for example, the number of customers (and consequently, demand) for these products will increase. One example is the use of calcium-channel blockers (originally used for treatment of angina) for prevention of migraine headaches. Another example is minoxidil, which was originally marketed as Loniten for treatment of hypertension, but reformulated as Rogaine for hair growth applications.

Attitudes, Tastes, and Preferences of the Consumer

Consumer attitudes, tastes, and preferences are affected greatly by advertising or by fashion changes. The manufacturer of NyQuil liquid cold medicine, for example, created a demand for its product by marketing it as a medication that works while a person is sleeping. This appeal, combined with the distinguishing characteristic that the medication was a liquid rather than a tablet or capsule, resulted in an increased demand for the product, and NyQuil's sales skyrocketed. Conversely, the environmental concerns associated with polystyrene containers for fast food decreased demand for products that use such materials.

Consumer Expectations

A good example of how consumer expectations of future prices and personal incomes affect demand was recently seen in the demand for oranges. Newspapers published articles reporting that Florida's orange crop had been badly damaged by freezing weather, and suggested this shortage of oranges would cause orange juice prices to rise in the United States. Consumers responded by immediately buying several cans of frozen orange juice concentrate to have on hand when orange juice prices were high. The grocers understood economics and had read the same newspaper articles, so they immediately raised the price of orange juice.

As another example, consider the housing market. Despite tremendous increases in the cost of building a home, the number of houses being built has tended to increase over the years. Two reasons underlie this increase: (1) Economists predicted that housing costs would continue to rise, so people are deciding to build now before costs go any higher; and (2) people anticipated a continual growth in their incomes, so they built homes based on what they expected to earn.

In summary, an increase in the demand for Product X can be caused by any of the following:

- An increase in the price of Product Y if it is a substitute for Product X
- A decrease in the price of Product Y if it is a complement to Product X
- A rise in one's income if Product X is a normal good
- A decrease in one's income if Product X is an inferior good
- An increase in the number of buyers for Product X in the market

- A favorable change in the consumer tastes for Product X
- Consumer expectation that the price of Product X will increase in the future

The case scenario at the beginning of this chapter described an increase in the demand for prescription drugs. This increase in demand could have been due to several factors: (1) an increase in enrollment in health plans, (2) an increase in the average age of enrollees, (3) an increase in the cost of alternative therapies such as surgery, or (4) an increase in physicians' and patients' tastes and preferences in response to the increase in drug advertising aimed directly at consumers. Examples of factors that can affect the demand for healthcare services are shown in **Table 13-3**.

Exercise 1: Change in Demand

A rightward shift in the demand curve for a commodity means that

a. Consumers' incomes may have fallen.
b. Supply conditions are more favorable.
c. Consumers are willing to buy more of the good at each price than previously.
d. The price of the commodity has decreased.

Answer

Answer "a" is incorrect because a drop in buyers' incomes would decrease their ability and willingness to pay and, therefore, decrease their demand, which would be represented by a leftward shift of the demand curve.

Answer "b" is incorrect because a change in supply does not cause a change in demand. Supply and demand are affected by different sets of factors.

Answer "c" is correct because a rightward shift in the demand curve represents an increase in demand. Because of this increase in demand, consumers are willing to buy more at each given price.

Answer "d" is incorrect because a change in price causes a change in the quantity demanded, not a change in demand. In other words, a given demand curve represents the various quantities that would be demanded by consumers for each of the prices that may be charged by the seller. A change in price simply moves you up and down the curve; it does not change the curve itself.

Exercise 2: Change in Demand

If the price of Product A decreases, what is the effect on Product B (a substitute)?

a. The quantity demanded for Product B increases.
b. The quantity demanded for Product B decreases.
c. The demand increases for Product B.
d. The demand decreases for Product B.
e. The supply increases.
f. The supply decreases.

Answer

Answers "a" and "b" are incorrect because a change in price of a product causes a change in the demand of a substitute product, not a change in quantity demanded. In other words, the demand curve itself is changed; you do not just move up and down the curve.

Answer "c" is incorrect because a decrease in the price of Product A means that more consumers will switch from B to A, thereby decreasing the amount of B that people buy at a given price.

Answer "d" is correct for the same reason.

Answers "e" and "f" are incorrect because a change in the price of Product A changes the demand but has no effect on the supply curves. A change in demand does not cause a change in supply. Supply and demand are affected by independent factors.

Table 13-3 Factors that Affect Demand for Healthcare Services

Cause for change in demand	Explanation	Examples
Prices of related goods 1) Substitutes 2) Complements	Assuming: A is a substitute for B and X is a complement of Y 1) ↑ price of product A = ↑ demand for B 2) ↑ price of product X = ↓ demand for Y	1) ↑ price of brand-name products = ↑ demand for generics 2) ↑ price of NSAIDs = ↓ demand for antacid
Consumers' incomes	↑ income = ↑ demand	↓ income = ↑ self treatment ↑ income = ↑ demand for physician visits and elective surgery
Number of consumers	↑ population = ↑ demand	New indications for old drugs = ↑ demand Aging of population = ↑ drug use
Attitudes, tastes, and preferences	↑ preferences = ↑ demand	↑ advertising of prescription drugs = ↑ drug use
Expectations	Expected shortage or price increase in future = ↑ demand	Fear of flu vaccine shortage = ↑ demand for flu vaccine

THE LAW OF SUPPLY

Supply, like demand, can be depicted as a schedule. A supply schedule shows the number of goods or services offered for sale at specific prices during some specified period of time. **Table 13-4** shows a hypothetical supply schedule for a producer of pizza. Again, only two variables are considered; all others are assumed to be held constant. The independent variable in this case is the price that consumers are willing to pay. Notice that there is a subtle difference between this variable and the independent variable for the demand schedule. For the demand schedule, the independent variable is the price charged; for the supply schedule, the independent variable is the price customers are willing to pay.

The dependent variable for the supply schedule is the quantity that sellers are willing to supply at each given price. As shown in Table 13-4, as the price that consumers are willing to pay increases, more pizzas are produced. This illustrates the *law of supply,* which states that as the price that people are willing to pay rises, the corresponding quantity supplied also increases. In short, a direct relationship exists between price and quantity supplied.

The Supply Curve

Just as the law of demand was illustrated by drawing a demand curve, so the law of supply can be illustrated with a supply curve. **Figure 13-3** illustrates the supply curve for the supply schedule given in Table 13-4. Supply curves slope upward to the right, in this case illustrating a direct relationship between the price that people are willing to pay for pizza and the quantity supplied to consumers.

Changes in Supply

The terms "change in quantity supplied" and "change in supply" are used similarly to those discussed under demand. Whereas changes in the quantity supplied are caused only by changes in prices people are willing to pay, changes in several factors can bring about a change in supply:

- Techniques of production, including technology
- Number of sellers in the market
- Resource costs (materials and wages)
- Prices for related goods
- Sellers' expectations

Table 13-4 A Supply Schedule for Pizza

Price per pizza	Pizzas produced per week
$ 6	24
$ 8	36
$10	48
$12	60
$14	72

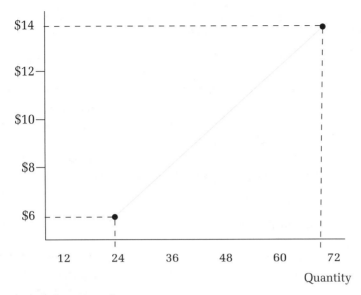

Figure 13-3 A Supply Curve for Pizza

Techniques of Production

When technology advances, the costs of production usually decrease. At a given price, suppliers will make more profits and, consequently, are willing to produce more. Technological advances could include equipment (e.g., more efficient tractors), supplies (e.g., genetically engineered seeds), methods of production (e.g., crop rotation), or management techniques (e.g., using the advice of agricultural experts).

Number of Sellers in the Market

More producers create more output. Therefore, as the number of sellers in a market increases, supply also increases. This outcome is represented by a rightward shift in the supply curve.

Resource Costs

As the costs of resources (e.g., materials, labor, rents, interest rates) increase, sellers cannot make as much profit at a given price. Companies therefore have less incentive to produce when input costs increase. However, a decrease in resource costs will cause supply to increase. Lower fertilizer prices, for example, can lead to an increase in agricultural production that will encourage farmers to produce more. Some employers have used this same principle to predict that increases in the minimum wage would hurt production levels.

Prices for Related Goods

Producers recognize two types of related goods: (1) substitute products and (2) joint products. Substitute products are those that are produced with the same, or similar, inputs. If the price of one product increases, it will affect the supply of another

Table 13-5 Factors that Affect Supply of Healthcare Services

Cause for change in supply	Explanation	Examples
Prices of related goods 1) Substitutes 2) Joint products	Assuming: A = substitute for B and W = joint product with Z 1) ↑ price of product A = ↓ supply of B 2) ↑ price of product W = ↑ supply for Z	1) ↑ reimbursement for generic substitutes = ↓ brand-name drugs supplied 2) ↑ reimbursement for teaching hospitals = ↑ amount of medical education
Resource costs	↑ production cost = ↓ supply	↑ wages = ↓ personnel hours
Production technology	↑ technology = ↓ production cost = ↑ supply	↑ department automation = ↓ cost to dispense a prescription and ↑ willingness to supply prescriptions
Number of sellers	↑ number of sellers = ↑ supply and ↓ price	↑ number of generic companies = ↑ number of generic products supplied and ↓ price for generic products

product. For example, if the price of wheat increases, farmers will start growing less corn and more wheat. Therefore, the price of wheat affects the supply of corn.

Goods that are almost always produced together are known as joint products. Leather and beef, for example, are joint products because they cannot be produced separately. An increase in the price of beef will induce a greater quantity of beef supplied; consequently, the supply of leather will increase even if the price of leather falls.

Seller Expectations

If sellers expect prices to increase in the near future, they may increase production now or withhold some product from the market. This happens in agriculture when farmers try to time their sales to obtain favorable prices. Examples of factors that affect the supply of healthcare services are shown in **Table 13-5**.

EQUILIBRIUM PRICE

The price system—the interaction of supply and demand—determines how economic resources are allocated. Because buyers in any market always want to demand more units of a good at a lower price and sellers always want to supply more units of that good at a higher price, a market equilibrium price can be achieved, which creates economic efficiency by exactly balancing these competing market forces. This market equilibrium price represents the point where the supply and demand curves intersect, as illustrated in **Figure 13-4**.

In this case, market equilibrium occurs when pizza is priced at $10. At that price, the quantity demanded equals the quantity supplied. At the equilibrium price of $10, both the seller and the buyer are satisfied with the price. At any price other than $10, economic forces will attempt to change the price. These economic forces can be illustrated with two cases.

Case 1: Price increases to $12. At a price of $12, pizza sellers produce 60 pizzas, whereas consumers want to buy only 32 pizzas. Thus a surplus (excess supply) of pizza exists. What happens? Consumers buy only 32 pizzas. Eventually, one pizza seller will lower the price to get rid of unsold pizza, which will increase the quantity demanded for the product. Other sellers also lower their prices until at $10 the demands of the consumers equal what the sellers are willing to produce at that price.

Case 2: Price decreases to $8. At a price of $8, pizza sellers produce 36 pizzas, whereas consumers want to buy 64. Thus a shortage (excess demand) for pizza exists. What happens? Consumers order a pizza, but the seller is sold out. The seller notices that each day every pizza produced is sold. Consumers might even be calling the seller to say they will pay extra if a pizza is saved for them. This increased demand and the opportunity to increase the price serve as incentives for the seller to produce more pizza. When the price reaches $10, both the seller and the buyer are satisfied. Everyone who wants to buy a pizza does, and the seller does not have any unsold pizza remaining.

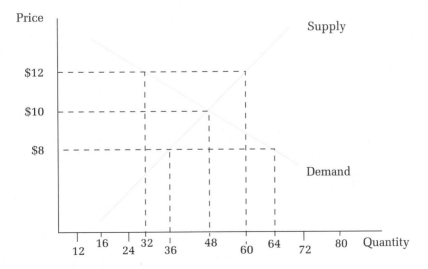

Figure 13-4 Supply and Demand Curve for Pizza

Exercise 3: Change in Equilibrium Due to an Increase in Supply

When supply increases in a competitive market:

a. Equilibrium price will fall.
b. Demand will fall.
c. Shortages will emerge.
d. Quantities sold will decrease.

Answer

Answer "a" is correct because the new supply curve will shift to the right and intersect with the demand curve at a new point that represents both a decrease in equilibrium price and an increase in equilibrium quantity (see **Figure 13-5**).

Answer "b" is incorrect because a change in supply does not cause a change in demand. Supply and demand are affected by independent factors.

Answer "c" is incorrect because an increase in supply will result in a temporary surplus, which will be corrected when prices drop to a new equilibrium point. At this new equilibrium point, the quantity demanded will equal the quantity supplied.

Answer "d" is incorrect for the same reason given for answer "a."

Note that the equilibrium would also change when there is a change in demand. The increased demand for prescription drugs discussed in the case scenario at the beginning of this chapter, for example, resulted in increases in both the price and the quantity of prescription drugs dispensed.

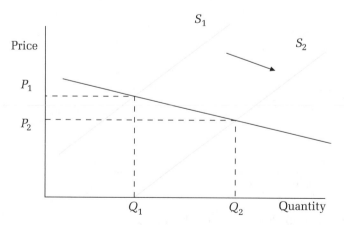

Figure 13-5 Change in Equilibrium for a Product with an Elastic Demand

ELASTICITY OF DEMAND

Elasticity is a widely used economic concept that measures the responsiveness of consumer demands to a change in price. As stated previously, the demand curve slopes downward because as the price of a commodity decreases, the quantity demanded increases. However, the degree (or angle) of this downward slope varies with different types of goods. Depending on the slope, a commodity is said to have an elastic demand, an inelastic demand, or a unitary demand.

The producers (or sellers) of any good typically can charge whatever price they desire. Naturally, they will try to sell the good at a price that maximizes their profits. If they think they can make more money by lowering the price, they will do so. Likewise, if they think they can make more money by raising the price, they will do so. The key factor in such an analysis is not the good's selling price, but rather the total revenue the producer receives. This total revenue equals the selling price multiplied by the quantity sold. Whether a change in the selling price will result in an increase or a decrease in total revenue depends on the elasticity of demand for the particular good.

Elastic Demand

Suppose a producer is faced with the demand schedule shown in **Table 13-6** for one of its goods. As the price of the good increases, the producer's total revenue decreases. This relationship characterizes a good with an elastic demand. Demand is elastic if an increase in price causes the quantity demanded to decrease enough to result in a decrease in total revenue. Conversely, a decrease in price causes the quantity to increase enough to result in an increase in total revenue. Thus, when a good has an elastic demand, the quantity demanded is sensitive to the price.

An example of a good with an elastic demand is a brand of gasoline. If a Shell Oil gas station proprietor lowered his or her price below the competitor's price, sales likely would increase so much that total revenue would increase. The opposite outcome will occur if prices are raised above other brands. That is why gasoline prices are often standardized within a community; the demand for any brand of gasoline is extremely sensitive to price. (Note that gasoline is narrowly and specifically defined here as a particular brand of gasoline at a particular station, and it is understood that this station's gasoline has interchangeable substitutes at many competing stations. When we look at prices for gasoline in general, rather than prices at particular stations, demand is more inelastic.)

Table 13-6 Demand Schedule for an Elastic Good

Price	Expected number to be sold	Total revenue
$2	56	$112
$3	36	$108
$4	26	$104
$5	20	$100

Inelastic Demand

Suppose a producer is faced with a demand schedule like the one shown in **Table 13-7** for one of its goods. As the price of the good increases, total revenue increases. This relationship characterizes a good with an inelastic demand. With inelastic demand, an increase in price causes only a slight decrease in the quantity demanded, resulting in an increase in total revenue. Conversely, a decrease in price causes the quantity demanded to increase, but the increase is so small that the result is a decrease in total revenue. Thus, when a good has an inelastic demand, the quantity demanded is relatively insensitive to price.

An example of a good with an inelastic demand is gasoline (when broadly defined as noted in the preceding section). An automobile will not operate without gasoline, so when the price of gasoline increases, people will buy a little less, but they will still buy enough to give the gas station proprietor an increase in total revenue. Thus gasoline has a relatively inelastic demand. Although the quantity of gasoline demanded by consumers does not tend to depend too much on price (inelastic demand), the quantity purchased at a particular station does depend on how prices at that station compare with the competitors' prices (elastic demand).

As described in the case scenario at the beginning of this chapter, studies show that the demand for healthcare services, including prescription drugs, is inelastic. People with true emergencies (such as a broken arm or a heart attack) will seek treatment without regard to the cost. Nevertheless, high prices may create an elastic demand for emergency treatment of routine problems or minor ailments. This explains the rationale behind patient cost-sharing mechanisms, which are designed to discourage unnecessary use of services while not inhibiting demand for truly necessary services.

A logical question to ask at this point is this: If total revenue increases every time the price of an inelastic good increases, what keeps the price from rising to infinity? Usually competition keeps prices in check or, in the case where not much competition exists (such as public utilities), government intervention may be needed to regulate prices. Although managed care organizations in the United States have controlled costs by facilitating competition among some pharmaceutical products through generic and therapeutic substitution, government agencies in Canada and Europe control costs by regulating pharmaceutical manufacturers' prices.

Unitary Demand

Suppose a producer is faced with a demand schedule like the one shown in **Table 13-8** for one of its goods. As the price of the good increases or decreases, the producer's

Table 13-7 Demand Schedule for an Inelastic Good

Price	Expected number to be sold	Total revenue
$2	45	$ 90
$3	31	$ 93
$4	24	$ 96
$5	20	$100

Table 13-8 Demand Schedule for a Unitary Good

Price	Expected number to be sold	Total revenue
$2	50	$100
$2.50	40	$100
$4	25	$100
$5	20	$100

total revenue remains the same. This relationship characterizes a good with a unitary demand. Unitary demand is not common in the actual marketplace; instead, products tend to have either an elastic or inelastic demand.

Exercise 4: Elasticity of Demand

If demand is price elastic, an increase in supply will cause a relatively

a. Large decrease in quantity demanded.
b. Large increase in quantity demanded.
c. Small decrease in quantity demanded.
d. Small increase in quantity demanded.

Answer

Answers "a" and "c" are incorrect because an increase in supply will result in an increase in quantity demanded.

Answer "b" is correct because an elastic demand curve, by definition, means that consumers are sensitive to changes in price and any change in price will result in a proportionately greater change in quantity demanded. Therefore, an increase in the supply of a product with an elastic demand curve will result in a large increase in quantity demanded (see Figure 13-5).

Answer "d" is incorrect for the reason explained for answer "c."

Determinants of Elasticity of Demand

What makes the demand for a particular good or service elastic or inelastic in the short run? To differentiate between the terms "short run" and "long run," consider that a consumer has two resources when shopping: money and time. In other words, a person can purchase a demanded good with money now or wait until a later time when more money is available, when the price of the demanded commodity decreases, or when the consumer's demand may change to favor another commodity. Elasticity of demand for a given commodity changes when one talks about the short run versus the long run because a longer time span allows people to pursue more alternatives (substitutes).

For example, when the price of gasoline increases, automobile owners continue to buy gas in the short run because they need their cars for business or other important purposes. In the long run, alternative means of transportation such as buses, commuter trains, or carpools may be sought as companies continue to work on developing a car that operates on some form of energy other than gasoline. The desired result, of course, is eventually to decrease one's need for—and thus one's demand for—gasoline.

Three determinants of elasticity exist: (1) the availability of substitutes for the commodity, (2) the price of a commodity relative to consumers' incomes, and (3) the number of alternative uses for the commodity.

The Availability of Substitutes

When the price of one good and the demand for another good are directly related, the two products are substitute goods, like beef and chicken. The greater the number of substitute goods available for a particular commodity, the more elastic the demand for that commodity.

The more narrowly and specifically a commodity can be described, the more substitutes it will have. Consequently, the demand for such a commodity will be more elastic. For example, when a person is suffering from athlete's foot, he or she probably has a strong desire for an antifungal. Because no other kinds of OTC drugs will help relieve athlete's foot, the demand for antifungals is inelastic. Because numerous antifungal products are available, however, the demand for any particular brand of antifungal is elastic.

Sellers have found that some customers have more substitutes available than other customers. For example, business travelers are not as flexible in their plans as individuals planning vacations. Therefore, vacation travelers have a more elastic demand for air travel and can obtain less expensive airfares.

Segregating customers and charging prices according to customers' elasticity of demand is known as differential pricing (also known as price discrimination). Because hospitals and managed care organizations use formularies (and consequently have more substitutes available), they can obtain larger discounts or rebates from pharmaceutical manufacturers. Another example of differential pricing is the higher long-distance telephone rates charged during working hours as opposed to weekends and evenings. For price discrimination to work, it must be difficult for buyers to resell to one another. Price differences reflecting actual production cost differences, such as volume discounts, do not represent true price discrimination.

The Price Relative to Consumers' Incomes

The demand for commodities that account for a large portion of a person's income will be more elastic than the demand for purchases that are relatively inexpensive. For example, most managers are more price conscious when they are shopping for a computer than when shopping for envelopes or paper clips. Because envelopes and paper clips account for a negligible fraction of a company's budget, changes in price likely will have little effect on the quantity demanded. Thus the demand for these products is relatively inelastic.

The Number of Alternative Uses

The fewer uses that a commodity has, the more likely that its demand will be inelastic. People tend to become more selective about a commodity's use as its price increases.

An example of this occurred several years ago when the price of sugar rose greatly. When the price of sugar increased, people found that they still needed it for some types of foods, but they could reduce the amount they used. Thus consumers were able to change the demand for sugar from elastic to inelastic.

Exercise 5

Elasticity of demand will increase as the

a. Number of available substitutes decreases.
b. Price of the good relative to income decreases.
c. Time horizon increases.

Answer

Answer "a" is incorrect because the greater the number of substitute goods available for a particular commodity, the more elastic the demand for that commodity.

Answer "b" is incorrect because those commodities that account for a large portion of a person's income will have a more elastic demand than those purchases that are relatively inexpensive.

Answer "c" is correct because the longer time frame allows consumers to consider more alternatives and find more substitutes for a product in the long run.

Elasticity of Demand for Prescription Drugs

The three determinants of elasticity can be applied to prescription drugs. First, when a physician writes a prescription order for a specific drug for an ambulatory patient, usually no substitute goods are involved. The patient has the choice of having the prescription filled. If he or she decides to have the prescription filled, the patient often has no choice as to which drug will be dispensed by the pharmacist. (Product selection legislation gives the patient some choices in certain cases, but this description is accurate for drugs protected by patents. This situation is altered to some degree by the adoption of formularies and the practice of therapeutic selection.)

Second, prescription drugs take up a relatively small portion of most people's income.

Third, prescription drugs have few alternative uses. An antibiotic is prescribed for a specific type of infection, but it has no value in treating most other types of physical or mental ailments.

In summary, prescription drugs have few—if any—substitutes; they take a relatively small portion of one's income (particularly if the patient pays only a co-payment); and they have few uses other than the purpose for which they are prescribed. Thus a prescription drug has an inelastic demand. As described in the case scenario at the beginning of this chapter, the quantity demanded is relatively insensitive to changes in price.

Three additional factors unique to the pharmaceutical industry contribute to the inelasticity of demand for prescription drugs. First, the decision maker (the physician) is not the payer (the patient and/or prescription benefit plan); consequently, price is not usually the primary consideration when prescribing a particular drug. Second, the industry promotes product differentiation between drug products, reducing the importance of price in selecting a particular drug to prescribe. Third, having a third-party plan pay all or part of the cost of a person's prescription drugs significantly increases the inelasticity of demand for those drugs.

CONCLUSION

This chapter introduced some basic economic concepts, such as supply, demand, equilibrium price, the price system, price discrimination, and elasticity of demand. Chapter 13 discusses how economic forces in the healthcare marketplace compare with those of other industries and how health care can be influenced by competition.

Healthcare professionals should understand and use economic principles to work effectively with healthcare organizations and health benefit programs. By understanding these basic principles, one can begin to appreciate the factors affecting the economics of the healthcare industry.

QUESTIONS FOR FURTHER DISCUSSION

1. For most products, when substitutes appear in the market, the innovator must usually decrease its price to be competitive. Why don't the prices of brand-name prescription drugs tend to decline when generic substitutes become available?
2. What steps can be taken to control the rapid increase in the quantity demanded for prescription drugs?
3. A demand for a product or service exists only if the potential customers have the ability and willingness to pay for it. What would pharmacists have to do to be reimbursed for nondispensing services?
4. If many healthcare products and services have inelastic demand, how might companies compete with one another to increase their market shares?
5. Give examples of healthcare products or services that have an elastic demand. Do competitors compete on price?

KEY TOPICS AND TERMS

Changes in demand
Changes in quantity demanded
Changes in quantity supplied
Changes in supply
Complements
Demand

Demand curve
Demand schedule
Economic resources
Economics
Elastic demand
Elasticity
Equilibrium point
Equilibrium price
Equilibrium quantity
Law of demand
Law of diminishing marginal utility
Law of supply
Marginal utility
Shortage
Substitutes
Supply
Supply curve
Supply schedule
Surplus
Utility

Unique Aspects of Health Economics

Kenneth W. Schafermeyer

Case Scenario

There has been a great deal of controversy and debate over how to control rapidly rising healthcare costs and expand healthcare services to the millions of Americans who do not currently have health insurance. Some observers believe that these problems can be resolved by encouraging more competition into the healthcare system. Others believe that health care is such a unique industry that more competition will not necessarily create efficiencies that will reduce costs and improve access. Some members of the latter group also question the morality of using the price system to allocate healthcare resources.

Using your knowledge of economics and the healthcare system, what do you think are some of the arguments that would be used by both sides in this debate?

LEARNING OBJECTIVES

Upon completion of this chapter, the student shall be able to:

- Give examples of how basic economic principles apply to contemporary healthcare issues
- Compare and contrast the various types of market structures: perfect competition, monopolistic competition, oligopoly, and monopoly
- Explain how the economics of health care is different from the economics of other industries
- Describe how economic performance of the healthcare system could be improved
- Explain the factors that can cause healthcare costs to increase
- Describe how various forms of reimbursement can create different incentives to control utilization of health care

CHAPTER QUESTIONS

1. To what extent is health care a competitive industry? Does competition always result in decreases in price?
2. How is the economics of health care different from the economics of other industries?
3. What factors can cause healthcare costs to increase?
4. How do various forms of reimbursement create different incentives to control utilization of health care?

INTRODUCTION

This chapter is designed to help students and practitioners understand and respond to the economic forces shaping the healthcare market. Chapter 12 presented the basic economic concepts of supply, demand, equilibrium price, the price system, price discrimination, and elasticity of demand. This chapter discusses some of the factors that influence supply and demand for healthcare services and describes how economic forces in the healthcare marketplace compare with those of other industries.

In recent years, there has been renewed interest in reforming the healthcare system through the use of market forces rather than government regulations. One example of such a "market-based policy" is the provision of subsidies to low-income patients for the purchase of health insurance rather than direct payments for healthcare services. Another example is the increased use of higher cost-sharing levels (Rice, 1997). The critical question, and the one discussed in this chapter, is this: Is the healthcare market a competitive market?

PERFECTLY COMPETITIVE INDUSTRIES

To describe the unique aspects of the healthcare market, it is helpful to compare it with the four basic types of market structures: (1) perfect competition, (2) monopolistic competition, (3) monopoly, and (4) oligopoly. First, this chapter describes a market structure known as perfect competition. Next, it contrasts the perfectly competitive market with the other types of market structures and discusses how the healthcare industry may or may not resemble one or more of these basic structures.

Perfect competition has the following characteristics:

- Many buyers and sellers
- Freedom of entry and exit
- Standardized products
- Full and free information
- No collusion

Many Buyers and Many Sellers

In perfect competition, the number of buyers and sellers has to be large enough so that the entry (or exit) of one firm or one customer into (or out of) the marketplace does not affect market prices. Companies in a perfectly competitive industry do not set prices;

instead, prices are set by the market. These firms are referred to as "price takers, not price makers." The demand curve for a company's product is horizontal and referred to as perfectly elastic. In other words, if a single company increased its price, customers would not demand the product from that company—they would just switch to another company.

Freedom of Entry and Exit

Most industries have barriers to entry or exit. Entry barriers may consist of patents, licenses, zoning, environmental regulations, or large investments in technology, training, inventories, or fixed assets such as buildings, specialized equipment, or research and development. Exit barriers exist when a firm's fixed assets cannot be transferred to another use, thereby preventing a company from easily switching to a more profitable industry. Low barriers to entry into and exit from an industry stimulate competition; high barriers inhibit it. In perfect competition, there are no barriers to entry or exit.

Standardized Products

By "standardized products," we mean all products are similar and interchangeable and, therefore, many substitutes exist. Clothing, building materials, gasoline, tires, and many other products have standard sizes or grades, so consumers can easily identify substitutes. In perfect competition, products are perfectly substitutable for each other.

Full and Free Information

In perfect competition, customers have complete information on the prices of goods and services and can compare the prices offered by competing sellers. Equally important, consumers can identify and compare the quality of these goods and services.

No Collusion

In perfect competition, companies in a given industry compete with each other rather than colluding or getting together to set prices. Collusion is more likely to be successful when there are few sellers, because the competitors know each other well and can easily retaliate against each other if the agreement is broken. Because of its anti-competitive nature, collusion is illegal in the United States. Collusion does occur in international trade, where it is referred to as a cartel. The most famous cartel is the Organization of Petroleum Exporting Countries (OPEC).

Although no industries fit the perfectly competitive model exactly, agriculture is usually cited as the industry that most closely matches this description. Although farmers can transfer their resources to producing different crops, they cannot usually do so in the short run. Also, products are fairly standardized, although some differentiation exists by grade and by production method (e.g., organically grown or genetically engineered). Most industries, however, can be categorized into one of the other market structures.

OTHER MARKET STRUCTURES

Monopolistic Competition

The market structure closest to perfect competition is known as monopolistic competition. Despite its somewhat confusing name, monopolistic competition is similar to perfect competition except that it does not have standardized and interchangeable products. In most cases, firms in this industry rely heavily on product differentiation. They minimize price competition by differentiating their products from those of their competitors by promoting perceived or real advantages in style, image, quality, or other attributes. The automobile industry is an example of monopolistic competition.

Monopoly

At the opposite extreme is a market structure known as monopoly, which features only one seller of a product that has no close substitutes. To maximize income, monopolists do not have to produce as much output as possible; they can accomplish this same purpose by producing less and charging higher prices. Some monopolies are formed by controlling the supply source. Barriers that prevent other firms from entering a market, such as legal restrictions (e.g., licenses, government approval, or patents), can also create monopolies. By granting patents, the government allows temporary monopolies to encourage research and innovation. According to Folland, Goodman, and Stano (1997), pharmaceutical firms that control patents for certain drugs that lack close substitutes may be considered monopolists during the life of the patent. With managed care formularies, however, competition can be created between some patented drugs and other therapeutic alternatives.

Other monopolies exist because the required infrastructure for the industry is so expensive that the presence of competing firms would increase—rather than decrease—prices. The prime example of these natural monopolies is utilities. To ensure adequate output at reasonable prices, natural monopolies are usually regulated by government agencies such as public service commissions.

Although a monopoly consists of only one seller, situations exist in which there is only one buyer. In this situation, which is known as a monopsony, the buyer sets the price. The federal government is often a monopsony for military hardware and for health care services for Medicare and Medicaid patients. Unlike private businesses, however, the government is sometimes unable to fully exploit its market power to set prices because it is subject to political pressure and due process.

Oligopoly

Between perfect competition and monopoly is a market structure known as oligopoly, which consists of a few sellers and many buyers. Firms in oligopolies are often interdependent, and a dominant firm can exert influence through price leadership. Although this situation falls short of meeting the definition for collusion, the pricing practices of the oligopolists tend to coincide, with one firm usually taking a leadership role. Oligopolists know that the firms in the industry will not benefit if all of them decrease their prices. However, a single firm that increases its price may lose business if the other firms do not follow suit. This factor usually restricts the ability of smaller companies to change prices unilaterally. If a dominant firm increases prices, however, the other competitors usually follow.

Cereal manufacturers constitute a well-known oligopoly: Four major companies have at least 80% of the market share for cereal. In medium-sized urban areas, hospitals may represent an oligopoly. Certain drug classes with market share concentrated among a few manufacturers may also be oligopolies.

Although an oligopoly consists of few sellers and many buyers, a market structure in which there are many sellers but only a few buyers is known as an oligopsony. To the extent that three large national pharmacy benefit managers (to be discussed in Chapter 17) pay for the large majority of prescriptions, they are considered by some to be an example of an oligopsony. As one might expect, oligopsonists are interdependent to the extent that they tend to offer similar products or services, copy each other's ideas, and take into account competitors' pricing structures when setting their own.

THE HEALTHCARE MARKET

Having just described the characteristics of the various market structures, we now consider whether the healthcare market fits these characteristics. As pointed out in the case scenario at the beginning of this chapter, this remains a highly debated issue in economic circles. In a survey of health economists, 50% thought the competitive model could apply to the healthcare industry, whereas 50% did not (Feldman & Morrisey, 1990). Those who did not believe that health care qualifies as a competitive market cited the following factors:

- Numbers of buyers and sellers
- Entry to and exit from the market
- Variation in products, services, and quality
- Full and free information
- Inelastic demand
- Universal demand
- Unpredictability of illness
- Health care as a "right"
- Supplier-induced demand
- Third-party insurance and patient-induced demand

Numbers of Buyers and Sellers

A maldistribution in the supply of healthcare services exists by geographic and specialty area. Although some healthcare markets are served by large numbers of sellers (e.g., retail pharmacies), some communities have a shortage of healthcare providers or healthcare facilities. In addition, although the United States as a whole has a sufficient supply of physicians, a shortage of primary care physicians (and an oversupply of specialists) exists. In some cases, the shortage exists because the market size is just too small to support enough hospitals or providers in each specialty to create a competitive market (e.g., transplant services).

Further, consolidation among buyers and sellers is occurring. The number of sole practitioners and small group practices is shrinking, while large medical groups are growing larger. Likewise, health maintenance organizations, pharmacy benefit managers, pharmaceutical manufacturers, and drug wholesalers are merging into fewer, but larger organizations. Employer groups have also pooled their purchasing power in many cities by forming employer health coalitions to negotiate better rates for healthcare services. Retail pharmacies have also participated in this trend through consolidation of chain pharmacies and by independent pharmacies forming volume purchasing alliances and cooperatives.

By consolidating, buyers and sellers find they can lower costs and have more market power to negotiate favorable prices. The concern is that too much consolidation could reduce competition. In some cases, the Federal Trade Commission has intervened to restrict or prevent acquisitions and mergers that it believed would unduly inhibit competition.

Entry to and Exit from the Market

High barriers to entry exist for suppliers of health care, whether they are individual providers or institutions. To pursue a career as a healthcare provider, one must apply to a limited number of schools and seek out one of a limited number of positions. Becoming a healthcare professional can require a great deal of education and compulsory licensure. These entry barriers effectively limit the number of new healthcare professionals who can be added to the labor force at any one time. Healthcare facilities must also be licensed, certified, and inspected and often require large capital investments. Pharmaceutical manufacturers face extremely large financial barriers to get new drugs approved by the Food and Drug Administration. These same barriers, however, can also inhibit potential competitors.

Because healthcare resources are not easily transferred to producing other products and services, exit barriers are also formidable. For example, closing a hospital is difficult in part because it is not always possible to convert the building and equipment to other uses.

Variation in Products, Services, and Quality

Instead of producing standardized products and services, health care is usually customized for individual patients. Well-documented variations exist in patterns of medical care. Quality, although hard to measure, also varies; that is why requesting a second opinion is common. For all these reasons, it can be difficult to identify true substitutes for a particular product or service.

Full and Free Information

Most healthcare services require specialized knowledge. Although patients have more sources of information available today than ever before, they nevertheless may have incomplete information about the prices and quality of healthcare services. Patients and other healthcare purchasers often do not know what constitutes good physician care or pharmaceutical care and cannot often tell when they are getting accurate information.

Inelastic Demand

In perfect competition, even small price increases may result in significant loss of quantity demanded and, therefore, losses in revenue; thus demand is relatively elastic. Demand for healthcare services, however, is relatively inelastic. In other words, patients who need healthcare services are usually not price sensitive, especially in emergency situations. In part because of this sensitivity, prices for healthcare services increase more rapidly than the prices for most consumer goods and services. According to the Bureau of Labor Statistics, the Consumer Price Index for Urban Consumers (CPI-U) has increased during the past decade at nearly twice the rate for medical care (49.5%) as it has for all items (28.4%). Demand, however, has not decreased. Per capita prescription utilization for non-Medicaid patients enrolled in health maintenance organizations has increased from 5.7 prescriptions per person per year in 1990 to 8.5 in 2004. Per capita prescription utilization for Medicare beneficiaries enrolled in HMOs increased from 16.5 prescriptions per year in 1994 to 21.3 prescriptions per year in 2004 (Aventis, 2001, 2005).

Universal Demand

Many products and services offered for sale in the United States are used by only part of the potential market (e.g., rollerblades, cordless power tools, high-adventure vacations). Healthcare products and services, however, are used by nearly everyone. Not only is demand universal, but it is also nearly insatiable. Because of the lack of complete knowledge, many people demand healthcare services that are of questionable value. Even those services that are usually helpful are sometimes used in inappropriate ways that produce little or no value (e.g., antibiotics for the common cold or heroic efforts to prolong the life of a patient who is in the last stages of a terminal illness). In some cases, too many services may produce net losses in value (e.g., antibiotic resistance, addiction, iatrogenic disease, or unnecessary pain and suffering).

Unpredictability of Illness

Given a large enough group of people, we can predict with some certainty the number of individuals who will need trauma care in the emergency department during a given time. We cannot, however, predict exactly which individuals will need this care. Because consumers are often unable to time their healthcare purchases, they are typically not in a negotiating position when they need services. An obvious implication of this unpredictability is the need to pool risk through health insurance, especially if done so through a managed care organization that is in a position to negotiate discounts before services are actually needed.

Health Care as a "Right"

Many people view health care as a "right" because it is a prerequisite for individuals to become useful, productive members of society (much like public education). Those who espouse this viewpoint also believe that the allocation of scarce resources should not be determined by people's ability and willingness to pay, as is the case with most goods and services in the United States; instead, some level of health care should be provided to everyone. This position holds, therefore, that the price system should not be the sole determining factor in deciding who will receive healthcare products and services.

Supplier-Induced Demand

Physicians are in the unique position of controlling both the supply of and the demand for healthcare services. Although patients do not usually gain financially from illness or injury, their physicians often do. Acting as the patients' agents, physicians can create demand for their services and, at the same time, supply the services. This potential conflict of interest is an inherent element of health care under fee-for-service reimbursement and is difficult to prevent completely. Many managed care organizations, however, have restricted physicians' abilities to create self-referrals for laboratory, radiology, and other healthcare services.

Chapter 12 illustrated that an increase in the supply of most goods and services will result in an increase in the equilibrium quantity and a decrease in the equilibrium price. This is not necessarily the case in health care, however. Studies conducted in 1959 and 1961 first illustrated the effect of what is now called supplier-induced demand by showing a close correlation between the number of hospital beds per 1,000 people and rates of utilization measured as hospital days per 1,000 people (Roemer, 1961; Shain & Roemer, 1959). This led to an observation known as Roemer's Law: "A bed built is a bed filled."

The effect of supplier-induced demand has also been demonstrated by the increases in utilization that often accompany attempts to impose controls on physician fees (Folland et al., 1997). Other studies have shown that physicians' clinical decisions can be influenced by financial incentives (Hemenway, Killen, Cashman, Parks, & Bicknell, 1990; Hillman, Pauly, & Kerstein, 1989). This may explain, in part, why increases in the supply of physicians during the 1980s and 1990s were accompanied by acceleration—rather than moderation—in the growth of healthcare costs. However, increases in the supply of healthcare services may be favorable if they allow more people to access care or if they lead to improvements in quality.

Third-Party Insurance and Patient-Induced Demand

The availability of insurance creates a form of induced demand that is initiated by patients. As discussed in Chapter 12, when the price of a product or service decreases, the quantity demanded tends to increase. By decreasing patients' out-of-pocket expenses, health insurance has encouraged patients to consume more healthcare services than they would if they had to bear the full cost of the product or service (Torrens & Williams, 1993). One concern with expanding Medicare coverage for outpatient prescription drugs, therefore, is the potential for growth in prescription drug utilization resulting from induced demand. A potential solution is patient cost sharing that—if structured properly—can reduce unnecessary utilization without decreasing the quality of care (Manning et al., 1987).

The open-ended nature of most health insurance coverage leads to a situation that economists call "moral hazard," where people overconsume health care. For health insurance plan enrollees, the out-of-pocket costs for healthcare services are generally much less than the actual cost for providing those services. At some point, the additional health benefits achieved from consuming additional health services are not really worth their full costs; nevertheless, because the enrollees are paying only a fraction of the costs, they still want to use these services. Overconsumption of health services from moral hazard increases total health expenditures and insurance premiums.

Not all induced demand is undesirable, of course. In some cases, reducing financial barriers to health care may encourage patients to seek healthcare services earlier, thereby avoiding more expensive health expenditures in the future, particularly for lower-income and more severely ill persons.

IMPROVING ECONOMIC PERFORMANCE OF THE HEALTHCARE SYSTEM

Using Market Forces

From the preceding discussion, it should be clear why many observers feel that the economic aspects of health care are unique. Strategies that successfully reduce costs in most industries (e.g., promoting an increase in supply or an increase in competition) are often not seen as effective in the healthcare industry. Some individuals and groups, however, believe that health care is more monopolistic than competitive, and consequently, advocate that healthcare services should be considered a public utility and regulated accordingly. Many industrialized nations have already adopted this stance and regulate both provider fees and manufacturers' prices for pharmaceuticals.

Recognizing that health care is unique, many public policy leaders and payers for healthcare services advocate instead that the healthcare industry be managed in a way that allows market forces to work more effectively. Some of the more common approaches are described next.

First, patients can be made aware of and sensitive to healthcare costs. For example, patients can be given itemized receipts showing the actual costs paid by their insurance programs. They can also be required to pay more through patient cost sharing, especially through tiered co-payments, which allow lower co-payments for preferred products, such as generic drugs, and require higher co-payments for nonpreferred drugs, such as expensive brand-name products.

Second, healthcare providers can be given feedback about variations in the cost, quantity, and quality of healthcare services through performance reports and academic detailing.

Third, managed care organizations can design physician and hospital reimbursement so as to create incentives for reducing costs. Because costs are a function of price and quantity, both factors need to be considered. Price (i.e., cost per unit) increases are attributable to inflation and can be controlled to some extent through contracting and competitive bidding. Increased utilization, by contrast, is a function of three separate components (as illustrated in **Table 14-1**): population effects, duration of treatment, and intensity of services.

Creating Incentives

As discussed in Chapter 12, managed healthcare plans have designed reimbursement methods that seek to reduce unnecessary hospital admissions, decrease hospital length of stay, and decrease the intensity of services provided to hospitalized patients. Similar steps have been implemented to control the cost and utilization of ambulatory services.

Table 14-1 Examples of Utilization Measurements for Various Types of Healthcare Services

	Hospital	Physician	Pharmacy
Population effects	Number of admissions	Number of new patients	Number of new prescriptions
Duration	Length of stay	Episode of care	Number of prescription drug refills
Intensity	Number and types of diagnostic tests	Number and types of treatments ordered	Relative expense of prescription drug or mix of brands versus generics

Table 14-2 Incentives under Various Forms of Hospital Reimbursement

	Number of admissions	Length of stay	Intensity of services
Discounted fee-for-service	↑	↑	↑
Per diem	↑	↑	↓
DRGs	↑	↓	↓
Capitation	↓	↓	↓

Healthcare providers, like everyone else, usually respond to incentives. **Table 14-2** shows the incentives created by each of the various types of hospital reimbursement. Discounted fee-for-service reimbursement (i.e., retrospective reimbursement based on a negotiated fee schedule), for example, creates incentives to increase admissions (population), length of stay (duration), and intensity of services. Per diem reimbursement (i.e., prospective reimbursement of a flat rate per day without regard to actual cost), the most common form of managed care reimbursement for hospitals (Kongstvedt, 1997), creates incentives for hospitals to increase admissions and length of stay but decrease the intensity of services. Prospective reimbursement of a flat rate based on the patient's admission diagnosis, known as diagnosis-related group (DRG) reimbursement, creates incentives to increase admissions but minimize length of stay and intensity of services. Capitation (i.e., prospective reimbursement of a fixed amount each month for each enrolled patient, regardless of the amount of healthcare services actually provided) creates incentives to minimize all three utilization measures.

Physicians and pharmacies that are paid under discounted fee-for-service systems have the same incentives to increase utilization as do hospitals. Per diems, however, are difficult to apply to outpatient care services. Capitation reimbursement can also be applied to outpatient services in the form of case management (or disease state management). As under DRGs, prospective payments for outpatient services are based on diagnosis but are known as ambulatory patient groups (APGs). Although these programs continue to evolve, they are expected to work best for chronic conditions with a wide range of costs. Again, healthcare providers in the outpatient setting would have the same types of incentives as would hospitals under prospective (APG) and capitation reimbursement.

Balancing Cost and Value

Another approach to improving the economic performance of the healthcare system is balancing the cost of healthcare services with the value received. As described in Chapter 12, most consumers make purchases only when the marginal value of those services meets or exceeds the marginal cost. This principle does not always apply in the healthcare industry, however. To illustrate, assume that the quantity of medical services (M) provided to a patient is compared with the patient's resulting health status (H) as shown in **Figure 14-1**. The curve in Figure 14-1 illustrates a variation of the law of diminishing marginal utility discussed in Chapter 12—marginal increases in the number of resources consumed result in ever smaller marginal increases in utility. Providing initial medical care services causes health status to improve rapidly at first; as more medical care is provided, however, health status increases more slowly. At some

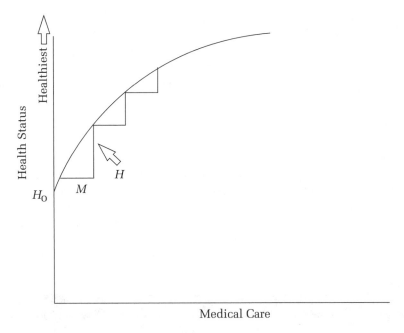

Figure 14-1 Hypothesized Relationship Between Health and Medical Care. In this representation, additional doses of medical care have diminishing impacts on health; eventually, a situation of low medical productivity, termed "flat of the curve medicine," is reached. *Source:* Reprinted from *The Economics of Health and Medical Care, Fourth Edition,* by P. Jacobs, p. 12, 1996, Jones and Bartlett Publishers.

point we will reach the "flat of the curve," where additional healthcare expenditures produce very little incremental benefit (Jacobs, 1991, 1996).

When patients are isolated from costs, they often demand additional services, even though these services may provide limited or no benefits. It is important to consider the marginal benefit of additional medical services and to determine whether increases in services will produce proportional increases in benefits. If a great deal must be spent to produce a small incremental benefit, this usage may be a waste of limited health care resources.

This concept was used by the state of Oregon when it faced a shortage of funds for its Medicaid program and needed to reform its healthcare system. Use of limited funds for some services meant that opportunities to help other patients had to be forgone. To minimize these opportunity costs, Oregon wanted to allocate resources in a manner that would maximize marginal outcomes. A decision was made to provide coverage for those treatments that provided the greatest benefits compared with the cost of services. By not covering procedures such as removal of benign skin cancer, removal of benign tumors in the gastrointestinal system, and liver transplants for liver cancer patients, the state expanded basic services to approximately 120,000 more uninsured patients (Clewer & Perkins, 1998; for a more detailed discussion of Oregon's Medicaid program, see Chapter 20.)

Although Oregon's experience has not been widely adopted, many other examples exist where this principle is applied to some degree. Managed care organizations are giving more attention to pharmacoeconomic considerations (e.g., cost-effectiveness, cost-benefit, and cost-utility analyses; see Chapter 18). Formulary decisions, step care protocols, and disease management, for example, all consider the incremental costs and outcomes of healthcare services. More attention will be given in the future to ways in which scarce healthcare resources can be applied more efficiently and effectively.

CONCLUSION

This chapter described some of the unique aspects of health economics and ways to enhance the economic performance of the healthcare system. Healthcare practitioners should understand and use these economic principles to work effectively with or for healthcare institutions and insurance programs. Because of the unique nature of the healthcare industry, payers are still investigating how they might better control healthcare costs and improve quality so that patients can receive more benefits from the limited resources available.

QUESTIONS FOR FURTHER DISCUSSION

1. To what extent is health care a monopoly or oligopoly?
2. What can be done to enhance competition in the healthcare industry? Are there cases where competition will not decrease prices?
3. If pharmacists are able to charge for nondispensing services, how might payers act to prevent or minimize potential supplier-induced demand?
4. In addition to the healthcare services listed in the text, what other types of healthcare services might be considered for elimination from health insurance coverage because their marginal cost is likely to exceed their marginal benefits?
5. Which disease states would lend themselves best to pharmacy reimbursement on a capitation basis through ambulatory patient groups (APGs)? Why?

KEY TOPICS AND TERMS

Ambulatory patient groups (APGs)
Capitation
Diagnosis-related groups (DRGs)
Discounted fee-for-service
Duration of treatment
Flat of the curve
Intensity of services
Market structure
Monopolistic competition
Monopoly
Monopsony
Oligopoly
Oligopsony
Patient-induced demand
Per diem

Perfect competition
Population effects
Roemer's Law
Supplier-induced demand
Tiered co-payments

REFERENCES

Aventis. (2001). *Managed care digest series, 2001.* Bridgewater, NJ: Aventis Pharmaceuticals, Inc.

Aventis. (2005). *Managed care digest series, 2005.* Bridgewater, NJ: Aventis Pharmaceuticals, Inc.

Clewer, A., & Perkins, D. (1998). *Economics for health care management.* Hertfordshire, UK: Prentice Hall Europe.

Feldman, R., & Morrisey, M. A. (1990). Health economics: A report on the field. *Journal of Health Politics, Policy and Law, 15,* 627–646.

Folland, S., Goodman, A. C., & Stano, M. (1997). *The economics of health and health care* (2nd ed.). Upper Saddle River, NJ: Prentice Hall.

Hemenway, D., Killen, A., Cashman, S. B., Parks, C. L., & Bicknell, W. J. (1990). Physicians' responses to financial incentives: Evidence from a for-profit ambulatory center. *New England Journal of Medicine, 322,* 1059–1063.

Hillman, A. L., Pauly, M. V., & Kerstein, J. J. (1989). How do financial incentives affect physicians' clinical decisions and the financial performance of health maintenance organizations? *New England Journal of Medicine, 321,* 86–92.

Jacobs, P. (1991). *The economics of health and medical care* (3rd ed.). Gaithersburg, MD: Aspen.

Jacobs, P. (1996). *The economics of health and medical care* (4th ed.). Sudbury, MA: Jones and Bartlett.

Kongstvedt, P. R. (1997). Negotiating and contracting with hospitals and institutions. In P. R. Kongstvedt (Ed.), *Essentials of managed health care* (2nd ed.). Gaithersburg, MD: Aspen.

Manning, W. G., Newhouse, J. P., Duan, N., Keeler, E. B., et al. (1987). Health insurance and the demand for medical care. *American Economic Review, 77,* 251–277.

Rice, T. (1997). Can markets give us the health system we want? *Journal of Health Politics, Policy and Law, 22,* 383–426.

Roemer, M. I. (1961). Bed supply and hospital utilization: A national experiment. *Hospitals, Journal of the American Hospital Association, 35,* 988–993.

Shain, M., & Roemer, M. I. (1959). Hospital costs relate to the supply of beds. *Modern Hospital, 92,* 71–73.

Torrens, P. R., & Williams, S. J. (1993). Understanding the present, planning for the future: The dynamics of health care in the United States in the 1990s. In S. J. Williams and P. R. Torrens (Eds.), *Introduction to health services* (4th ed.) (pp. 421–429). Albany, NY: Delmar.

ACKNOWLEDGMENT

Adapted with permission from the Academy of Managed Care Pharmacy. Copyright 2000. All rights reserved.

Private Health Insurance

Kenneth W. Schafermeyer and Brenda R. Motheral*

Case Scenario

Barb Ital recently graduated from pharmacy school and is considering a job offer from a large pharmacy chain. As part of her benefits package, the company will pay one half of the premium for Barb's health insurance coverage. Barb knows that this is a good deal. Even if she paid 100% of the premium, the group policy would be much less expensive than a policy that she could buy on her own. Barb also knows that if she does not elect to participate in the plan when she begins her employment, she will have to wait until next year before she can join the plan during another open enrollment period. Also, if she joins later, there will be an elimination period; she will have to wait a specified period of months before any preexisting health conditions are covered. Upon reading the policy, Barb discovers that she is required to pay part of the cost for most healthcare services and that some healthcare procedures, such as cosmetic surgery, are not covered.

Questions
1. Why are group policies less expensive than individual policies?
2. What is the purpose of the open enrollment period and the elimination period?
3. Why are patients required to pay part of the cost of most healthcare services?
4. Why are some procedures not covered?

LEARNING OBJECTIVES

Upon completion of this chapter, the student shall be able to:

- Identify the factors that determine whether an event is insurable
- Describe the original purpose of health insurance
- List and define the various parties involved in the health insurance industry

---

*The authors wish to express appreciation to Evan S. Schnur for his assistance gathering information for this chapter.

- Explain how prepaid prescription programs are inconsistent with the principles of health insurance
- Explain why health insurance plans cover prescriptions despite their incompatibility with some risk management principles
- Outline the advantages and disadvantages of the U.S. practice of offering health insurance as an employee benefit
- Describe the potential risk management problems faced by health insurance programs, and explain how insurance companies try to minimize these risks
- Describe the purpose of pharmacy benefit managers and the types of services they provide to control prescription cost and quality
- Given a third-party plan's reimbursement formula, the pharmacy's actual acquisition cost, and the pharmacy's cost of dispensing the prescription, calculate the pharmacy's earned discount, gross margin, and net profit for that prescription when reimbursed by the third-party plan
- Describe how private health insurance has affected pharmacy practice

CHAPTER QUESTIONS

1. What determines whether an event is insurable or uninsurable?
2. What was the original purpose of health insurance?
3. How are prepaid prescription programs inconsistent with the principles of health insurance?
4. Why do health insurance plans cover prescriptions despite their incompatibility with some risk management principles?
5. Why are most private health insurance policies offered through employers?
6. What can insurance programs do to reduce their risk?

INTRODUCTION

The last half of the 20th century witnessed dramatic changes in the way health care is provided, paralleled by equally profound transformations in the way health care is financed. Although health insurance has preserved financial security and improved access to health care for millions of Americans, it has also ensured payment for health-care providers and fueled the growth of hospitals and the development of new health services. Without health insurance, many Americans could not afford the services they need to stay healthy and to continue working as productive members of society.

THE UNINSURED

In 2008, 46.3 million Americans (15.4% of the population) lacked health insurance—600,000 more people than in 2007 (DeNavas-Walt, Proctor, & Lee, 2009). These uninsured individuals face greater barriers to receiving healthcare, are generally in poorer health, and have shorter life expectancies than do individuals with health insurance coverage.

Catastrophic medical bills also are a major cause of personal bankruptcies in the United States, accounting for about 62.1% of these filings in 2007 (Himmelstein, Thorne, Warren, & Woolhandler, 2009). Financial difficulties resulting from such healthcare expenses affect not only the uninsured, but also individuals with inadequate insurance coverage. The demographic groups most likely to be financially devastated by noncovered medical expenses are the elderly, women, and families headed by single women.

Surprisingly, the individuals most likely to be uninsured are not the groups that were traditionally considered uninsurable—the poor, the disabled, and the elderly. These groups are provided some protection by the public sector through Medicare and Medicaid (discussed in Chapter 18). Who, then, are the uninsured? Following are some of the highlights from a U.S. Census Bureau report shown in **Table 15-1** (DeNavas-Walt et al., 2009):

- Among adults, the largest group of uninsured comprises the working poor—individuals who are working in low-paying jobs that either do not offer health insurance benefits or require workers to pay premiums that are unaffordable.
- Foreign-born U.S. residents are about 2.6 times as likely as U.S.-born individuals to be uninsured (33.5% versus 12.9%). The highest rate of uninsured status is found among foreign-born Hispanics. This finding has serious public health implications for areas of the country with large numbers of immigrants (Thamer, Richard, Casebeer, & Ray, 1997).
- Almost one third (28.6%) of young adults between the ages of 18 and 24 are uninsured (about twice the rate of the general population). Young adults who are full-time students fare better because many stay on their parents' health insurance policies through college. As discussed in Chapter 21, however, this may change with full implementation of healthcare reform, which would allow children to be covered their parents' health insurance policy up to age 26. A disproportionately large percentage (more than one fourth) of adults between the ages of 25 and 34, however, are also uninsured.
- As might be expected, the proportion of individuals with health insurance increases with household income; only 8.2% of individuals living in households with incomes greater than $75,000 lack health insurance.

Removing financial barriers by providing universal health insurance coverage will not, by itself, eliminate all of the barriers to receiving high-quality health care. For example, insurance coverage was not found to be an independent predictor of vaccination in a study of preschool children (Santoli et al., 2004). An earlier study showed that the barriers to immunization reported by middle/upper income parents are similar to those reported by lower income parents. Only about one third identify cost and lack of insurance coverage as problems (Salsberry, Nickel, & Mitch, 1994). Greater health problems faced by poor people are attributable not only to lack of adequate insurance coverage but also to organizational barriers, such as a lack of flexibility in scheduling, long waiting times, and personal barriers such as a lack of reliable transportation, chaotic home environments, and employment conflicts. Other obstacles include lack of knowledge of healthcare needs and misperceptions about the safety of healthcare services (Lannon et al., 1995). Although attempts to reform health care in the United States must focus first on providing adequate insurance coverage, other barriers, such as education and transportation, must be addressed as well.

Table 15-1   People Without Health Insurance Coverage by Selected Characteristic, 2008

Category	Percentage
Total population	15.4
Race	
White, not Hispanic	10.8
Black	19.1
Asian	17.6
Hispanic	30.7
Age	
Under 18 years	9.9
18–24 years	28.6
25–34 years	26.5
35–44 years	19.4
45–64 years	14.4
65 years or older	1.7
Nativity	
Native born	12.9
Foreign born	33.5
Region	
Northeast	11.6
Midwest	11.6
South	18.2
West	17.4
Household income	
Less than $25,000	24.5
$25,000–$49,999	21.4
$50,000–$74,999	14.0
$75,000 or more	8.2

Source: U.S. Census Bureau, current population survey, 2008 and 2009 annual social and economic supplements. From *Income, Poverty, and Health Insurance Coverage in the United States: 2008.*

More discussion about covering the uninsured and reforming the healthcare system is included in Chapter 21.

Health insurance is a vital component of the U.S. healthcare system, and yet, many individuals—including both healthcare providers and consumers—do not have a clear understanding of how it works. The difficulty of understanding health insurance may be due in part to a number of interesting paradoxes, such as:

- Health insurance ensures payment for healthcare providers, yet it restricts provider reimbursement.
- Health insurance creates patient access to healthcare services by reducing financial barriers, yet it restricts utilization of those services.
- Healthcare providers supply services, yet they create the demand for these services—an inherent conflict of interest that can drive up healthcare costs.

- Health insurance increases access to health care, yet it can encourage unnecessary use of healthcare services.
- Groups of patients who were once thought of as uninsurable (the poor, the disabled, and the elderly) are now covered through Medicaid and Medicare, yet millions of working poor and their families remain uninsured.
- Individuals with chronic or expensive health problems have the greatest need for health insurance, yet they have the most difficulty obtaining it.

Health insurance has been roundly maligned because of these problems, especially by pharmacists and other healthcare providers who depend on health insurance for payment for services rendered. These paradoxes do make sense, however, when one understands the basic principles of insurance and the needs of the insurance industry. This chapter dispels some of the mystery of health insurance by explaining some of the principles of insuring risk. First, the chapter explains the evolution and structure of the health insurance industry, especially as it relates to prescription drug programs. Next, it outlines the basic principles of insurance and highlights the tools that insurers use to manage risk. The impact of health insurance on pharmacy and strategies for working with insurance programs are also discussed.

HISTORY OF HEALTH INSURANCE

Early Health Insurance Programs

Health insurance has a long history in the United States, beginning with the federal Marine Hospital Service, which was first authorized in 1798. Starting in the mid-19th century, accident insurance and life insurance companies began entering the field of health insurance. The Massachusetts Health Insurance Company of Boston was incorporated in 1847, and several health insurance plans were offered for California gold rush workers in 1849 and for railroad workers in 1860 (Campbell & Newsome, 1995).

Most early health insurance plans were really disability insurance—that is, they did not cover health expenses, but instead protected individuals from the loss of income resulting from illness. At first, only specified diseases such as diabetes, diphtheria, scarlet fever, and typhus were covered. Coverage was later expanded to include more diseases and to reimburse individuals for certain out-of-pocket health expenses. The emphasis, however, remained on protecting income.

Hospital Insurance

In 1929, Baylor University Hospital offered hospital care to a group of Dallas teachers on a prepaid basis. The plan collected premiums of $6 per year for each covered person and then reallocated those funds to the small portion of the group that had hospital expenses.

With fewer financial barriers to hospital care, the demand for hospital services eventually increased. As hospitals experienced empty beds and declining revenues during the Great Depression, the increased revenue and financial stability promised by insurance became increasingly attractive. One problem, however, was that these plans restricted care to a particular hospital. This problem was resolved when the American Hospital Association expanded the prepayment concept by establishing statewide Blue

Cross hospital insurance plans allowing free choice of hospitals. These plans did not pay hospitals directly; instead, patients were expected to pay their bills and then were reimbursed by the plan for 80% of the first 21 days of hospital expenses. It should be noted that this insurance program was designed to increase the *demand* for healthcare services (i.e., the ability and willingness of consumers to pay); it did not address the issue of *supply* (i.e., the extent to which healthcare services were available).

Medical Insurance

At the same time that Blue Cross was being created, a medical group practice in Los Angeles organized a similar program to cover medical services. Not only did this plan create insurance for physician services, but it also organized physicians into a large group practice—a unique arrangement at the time that became a model for today's medical foundations and health maintenance organizations (Pharmaceutical Manufacturers Association, 1973). In 1939, the California Medical Association established the first Blue Shield plan to facilitate payment for medical services. Like Blue Cross, Blue Shield focused on reimbursing patients for a portion of their medical expenses, not on organizing or providing health services directly.

The rapid adoption of health insurance occurred in the 1940s, fueled by government policy. Health insurance benefits became an important part of labor negotiations during World War II; the reason being that government wage and price controls prohibited wage increases during the war so companies that wanted to attract workers began offering additional benefits, especially health insurance. Before World War II, health insurance was an occasional employee benefit, covering about 5% of the U.S. population; in just a few years, however, it became commonplace, covering more than 50% of the population (Institute of Medicine, 1993).

Health insurance remains a standard employee benefit today, with 90% of workers in manufacturing jobs covered; it is less common in the service sector (75%) and in agriculture (70%) (Lee, Soffel, & Luft, 1992). Evidence suggests, however, that the percentage of workers covered by employment-based health insurance is declining because of decreased unionization, the trend toward using part-time workers, and the decreased percentage of employers sponsoring health insurance plans (Fronstin & Snider, 1996).

Major Medical Insurance

With the merger of Blue Cross and Blue Shield and the formation of several other commercial insurance companies, hospital coverage and medical coverage were combined into more comprehensive insurance plans. By the early 1950s, most employee health benefit plans took the form of major medical insurance. These policies were designed to help offset expenses incurred because of catastrophic illness or injury. Until major medical insurance was developed, insurance policies generally limited coverage to a specific dollar amount that was relatively modest and/or limited coverage to specific types of services. Also in the 1950s, the health insurance industry came full circle by reemphasizing income replacement through long-term disability insurance policies.

Indemnity Versus Service Benefit Insurance

Blue Cross, Blue Shield, and other health insurers initially reimbursed subscribers—not providers—for a portion (usually 80%) of their medical expenses. These plans, which were known as indemnity insurance, represented the dominant form of health insurance for decades because they were simple and effective in achieving their objectives—to protect both patients and healthcare providers from financial loss and bankruptcy. Indemnity plans, however, also presented some problems. Patients found it inconvenient to collect receipts and complete claim forms. In turn, insurance companies found the individual claims submitted by thousands of policyholders expensive to process. Premiums for these plans increased rapidly because insurance companies reimbursed on a fee-for-service basis and, consequently, were relatively ineffective at controlling expenditures for reasons discussed later in the chapter. Today, the term *indemnity* is used loosely to refer to any health insurance program reimbursing on a fee-for-service basis with few cost controls.

Most health insurance programs have discontinued the indemnity approach in favor of service benefit programs, in which healthcare providers submit claims and are paid directly by the insurance plan. This arrangement allows standardization and automation of claims processing and better control of costs through contractual agreements between the insurance plans and healthcare providers.

Current Trends

Private health insurance has primarily supported and reinforced existing patterns of health services rather than address gaps in care. Those areas that were neglected by the private sector—prevention, control of communicable diseases, and care for segments of society that have the highest incidence of disease and the greatest need for care (persons who are poor, disabled, chronically ill, mentally ill, retarded, and elderly)—have become the responsibility of the public sector (Litman, 1994). This problem was addressed in 1965 when the Social Security Act was amended to provide government-sponsored health insurance coverage for the poor (Medicaid) and for older and disabled persons (Medicare). Medicare and Medicaid are discussed in more detail in Chapter 18 of this book.

Because early health insurance programs, such as Blue Cross and Blue Shield, were controlled by hospitals and physicians, the primary goal was to protect providers—not patients—from financial loss. The form of insurance preferred by these indemnity plans guaranteed that reimbursement would be generous and that little attention would be given to controlling costs (Starr, 1982). Until recently, most healthcare providers have been reimbursed on a fee-for-service basis—that is, they received a fee for each service performed. This system offered little financial incentive to control utilization, reduce costs, or enhance quality of care.

As healthcare costs increased rapidly during the 1970s, employer groups that paid for health benefits demanded that health insurance programs control costs and change their governing bodies to reduce the extent of provider control. Health insurance companies responded by restricting reimbursement to providers and by controlling the use of healthcare services. However, until more recently, there was little desire or perceived need to improve quality or ensure positive outcomes—ordinary management functions for most businesses. In other words, healthcare services were not managed.

In the past few decades, traditional health insurance programs have evolved into managed healthcare plans through the implementation of extensive cost controls and through the use of patient information and claims databases to improve the quality of healthcare services in an attempt to enhance patient outcomes. Managed care is discussed in more detail in Chapter 17.

Evolution of Prepaid Prescription Drug Programs

Until the early 1970s, most insurance coverage for prescription drugs was offered through major medical insurance programs. The first program to focus primarily on pre-payment of prescription drug expenses was the Green Shield plan offered in Ontario, Canada, in the 1950s. Outpatient coverage of prescription drugs through insurance pro-grams other than major medical plans grew slowly in the United States, however, for several reasons. First, other healthcare services, such as hospital and medical services, historically accounted for a much larger portion of health expenditures; prescription drug coverage, therefore, was a much lower priority. Second, because prescriptions result in a large number of small claims, prescription coverage is not consistent with some of the principles of insurance and risk management. (This point is discussed later in this chapter.) Third, antitrust laws prohibit U.S. pharmacists from doing what Canadian pharmacists had done—working together to negotiate fees.

After the United Auto Workers Union negotiated a prescription drug plan adminis-tered by Blue Cross in 1969, labor unions became the major catalyst driving the growth of prepaid prescription plans. In response to this trend, a new industry of fiscal inter-mediaries was created in the early 1970s to help employer groups provide these pre-scription benefit programs to their employees. These fiscal intermediaries, which are described in more detail in the next section of this chapter, made it easier for employee benefit plans to include prescription drug coverage.

Private insurance coverage for prescription drugs has continued to grow and represented 42% of all prescription expenditures in 2008. Public insurance programs (e.g., Medicare and Medicaid) covered about 37% of expenditures, and the remaining 21% were paid by patients out of pocket, commonly as a part of a patient cost-sharing requirement (Kaiser Family Foundation, 2010).

THE HEALTH INSURANCE INDUSTRY

Structure of the Industry

Although the term third party implies that only three individuals or companies are involved in a transaction (in this case, the patient, the healthcare provider, and the payer), the health insurance industry actually includes many different participants, each with its own specific function. To work successfully with third-party programs, healthcare providers need to understand the structure of the industry and the objec-tives of each of the participants.

Figure 15-1 outlines the most important participants in employer-sponsored group health insurance. At the top of the diagram is the patient—either an employee of a company that sponsors the health insurance plan or a family member of the covered employee. Sometimes employees are represented by labor unions that negotiate ben-efits on their behalf. The labor contract may specify the type of health care and pre-scription coverage that employees and their families receive.

As shown in Figure 15-1, patients often have to pay a portion of the cost of health services received. This patient cost sharing is designed to control utilization of health services by making patients more cost conscious. As discussed later in this chapter, patient cost sharing can take one of the following three forms: a co-payment, a deduct-

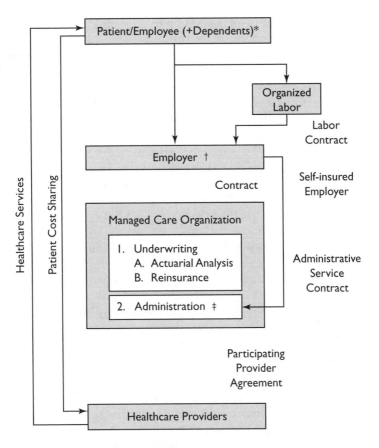

* For public programs = Patient/Qualified Beneficiary
† For public programs = Government Agency (e.g., Medicaid)
‡ Some administrative duties may be assumed by a PBM

Figure 15-1 The Third-Party Prescription Industry
Source: Schafermeyer, K. W. (1996). Third-party prescription program evaluation.
In *Effective Pharmacy Management,* 8th ed., p. 322. Alexandria, VA: National
Community Pharmacists Association.

ible, or coinsurance. Most plans use patient cost sharing as a financial incentive to avoid using unnecessary healthcare services. To be effective, however, patient cost-sharing provisions should not be so high as to discourage use of truly necessary health services.

Figure 15-1 also shows the sponsor of the insurance program—usually an employer that assumes responsibility for obtaining coverage and pays some or all of the premiums. Because healthcare costs for small groups (several hundred persons or fewer) can be unpredictable, and the payment of claims for health expenditures is complex, most employer groups seek professional help from fiscal intermediaries—companies that provide underwriting and/or administrative services.

Underwriting is the process of insuring someone. The underwriter assumes the financial risk for health services in return for premiums paid by an individual or by an employer for a group of employees. To limit their own risk, most insurance companies purchase reinsurance to cover losses that exceed a specified amount. For health insurance programs, this means that both underwriters and reinsurance companies must agree that a health insurance program is designed properly with minimum expenses (known as losses). Consequently, insurance programs tend to limit the types of claims that may be billed by providers unless they determine them to be necessary or that they will reduce costs elsewhere in the program. Estimating the amount of risk assumed by an insurance company is known as actuarial analysis. An actuary conducts a statistical analysis of the population served and estimates the income (premiums) that must be earned to cover the estimated expenses, usually expressed as cost per member per month. An actuary estimates these three expenses: (1) the cost for each type of service; (2) the projected number of services that will be received by the group as a whole (the utilization rate); and (3) the administrative expenses that the fiscal intermediary incurs by insuring and administering the healthcare benefit program. Actuaries may then adjust their estimates based on the insurance company's overall expenses for a specific geographic area during the previous year (community rating) or adjust the rates for a specific subset of insured individuals—usually an employer group—based on the group's experience for the previous year (experience rating). These adjustments affect premiums for the next year, depending on whether the claims expenses were higher or lower than the actuary's estimate.

Sometimes a large corporation decides that it is unnecessary to use an insurance company to underwrite a health benefit program and decides to self-insure instead. Laws in most states require employers that self-insure healthcare benefits to place a large sum of money aside into a restricted account that can be used only to pay for employees' health benefits. This restricted account (escrow account) must be large enough to pay any unexpected future health benefit claims. Because self-insurance is a risky strategy and ties up a considerable amount of cash, most smaller employers prefer to use the underwriting services of an insurance company.

Some fiscal intermediaries specialize in providing only underwriting services; others provide only administrative services, meaning that they do not take on the risk. Some fiscal intermediaries, such as Blue Cross/Blue Shield, provide both underwriting and administrative services. Because healthcare providers and administrators are linked through contractual arrangements, administrators are the component of the healthcare industry that is most visible to healthcare providers. The elements of this contractual arrangement are discussed later in this chapter.

Viewpoints of the Participants

The various groups involved in the health insurance industry often have competing goals. Employees are interested primarily in having convenient access to healthcare providers, quality services, and reduced out-of-pocket costs. Employers want healthy, satisfied employees but also want to reduce or control the amount they spend on health benefits. Administrators need to satisfy their customers—employer groups—by maintaining an adequate network of participating healthcare providers and helping employers manage their health benefit programs at a reasonable cost.

Healthcare providers, however, often see third-party programs as an unnecessary and unwelcome intrusion into the provider–patient relationship and as an unfair market force that controls their practice and limits their earnings. Individual providers do not like to be viewed as commodities to be purchased at the lowest price. Although providers express concern that cost-containment efforts are frequently imposed at the expense of quality, this concern is difficult to document.

BASIC PRINCIPLES AND STRATEGIES OF HEALTH INSURANCE

Principles of Risk Management

To understand insurance and its effect on the provision of health care in the United States, it is helpful to first understand the principle of risk and how it can be managed. The purpose of insurance is to help individuals and businesses manage certain types of unanticipated risk. Death, for example, is inevitable; because it can be sudden or unexpected (unanticipated), however, it is insurable. Most accidents and many other perils are also unanticipated and, therefore, insurable. In contrast, risk that can be anticipated is not insurable (for example, spoilage of products, depreciation of buildings and equipment, or expiration of drugs).

Risk can be described as pure or speculative. Pure risk occurs in situations where a person faces the possibility of loss but no gain. Illness, fires, or storms are unpredictable perils and are often unavoidable. Because these events can cause significant loss but seldom result in any type of gain, they are referred to as pure risk. Speculative risk involves a chance of gain as well as a chance for loss. Gambling is a classic example of speculative risk. Pursuing a business venture also involves speculative risk because an individual accepts the risk of losing money while pursuing the chance of making profits. Speculative risk cannot be insured because risk takers can usually choose the amount of risk they are willing to assume; removing the risk would encourage overspending or careless behavior.

Insurance is designed to help people to reduce pure risk, not speculative risk. Pure risk becomes an insurable hazard when all six of the following elements are present:

1. The probability of a peril occurring in a population can be accurately determined. We can predict with reasonable certainty, for example, the percentage of 60-year-old women who will develop breast cancer in a given year and the percentage of 19-year-old men who will have traffic accidents during a given year.
2. The peril is an irregular event on an individual basis. Although we can predict approximately how many breast cancer cases or traffic accidents will occur in a population, we cannot determine to whom these events will occur.
3. The loss must be accidental. For example, arson committed by the insured party is not covered by insurance; neither is murder by a beneficiary of a life insurance policy. This requirement is essential to avoid creating profit-making incentives for purchasing insurance.
4. The event must result in a substantial loss. Insurance is designed to protect a person's financial security. Although most people can sustain small losses, insurance is needed to cover the large, unexpected losses that can overwhelm an individual's income stream or wipe out a family's accumulated resources.
5. The loss must be measurable. For a loss to be measurable, the following two conditions must be met: the loss must be attributable to a specific event, and the monetary value of the loss must be relatively easy to determine. For example, normal

wear and tear for an automobile does not come from a specific event. In contrast, the loss from a theft or a hailstorm is the result of a specific incident and, therefore, can be insured. Insurance policies state the basis under which the amount of loss will be measured. For personal property, insurance coverage is set at either market value (the amount for which the item could have been sold before it was damaged) or replacement value (the amount it would cost to fix or replace the item). Insurance companies may also establish schedules stipulating the amount they will pay for various services. The intrinsic value of a lost heirloom or a favorite photograph, however, cannot be measured in monetary terms and, therefore, is difficult to insure.

6. The individual must have an insurable interest. Because insurance is designed to compensate for loss, an individual who does not suffer the loss personally usually cannot receive insurance compensation. A person cannot, for example, be reimbursed when a neighbor's house burns down. Likewise, whereas people can purchase life insurance for family members or business partners (with their permission), they cannot purchase insurance on an acquaintance who is a poor driver, thereby speculating that they can cash in when the acquaintance finally has an accident.

Purchasing insurance involves incurring a small, certain loss (prepayment of an annual or monthly premium) in exchange for the possibility of a large, unpredictable loss. Trading uncertainty for certainty reduces risk. Insurance has several other equally valuable benefits; it reduces worry, it makes it easier to borrow money, and it frees up capital for investment.

Insurance does not make risk disappear, but rather transfers risk from individuals to the insurance company for a fee. The insurance company then pools the risk with that assumed from many other insurance policyholders. Transfer of risk and risk pooling are based on the law of large numbers; the larger the number of insured persons, the more accurate the predictions regarding losses. When losses are more predictable, the predicted risk of a loss actually decreases, which is important because the underwriter estimates the predicted amount of loss and sets premiums accordingly.

Premiums are based on the claims experience of the policyholders who make up the risk pool. If claims are higher than anticipated, next year's premiums will increase to make up for this loss. In these experience-rated pools, each insurance subscriber is affected by the aggregate claims experience of the group. A large amount of bad risk that results in a high number of claims leads to large premium increases; good risk with fewer claims results in lower premium levels.

Prescription Coverage: An Exception to the Principles of Risk Management

The need for health insurance is obvious. Unexpected injury or hospitalization costing tens of thousands of dollars (or more) can quickly exceed a family's annual income or accumulated savings. Most families consider the financial security provided by health insurance to be a necessity. Insurance coverage for pharmaceuticals, however, is not consistent with all of the requirements of an insurable hazard as described previously. Compared with other health expenditures, the cost of a prescription usually does not represent a substantial loss, the exception being some specialty medications. In addition, for some medications, such as oral contraceptives, the prescriptions do not represent an accidental or unpredictable hazard. Also, because prescriptions represent a large number of relatively small claims, administrative costs represent a significant percentage of total expenditures.

If prescription coverage is inconsistent with some of the basic principles of insurance, why, then, are prescriptions covered by most health insurance programs? One explanation is that drug therapy is often preventive in nature and is less expensive than other medical alternatives such as surgery. If medications can keep patients out of the hospital, it is theorized, encouraging proper use of medications may reduce overall healthcare costs. Another explanation is that the growth in prescription coverage may have been driven by an entitlement mentality of employees as well as a lack of understanding of the insurability of pharmaceuticals on the part of corporations' employee benefit managers. However, rising prescription expenditures are starting to make prescription drugs more of an insurable risk for some groups of patients, especially older persons and those with rare, chronic conditions that require specialty medications.

Potential Risk Management Problems

Theoretically, the law of large numbers allows accurate prediction of losses for insured populations. A number of potential risk management problems, however, can make it difficult for insurance companies to predict losses accurately. They include catastrophic hazard, adverse selection, supplier-induced demand, and moral hazard.

Catastrophic Hazard

One of the most important risks to avoid is catastrophic hazard. Most insurance policies exclude coverage for widespread, catastrophic events that, if covered, would exceed the company's ability to pay and could, consequently, bankrupt the company. Property insurance policies, for example, exclude coverage for damages caused by earthquakes. Earthquakes are, however, sometimes covered under special addenda (riders) to homeowners' policies. As another example, both health insurance and casualty insurance policies exclude catastrophic losses caused by acts of war.

Adverse Selection

If individuals could predict future losses accurately, they would be more likely to purchase insurance coverage only when they knew they were going to need it and to drop coverage when they did not need it. The situation in which individuals or companies purchase insurance because they expect a loss is known as adverse selection. This practice, of course, makes it difficult for insurers to raise enough premium income from individuals who do not have losses to cover those who do. Adverse selection inevitably results in premium increases for future policyholders.

Flood insurance is notorious for being subject to adverse selection; only policyholders residing in flood plains buy it. Therefore, premiums would be extremely high, and flood insurance probably would not be available without federal subsidies. Adverse selection is also a problem inherent in health insurance; older or sicker individuals are more likely to use insurance and, therefore, more likely to purchase it. Because large, employer-sponsored groups usually include many healthy individuals, adverse selection is not likely to be a problem, and, consequently, premiums for group policies are usually less expensive than individual policies. Dental insurance is also subject to adverse selection because individuals can obtain coverage only when they know they will need it.

For the benefit of insurance companies and policyholders, it is important to avoid adverse selection. Many restrictions in insurance policy contracts (discussed later in this chapter) are aimed at avoiding the problems associated with adverse selection.

Incentives to Create Losses and Supplier-Induced Demand

A third potential risk management problem occurs when an individual actually gains from an apparent loss. For example, insuring a car for more than its value could give the policyholder an incentive to destroy the car. Insurers try to prevent this kind of profiteering by limiting the amount of insurance coverage to the market value of the insured item. For health insurance, however, it is more difficult to avoid incentives to incur losses (i.e., medical claims). Physicians, who serve as the patients' agents, can always create a demand for the same services that they supply. This potential conflict of interest, known as supplier-induced demand, is an inherent element of health care under fee-for-service reimbursement and is difficult to avoid completely. The issue of supplier-induced demand is discussed in more detail in Chapter 14.

Moral Hazard

Health insurance is often subject to a problem known as moral hazard, where people overconsume health care when they have health insurance. As all consumers know, when the price of a product or service decreases, the quantity demanded tends to increase. This is also true of healthcare services. By decreasing patients' out-of-pocket expenses for health services, health insurance has encouraged patients to use services that they might not seek out otherwise and has contributed to a dramatic increase in healthcare expenditures (Torrens & Williams, 1993).

If a person has health insurance coverage, then his or her out-of-pocket costs are generally much less than the true cost of providing the individual's health care. At some point, the benefits of additional health services in terms of improving one's health are not really worth their full costs. Overconsumption of health services can drive up health expenses and health insurance premiums for everyone. As presented in the case scenario at the beginning of this chapter, insurers often mandate cost sharing (deductibles, coinsurance, or co-payments) as a means to decrease unnecessary demand.

Strategies for Avoiding Risk Management Problems

Insurers must be careful to avoid the problems discussed previously. Failure to do so may result in large increases in premiums or—even worse—make insurance coverage difficult or impossible for individuals or even groups to obtain. Fortunately, insurance companies have developed a variety of strategies to overcome potential risk management problems and to limit their own risks.

Group Policies

To avoid adverse selection, insurance companies use group policies, which are usually sponsored by employer groups and provided to employees and their dependents. As highlighted in the case scenario at the beginning of this chapter, group policies are usually less expensive than individual policies for two reasons. They are less prone to adverse selection, and they are less expensive to sell and administer. Employer groups assume many of the administrative costs associated with enrolling policyholders and explaining the plan's benefits. Selling costs are lower because the insurance company only has to negotiate a master contract with the employer group; it does not have to sign individual contracts with each insured person. Obviously, for a group policy to be cost effective for the insurer, enough policyholders must be in the risk pool so that the law of large numbers allows accurate prediction of losses.

Employer-sponsored group health insurance is popular with workers because it reduces their tax liability; if the amount paid in premiums had been given to employees as salary instead, the workers would have paid income tax and Social Security tax on this income first and then purchased premiums out of their own pockets. Employers also benefit because their payroll taxes, such as the employers' Social Security matching payments and federal and state unemployment taxes, are not paid on the amount of compensation given as employee benefits.

Elimination Period

As introduced in the case scenario at the beginning of this chapter, another contract restriction aimed at avoiding adverse selection is the elimination period (also known as an exclusionary period), in which preexisting health problems are not covered by a new health insurance policy until after the policyholder has been covered for a given period of time. Expenses related to pregnancy and childbirth, for example, may not be covered for the first 9 months of a new policy. Elimination periods are often waived for a short period of time after new employees begin their employment. Thereafter, many policies either impose an elimination period for preexisting health problems or require a health test to demonstrate that the patient does not have preexisting health problems that would result in adverse selection.

Coverage Limitations

Even when a given service is covered, the insurance contract will restrict losses by limiting the amount paid for certain covered expenditures and/or what services are covered. Health insurance policies commonly limit payments for physician office visits or prescriptions and state that they will not pay the extra cost for a private hospital room unless isolation of the patient is medically necessary.

Insurance companies carefully restrict the perils covered to reduce costs and, more importantly, to avoid adverse selection. This is why health insurance policies, such as the one described in the chapter-opening case scenario, often exclude elective treatments such as cosmetic surgery, fertility treatment, abortion, childbirth, and dental care. Mental health and drug and alcohol rehabilitation were commonly excluded until many states adopted laws requiring insurers to cover these services. The perils associated with some injury-prone activities, such as contact sports, aviation, and military service, are also commonly excluded from coverage.

Coordination of Benefits

Occasionally individuals have overlapping coverage from two insurance policies, and questions may arise about which insurance company should be responsible for payment. This can happen, for example, when a person with health insurance is injured in an auto accident or on the job. In these cases, medical expenses may also be covered by the auto insurance policy or by the employer's workers' compensation policy. To avoid the case in which multiple payments are made for the same care, insurance policies usually include a coordination of benefits provision that limits total reimbursement of all insurance to the amount of loss. An insurance policy's subrogation provision states which company pays first. In the examples cited previously, health insurance policies usually pay after auto, homeowner's, or workers' compensation insurance policies have paid their portion.

Other Strategies

The risk management techniques discussed previously are designed to prevent some of the most common risk management problems and are aimed primarily at policyholders. Reducing risk is extremely important because it is a prerequisite for achieving the basic financial objective of all insurance companies—generating revenues in excess of expenses. (Even nonprofit companies need to avoid losses and build reserves.)

Risk can also be reduced by controlling underwriting—avoiding bad risks by refusing coverage to those individuals who are most likely to incur high costs. In the past, some insurance companies have canceled or refused to renew policies for policyholders who incurred major healthcare expenses. Most states now prohibit this practice. Insurance companies have also refused new coverage to people with certain preexisting health problems; this practice makes it difficult for some workers to change jobs because they cannot afford to lose their health insurance coverage. Some of these problems were addressed by the Health Insurance Portability and Accountability Act (HIPAA), discussed in Chapter 21.

The facts that health insurance premiums have increased faster than the cost of other goods and services in the United States and that more than 45 million Americans do not have health insurance are evidence that risk management is a complex endeavor and risk management problems are difficult to overcome.

ADMINISTRATION OF PRESCRIPTION DRUG PROGRAMS

Pharmacy Benefit Manager

Given that the administration of prepaid pharmacy programs is complex and requires a large prescription volume to be conducted efficiently, third parties often separate (or carve out) prescription programs from other health benefits and contract with a type of administrator known as a pharmacy benefit manager (PBM) to manage them. Using a PBM isolates cost centers and concentrates a workforce of prescription benefit experts to manage the prescription program. The administrative services provided by PBMs usually include the following:

- Contracting with healthcare providers to supply specified services
- Communicating with both patients and providers to explain and update administrative policies
- Providing reports to plan sponsors
- Identifying eligible beneficiaries
- Maintaining formulary systems
- Conducting drug utilization reviews
- Processing claims submitted by providers
- Reimbursing providers
- Auditing providers

- Controlling costs
- Controlling utilization
- Ensuring program quality

Participating Pharmacy Agreement

Even health insurance contracts that are carefully crafted to minimize risk manage-ment problems include provisions to control healthcare expenditures by reducing the costs per claim and the overall number of claims. Many cost-control provisions for prescription drug programs are specified in participating pharmacy agreements—con-tracts that stipulate the services to be provided by contracting pharmacies in exchange for a specified reimbursement. (These contracting pharmacies are sometimes referred to as "participating pharmacies" or "network pharmacies." If only a selected group of pharmacies is allowed to contract, these entities are known as "preferred pharmacies" or "preferred providers.")

Plan administrators recruit healthcare providers who are willing to sign participating provider agreements. A clear understanding of the terms of these contracts is impor-tant for pharmacy managers and other key employees. Following is a description of some of the most important elements of the participating pharmacy agreement.

Reimbursement

The participating pharmacy agreement specifies the amount and frequency of pay-ment. For pharmacies that dispense large numbers of third-party prescriptions, timely reimbursement is vital. Even more important is the amount of reimbursement. Pre-scription reimbursement consists of three components: the PBM's cost for the drug ingredients, the dispensing fee, and the amount paid by the patient in the form of co-payments, coinsurance, or deductibles. These factors are shown in **Equation 15-1**.

$$\text{Rx payment} = \text{ingredient cost} + \text{dispensing fee} - \text{patient cost sharing} \qquad (15\text{-}1)$$

Ingredient Costs

Ingredient costs (also known as the cost of goods sold) represents between 75% and 80% of the cost of the average prescription. Pharmacy reimbursement for drug ingre-dient costs has traditionally been based on the average wholesale price (AWP)—that is, the list price established by the manufacturer. The AWP is higher than the actual acquisition cost (AAC) that pharmacies pay for drug products. As shown in **Equation 15-2**, the difference between the average wholesale price and the pharmacy's actual acquisition cost is known as the earned discount.

$$\text{AWP} - \text{AAC} = \text{earned discount} \qquad (15\text{-}2)$$

As shown in **Equation 15-3**, the amount of the pharmacy's earned discount varies depending on the pharmacy's purchasing volume (volume discount), its ability to pay early (cash discount), and special deals and promotions the pharmacy is able to take advantage of (trade discounts).

$$\text{Earned discount} = \text{volume discount} + \text{cash discount} + \text{trade discount} \qquad (15\text{-}3)$$

Earned discounts are very important because they decrease the pharmacy's AAC. A lower AAC, of course, results in a higher gross margin (the difference between the selling price and the cost to the pharmacy for the product that was sold; see **Equation 15-4**). By supplementing low dispensing fees, earned discounts allow pharmacies to participate in managed care plans that would otherwise have been unprofitable.

$$\text{Gross margin} = \text{reimbursement} - \text{AAC} \qquad (15\text{-}4)$$

Because earned discounts vary among pharmacies and even for the same pharmacy from time to time, managed care plans usually do not reimburse pharmacies for their AAC. Instead, the participating pharmacy agreement usually specifies that reimbursement for drug ingredient costs will be based on an estimated acquisition cost, which is usually calculated as a percentage of the average wholesale price (**Equation 15-5**).

$$\text{Estimated acquisition cost} = \text{AWP} - (x\% \text{ of AWP}) \qquad (15\text{-}5)$$

Of course, because AWP is a reference price rather than a transaction price, payers are looking for a better way to estimate actual acquisition costs. Instead of calculating the estimated acquisition cost as a percentage of the AWP, some payers have begun using alternative methods of calculating estimated acquisition cost such as wholesale acquisition cost (WAC). WAC is defined in federal statutes as "The manufacturer's list price for the drug ... to wholesalers or direct purchasers in the United States, not including prompt pay or other discounts, rebates or reductions in price ... as reported in wholesale price guides or other publications of drug ... pricing data" (42 USCA1395w-3a). Estimated acquisition cost is often calculated as WAC plus a specified percentage, as shown in **Equation 15-6**.

$$\text{AAC} = \text{WAC} + X\% \qquad (15\text{-}6)$$

When a drug product has chemically equivalent generics, managed care plans often limit reimbursement to the price of a commonly used generic product, referred to as the maximum allowable cost. Each managed care plan creates its own maximum allowable cost list. On those occasions when a physician requires the pharmacy to dispense the brand-name version of a multiple-source product, some managed care plans allow full reimbursement for the higher-cost branded product if the pharmacist indicates that the physician specified that the prescription was a dispense-as-written order. Medicaid also sets upper limits for reimbursement of multiple-source drugs but uses the term *federal upper limit* instead of *maximum allowable cost.*

For generic drugs, the federal government has proposed using a new cost basis known as average manufacturer's price (AMP) for prescriptions covered by government-sponsored plans. AMP is defined as, "The price at which drugs are sold by the manufacturer to purchasers. For sales to wholesalers, AMP represents the Wholesaler Acquisition Cost (WAC after all discounts); for sales directly to pharmacies, AMP represents the net 'direct' price after discounts" (Kreling, Mott, & Wiederholt, 2001, p. 56)

The Deficit Reduction Act of 2005 instructed Medicaid and Medicare to change the pharmacy reimbursement formula for multisource drugs from its current use of AWP to AMP. To implement the Deficit Reduction Act changes, the Centers for Medicare and Medicaid Services issued final rules that created a new formula for calculating the maximum prices paid for multisource drug products.

Significant reductions in the reimbursement for drug acquisition costs are likely to create financial problems for pharmacies (and, consequently access problems for patients) unless payers such as Medicaid take steps to increase dispensing fees to make up for the lower reimbursement for drug ingredient costs. Consequently, the methods used to calculate AMP have been the source of significant concern for the pharmacy industry. Pharmacy associations were successful in blocking implementation of the Deficit Reduction Act provisions in court; then the Patient Protection and Affordable Care Act, passed in 2010, redefined how AMP prices are to be determined. As a result of this fix, it appears that AMP prices will not reduce overall expenditures to the extent expected and, consequently, it appears that the Centers for Medicare and Medicaid Services may abandon AMP as a method for calculating reimbursement for multiple-source drug products.

Dispensing Fees

The second part of the reimbursement for a managed care prescription (Equation 15-1) is the dispensing fee paid to the pharmacy. It is a fixed amount that is paid to the pharmacy for each prescription dispensed. PBMs, of course, try to keep total reimbursement for ingredient costs and dispensing fees as low as possible while still maintaining an adequate provider network.

Patient Cost Sharing

The third component of the reimbursement for a managed care prescription (Equation 15-1) is patient cost sharing. Patient cost sharing effectively decreases managed care organizations' prescription costs by shifting some responsibility for payment directly to the patient. This practice is designed to not only decrease prescription costs, but to also decrease the utilization rates. Patient cost sharing can take one of three forms: (1) a co-payment, (2) a deductible, or (3) coinsurance. Cost-sharing provisions may also include out-of-pocket limits (i.e., a stop-loss provision) or maximum benefit limits.

Under a co-payment system, patients pay a specified dollar amount every time a service is received (for example, $50 per hospital admission or $5 per prescription). Co-payments are the most common form of patient cost sharing for prescription benefits.

A deductible requires patients to cover their own healthcare expenses until a specified dollar amount has been paid out of pocket during a given period of time, usually a year. (For example, the insurance company might begin paying health expenses once a patient has paid $200 of out-of-pocket healthcare expenses during the policy year.) Because patients may receive health services from several different providers, in the past it has sometimes been difficult to determine exactly when the deductible requirement has been met. The expansion of online computerized claims processing makes it easier to keep track of expenses, encouraging more plans to use deductibles in their programs.

The third form of patient cost sharing, coinsurance, requires the patient to pay a specified percentage (often 20%) of the cost of the service; the plan pays the remainder. Although co-payments are the most common type of patient cost sharing, the use of coinsurance increased over the last decade and was used by about 18% of plans in 2007. (*The Takeda Prescription Drug Benefit Cost and Plan Design Survey Report*, 2009). Co-payment levels have been increasing significantly since the mid-1990s to reflect rising drug prices; coinsurance levels, by contrast, have not changed because the actual dollar amount paid by patients automatically increases as the price of prescriptions increases.

To encourage patients to ask for generic prescriptions, many prescription plans require patients to pay a tiered co-payment, which is a relatively low co-payment for generic drugs, a higher co-payment for preferred brand-name drugs, and an even higher co-payment for nonpreferred brand-name products. A small number of employers have created a fourth tier for certain "lifestyle" drugs (e.g., Viagra) that are subject to very high co-payments or 50% coinsurance. A fifth tier is sometimes reserved for nonformulary products, euphemistically referred to as a "100% co-payment." Multitiered cost-sharing levels are often coordinated with formulary systems to encourage patients to request that their physicians prescribe lower cost medications.

Plans without patient cost sharing offer first-dollar coverage. Although first-dollar coverage once was common, most plans now see patient cost sharing as a financial incentive that encourages enrollees to avoid using unnecessary healthcare services (i.e., moral hazard). To be effective, however, patient cost-sharing provisions should not be so high as to discourage use of truly necessary health services.

Payment

To be adequate, the total reimbursement should cover the cost of drug ingredients dispensed (the cost of goods sold or AAC) plus the overhead cost incurred by the pharmacy in dispensing the prescription (the cost of dispensing) and a reasonable return on the pharmacy's investment (the net profit); see **Equation 15-7**. If reimbursement covers only the pharmacy's cost without any profit, then it pays at the break-even point. The gross margin is the portion of the reimbursement that exceeds the pharmacy's actual acquisition cost for drug ingredients.

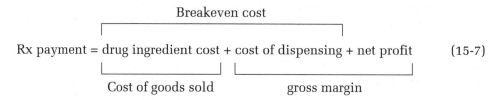

Rx payment = drug ingredient cost + cost of dispensing + net profit   (15-7)

For most plans, total reimbursement for a managed care prescription will not exceed the pharmacy's usual and customary price (i.e., the price charged most commonly to private-pay patients). Third-party pharmacy contracts typically state that pharmacy reimbursement is usually the lower of

1. The specified estimated acquisition cost plus the dispensing fee
2. The specified maximum allowable cost plus the dispensing fee
3. The pharmacy's usual and customary charge

Other Contract Provisions

The participating pharmacy agreement tells the pharmacy how to determine whether a person is eligible for benefits. Usually, eligible beneficiaries receive some form of identification card. Because cardholders often change jobs or insurance plans, the card itself may not be a guarantee of payment; pharmacies typically confirm eligibility through a computerized eligibility verification system.

The participating pharmacy contract also specifies how pharmacies are to submit claims for reimbursement. In most cases, this step involves submitting electronic claims through the pharmacy's computer at the time the prescription is dispensed. Such an online adjudication system is a major improvement over the old paper claims system because it is faster and less expensive and tells the pharmacy immediately whether the claim will be accepted, the amount of co-payment that should be collected, and the amount that the plan will reimburse for the prescription.

Not all third-party programs cover the same products. A section of the contract titled "limitations" or "exclusions" specifies what is not covered. Some common exclusions are nonprescription drugs (other than insulin), compounded prescriptions, devices (such as syringes), and products used for cosmetic purposes (such as hair growth or wrinkle removal). There may be a maximum quantity that can be dispensed for some products (for example, a 30-day supply). However, some contracts specify a minimum quantity (such as a 3-month supply) that may be dispensed for certain maintenance medications used for chronic conditions.

Almost all contracts reserve the right to audit the pharmacy's records as a deterrent to fraudulent claims. Preferably, the contract specifies the auditing procedures that will be used.

IMPACT OF HEALTH INSURANCE ON PHARMACY

Health insurance has profoundly affected the profitability of pharmacies. In the past decade, dispensing fees have declined while inventory costs have increased. This has contributed to a decline in the average pharmacy's gross margin from 32.2% of sales in 1986 to 23.2% of sales in 2008—a drop of 9 percentage points (West, 2009). As shown in **Table 15-2**, those pharmacies that have survived have maintained net profits at 3% to 4% of sales. They have done so by becoming more efficient and by decreasing their expenses. These efficiencies have been achieved primarily through aggregation of buying power, automation, and increased use of pharmacy technicians.

As shown in **Table 15-3**, there is evidence that pharmacies whose prescription volumes are dominated by third parties and managed care organizations (accounting for 80% or more of their total volume) have significantly lower gross margins and lower proprietor's incomes than do pharmacies with lower third-party prescription volumes

Table 15-2 Changes in Pharmacy Operations, 1986–2008

	1986 (%)	1996 (%)	2008 (%)	Change 1986–2008 (%)
Sales	100	100	100	0
Cost of goods sold	67.8	74.4	76.8	+9.0
Gross margin	32.2	25.6	23.2	−9.0
Expenses	29.5	22.5	20.0	−9.5
Net profit	2.7	3.1	3.2	+0.5

Source: Data from Dankmeyer, T. (Ed.). (1997). *1997 NCPA-Searle Digest*. Alexandria, VA: National Community Pharmacists Association; West, D. S. (Ed.). (2009). *2009 NCPA Digest*. Alexandria, VA: National Community Pharmacists Association.

Table 15-3 Effect of Third-Party Prescription Volume on Pharmacy Operations, 2007

	Less than 80% third party	80–90% third party	90% or more third party
Sales	100	100	100
Cost of goods sold	74.8	76.6	77.2
Gross margin	25.2	23.4	22.8
Expenses	21.2	20.4	19.9
Salaries	11.6	11.7	11.6
Net profit	4.0	3.0	2.9

Source: Data from West, D. S. (Ed.). (2009). *2009 NCPA Digest*. Alexandria, VA: National Community Pharmacists Association.

(less than 80%) (West, 2009). Lower reimbursement requires higher volume to maintain profits. This shift to an economy-of-scale business requires that pharmacies operate very efficiently and reduce unnecessary costs whenever possible.

Why do pharmacies participate in third-party plans that offer low reimbursement? The answer to this question is not simple and varies from pharmacy to pharmacy. Some pharmacies accept third-party plans because they are reluctant to lose customers who may be buying over-the-counter products and other goods from the front of the store. For others, as long as reimbursement covers the variable costs of the dispensed prescription, fixed expenses can be spread among the larger percentage of private-pay prescriptions. However, this strategy is effective only as long as third-party prescriptions represent a minority portion of a pharmacy's business. Given that the majority of prescriptions are now paid for by third parties, such cost shifting will not be feasible as a long-term strategy.

To survive or prosper in the managed care environment, all community pharmacies— both chains and independents—need to be run by good managers. Community pharmacy managers must know their costs and lower them to the greatest extent possible by managing their operations efficiently, and they must be familiar with the prescription benefit plans sponsored by major employer groups. Pharmacists in all settings should also be prepared to document the value of their services.

Pharmacists have tried to work together through a variety of pharmacy organizations, such as volume purchasing groups and pharmacy associations to help pharmacists succeed in this environment. (There is a limit, however, to the extent to which pharmacies can work together. Because of antitrust laws, they cannot collectively boycott undesirable plans, nor can they collectively negotiate fees with third parties.) Above all, pharmacy managers must understand the healthcare marketplace and the roles of the various participants in the health insurance industry. Without this knowledge, even the best manager will be unprepared to work effectively in today's rapidly changing healthcare environment.

CONCLUSION

Health insurance has profoundly changed how health care is financed and delivered in the United States. The health insurance industry has grown rapidly during the last century and will continue to evolve toward managed care. Although health insurance presents some formidable challenges for pharmacists and other healthcare providers, it also presents some promising opportunities. All pharmacists—whether staff or managers, community or institutional—must understand the principles and dynamics of the health insurance industry to be effective in their position. Those pharmacists who strive to genuinely understand the needs and perspectives of insurance plan sponsors, underwriters, and administrators and are able to identify new opportunities for pharmacists and pharmacies will help determine the profession's future success.

QUESTIONS FOR FURTHER DISCUSSION

1. What is the difference between controlling costs and managing care? What are some examples of each?
2. How can experience rating decrease premiums and at the same time increase the number of uninsured?
3. How can health insurance companies reduce or prevent problems associated with adverse selection and moral hazard?
4. What is the traditional role of public insurance programs? How might this role change in the future?

KEY TOPICS AND TERMS

Actual acquisition cost (AAC)
Actuary
Adjudication
Adverse selection
Average manufacturer's price (AMP)
Average wholesale price (AWP)
Catastrophic hazard
Coinsurance
Community rating
Coordination of benefits
Co-payment
Deductible
Dispense as written
Earned discount
Elimination period
Estimated acquisition cost
Experience rating
First-dollar coverage
Fiscal intermediary
Gross margin
Group policies
Health Insurance Portability and Accountability Act (HIPAA)
Indemnity
Induced demand
Insurable hazard

Insurable interest
Law of large numbers
Major medical insurance
Maximum allowable cost
Moral hazard
Open enrollment period
Participating pharmacy agreement
Patient cost sharing
Pharmacy benefit manager (PBM)
Pure risk
Reinsurance
Risk pool
Service benefit
Speculative risk
Subrogation
Supplier-induced demand
Underwriting
Wholesale acquisition cost (WAC)

REFERENCES

42 USCA1395w-3a.

Campbell, W. H., & Newsome, L. A. (1995). The evolution of managed care and practice settings. In S. M. Ito & S. Blackburn (Eds.), *A pharmacist's guide to principles and practices of managed care pharmacy* (pp. 1–14). Alexandria, VA: Foundation for Managed Care Pharmacy.

DeNavas-Walt, C., Proctor, B. D., & Lee, C. H. (2009). *Income, poverty, and health insurance coverage in the United States: 2008. Current population reports* (p. 20). Washington, DC: U.S. Government Printing Office.

Fronstin, P., & Snider, S. C. (1996). An examination of the decline in employment-based health insurance between 1988 and 1993. *Inquiry, 33,* 317–325.

Himmelstein, D. U., Thorne, D., Warren, E., & Woolhandler, S. (2009). Medical bankruptcy in the United States, 2007: Results of a national study. *American Journal of Medicine, 122*(8), 741–746.

Institute of Medicine. (1993). *Employment and health benefits: A connection at risk.* Washington, DC: National Academy Press.

Kaiser Family Foundation. (2010, May). *Prescription drug trends.* Retrieved from http://www.kff.org/rxdrugs/3057.cfm

Kreling, D. H., Mott, D. A., & Wiederholt, J. B. (2001, November). *Prescription drug trends—A chartbook update.* Kaiser Family Foundation, p. 56.

Lannon, C., Brack, V., Stuart, J., Caplow, M., NcNeill, A., Bordley, W. C., & Margolis, P. (1995). What mothers say about why poor children fall behind on immunizations. A summary of focus groups in North Carolina. *Archives of Pediatric Adolescent Medicine, 149,* 1070–1075.

Lee, P. R., Soffel, D., & Luft, H. S. (1992). Costs and coverage: Pressures toward health care reform. *Western Journal of Medicine, 157,* 576–583.

Litman, T. L. (1994). Government and health: The political aspects of health care—A sociopolitical overview. In P. R. Lee & C. L. Estes (Eds.), *The nation's health* (4th ed., pp. 107–120). Sudbury, MA: Jones and Bartlett.

Pharmaceutical Manufacturers Association. (1973). *Pharmaceutical payment programs: An overview.* Washington, DC: Pharmaceutical Manufacturers Association.

Salsberry, P. J., Nickel, J. T., & Mitch, R. (1994). Immunization status of 2-year-olds in middle/upper- and lower income populations: A community survey. *Public Health Nurse, 11,* 17–23.

Santoli, J. M., Huet, N. J., Smith, P. J., Barker, L. E., Rodenwald, L. E., Inkelas, M., ... Halfon, N. (2004). Insurance status and vaccination coverage among U.S. preschool children. *Pediatrics, 113,* 1959–1964.

Starr, P. (1982). *The social transformation of American medicine.* New York, NY: Basic Books.

The Takeda prescription drug benefit cost and plan design survey report. (2009). Scottsdale, AZ: The Pharmacy Benefit Management Institute.

Thamer, M., Richard, C., Casebeer, A. W., & Ray, N. F. (1997). Health insurance coverage among foreign-born U.S. residents: The impact of race, ethnicity, and length of residence. *American Journal of Public Health, 87,* 96–102.

Torrens, P. R., & Williams, S. J. (1993). Understanding the present, planning for the future: The dynamics of health care in the United States in the 1990s. In S. J. Williams & P. R. Torrens (Eds.), *Introduction to health services* (4th ed., pp. 421–429). Albany, NY: Delmar.

West, D. S. (Ed.). (2009). *2009 NCPA Digest.* Alexandria, VA: National Community Pharmacists Association.

CHAPTER 16

Government Involvement in Health Care

Earlene E. Lipowski and Marcus Long

Case Scenario

Tobacco use has been a major public health concern for over half a century. Although it is expected that the healthcare system will treat individuals with diseases and conditions related to tobacco use, the role of government in regulating the sale and use of tobacco products is a contentious issue. Those who grow, sell, and use tobacco products maintain their right to these pursuits, while the rights of others are allegedly infringed by the choices of tobacco users. The tension between individual rights and collective good is the heart of the debate about the role of government.

Public sentiment shifted as evidence accumulated on the adverse health effects of tobacco. Furthermore, investigation showed that while the industry resisted government regulation, it manipulated nicotine levels to promote addiction and targeted advertising toward youngsters not capable of making a truly informed decision about smoking (Bayer & Colgrove, 2002, 2004). Government involvement gradually shifted from informing the public about risks to exerting pressure on smokers and finally to prohibiting the activity in public spaces (Feldman & Bayer, 2004).

Three government interventions are credited with having the greatest influence on modifying smoking, including restricting advertising and promotion, particularly to youth; prohibiting smoking in public places as a matter of environmental protection; and imposing taxes that increase the cost of smoking while funding tobacco cessation programs and health care (Gostin, 2007, 2009). The shift in public sentiment over time culminated in the passage of the Family Smoking Prevention and Tobacco Control Act of 2009. The act gives the Food and Drug Administration (FDA) the authority to regulate tobacco products.

LEARNING OBJECTIVES _____

Upon completion of this chapter, the student shall be able to:

- Review the evolution of the government's role in health care during the 20th century
- Explain the system of checks and balances among the three branches of government and cite the benefits of that system with regard to government involvement in health care
- Identify the three basic functional roles of government in the U.S. healthcare delivery system
- List the major federal agencies involved in healthcare delivery and give examples of the services each provides
- Compare and contrast the roles of the federal, state, and local governments in the U.S. healthcare system

CHAPTER QUESTIONS

1. Give at least one example of a government function in healthcare delivery where the federal government takes primary responsibility. Give at least one example where state and local government agencies have primary responsibility.
2. How does government use its police power in ensuring the health of the population? Propose a definition of police power in the context of health care.
3. What are the advantages and disadvantages of dividing the primary responsibilities for health care among multiple levels of government? How is this division consistent with the philosophy of government in the United States?
4. The U.S. Food and Drug Administration (FDA) must balance concerns for patient safety with the demand for timely access to needed medications. How does the FDA attempt to balance these competing objectives?
5. Cite a recent example from the news that illustrates government involvement in the delivery of health care.

INTRODUCTION

"We the People of the United States, in Order to form a more perfect Union, establish Justice, insure domestic Tranquility, provide for the common defense [and] promote the general Welfare ... do ordain and establish this Constitution." (Preamble to the U.S. Constitution, 1787)

Duty, Authority, and Limits

At the most fundamental level, the role of any government is to provide the foundation for social interaction and mutual security. The founding principles of the U.S. government are affirmed in its Constitution. For the United States, the purpose of the union is to guard the common good, including defense, economic welfare, and social well-being. The Tenth Amendment reserves to the states all powers that are not given to the federal government or prohibited by the Constitution. In exchange for the good of the community, member states agree to subordinate their self-interests to that of the federal government.

The U.S. Constitution and its first 10 amendments, the Bill of Rights, make no specific reference to health care. The government claims authority over health matters at the national and state levels because it is reasonable and consistent with the intent of the Constitution. No individual or set of individuals can protect and assure the health of the entire population, so promoting the health and well-being of the public is considered to be a common good. An individual may procure some of the necessities of living, including food, shelter, clothing, and even personal medical services. However, it is organized action on behalf of the community that sets limits on individuals as a means of controlling infectious diseases or ensuring safe and clean water, air, and food. It is government that holds the power and duty to provide for the well-being of the people.

The Constitution also is the basis for assigning jurisdiction of power among federal, state, and local governments and for setting limits on that power to protect individual liberties. Limits to government rest on the rights of individuals to autonomy, liberty, privacy, personal expression, property, and economic freedom of contract and uses of property (Gostin, 2001).

Another important power the U.S. Constitution has granted to the federal government, and one the Supreme Court has strengthened in the 19th and 20th centuries, is the power to regulate interstate commerce. The regulation of commerce is the basis for environmental protection, occupational health, food and drug purity, and safe drinking water. The power to tax and spend gives the federal government the means to exercise its duties and responsibilities (Gostin, 2001).

State and local governments retain police power to enforce laws and restrict behaviors. In matters of health, the states may limit proprietary freedoms through inspections of health institutions and licenses for professionals. States control the actions of individuals to prevent nuisances that threaten health by regulating smoking, inspecting commercial establishments for fire hazards and environmental contaminants, and checking residential property for unsanitary conditions and pests. State authority also limits personal freedoms in the interest of public health through mandatory vaccination and diagnostic screening programs. The right to personal privacy is subordinate to state requirements for reporting sexually transmitted diseases and partner notification, and individual liberties may be curtailed through isolation and quarantine.

Evolution of Government Role in the 20th Century

It is not surprising that the Constitution did not make specific references to the role of government in health matters. When the Constitution was written and for the first 150 years after its adoption, citizens did not look to government to get involved in their healthcare needs. Government intervention was limited to protecting the populace from epidemics and meeting the most basic needs of the poor. That situation changed when the Great Depression in the 1930s affected all levels of society and dramatically altered public sentiment. Americans turned to government to help them deal with immediate needs and to protect them against future uncertainties. The system of healthcare delivery in the United States evolved slowly from that point, accompanied by many shifts in the government's role and influence (Litman & Robins, 1997; Turnock, 2001).

The Sixteenth Amendment to the Constitution gave the federal government the authority to levy a tax on income early in the 20th century. The states turned to the federal government for assistance because they did not have the same authority to raise the sum of money needed to address health problems (Turnock, 2001). Federal grants beginning in 1935 made it possible for states to establish maternal and child healthcare services, public health laboratories, and public health departments. The federal government then gained additional power and influence over healthcare delivery through a succession of programs, including the establishment of the National Institutes of Health in the 1930s, the Centers for Disease Control and Prevention in 1946, the Hospital Survey and Construction Act (Hill-Burton) of 1946, and Medicare and Medicaid in 1965. (For more information, see Chapter 1.)

The states enjoy some measure of flexibility in meeting their own priorities through the distribution of funds provided by the federal government for state healthcare initiatives such as Medicaid. However, the federal government exerts considerable influence over the states through its significant involvement in research, regulation, education and training, and technical assistance in healthcare delivery.

Responsibilities of the Three Branches of Government

Government power at all levels in the United States is divided among three branches of government in accordance with the Constitution. The responsibilities defined by the Constitution are among the legislative, executive, and judicial branches.

Legislative Branch

The first charge that the Constitution gives to the legislative branch is to provide for the common defense and general welfare of the United States. Congress has the sole authority to decide matters of public policy—that is, to organize, fund, and implement government programs. Members of Congress are accountable to their constituents for securing public health and welfare; in turn, their constituents are committed to accepting the responsibility for programs that result from congressional action (Gostin, 2000a).

Congress serves as the forum for identifying problematic conditions or situations in need of change, debating alternative arrangements, and exhorting others to take action to create change. It is the place where antagonists challenge the diagnosis or the prognosis of alleged problems. Elected representatives pay particular attention to disagreements and the intensity of conflict between or among special-interest groups or to issues that set the special interests of a group against the larger public interest. Congress attends to public opinion and often learns more about matters by convening public hearings. Secondary problems often come to light in Congress and are placed on the political agenda because they are closely linked to a primary problem that is under examination (Longest, 2002).

The legislative role in the healthcare system is to enact laws necessary to safeguard the population from harm and to promote health. A member of Congress can propose new legislation or modify existing law by introducing a proposal in the form of a bill. Most general health bills are referred to the House Committee on Energy and Commerce and to the Senate Committee on Health, Education, Labor and Pensions for further investigation and deliberation. Any bills involving taxes and expenditure of public funds must also be referred to the House Committee on Ways and Means and to the Senate Committee on Finance.

The Congressional Budget Office plays a role at this point as well (www.cbo.gov). Its purpose is to help Congress formulate budget plans, stay within those plans, assess the effects of federal laws, and estimate the impact of proposals on the federal budget—a process known as "scoring" the bill. The Congressional Budget Office does not offer recommendations on legislative options but merely evaluates their economic impact.

A bill that survives committee deliberation on its merits and economic impact is placed on the calendar for a formal vote by the respective body of Congress. Both the House of Representatives and the Senate must approve identical bills before a bill passes to the president for his signature and adoption into law.

Executive Branch

The executive branch is the administrative arm of government under the direction of the Office of the President of the United States. The president is charged with implementing and enforcing the laws passed by the legislative branch. His advisors make up the cabinet, which includes the heads of 15 executive departments and the vice president. Currently, the White House chief of staff, the administrator of the Environmental Protection Agency, the director of the Office of Management and Budget, the chairman or chairwoman of the Council of Economic Advisors, the U.S. trade representative, and the U.S. ambassador to the United Nations also serve in the president's cabinet.

Administrative agencies of the executive branch promulgate the regulations needed to implement laws. Reliance on the regulatory process allows for greater flexibility in the design and subsequent revisions needed to keep the law functional in the face of social and technological change.

Administrative agencies issue regulations through the notice-and-comment rule-making process that is specified by federal law. The statutes require agencies to include the public in the regulatory process. A governmental agency that proposes a new regulation must solicit public commentary that is typically open to any person or any organization (Roth, Dunsby, & Bero, 2003). Administrative agencies are charged with giving each individual comment full and serious consideration. Officials must incorporate valid comments into the revised rule and explain why they rejected others. At the conclusion of the public commentary period, agency staff review, categorize, and analyze each comment on the proposed rule and publish their findings in the *Federal Register*.

Public comment is an important requirement that allows for public participation in the development of regulations. Even if there is widespread agreement on the scientific evidence, the role of science in health regulation is not independent of politics, law, and the mass media (Abraham & Sheppard, 1999). In 1995, the FDA attempted to promulgate regulations to control tobacco as rational policy based on scientific evidence. The FDA, however, found the nature of public response rested almost exclusively on political ideology irrespective of whether individuals were in support or opposition to the proposed rule (Roth, Dunsby, & Bero, 2003).

Public comments shape the final version of the proposed regulation, increase its public acceptability, and reduce the risk that special-interest groups will unduly influence the regulatory process. If the regulations are formally challenged, the courts generally hold an agency's interpretation of a statute in high regard because regulation is developed through the open rule-making process. Executive agencies may issue manuals, memos, and guidance to accompany laws and regulations. These documents often specify details, which, in effect, have nearly the same force as regulation (Keough & Greene, 2003).

Federal agencies need the capacity to investigate, impose penalties, or grant rewards to enforce regulatory policies. Government agencies need resources to target beneficiaries, validate eligibility for benefits, manage the supply and quality of goods and services, and deliver the goods, services, and payments. The success of a law can depend on whether the executive agency has the necessary resources to enforce it, including the authority, money, personnel, status, prestige, information, expertise, technology, physical facilities, and equipment.

The Office of Management and Budget (www.whitehouse.gov/omb) is the executive branch's counterpart to the Congressional Budget Office. Office of Management and Budget staff members evaluate the effectiveness of agency programs, analyze competing demands for funding, set funding priorities, and formulate annual budget plans. In accordance with the Constitution, the president must report to Congress from time to time on the state of the union and recommend laws for consideration that the president believes to be necessary, useful, or expedient.

Judicial Branch

The role of the judicial branch is to interpret the law and ensure that actions of the legislative and executive branches conform to the Constitution. The courts provide oversight when the effects of one policy infringe on or conflict with the desired outcomes of other policies. In the case of tobacco control, in 2001 in the case of Lorillard Tobacco Co. v. Reilly, the U.S. Supreme Court ruled in support of tobacco companies' right to advertise as a matter of free speech. In that case the plaintiff did not convince the justices that proposed restrictions were sufficiently narrow; therefore, the court determined that a total ban on advertising would be an unnecessarily restriction of freedom of expression (Bayer, 2002).

Where protection of the public health is concerned, the courts consistently have upheld the right of government to compel adherence to laws and regulations. For example, court rulings permit government to collect taxes and expend public resources, and to require members of the community to submit to licensing, inspection, and regulation (Gostin, 2000b). Three general justifications are commonly cited to uphold any intrusion on the rights of a single individual or to force a person to incur economic costs or take other actions that may not be in the individual's self-interest. The courts authorize restraining an individual when (1) there is a risk to the individual, (2) there is a risk to others, or (3) protection is needed for individuals who are judged incompetent or incapable of protecting themselves.

Judicial standards for government actions that affect organizations or groups of individuals require that the government demonstrate (1) a legitimate health threat, (2) compelling reasons for the invasion of personal rights, and (3) use of the least restrictive intervention needed to substantially reduce the health threat and avoid harm (Gostin, 2001).

Evolution of Government Role in the 21st Century

Responsibility for securing the public health and welfare assures widespread government regulatory involvement in modern society. Tobacco legislation and regulation illustrate the difficulty achieving the appropriate balance between individual liberty, privacy, and ensuring public health.

Concerns about bioterrorist threats prompted legislative proposals that give the authorities the right to restrict individual freedom by monitoring individuals who may have conditions that could lead to a sudden outbreak of an infectious disease. The threat of a pandemic generates additional calls for stringent public health surveillance, isolation, and quarantine. Events like these underscore the tension between the threat of uncertain but potentially catastrophic events and limits to individual liberty.

Efforts to curb tobacco use and to deal with the threat of a pandemic demonstrate arduous process involved in resolving tensions between public and private concerns. The leading causes of death in the world today are no longer acute infectious diseases, but rather chronic illnesses that are related to environmental, social, and behavioral factors such as diet, exercise, smoking, environmental toxins, alcohol and drug abuse, sexual practices, motor vehicle accidents, and firearms. There is broad support for the government's role in restricting individuals when they pose a risk to others. Restrictions imposed on individuals who are at substantial risk to themselves but represent significantly less risk to others are suggestive of paternalism on the part of government. Is it an appropriate role of government to prohibit smoking outdoors, mandate motorcycle helmets and seat belts, or regulate fast-food restaurants that allegedly are fueling an epidemic of obesity (Bayer & Fairchild, 2004)? Some view this debate as a matter of moral judgment rather than ethics (Hall, 2003). Other legal scholars argue that it is not a matter of justice if any restrictions on civil liberties are applied equally to all for the good of society as a whole (Epstein, 2003).

The irony is that the current debate has forged strange ideological alliances—for example, libertarians may side with tobacco and other business interests in support of individual rights and go against social welfare concerns of modern society (Bayer & Colgrove, 2002). Public policy debates of the 21st century will continue to sort out the circumstances in which the rights of the individual must be subordinated to the needs of the community (Gostin & Blochet, 2003; Gostin & Powers, 2006).

GOVERNMENT HEALTH FUNCTIONS AND ORGANIZATION

Functional Roles

The involvement of the U.S. government in the delivery of health care is currently geared toward the identification, formation, and implementation of health policy. Some policies lead to health delivery functions that are funded, organized, and executed by the private sector without direct government intervention. At other times, and in certain circumstances, the government has faced the necessity to fund and organize the delivery of health care itself.

Payer

Government decisions in the financing of health care are meant to satisfy three objectives: (1) ensure adequate funding, while avoiding excessive expenditures; (2) regulate the health insurance market and pool risk when market failure causes uneven distribution of goods and services; and (3) subsidize care for the poor and disadvantaged.

The government is the largest purchaser of healthcare services in the United States, accounting for nearly half (48%) of all national expenditures related to health (U.S. Census Bureau, 2010). The major share, representing more than 50% of total federal expenditures, is spent on the Medicare program, which serves 47 million elderly and permanently disabled individuals, and the Medicaid program, which serves an additional 47 million economically disadvantaged persons. The addition of the Medicare Part D prescription drug benefit in 2006 represented a significant expansion of Medicare. Medicare's share rose from 7% of federal expenditures for prescription drugs in 2005 to 60% in 2008 (Kaiser Family Foundation, 2010).

The government also is a significant purchaser of health insurance coverage as an employer. Government, including state and local units, school districts, and public utilities, employed about 20 million people in 2008, more than 15% of the total U.S. workforce (U.S. Census Bureau, 2010). Other significant expenditures include the purchase of health care for military personnel and their dependents through the Department of Defense and programs for retired and former members of the military conducted through the Department of Veterans Affairs.

The United States is unique in being the only major developed country that does not provide universal healthcare coverage for its citizens. Government financing of health care has moved forward in incremental steps in response to concerns about the significant proportion of the population without health insurance coverage.

One of the programs that expand the government's role as a payer is the Children's Health Insurance Program. Federal funds are available to states for expansion of Medicaid eligibility to children younger than 19 years of age who otherwise would not qualify for coverage because their family income exceeds the Medicaid threshold.

Provider

Whereas Medicare and Medicaid are financed by the government, the health care delivered through these programs is purchased from providers in the private sector. For active-duty members of the armed forces and for veterans, health services are not only financed but also provided directly by government employees at government-owned facilities. The Veterans Health Administration operates one of the largest integrated health services systems in the United States, involving 1,400 facilities that include 153 hospitals and 773 outpatient clinics. More than 5.7 million people received care in Veterans Administration (VA) health care facilities in 2009 (U.S. Department of Veterans Affairs, 2011a).

Originally, the Veterans Administration healthcare system was created to treat injuries and provide rehabilitation services for disabilities resulting from military service. Although these services remain priorities, the Veterans Administration now extends care to veterans with low incomes or special healthcare needs if they can be accommodated using existing resources. As a result, the Veterans Administration is supplying increasingly more care for conditions not related to military service. The Veterans Administration system is used by roughly 60% of all disabled and low-income veterans annually (U.S. Department of Veterans Affairs, 2011b).

The Department of Defense operates a substantial healthcare program that provides medical services to active-duty members and retired personnel of the armed forces, their dependents, and their survivors. The hospitals and clinics for active-duty members are primarily staffed by military personnel. Dependents of active-duty troops and retirees receive medical care under managed care and fee-for-service plans through TriCare. TriCare combines the medical resources of the Army, Navy, and Air Force and supplements them with networks of civilian healthcare professionals and facilities (Kaiser Family Foundation, 2011).

In addition to directly providing health care, the government serves an important function as a provider of healthcare information through agencies at all levels of government and through the public education system (Novick & Mays, 2001). This information ranges from basic scientific research with applications in health care to consumer-friendly health promotion and guidance about self-care practices.

Regulator

Laws and regulations are the tools that the government uses to control the public environment and protect it from threats created by the actions of groups and individuals. The government performs surveillance and enforcement functions in addition to carrying out development and implementation of laws and regulations.

When members of the public seek health care, both state and federal governments regulate the services that are provided and the education and certification of those who provide the services. Government agencies also ensure fair and adequate access to services and basic standards of quality. Finally, the government monitors the healthcare marketplace to address adverse consequences of market failures that might endanger the availability, cost, or quality of medical care.

A Multilayered, Multifaceted Organizational Structure

Healthcare delivery rests on many supporting elements, ranging from the discovery, application, and dissemination of scientific research, to the inspection and enforcement of law and regulations, to education of the public and healthcare professionals, to deploying and monitoring the impact of changing technology. All three branches of government at the federal, state, and local levels have roles to play in healthcare delivery, including the roles of payer, provider, and regulator.

Other chapters in this book describe in greater detail how the government carries out many of its most important responsibilities. This chapter provides an overview of the organizational structure that houses the various government functions at the federal, state, and local levels. At the federal level, this chapter can be quite specific in describing the organization and delivery of an agency's specific functions. By its very nature, however, health care is delivered to individual persons by individual organizations in specific locales. Each state and territory is free to organize its functions in a way that is consistent with the distribution, size, and needs of its population. Needs and resources are most closely specified at the level of state and local governments. Consequently, the organizations that deploy health services are highly varied and difficult to characterize in detail. For this reason, the involvement of government in health delivery at the state level is described here in more general terms.

A policy is rarely implemented by a single organization; instead, when the scope of the policy is broad, a myriad of organizations are involved in turning the policy into reality. The healthcare system is so complex that many different agencies inevitably come in contact with people. Furthermore, the determinants of health are not confined to the healthcare sector but require government programs in many areas (Koop, Pearson, & Schwarz, 2002). Overlap is present at the interface between agencies. The flow of goods and services through the healthcare system generates effects that ripple across organizational charts and geographical divisions. Some degree of overlap is desirable as well as inevitable.

Our brief review focuses on the more particular assignments of responsibilities rather than the interfaces between government entities. Students of the healthcare delivery system will undoubtedly encounter apparent duplications of efforts across organizational and geographical boundaries, just as the roles and responsibilities of various healthcare professionals overlap to ensure continuity of care.

FEDERAL GOVERNMENT

Department of Health and Human Services

The Department of Health and Human Services (DHHS) is home to many government programs whose functions are related to health care. The secretary of DHHS is responsible for roughly 23% of government spending, both discretionary and by entitlement. **Figure 16-1** shows the major offices within DHHS. Other chapters in this book

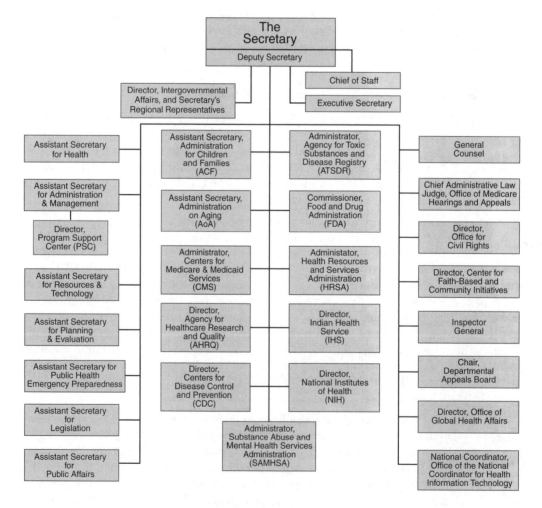

Figure 16-1 Department of Health & Human Services Organizational Chart
Source: U.S. Department of Health & Human Services

describe many of the offices within DHHS that are engaged in the delivery of health services and directly involved in the formation of health policy. Some DHHS offices and agencies provide social services or deliver administrative and support functions. DHHS also assumes a significant role in the research and development activities of the healthcare system, by conducting and sponsoring fundamental research, assuring the safety of food and drugs, and monitoring the adoption of information technology.

Centers for Medicare and Medicaid Services

The Centers for Medicare and Medicaid Services is the largest agency within DHHS. Altogether about one of four Americans is covered through health programs operated by the Centers for Medicare and Medicaid Services, which has three operating divisions: the Center for Medicare Management, which oversees the traditional Medicare program; the Center for Beneficiary Choices, which administers Medicare's managed care options; and the Center for Medicaid and State Operations, which has responsibility for state-administered programs including the survey and certification of Medicare providers, operation of the Children's Health Insurance Program, and regulation of self-insured employers. Chapter 18 describes the Medicare and Medicaid programs in greater detail.

Health Resources and Services Administration

The Health Resources and Services Administration assures access to healthcare services for people who have low incomes, are uninsured, or live in rural areas or urban neighborhoods where health resources are scarce. Health Resources and Services Administration provides services to people with AIDS under the Ryan White Care Act, works to improve the health of mothers and children, and offers primary care to 14 million people annually through a national network of 3,700 community and migrant health centers or in clinics for the homeless and residents of public housing. Health Resources and Services Administration also oversees the U.S. organ transplantation system.

Indian Health Service

The Indian Health Service works with tribes to make health services available to nearly 1.9 million American Indians and Alaska Natives from 564 federally recognized tribes who live on reservations, often in rural and sparsely populated areas. The Indian Health Service provides primary and specialized healthcare services that would otherwise be unavailable, such as dental clinics and residential substance abuse treatment centers.

Food and Drug Administration

The Food and Drug Administration (FDA) is responsible for assuring the safety of foods and cosmetics and the safety and efficacy of pharmaceuticals, biologic products, and medical devices. This agency traces its history to 1906, when Congress passed the Pure Food and Drug Act.

Because drugs have been the fastest-growing cost component of health care in the past decade, and because prescription drugs represent the single most important out-of-pocket medical expense for most Americans, the role of the FDA has come under intense scrutiny. Its role offers a prime example of the tension that exists between government paternalism and individual autonomy. Many citizens misunderstand the function of the FDA and incorrectly believe that the agency itself tests drug products. For all of these reasons, the drug approval process is described here in some detail.

The FDA reviews new molecular entities (NMEs), which are drugs that have never been marketed in the United States. A streamlined application process is in place for generic equivalents of drugs that are already approved for marketing in this country. The FDA issues guidelines for basic research and safety testing in animals before clinical testing may begin. Human testing is conducted in phases, involving progressively greater numbers of people at each phase, as a way to limit exposure to dangerous products. The review process can be halted at any point if findings suggest that the drug lacks efficacy or safety.

In the preclinical (animal) testing phase, scientists study the chemical and physical properties of the molecular entity. Dosage forms are designed and tested, and chemical engineers develop optimal ways to manufacture adequate quantities of the drug product. Patents are filed to protect the intellectual property rights of the inventor.

The approval process begins with the investigational new drug (IND) application, which is filed following toxicology and safety testing of the drug in animals. An investigational new drug application includes the results of preclinical tests, research protocols for the initial clinical trials, and a general overview of studies to follow. The applicant also details the manufacturing process—facilities, equipment, and techniques—needed to produce the drug. FDA approval of the investigational new drug allows the manufacturer to proceed with clinical trials in humans. At this point, the FDA rates the drug as either standard or priority to distinguish those chemical entities that will receive priority attention because they may represent a significant therapeutic improvement over existing treatments.

FDA staff members review the procedures and scrutinize data from the trials submitted by the manufacturer. The agency's procedures are intended to ensure that all research participants are well informed of potential benefits and risks and that their decision to participate in a clinical trial is freely given and documented. The first human trials (Phase I) are small, generally including 20–100 healthy volunteers, with the goals of assessing safety, studying drug metabolism and excretion, and documenting pharmacologic response. Phase I results are used to calculate the sample size and length of testing needed to establish efficacy in the next phase of clinical studies.

In Phase II trials, the drug is administered to several hundred individuals who are representative of the patients the drug is intended to treat. Response to most new drugs is compared to placebo and less often to existing treatment. Studies are double blind to reduce the likelihood of bias. Neither the patient nor the caregivers know whether the subject receives the experimental drug or the comparison drug or placebo. When the drug is intended for the treatment of chronic diseases, investigators seek data about clinical end points including morbidity, mortality, or quality of life in addition to changes in biochemical, physiologic, or anatomic attributes. Various doses are compared, and additional safety data are gathered. Phase II trials generally last about 2 years.

Phase III trials are controlled clinical studies that are conducted with several hundred to thousands of persons and are intended to demonstrate that the drug has statistically significant safety and effectiveness. Information gathered through these clinical trials determines the content of the product label and package insert required by the FDA.

Phase III trials may last as long as 3 years or more so that they can establish the longer term safety and efficacy of the product.

The drug developer files a new drug application (NDA) after it completes Phase III trials with the drug. The FDA reviews a summary of results from all clinical trials and the procedures planned for the drug's manufacture, formulation, and quality control. The agency may then issue an approval letter, specify conditions under which approval might be granted, or grant no approval. In the latter cases, the sponsor of the NDA may respond to FDA requests for additional information or withdraw the NDA from further consideration. For most NDAs, the FDA requires at least one amendment to the original application, and it may often require several such changes.

FDA approval gives the applicant the right to market the new drug as safe and effective for specific indications supported by evidence. Although individual physicians retain the right to prescribe a drug for off-label uses, the manufacturer may promote only the approved uses.

The FDA includes two review centers. The Center for Drug Evaluation and Research grants approval to new chemical entities, antibiotics, hormones, and enzyme products pursuant to an NDA. The Center for Biologics Evaluation and Research reviews biotechnologic drug products and vaccines and grants approval for both a product license to cover the drug and an establishment license to cover safety and quality assurance procedures for facilities where the product will be manufactured.

After a drug is marketed to the public, the manufacturer is required to notify FDA about uncommon, yet serious, adverse reactions that were not found in the clinical trial phases but become evident when the drug is used in a broader population. This stage, known as Phase IV or postmarketing surveillance, is especially critical in cases when a priority drug undergoes an accelerated approval process. If the FDA judges a drug to be too hazardous after its original approval, it may request the manufacturer to issue a warning, revise the product label, or withdraw the product from the market.

The FDA regulates all aspects of pharmaceutical marketing. Its regulations aim to assure health professionals and the public that all promotional claims are based on scientific evidence and that the information presented is complete, truthful, and balanced with regard to risks and benefits.

The availability of new drugs has important implications for the nation's overall health status, health expenditures, social equity, and economic growth (Schweitzer, 1997). In 1994, Congress responded to manufacturer complaints about excessive FDA review times by passing the Prescription Drug User Fee Act. The act authorized the FDA to collect fees from the companies submitting applications and hire more reviewers, improve computer support, and reduce review time. As a result of these measures, FDA review time fell and Congress has continued to reauthorize the collection of user fees.

In the case of the FDA, the role of government involves maintaining a delicate balance between safety and access to potentially beneficial treatments. Criticism of the process is frequent and inevitable from those with competing interests.

National Institutes of Health

The National Institutes of Health (NIH) comprises 27 health institutes and centers that support some 38,000 medical and social science research projects nationwide. In addition, a large research and treatment program is under way at NIH headquarters in Bethesda, Maryland.

Government involvement is particularly critical for the support of health research in cases where economic incentives are lacking or risky. For example, drugs to treat conditions that are poorly understood or that affect small numbers of people have limited appeal to commercial firms. NIH also funds basic research where the commercial application of knowledge to be gained is unclear, uncertain, or unlikely in the short term (Koop et al., 2002).

The National Library of Medicine is a part of the NIH. The National Library of Medicine is the world's largest medical library. Internet access and services like PubMed provide worldwide access to peer-reviewed literature.

Agency for Healthcare Research and Quality

The mission of the Agency for Healthcare Research and Quality is the creation and dissemination of knowledge that enhances the quality, appropriateness, and effectiveness of health services and access to services. The Agency for Healthcare Research and Quality supports researchers who study the organization, financing, delivery, quality assessment, and improvement of the health delivery system through basic research, evaluation studies, and demonstration projects.

Centers for Disease Control and Prevention

The Centers for Disease Control and Prevention (CDC) works to prevent and control infectious and chronic diseases, injuries, workplace hazards, disabilities, and environmental health threats. It sets national health status goals through its *Healthy People* program and maintains the National Center for Health Statistics from its headquarters in Atlanta, Georgia. Centers for Disease Control and Prevention personnel are stationed in more than 25 different countries.

The Agency for Toxic Substances and Disease Registry is closely affiliated with the Centers for Disease Control and Prevention. The Agency for Toxic Substances and Disease Registry coordinates programs that aim to prevent exposure to hazardous substances and conducts public health assessments, studies, and surveillance for persons who are exposed to hazardous materials. The agency maintains exposure and disease registries for study and long-term follow-up.

Office of the Assistant Secretary for Planning and Evaluation

The Office of the Assistant Secretary for Planning and Evaluation has an important role in health policy formation within DHHS. This office advises department agencies on policy needs in health, disability, human services, and science. The Office of the Assistant Secretary for Planning and Evaluation coordinates the evaluation, research, and demonstration activities of DHHS; it also directly performs some studies and leads other demonstration projects. The Office of the Assistant Secretary for Planning and Evaluation staff manages strategic planning, legislative planning, and review of regulations, including policy analyses and cost-benefit evaluations of policy options.

Substance Abuse and Mental Health Services Administration

The Substance Abuse and Mental Health Services Administration gathers and disseminates information on health problems related to the use and abuse of drugs and alcohol and the mental health condition of the U.S. population. The Substance Abuse and Mental Health Services Administration's work is conducted primarily through block grants to states, which then direct the distribution of funds for substance abuse and mental health services at the local level.

Administration on Aging

The Administration on Aging works to provide services that enable elders to live independently—especially those who are disadvantaged. The Administration on Aging network provides home-delivered meals, preventive healthcare services, transportation to medical appointments and shopping, personal care services, adult day care, and caregiver support. In addition, Administration on Aging provides health insurance and pension counselors and ombudsmen to serve older persons in long-term care institutions.

Other Executive Agencies

DHHS is, by far, the largest of the federal departments concerned with the U.S. healthcare system. Nevertheless, other cabinet-level departments and agencies play a role in the provision of health care and protection of national resources that are essential to the health of the nation. Because health matters are so pervasive, some degree of overlap is inevitable among government functions.

Oversight and Advisory Bodies

Congressional Committees

After Congress enacts a law and the president signs it, one of the executive agencies promulgates regulations to implement the law and then enforces both the law and its corresponding regulations. However, Congress does provide oversight in the implementation of laws ensuring consistency with its intent. Responsibility is assigned to the committee that has jurisdiction over the policy area and to specific oversight committees or subcommittees. Congressional staff members may undertake investigations, subpoena witnesses, and conduct hearings to document these activities.

Government Accountability Office

The Government Accountability Office is the investigative arm of Congress. Government Accountability Office staff evaluates federal programs and activities, examines the use of public funds, and provides the office's analyses, options, and recommendations to Congress. The Government Accountability Office issues public reports of their investigations and frequently testifies before Congress.

Office of the Inspector General

The Office of the Inspector General within the DHHS reports to both the secretary of the DHHS and Congress about program and management problems, and makes recommendations for improvements. Office of Inspector General staff conducts nationwide audits, investigations, inspections, and other project-specific strategies.

STATE GOVERNMENTS

Although the federal government is the primary payer for Medicaid, states share costs and the administration of the program. Medicaid represents a substantial and ever-increasing portion of individual state budgets (see Chapter 18). In addition to Medicaid, state and local governments administer a small number of programs that provide direct care for persons who do not qualify for any of the federal healthcare programs. State services frequently include hospitals for the mentally ill and developmentally disabled, general hospitals operated by county and municipal governments, community health centers, and health departments. In recent years, states have taken on an important role in experimenting with innovative health reform strategies in an effort to ensure availability of healthcare services to the uninsured.

Although each state establishes its own organizational structure for carrying out its responsibilities for healthcare delivery systems, programs and services are similar across states. Two important functions of state governments are (1) professional regulation and licensure, and (2) regulation of the health insurance industry.

Professional Regulation and Licensure

Each state has boards that administer a licensure system responsible for controlling entry into the medical professions. Licensure statutes date back to the late 19th century, when allopathic physicians established their control over medical practice. Most state boards of pharmacy were instituted a few years later. Many other health professions achieved license status during the 20th century. Initially, the boards were constituted solely of members of the regulated profession, but today many state boards include consumer members. State boards are subject to legislative oversight.

Licensure assures that applicants to a profession have completed basic educational requirements and demonstrated knowledge by examination. Licensure boards do little at present to assure continuing competency. Instead, they act in response to complaints of incompetence or unprofessional or unethical conduct. The boards take disciplinary action when allegations are substantiated. The most common disciplinary power is the power to revoke or suspend licenses (Jost, 2003).

Most states also license healthcare institutions. However, institutions may be exempt from further state inspection if they are accorded accreditation status from a private agency. Because many hospitals are accredited by a private, nonprofit agency (e.g., the Joint Commission), state licensure plays a secondary role in this area (Pawlson & O'Kane, 2002).

Health Insurance

Employers provide health insurance benefits for the majority of Americans. The federal Employee Benefits Security Administration within the Department of Labor is charged with protecting the integrity of health plans, pensions, and other employee benefits by assisting employers in understanding and meeting their legal responsibilities, and providing workers with information about their benefit rights. State governments operate offices that respond to threats on workers' benefits and encourage sound benefits programs.

Through a state commissioner of insurance or similar agency, states monitor health insurance companies, their organizations, marketing practices, and the products they sell. States require insurance companies to establish capitalization and financial reserves to meet their obligations to the insured. State regulations control the marketing and enrollment activities of insurance companies and the establishment of insurance rates. States often mandate that health insurance plans cover specific medical services, such as treatment for alcohol abuse, mental health services, preventive care, and diagnostic services. Finally, states support the rights of consumers to file malpractice claims or other actions that hold insurers and contracted providers accountable for quality care.

Workers' Compensation Funds

Although U.S. workers generally rely on their employers as a source of healthcare insurance, injuries and illnesses that occur in the workplace or are related to workers' employment or occupation are traditionally considered a separate responsibility of industry. An employer is held financially responsible for the treatment of injury or illness regardless of how fault is assigned. Workers' compensation funds are used primarily as a method to provide payment for medical treatment. There are also provisions for cash payments to replace lost wages, provide benefits to survivors in the event of an employee's death, and compensate workers who are disabled and unable to return to work.

Employers are required by law to fully fund workers' compensation insurance. Employees have no responsibilities for sharing the costs. The federal government operates separate compensation programs for coal miners and for railroad workers who suffer injuries linked to these particular occupations. All other workers' compensation programs are operated by the states and vary considerably in terms of the financing mechanisms and levels of benefits they deliver. Depending on the state, the employer may self-insure by creating its own workers' compensation fund, purchase private insurance to cover workers' claims, contribute to a fund established and maintained by the state for this purpose, or participate in some combination of these mechanisms.

Other State Programs

Other activities under state control ensure the public health by taking the following steps:

- Monitoring the environment, the workplace, and establishments that provide food services
- Providing or supporting disease prevention activities that include nutritional services, school health, and campaigns to promote healthy behavior regarding tobacco use and traffic safety, and communicable disease control
- Supporting public health nursing services, including family planning and prenatal care

Although a state may organize and coordinate these services, their delivery is often the responsibility of the local government.

LOCAL GOVERNMENTS

National health policy identifies the range of health, morbidity, disability, and mortality issues it intends to address as well as the relevant settings covered by the policy and the framework for implementing it—for example, health services, social services, the education sector, and the workplace. The individual states have their own priorities and create political subunits to make both the national and state services available to the residents of a particular jurisdiction. Good public policy at the national level specifies the desired goals and the adverse events it intends to minimize, but this merely sets the agenda for planning and delivery of care at a local level (Jenkins, 2001).

The most significant role for local government in the past century centered on the following three activities: (1) assessing the health needs of the community; (2) devising policies to address those needs; and (3) providing primary and preventive care to all persons without alternative resources. Local emergency situations, including both natural and human-made disasters, also rely on properly trained healthcare personnel and readily available healthcare services to meet the immediate needs of citizens. In addition, many localities provide emergency transportation by ambulance as a complement to local fire and rescue services.

Local health department officials are responsible for collecting data on the frequency, trends, and patterns of disease and for maintaining general public health functions such as testing and regulating water quality. They enforce local health codes for sanitation and food safety, implement health education campaigns, and supply population-based preventive care through immunization campaigns, mosquito control programs, and routine healthcare services for children.

WHAT SHOULD BE THE ROLE OF GOVERNMENT IN HEALTH CARE?

This chapter describes the role that government plays in the U.S. healthcare system. It takes the perspective that the U.S. Constitution is the definitive statement of principles on which the government acts. Other texts are devoted to discussions about what the role of government *ought to be.* The basis for a difference of opinions about the appropriate role of government rests on other sets of principles.

A common approach looks to the principles of economics and takes the stance that markets functioning with little or no government interference will assure the most productive use of societal resources. Those who disagree with this perspective may believe that health care lacks many of the characteristics of a competitive market and that government intervention is necessary (see Chapter 14 for more details.) Others may support government intervention for other reasons. For example, markets may assure the efficient allocation of resources but not achieve the goal of social justice.

One's beliefs about the proper role of government are connected to political ideology (Jost, Federico, & Napier, 2009). Conservative governments tend to favor free-market principles and limit the role of government in regulation. The more liberal a government's policies, the more inclined it is for governmental regulation. Much of the public attention on political ideology in the United States focuses on the difference between Democrats and Republicans and the beliefs they espouse.

For example, during the healthcare reform debates of 2009–2010, President Barack Obama and Democratic leaders in Congress believed that it was the responsibility of government to ensure that every American had access to health care—that is, pursuit of the goal of social justice (Gostin & Powers, 2006). Republicans in Congress worked for healthcare reform, but they believed that more moderate steps, such as allowing people to invest in health savings accounts, would achieve allocative efficiency and would be more fiscally prudent for the U.S. treasury.

One of the most poignant ideologic rifts between Democrats and Republicans over health reform options was universal insurance coverage. The Democrats proposed banning insurance companies from denying coverage, while Republicans preferred to provide money to assist uninsured individuals in obtaining coverage (Murray & Bacon, 2010). In the end the Democrats, with majorities in both houses of Congress, prevailed. Their version of healthcare reform was signed into law by President Obama.

The dominant political ideology provides only a general guide to government policies, however. Elections, interest groups, grassroots efforts, and other forces can compel governments to adopt policies that might be viewed as contrary to the fundamental ideology of the party in power. In 2003, President George W. Bush, a Republican, led a revision of Medicare that included the Part D drug benefit, which was the largest expansion of government healthcare since Medicare was first introduced in 1965. By increasing drug benefits for seniors, who vote in larger percentages than other age groups, Republicans were able to deflect charges that they were unfriendly to Medicare during the 2004 election year (Inglehart, 2004).

CONCLUSION

The government's role in health care in the United States is very different from that of other developed nations; nevertheless, it is extensive. Federal, state, and local governments in the United States serve as providers, financers, and regulators of healthcare services, information, and research. While the federal government's role as a provider of health care is much more limited than that of national governments in other countries, it does provide healthcare services through the Department of Defense, Department of Veterans Affairs, and the Indian Health Service.

Rather than providing direct services, the U.S. federal government is more involved in financing healthcare services through programs such as Medicare and Medicaid, and research and information services through the NIH, the Agency for Healthcare Research and Quality, the Health Resources and Services Administration, and other programs. The federal government, through administrative agencies such as the FDA, the Centers for Disease Control and Prevention, and the Centers for Medicare and Medicaid Services, provides regulation and oversight of health care.

State and local governments also fulfill important roles, sometimes in collaboration with the federal government and sometimes independently. States collaborate with the federal government by administering and partially funding Medicaid. Independent functions include licensure of healthcare professionals and institutions, regulation of the health insurance industry, protection of public health, and other programs. State governments directly provide healthcare services through state hospitals for specific purposes such as mental illness and mental retardation. Local governments provide care through county and city hospitals and health clinics.

The extent of the government's role in health care has always been a matter of controversy. Government success in matters of public policy depends on having a well-defined problem, workable solutions, and a clear direction for developing effective interventions. All three criteria for success require clear consensus. Even when there is a clear mandate and correct decisions are made, circumstances may change over time. Changes that are biologic, cultural, demographic, ecologic, economic, ethical, legal, psychologic, social, and technologic in nature make laws and regulations outdated. Indeed, the rise of obesity as a major health concern has already driven political pundits to speculate that obesity may replace tobacco as a target of government action (Gostin, 2007; Klein & Dietz, 2010). There is an unrelenting pressure to modify policies and programs.

QUESTIONS FOR FURTHER DISCUSSION

1. Does form follow function in the government's organization of its healthcare activities? That is, are U.S. government agencies organized around healthcare activities that have similar functions, similar resource needs, or overlapping jurisdictions? What are the advantages and disadvantages of this organizational structure?

2. Imagine that scientists discover a vaccine for HIV.
   a. What government activities do you think would be involved in public immunization programs?
   b. What issues might the government face in an effort to establish public policy in this area? Which stakeholders and special-interest groups are apt to be involved in the debate?

3. Should the federal government regulate the prices of drugs? If the government were to set prices for drugs, what changes could occur in the market for pharmaceuticals in the United States?

4. What are the advantages and disadvantages of having different roles and responsibilities for federal, state, and local governments with regard to health care?

5. Liberal and conservative perspectives are the dominant political ideologies in the United States. What differences in beliefs and attitudes are held by each regarding justice, fairness, citizens' rights, and responsibilities?

KEY TOPICS AND TERMS

Administration on Aging
Administrative agencies
Agency for Healthcare Research and Quality
Centers for Disease Control and Prevention
Centers for Medicare and Medicaid Services
Commissioner of insurance
Congressional Budget Office
Department of Health and Human Services (DHHS)
Food and Drug Administration (FDA)
Government Accountability Office
Human trials—Phases I, II, III, and IV
Indian Health Service
Investigational new drug
Medicaid
Medicare
National Institutes of Health (NIH)
National Library of Medicine
New drug application (NDA)
Office of the Inspector General
Preclinical testing phase
TriCare
Veterans Administration
Workers' compensation

REFERENCES

Abraham, J., & Sheppard, J. (1999). Complacent and conflicting scientific expertise in British and American drug regulation: Clinical risk assessment of triazolam. *Social Studies of Science, 29*(6), 803–843.

Bayer, R. (2002). Tobacco, commercial speech, and libertarian values: The end of the line for restrictions on advertising? *American Journal of Public Health 92,* 356–359.

Bayer, R., & Colgrove J. (2002). Bioterrorism, public health, and the law. *Health Affairs, 21*(6), 98–101.

Bayer, R., & Colgrove, J. (2004). Children and bystanders first: The ethics and politics of tobacco control in the United States. In E. A. Feldman & R. Bayer (Eds.), *Unfiltered: Conflicts over tobacco policy and public health* (pp. 8–26). Cambridge, MA: Harvard University Press.

Bayer, R., & Fairchild, A. L. (2004). The genesis of public health ethics. *Bioethics, 18*(6), 473–492.

Epstein, R. A. (2003). Let the shoemaker stick to his last: A defense of the "old" public health. *Perspectives in Biology and Medicine, 46*(3 suppl), S138–S159.

Feldman, E. A. & Bayer, R. (2004). Introduction. In E. A. Feldman & R. Bayer (Eds.), *Unfiltered: Conflicts over tobacco policy and public health* (pp. 1–7). Cambridge, MA: Harvard University Press.

Gostin, L. O. (2000a). Public health law in a new century. Part I: Law as a tool to advance the community's health. *Journal of the American Medical Association, 283,* 2837–2841.

Gostin, L. O. (2000b). Public health law in a new century. Part III: Public health regulation: A systematic evaluation. *Journal of the American Medical Association, 283,* 3118–3122.

Gostin, L. O. (2001). Public health theory and practice in the constitutional design. *Health Matrix, 11*(2), 265–326.

Gostin, L. O. (2007). Law as a tool to facilitate healthier lifestyles and prevent obesity. *Journal of the American Medical Association, 297,* 87–90.

Gostin, L. O. (2009). FDA regulation of tobacco. Politics, law, and the public's health. *Journal of the American Medical Association, 302,* 1459–1460.

Gostin, L. O., & Blochet, M. G. (2003). The politics of public health. A response to Epstein. *Perspectives in Biology and Medicine, 46,* S160–S211.

Gostin, L. O., & Powers, M. (2006). What does social justice require for the public's health? Public health ethics and policy imperatives. *Health Affairs, 25,* 1053–1060.

Hall, M. A. (2003). The scope and limits of public health law. *Perspectives in Biology and Medicine, 46*(3 suppl), S199–S209.

Inglehart, J. K. (2004). The new Medicare prescription-drug benefit—A pure power play. *The New England Journal of Medicine, 350*(5), 826–833.

Jenkins, R. (2001). Making psychiatric epidemiology useful: The contribution of epidemiology to government policy. *Acta Psychiatrica Scandanavica, 103,* 2–14.

Jost, J. T., Federico, C. M., & Napier, J. L. (2009). Political ideology: Its structure, functions, and elective affinities. *Annual Review of Psychology, 60,* 307–337.

Jost, T. S. (2003). Legal issues in quality of care oversight in the United States: Recent developments. *European Journal of Health Law, 10,* 11–25.

Kaiser Family Foundation. (n.d.) Military and Veterans' Healthcare. Background Brief. Retrieved from http://www.kaiseredu.org/Issue-Modules/Military-and-Veterans-Health-Care/Background-Brief.aspx

Kaiser Family Foundation. (2010, May). *Prescription drug trends.* Retrieved from http://www.kff.org/rxdrugs/upload/3057-08.pdf

Keough, C. L., & Greene, A. (2003). Judicial review of CMS policies: An evolving doctrine. *Healthcare Financial Management, 57*(2), 76–80.

Klein, J. D., & Dietz, W. (2010). Childhood obesity: The new tobacco. *Health Affairs 29,* 388–392.

Koop, C. E., Pearson, C. E., & Schwarz, M. R. (2002). *Critical issues in global health.* San Francisco, CA: Jossey-Bass.

Litman, T. J., & Robins, L. S. (1997). *Health politics and policy* (3rd ed.). Albany, NY: Delmar.

Longest, B. B., Jr. (2002). *Health policymaking in the United States* (3rd ed.). Chicago, IL: Health Administration Press.

Murray, S., & Bacon, P., Jr. (2010). GOP plans own pitch for health summit: Delegation prepares a high-stakes challenge to Obama's proposal. *The Washington Post,* p. A04.

Novick, L. E., & Mays, G. P. (2001). *Public health administration: Principles for population-based management.* Gaithersburg, MD: Aspen.

Pawlson, L. G., & O'Kane, M. E. (2002). Professionalism, regulation, and the market: Impact on accountability for quality of care. *Health Affairs, 21*(3), 200–207.

Roth, A. L., Dunsby, J., & Bero, L. A. (2003). Framing processes in public commentary on U.S. federal tobacco control regulation. *Social Studies of Science, 33*(1), 7–44.

Schweitzer, S. O. (1997). *Pharmaceutical economics and policy.* New York, NY: Oxford University Press.

Turnock, B. J. (2001). *Public health: What it is and how it works* (2nd ed.). Gaithersburg, MD: Aspen.

U.S. Census Bureau. (n.d.). National Health Expenditures—Summary, 1960 to 2007, and Projections, 2008 to 2018. Retrieved from http://www.census.gov/compendia/statab/2010/tables/10s0127.pdf

U.S. Census Bureau. (2010). *Government employees & payroll.* Retrieved from http://www.census.gov/govs/

U.S. Department of Veterans Affairs. (2011a). About VA—History. Retrieved from http://www.va.gov/about_va/vahistory.asp

U.S. Department of Veterans Affairs. (2011b). National Center for Veterans Analysis and Statistics. Retrieved from http://www.va.gov/VETDATA/Utilization.asp

CHAPTER

17

Managed Health Care

Kenneth W. Schafermeyer and Brenda R. Motheral*

Case Scenario

Viagra, which was approved by the Food and Drug Administration in early 1998, is indicated for the treatment of erectile dysfunction but may also improve healthy men's sexual performance. Initial sales of this drug were staggering, with doctors writing as many as 40,000 prescriptions per day (Gillis, 1998b). With such prescription volume, Viagra was on pace to become the best-selling drug in history. Urologists established waiting lists for men seeking appointments that would lead to prescriptions. At a Georgetown University clinic, the phone system was modified to "press 3 for Viagra," creating a waiting list of more than 300 (Gillis, 1998a).

The controversy surrounding insurance coverage of Viagra transcends private and public healthcare institutions. In July 1998, the U.S. Department of Health and Human Services notified state Medicaid agencies that they had to cover Viagra if their Medicaid programs covered prescription medications. The director of the American Public Welfare Association argued that Viagra, at $10 per tablet, would add $100 million to $200 million to Medicaid expenses across the country and that to insist on coverage without consultation with the states was unacceptable (Goldstein, 1998). The head of the Health Care Financing Administration responded that a 1990 law mandates coverage of any prescription drug that has been approved by the Food and Drug Administration with few exceptions, which include diet pills, smoking cessation products, and fertility treatments.

Suppose you work for a pharmacy benefit manager and clients are asking about your company's recommendation concerning Viagra coverage. What are the key ethical, political, clinical, financial, and equity issues to consider in deciding whether to cover Viagra? What is your recommendation and why?

How would your recommendation change, if at all, if the client already covers other impotence medications? What if the client currently does not cover oral contraceptives or infertility medications?

One client has decided to cover Viagra but has indicated that it does not want the drug's utilization, and hence its costs, to skyrocket out of control. What are your recommendations in regard to plan design for Viagra (e.g., prior authorization, quantity limits, and cost-sharing levels)?

*The authors wish to express appreciation to Evan S. Schnur for his assistance gathering information for this chapter.

LEARNING OBJECTIVES

Upon completion of this chapter, the student shall be able to:

• Describe the objectives of managed health care (i.e., access, quality, and cost)
• Differentiate between insuring health and managing health care
• Differentiate between retrospective and prospective payment for services
• Compare and contrast fee-for-service and capitation reimbursement
• Describe and differentiate among the major types of managed care organizations (MCOs)
• Describe the market power of managed care organizations
• List the functions of a pharmacy benefit manager
• Describe MCO tools used to control costs and enhance quality
• Describe the impact of managed care on pharmacy
• Suggest approaches for pharmacists to work successfully with MCOs
• Define third-party and managed care terminology
• Define the organization and method used to accredit MCOs

CHAPTER QUESTIONS

1. What factors have encouraged or hindered the growth of managed care?
2. How do staff-, group-, network-, and independent practice association–model health maintenance organizations (HMOs) differ?
3. Since 1980, what have the enrollment trends been for the four basic types of HMOs?
4. What are the characteristics of the four major tools used to manage the pharmacy benefit?
5. What measures are considered in National Committee for Quality Assurance accreditation?

INTRODUCTION

Managed care has profoundly affected the way in which medical care is delivered, consumed, and perceived. While there is no universally accepted definition of managed care, most would agree that any movement away from strict payment of services and toward governing of the provision of medical services is a form of managed care. Managed care organizations (MCOs) provide healthcare services, including prescriptions, to defined populations such as employer groups on a prepaid basis. Because MCOs assume financial risk for expenditures, they have strong incentives to control costs and utilization of healthcare services. A major challenge facing MCOs continues to be the need to balance advocacy for patient care against the efficient allocation of scarce resources.

THE HISTORY OF MANAGED CARE

Managed care's roots can be traced to the lodges, fraternal orders, and benevolent societies established in the 1800s by European immigrants to care for their sick and disabled. The first organized health delivery services were offered to recruit employees to work in isolated areas such as pineapple plantations in Hawaii, lumber camps in Michigan, iron ranges in northern Minnesota, and railroads in isolated pockets across the country. Physicians were usually on contract or salary because the best way to recruit physicians was to provide them with a guaranteed income. Hospital beds were either owned or under contract (Friedman, 1996).

The American Medical Association (AMA) did not object to these plans in the rural areas, considering them an economic necessity. However, the AMA continued to object to any other form of organized medicine that involved a third-party intermediary (Jecker, 1994). By the 1920s, the AMA had established the solo practitioner with a fee-for-service (FFS) reimbursement (where a fee was paid for each service performed) as the predominant model of medical practice (Miller & Luft, 1994). Despite the AMA's opposition, numerous state courts ruled that medical societies could not take actions against physicians who participated in prepaid plans (plans in which patients paid in advance of receiving service for the cost of predetermined benefits) (Jecker, 1994).

The availability of prepaid plans expanded during World War II. Many of the plans formed during that era still exist today (such as Group Health Cooperative of Puget Sound and Kaiser Permanente), but in the early years they generally had some advantage that allowed them to survive in the antimanaged care environment that prevailed at the time (Miller & Luft, 1994).

Perhaps the most famous MCO was, and is, Kaiser Permanente. Henry J. Kaiser, an industrial contractor, called upon Dr. Sidney Garfield to develop a system for providing medical care to his 15,000 workers and dependents who were building the Grand Coulee Dam in Washington. The Kaiser Company financed everything from hospital equipment to nurses and staff for outpatient clinics, thereby creating an entire medical delivery system. Kaiser covered workers' industrial injuries and illnesses, and employees had the option of contributing 50 cents per week for themselves, 50 cents per week for each adult dependent, and 25 cents per week for each child to cover nonindustrial injuries and illnesses (Campbell & Newsome, 1995).

The passage in 1973 of the Health Maintenance Organization Act was a major catalyst in the growth of managed care (Davis, Collins, & Morris, 1994). The legislation supported start-up grants and loans for health maintenance organizations (HMOs), a type of MCO, and required employers with 25 or more employees to provide HMO enrollment as an alternative to traditional indemnity insurance for their employees where it was available (see Chapter 15 for a description of indemnity insurance). These factors, taken collectively, had a tremendous effect on the growth of managed care. In 1970, there were 3 million enrollees in HMOs; in 1980, there were 9 million HMO members (Miller & Luft, 1994). In 1989, HMO enrollment had grown to 35 million enrollees; by 1998, the number had tripled to 105.3 million participants (Hoechst Marion Roussel, 1999). Since the early 2000s, HMO popularity has declined significantly. In 2008 there were only 77 million Americans enrolled in HMO plans (Sanofi-Aventis, 2010). This decline may be a reflection of employers' growing inability to afford the state-mandated comprehensive healthcare benefits that are typical of HMO offerings. While employers still use many of the principles and tools conceived in early managed care, they have more flexibility in cost sharing and service coverage by steering away from the heavily regulated HMO offerings with higher premiums.

TYPES OF MANAGED CARE ORGANIZATIONS

While the term *managed care* can be defined in many ways and is constantly evolving to meet the demands of the healthcare market, the differentiating feature of managed care relative to FFS plans is the use of provider networks (Miller & Luft, 1994). A network is a defined group of providers, typically linked through contractual arrangements, who supply a full range of primary and acute healthcare services (Medicom International, n.d.). Managed care enrollees who use providers outside the network may receive reduced coverage or even no coverage. Four characteristics differentiate the various managed care plans (see **Table 17-1**):

- *Risk bearing* refers to the amount of risk borne by the providers, which can range from full risk to no risk.
- *Physician type* refers to the relationship between the MCO and the physician(s).
- *Relationship exclusivity* addresses whether the physician provides care to patients from one MCO only or to patients from multiple MCOs.
- *Out-of-network coverage* identifies whether care received from a provider who is not in the MCO's network is a covered benefit. Types of MCOs are discussed below in terms of these distinguishing characteristics (see Miller & Luft, 1994, for a thorough discussion).

Health Maintenance Organizations

The distinguishing characteristics of HMOs are that they place providers at risk, either directly or indirectly, and generally do not provide coverage for medical care that is received out of network. The risk arrangement can take many forms. In capitation, costs of care for a given population are estimated for some time span (typically 1 year),

Table 17-1 Characteristics of Managed Care Plans

Type	Physician risk bearing	Physician type	Exclusivity of relationship with physician	Out-of-network coverage
HMO				
Staff	No	Staff	Yes	No
Group	Yes	Large group	Yes	No
Network	Yes	Large group	No	No
IPA	Yes	Solo/small group	No	No
PPO	No	Solo or group	No	Yes
EPO	No	Solo or group	No	No
POS	Varies	Varies	Varies	Yes

HMO—health maintenance organization
IPA—independent practice association
PPO—preferred provider organization
EPO—exclusive provider organization
POS—point of service

Source: Adapted and reprinted with permission from the *Annual Review of Public Health,* Volume 15, copyright 1994, by Annual Reviews, Inc., www.annualreviews.org.

and physicians are prospectively paid this set amount of money to provide agreed-upon services (Rognehaugh, 1996). The provider keeps the capitation payment, regardless of whether a patient actually receives any services during the year. The provider is, however, obligated to provide any services—no matter how many—needed by the patient. Thus the physician is taking the risk that the capitation rate will be sufficient to cover all the costs of care for the population. In this way, the provider assumes risk that traditionally was underwritten by the insurance company.

Risk pools, in which a portion of payments for services rendered (i.e., a withhold) is placed in a pool as a source for any subsequent claims that exceed projections (Rognehaugh, 1996), have been implemented for hospitals and other high-risk services. In these schemes, the physician and the HMO share the surplus or loss from the risk pool at the end of the year (Mack, 1993). The use of this strategy peaked in 2003 with 32.1% of plans using risk pools, then the usage rate declined until 2007, with a slight increase in 2008 to 29.9% (Sanofi-Aventis, 2009).

The gatekeeper is a central component of most HMOs. Gatekeepers, who are typically primary care physicians, must coordinate and authorize all medical services, including laboratory services, specialty referrals, and hospitalizations (Medicom International, n.d.). In many gatekeeper systems, a patient must receive a referral from his or her primary care physician to receive coverage for a specialist's care. The rationale behind this approach is that it avoids unnecessary and often expensive referrals to specialists. The gatekeeper may be financially at risk—not only for the services that he or she provides, but also for the medical services provided by specialists to whom a patient is referred.

Traditionally, HMOs were classified into four major types:

1. *Staff-model HMO:* a type of HMO characterized by direct ownership of healthcare facilities and direct employment physicians. Physicians in a staff-model HMO typically bear no direct risk, but the HMO can influence the care given by the physicians through utilization review (the review of the necessity and efficiency of patients' utilization patterns). In addition, because the HMO pays most or all of the physicians' salaries, these providers risk termination of their contracts if their treatment patterns do not meet administrators' expectations.
2. *Group-model HMO:* a type of HMO characterized by contracts with large, multispecialty medical groups offering services exclusively to the HMO on a capitated basis.
3. *Network-model HMO:* a type of HMO characterized by nonexclusive contracts with large medical groups. While networks typically bear risk, the nonexclusivity of the arrangement reduces the influence of the risk on the physician's behavior.
4. *Independent practice association (IPA)-model HMO:* a type of HMO in which physicians form a separate legal entity, usually a corporation or partnership, that then contracts with the MCO. The IPA usually shares risk with the MCO, and then individual providers are paid by the IPA for services provided to enrolled patients for a negotiated fee. The IPA may reimburse physicians on a discounted FFS basis or may share some risk with them. These physicians typically maintain their own private practices and are allowed to provide services to patients enrolled in other MCOs.

While these four models represent the traditional categories into which HMOs are classified, recent innovations in plan designs have blurred the distinctions among these models. Plans can have elements of two or more of these categories and, therefore, be difficult to classify as fitting into any single model.

Preferred Provider Organizations

Preferred provider organizations (PPOs) are affiliations of providers that seek contracts with insurance plans. The physicians are usually from solo or small-group practices and have nonexclusive arrangements with the PPO. Under a PPO plan, individuals are free to see any provider they choose but have a financial incentive (i.e., lower out-of-pocket expenses) to receive care from providers in the preferred network. PPOs generally do not capitate physicians who are members of their network. Rather, physicians accept discounted FFS payment in exchange for increased patient volume and a quick turnaround on claims payment. Because physicians bear no risk, plan administrators emphasize fee reduction and case-by-case utilization management to control costs. PPOs have proved more popular than HMOs with sponsors, providers, and patients because they are perceived to be less restrictive, with enrollment at nearly 150 million people in 2008 (Sanofi-Aventis, 2009). Nevertheless, the number of operating PPO plans has decreased each year since 1998 (Sanofi-Aventis, 2009).

Hybrid Plans and Categorical Limitations

Many plans combine two or more of the previously described organizational models and, accordingly, are referred to as hybrid plans. An example of a hybrid plan is a point-of-service (POS) plan. POS plans allow patients to select providers at the time a service is needed rather than when they join the plan. As with PPOs, when care is received from a provider outside the network, partial coverage is provided. As with HMOs, physicians may be at risk or contract exclusively with the plan.

With the rapidly changing healthcare market, the categorization of the various types of MCOs can become quickly outdated. As HMOs provide more diversified products, the lines of distinction become blurred. For example, mixed-model HMOs, which contract with more than one type of physician organization, are becoming more prevalent as the arrangements among the organizations grow increasingly complex (Miller & Luft, 1994).

Growth and Composition of Managed Care Plans

Early on, managed care plans were predominantly not-for-profit, operating as either staff- or group-model HMOs. IPAs and network-model HMOs appeared in the 1950s in response to physicians' feeling threatened by the staff and group models (Davis et al., 1994). Since then, growth in this market has been greatest in IPA models and slowest in staff and group models. In recent years, however, both the number of HMOs and HMO enrollment have declined. For example, in 1998, there were 902 HMOs licensed in the United States; by 2008, the number dropped to 440. Although IPAs are still the predominant HMO model—accounting for 54% of all HMOs in 2008—the number of plans declined from 606 in 1998 to 238 in 2008 (Aventis, 2002; Sanofi-Aventis, 2009). Group and staff models remain the least popular options, accounting for 8% and 3% of all HMOs in 2008, respectively (Sanofi-Aventis, 2009).

In 2001, 31.7% of the U.S. population was enrolled in some kind of HMO; by 2008, that percentage had dropped to 25.4%. There were, however, some significant regional differences in acceptance of HMOs. The highest enrollment is in California and Hawaii;

in both states, more than 40% of patients belong to an HMO. By contrast, the following 10 states posted HMO penetration rates of less than 10%: Alabama, Alaska, Arkansas, Idaho, Mississippi, Montana, North Dakota, South Carolina, South Dakota, and Wyoming (Aventis, 2002; Sanofi-Aventis, 2009).

Managed health care continues to evolve rapidly. While HMO enrollment has declined in recent years, enrollment in other types of MCOs has increased. Managed health care has also shifted from being predominantly a not-for-profit industry to a for-profit sector (Davis et al., 1994). Concurrently, there has been a marked expansion of managed care to the Medicaid and Medicare populations.

MANAGING THE PHARMACY BENEFIT

Much emphasis is placed on managing the pharmacy benefit in MCOs, given the large expenditure growth in this sector over the last fifteen years. Companies that manage the pharmacy benefit may offer performance guarantees. If they do not achieve a certain level of performance, they are subject to financial penalties. Performance guarantees can relate to cost savings (e.g., generic substitution rates), customer service (e.g., wait time on calls to customer service), or client reporting (Lipton, Kreling, Collins, & Hertz, 1999).

Pharmacies are rarely reimbursed on a capitation basis because it is physicians—not pharmacists—who have the greatest influence over prescription utilization and costs. Physicians, therefore, are more likely to be held responsible for prescription costs. An effective way to influence prescribing practices is to give physicians financial incentives to control drug costs. Traditionally, these incentives took the form of performance bonuses or withholds and risk pools. While physicians are most commonly reimbursed retrospectively on a discounted fee-for-service basis, prospective payment methods that encourage cost control (e.g., capitation) are gaining more acceptance among PPOs (Sanofi-Aventis, 2010).

Because managed care prescription programs reimburse pharmacies on an FFS basis, health plans' cost-containment efforts are directed to the following three types of costs incurred whenever a prescription is dispensed:

1. *Unit cost,* which refers to the amount paid for each prescription, consists of reimbursement for drug ingredient costs and a dispensing fee.
2. *Utilization rate,* which refers to the number of prescriptions dispensed per patient.
3. *Administrative costs,* which are the charges for processing a claim and managing the prescription benefit program. These costs are greatly reduced by having pharmacies submit claims for reimbursement electronically, thereby eliminating most, if not all, paperwork. While administrative costs are commonly paid on a per-claim-processed basis, some are paid on a per-enrollee basis.

Pharmacy Benefit Managers

In 2008, approximately 88% of retail prescription claims were paid for by a third party rather than by individual patients (West, 2009). Most often, the payer was a specialized organization known as a pharmacy benefit manager (PBM). Even the largest managed care organizations commonly outsource management of the pharmacy benefit to a PBM. As explained in Chapter 15, PBMs administer the prescription drug part of health insurance plans on behalf of plan sponsors, which could be HMOs, self-insured employers, PPOs, or indemnity insurers.

While not always considered a type of MCO, PBMs have many of the characteristics of managed care, including having a provider network of pharmacies. Typically, PBMs contract with existing community pharmacies to create a network of pharmacies from which patients can receive prescriptions at the rate established by the plan sponsor. PBMs negotiate with network pharmacies for decreased product reimbursement prices in exchange for an increased volume of prescriptions to be dispensed through their pharmacies.

Because the administration of pharmacy programs is rather complex and requires a claims-processing system and large prescription volume to be handled efficiently, PBMs typically can offer lower costs and patient access to a greater number of pharmacies than can an individual plan sponsor. Services offered by most PBMs include pharmacy network development, claims processing, eligibility maintenance, client reporting, rebate contracting, generic use programs, formulary management, therapeutic interchange, mail service, drug utilization review (DUR), patient and provider education, step therapy, and medication adherence programs. The following sections describe some of these tools.

Limited Networks

As previously mentioned, PBMs contract with community pharmacies to create a network of pharmacies from which patients can receive prescriptions. In selecting a network, considerations include location, cost, and quality, which are interrelated (Sterler & Stephens, 1999). For example, plans can simultaneously reduce administrative expenses and negotiate greater fee reductions by contracting with fewer pharmacies in return for increased prescription volume. Location is a key consideration in network development because it determines the ease with which patients can access a pharmacy. When developing a network, the PBM will model the average distance between pharmacies and patients in the area using geographic information systems that are based on the pharmacies' and the patients' ZIP codes. An example of a common target is that a pharmacy provider be located within 1 to 5 miles of each enrollee's home in metropolitan areas, within 5 miles in suburban areas, and within 10 miles in rural areas (Sterler & Stephens, 1999).

Cost is the second critical element in network development and requires negotiation of multiple reimbursement rates for the various types of medications dispensed. Pharmacy benefit managers often lack data on actual pharmacy drug costs and, instead, determine an estimated acquisition cost (EAC) based on a discount from published pricing data such as the average wholesale price (AWP). AWP is a published reference price from which pharmacies obtain significant discounts; it is not based on actual selling prices. Studies have shown actual acquisition cost for brand-name drugs to be about 79% of AWP (Myers & Stauffer, 2007), and pharmacies are typically reimbursed by private plans for brand medications in the range of AWP minus 14–18%. Wholesale acquisition cost (WAC) is a more accurate estimate of prices charged by wholesalers for brand-name drugs before applying certain discounts based on volume and prompt payment; it is not, however, a uniformly accurate estimate of generic prices.

Rather, the vast majority of plans use maximum allowable cost (MAC) in setting generic prices. MAC is a maximum ingredient cost that will be paid for a drug, independent of the manufacturer's AWP. The use of MAC incentivizes retail pharmacies to purchase from lower cost generic providers as there are typically multiple manufacturers of generics, and price competition is significant. Regardless of the discount that is stipulated for brands and generics, most contracts require that the payment be the lowest of the following three measures:

1. The contract rate—usually stated as an EAC plus a dispensing fee
2. The MAC plus a dispensing fee
3. The usual and customary price charged to a cash-paying customer

Thus, in those cases where the pharmacy's usual and customary price is less than the contract rate, the pharmacy is paid the lower usual and customary price.

Once a network has been established, ongoing network communication and provider performance (i.e., quality) are key issues. The PBM can use a variety of methods to communicate with network providers, including newsletters, online communications, and Internet websites (Sterler & Stephens, 1999). Audits are a key tool that is used in pharmacy network performance. While online adjudication systems help minimize fraud and abuse problems, audits serve as an additional quality control technique. Electronic audits (i.e., automated algorithms that look for outlier patterns of prescription utilization that may be indicative of potential fraud problems) are very common. An electronic audit may trigger an on-site audit in which the auditor visits the pharmacy and examines its prescription records (Sterler & Stephens, 1999). On-site audits may result in no action, termination from the network, a request for reimbursement for select claims, or other actions.

Claims Adjudication

PBMs use online electronic claims submission systems to adjudicate claims for prescriptions dispensed by network pharmacies. This electronic data interchange has been standardized and is maintained by the National Council for Prescription Drug Programs. Electronic claims systems can carry out distinct administrative functions, including eligibility verification and claims adjudication. The pharmacy is notified of the formulary status of the prescribed medication, and any limits on medication quantities or refills are addressed. The amount to be remitted to the pharmacy and the patient's co-payment are also determined.

In addition, electronic claims systems can review the prescribing, dispensing, and usage patterns for given patients or drug products and suggest improvements (see "Drug Utilization Review" later in this chapter). They may also suggest therapeutic alternatives and provide information regarding physician network status and various patient and provider characteristics.

A transaction can be rejected by the PBM during adjudication if the pharmacy violates a clinical or administrative requirement. An online dispensing message that can be overridden by the pharmacist is known as a soft-edit message; a hard-edit message cannot be overridden without approval of the plan/PBM or an appropriate change to one or more components of the submitted claim. Under the latest National Council for Prescription Drug Programs guidelines, intervention/outcome codes allow pharmacists to override certain edits by indicating which intervention took place to address the identified issue (e.g., the pharmacist called the doctor to notify him or her about a potentially serious drug–drug interaction).

Mail Service

Most PBMs offer mail service pharmacies—either through their own mail-order facility or by contracting with one. As a result of their large prescription volumes, these mail service pharmacies are able to negotiate discounts on product costs and achieve economies of scale that reduce their dispensing costs. Because of the scale advantage, mail service pharmacies usually provide deeper discounts (when measured as cost per dose) to plan sponsors than retail pharmacies can, and they also represent the greatest profitability per prescription for PBMs. Accordingly, with the approval of the plan sponsor, PBMs may require members to use only a mail service pharmacy for certain prescriptions (usually refills of maintenance medications for chronic conditions), or at least give incentives, such as discounted co-payments, to encourage patients to use the mail service pharmacy. As a result of the continued focus on mail order by PBMs, its use has continued to grow over the last decade, representing about 18% of all prescriptions as of 2009 (Fein, 2009).

Generic Promotion, Formularies, and Utilization Management

Plan sponsors use a variety of tools to promote use of lower cost generic and brand medications and to reduce unnecessary use of medications. Generics have represented one of the greatest opportunities for savings in the pharmacy benefit over the last decade as the number of generic alternatives has grown. Generic fill rates are calculated as: (number of generic claims) ÷ (number of generic claims + number of brand claims). PBMs frequently report that 50–60% of prescriptions reimbursed are for generic drug products; some closed-model plans report rates of 70% or more (Navarro & Hailey, 2009). To promote use of generics, PBMs recommend lower co-payments for generics than brands and offer a variety of educational tools to help promote generics, such as online tools that identify generic alternatives to brand medications, letter- or telephone-based outreach programs that identify generic alternatives to brand medications that a patient is currently taking, and physician education programs aimed at increasing the writing of prescriptions for generic alternatives.

The use of lower cost brand medications also represents a significant savings opportunity for plan sponsors, which is typically achieved through the use of a formulary. PBMs generate significant savings from the rebates received from pharmaceutical manufacturers in return for placing specific drugs on the formulary or giving these drugs preferred status. The amount of these rebates may be based on the plan sponsor's benefit design (e.g., open, three-tier, or closed formulary and number of drugs on formulary) or strictly on market share (i.e., the percentage of all prescriptions within a given therapeutic class that are dispensed for the company's product) relative to national market share. When a PBM is administering the plan sponsor's pharmacy benefit, the rebate may be shared between the PBM and the plan sponsor or may be awarded solely to one party, depending on the contract between the plan sponsor and the PBM. Due to a greater push for transparency in PBM pricing, rebates are generally passed on to clients or are used to reduce pharmacy program costs (Navarro & Hailey, 2009). As described in the case scenario at the beginning of this chapter, formulary development and management is a core function of PBMs. Formularies can be described as open, closed, or incented, and plan sponsors choose which type of formulary design they want to offer. In an open formulary, all drugs are covered, regardless of their formulary status. In a closed formulary, drugs not on the formulary are not covered by the health plan. In an incented formulary, patients are provided with financial incentives (i.e., lower co-payments) to use preferred drugs; coverage is also provided for nonpreferred products, albeit at higher co-payments. Incented formularies are often referred to as multiple-tiered formularies or described as having tiered co-payments. (Tiered co-payments are discussed in more detail in the "Cost Sharing" section of this chapter.) In recent years, traditional open or closed formularies have been replaced for the most part by incented formularies.

As in the Viagra case scenario at the beginning of this chapter, plan administrators have debated whether they should cover lifestyle drugs and, if so, whether they should be subject to higher co-payments or require approval from the PBM. Plan sponsors often exclude specific classes of drugs from coverage, such as the following:

- Nonprescription drugs (other than insulin)
- Parenteral products (other than insulin)
- Compounded prescriptions
- Devices (e.g., syringes, blood glucose monitors, blood pressure machines, and glucose test strips)
- Appetite suppressants
- Products for smoking cessation
- Drugs for erectile dysfunction
- Oral contraceptives
- Growth hormone
- Fertility agents
- Products used for cosmetic purposes (such as hair growth or wrinkle removal) (Takeda Pharmaceuticals, 2007)

In addition to benefit exclusions, plan sponsors frequently ask PBMs to employ utilization management tools such as limiting the quantity of a particular prescription or the number of refills, to mitigate fraud and waste. Quantity may be limited to a specified number of dosage units or, more commonly, to a specified day's supply. Usually the day's supply is limited to 30 days. Early refills may not be allowed unless the PBM gives authorization to do so (e.g., if the patient is going on vacation). Some plan sponsors, however, specify a minimum quantity (such as a 3-month supply) that may be dispensed for certain maintenance medications used for chronic conditions.

Most plans incorporate a prior authorization (PA) program, another type of utilization management tool, into their pharmacy benefit. A PA program, which allows a patient's physician to request coverage of nonpreferred or noncovered medications such as those listed previously, provides access to certain drugs when they are needed without covering the drug for the general population. A variation on the formulary and prior authorization is step therapy. With step therapy, the use of the more expensive agent is reserved for second-line treatment if treatment with the less expensive agent, commonly a generic, proves unsuccessful. For example, a patient with heartburn might be required to try a generic proton pump inhibitor (PPI) before a more expensive brand-name PPI will be covered. Some staff- and group-model HMOs authorize pharmacists to dispense therapeutic alternatives in accordance with previously established formulary guidelines to promote either generic or lower cost brand alternatives. This practice, known as therapeutic interchange, is used by some PBMs for the following two reasons: (1) therapeutic categories are becoming more crowded with very similar drugs and generic alternatives, and (2) there is growing pressure to increase the market share of particular products so that the payer can receive manufacturer rebates.

Outside of these tightly managed environments, the term *therapeutic interchange* takes on a somewhat different meaning because the pharmacist contacts the physician to request approval for a switch in medication. Depending on the particular plan, the pharmacist may also contact the patient to get his or her permission before making the switch. Such programs, which are also called therapeutic conversion, therapeutic substitution, or switch programs, have been more commonly administered in mail-service pharmacies than in the retail networks because of the efficiencies that can be achieved in the mail-order setting (Kreling, Lipton, Collins, & Hertz, 1996). Controversy surrounds these therapeutic conversion programs, however. Opponents argue that these programs have negative effects on patients' health and are motivated by rebate revenues; proponents advocate their use as a way to control the growth in drug costs without compromising quality of care as promoted alternatives must be therapeutically equivalent. Research is beginning to emerge on these programs. For example, Cheetham and colleagues found that patients converted from simvastatin to generic lovastatin had an improvement in their lipid profile without evidence of hepatic or muscle enzyme elevations (Cheetham et al., 2005).

Drug Utilization Review

The review of physician prescribing, pharmacist dispensing, and patient use of drugs is known as drug utilization review (DUR) (Palumbo & Ober, 1995). The goal of DUR is to ensure that drugs are used appropriately, safely, and effectively.

Reviews based on claims data for prescriptions that have already been dispensed are known as retrospective DUR. The primary goal of a retrospective DUR is educational—to find ways in which drug therapy can be improved and inform prescribers and dispensers about these findings. Retrospective DUR may focus on physicians' prescribing patterns, individual patients' patterns, or patterns of use for certain therapeutic categories—especially for drugs that may be subject to abuse.

Prospective DUR is conducted at the time the prescription is dispensed via the electronic claims adjudication system. Patients' medication records are reviewed during the dispensing process to determine whether the prescriptions are appropriate. If a problem is identified, a message describing the problem is returned to the pharmacy through the computer system before the prescription is dispensed. Examples of reviews performed by these systems include appropriateness of dose, drug interactions, duplication of therapy, and drug–allergy interactions. Online prospective DUR programs may duplicate pharmacists' reviews of their own records but have the added benefit of screening prescription claims from other pharmacies that may have filled prescriptions for the same patient.

Cost Sharing

Cost sharing requires the patient to share in the cost of a medication based on some predetermined rate schedule established by the plan sponsor. It tries to optimize utilization by requiring patients to consider the cost of the medication (at least part of the cost), just as they would in any other purchasing transaction. Cost sharing can take many forms, including co-payments, coinsurance, deductibles, out-of-pocket limits, or maximum benefits. Many health plans use a combination of deductibles and co-payments or coinsurance when designing their pharmacy benefits. These techniques are fully described in Chapter 15.

PBMs commonly use tiered co-payments to promote utilization of lower cost alternatives in place of high-cost brand-name medications. In the very common three-tier pharmacy benefit, generic drugs are placed on the first tier of the formulary and have the lowest co-payment; preferred brand-name drugs are placed on the second tier with a higher co-payment; and nonpreferred brand-name drugs are placed on the third tier and have the highest co-payment. Some plans specify four-tier co-payments, with certain lifestyle drugs (e.g., drug products for erectile dysfunction) or nonformulary drugs appearing on the fourth tier. This fourth tier often has a coinsurance requirement ranging from 50% to 100%.

Provider and Patient Education

Physician profiling is a tool for comparing the practice patterns of providers on cost and quality dimensions. Measures are generally expressed as a rate over a specific period of time within the physician's patient population (e.g., the average dollars spent per patient per month). Report cards are then provided to individual physicians. These reports show not only the specific physician's practice patterns but also the average practice patterns of their physician counterparts, thereby providing a benchmark for comparison. The information on a report card typically includes healthcare and prescription costs per patient per month, number of prescriptions per patient per month, percentage of brand-name versus generic prescriptions, compliance with formulary guidelines, and prescribing patterns for selected prescription drugs.

As a follow-up to physician profiling, some health plans and PBMs provide counterdetailing (also known as academic detailing). Plans monitor physicians' prescribing patterns to identify those physicians who are prescribing inappropriately as viewed by the health plan. A health plan representative (or the contracting PBM) then visits targeted physicians to provide information regarding the most cost-effective use of selected drugs and to encourage physicians to prescribe in ways that will reduce overall costs while maintaining program quality. The targeted physicians are usually identified by the practice profiling program as ones with higher than average costs or unusual prescribing patterns. As discussed previously, the ability to influence providers' behavior depends greatly on how much of the contracted provider's business the organization controls.

With the growing emphasis on consumerism in health care, patient education is becoming more prevalent in PBMs and health plans. The goal of these programs is to produce voluntary changes in patients' behavior that will improve their health. Such efforts take a variety of forms, from passive educational mailing to more active educational efforts through telephone call centers. More encompassing patient education programs are sometimes referred to as disease management programs. The idea behind disease management is to take a broad view of a disease, focusing on how it is treated across the continuum of care. Often disease management programs target high-cost or high-prevalence diseases for which pharmaceutical therapy plays a central role, with the goal of improving how patients and physicians manage the disease. Examples include asthma, diabetes, heart disease, and depression.

ETHICAL ISSUES IN MANAGED CARE

Managed care takes an active approach to managing health, and this approach frequently intervenes in the physician–patient relationship. Considering the historical perspective discussed at the beginning of the chapter (see "The History of Managed Care"), it should not be surprising that the growth of managed care has fueled many ethics debates almost since its inception (Jecker, 1994). Ethical concerns related to managed care revolve around four central themes: the sanctity of the physician–patient relationship, the ethics of medicine, the quality of care, and freedom of choice for patients and providers (see **Table 17-2**). The challenge for managed care is to balance these concerns against the limited amount of resources that can be devoted to medical care spending.

Table 17-2 Summary of the Ethical Issues in Managed Care

Anti-managed care position	Pro-managed care position
The financial incentives of managed care threaten the role of physician as the patient advocate, undermining the patient's trust and jeopardizing the oath of doing good while avoiding harm.	The financial incentives of FFS resulted in overtreatment of patients, which can also be detrimental to the patient.
The ethics of medicine will be replaced with the ethics of business.	The ethics of medicine are not as superior as perhaps believed. Physicians do not take vows of poverty. In addition, businesses are increasingly being held to ethical standards. By considering medicine to be both a profession and a business, society will not overlook the ethical issues that can arise as a result of these conflicting agendas.
Physicians' autonomy is removed, which will eventually harm patients.	Physicians did not have complete autonomy under FFS. Nonetheless, reducing physician autonomy is not necessarily a bad thing. Who is to say that physicians are the experts or have special authority about the ethical values that should be considered in making resource allocation decisions? Further, empirical evidence does not show that managed care results in a lower quality of care. Rather, it can provide numerous benefits, such as an emphasis on preventive care.
Patients' freedom to choose providers and obtain medical services is limited, resulting in decreased patient satisfaction.	Patients have limits under FFS. Further, as managed care grows, a greater number of providers will be included in managed care, increasing patients' choice of providers.

Source: Reprinted from *Clinics in Geriatric Medicine*, Vol 10(3), N. S. Jecker, "Managed Competition and Managed Care: What are the Ethical Issues?", pp. 527–540, ©1994 with permission from Elsevier.

QUALITY IN MANAGED CARE

Background

While much of the interest in managed care has traditionally focused on controlling costs, today there is a growing emphasis on ensuring the quality of care. A major difficulty facing those who attempt to measure quality is that there is no universally agreed-upon definition of quality. Which variables should be measured, and how should they be weighed? Donabedian (1978) identified the following three measures for the assessment of quality that are still used today: structure, process, and outcomes.

Structure refers to the personnel and other resources used to provide care as well as the policies and procedures that govern the use of resources and providers' decision making. Examples include availability of X-ray equipment, the type of information system used, the number of physicians and their credentials, and the policy for receiving prior authorization for noncovered services. Structural criteria are generally easy to measure and document, but their relationship to other measures of quality is not always clear.

Process refers to the interactions that occur between practitioners and patients or what was done to the patient. Examples in a community pharmacy include the percentage of patients counseled per day and the number of dispensing errors as a percentage of prescriptions dispensed. For a PBM, a process measure may include the number of patients switched to a preferred medication.

Outcomes are the end results of medical care—that is, what happened to the patient. Examples of outcomes include stroke, death, quality of life, and patient satisfaction. While most would agree that outcomes are the best indicators of quality, quality assessment efforts often focus on the structure and process of care because they are much easier to measure and interpret.

Oversight and Accreditation

Oversight is the process of reviewing and monitoring managed care organizations to determine whether they meet specified structure, process, and/or outcome criteria. Government agencies, such as state insurance departments, are responsible for ensuring compliance with state laws and regulations regarding issues such as financial solvency, enrollment procedures, and patient rights. Accreditation, by contrast, is a voluntary form of oversight involving independent, nonprofit, nongovernment entities. Accreditation goes beyond oversight in that it evaluates and reports on the quality and performance of MCOs, thereby enabling purchasers and consumers of managed health care to make comparisons and more informed healthcare purchasing decisions. Accreditation, therefore, serves as a seal of approval that is relied upon by employers, patients, and, sometimes, government agencies (Kongstvedt, 2007).

There are three major accreditation agencies in the United States, which include:

1. The National Committee for Quality Assurance (NCQA)
2. The Joint Commission for the Accreditation of Healthcare Organizations (JCAHO)
3. The Utilization Review Accreditation Commission (URAC)

The majority of HMOs voluntarily submit to accreditation—more than any other type of MCO. NCQA is the dominant accreditation agency for HMOs. Accreditation of PPOs is increasing but still is not as common as for HMOs. URAC is the main accreditation agency for PPOs; and more recently, URAC has also begun to accredit PBMs. Generally speaking, the accreditation process looks at utilization management, patient satisfaction, access, financial performance, provider credentialing, treatment of specific diseases and outcomes achieved, and other measures (Kongstvedt, 2007). The accreditation survey process involves both on- and off-site components that are assessed by a team of reviewers.

In addition to accrediting HMOs, NCQA promotes performance standards, quality assurance, and review standards. It has also developed the Healthcare Effectiveness Data and Information Set (HEDIS), a group of measures that gives plan sponsors objective information that they can use to evaluate MCOs. The 71 HEDIS measures are divided into eight domains of care as described in **Table 17-3**. Examples of healthcare areas measured by HEDIS include immunization rates, cancer screening, mental health services, and treatment of diabetes, asthma, and heart attacks. Measures are frequently revised, added, or deleted. Some recently added measures, for example, focus on areas such as glaucoma screening and osteoporosis treatment for older adults.

Table 17-3   Major Categories of HEDIS Measures

Area measured	Examples
Effectiveness of care	Childhood immunization rates
	Mammography rates
	Response to those who are ill
Access/availability of care	Availability of care when needed
	Call answer timeliness
Satisfaction with the experience of care	Average office wait times
	Difficulty receiving care
	Satisfaction with choice of provider
	Overall satisfaction
Use of services	Mental health utilization
	Well-child visits
	Cesarean section rates
	Frequency of selected procedures
Cost of care	Frequency of high-cost procedures
	Cost trends
Health plan descriptive information	Board certification
	Race/ethnicity diversity of membership
	General questions about patient perceptions of the health plan
Health plan stability	Years in business
	Total membership
Informed healthcare choices	Patients' active involvement in making informed choices among treatment options

IMPACT OF MANAGED CARE ON PHARMACISTS

As discussed in Chapter 15, the growth of health insurance coverage for prescription drugs has resulted in extra work (e.g., prior authorization, online prospective DUR, and formulary restrictions) and reduced reimbursement for pharmacists. Nevertheless, the concept of pharmaceutical care is consistent with the goals of managed care. Changes in pharmacy education are preparing pharmacists to manage care and affect positive patient outcomes. Taking a broader perspective, greater focus on patient outcomes and cost-effectiveness will encourage pharmacists, physicians, and other healthcare providers to collaborate for the benefit of the patient to realize the goal of optimally managed health care.

Managed care has also expanded the roles played by pharmacists. New opportunities include roles as formulary managers, drug utilization reviewers, clinical specialists in disease management programs, outcomes researchers, and numerous other positions that combine the clinical and business aspects of pharmacy benefit management.

CONCLUSION

Managed care organizations continue to evolve in response to consumer and payer preferences and regulatory initiatives, and it is expected that they will continue to invest in data management and experiment with benefit designs that will enhance quality and cost controls. Plan sponsors can customize managed care benefits by designing the scope of coverage, provider incentives, and the various quality and cost-control options that they want to implement. When plan benefits are designed optimally, managed healthcare plans can contribute to better clinical outcomes and reduce healthcare costs.

QUESTIONS FOR FURTHER DISCUSSION

1. Bad publicity continues to plague managed care. To what extent is the current trashing of managed care an unavoidable cost of bringing change to the U.S. medical system? How much, if any, are the media to blame?
2. What are the strengths and limitations of prospective DUR systems from the perspectives of the PBM and the retail pharmacist? Given your explanation, what could be done to improve prospective DUR?
3. Describe some of the new and innovative career opportunities that have developed for pharmacists as managed care enrollment has grown.

KEY TOPICS AND TERMS

Academic detailing (counterdetailing)
Capitation
Cost sharing
Fee-for-service (FFS)
Gatekeeper

   Group-model HMO
   Health maintenance organization (HMO)
   Healthcare Effectiveness Data and Information Set (HEDIS)
   Independent practice association (IPA)-model HMO
   Managed care organization (MCO)
   National Committee for Quality Assurance (NCQA)
   Network
   Network-model HMO
   Pharmacy benefit manager (PBM)
   Point-of-service (POS) plan
   Preferred provider organization (PPO)
   Prospective drug utilization review
   Rebates
   Report cards
   Retrospective drug utilization review
   Risk bearing
   Risk pool
   Staff-model HMO
   Tiered co-payments
   Utilization review

REFERENCES

Aventis. (2002). Managed care digest series. Bridgewater, NJ: Aventis Pharmaceuticals.

Campbell, W. H., & Newsome, L. A. (1995). The evolution of managed care and practice settings. In S. M. Ito & S. Blackburn (Eds.), *A pharmacist's guide to principles and practices of managed care pharmacy* (pp. 1–14). Alexandria, VA: Foundation for Managed Care Pharmacy.

Cheetham T. C., Chan, J., Benson, V., Richmond, C., Levin, E., & Campen, D. (2005). Successful conversion of patients with hypercholesterolemia from a brand name to a generic cholesterol-lowering drug. *American Journal of Managed Care, 11,* 546–552. Retrieved from http://www.ajmc.com/issue/managed-care/2005/2005-09-vol11-n9/Sep05-2126p546-552

Davis, K., Collins, K. S., & Morris, C. (1994, Fall). Managed care: Promise and concerns. *Health Affairs, 13*(4), 178–185.

Donabedian, A. (1978). The quality of medical care. *Science, 200*(4344), 856–864.

Fein, A. (2009). Chains win big in 2009. *Drug Channels.* Retrieved from http://www.drug channels.net/2010/04/chains-win-big-in-2009.html

Friedman, E. (1996). Capitation, integration, and managed care lessons from early experiments. *Journal of the American Medical Association, 275*(12), 957–962.

Gillis, J. (1998a, April 22). The impotence pill: Who will pay? *The Washington Post,* p. A1.

Gillis, J. (1998b, April 26). Prescriptions for a better life. *The Washington Post,* p. AO1.

Goldstein, A. (1998, July 3). U.S.: Medicaid must cover Viagra. *The Washington Post,* p. A21.

Hoechst Marion Roussel. (1999). *HMO-PPO/Medicare–Medicaid digest.* Kansas City, MO: Hoechst Marion Roussel.

Jecker, N. S. (1994). Managed competition and managed care: What are the ethical issues? *Clinics in Geriatric Medicine, 10*(3), 527–540.

Kongstvedt, P. R. (2007). *Essentials of managed health care* (5th ed.). Sudbury, MA: Jones and Bartlett, p. 521-551.

Kreling, D. H., Lipton, H. L., Collins, T. C., & Hertz, K. C. (1996). *Assessment of the impact of pharmacy benefit managers: Final report to the Health Care Financing Administration* (Pub. No. PB97-103683). Springfield, VA: National Technical Information Service.

Lipton, H. L., Kreling, D. H., Collins, T., & Hertz, K. C. (1999). Pharmacy benefit management companies: Dimensions of performance. *Annual Review of Public Health, 20,* 361–401.

Mack, J. M. (1993). Managed care relationships from the physician's perspective. *Topics in Health Care Financing, 20*(2), 38–52.

Medicom International. (n.d.). *Medical interface. A thru Z. Managed care terms.* Bronxville, NY: Medicom International.

Miller, R. H., & Luft, H. S. (1994). Managed care plans: Characteristics, growth, and premium performance. *Annual Review of Public Health, 15,* 437–459.

Myers & Stauffer. (2007). *Survey of dispensing and acquisition costs of pharmaceuticals in the state of California.* California Department of Health Services, pp. 39–40.

Navarro, R. P., & Hailey, R. (2009). Overview of prescription drug benefits in managed care. In R. P. Navarro (Ed.), *Managed care pharmacy practice* (2nd ed.) (pp. 17–45). Sudbury, MA: Jones and Bartlett.

Palumbo, F. B., & Ober, J. (1995). Drug use evaluation. In S. M. Ito & S. Blackburn (Eds.), *A pharmacist's guide to principles and practices of managed care pharmacy* (pp. 51–59). Arlington, VA: Foundation for Managed Care Pharmacy.

Rognehaugh, R. (1996). *The managed health care dictionary.* Gaithersburg, MD: Aspen.

Sanofi-Aventis. (2009). *Managed care digest series.* Bridgewater, NJ: Sanofi-Aventis Pharmaceuticals. Retrieved from http://www.managedcaredigest.com/hmo/default.aspx

Sanofi-Aventis. (2010). *Managed care digest series.* Bridgewater, NJ: Sanofi-Aventis Pharmaceuticals. Retrieved from http://www.managedcaredigest.com/hmo/default.aspx

Sterler, L. T., & Stephens, D. (1999). Pharmacy distribution systems and network management. In R. P. Navarro (Ed.), *Managed care pharmacy practice* (pp. 89–123). Sudbury, MA: Jones and Bartlett.

Takeda Pharmaceuticals of North America, Inc. (2007). *The prescription drug benefit cost and plan design survey report.* Retrieved from http://www.pbmi.com/2007report/utilization_management/index.html

West, D. S. (2009). *NCPA–Digest.* Alexandria, VA: National Community Pharmacists Association.

Medicare and Medicaid

Alan P. Wolfgang

Case Scenario: Medicare

Helen is a retired bank teller, 67 years of age, who was recently afflicted with a serious illness. After spending 10 days in the hospital, she spent 4 weeks in a skilled nursing facility before being discharged to her home. During her recuperation, Helen often reflected on how lucky she was to be enrolled in Medicare. Because of her limited income, it was reassuring to know that Medicare would take care of her substantial healthcare expenses. Helen was shocked, however, when she began receiving bills that Medicare did not pay. Adding up the bills from the hospital, skilled nursing facility, pharmacy, and her physician, she owed more than $2,500! Helen could not understand how she could owe so much money when she had health insurance through Medicare.

LEARNING OBJECTIVES

Upon completion of this chapter, the student shall be able to:

- Explain the eligibility requirements of the Medicare program
- Describe the sources of funding for Medicare
- Describe the benefits provided under Medicare Parts A and B
- Describe the types of cost sharing required for Medicare patients
- Explain the concepts of approved charges and assignment
- Explain the benefits provided under Medicare Part C
- Describe the major provisions of the Medicare Part D prescription drug benefit
- Describe the magnitude of Medicare enrollment and spending
- Explain the need for and types of Medicare supplement policies
- Describe the three broad groups of people who may be eligible for Medicaid
- Describe the roles of state and federal governments in financing and administering Medicaid
- Describe the mandatory and optional benefits provided under Medicaid
- Describe the types of cost sharing required for Medicaid patients
- Describe the magnitude of Medicaid enrollment and spending
- Explain the role of waivers in encouraging innovation in Medicaid programs

CHAPTER QUESTIONS: MEDICARE

1. Which groups of people are eligible to be covered by Medicare?
2. How is Medicare financed?
3. What services are covered by Parts A and B of Medicare?
4. What types of cost sharing are imposed on Medicare beneficiaries?
5. What is *assignment*, and why is it important to Medicare beneficiaries?
6. What is a Medicare supplement insurance policy?

CHAPTER QUESTIONS: MEDICAID

1. What are the characteristics of the persons mandated categorically needy, optionally eligible, and medically needy?
2. What are the roles of federal and state governments in financing and administering Medicaid?
3. Which services must be covered by state Medicaid programs?
4. What are examples of optional services in Medicaid programs?
5. What types of cost sharing are imposed on Medicaid beneficiaries?
6. How have waivers been used by states to test innovative Medicaid programs?

MEDICARE: LEGISLATIVE HISTORY

The development of the Medicare program can be traced back to the 1935 Social Security Act (SSA). Although Medicare was not enacted at that time, this landmark legislation marked the beginning of the federal government's central role in the area of social insurance (Longest, 1994). Passed by Congress during President Franklin Roosevelt's first term, the SSA was designed to provide for the material needs of Americans (Hellman & Hellman, 1991). Title XVIII of the SSA, "Health Insurance for the Aged and Disabled," was established as part of the Social Security Amendments of 1965. More commonly known as Medicare, Title XVIII launched a health insurance program that complemented the SSA's retirement, survivors, and disability insurance benefits (Medicare and Medicaid Statistical Supplement, 1995).

The concept of Medicare was introduced early in 1952, during the Harry Truman administration. Abandoning his advocacy of a universal health program, President Truman suggested a more limited health insurance plan that would cover all Social Security beneficiaries (Ball, 1995). However, Truman's plan received little serious consideration. Fein (1989) believes that the introduction of a bill by Representative Aimee Forand of Rhode Island in August 1957 initiated the legislative activity that led to the enactment of Medicare. This bill, which proposed a social insurance program of health insurance for the aged, and its legislative successors received sustained attention in Congress for the next 8 years. Hearings on the bill held in 1959 helped build a consensus for the belief that many aged Americans faced severe difficulties in obtaining health insurance and that federal action in this arena was necessary.

Health insurance for the elderly was at the top of the federal legislative agenda in 1965 following the reelection of Lyndon Johnson as president in November 1964. During the early months of 1965, Representative Wilbur Mills of Arkansas, chairman of the House Ways and Means Committee, designed a compromise that encompassed three major proposals that were under consideration at that time: (1) a compulsory health insurance program for the elderly, which was to be financed by payroll taxes; (2) a voluntary insurance program for physician services, which was to be subsidized with general tax revenues; and (3) a means-tested health insurance program for the poor, which was to be administered by the states (Ginsburg, 1988). The first two proposals were combined in the Mills compromise to form the Medicare program; the third proposal was addressed through development of the Medicaid program.

After many years of often acrimonious debate about the government's responsibility for ensuring Americans' access to health services, passage of the 1965 SSA amendments was made possible by Johnson's landslide victory in the 1964 election and the accompanying large Democratic majority in Congress (Longest, 1994). If not for these unique circumstances that existed in 1965, it is unlikely that Medicare could have mustered the votes necessary for passage (Ball, 1995). In fact, some have argued that this comprehensive program could not have been enacted at any time except in 1965. The legislation was signed into law by President Johnson on July 30, 1965, with Medicare's implementation set for July 1, 1966 (Fein, 1989).

PROGRAM STRUCTURE

Medicare was traditionally a two-part insurance program. Part A, also known as Hospital Insurance, pays for care provided to patients in hospitals, skilled nursing facilities, hospices, and home healthcare programs. Part B, or Supplementary Medical Insurance, provides coverage for physicians' services, outpatient hospital care, and a variety of other medical services not covered under Part A (Centers for Medicare and Medicaid Services, 2010c). Part C, which was added in 1997, was originally known as the Medicare + Choice program, but now is called Medicare Advantage. It expanded beneficiaries' ability to participate in a wide variety of private health plans, including health maintenance organizations (HMOs) and preferred provider organizations (PPOs). The Medicare Prescription Drug, Improvement, and Modernization Act of 2003 established a new prescription drug benefit, also known as Part D (Centers for Medicare and Medicaid Services, 2005a; Henry J. Kaiser Family Foundation, 2003).

ELIGIBILITY

Part A

In 2010, approximately 46 million people were enrolled in Medicare (Henry J. Kaiser Family Foundation, 2010e). Most of these people qualify for Medicare by virtue of the fact that they or their spouse worked for at least 10 years in Medicare-covered employment, they are citizens or permanent residents of the United States, and they are at least 65 years old. Persons who are 65 or older are entitled to receive Part A automatically without paying any premium if they (1) are receiving or are eligible to receive retirement benefits from either Social Security or the Railroad Retirement Board, or (2) had Medicare-covered government employment. People age 65 or older who do not meet these criteria can purchase Part A by paying a monthly premium (Health Care Financing Administration, 1996, 1998, 2009a; Medicare and Medicaid Statistical Supplement, 1995). This premium, which varies based on an individual's length of Medicare-covered employment, ranged between $254 and $461 per month in 2010 (Centers for Medicare and Medicaid Services, 2009a).

Two groups of people younger than age 65 can receive Part A without paying a monthly premium: (1) individuals who have received disability benefits from Social Security or the Railroad Retirement Board for at least 24 months, and (2) patients with end-stage renal disease who require dialysis or a kidney transplant (Health Care Financing Administration, 1996; Medicare and Medicaid Statistical Supplement, 1995). Legislation enacted in 2000 allows persons with amyotrophic lateral sclerosis (also known as Lou Gehrig's disease) to waive the 24-month waiting period for Part A coverage. Overall, the nonelderly account for about 17% of the Medicare population (Centers for Medicare and Medicaid Services, 2005a, 2009a).

Part B

Although most Medicare patients do not pay a premium for Part A coverage, everyone who wishes to be covered by Part B is charged a monthly premium, and for most individuals this amount is deducted from the monthly Social Security benefit checks. For 2010, the standard Part B was set at $110.50 per month. However, about three quarters of Part B enrollees paid only the 2009 premium of $96.40 due to a hold-harmless provision. This provision prohibits states from increasing the standard Part B premium to an amount that exceeds an individual's Social Security cost-of-living adjustment. Since there was no cost-of-living adjustment in 2010, this meant that enrollees' Part B had to remain at the same level as the previous year. Certain individuals, such as first-time enrollees and those whose Part B is paid by a state Medicaid program, are not protected by the hold-harmless provision and thus were charged the higher Part B premium. Approximately 93% of the Medicare population voluntarily enrolls in Part B (Centers for Medicare and Medicaid Services, 2009a). Individuals who would have to pay a premium for Medicare Part A can purchase Part B even if they do not enroll in Part A.

Beginning in 2007, higher-income Medicare beneficiaries began paying a higher, income-related Part B premium. For 2010, the higher premium was triggered when annual income exceeded $85,000 for an individual or $170,000 for a couple, with the minimum premium being $154.70 per month. The premium increases on a sliding scale, with the maximum premium of $353.60 per month being paid when income exceeded $214,000 for an individual or $428,000 for a couple. Higher-income beneficiaries are not protected by the hold-harmless provision described above (Centers for Medicare and Medicaid Services, 2009a). It is estimated that 5% of Medicare beneficiaries pay this income-related Part B premium (Henry J. Kaiser Family Foundation, 2009f).

FINANCING

The expenses of providing the benefits and administration of Parts A and B are paid from separate trust funds. Part A expenses are paid from the hospital insurance trust fund, which is financed primarily through payroll taxes paid by employees, employers, and self-employed individuals. At present, employees and employers each contribute

1.45% of earnings to the trust fund; self-employed individuals pay 2.9% of earnings. Additional funding is provided by beneficiary cost-sharing mechanisms (such as premiums, deductibles, and coinsurance) that are required for most Part A and B services (Centers for Medicare and Medicaid Services, 2009a; Davis & Burner, 1995; Medicare and Medicaid Statistical Supplement, 1995). Approximately 25% of the contributions to the hospital insurance fund come from beneficiary cost sharing. Most of the income for the supplementary medical insurance trust fund is provided from general revenues of the federal government (Davis & Burner, 1995; Zarabozo, Taylor, & Hicks, 1996).

ADMINISTRATION

Administration of the Medicare program is the responsibility of the U.S. Department of Health and Human Services. Within the Department of Health and Human Services, Medicare eligibility and enrollment are the responsibility of the Social Security Administration. The Centers for Medicare and Medicaid Services (CMS), formerly the Health Care Financing Administration, is charged with carrying out most other duties pertaining to Medicare, including developing operational policies and guidelines, formulating conditions of participation for providers, maintaining and reviewing utilization records, and overseeing general financing of the program. The U.S. Department of the Treasury manages the hospital insurance and supplementary medical insurance trust funds (Medicare and Medicaid Statistical Supplement, 1992, 1995).

To be reimbursed for providing services to Medicare patients, healthcare providers must comply with the program's conditions of participation, which are requirements relating to the health and safety of Medicare beneficiaries. Agencies of state governments assist CMS in the certification process by surveying and inspecting potential providers (Medicare and Medicaid Statistical Supplement, 1995).

Providers are paid for services delivered to Medicare patients after they file claims with designated administrators (such as Blue Cross/Blue Shield associations and commercial insurers), which are organizations that contract with CMS to administer Part A and B claims. These administrators determine reasonable charges for covered services, make payments to providers, and guard against unnecessary utilization of services. Providers are required to file claims with the administrators on patients' behalf (Medicare and Medicaid Statistical Supplement, 1995).

MEDICARE SERVICES AND COST SHARING

Part A

Inpatient Hospital Care

Services for inpatient hospital care are based on the concept of a benefit period. A benefit period begins on the day an individual enters the hospital and ends when that person has not been a patient in either a hospital or skilled nursing facility for 60 consecutive days. It also ends if the person resides in a nursing home for 60 consecutive days without receiving skilled care. A Medicare beneficiary can have several benefit periods during a given year, and there is no lifetime limit on the number of benefit periods available to individuals (Centers for Medicare and Medicaid Services, 2003c).

Part A covers 90 days of medically necessary inpatient hospital care per benefit period. Each patient also has a lifetime reserve of 60 days that can be used if he or she needs to be hospitalized for more than 90 days in one benefit period. This lifetime reserve is not renewed at the beginning of each benefit period. The services that Medicare covers for hospital inpatients include a semiprivate room, meals, nursing care, operating and recovery room, drugs, laboratory tests, and X-rays. Medicare does not cover extra charges such as those for a private room or the cost of amenities such as a television or telephone.

A separate limit applies to inpatient services received in psychiatric hospitals; each Medicare beneficiary is entitled to just 190 days of inpatient psychiatric care during his or her lifetime. Psychiatric care provided in a general hospital does not count toward this 190-day limit (Centers for Medicare and Medicaid Services, 2003c).

Hospitalized Medicare patients are subject to a schedule of deductibles and co-payments, the amount of which changes each year. For days 1 through 60 of hospitalization during a benefit period, the patient is responsible for paying a deductible ($1,100 in 2010). Regardless of how many times a person might be admitted to the hospital, as long as he or she has not received more than 60 days of care within the benefit period, he or she pays only this deductible. The patient is not required to pay for any other portion of the costs of covered services during that time period. If, however, a patient is hospitalized for more than 60 days in a benefit period, further cost sharing is required in the form of daily co-payments. For days 61 through 90 of a benefit period, the co-payment amount ($275 per day in 2010) equals one fourth of the inpatient hospital deductible; for the lifetime reserve days, the co-payment ($550 per day in 2010) is one half of that deductible (Centers for Medicare and Medicaid Services, 2009a).

The other form of cost sharing that may be imposed on hospitalized Medicare patients is the blood deductible. Patients are required to pay for or replace (either by themselves or another person on their behalf) the first three pints of blood used each year. Both Parts A and B cover blood. Thus, to the extent that the blood deductible is met under one part of Medicare, it does not have to be met under the other part (Centers for Medicare and Medicaid Services, 2003c).

Skilled Nursing Facility Care

Medicare patients are entitled to 100 days of care in a skilled nursing facility (SNF) per benefit period. During stays in such facilities, covered services include a semiprivate room, nursing care, meals, drugs, medical supplies and equipment, and rehabilitation services (such as physical therapy and speech therapy). A number of criteria must be met before a Medicare patient can qualify for these services. Perhaps most important is the requirement that the patient require daily skilled nursing or rehabilitation services that can be provided only in a skilled nursing facility. Because this benefit is intended to serve acutely ill patients who can be cured or improved by short-term, daily, skilled services, Medicare will not cover SNF care for patients who need only custodial care (such as assistance with eating, toileting, or taking medication). In addition to the requirement regarding level of care, admission to an SNF must be preceded by a hospital stay of at least 3 days, and it typically must occur within 30 days of hospital discharge (Centers for Medicare and Medicaid Services, 2003c; Hellman and Hellman, 1991).

There is no charge to the patient for the first 20 days of care in an SNF. For days 21 through 100 of care within a benefit period, however, Medicare patients are responsible for a daily co-payment. This co-payment ($137.50 per day in 2010) is set at one eighth of the inpatient hospital deductible (Centers for Medicare and Medicaid Services, 2009a).

Home Health Care

Like the skilled nursing care benefit, Medicare's home healthcare coverage is designed to help people recover from illnesses through the provision of skilled services—not to provide long-term, unskilled care. Part A and Part B actually share responsibility for home healthcare services. Part A covers a maximum of 100 home health visits following a hospital or SNF stay of at least 3 days. Thereafter, visits are covered by Part B, as is home health care not associated with a hospital or SNF stay. Homebound patients may continue to receive home healthcare benefits as long as they require intermittent skilled nursing care, physical therapy, occupational therapy, or speech therapy. If a patient receives any of those services, he or she is entitled to a variety of other services, including home health aide services, medical social services, medical supplies (such as bandages or incontinence pads), and durable medical equipment (such as wheelchairs and walkers). Services not covered include meal preparation and delivery and full-time nursing care.

Medicare Part A pays the entire bill for most covered services provided by approved home health agencies without requiring any patient cost sharing. The one exception concerns durable medical equipment, for which the patient must pay a 20% coinsurance (Centers for Medicare and Medicaid Services, 2003c, 2005a; Hellman & Hellman, 1991).

Hospice Care

The hospice benefit provides care to patients who have life expectancies of 6 months or less (as certified by a physician) and who voluntarily waive their right to traditional treatment of their terminal illnesses (such as cancer chemotherapy). Hospice services, which primarily are delivered in a home setting, can include relief of pain and other symptoms (such as nausea or diarrhea), physician services, nursing care, counseling, and homemaker services. Short-term respite care in a nursing home or hospital, which provides temporary relief for the family members who regularly assist with home care, is also covered for a maximum of 5 consecutive days. If a hospice patient requires care for conditions not related to his or her terminal illness, these services may be covered under the standard Medicare plan (Centers for Medicare and Medicaid Services, 2003c; Hellman & Hellman, 1991).

Very little patient cost sharing is required for covered services provided under the hospice benefit. Patients pay small coinsurance amounts for outpatient prescription drugs and inpatient respite care (Centers for Medicare and Medicaid Services, 2005a).

Other Services

Medicare Part A covers emergency services received in all hospitals, even those that do not participate in the Medicare program, including hospitals in Canada and Mexico under some circumstances. In general, Medicare does not pay for healthcare services received outside the United States and its territories (Centers for Medicare and Medicaid Services, 2003c). Therefore, elderly patients are advised to obtain other health insurance when they travel outside the country.

Part B

Services Covered

Part B covers services provided by physicians in a wide variety of settings, including hospitals, physicians' offices, nursing homes, and patients' homes. Thus, when a Medicare patient undergoes an inpatient surgical procedure, Part A pays the hospital charges and Part B pays for the surgeon's services. Also covered are services provided by nonphysician providers such as physician assistants, nurse practitioners, and certified registered nurse anesthetists (Centers for Medicare and Medicaid Services, 2009a).

Other services covered under Part B include outpatient hospital services, X-rays and laboratory tests, physical and occupational therapy, home health care (if not covered under Part A), drugs that are usually not self-administered, immunosuppressive drugs subsequent to a transplant, kidney dialysis, durable medical equipment, and ambulance transportation. A variety of other preventive services are covered under Part B, including bone mass measurements, colorectal cancer screenings, diabetes screening and supplies, mammograms, Pap tests, and prostate cancer screenings. Limited coverage is available for services provided by chiropractors, podiatrists, optometrists, and dental surgeons (Centers for Medicare and Medicaid Services, 2009a, 2010c).

Although a wide variety of physician and outpatient services are covered by Part B, many services are not covered. Services not covered by Medicare Part B include routine physical examinations, routine vision and hearing tests, hearing aids, routine dental care, homemaker services, and most healthcare services received while traveling outside the United States (Centers for Medicare and Medicaid Services, 2003c; Hellman & Hellman, 1991).

Cost Sharing

Each calendar year, Medicare patients pay a deductible ($155 in 2010) for Part B services. After that deductible has been met, Medicare typically pays 80% of the approved charge for most services; this approved charge may be lower than the amount actually billed by the healthcare provider. The patient is responsible for paying the other 20% of approved charges and may be financially responsible for the difference between Medicare's approved charge and the provider's actual charge, depending on whether the provider accepts assignment (Centers for Medicare and Medicaid Services, 2009a).

When a provider accepts assignment, it means that his or her actual charge will equal Medicare's approved charge (i.e., no balance billing). In such cases, Medicare patients are assured that they will be billed only for 20% of the approved charge. However, when patients receive services from providers who do not accept assignment, they can also be billed for the difference between actual and approved charges (see **Table 18-1**). The amount of this balance billing is limited, as federal law prevents providers who do not accept assignment from charging Medicare patients more than 115% of Medicare's approved charges (Centers for Medicare and Medicaid Services, 2003c). States may place even further restrictions on providers' ability to balance bill.

Physicians can agree on an annual basis to accept assignment for all services provided to Medicare beneficiaries; they are then referred to as Medicare participating physicians. To encourage physicians to sign up for this program, payments for participating

Table 18-1 Impact of Assignment on Total Payment by Medicare Patients

Assignment accepted		Assignment not accepted
$200	Approved charge	$190
$215	Actual charge	$215
$200	Approved charge	$190
$160	80% of approved charge, paid by Medicare	$152
$ 40	20% of approved charge, paid by patient	$ 38
$ 0	Balance billing (actual charge minus approved charge)	$ 25
$ 40	Total payment due from patient (20% of approved charge plus balance billing)	$ 63

physicians are set approximately 5% higher than payments for nonparticipating physicians (Coleman, 1990). More than 90% of physicians and other medical practitioners are Medicare participating (Henry J. Kaiser Family Foundation, 2010f).

Part C

One solution to controlling Medicare spending might be to implement the types of managed care innovations that appear to have been successful in constraining healthcare costs in the private sector. Encouraging more Medicare enrollees to obtain their healthcare services through managed care organizations might allow the federal government to maintain—if not improve—the level of service provided to older Americans while assisting in its efforts to control expenditures. Even though Medicare does not require its beneficiaries to enroll in managed care plans, Medicare managed care enrollment nevertheless increased tremendously beginning in the later half of the 1990s. The number of Medicare beneficiaries in HMOs increased from fewer than 2 million in 1995 to 6.3 million (16% of all Medicare beneficiaries) in 1999 (Henry J. Kaiser Family Foundation, 1999, 2005a).

Enrollment in traditional HMOs was the only managed care option available to Medicare beneficiaries from 1985 until implementation of the Balanced Budget Act of 1997. Under the new Part C (Medicare Advantage) program, an expanded set of options for the delivery of healthcare services became available to Medicare beneficiaries, including PPOs and other types of managed care plans. The addition of these new managed care options made the variety of plans available under Medicare similar to those available to non-Medicare patients. By 2009, 22% of Medicare beneficiaries were enrolled in Medicare Advantage plans (Henry J. Kaiser Family Foundation, 2009b).

Medicare Advantage plans are required to provide a benefit package that is actuarially equivalent to traditional Medicare. If plan costs are lower than Medicare payments, plans are required either to pass those savings along to beneficiaries in the form of lower premiums, reduced cost sharing, and/or additional benefits (e.g., preventive dental care, eyeglasses, hearing aids), or to return the excess payments to Medicare. In 2010, 90% of Medicare Advantage plans imposed no cost sharing for preventive services, almost 80% limited out-of-pocket spending for covered services, and more than 90% provided unlimited days of inpatient hospital care (Henry J. Kaiser Family

Foundation, 2010d). It has been estimated that the value of these enhanced benefits, for the average enrollee, is $79 per month (Medicare Payment Advisory Commission, 2009).

Part D

Since January 1, 2006, prescription drug coverage has been available to Medicare beneficiaries through voluntary enrollment in Part D. Individuals obtain this coverage in one of two ways: (1) by enrolling in a freestanding prescription drug plan while getting other Medicare benefits through the traditional fee-for-service program or (2) by joining a Medicare Advantage plan that covers all Medicare benefits, including prescription drugs. Beneficiaries will pay an additional premium for Part D benefits. This premium, estimated to have averaged about $30 per month in 2010, is designed to cover approximately 25% of the cost of the standard drug benefit. Other sources of funding for Part D include contributions from the general fund of the U.S. Treasury and payments from states, which must offset some of the cost of prescription drugs for Medicaid beneficiaries who also are enrolled in Medicare (Centers for Medicare and Medicaid Services, 2005a, 2009a; Henry J. Kaiser Family Foundation, 2005b).

Under the Part D standard benefit, beneficiaries paid a $310 deductible for prescription drugs in 2010, after which they paid 25% of the next $2,520 of drug costs. Thus, in total, patients paid $940 of the first $2,830 in prescription drug costs. At that point, there is a coverage gap (or "doughnut hole") in Medicare coverage that requires Medicare patients to pay 100% of the next $3,610 in prescription drug costs out of their own pockets. In 2010, after beneficiaries had reached a catastrophic threshold by spending some $4,550 out of pocket, Medicare's catastrophic coverage kicked in; beneficiaries then paid the greater of either a 5% coinsurance charge or co-payments of $2.50 for generic or preferred multisource drugs and $6.30 for other drugs (Centers for Medicare and Medicaid Services, 2009a). The annual deductible, benefit limits, and catastrophic threshold are indexed to rise with Part D spending.

As long as their designs are at least actuarially equivalent to this standard benefit, prescription drug plans are given the flexibility to offer alternative benefit designs. For example, in 2010 only 36% of stand-alone prescription drug plans charged a $310 deductible, and another 40% of those plans charged no deductible at all. Similarly, only 11% of plans utilized the standard 25% coinsurance; the vast majority used a tiered cost-sharing structure instead (Henry J. Kaiser Family Foundation, 2009c).

Part D coverage includes most FDA-approved prescription drugs (drugs currently covered under Parts A and B are still covered by these Medicare components). However, although they must provide a broad range of drugs, plans are allowed to have formularies under Part D. Likewise, plans can use tiered cost sharing, prior authorization, and other cost-containment tools, so long as they are not deemed unduly restrictive. While the law that created Part D prevents Medicare from negotiating drug prices with manufacturers, individual drug plans can use such tactics to produce savings in their drug expenditures (Centers for Medicare and Medicaid Services, 2005a; Henry J. Kaiser Family Foundation, 2005c). Because formularies and cost-containment strategies differ among drug plans, as do premiums and cost-sharing requirements, patients' actual out-of-pocket expenses can vary considerably among plans, and it is important for Medicare beneficiaries to shop wisely when selecting plans.

Medicare provides a variety of subsidies for low-income beneficiaries who enroll in Part D. For example, individuals with both Medicare and Medicaid (those who are "dual eligibles") pay no monthly premium or deductible, and their co-payments are $1.10 or $2.50 for generic drugs and $3.30 or $6.30 for brand-name drugs, depending on income; dual eligibles in nursing homes have no co-payments. Numerous other groups of Medicare beneficiaries with limited incomes and resources also qualify for some type of assistance with Part D premiums, deductibles, and co-payments. In 2009, more than one third of Medicare Part D enrollees received some form of low-income subsidy (Henry J. Kaiser Family Foundation, 2009a).

The Patient Protection and Affordable Care Act (known informally as the healthcare reform act) enacted in March 2010 brought important changes to the Part D drug benefit. This healthcare reform law provided for a $250 rebate to Part D enrollees to cover spending in the coverage gap during 2010. Additional subsidies in the coverage gap will be phased in for generic drugs beginning in 2011 and for brand-name drugs beginning in 2013, eventually reducing the coinsurance rate in that gap from 100% to 25% by 2020. The law also reduces the level of out-of-pocket spending required for catastrophic coverage between 2014 and 2019 (Henry J. Kaiser Family Foundation, 2010a).

Part D was not launched without its share of problems. Most notably, widespread eligibility verification problems frustrated both Medicare patients and the community pharmacists who served them (Pharmacy Times, 2006; Ukens, 2006). Despite what many viewed as a rough start, however, enrollment has continued to increase, and by 2009 almost 27 million Medicare beneficiaries were enrolled in Medicare Part D plans. Combined with another 14 million individuals who had drug coverage through retiree health plans or systems such as the Indian Health Service or Veterans Affairs, approximately 90% of Medicare beneficiaries had some form of prescription drug coverage (Henry J. Kaiser Family Foundation, 2009d).

EXPENDITURES

Growth in Medicare Spending

Medicare has witnessed tremendous growth since its inception. When this program was first implemented, Medicare served some 19 million enrollees; by 2010, some 46 million Americans were enrolled in Medicare (Centers for Medicare and Medicaid Services, 2008; Henry J. Kaiser Family Foundation, 2010f).

Accompanying this expansion in the Medicare population has been rapid growth in Medicare program spending. Between 1968 and 2010, expenditures increased from $6 billion to more than $500 billion. The important role of this program in the American healthcare system is illustrated by the fact that Medicare accounts for 23% of all national personal healthcare expenditures (Centers for Medicare and Medicaid Services, 2003a; Henry J. Kaiser Family Foundation, 2009e, 2010d).

SPENDING BY TYPE OF SERVICE

Inpatient hospital services and physician services are two of the largest individual components of total Medicare payments (see **Table 18-2**), but the proportion of Medicare spending attributable to these two types of services has decreased markedly over

Table 18-2   Estimated Medicare Expenditures by Service, 2010

Service	% of expenditures
Inpatient hospital	27.0
Managed care	24.2
Physician/other suppliers	17.6
Prescription drugs	11.0
Outpatient care	8.6
Nursing homes	5.2
Home health	3.8
Hospice	2.6

Source: Congressional Budget Office, 2009.

time due to various payment reforms and cost-containment efforts. While inpatient hospital services and physician services accounted for more than 90% of Medicare payments in 1967, they accounted for just 45% of such payments in 2010. Conversely, the proportion of payments attributable to home health care and other outpatient benefits has increased substantially since 1967, and managed care, which was virtually nonexistent in 1967, accounted for almost one quarter of Medicare payments (Henry J. Kaiser Family Foundation, 2010c; Medicare and Medicaid Statistical Supplement, 2001).

MEDICARE SUPPLEMENT (MEDIGAP) INSURANCE

Need for Supplemental Insurance

Although some Medicare beneficiaries, such as Helen in the case scenario at the beginning of this chapter, may be under the impression that Medicare will pay for all of their healthcare bills, it does not. Medicare pays less than half of the average beneficiary's medical expenses (Henry J. Kaiser Family Foundation, 2009e). Substantial patient cost sharing is required in the form of deductibles, co-payments, coinsurance, and premiums. As an extreme example, a seriously ill Medicare patient who stayed 150 consecutive days in the hospital during 2016 would have been responsible for more than $42,000 in hospital deductibles and co-payments. But even relatively healthy Medicare enrollees who visit their physicians a few times per year will be liable for the premiums, deductibles, and coinsurance associated with Part B, as well as the full cost of services that are not covered by Medicare. Medicare beneficiaries paid 16.5% of their incomes for out-of-pocket healthcare expenses in 2006 (Henry J. Kaiser Family Foundation, 2010d).

Several options are available to help Medicare beneficiaries meet these cost-sharing requirements, aside from paying these expenses out of their own pockets. First, some patients might have additional retiree health insurance through a former employer or union. Second, they might be poor enough to qualify for assistance from Medicaid, which would help pay for their care. Third, they might enroll in a Medicare Advantage plan that covers more services than does traditional Medicare. Lastly, Medicare beneficiaries can purchase additional private insurance, known as Medicare supplement or Medigap insurance, which is designed to pay for many of the charges for Medicare-covered services for which the beneficiary is responsible (Centers for Medicare and Medicaid Services, 2011).

Types of Medigap Policies

Most states have adopted regulations designed to make it easier for consumers to comparison shop for a Medigap policy. Standardized policies, which were developed by the National Association of Insurance Commissioners and incorporated into state and federal laws, are assigned letter designations from A through N. To further enhance comparison shopping, insurers must use the same format, language, and definitions in describing their plans. In accordance with federal regulations, each state must allow the sale of Plan A, the most basic type, and all Medigap insurers must offer Plan A. Beyond this requirement, states may restrict the number of other plans that may be sold, and insurers are not obligated to sell any other Medigap plans (Center for the Study of Services, 1995; Centers for Medicare and Medicaid Services, 2010a).

Plan A consists of five basic benefits, which cover:

1. Part A coinsurance hospital costs up to an additional 365 days after Medicare benefits are used up
2. Part B coinsurance or co-payment
3. Part A hospice care coinsurance or co-payment
4. Three-pint blood deductible
5. Preventive care Part B coinsurance

Other plans offer combinations of other benefits in addition to those provided in Plan A. These additional benefits can include coverage of the SNF co-payment, the Part A hospital deductible, the Part B deductible, and foreign travel emergency care. Two plans, K and L, include an annual limit on beneficiaries' out-of-pocket spending; once it is met, the plan pays for 100% of covered services for the rest of the calendar year (Centers for Medicare and Medicaid Services, 2010a).

Case Scenario: Medicaid

Charlotte is a single parent of two children younger than age 6, and her annual income is about 10% above the federal poverty level for a family of three. She and her children receive health insurance through her state's Medicaid program.

In a nearby state, Ed and Teresa are married and have an infant daughter. Ed and Teresa both work at low-wage jobs, providing a family income equal to the federal poverty level, but neither of their employers offers a health insurance benefit. While their daughter is covered by the state's Medicaid program, Ed and Teresa have no health insurance.

In yet another state, Jack is an agricultural worker with an annual income that is less than half the federal poverty level. Despite his extremely low income, Jack does not qualify for health insurance through his state's Medicaid program.

How can some, but not all, of these people be covered by Medicaid? Why is Medicaid eligibility not uniform across the United States?

MEDICAID: LEGISLATIVE HISTORY

In addition to initiating the Medicare program, the 1965 amendments to the Social Security Act (SSA) established a program popularly known as Medicaid. Officially designated as Title XIX of the SSA, Grants to the States for Medical Assistance Programs, Medicaid was designed to provide medical assistance to eligible needy Americans and is now the largest source of funding for the provision of health-related services to the United States' poorest people (Medicare and Medicaid Statistical Supplement, 1995).

Medicaid remained a rider on the Medicare bill until late in the 1965 legislative debate, when it became a separate title at the last minute. For this reason, Medicaid has been referred to as Medicare's "kid brother." Some have suggested that no one knew enough in 1965 to predict accurately how large the Medicaid program would become. Of course, Medicaid proponents may have also provided unrealistically low estimates of the program's cost and eligibility to ensure its passage in Congress (Friedman, 1987). Many people viewed the legislation that created Medicaid and Medicare as a stopgap measure. Democrats assumed that either Lyndon Johnson or Hubert Humphrey would be elected president in 1968 and that a universal health plan for all Americans would become a reality soon thereafter. After Richard Nixon's election, however, movement toward a universal health plan stalled and these temporary measures became permanent fixtures in the U.S. healthcare market (Friedman, 1990).

ELIGIBILITY

Three broad groups of people may be covered by a state's Medicaid program: the mandated categorically needy, the optionally categorically needy, and the medically needy (Oberg & Polich, 1988). Because Medicaid is a joint state–federal program, states have some flexibility in determining criteria for Medicaid eligibility. States establish their own criteria within federal guidelines, so eligibility for each of these groups may vary considerably from state to state.

Mandated Categorically Needy

If a state has a Medicaid program and wishes to receive matching federal funding, it must provide coverage for several groups of people. Federal welfare reform legislation enacted in the later half of the 1990s made a major change with respect to individuals who must be provided Medicaid coverage. Prior to enactment of the Personal Responsibility and Work Opportunities Act of 1996, individuals who received cash assistance (welfare) through Aid to Families with Dependent Children (AFDC) were automatically eligible for Medicaid. The 1996 welfare reform act, however, cut the link between Medicaid and cash welfare by replacing the AFDC program with the Temporary Assistance for Needy Families (TANF) program, which provides block grants to states to be used for time-limited cash assistance. TANF generally allows a family to receive cash welfare (income maintenance) benefits for no more than 5 years and allows states to impose other requirements related to employment. Even if they are not receiving welfare, families are still eligible for Medicaid if they meet the AFDC eligibility criteria that were put in place in July 1996 (Centers for Medicare and Medicaid Services, 2009a; FamiliesUSA, 1999).

While those eligible for Medicaid must fall below income and financial resources thresholds, Medicaid is not designed to provide assistance to all poor Americans. Even for very poor individuals, Medicaid covers healthcare services only if they fall into certain categories. Several eligibility groups of families and children are considered to be mandatory categorically needy, including (Centers for Medicare and Medicaid Services, 2009a) the following:

- Low-income families with children, with limits on income and resources determined by individual states. In 2009, for example, the maximum annual income limit for working parents to be eligible for Medicaid ranged from 17% to more than 200% of the federal poverty level (FPL) (Kaiser Commission on Medicaid and the Uninsured, 2009).
- Children under age 6 and pregnant women whose family income is below 133% of the FPL.
- Children under age 19 in families with incomes below the FPL.

A second mandatory group of individuals qualifies for Medicaid because they receive government cash assistance through the Supplemental Security Income program (Centers for Medicare and Medicaid Services, 2009a). This program provides assistance to persons who are poor and either elderly, blind, or disabled. As with TANF, eligibility for the Supplemental Security Income program is based on income and asset limits.

States must also provide limited Medicaid coverage to certain groups of low-income Medicare enrollees. Medicare-eligible individuals with incomes below the FPL and limited assets are known as qualified Medicare beneficiaries. Medicaid must pay the premiums and other cost-sharing expenses (such as deductibles and coinsurance) incurred with Part A and Part B of Medicare for qualified Medicare beneficiaries. For low-income Medicare beneficiaries with incomes between 100% and 120% of the FPL, Medicaid must pay only the Part B premiums. Individuals who have lost their Medicare disability benefits because they returned to work but are allowed to purchase Medicare coverage (called qualified disabled and working individuals) can qualify to have Medicaid pay their Medicare Part A premiums if their incomes are less than twice the FPL (Centers for Medicare and Medicaid Services, 2009a).

One provision of the Patient Protection and Affordable Care Act expands Medicaid coverage to all non-Medicare eligible individuals under age 65 with incomes up to 133% of the federal poverty level, effective January 1, 2014. To assist with financing for these newly eligible Medicaid recipients, states will receive 100% federal funding for these individuals for 2014 through 2016. This percentage will decline thereafter and stabilize at 90% federal financing for 2020 and subsequent years (Henry J. Kaiser Family Foundation, 2010g).

Optional Eligibility Groups

States have the option of providing coverage for other groups of needy individuals who do not meet the requirements for mandated coverage, although they may share certain characteristics with people in the aforementioned categories. Many of those considered optionally eligible are children or pregnant women. For example, states may cover infants up to 1 year of age and pregnant women in families not qualifying for mandated coverage but with incomes below 185% of the FPL. Likewise, children younger than age 21 who meet the income and asset requirements for TANF, but not the family status requirements, can be covered by state Medicaid programs (Centers for Medicare and Medicaid Services, 2005a). Another example of an optional eligibility group is persons with tuberculosis who would be financially eligible for Medicaid if they were in a Medicaid-covered category; their coverage is limited to tuberculosis-related services (Centers for Medicare and Medicaid Services, 2009a). If a state program does include the optionally categorically needy, it must provide these individuals with the same Medicaid benefits as those provided to people in the mandatory categories (Oberg & Polich, 1988).

Medically Needy Groups

At their option, state Medicaid programs may elect to cover a group known as the medically needy. These individuals include people who would be eligible for Medicaid under one of the mandated or optional groups, except for the fact that their income and/or assets are higher than allowed by the state. Such individuals become Medicaid eligible under the medically needy provision if their medical expenses reduce their net income to the Medicaid eligibility threshold or less. Thus the medically needy consist of families and children, or elderly, blind, or disabled individuals, who spend down to Medicaid eligibility by incurring high out-of-pocket medical expenses (Medicare and Medicaid Statistical Supplement, 1995). This spending-down process is especially important for granting Medicaid eligibility to institutionalized persons who incur extremely large medical expenses (Medicare and Medicaid Statistical Supplement, 1992).

Thirty-four states and the District of Columbia cover medically eligible persons in their Medicaid programs. When a state chooses to have a program for the medically needy, it must cover certain groups of people (e.g., children younger than age 19 and pregnant women who are medically needy) and services (e.g., prenatal and delivery care for pregnant women). States may include other groups and may offer different benefits to different groups under the medically needy option (Centers for Medicare and Medicaid Services, 2009a).

FINANCING AND ADMINISTRATION

Because Medicaid is funded by both federal and state governments, these entities share responsibility for administering this program. Through the CMS, the federal government establishes broad guidelines under which states must design and operate their individual programs. At the state level, a single agency must be designated as responsible for the Medicaid program. Within the federal guidelines, states have responsibility for establishing eligibility criteria, determining the type and scope of services to be covered, setting rates of payment for services, and administering their programs. Because states differ in exactly how they carry out these responsibilities, Medicaid programs vary considerably from state to state. A person who is Medicaid eligible in one state may not be eligible in nearby states, and the services provided may differ considerably between states (Centers for Medicare and Medicaid Services, 2009a; Medicare and Medicaid Statistical Supplement, 1995). Thus, while one may speak of Medicare as a program that is essentially uniform across the entire United States, there are actually 56 different Medicaid programs (one for each state, territory, and the District of Columbia).

Medicaid is entirely optional in the sense that the federal government does not require any state to have a Medicaid program. All 50 states do have Medicaid programs, of course, but they do so at their own discretion. Medicaid does not provide healthcare services for all poor Americans. Even in states with the broadest eligibility provisions, as illustrated by the case scenario presented above, Medicaid is unlikely to provide care for poor individuals unless they are children, parents, pregnant, elderly, blind, or disabled. As a consequence, it is important to recall that low income is only one criterion determining Medicaid eligibility (Centers for Medicare and Medicaid Services, 2003b). It has been estimated that only 45% of Americans living in poverty are covered by Medicaid (Galewitz, 2009).

The portion of Medicaid program costs that is paid by the federal government for provider services is known as the Federal Medical Assistance Percentage (FMAP). Each state's FMAP is determined annually through the use of a formula that compares a given state's average per capita income to the national average. By law, the FMAP can be no greater than 83% and no less than 50% for any given state. States that are wealthier in terms of average per capita income have a smaller share of their Medicaid costs paid by the federal government than do relatively poorer states. In 2009, the FMAP ranged from a high of almost 76% in Mississippi to 50% in 13 states. There are some exceptions to the FMAP rules. For example, the federal government reimburses states at a higher rate for family planning services and for healthcare services provided through Indian Health Service facilities. Most administrative costs are matched at 50%, but higher than normal matching rates are allowed for certain activities and functions, such as the costs of developing mechanized claims processing systems (Centers for Medicare and Medicaid Services, 2009a).

The American Recovery and Reinvestment Act of 2009, the so-called stimulus package, provided a temporary change to states' FMAPs. For a 9-quarter period, beginning in October 2008 and ending in December 2010, states were provided with an increase in their Medicaid FMAP, which ranged from 6.2% to almost 14%, depending on each state's unemployment rate. This increase in the FMAP was designed to help states during the recession, when demand for Medicaid services increased at a time when state budgets were under tremendous pressure. As a condition for receiving these additional funds, states could not restrict eligibility further or make it more difficult for people to apply for Medicaid benefits (Centers for Medicare and Medicaid Services, 2009a; Henry J. Kaiser Family Foundation, 2010b).

The total amount of money that the federal government spends on Medicaid has no set limit. It must match state government spending at the percentages established by law (Centers for Medicare and Medicaid Services, 2005b, 2009a). Thus, as state spending on Medicaid has escalated over time, so has the amount of money that the federal government contributes to the program.

State programs make payments directly to participating healthcare providers for services delivered to Medicaid patients. These providers must accept the amount of Medicaid reimbursement as payment in full; they may not bill patients for any difference between actual charges and Medicaid's approved charges (i.e., no balance billing). Payment levels are subject to federally mandated conditions to which states must adhere. For example, payments must be high enough to attract sufficient numbers of providers so that services will be available to Medicaid recipients to the same extent that those services are available to the general population in a given geographic area. As another example of the conditions that must be met, Medicaid payments for institutional services may not exceed the amounts that would be paid by Medicare (Medicare and Medicaid Statistical Supplement, 1995).

MEDICAID SERVICES AND COST SHARING

Services Covered

To receive federal matching funds, state Medicaid programs are required to offer a specified list of services to the mandatory and optional categorically needy groups. These required services include the following:

- Inpatient hospital services
- Outpatient hospital services
- Physician services
- Rural health clinic services
- Federally qualified health center services
- Laboratory and X-ray services
- Nursing facility services for individuals age 21 or older
- Early and periodic screening, diagnosis, and treatment services for individuals younger than 21 years of age
- Family planning services and supplies
- Home health services for persons eligible for skilled nursing services
- Nurse-midwife services
- Pediatric nurse practitioner and certified family nurse practitioner services
- Pregnancy-related services (Centers for Medicare and Medicaid Services, 2009a)

States also may receive federal funding for provision of a variety of optional services. States are under no obligation to cover any of these additional services, and the number of optional services provided by Medicaid programs varies widely. Outpatient prescription drugs are an optional service, for example, although they are covered by Medicaid programs in all 50 states. The following are examples of other optional services that are commonly covered:

- Prosthetic devices
- Physical and rehabilitative therapy
- Optometrist services and eyeglasses
- Services in an intermediate care facility for the mentally retarded
- Transportation services
- Hospice care
- Dental services (age 21 and older)
- Home and community-based care for certain persons with chronic impairments (Centers for Medicare and Medicaid Services, 2009a, 2010b)

Cost Sharing

States have broad discretion in determining reimbursement methodologies and payment rates within federal guidelines. Many states require Medicaid recipients to contribute to the cost of their health care in the form of deductibles, co-payments, or coinsurance (Centers for Medicare and Medicaid Services, 2009a). However, the magnitude of this cost sharing cannot be so great that it would present a serious barrier to receiving needed services. For example, in 2008, 80% of states imposed co-payments on outpatient Medicaid prescriptions, but most ranged between $0.50 and

$3.00 (Kaiser Commission on Medicaid and the Uninsured, 2008). Likewise, nursing home patients are expected to contribute most of their income to help pay for their care. There are certain services, however, for which cost sharing cannot be required (for example, emergency care, family planning services, pregnancy-related services, and services provided to children younger than age 18) (Centers for Medicare and Medicaid Services, 2009a).

EXPENDITURES

Growth in Medicaid Enrollment and Spending

In terms of both the number of beneficiaries and total expenditures, Medicaid has experienced tremendous growth since its inception. In 1972, Medicaid covered 17.6 million poor Americans, about 8.5% of the U.S. population, with total expenditures of less than $10 billion (National Center for Health Statistics, 1993). By 2010, the Medicaid program covered about 60 million persons, almost 20% of the population, and expended more than $400 billion annually (Centers for Medicare and Medicaid Services, 2009a; Truffer et al., 2010).

Spending by Eligibility Group

There are considerable differences between the proportion of beneficiaries and the proportion of expenditures accounted for by the major enrollment groups. Although 52% of all Medicaid beneficiaries in 2006 were children, less than 20% of Medicaid spending went to provide care for children. By comparison, the elderly represented only 8% of Medicaid beneficiaries but accounted for more than 22% of total spending. Similarly, blind and disabled persons made up just 16% of recipients, but they were responsible for 45% of expenditures. This disparity is explained by the fact that average Medicaid payments for children, the elderly, and the disabled were $1,752, $12,712, and $13,409, respectively (Centers for Medicare and Medicaid Services, 2009a).

Spending by Type of Service

Medicaid spending also varies by type of healthcare service. Substantial portions of Medicaid payments are associated with managed care, inpatient hospitals, nursing homes, and home health care, with each segment accounting for at least 14% of total payments in 2008 (see **Table 18-3**). These proportions have changed considerably for some services since the mid-1970s. Inpatient services (e.g., those delivered in inpatient hospitals, nursing homes, and intermediate care facilities for the mentally retarded) accounted for 66% of all Medicaid payments in 1975 but only about 33% in 2008. Similarly, payments for physician services declined from 10% to about 4% over the same period. Prescripton drugs accounted for less than 5% of Medicaid spending in 2008, a reduction from previous years due to enactment of Medicare Part D. The greatest change has been in managed care, which was essentially nonexistent in Medicaid in 1975 but now accounts for about 20% of Medicaid expenditures. Like Medicare, Medicaid has become a vital part of the U.S. healthcare system, accounting for 16% of all personal healthcare spending and 42% of nursing home expenditures (Centers for Medicare and Medicaid Services, 2009a, 2009b; Henry J. Kaiser Family Foundation, 2010c).

Table 18-3 Medicaid Expenditures by Service, 2008

Service	% of expenditures
Managed care	19.0
Inpatient hospital	15.0
Home health	15.0
Nursing homes	14.8
Outpatient care	7.4
Prescription drugs	4.7
ICF/MR*	3.8
Physician/lab/X-ray	3.7
Other	16.6

* ICF/MR = intermediate care facility/mentally retarded.
Source: Data from Henry J. Kaiser Family Foundation, 2010c.

STATE FLEXIBILITY

General Requirements for Medicaid Programs

State Medicaid programs must operate within broad guidelines established by the federal government. In addition to meeting the eligibility and services restrictions already described, the 1965 legislation required that states adhere to three other general requirements:

1. *Statewideness.* A state's Medicaid plan must be in effect across the entire state; the services covered in one part of a state generally cannot differ from those covered in another part of the state.
2. *Freedom of choice.* Medicaid recipients must be allowed to obtain covered services from any qualified participating provider.
3. *Comparability of services.* The amount, duration, and scope of services must be equal for all persons in the mandatory and optional eligibility categories (Medicare and Medicaid Statistical Supplement, 1992).

Section 1115 and 1915b Waivers

Under the SSA, CMS is given the power to grant two types of waivers of these requirements: (1) Section 1115 waivers, which allow statewide demonstration projects aimed at covering additional uninsured individuals and testing new budget-neutral delivery systems, and (2) Section 1915b waivers, which allow states to implement innovative delivery and reimbursement systems. These waivers were extremely important in allowing states to begin experimenting with managed care options for their Medicaid beneficiaries. The Balanced Budget Act of 1997 eliminated the need for states to request a waiver to implement Medicaid managed care programs (Centers for Medicare and Medicaid Services, 2009a; Muirhead, 1996).

Managed Care

As evidenced by these waiver programs, many of the efforts aimed at reforming Medicaid have involved greater utilization of managed care organizations for delivery of healthcare services. As a result of a number of factors, including the need for cost containment in light of Medicaid's cost explosion, the proliferation of managed care in the private sector, and changes in federal policy that have promoted the expansion of Medicaid-managed care through the waiver process, there has been tremendous growth in the number of Medicaid beneficiaries who are enrolled in managed care programs (Kaiser Commission on the Future of Medicaid, 1995). By 2008, almost 71% of Medicaid beneficiaries were enrolled in some form of managed care (Centers for Medicare and Medicaid Services, 2009a).

COMPARISON OF MEDICARE AND MEDICAID

Medicare and Medicaid are similar in the sense that both are health insurance programs financed and administered by government entities, and that both are roughly equivalent in terms of the number of beneficiaries and total expenditures. In many ways, however, Medicare and Medicaid are very different. Philosophically, Medicare is a social insurance policy for which beneficiaries have paid through taxes; Medicaid is based on a welfare concept of redistributing wealth among citizens of the United States. There also are differences between the two programs with respect to financing, administration, eligibility, and benefits. Thus these two government programs actually represent two very different mechanisms for delivering healthcare benefits to selected segments of American society, thereby providing a vital safety net for many of the nation's most vulnerable citizens.

QUESTIONS FOR FURTHER DISCUSSION

1. If Medicare did not exist today, do you believe such a program would be enacted by Congress? Why or why not?
2. If you were speaking to a group of senior citizens, how would you explain the importance of Medicare supplemental insurance?
3. What do you see as the advantages and disadvantages of delivering services to Medicare beneficiaries through managed care plans?
4. What do you believe are the primary strengths and weaknesses of the Part D prescription drug coverage?
5. Should Medicaid be expanded to cover more low-income people? Why or why not?
6. Do you believe Medicaid eligibility criteria should be uniform from state to state? Why or why not?
7. In the long term, do you believe that managed care will have a positive or negative effect on Medicaid and its recipients? Why?
8. How would you restructure Medicaid to ensure that it best meets the needs of low-income Americans at a reasonable cost?

KEY TOPICS AND TERMS

Assignment
Cost sharing
Federal Medical Assistance Percentage
Managed care
Mandated categorically needy
Medicaid
Medically needy
Medicare
Medicare Advantage
Medicare Part A
Medicare Part B
Medicare Part C
Medicare Part D
Medicare supplement (Medigap) insurance
Optionally categorically needy
Temporary Assistance for Needy Families
Waiver

REFERENCES

Ball, R. M. (1995). What Medicare's architects had in mind. *Health Affairs, 14*(4), 62–72.

Centers for Medicare and Medicaid Services. (2003b). *Medicaid eligibility.* Retrieved from http://www.cms.hhs.gov/medicaid/eligibility/criteria.asp

Centers for Medicare and Medicaid Services. (2003c). *Your Medicare benefits.* Baltimore, MD: U.S. Department of Health and Human Services.

Centers for Medicare and Medicaid Services. (2005a). *Brief summaries of Medicare & Medicaid.* Retrieved from http://www.cms.hhs.gov/MedicareProgramRatesStats/downloads/Medicare MedicaidSummaries2005.pdf

Centers for Medicare and Medicaid Services. (2005b). *Medicaid at-a-glance 2005.* Baltimore, MD: U.S. Department of Health and Human Services.

Centers for Medicare and Medicaid Services. (2008). *Medicare enrollment: National trends 1966–2008.* Retrieved from http://www.cms.gov/MedicareEnRpts/Downloads/HI08.pdf

Centers for Medicare and Medicaid Services. (2009a). *Brief summaries of Medicare and Medicaid.* Retrieved from http://www.cms.gov/MedicareProgramRatesStats/Downloads/Medicare MedicaidSummaries2009.pdf

Centers for Medicare and Medicaid Services. (2009b). *Medicare and Medicaid statistical supplement, 2009.* Retrieved from http://www.cms.gov/MedicareMedicaidStatSupp/10_2009. asp#TopOfPage

Centers for Medicare and Medicaid Services. (2010a). *Choosing a Medigap policy: A guide to health insurance for people with Medicare.* Retrieved from http://www.medicare.gov/Publications/Pubs/pdf/02110.pdf

Centers for Medicare and Medicaid Services. (2010b). *Medicaid dental coverage: overview.* Retrieved from https://www.cms.gov/MedicaidDentalCoverage/

Centers for Medicare and Medicaid Services. (2010c). *Medicare & you 2010.* Retrieved from http://www.medicare.gov/Publications/Pubs/pdf/10050.pdf

Centers for Medicare and Medicaid Services. (2011). *Choosing a medigap policy: a guide to health insurance for people with Medicare.* Retrieved from http://www.medicare.gov/Publications/Pubs/pdf/02110.pdf

Center for the Study of Services. (1995). *Consumers' guide to health plans.* Washington, DC: Center for the Study of Services.

Coleman, T. S. (1990). *Legal aspects of Medicare & Medicaid reimbursement: Payment for hospital and physician services.* Washington, DC: National Health Lawyers Association.

Congressional Budget Office. (2009). *March 2009 baseline: Medicare.* Retrieved from http://www.cbo.gov/budget/factsheets/2009b/medicare.pdf

Davis, M. H., & Burner, S. T. (1995). Three decades of Medicare: What the numbers tell us. *Health Affairs, 14*(4), 231–243.

FamiliesUSA. (2000). *Welfare–Medicaid links: What every welfare advocate should know about Medicaid.* Retrieved from http://www.familiesusa.org/resources/publications/fact-sheets/what-every-welfare-advocate-should-know-about-medicaid.html

Fein, R. (1989). *Medical care, medical costs* (2nd ed.). Cambridge, MA: Harvard University Press.

Friedman, E. (1987). Medicaid's overload sparks a crisis. *Hospitals, 61*(2), 50–54.

Friedman, E. (1990). Medicare and Medicaid at 25. *Hospitals, 64*(15), 38, 42, 46, 48, 50, 52, 54.

Galewitz, P. (2009). Medicaid: True or false? *Kaiser health news.* Retrieved from http://www.kaiserhealthnews.org/Stories/2009/July/01/Medicaid-True-or-False.aspx

Ginsburg, P. B. (1988). Public insurance programs: Medicare and Medicaid. In H. E. Frech III (Ed.), *Health care in America* (pp. 179–218). San Francisco, CA: Pacific Research Institute for Public Policy.

Health Care Financing Administration. (1996). *Your Medicare handbook, 1996.* Baltimore, MD: U.S. Department of Health and Human Services.

Health Care Financing Administration. (1998). *A profile of Medicare chart book.* Baltimore, MD: U.S. Department of Health and Human Services.

Hellman, S., & Hellman, L. H. (1991). *Medicare and Medigaps: A guide to retirement health insurance.* Newbury Park, CA: Sage.

Henry J. Kaiser Family Foundation. (1999). *Analysis of benefits offered by Medicare HMOs, 1999: Complexities and implications.* Menlo Park, CA: Henry J. Kaiser Family Foundation.

Henry J. Kaiser Family Foundation. (2003). *Medicare+Choice.* Menlo Park, CA: Henry J. Kaiser Family Foundation.

Henry J. Kaiser Family Foundation. (2005a). *Medicare at a glance.* Menlo Park, CA: Henry J. Kaiser Family Foundation.

Henry J. Kaiser Family Foundation. (2005b). *Medicare chart book 2005.* Menlo Park, CA: Henry J. Kaiser Family Foundation.

Henry J. Kaiser Family Foundation. (2005c). *The Medicare prescription drug benefit.* Menlo Park, CA: Henry J. Kaiser Family Foundation.

Henry J. Kaiser Family Foundation. (2009a). *Low-income assistance under the Medicare drug benefit.* Menlo Park, CA: Henry J. Kaiser Family Foundation.

Henry J. Kaiser Family Foundation. (2009b). *Medicare Advantage.* Menlo Park, CA: Henry J. Kaiser Family Foundation.

Henry J. Kaiser Family Foundation. (2009c). *Medicare Part D 2010 data spotlight: Benefit design and cost sharing.* Menlo Park, CA: Henry J. Kaiser Family Foundation.

Henry J. Kaiser Family Foundation. (2009d). *The Medicare prescription drug benefit.* Menlo Park, CA: Henry J. Kaiser Family Foundation.

Henry J. Kaiser Family Foundation. (2009e). *Medicare spending and financing.* Menlo Park, CA: Henry J. Kaiser Family Foundation.

Henry J. Kaiser Family Foundation. (2009f). *The Social Security COLA and Medicare Part B premium: Questions, answers, and issues.* Menlo Park, CA: Henry J. Kaiser Family Foundation.

Henry J. Kaiser Family Foundation. (2010a). *Explaining health care reform: Key changes to the Medicare Part D drug benefit coverage gap.* Menlo Park, CA: Henry J. Kaiser Family Foundation.

Henry J. Kaiser Family Foundation. (2010b). *Explaining health care reform: Questions about Medicaid's role.* Menlo Park, CA: Henry J. Kaiser Family Foundation.

Henry J. Kaiser Family Foundation. (2010c). *Medicaid at a glance.* Menlo Park, CA: Henry J. Kaiser Family Foundation.

Henry J. Kaiser Family Foundation. (2010d). *Medicare Advantage 2010 data spotlight: Benefits and cost sharing*. Menlo Park, CA: Henry J. Kaiser Family Foundation.

Henry J. Kaiser Family Foundation. (2010e). *Medicare at a glance*. Menlo Park, CA: Henry J. Kaiser Family Foundation.

Henry J. Kaiser Family Foundation. (2010f). *Medicare chartbook, fourth edition*. Menlo Park, CA: Henry J. Kaiser Family Foundation.

Henry J. Kaiser Family Foundation. (2010g). *Summary of new health reform law*. Menlo Park, CA: Henry J. Kaiser Family Foundation.

Kaiser Commission on the Future of Medicaid. (1995). *Medicaid and managed care: Lessons from the literature*. Washington, DC: Henry J. Kaiser Family Foundation.

Kaiser Commission on Medicaid and the Uninsured. (2008). *Medicaid benefits: Online database*. Retrieved from http://www.kff.org/medicaid/benefits/service.jsp?gr=off&nt=on&so=0&tg=0&yr=4&cat=5&sv=32

Kaiser Commission on Medicaid and the Uninsured. (2009). *Where are states today? Medicaid and state-funded coverage eligibility levels for low-income adults*. Washington, DC: Henry J. Kaiser Family Foundation.

Longest, B. B., Jr. (1994). *Health policymaking in the United States*. Ann Arbor, MI: Association of University Programs in Health Administration Press/Health Administration Press.

Medicare Payment Advisory Commission. (2009). *Report to the Congress: Medicare payment policy*. Retrieved from http://www.medpac.gov/documents/Mar09_EntireReport.pdf

Medicare and Medicaid Statistical Supplement. (1992). *Health Care Financing Review, 14*(suppl).

Medicare and Medicaid Statistical Supplement. (1995). *Health Care Financing Review, 16*(suppl).

Medicare and Medicaid Statistical Supplement. (2001). *Health Care Financing Review, 21*(suppl).

Muirhead, G. (1996). More Medicaid programs turning to managed care. *Drug Topics, 140*(8), 50–51.

National Center for Health Statistics. (1993). *Health, United States, 1992*. Hyattsville, MD: Public Health Service, U.S. Department of Health and Human Services.

Oberg, C. N., & Polich, C. L. (1988). Medicaid: Entering the third decade. *Health Affairs, 7*(4), 83–96.

Pharmacy Times. (2006). *Medicare offers seniors advice for dealing with Part D glitches*. Available at http://www.pharmacytimes.com/article.cfm?ID=3327

Truffer, C. J., Keehan, S., Smith, S., Cylus, J., Sisko, A., Poisal, J. A., Lizonitz, J., & Clemens, M. K. (2010). Health spending projections through 2019: The recession's impact continues. *Health Affairs, 29*(3), 522–529.

Ukens, C. (2006). *Medicare Part D off to rocky start*. Retrieved from http://www.drugtopics.com/drugtopics/article/articleDetail.jsp?id=283609

Zarabozo, C., Taylor, C., & Hicks, J. (1996). Medicare managed care: Numbers and trends. *Health Care Financing Review, 17*(3), 243–261.

Pharmacoeconomics

Kenneth W. Schafermeyer and Craig I. Coleman*

Case Scenario

Psoriasis is a common, chronic inflammatory skin disease with a prevalence of about 2–3% in the general population. It typically presents as thickened, erythematous, scaling plaques, which are often pruritic. Psoriasis has been associated with markedly elevated healthcare utilization, work limitations, and productivity loss. This, along with the clinically relevant reductions in health-related quality of life (HrQoL) experienced by many psoriasis patients, underscores the need for effective management with one of a number of potential drug therapies.

While mild or localized disease may be managed effectively with topical agents (emollients, vitamin A and D, and corticosteroids), patients with moderate-to-severe disease often require systemic treatment. In the United States, there are two broad classes of systemic drugs to treat chronic plaque psoriasis—nonbiologic agents and biologic agents. A nonbiologic systemic agent (such as methotrexate, cyclosporine, or acitretin) is often effective but may be associated with significant long-term toxicity. Furthermore, some patients have disease resistant to such agents or become refractory to treatment. As a result, patients often report high levels of dissatisfaction with such drugs. Numerous biologic agents have also gained United States Food and Drug (FDA) approval for psoriasis treatment. These agents, however, are associated with toxicities of their own, including an increased risk of significant infection. Biologic agents also have an annual cost that far exceeds that of nonbiologics such as methotrexate (a recommended gold-standard agent) ($18,000 to $28,000 for biologics vs. $1,200 for methotrexate).

A well-done randomized controlled trial is published in a respectable medical journal that demonstrates for the first time that a biologic agent, adalimumab, is more efficacious then methotrexate for treatment of moderate-to-severe chronic plaque psoriasis (Saurat et al., 2008; Revicki et al., 2008). Specifically, a greater proportion of patients taking adalimumab achieved the trial's primary efficacy end point, a 75% reduction in psoriasis area and severity index score (a psoriasis symptom score)

---

*The authors wish to express appreciation to Emily R. Cox, PhD, for her contributions on pharmacoeconomics published in previous editions of this text.

compared to those receiving methotrexate. The trial further demonstrates that patients receiving adalimumab have better HrQoL (measured as utilities), but also a greater theoretical risk of severe infections.

As a result of these new findings, Bob, the chairman of a large managed care organization's (Husky Health) pharmacy and therapeutics committee, is asked to consider the economic impact of adding biologic agents (such as adalimumab) to the formulary for this purpose. He needs to conduct a pharmacoeconomic evaluation to aid him in his decision-making process.

LEARNING OBJECTIVES

Upon completion of this chapter, the student shall be able to:

- Define pharmacoeconomics and explain how it is used
- Explain how perspective can affect a pharmacoeconomic study
- Define and differentiate among cost-minimization analysis (CMA), cost-benefit analysis (CBA), cost-effectiveness analysis (CEA), cost-utility analysis (CUA), cost-of-illness (COI) analysis, and cost-consequence analysis (CCA) (when should each be used, how they differ with regard to measuring costs and outcomes, and so on). Given a case study or a scenario, be able to calculate each and use them to decide among alternatives.
- Define, differentiate, and give examples of inputs, outputs, and outcomes
- Compare and contrast efficiency, efficacy, and effectiveness
- Define, differentiate, and give examples of the four types of costs used in pharmacoeconomic analyses
- Differentiate between a clinical end point and an outcome
- Critically appraise a pharmacoeconomic study

CHAPTER QUESTIONS

Begin formulating in your mind how Bob might begin to assess whether he should make this formulary addition.

1. Should Bob recommend these products be covered?
2. Upon what criteria should he base his decision?
3. What therapies should be compared to biologic agents?
4. What would the impact of adding biologic agents be to Husky Health's pharmacy budget?

INTRODUCTION

In 2008, overall spending for pharmaceuticals in the United States grew by 3.2% and average drug prices increased by 2.5% (Hartman, Martin, Nuccio, Caitlin, & the National Health Expenditure Accounts Team, 2010). Those most alarmed by rising pharmaceutical costs are, of course, those responsible for paying for and managing these costs. Payers of pharmaceuticals include employers, managed care organizations, and a myriad of healthcare institutions such as inpatient hospitals and the Veterans Administration. Those responsible for managing these costs are the individuals within these institutions who, through their own expertise and with the help of outside management organizations, such as pharmacy benefit management companies, attempt to constrain pharmacy costs in the face of limited budgets.

Decision makers charged with managing pharmacy costs have historically focused on the ingredient cost of the product along with its clinical profile in assessing a product's value. This is often referred to as the silo approach to evaluating pharmaceuticals. However, this approach does not consider how pharmaceuticals affect other healthcare costs, such as hospitalizations, physician visits, or laboratory services. All of these are important aspects to consider so as to capture the true value of pharmaceuticals.

Pharmacoeconomics is a term used to describe a compilation of methods that evaluate the economic, clinical, and humanistic dimensions of pharmaceutical products and services. More formally, pharmacoeconomics identifies, measures, and compares the costs and consequences of the use of pharmaceutical products and services (Bootman, Townsend, & McGhan, 1996). In its most simplistic form, a pharmacoeconomic evaluation compares the economic resources consumed (inputs) to produce the health and economic consequences of products or services (outcomes). This relationship is presented graphically in **Figure 19-1.**

The economic evaluation of health care began to take shape in the late 1970s with the writings of Weinstein & Stason (1977). The techniques used were taken from the field of public economics, particularly methods related to cost-benefit analysis. The application of economic evaluation to pharmacy began around the same time. These early writings and studies on the subject did not evaluate pharmaceuticals, but rather pharmacy services (Bootman, McGhan, & Schondelmeyer, 1982; Bootman, Wertheimer, Zaske, & Rowland, 1979). The focus shifted to evaluation of products after the term *pharmacoeconomics* appeared in the literature in 1986 (Townsend, 1986). A tremendous growth in the number of pharmacoeconomic studies appearing in the literature has occurred since that time.

Pharmacoeconomic evaluations have been used as a tool in selecting formulary products, developing treatment guidelines, conducting disease-management programs, establishing prior authorization policies, implementing step-therapy programs, and designing prescription drug benefit programs (Motheral, Grizzle, Armstrong, Cox, & Fairman, 2000). Together with information on a product's clinical efficacy, effectiveness, and safety, pharmacoeconomic information assists decision makers in optimizing the use of prescription therapy.

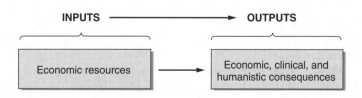

Figure 19-1 Pharmacoeconomic Evaluation of Health Care

The economic evaluation of pharmaceuticals and pharmacy services grew out of the need to establish value or to respond to the question of value. Statements of product or service value center on the following two attributes: cost and benefit. From the consumer's perspective, the price paid should reflect the benefit gained from use of the product or service. Several factors have created the need to monitor the value of pharmaceuticals more closely, including increased cost and thus growing concern on the part of payers, increased number of alternatives available to treat illness and disease, growing demand for pharmaceuticals, and the introduction of high-cost biotechnology products (Hartman et al., 2010).

To conduct pharmacoeconomic evaluations, the following six common methodological approaches are used: (1) cost-minimization analysis (CMA), (2) cost-benefit analysis (CBA), (3) cost-effectiveness analysis (CEA), (4) cost-utility analysis (CUA), (5) cost-of-illness (COI) analysis, and (6) cost-consequence analysis (CCA). This chapter covers each of these methods, including their advantages and disadvantages and their application to pharmaceutical products and services.

First, however, it is important to distinguish between several terms that are often confused with one another: efficiency, efficacy, and effectiveness. Efficiency can refer to a number of economic goals, such as properly allocating resources or increasing production. In our context, efficiency refers to the lowest cost per unit of output (or the biggest bang for the buck). It should be noted that an output is not the same as an outcome. For example, reducing the cost of prescriptions (outputs) may be efficient but it does not necessarily improve health outcomes.

Efficacy and effectiveness address outcomes. Efficacy answers the question, *Does the product work?* This question is answered through the clinical trial process, where it is determined whether the product does more good than harm. Effectiveness, however, seeks to determine whether the product works in real-world practice settings. Effectiveness answers the question, *Does the product work in those individuals it was designed to treat?*

COMPARING PHARMACOECONOMIC METHODOLOGIES

As shown in **Table 19-1,** each pharmacoeconomic method measures costs in monetary units (e.g., U.S. dollars). The methods differ from each other, however, in how (if at all) consequences are measured.

In both CMA and CEA, the consequences or outcomes of the intervention being evaluated are measured in natural units of effectiveness. Natural units of effectiveness are typically clinical measures of a product's efficacy or effectiveness, such as mm Hg or blood glucose levels, or in our plaque psoriasis scenario, improvement in psoriasis area and severity index score. Natural units of effectiveness also include years of life saved, judgments of clinical success, or cases averted because of an intervention.

CBA measures the consequences of the intervention in dollars, whereas CUA (often considered a special type of CEA) measures the consequences of therapy in quality-adjusted life years (QALYs). CCA also measures costs in dollars, but is different from the other methods in that multiple outcome measures are presented to the decision maker. COI analyses do not aim to compare treatment alternatives, but rather estimate the cost burden of a disease in a specific population. Each of these methods will be covered in greater detail later in the chapter.

Table 19-1 Measurement of Costs and Consequences Under Different Pharmacoeconomic Methodologies

Methodology	Cost	Outcomes	Calculation	Decision rule	Application
Cost-minimization analysis (CMA)	$	Proven equivalent	$Costs_1 - Costs_2$	Choose the alternative with the lowest total cost.	To compare alternative products or services that have equal efficacy and safety (e.g., brand versus generic substitution)
Cost-benefit analysis (CBA)	$	Outcomes converted into dollars	$NB = \Sigma$ benefits − Σ costs	Choose alternatives where the net benefits are positive, or if more than one alternative is being compared and resources are limited, choose the alternative with the greatest net benefit.	To compare programs with different outcomes (e.g., a vaccination program and a colon cancer screening clinic)
Cost-effectiveness analysis (CEA)	$	Natural units (e.g., achievement of PASI75)	$ICER = (costs_1 - costs_2)/(cure_1 - cure_2)$	$\leq$ \$20,000/additional outcome gained would be considered cost effective, whereas an intervention with an ICER $\geq$ \$100,000/additional outcome gained may not be.	To compare alternatives with similar indications or goals measured in the same unit of consequence (e.g., number of patients achieving PASI75 goal)
Cost-utility analysis (CUA)	$	Quality-adjusted life years (QALYs)	$ICUR = (costs_1 - costs_2)/(QALY_1 - QALY_2)$	> \$50,000 to \$100,000/QALY gained may not be considered cost effective.	To compare alternatives that results in changes in both quantity and quality of life (e.g., chemotherapy regimen)

(continues)

Table 19-1 Measurement of Costs and Consequences Under Different Pharmacoeconomic Methodologies (*Continued*)

Methodology	Cost	Outcomes	Calculation	Decision rule	Application
Cost-of-illness (COI) analysis	$	Not assessed	N/A	N/A	Determine the total economic burden of a disease on society (e.g., the economic burden of treating chronic plaque psoriasis)
Cost-consequence analysis (CCA)	$	Natural units, QALYs	No calculations performed	N/A	To present all costs and effects in a disaggregated format so that decision makers can choose among those that best fit their perspective

ICER = incremental cost-effectiveness ratio; ICUR = incremental cost-utility ratio; NB = net benefit; PASI75 = relative reduction in Psoriasis Area and Severity Index of 75%; QALY = quality-adjusted life year; Σ = sum.

The remainder of this chapter will not only familiarize readers with the terminology and concepts of pharmacoeconomics, but also present some of the basic guidelines for conducting pharmacoeconomic studies and equip students and practitioners for critical appraisal of the literature.

STEPS FOR CONDUCTING A PHARMACOECONOMIC EVALUATION

Before the specifics of each method are presented, some important points need to be considered. When conducting a pharmacoeconomic evaluation, it is important to (1) define the problem and state the objective; (2) identify the perspective and the alternative interventions to be compared; (3) identify and measure the outcomes of each alternative; and (4) identify, measure, and value the costs of all alternatives. Other important aspects of pharmacoeconomic evaluations to be discussed are discounting and performing sensitivity analysis.

Define the Problem and State the Objective

All pharmacoeconomic evaluations should begin with a clear and concise statement of the problem or question to be addressed. In the chapter-opening case scenario, Bob could evaluate the alternative systemic drug therapies (biologics and nonbiologics) for a specific indication or patient population, or he could compare the biologic agents to no therapy for a specific study population such as newly diagnosed patients. Examples of problem statements include "Are biologic agents cost effective for the treatment of moderate-to-severe plaque psoriasis?" and, more broadly, "What is the most cost-effective regimen for the treatment of moderate-to-severe plaque psoriasis?"

Identify the Perspective

Establishing the perspective of a study is an important step in pharmacoeconomic evaluation. Pharmacoeconomic evaluations can be conducted from several different perspectives, including those of the employer, the patient, the health insurance plan, society, and the government. For example, the perspective of the case scenario could be that of either Husky Health or the managed care organization's major employer group. The study perspective is an important factor in determining the costs considered relevant (i.e., cost of lost productivity is pertinent to the employer's perspective, but not to the healthcare provider's perspective), how costs are valued (i.e., the cost of a drug might be valued at actual acquisition cost from the provider's perspective, but as out-of-pocket costs or co-payment amount in the patient's perspective), the choice of outcomes measured (e.g., HrQoL or patient satisfaction is often only included in analyses conducted from the patient or societal perspective), and the time period over which the product or service will be evaluated.

An example from the literature highlights the importance of perspective and how it can influence the results of the study. A cost-benefit analysis of a routine varicella (chickenpox) vaccination program for healthy children was conducted from two perspectives—that of society and that of the payer of health services (e.g., a health plan) (Lieu et al., 1994). The study found that from a payer's perspective, the vaccine had a benefit-to-cost ratio that was less than 1:1 (i.e., the benefits were less than the costs). However, when conducted from a societal perspective, the benefit-to-cost ratio was greater than 1:1, suggesting that the program should be implemented. The difference in findings derived from which costs were considered relevant from the different perspectives. From society's perspective, costs related to lost workdays avoided because of the vaccine were relevant and, therefore, were included. From a payer's perspective, these costs were not considered relevant and, therefore, were not included in the analysis.

Identify Alternative Interventions

The decision as to which alternatives should be compared in pharmacoeconomic evaluations is important. A simple question to ask when considering which alternatives to compare is, *Have all relevant treatment alternatives been considered in addressing the research question?* In many studies, as in our case scenario, the alternatives involve drug-to-drug comparisons; in other situations, drug therapy is compared to no or nonpharmacologic therapies.

Alternatives are compared only when one of the alternatives is both more costly and more effective than the other options. **Figure 19-2** represents what is commonly referred to an incremental cost-effectiveness plane, with the horizontal axis representing the effect of a therapy and the vertical representing the cost. Four scenarios exist when comparing two different therapies (alternatives A and B). Alternative A is either

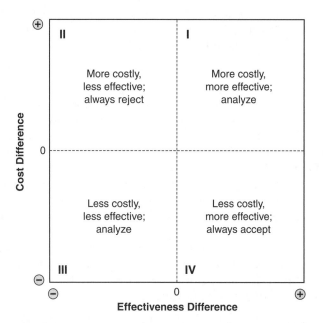

Figure 19-2 Incremental Cost-Effectiveness Plane and the Decision to Conduct a Pharmacoeconomic Evaluation. The incremental cost-effectiveness plane can be broken into four quadrants (I-IV). When comparing two agents, quadrants I and III represent scenarios where pharmacoeconomic analysis is helpful to determine how much additional money needs to be spent to get additional benefit. Quadrants II and IV represent scenarios were one agent dominates (is more effective and less costly or less effective and less costly) the other and analysis would be pointless.

more costly than B or less costly than B. The same relationship applies to the degree of effectiveness. In our case scenario, it is believed that the biologic agents are more effective but also more costly. If alternative A represents the biologic agents and alternative B the older nonbiologic agents such as methotrexate, this scenario would fall in the upper-right cell (quadrant I) of Figure 19-2. The researcher would then analyze the differences in costs and effects between these two alternatives. The same comparison could also be interpreted as methotrexate being less costly and less effective (quadrant III). In these scenarios, the question then becomes, *Is the additional gain in benefit or effectiveness worth the additional cost?* In those scenarios where one alternative dominates the other, such as in the upper-left and lower-right quadrants (quadrants II and IV) of the incremental cost-effectiveness plane, no analysis is necessary, since such analysis would provide little additional information.

Identify and Measure Outcomes of Each Alternative Intervention

When a clinician thinks about evaluating pharmaceutical products, the products' clinical effects immediately come to mind. In general terms, treatment could result in one of several outcomes (listed in order from most desirable to least desirable):

- A cure (health is restored)
- Improved quality of life
- Decreased incidence of morbidity
- Extended life
- Relief or reduction in symptoms
- No effect
- Increased morbidity (e.g., drug interactions or adverse drug reactions)
- Death

Some of these outcomes are easier to measure than others. Death, for example, is easy to measure and quantify. In contrast, measures such as decreased risk of morbidity and improved HrQoL are less exact. Outcomes may be difficult to measure because of the long follow-up required to determine whether the outcome has been achieved. For example, the desirable outcome for treatment of hypertension would be prevention of strokes or heart attacks (i.e., decreased incidence of morbidity). Achieving a normal blood pressure reading (e.g., diastolic reading < 90 mm Hg) is not, in itself, the desired outcome; it is merely an intermediate or surrogate measure or clinical indicator.

Although we would prefer to measure final or terminal outcomes, this process can require years, even decades. However, given that normal blood pressure is correlated with fewer heart attacks and strokes, we often accept intermediate measures as surrogate indicators of outcomes. For diabetes, for example, the desirable outcomes are prevention of complications (e.g., retinopathy, neuropathy, nephropathy). Because these outcomes also occur over the long term, we use intermediate measures such as blood glucose and glycosylated hemoglobin (HbA1c) levels as predictors of risk for complications of diabetes. For patients with asthma, we might desire an outcome of fewer complications (e.g., respiratory infections) or fewer emergency department visits or hospitalizations; the clinical indicators correlated with these outcome measures are peak-flow meter readings.

The outcomes discussed in the preceding paragraph were described in clinical terms. In fact, outcomes can also be described in humanistic terms (e.g., patient HrQoL or patient satisfaction) or in economic terms such as cost per day, cost per course of therapy, or cost per member per month. For a patient with asthma, for example, we could measure outcomes not only as the clinical end point peak-flow rate but also in terms of the patient's HrQoL or the cost of treatment over a given period of time. Using economic measurement assumes that a patient who is achieving the desired outcomes will need less intervention and treatment, such as physician visits, antibiotics, emergency department visits, or hospital admissions.

Identify, Measure, and Value Costs

As stated previously, the principles of pharmacoeconomics require one to identify, measure, and compare the costs and consequences of the use of pharmaceutical products and services. From a measurement aspect, two components exist—costs and consequences. Some of the issues related to identifying and measuring consequences or outcomes of therapy have been covered already. Our focus now shifts to the following three considerations that affect the cost side of the equation: identifying, measuring, and placing a value on resources or costs.

Identifying Relevant Costs

The first step in measuring costs is identifying all relevant resources consumed in association with the product or service under evaluation. To determine whether a cost is relevant, consider this question: *Would this cost have been incurred had the program not been implemented?*

As a method of identification, costs are often categorized as direct medical, direct nonmedical, indirect, or intangible costs.

Direct medical costs are resources consumed for medical services or products that are directly related to the product or service being evaluated. They include physician services, emergency department visits, laboratory services, prescribed medications, and hospitalizations. These costs are typically services covered by third-party payers, such as insurance companies, managed care organizations, or the government.

Direct nonmedical costs are those nonmedical resources consumed as the result of providing the product or service. They include transportation to treatment facilities and additional housing expenses incurred by the patients and their family when traveling to healthcare facilities outside their hometown. Other examples are special diets and exercise equipment required as a component of treatment or rehabilitation. These costs are not typically covered by third-party payers and are usually the responsibility of the patient.

Indirect costs are those costs indirectly associated with the product or service under evaluation. Illness and disease have an impact on resources outside the medical sector. For example, people who are sick may be unable to work or may be less productive. This loss of productivity is an important cost that should be captured in an evaluation. The inclusion of indirect costs is controversial in the literature, primarily because of the difficulty in measuring lost productivity and establishing causal links between illness and lost productivity. Nevertheless, many pharmacoeconomic studies attempt to measure the impact of morbidity or the ill effects of the treatment or health condition on worker productivity. These costs are often borne by patients, caregivers, employers, the government, and society.

Intangible costs are costs associated with pain and suffering resulting from treatment or the illness itself. Whereas these costs are important aspects of the product or service being evaluated, they can be very difficult to measure or quantify. Nevertheless, from the patient's perspective, these are real costs that the individual must bear.

Different types of costs are borne by different parties, and, consequently, the responsibility for payment of healthcare expenditures is fragmented. Managed care organizations, for example, determine what they will pay for in their statement of benefits; the patient then pays the remaining costs. In some cases, either patients or payers may try to shift costs to each other. When reviewing a pharmacoeconomic study, one should be aware of whether true cost savings have occurred or just cost shifting.

Measuring Costs

Once costs have been identified, the next step is to measure them. Depending on the type of cost, measurement often involves counts of units of resources consumed. These units can be amount of time or occurrence of certain events, such as hospitalizations or physician visits. For example, the number of office visits, hospitalizations, or laboratory services would be counted per patient over the time period of the evaluation. Measuring the cost of personnel services, whether it is nursing or pharmacist time, involves counts in units of time (often measured in what is commonly referred to as a time-motion study). However, some would argue that personnel time is a fixed cost and would be incurred whether the program was implemented or not. The inclusion of this cost is warranted if the time spent on the program detracts from other required responsibilities.

Valuing Costs

Once costs have been measured, the final step involves placing a dollar value on the resource or service. In a perfectly competitive market, the value of the resource would be based on the market price of the commodity or service. Of course, the price does not reflect the true opportunity cost for many healthcare products or services. Opportunity cost—an important concept in the valuation of resources—is defined as the value of a resource in its next best use.

To illustrate the idea of opportunity cost, consider a pharmacist who owns and operates his own independent pharmacy. The pharmacist has decided to expand the pharmaceutical care services he provides by offering flu vaccines to local senior citizens. As part of the proposal he has developed, he needs to estimate the additional hours he will spend on this service and place a value on these hours. The value of his time would not be based on the wages the pharmacist pays himself (which often vary based on the profitability of the business), but rather would be based on wages he would earn if he were employed elsewhere. In other words, his time should be valued based on the market price he could obtain if he were employed as a pharmacist at another local community pharmacy.

A critical component in the valuation of resources goes back to the issue of perspective. Perspective is important in health care, as in other sectors of the economy, because of the many ways in which the price of a commodity can vary by consumer. Consider the difference in price paid by a teaching hospital and the price paid by an independent pharmacy for the same pharmaceutical product. As discussed earlier, the resource should be valued based on its opportunity costs. However, because opportunity costs are often difficult to infer, researchers often use reference prices or reimbursement rates.

Reference prices are published list prices that serve as a reference for providers of those services or products. For example, a reference price for pharmaceuticals is the average wholesale price assigned to products by the manufacturer. Many reference price lists are publicly available for a myriad of healthcare products and services (Else, Armstrong, & Cox, 1997).

Another method of valuing resources is by identifying actual reimbursement rates for services. Actual reimbursement rates are difficult to obtain because they are considered proprietary and thus are not publicly available. Comprehensive sources of healthcare reimbursement rates that are publicly available are those for the Centers for Medicare and Medicaid Services. Through commonly used methods (Tumeh, Moore, Shapiro, & Flowers, 2005), those conducting pharmacoeconomic evaluations can use Healthcare Common Procedure Coding System (HCPCS)/Current Procedural Terminology (CPT) codes, Ambulatory Payment Classifications (APCs), International Classification of Disease (ICD) codes, and Diagnosis Related Groups (DRGs) to assign value to inpatient and outpatient physician, procedure and laboratory test, and inpatient and outpatient healthcare utilization.

What is controversial about using reference price lists or reimbursement rates as a proxy for actual cost is that these costs do not reflect the opportunity costs of using that resource elsewhere. Thus cost data should be adjusted when they are known to be very different from market prices. This adjustment ensures that costs are a true reflection of the opportunity cost of using those resources. Many methodological issues exist regarding valuation of costs, and readers should be aware of these controversies in conducting any economic evaluation (Copley-Merriman & Lair, 1994).

Sensitivity Analysis

Sensitivity analysis involves testing key outcomes or cost assumptions of an analysis to determine how sensitive the results are to variation or uncertainty in these estimates. In many pharmacoeconomic evaluations, the accuracy with which costs can be identified, measured, or valued will vary. Variation around the measurement of outcomes also exists. In critiquing studies, it is important to determine the key areas of uncertainty within a study and note whether researchers addressed areas of uncertainty through sensitivity analysis.

Numerous methods are available to test the impact of uncertainty within pharmacoeconomic evaluations (Briggs, Sculpher, & Buxton, 1994). Simple sensitivity analysis is the most commonly used and involves varying study assumptions (either cost or outcome) within the range of plausible values to determine if the original conclusions remain sound. When only one variable is altered at a time, this is called one-way simple sensitivity analysis. For example, a new biologic agent such as adalimumab to treat moderate-to-severe chronic plaque psoriasis, which was valued using a hospital's actual acquisition cost in the base-case economic evaluation, might be valued as high as its average wholesale price and as low as the cost of infliximab (an older biologic agent sold at a significantly lower cost). If the pharmacoeconomic evaluation's conclusions remain similar, they could be considered robust to changes in biologic drug cost, and the researcher can more easily defend his or her conclusions. If more than one variable is altered at a time, this is called multiple-way simple sensitivity analysis and is conducted and interpreted in the same fashion as a simple sensitivity analysis.

Analysis of extremes is conducted by reassigning values of both cost and effectiveness variables concurrently to their highest and lowest extremes in order to determine the robustness of the conclusions in the best and worst case situations. The best-case scenario is depicted by the highest effectiveness and lowest cost estimates, and the worst-case scenario is the lowest effectiveness and highest costs estimates. In order for this analysis to be useful to decision makers, sufficient detail of the extremes must be provided to determine whether the extremes being evaluated are near their own health plan's resource cost. The usefulness of analysis of extremes is questionable because it is doubtful that all worst-case or best-case findings will occur at the same time.

Threshold sensitivity analysis requires that a single assumption in the analysis be varied until the alternative treatment option has the same outcome and there is no advantage between the treatment options. The value determined by conducting such an analysis is often referred to as a break-even point. This break-even point can then be compared by decision makers to their value to make decisions concerning the validity of the evaluation's results to their institution.

Probabilistic sensitivity analysis allows researchers to assign plausible ranges for variables and an estimate of the distribution of the data points for each variable. The most common type of probabilistic sensitivity analysis is Monte Carlo simulation, which uses computer simulation to randomly assign values from inputted variable ranges and estimating outcomes from models with large numbers of hypothetical patients.

Discounting and Inflation

The final step in calculating costs relates to the issue of discounting. In those instances where the program or service being evaluated extends beyond one year, adjustment should be made for differences in timing that may occur between alternatives. The purpose of discounting is to determine the present value of all costs and to incorporate society's time preference for money. We all have a preference for when we would like to receive money. Most, if not all, of us would rather receive $10 today than $10 a year from now. Because money can generate interest income, $10 received today is worth more than $10 received 1 year from now. In most, if not all, cases, people prefer to incur costs later and reap benefits earlier. This same time preference applies to healthcare costs. Thus costs or benefits of alternatives realized at different times should be discounted to a present value to make valid comparisons.

The effects that discounting, or failure to discount, can have on study results are presented in **Table 19-2.** In this example, the total costs of two competing programs, A and B, are the same ($85,000), but the costs occur at different time periods. Assuming that money received today is worth 4% more than money received 1 year later (a 4% discount rate), the present value of costs are $75,022 for program A and $81,318 for program B, a difference of more than $6,000.

Table 19-2 Discounted Versus Undiscounted Costs

Program	Year					Undiscounted	Discounted at 4%
	0	1	2	5	10		
A	$25,000	$15,000	$15,000	$10,000	$20,000	$85,000	$75,022
B	$40,000	$20,000	$15,000	$10,000		$85,000	$81,318

The choice of a discount rate is important, as it can significantly affect the results of the evaluation. The U.S. Public Health Service Panel on Cost-Effectiveness in Health and Medicine recommends using a discount rate of 3% (Gold, Siegel, Russell, & Weinstein, 1996). Drummond and colleagues suggest several other factors to consider when discounting (Drummond, O'Brien, Stoddart, & Torrance, 1998), including:

- Presenting results in their undiscounted form so that the reader can evaluate the impact of discounting
- Using sensitivity analysis to vary the discount rate over a range of values
- When discounting affects the results, being clear with readers so that they are aware of its influence on the study's findings

Alternatively, evaluations often have cost or outcome data that were assigned a value at a point in the past. For example, when a retrospective pharmacoeconomic evaluation is undertaken, the value of both costs and outcomes were likely assigned at the time the resource was consumed or outcome realized. When conducting a study in 2010, the cost of a hospitalization occurring in 2009 (say $10,000) must be adjusted to reflect 2010 dollars. In these situations, the cost must be inflated to represent present-day value. Many investigators have chosen to use the Consumer Price Index (CPI) for Medical Care to represent this inflation rate. The CPI, which is calculated by the U.S. Bureau of Labor Statistics, represents the percentage change in the prices paid by urban consumers for medical care related products and services. Thus, the $10,000 hospitalization in 2009 is valued at $10,320 in 2010 dollars ($10,000 × 1.032 [the 2009 CPI for Medical Care was 3.2%]) (Gold et al., 1996).

PHARMACOECONOMIC METHODOLOGIES

Cost-Minimization Analysis

Cost-minimization analysis (CMA) compares the costs and consequences of two or more therapeutic interventions that are equivalent in terms of their outcomes or consequences. Thus the purpose of CMA is to choose the least costly alternative among interventions with equivalent outcomes. CMA is often confused with cost analysis, in which only the costs of therapy are evaluated. However, consequences are also evaluated in CMA to show or prove equivalency.

The requirement of equivalent outcomes limits the application of CMA to those situations where equivalency of both effectiveness and safety consequences has been established. They include, but are not limited to, comparisons between branded and generic products, comparisons of different routes of administration of the same drug, and comparison of different settings for the administration of the same drug therapy—for example, inpatient versus home therapy. In all of these instances, the evidence supporting equivalent outcomes should be clearly stated and, where appropriate, statistically confirmed.

Because the consequences of alternatives being compared are shown to be equivalent, CMA focuses on cost differences. These differences in cost can be presented as average cost per patient or average total cost of care if the number of patients is the same under each alternative. When choosing between alternatives, decision makers will then choose the alternative with the lowest total cost.

Cost-Benefit Analysis

Cost-benefit analysis (CBA) was first defined as:

> a way of assessing the desirability of projects, where it is important to take a long view (in the sense of looking at repercussions in the future) and a wide view (in the sense of allowing for side effects of many kinds on many persons, industries, regions, etc.), i.e., it implies the numeration and evaluation of all relevant costs and benefits. (Prest & Turvey, 1965, p. 721)

The two aspects of CBA—taking a long and wide view—have made it most applicable to decisions with a broad societal impact, such as whether to fund immunization programs or whether to implement child safety seat legislation. In evaluating each of these programs, researchers would take a long view (estimating the value of the lives lost in terms of future productivity on the community) and the wide view (estimating not only the direct benefits but also the indirect benefits to the community from reduced risk of illness to those not immunized).

In measuring outcomes in dollars, CBA enjoys an advantage over other economic evaluations. It can compare alternatives that are not measured using the same natural unit of effectiveness. For example, CBA could compare an immunization program to child safety seat regulations to determine which program would yield the highest net benefit (benefits minus costs).

One of the methodologically challenging aspects of CBA is measuring and valuing benefits in dollars. Two broad categories of direct benefits can be measured in CBA—personal health benefits and medical resource benefits. The measurement and valuation of medical resource benefits have already been discussed. The measurement of personal health benefits is more challenging. Personal health benefits include the alternative's effects on morbidity or mortality. Changes in morbidity are reflected in the following two ways: changes in medical resource consumption for treatment of illness, and intangible benefits such as reduction in pain and suffering. The impact on mortality is captured as the number of lives saved. Two methods are commonly used to value lives saved: the human capital approach and the willingness-to-pay approach.

The human capital approach measures the value of a life saved in terms of the income that the person could have earned over his or her remaining productive years. The criticism of the human capital approach of valuing human life is that it focuses on the productivity of the individual and not his or her value to family and friends. Also, because of imperfections in the labor market, this method tends to undervalue women, the elderly, and minorities.

Willingness to pay values both the intervention's impact on lives saved and intangible benefits. In measuring willingness-to-pay values, individuals are presented with a hypothetical statement describing the illness or disease and asked to express their willingness to pay to reduce the risk of death, pain, or suffering (Gafni, 1991). The advantage of willingness to pay is that, in theory, it measures the full range of benefits, including productivity and intangible benefits. The disadvantage is that the willingness-to-pay approach is a difficult method to apply and relies on individuals' abilities to comprehend and respond to hypothetical statements regarding small changes in health risks.

Presentation of Results

Two methods are most commonly used to present results in CBA. Those methods are net benefit and cost-to-benefit or benefit-to-cost ratios.

Net Benefit

The formula for calculating net benefits when costs and benefits do not extend beyond 1 year is presented in **Equation 19-1**. The formula for calculating the net benefit when either costs and/or benefits extend beyond one year, also known as net present value, is presented in **Equation 19-2**. If the project lifetime extends beyond 1 year, the net benefits should be adjusted using an appropriate discount rate (r).

$$NB = \sum_{i=1}^{x} B_i - \sum_{i=1}^{y} C_i \tag{19-1}$$

$$NPV_i = \sum_{t=0}^{n} \frac{B_t - C_t}{(1 + r)^t} \tag{19-2}$$

where:

NB = net benefit

NPV_i = present value of net benefit received from project i

B_t = benefits received from the project in year t

C_t = costs of the project in year t

$1/(1 + r)$ = discount factor at rate of interest r

n = lifetime of the project

Equation 19-1 calculates the net benefit (NB) as the sum of all benefits (B), minus the sum of all costs (C). Equation 19-2 discounts costs and benefits to their net present value using the appropriate discount rate.

The decision rules for determining cost benefit are definite. The decision criteria when results are presented as net benefit, assuming a limited budget, would be to choose the project that provides the greatest net benefit or—if funds allow—to choose those projects that provide a positive net benefit.

Ratio Analysis

The formulas used in calculating benefit-to-cost ratios when costs and benefits are measured within a 1-year period and when they extend beyond 1 year are presented in **Equations 19-3 and 19-4**, respectively.

$$\text{BC ratio} = \sum_{i=1}^{x} B_i \div \sum_{i=1}^{y} C_i \tag{19-3}$$

$$\text{BC ratio} = \sum_{t=0}^{n} \frac{B_t}{(1 + r)^t} \div \sum_{t=0}^{n} \frac{C_t}{(1 + r')^t} \tag{19-4}$$

where:

$$B_t = \text{benefits received from the project in year } t$$
$$C_t = \text{costs of the project in year } t$$
$$1/(1 + r) = \text{discount factor at rate of interest } r$$
$$n = \text{lifetime of the project}$$

The decision rule for choosing among projects when results are presented as ratios would be to choose those projects with a benefit-to-cost ratio greater than 1:1, or inversely where the cost-to-benefit ratio is less than 1:1. Assuming limited resources, the task would then be to select the project or projects with the highest benefit-to-cost ratio or lowest cost-to-benefit ratio.

How results are presented (net benefit versus ratios) can influence the decision. As an example, **Table 19-3** presents four hypothetical program options with their costs and benefits. Results are calculated both as net benefit and benefit-to-cost ratios.

Based on the information in Table 19-3 and assuming unlimited resources, the free oral contraceptives, the statewide drug abuse program, and the smoking cessation programs would be considered because their benefits are greater than their costs and the benefit-to-cost ratios are all greater than 1:1. Under conditions of limited resources, if one were to choose the project with the greatest net benefit, the choice would be the drug abuse treatment program. If the decision were based on benefit-to-cost ratio, however, the choice would be the free oral contraception program.

It is generally agreed that presenting results in terms of the net benefit provides decision makers with more information. For example, presenting results as a ratio does not provide information on the magnitude of both costs and benefits. Although the drug abuse treatment program included in Table 19-3 provides the greatest net benefit, it also requires an outlay by the state of $2 million.

Summary

Cost-benefit analysis remains a unique method of assessing the costs and benefits of programs and therapy interventions. However, it is applicable only when outcomes

Table 19-3 Presentation of Results in Hypothetical Cost-Benefit Analysis

Option	Benefits ($)	Costs ($)	Net benefit	Benefit-to-cost ratio
Free oral contraceptives at County Health Department	$45,000	$20,000	$25,000	2.25
Statewide drug abuse treatment program	$2 million	$1.5 million	$500,000	1.33
Additional police protection in high-crime neighborhoods	$85,000	$90,000	−$5,000	0.94
Smoking cessation program	$200,000	$100,000	$100,000	2.00

are easily converted to dollars and is most appropriate in situations where the objectives are broad in scope.

Cost-Effectiveness Analysis

Cost-effectiveness analysis (CEA) is the most commonly used pharmacoeconomic method. Its popularity is attributable in part to the way in which outcomes or consequences are measured (e.g., natural units of effectiveness). CEA is restricted to those situations in which the outcomes of the alternatives are all measured on the same scale, such as mm Hg or serum cholesterol levels. The purpose of CEA is to compare the costs and consequences of two or more alternatives to determine which alternative can achieve the best outcome at the lowest cost.

The term *cost effective* is often misused in the literature. The judgment of whether a product is cost effective is relative and often subjective. It is relative in the sense that when a product or service is deemed cost effective, this distinction is made in comparison to the costs and outcomes of other alternatives. It is subjective in the sense that the decision maker determines whether the additional cost is worth the additional gain in effectiveness. Some guidelines exist to determine under what range of values a product would be considered cost effective (for example, cost per QALY gained). In many other situations, it is left to the decision maker to determine what qualifies as cost effective. Unlike CBA where the decision rules for determining cost benefit are definite, the decision rules in CEA can be subjective.

Results of a CEA take the form of an incremental ratio of costs to outcomes. **Table 19-4** presents the average total costs per patient and the average outcome per patient for three therapies used to treat a common toenail fungus. Also shown in the table are the average cost-effectiveness ratios and the incremental ratios. The outcome is measured simply as number of successful cases. When determining whether an alternative is cost effective, one has to ask, "Are you willing to pay $122, $155, or $187 per successfully treated patient?" The investigator might be willing to pay all three prices, but certainly $122 per successful treatment appears to be the more efficient treatment regimen when compared to doing nothing. Of course, comparing an alternative to doing nothing is not a realistic approach.

Incremental cost-effectiveness ratios are a more appropriate way to compare product alternatives in cost-effective analysis. What additional amount must be paid to obtain the additional successfully treated cases? Comparing alternatives A and B (because B is both more costly and more effective), we see the additional cost of $65 would pro-

Table 19-4 Average and Incremental Cost-Effectiveness Ratios

Alternative	Average cost per patient	Outcome (success rate)	Average cost-effectiveness ratio	Incremental cost-effectiveness ratio
A	$ 85	0.55	$155/successful case	
B	$150	0.80	$187/successful case	$260/additional successful case treated
C	$ 95	0.78	$122/successful case	$43/additional successful case treated

vide an additional gain in the rate of successfully treated cases of 0.25. The cost per additional successfully treated case is $260 ($65 ÷ 0.25). Comparing alternatives A and C shows that the incremental ratio is $43 per additional successfully treated case. Based on this information, alternative C appears to be the most cost-effective alternative, given that the additional successfully treated cases cost less, on average, than the average cost of treatment under alternative A ($155 per successful case).

No established guidelines exist to determine whether an alternative is cost effective in this example of antifungal therapies. In this scenario, decision makers may have been willing to pay $155 or even $187 per successfully treated case because the idea of cost-effectiveness is value for money. They may have been willing to pay these costs to obtain the benefit of successful treatment. In comparing all three alternatives, however, they discovered that alternative C is the most efficient (i.e., least costly for a given level of output) and most cost-effective option.

Budget impact analysis is increasingly being considered an integral companion to a comprehensive CEA (Mauskopf et al., 2007). Budget impact analyses aim to estimate the financial impact of adoption and diffusion of a new healthcare intervention (deemed cost effective in a CEA) within a specific healthcare setting. Specifically, budget impact analyses predict how a change in the formulary mix of drugs used to treat a disease state will affect healthcare spending for that disease state, and therefore, can be used for budget planning. Many managed care organizations in the United States now require pharmaceutical companies to submit budget impact analyses along with cost-effectiveness data to support their requests for formulary inclusion.

Cost-Utility Analysis

While CEA is the most popular pharmacoeconomic methodology, in certain healthcare decision-making situations, CEA may not provide a sufficient or optimal to answer the question at hand. For example, suppose a patient with cancer has a choice of two chemotherapy agents. The newer, more expensive chemotherapy agent is expected to increase the patient's life span modestly more than an older and cheaper agent. However, during treatment with the newer agent, the patient is expected to experience greater discomfort than with the older agent, and as a result, be unable to carry out activities of daily living such as bathing or dressing. Thus, while the newer chemotherapy agent will extend the patient's life, the patient's preference for those extended years of life may be diminished when the quality of those additional years of life is considered.

CUA, often considered a subtype of CEA, measures both the quantity and quality aspects of two or more therapies. Most commonly in CUA, the natural effectiveness units of life years saved are converted to quality-adjusted life years (QALYs) by multiplying life years saved by a utility value. Utility is often perceived as preference, and it is measured on a scale of 0.0 to 1.0, where 0 represents death and 1 represents perfect health. Most health states fall somewhere between these extremes. Therefore, 1 life year multiplied by a utility of 1.0 equals 1.0 QALY, as does 2 life years with a utility of 0.5 (2 life years saved × 0.5 = 1 QALY). Utility scores are elicited from patients through a number of methodologies including visual analog scales, validated questionaires, and by employing standard gamble or time trade-off game theories. All are similar in that they assume that when given a choice, patients will choose the health state with the highest utility score assigned to it.

An interactive example demonstrating how a visual analog scale can be used to elicit a utility score is provided in **Exhibit 19-1.**

As in CEA, both average and incremental cost-utility ratios are calculated in CUA. The additional cost of a given treatment is divided by the additional effectiveness. The only difference is that effectiveness is measured as a QALY rather than in life years alone or other natural units of effectiveness. To continue our example, consider that patients with moderate-to-severe plaque psoriasis could be treated with a biologic agent or a nonbiologic agent such as methotrexate. In this scenario, we could use CUA to assess the cost-effectiveness of choosing one treatment strategy over the other. Let's assume that to administer a biologic agent to patients for 5 years costs $100,000. Treatment with methotrexate for the same period of time (we will assume that all patients will survive the entire 5 years in both groups, since neither moderate-to-severe plaque psoriasis nor the treatments are associated with a change in risk of death) and costs only $6,000. Assume further that the biologic agent results in patients having an average utility value of 0.9 and methotrexate a utility value of 0.8. Would biologic agents be considered a cost-effective treatment? Would their use be preferable to methotrexate?

Exhibit 19-1 Visual Analog Scale

Imagine you suffered from moderate-to-severe chronic plaque psoriasis as described below:

You are a 31-year-old male with thick, well-defined, erythematous plaques covered with silvery scales on both arms and legs and a dense scale evident on your scalp. Altogether, approximately 25% of your body is covered with psoriasis plaques. For the past year you have been applying a corticosteroid cream to affected areas twice a day. Although you enjoy being outside, you have started to feel quite emotionally distraught in public places because you sense that other people are staring at you. Recently, you have begun to go to your dermatologist's office every other week to receive subcutaneous injections. This has reduced the redness and scaling some, but you dislike getting injections and having to waste time going back and forth to the dermatologist's office. You also worry about the side effects of this new drug because it predisposes you to serious infections.

If 0.0 represents death and 1.0 represents perfect health (the best health imaginable for a person your age), please mark on the line the level of health described above.

0.0   1.0

The literature would suggest that the average patient with moderate-to-severe plaque psoriasis as described above would provide a utility score around 0.7 (Revicki et al., 2008).

If you live for 4 years with plaque psoriasis as described above and have a utility value of 0.7 during those years, then you have accumulated 2.8 QALYs.

If we conducted a cost-utility analysis, the incremental cost utility ratio would be:

Incremental CU ratio = Additional cost of biologics ÷ additional QALYs with biologics

$$= (\$100,000 - \$6,000) \div [(5 \text{ years} \times 0.90 \text{ utility}) - (5 \text{ years} \times 0.80 \text{ utility})]$$

$$= \$94,000 \div (4.5 \text{ QALY} - 4.0 \text{ QALY})$$

$$= \$94,000 \div 0.50 \text{ QALY}$$

$$= \$188,000 \text{ per additional QALY gained}$$

Although this is somewhat arbitrary, many have concluded that an intervention that results in an incremental CU ratio > $50,000 to $100,000 per QALY gained may not be considered cost effective (Harvard Public Health Review, 2004; Weinstein & Skinner, 2010). The $188,000 additional cost per QALY calculated in our scenario is above this threshold and consequently, suggests that the extra benefits of biologic agents to treat moderate-to-severe plaque psoriasis may not be worth the extra cost. While in our scenario, biologic agents were not found to be cost effective, many therapies have been found to have incremental CU ratios that fall significantly below this threshold. These include influenza vaccination in the elderly, beta blockers in patients postmyocardial infarction, combination antiretroviral therapy in HIV patients, and the use of antihypertensive agents in adults 35–64 years of age with high blood pressure but no coronary disease.

Cost-of-Illness Analysis

Cost-of-illness (COI) analyses (also commonly referred to as burden-of-illness analyses), attempt to estimate the magnitude of resources needed for a specific disease state in a defined population. COI analyses include both direct and indirect costs associated with prevention, treatment, and disease-related morbidity and mortality. Such analyses provide a unique benefit to healthcare decision makers because these analyses do not compare competing treatment alternatives but rather provide insight into the value of disease prevention or treatment of an illness. They can also be used to compare the relative economic burden of one disease state compared to another to aid decision makers in allocating limited healthcare resources and research funding monies.

COI analyses have been used to estimate the economic burden of many different chronic diseases in the United States, such as type 2 diabetes mellitus. Related to the chronic plaque psoriasis case scenario at the beginning of this chapter, a COI published in 2008 found the cost of psoriasis to be approximately $1,500 per patient per year, with indirect (work loss) costs accounting for 40% of the cost burden (Fowler et al., 2008).

Cost-Consequence Analysis

Cost-consequence analysis (CCA) has been defined as an analysis that presents all costs and effects in a disaggregated format (Mauskopf, Paul, Grant, & Stergachis, 1998). Costs are listed in table format by type of costs (e.g., direct medical, direct nonmedical, indirect costs, and intangible costs) as are outcomes (e.g., clinical intermediaries, dollars, and QALYs). Decision makers can then choose among the costs and outcomes that best fit their perspective. The advantage of CCA lies in its comprehensiveness and

Table 19-5 Presentation of Costs and Consequences in Cost-Consequence Analysis

| | Drug A | | Drug B | |
	Units	Costs	Units	Costs
Costs (per patient)				
Direct medical	—	—	—	—
Drug therapy	—	—	—	—
Physician costs	—	—	—	—
Hospitalizations	—	—	—	—
Direct nonmedical				
Transportation	—	—	—	—
Caregiver time	—	—	—	—
Indirect				
Productivity (lost days/episode)	—	—	—	—
Consequences				
Clinical				
Cases successfully treated	—	—	—	—
Quality-of-life (QALY)	—	—	—	—

transparency for decision makers. The disadvantage of CCA is that the researcher must identify, collect, and value costs and outcomes salient to a variety of perspectives. This burden of analysis, however, far outweighs the potential gain for decision makers.

Table 19-5 provides a framework for how costs and consequences would be presented in a CCA. All costs and consequences are identified and measured in units, and a cost is assigned to each unit. Based on this information, decision makers can choose the costs and consequences that are relevant for their purposes. They can then calculate average and incremental ratios for each alternative.

Figure 19-3 depicts a decision algorithm to assist decision makers in selecting the most appropriate pharmacoeconomic methodology.

APPROACHES TO CONDUCTING PHARMACOECONOMIC STUDIES

Pharmacoeconomic evaluations can be conducted using several approaches, including randomized controlled trials, naturalistic designs, decision analysis, and retrospective claims analysis.

Randomized Controlled Trials

Randomized controlled trials involve randomly assigning patients to the alternative therapies being considered. A standard protocol is established, and patients are followed over a specified time period. Patients and investigators are blinded as to which alternative they receive. The advantage of this design is that it has strong internal validity—that is, the results are attributable to the intervention and not to other extraneous factors. The disadvantage is that randomized controlled trials can be costly, and the strict adherence to treatment protocols is not reflective of real-world practice settings.

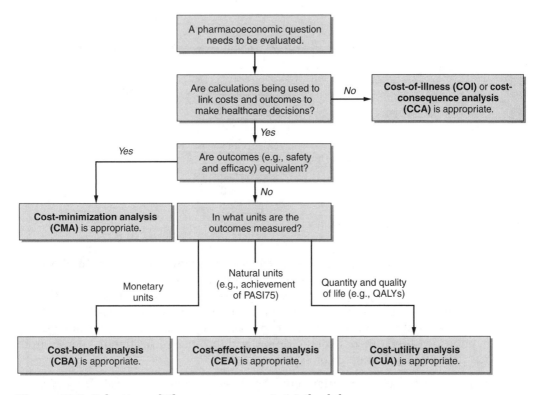

Figure 19-3 Selection of Pharmacoeconomic Methodology

Naturalistic Designs

Naturalistic designs are similar to clinical trials in that patients are randomly assigned to treatment groups, but the patients recruited and the follow-up care delivered would be representative of routine clinical care (Simon, Wagner, & Vonkorff, 1995). Whereas this type of study design does have its advantages, it can be expensive.

Decision Analysis

Decision analysis is a systematic approach to decision making under conditions of uncertainty. Rather than conducting the study prospectively or collecting data on individual patients, decision analysis synthesizes clinical data from the literature with data on resource use to simulate or model the question or problem. The following two modeling types are often used to represent the decision process: decision analysis and Markov models. Decision analysis is employed when direct observation is not feasible or when time or money constraints prohibit collecting data prospectively. The advantage of decision analysis as compared to clinical or naturalistic trial study designs is that results can be obtained in a timely and cost-efficient manner.

The use of decision analytic models (also known as decision trees) is becoming increasingly popular in the literature. **Figure 19-4** depicts a simplified decision tree for the decision of whether to treat a particular disease with drug therapy. The decision node, represented by the square (□), designates the point at which the decision to treat or not to treat is made. If the decision is to treat, the process follows the branch of the tree for drug therapy. The branch then comes upon a chance or probability node, represented

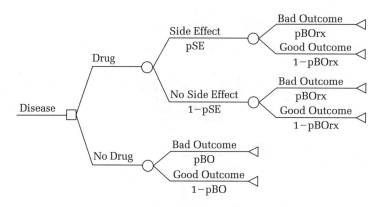

Figure 19-4 Decision Analysis Tree

by a circle (○), at which point a probability of experiencing a side effect (pSE) exists. Patients must either experience a side effect or not experience a side effect, so the probability of no side effect is therefore 1 minus the probability of a side effect (1 − pSE). The terminal branch for each alternative (drug or no drug) is the chance of a bad outcome (pBOrx) or a good outcome (1 − pBOrx). The probabilities used in the model are derived from the published literature or expert opinion, and resource utilization is inferred from either accepted practice standards or expert opinion.

As an example, assume three antiepileptic medications could be used. Drug A costs $120 per month, Drug B costs $160 per month, and Drug C costs $230 per month. Assume also that Drug A is 60% effective, Drug B is 80% effective, and Drug C is more than 90% effective. The managed care organization has already decided that Drug C should be used only in those cases in which either Drug A or Drug B has been tried unsuccessfully. An unsuccessful trial of either Drug A or B will result in an additional physician office visit costing $30 plus the cost of Drug C. Which drug, A or B, would be more cost effective?

One way to answer this question is to use a decision tree like the one depicted in **Figure 19-5.** For Drug A, the cost of effective treatment is multiplied by the probability of effectiveness (pE), whereas the cost of unsuccessful treatment ($120 for Drug A, plus $30 for the additional office visit, plus $230 for the new Drug C) is multiplied by the

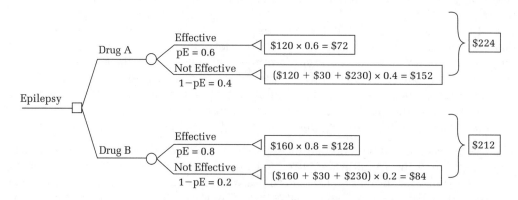

Figure 19-5 Hypothetical Decision Tree for First Line Epilepsy Treatment

probability that Drug A is not effective (1 − pE). The sum of these costs is compared to the sum of the same costs for Drug B. The results show that although Drug B costs more than Drug A, it is actually more cost effective. Therefore, based on this information, Drug B would be preferred. As presented, the assumption is made that the products do not differ substantially in any other aspect, such as their side-effect profiles.

Markov Modeling

Decision trees are difficult to use for modeling chronic disease states in which patients may experience intermittent relapses and remissions. A convenient solution to this problem is to use Markov models. Markov models offer advantages when a problem involves risk that is continuous, when the timing of events is important, and when important events may happen more than once (Sonnenberg & Beck, 1993). The Markov model frames the decision in terms of health states and follows patients as they transition from one state to another.

Figure 19-6 illustrates a three-state Markov model in which the health states are well, ill, or dead. When patients are well, there is a probability that they will become ill, stay symptom free, or die. When they experience symptoms, there is a probability that they could go into remission, stay symptomatic, or die. Of course, when they die, patients cannot change to other health states. In this way, Markov models simulate the natural progression of chronic diseases (Elliott & Payne, 2005).

The probabilities of moving from one state to the other are usually included in Markov models based on data published in the literature. (For example, a researcher could determine from the literature the probability that a patient with multiple sclerosis will either experience an asymptomatic period or die.) More sophisticated analyses may recognize that the probability of illness and death increases according to the duration of the disease, the age of the patient, and other variables. To the extent possible, these factors could also be included to determine probabilities of events. While pharmaco-economics calculations using Markov models are beyond the scope of a single-chapter

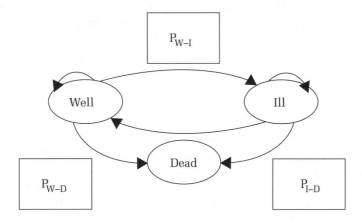

Figure 19-6 Three-State Markov Model. *Source:* Sonnenberg, F. A., & Beck, J. R. (1993). Markov models in medical decision making: A practical guide. *Medical Decision Making, 13*(4), 322–338. Reprinted by permission of Sage Publications, Inc.

overview of pharmacoeconomics, it is useful for students to know that Markov models are a better choice than decision trees for analysis of certain chronic diseases such as multiple sclerosis, osteoporosis, and arthritis.

Retrospective Claims Analysis

Retrospective analysis of claims data (also known as observational data) can also be used to evaluate the costs and consequences of drug therapy. The advantages of using claims data are that they reflect routine clinical care, are comprehensive, and provide a large sample of patients to evaluate. Additionally, the evaluations often involve less time and lower costs than randomized controlled trials or naturalistic designs. However, claims data were developed for billing and reimbursement purposes rather than to monitor and track healthcare costs and outcomes. As a consequence, several limitations apply to their use in pharmacoeconomic research—namely, the lack of information regarding clinical indicators, incompleteness of data, inaccuracies in coding of diagnoses and procedures, and the valuation of healthcare utilization as charges (what the patient paid) and not costs (what the true value of the utilization was). This latter concern can often be overcome by obtaining cost-to-charge ratios from the healthcare provider (Gold et al., 1996). Cost-to-charge ratios, which are simply the ratio of the cost of providing services and the reimbursement obtained for those same services, are used to adjust available charge data to better reflect actual costs.

No particular study design is inherently superior to another. Each design approach has its advantages and disadvantages, and the final choice will depend on many factors. In critiquing a study with respect to study design, it is important to determine whether the disadvantage of a particular method affects the results.

CRITICAL APPRAISAL OF A PHARMACOECONOMIC STUDY

Many articles in the literature claim to study the cost effectiveness or cost benefit of alternative treatments. Readers should be cautioned, however, that many of these articles are flawed because they do not adequately identify, measure, or value costs and consequences. A number of guidelines have been published to assist researchers in conducting evaluations or evaluating the pharmacoeconomic literature (Dao, 1985; Jolicoeur, Jones-Grizzle, & Boyer, 1992; Task Force on Principles for Economic Analysis of Health Care Technology, 1995). Following is a list of questions that readers should ask when appraising a pharmacoeconomic study:

1. What is the perspective of the study?
2. What pharmacoeconomic methodology was utilized?
3. Were the competing treatment alternatives described and compared?
4. Were the relevant costs and consequences for each alternative properly identified?
5. Were the relevant costs and consequences for each alternative properly measured?
6. Were the relevant costs and consequences properly valued?
7. Were the instruments used to measure patient preferences or quality of life validated?
8. What are the assumptions and limitations of the study?
9. Were costs and consequences adjusted for different time periods?

10. Was a sensitivity analysis performed?
11. Are the conclusions appropriate and not overgeneralized?

CONCLUSION

As a larger number of students of pharmacy and practitioners become familiar with the concepts of pharmacoeconomics, the application of these tools in everyday practice will grow. The potential exists for pharmacoeconomic information to aid greatly in decision making in the ever more cost-conscious field of health care.

QUESTIONS FOR FURTHER DISCUSSION

1. Clinicians tend to focus their efforts on the measurement of outcomes of clinical therapy, including measures of clinical effectiveness or side effects. Discuss the importance of measuring the inputs of clinical therapy.
2. Discuss the reasons why a pharmaceutical company might use one methodological approach over another (e.g., decision analysis, naturalistic design, or retrospective analysis) in conducting a pharmacoeconomics evaluation for its product. How might this differ based upon where the product is in its life cycle (e.g., products at market maturity or products yet to be launched)?
3. Discuss how pharmacists in various practice settings (e.g., retail, hospital, or managed care) might apply pharmacoeconomic principles.
4. Discuss why various decision makers might be more inclined to select one pharmacoeconomic method over another. Various decision makers could include managed care organizations, public health officials, pharmacy benefit managers, physicians, hospital pharmacists, or members of a pharmacy and therapeutics committee.

KEY TOPICS AND TERMS

Analysis of extremes
Benefit-to-cost ratio
Break-even point
Budget impact analysis
Consumer Price Index
Cost-benefit analysis (CBA)
Cost-consequence analysis (CCA)
Cost-effectiveness analysis (CEA)
Cost-minimization analysis (CMA)
Cost-of-illness analysis (COI)
Cost-to-charge ratio
Cost-utility analysis (CUA)
Decision analysis
Decision tree
Direct medical costs

Direct nonmedical costs
Discounting
Effectiveness
Efficacy
Efficiency
Health-related quality of life (HrQoL)
Human capital approach
Incremental cost-effectiveness plane
Incremental cost-effectiveness ratio
Incremental cost-utility ratio
Indirect costs
Inflation
Inputs
Intangible costs
Markov model
Naturalistic designs
Net benefit
Net present value
Opportunity cost
Outcome
Perspective
Pharmacoeconomics
Probabilistic sensitivity analysis
Quality-adjusted life year (QALY)
Randomized controlled trials
Retrospective claims analysis
Simple sensitivity analysis
Threshold sensitivity analysis
Utility score
Willingness-to-pay approach

REFERENCES

Bootman, J. L., McGhan, W. F., & Schondelmeyer, S. W. (1982). Application of cost-benefit and cost-effectiveness analysis to clinical practice. *Drug Intelligence and Clinical Pharmacy, 16,* 235–243.

Bootman, J. L., Townsend, R. J., & McGhan, W. F. (1996). *Principles of pharmacoeconomics* (2nd ed.). Cincinnati, OH: Harvey Whitney Books.

Bootman, J. L., Wertheimer, A., Zaske, D., & Rowland, C. (1979). Individualizing gentamicin dosage regimens on burn patients with gram negative septicemia: A cost-benefit analysis. *Journal of Pharmacy Science, 68,* 267–272.

Briggs, A., Sculpher, M., & Buxton, M. (1994). Uncertainty in the economic evaluation of health care technologies: The role of sensitivity analysis. *Health Economics, 3,* 95–104.

Copley-Merriman, C., & Lair, T. J. (1994). Valuation of medical resource units collected in health economic studies. *Clinical Therapy, 16*(3), 553–567.

Dao, T. D. (1985). Cost-benefit and cost-effectiveness analysis of drug therapy. *American Journal of Hospital Pharmacy, 42,* 791–802.

Fowler, J. F., Duh, M. S., Rovba, L., Buteau, S., Pinheiro, L., Lobo, F., ... Kosicki, G. (2008). The impact of psoriasis on health care costs and patient work loss. *Journal of the American Academy of Dermatology, 59,* 772–780.

Drummond, M. F., O'Brien, B. J., Stoddart, G. L., & Torrance, G. W. (1998). *Methods for the economic evaluation of health care programmes* (2nd ed.). New York, NY: Oxford University Press.

Elliott, R., & Payne, K. (2005). *Essentials of economic evaluation in healthcare.* London, England: Pharmaceutical Products Press, p. 163.

Else, B. A., Armstrong, E. P., & Cox, E. R. (1997). Data sources for pharmacoeconomic and health services research. *American Journal of Health-Systems Pharmacy, 54,* 2601–2608.

Gafni, A. (1991). Willingness-to-pay as a measure of benefits: Relevant questions in the context of public decision making about health care programs. *Medical Care, 29*(12), 1246–1252.

Gold, M. R., Siegel, J. E., Russell, L. B., & Weinstein, M. C. (Eds.). (1996). *Cost-effectiveness in health and medicine.* New York, NY: Oxford University Press.

Hartman, M., Martin, A., Nuccio, O., Catlin, A., & the National Health Expenditure Accounts Team. (2010). Health spending growth at a historic low in 2008. *Health Affairs, 29,* 147–155.

Harvard Public Health Review. (2004, Winter). *What price health?* Retrieved from http://www.hsph.harvard.edu/review/review_fall_04/risk_pricetxt.html

Jolicoeur, L. M., Jones-Grizzle, A. J., & Boyer, J. G. (1992). Guidelines for performing a pharmacoeconomic analysis. *American Journal of Hospital Pharmacy, 49,* 1741–1747.

Lieu, T. A., Cochi, S. L., Black, S. B., Halloran, M. E., Shinefield, H. R., Holmes, S. J., ... Washington, A. E. (1994). Cost effectiveness of a routine varicella vaccination program for US children. *Journal of the American Medical Association, 271,* 375–381.

Mauskopf, J. A., Paul, J. E., Grant, D. M., & Stergachis, A. (1998). The role of cost-consequence analysis in healthcare decision making. *Pharmacoeconomics, 13*(3), 277–288.

Mauskopf, J. A., Sullivan, S. D., Annemans, L., Caro, J., Mullins, C. D., Nuijten, M., ... Trueman, P. (2007). Principles of good practice for budget impact analysis: Report of the ISPOR task force on good research practices-budget impact analysis. *Value Health, 10,* 336–347.

Motheral, B. R., Grizzle, A. J., Armstrong, E. P., Cox, E., & Fairman, K. (2000). Role of pharmacoeconomics in drug benefit decision-making: Results of a survey. *Formulary, 35,* 412–421.

Prest, A. R., & Turvey, R. (1965). Cost-benefit analysis: A survey. *Economics Journal, 75*(12), 683–735.

Revicki, D., Willian, M. K., Saurat, J. H., Papp, K. A., Ortonne, J. P., Sexton, C., & Camez, A. (2008). Impact of adalimumab treatment on health-related quality of life and other patient-reported outcomes: Results from a 16-week randomized controlled trial in patients with moderate to severe plaque psoriasis. *British Journal of Dermatology, 158,* 649–557.

Saurat, J. H., Stingl, G., Dubertret, L., Papp, K., Langley, R. G., Ortonne, J. P., ... CHAMPION Study Investigators. (2008). Efficacy and safety results from the randomized controlled comparative study of adalimumab vs. methotrexate vs. placebo in patients with psoriasis (CHAMPION). *British Journal of Dermatology, 158*, 558–566.

Simon, G., Wagner, E., & Vonkorff, M. (1995, March). Cost-effectiveness comparisons using "real world" randomized trials: The case of new antidepressant drugs. *Journal of Clinical Epidemiology, 48*(3), 363–373.

Sonnenberg, F. A., & Beck, J. R. (1993, October–December). Markov models in medical decision making: A practical guide. *Medical Decision Making, 13*(4), 322–338.

Task Force on Principles for Economic Analysis of Health Care Technology. (1995). Economic analysis of health care technology: A report on principles. *Annals of Internal Medicine, 122,* 61–70.

Townsend, R. J. (1986). Post marketing drug research and development: An industry clinical pharmacist's perspective. *American Journal of Pharmacy Education, 50,* 480–482.

Tumeh, J. W., Moore, S. G., Shapiro, R., & Flowers, C. R. (2005). Practical approach for using Medicare data to estimate costs for cost-effectiveness analysis. *Expert Review of Pharmacoeconomics Outcomes Research, 5,* 153–162.

Weinstein, M. C., & Skinner, J. A. (2010). Comparative effectiveness and health care spending—implications for reform. *New England Journal of Medicine, 362,* 460–465.

Weinstein, M. C., & Stason, B. (1977). Foundations and cost-effectiveness analysis for health and medical practitioners. *New England Journal of Medicine, 296,* 716–721.

International Healthcare Services

Ana C. Quiñones-Boex*

Case Scenario

Jane has recently accepted a position as a health policy analyst and will be in charge of following the implementation of the Patient Protection and Affordable Care Act of 2010 (also known as the healthcare reform act), which promises to increase patient access to healthcare services. In order to have comparison data, Jane decides to look at the healthcare systems of other countries with universal healthcare coverage to evaluate which types of healthcare services they cover and how this coverage is financed. What data would Jane need to gather?

BACKGROUND

A health policy analyst who wants to determine how other countries have provided universal access to healthcare services at a reasonable cost might start by looking at the World Health Organization's (WHO) *World Health Report 2000, Health Systems: Improving Performance,* which compares healthcare systems around the world (World Health Organization, 2000a). The comparative analysis of health systems helps policy makers (and policy analysts like Jane) know how health systems perform and what they can do to improve those systems. The report asserts that much of the widening gap in death rates between the rich and poor, both within and among countries around the world, is explained by the differing degrees of efficiency with which health systems organize and finance themselves and react to the needs of their populations. This may explain, for instance, why countries with similar income levels and health expenditures vary greatly with regard to health outcomes. The WHO report finds that inequalities in life expectancy persist and are strongly associated with socioeconomic class, even in countries that enjoy good health.

*The author wishes to express appreciation to Linda E. Barry Dunn, MPP, for her contributions to this chapter as coauthor for the *Fourth Edition* of this text.

To compare health systems, an analyst would review basic data such as per capita expenditures on health, immunization rates, infant mortality rates, mortality rates, or healthcare expenditures as a percentage of gross domestic product (GDP). The rankings contained in WHO's *World Health Report 2000* measure health systems' ability to achieve their goals (World Health Organization, 2000a). Achievement of these goals is based on the following measurements: (1) overall level of health or life expectancy; (2) responsiveness of how well people rated performance of their healthcare system; (3) fairness in responsiveness among different groups in the same country; and (4) fairness of financing among different groups, which looks at what proportion of income is devoted to health care (Hilts, 2000).

Based on this ranking system, the *World Health Report 2000* indicates that overall most European health systems perform the best. Among the highest-ranking countries are France, Italy, Singapore, Spain, Austria, and Japan (World Health Organization, 2000b). The United States outspends all other countries and ranks near the top on average health measures, but fails to deliver good health care to a large proportion of its population and distributes the cost relatively unfairly, leaving it ranked 37th on the WHO list (World Health Organization, 2000b).

Jane decides to start by researching four countries, each with a different type of healthcare delivery system. Three of those countries—Canada, Germany, and the United Kingdom—represent developed nations that fared better than the United States in the *World Health Report 2000* rankings. The fourth country, Cuba, received a health systems performance score of 39 but is worthy of examination because of its extraordinary health outcomes despite its developing nation status.

In her analysis, Jane would want to answer the following questions:

1. Is a ranking of a country's healthcare system based on how equitably resources are distributed a fair measurement of how a healthcare system performs?
2. Which factors, other than the amount of money spent on health care, could affect the overall health of a particular country?
3. Which aspects of various healthcare systems could be effectively applied in the United States?

LEARNING OBJECTIVES

Upon completion of this chapter, the student shall be able to:

- Describe the differences between the following healthcare models: socialized insurance program, decentralized national health program, and socialized medicine
- Compare and contrast the healthcare delivery systems of a developing country and a developed country
- Describe several factors that affect the health of a country's population
- Describe the main characteristics of the healthcare plans of Canada, Germany, the United Kingdom, and Cuba
- Describe some of the healthcare delivery strategies employed by other countries that might be useful to the United States

CHAPTER QUESTIONS

1. What are the general features of the healthcare systems of
   a. Canada?
   b. Germany?
   c. The United Kingdom?
   d. Cuba?
2. How does the healthcare delivery system of a developing country differ from that of a developed country?
3. Describe several factors that affect the health of a country's population.
4. Describe some of the healthcare delivery strategies employed by other countries that might be useful to the United States.

INTRODUCTION

The failure of the U.S. healthcare system to provide universal access to healthcare services at a reasonable cost has prompted many observers to examine the healthcare systems of other countries for possible solutions. This chapter, therefore, highlights different methods of structuring and financing healthcare services. It provides an overview of the unique features of the healthcare systems of several countries and discusses the characteristics of and issues faced by healthcare systems in both developed and developing countries.

The chapter analyzes the major features of four healthcare systems that illustrate the variety of models of healthcare delivery available—namely, the healthcare systems of Canada, the United Kingdom, Germany, and Cuba. The discussion of each of these systems includes a brief description of the history of each country's healthcare system, the system's main features, the health status of the population, the structure of the healthcare system (e.g., healthcare facilities and workforce, with a focus on hospitals, physicians, and pharmaceuticals), healthcare financing (i.e., how the system is funded and what contributions are rendered by the government, citizens, and employers), and issues that appear to present concerns for each system. **Table 20-1** summarizes the key aspects of these systems, comparing them to the features of the U.S. healthcare system.

Healthcare systems for different countries can be classified as belonging to four broad models:

1. The Beveridge model, also known as socialized medicine, in which health care is both financed by and provided by the government. The government employs healthcare practitioners, owns healthcare facilities, and administers the healthcare system. The health systems of Cuba and the United Kingdom are examples of the Beveridge model, which is named after the British social reformer who inspired the United Kingdom's National Health Service (Reid, 2009a).
2. The Bismark model, also referred to as a decentralized national health program, in which employers and employees are required to obtain private health insurance, usually provided by nongovernment insurance companies. Hospitals and clinics

Table 20-1 Summary of Healthcare Delivery Systems' Key Aspects

	United States	Canada	Germany	United Kingdom	Cuba
Total population (2008)	311,666,000	33,259,000	82,264,000	61,231,000	11,205,000
% of GDP devoted to health (2007)	15.7%	10.1%	10.4%	8.4%	10.4%
Total health expenditure per capita (2007)	$7,285	$4,049	$4,209	$3,867	$585
Life expectancy at birth (years, 2008)	Males: 76 Females: 81	Males: 79 Females: 83	Males: 77 Females: 83	Males: 78 Females: 82	Males: 76 Females: 79
Infant mortality rate per 1,000 (2008)	Males: 9 Females: 6	Males: 6 Females: 5	Males: 4 Females: 4	Males: 5 Females: 5	Males: 5 Females: 5
Universal coverage?	By 2019?	Yes	Yes	Yes	Yes
Hospital beds per 10,000 (2008)	31 (2002)	34	83	39	60
Physicians per 10,000 (2008)	27	19	35	21	64
Pharmacists per 10,000	7.7 (2004)	2.9 (2005)	6.5 (2004)	7.8 (2004)	1.4 (2003)

Public health expenditure as % of health spending (2007)	45.5%	70.0%	76.9%	87.1%	95.5%
Hospital payment	Contracted-prospective DRGs; per diem; and discounted fee for services	Global budget	Cost-per-case prospective budget DRGs	Annual block contracts HRGs	National budget
Physician payment	Mix of fee-for-service and capitation	Fee for service Fee schedule	Capitation and service complex payments DRGs Negotiated fee	Mix of fee for service and capitation	Salary
Drugs	Coverage by Medicare, Medicaid, and most private insurance; high cost-sharing requirements	Limited coverage; varies by province; some employer coverage	Coverage through sickness funds (copayments required)	Through NHS	Full coverage

DRG = Diagnosis related group; HRG = Healthcare resource group; NHS = National Health Service.

Note: This table was compiled from various sources included in the references. Most statistics are available at World Health Organization, *World Health Statistics, 2010–Part II: Global Health Statistics* (http://www.who.int/whosis/whostat/2010//en/index.html) and the *Global Pharmacy Workforce and Migration Report* (http://www.fip.org/hr/)

are privately owned. Germany created the first decentralized national health program (Reid, 2009a).

3. The national health insurance model, also known as a socialized insurance model, in which a single, government-run insurance program finances healthcare services that are provided by private payers with negotiated reimbursement. Canada is an example of a country with a socialized insurance model.

4. The out-of-pocket model is common in developing countries in which there is a lack of private health insurance and no government-sponsored healthcare system. This lack of private or government health insurance is usually accompanied by shortages of healthcare facilities, low expenditures, and poor health outcomes.

DEVELOPED AND DEVELOPING COUNTRIES

Based on per capita income, the world can be divided into developed and developing countries. Developed nations (i.e., mostly capitalistic and social democratic societies in industrialized countries) have per capita incomes of more than $8,260 (Boyes & Melvin, 1999) and tend to have strong health infrastructures and positive healthcare outcomes. Developing nations account for 84% of the world's population but only 11% of global health expenditures.

The income and health expenditures gap between developing and developed countries underscores the enormous difference in terms of capacities and types of health services that can be provided. This translates into large differences in the health infrastructure and the health outcomes of populations in developing countries. A limiting factor for developing countries is the large portion of their budgets required to finance the most basic of primary healthcare services. If a basic package of healthcare services is estimated to cost approximately $15 to $20 per person, then a low-income country would be required to devote one quarter to one third of its government budget to the health sector just for these basic services (Schieber & Maeda, 1999).

Lack of resources, poor administrative capacity, and the competing needs for other social and economic programs have a profound effect on the burden of disease in developing countries (Schieber & Maeda, 1999). Worldwide, one death in every three is attributable to largely preventable communicable diseases such as infectious disease, maternal and perinatal conditions, and nutritional deficiencies. Communicable diseases that are mainly preventable remain the leading causes of death in developing countries; indeed, almost all deaths from communicable diseases occur in developing countries (Harvard School of Public Health, 2000). In developing countries, mortality for individuals younger than age 5 (i.e., the probability of a child dying before reaching his or her 5th year) is almost 10 times the level found in developed countries (Schieber & Maeda, 1999). Approximately 1 in every 500 women in developing countries dies from complications related to pregnancy and childbirth, compared with only 1 in 27,000 women in the established market economies (UNICEF, 1995).

In the next 30 years, important demographic and epidemiologic changes are expected to occur in developing countries. These changes will alter the demand for health services and increase the pressure to make new investments in their healthcare systems (Harvard School of Public Health, 2000; Schieber & Maeda, 1999). Life expectancy at birth is expected to increase for women in all regions. Men are not expected to do as well on the longevity front, partly because of the effects of tobacco use on their life expectancy (Harvard School of Public Health, 2000).

Although overall deaths from communicable diseases are expected to decline, a steep increase is expected in the number of deaths resulting from noncommunicable diseases (e.g., heart disease, stroke, cancer, diabetes) as well as the number of deaths from injuries. In part, the projected reduction in deaths from communicable diseases reflects increased income, education, and technological progress in the development of antimicrobials and vaccines. The expected increase in deaths from noncommunicable diseases and injury is largely driven by aging of the population as well as exposure to tobacco. By 2020, the burden of disease attributed to tobacco is expected to outweigh that caused by any single disease (Harvard School of Public Health, 2000). In the future, health systems in developing countries will need to change their health systems to focus on treatment and prevention of noncommunicable diseases instead of the more cost-effective and lower cost interventions targeted toward communicable diseases—a trend that will further strain these already fragile health systems (Schieber & Maeda, 1999).

The health of a population or country is also influenced by a number of socioeconomic variables, such as the distribution of resources within a country, income per capita, the number of years of schooling in adults, and—to some extent—the ability to adopt new health technologies. Studies have also found the educational level and status of women to be indicators of the health outcomes in a household. Women are often the primary caregivers for the health and nutritional needs of other family members. As a consequence, greater educational attainment in women can contribute to improved understanding of disease prevention and better nutritional health within a household. When girls are offered educational opportunities, their value within the household increases. Thus the allocation of resources such as food and medicine within a household tends to be more equitable when parents place equal value on their children regardless of their gender.

A strong inverse relationship exists between per capita income and child mortality under 5 years of age. That is, as per capita income increases, infant mortality rates tend to decrease. However, variability exists among countries, indicating that social and cultural factors strongly influence these mortality rates, as do differences in the use of maternal and child health programs and the extent to which they achieve equity and efficiency in the delivery of health services (Schieber & Maeda, 1999). The distribution of limited health resources is also affected by whether services are administered through a public or private system. A strong direct relationship exists between an economy's health spending and its per capita gross domestic product (GDP—a measure of the value of the final goods and services produced in a given country). On a worldwide basis, for every 10% increase in per capita GDP, health spending increases by 13% (Schieber & Maeda, 1999).

Public health expenditures tend to be more responsive to income differences than private health expenditures. Thus, as countries' incomes increase, a larger share of total health spending tends to come from public sources. Public health expenditures account for 47% of health spending in low-income countries, 57% in middle-income countries, and 67% in high-income countries. These differing rates may be attributable to the relatively greater ability to tax and generate revenue in higher-income countries as well as governments' decisions to address health sector and health insurance market failures through public rather than private financing. The fact that such a large portion of health expenditures is privately financed in developing countries has important implications for both equity and efficiency in health care, because governments need to focus on efficient allocation of combined public and private resources (Schieber & Maeda, 1999). Typically, those countries with a higher proportion of publicly financed healthcare systems have also achieved better and more equitable health outcomes primarily through a more equitable distribution of scarce health resources. For this reason, certain socialist economic systems, even in developing countries, have achieved health outcomes that are comparable to those found in many industrialized countries.

Other factors—for example, public health improvements in drinking water, access to prenatal and perinatal care, population planning, immunizations, and the allocation of food supplies—also directly affect the health of a population. Rational and efficient investments in primary healthcare services could afford most developing countries a cost-effective package of basic primary care and emergency services, although data reveal that a disproportionate share of limited public health spending is allocated to tertiary care instead of primary care (Schieber & Maeda, 1999). In most developing countries, individuals in the highest income brackets can still enjoy access to health services (either within their country or by traveling outside the country) that is comparable to the best healthcare services available in higher-income countries. Nevertheless, the majority of people living in developing countries lack access to even basic primary healthcare services.

HEALTHCARE DELIVERY SYSTEMS IN SELECTED NATIONS

Canada's Healthcare System

The origins of Canada's current healthcare system date back to the 1940s, when the first government-financed insurance was established for hospital services in Saskatchewan (Organization for Economic Cooperation and Development, 1994). In 1957, the Hospital Insurance and Diagnostic Service Act established public insurance that provided inpatient hospital care coverage for all Canadians. In 1966, the Medical Care Act established the main principles of Canada's current healthcare system, which include:

1. Portability of benefits: Coverage is kept, even when the individual is absent from the province.
2. Comprehensiveness: All necessary physician and hospital services are covered.
3. Universality: All citizens of a province are entitled to the same services.
4. Accessibility: Reasonable access to services is assured.
5. Public administration: A nonprofit, public organization accountable to the provincial government runs the plan (Rozek & Mulhern, 1994).

This legislation was implemented on a province-by-province basis. By 1972, Canada's 10 provinces and 2 territories had implemented medical insurance measures, realizing the goal of national health insurance for the country. In 1984, the Canada Health Act aggregated the provisions of the Medical Care Act and Hospital Insurance and Diagnostic Service Act into one updated piece of legislation.

As a consequence of these measures, Canada has 13 different health insurance plans (a new territory was created in 1999). These plans are kept consistent through adherence to the five main principles of portability, comprehensiveness, universality, accessibility, and public administration. Failure to ensure that these principles are maintained would prevent a province from qualifying for federal subsidies (Rozek & Mulhern, 1994).

The Canadian system has been successful in providing universal access to care regardless of patients' ability to pay, and the services covered are extensive. As a result, the health status of the Canadian population is good. In 2007, life expectancy at birth was 79 years for men and 83 years for women—about 3 years longer than in the United States. That same year, infant mortality was 6 deaths per 1,000 births—compared to about 7 deaths per 1,000 births in the United States (World Health Organization, 2010). Canada's success in providing universal access and caring for the less fortunate has been a great source of pride for its citizens, who view it as presenting a striking contrast to the U.S. system that has left over 46 million people uninsured. However, recent polls indicate that public confidence in the system is eroding as waiting lists increase and availability of physicians and services becomes more limited.

Structure: Healthcare Facilities and Workforce

Although Canada has socialized health insurance, healthcare delivery systems in the country are mostly private. Hospitals are primarily nonprofit community and teaching hospitals, although 4% of hospitals belong to the federal government. Provinces set the standards for hospital facilities and staffing.

The Canada Medical Care Act explicitly prohibited private hospitals or insurance companies from providing or financing core medical services provided by the Canada Medical Care Act. However, a recent Canadian Supreme Court ruling struck down a Quebec law banning private medical insurance and private medical clinics. The court ruled that waiting lists at publicly financed hospitals had become so long that "the prohibition on obtaining private health insurance is not constitutional where the public system fails to deliver reasonable services" (Krauss, 2005). Supporters of the publicly financed system fear that the introduction of privately financed services will encourage physicians and private clinics to leave the publicly financed system for higher reimbursement—a system that favors better access to treatments for individuals with higher incomes (Canadian-healthcare, 2006).

The national health insurance program, called Medicare, covers physician care and the following hospital services: room and meals, nursing services, diagnostic procedures, and medications prescribed for inpatient use. Private insurance is available only as a supplement to the national health insurance. Until the recent court decision regarding private insurance, private policies provided coverage only for private or semiprivate rooms in a hospital and other services not covered through Medicare, such as cosmetic surgery, dental services, and outpatient medications for those not covered under the Canadian law (Rozek & Mulhern, 1994). Most Canadians have supplemental private insurance. Delivery systems other than hospitals are available to Canadians, but these options vary from province to province. These systems, which include community health centers and long-term care, aim to provide preventive care and other services for which an acute care hospital setting is not necessary (Rozek & Mulhern, 1994).

Under the Canada Health Act, primary care doctors, specialists, and dental surgery are all covered by provincial policies. Approximately half of all Canadian physicians are primary care doctors (e.g., general practitioners or family physicians) (Canadian Institute for Health Information, 2010). Primary care physicians function as gatekeepers, serving as the initial point of contact for patients at the forefront of Canadian health care. Patients have free choice of physicians. Typically, patients are referred to specialists by their primary care physicians.

The distribution of physicians across Canada is not homogeneous, and there is an undersupply in rural areas. A decrease in the supply of physicians is one of the latest concerns to arise regarding the country's healthcare resources (Iglehart, 2000). The government statistical agency estimates that more than 15% of the population does not have a primary care physician (Krauss, 2004). This compares to an estimated 20% of U.S. residents who do not have a primary care physician (Krauss, 2004).

Canada's physicians are paid lower salaries than their U.S. counterparts, with the average salary for a Canadian physician being about one third less than that for a U.S. physician. Even so, physicians are the highest-paid professionals in Canada. Their salaries are higher than those of British and Japanese physicians and similar to those of German physicians. In 2008, there were approximately 1.9 physicians for every 1,000 residents in Canada—far less than in the United States (Anderson, Hussey, Krogner, & Waters, 2005).

Medicare covers outpatient prescription drugs for senior citizens, individuals with low incomes, and patients with specific disease states. Four provinces have implemented universal prescription plans called pharmacare (Naylor, 1999). Most of the population relies on private insurance for outpatient prescription drug coverage, but subscribing to such supplemental coverage is often dependent on income.

Financing

The Canadian system is not one centralized plan, but rather 13 separate systems that are controlled by the provinces and territories. The universal insurance is paid for by personal and corporate taxes and distributed to each province according to budgets established on both national and provincial levels. Provinces may obtain additional funds from other sources such as lottery proceeds and sales taxes. The provinces of Alberta, British Columbia, and Ontario also charge health premiums to supplement health spending (Canadian-healthcare, 2006).

The provincial governments carefully plan how to allocate resources within their budgets. Because the government is the only insurer, administrative overhead is tightly controlled in Canada. Health administrative costs in Canada were less than one third of the *per capita* cost in the United States (Woolhandler, Campbell, & Himmelstein, 2003). The additional administrative costs in the U.S. system can be attributed to the nature of a pluralistic insurance system that has complex billing and reimbursement procedures that vary considerably among payers.

Costs are controlled through set fees for medical services. Every year, the government publishes a list of the fees that physicians are permitted to charge the government for treating patients. Physicians are then paid directly by the provincial government on a fee-for-service basis. Hospitals in Canada work on a budget that cannot be exceeded, which not surprisingly results in some strain on the system. Many hospitals have closed or merged, causing a shrinking hospital sector (Naylor, 1999). Because most hospitals are run at capacity in Canada, waiting lists are commonplace. For example, the waiting period for a coronary bypass in Canada can range from 3 to 6 months, compared with 1 day to a week in the United States.

While all inpatient prescription expenses are covered under the Canada Health Act, each province may offer varying levels of coverage for drugs prescribed on an out-patient basis. The publicly funded drug programs are generally established based on patients' age, income, and medical condition (Health Canada, 2006a). Only those medications listed on the Medicare formularies are covered. In recent years, drug spending has been increasing and has become the second largest category of health care–related expenditures in Canada, after hospital services.

Although drug prices are set at the federal level, purchasing takes place at the provincial level. Provinces, therefore, face the responsibility of controlling increasing drug expenditures without having direct control over pricing (Anis, 2000).

Current Status

In recent years, Canada has struggled with increased waiting times for diagnostic tests, hip and knee replacements, cancer treatments, and elective surgeries, among other things. In addition to the difficulties attributable to the maldistribution of physicians and long waiting lists for certain services, the federal government has decreased its contribution to provincial plans significantly, increasing the pressure on provincial governments. Coverage for services varies among the provinces, which can make it difficult for patients to receive care in provinces other than their own (Chidley, 1996). Moreover, the single-payer structure prevents the system from rapidly responding to local changes in the healthcare environment.

Dissatisfaction with the current waiting lists for services and the shortage of primary care physicians in some areas has grown sharply as well. With the recent ruling by the Canadian Supreme Court that allows residents to purchase health services privately, some predict the creation of a two-tiered healthcare system—where one branch is privately financed for those who can afford it and the other branch remains publicly financed. However, the current system has generally been strongly supported by most of the public, and most Canadian citizens identify with it as part of the Canadian national character (Krauss, 2005).

In 2003, the First Ministers' Accord on Health Care Renewal was adopted. This accord consisted of an agreement on a vision, principles, and action plan for renewal of the Canadian health system (Health Canada, 2006b). It incorporated an agreement on the value of a publicly funded health system, the need for reform, and the priorities for reform. The priorities established included additional investments in primary health care, home care, and catastrophic drug coverage to create a long-term, sustainable public healthcare system in Canada (Health Canada, 2006b). The federal government agreed to establish a health reform fund by 2004 for use by the provinces and territories to achieve the reform objectives. The health reform funding will eventually be integrated into the general health funding provided to each province (Health Canada, 2006b).

Recently, Canada's three largest provinces have approved healthcare reform measures in order to control rising healthcare costs (Newman, 2010). Quebec has proposed to charge a $25 co-payment per doctor visit while British Columbia is considering changing hospital global budgets to a payment scheme based on the procedures each hospital performs. It remains to be seen whether Canada's reform efforts will enable it to continue to achieve the health outcomes it has experienced in the past, but so far it continues to surpass the United States in terms of its national health coverage.

Germany's Healthcare System

Germany's current healthcare system has its roots in the statutory health insurance system (sickness funds) for manual industrial workers instituted by Chancellor Bismarck in 1883 (Beske, 1988). It constitutes the world's oldest national healthcare system (Reid, 2009b). This law, in conjunction with the accident insurance law of 1884 and the disability and old-age pension insurance law of 1889, remains the backbone of Germany's social security system. Although sickness funds started as coverage for certain occupations, they evolved to accept all qualified persons whose place of work fell within the geographical boundaries covered by the fund. During the 1990s, occupational and geographical limits on most of the sickness funds were lifted (Jackson, 1997). Today, only funds for small farmers, miners, and sailors remain closed (Busse, 2004). Moreover, potential enrollees cannot be discriminated against based on their age, gender, or other risk factors.

Thus Germany has no comprehensive national health plan. Instead, German citizens are covered by either the health insurance system (*Krankenkasse*, or sickness funds) or the social welfare program for the unemployed. The sickness funds are considered private corporations under public law (Hoffmeyer, 1994), so the statutory system is decentralized. In 2003, 319 self-governing sickness funds were in charge of the healthcare insurance of the individuals they covered (Busse, 2004). It is expected that mergers will decrease the number of sickness funds to 200 by 2010 (Reid, 2009b). Although insured individuals are allowed to change sickness funds at any time, when they do, they have to stay with their new fund for the next 18 months unless the new fund increases its contribution rate. This rule has recently been adopted because evidence has shown that healthier Germans consistently switched to funds with lower than average contribution rates.

Sickness funds can be classified in four main types. Most are company-based funds; the rest are either guild funds, general regional funds, or substitute funds (which originally covered white-collar groups) (Busse, 2004). Of those persons covered by sickness funds, 7% also carry supplemental private insurance for ambulatory and dental care (Beske, 1988).

By 1990, approximately 90% of the German population was covered through this statutory health insurance system, which provides a guaranteed healthcare package of comprehensive services (Hoffmeyer, 1994). Since 1994, this package has included long-term care, nursing home care, and home health care (Evans-Cuellar, & Wiener, 2000). The remaining 10% of the population had either private insurance (8%) or received free medical services (2%). The police, members of the armed forces, and welfare recipients all qualify for free medical care (Beske, 1988). Germans who earn more than a certain level of income have a choice of private insurance or voluntary membership in the sickness funds. Approximately 14% of the population covered through sickness funds joined voluntarily on this basis (Busse, 2004). Persons who elect to purchase private insurance, however, cannot switch back to a sickness fund (Jackson, 1997).

Three main values underlie the German healthcare system:

1. Self-governance: The system is administered by a self-managing organization (for example, the sickness funds).
2. Social partnership: Both the employer and the employee have a share in the system.

3. Social solidarity: Ensuring equality in health care through some members of society subsidizing other members' healthcare costs (Hoffmeyer, 1994). A strong commitment to social solidarity exists in Germany (Jackson, 1997).

Germany's decentralized system appears to be successful in keeping its population healthy. The country's infant mortality rate was 4 deaths per 1,000 live births in 2008—almost half of the rate in the United States (World Health Organization, 2010). Moreover, the percentage of infants with a low birth weight is smaller than that in the rest of Europe or the United States. In 2008, life expectancy was 77 years for men and 83 years for women in Germany (World Health Organization, 2010). These and other health status indicators are similar to those associated with other industrialized countries but significantly better than the indicators for the United States.

Structure: Healthcare Facilities and Workforce

In 2008, Germany had a ratio of 8.3 hospital beds per 1,000 persons. This ratio is high—over twice that of the United Kingdom, 2.4 times than that of Canada and 2.7 times that of the United States (World Health Organization, 2010)—and this has resulted in a surplus of hospital beds and consequently high operating costs for some hospitals (Beske, 1988). In recent years, the number of hospitals has been decreasing, but it is still high. Government and nonprofit organizations own the majority of German hospitals.

There were approximately 35 physicians for every 10,000 people in Germany in 2008—a significantly higher rate than in the United States and about twice the rate in Canada (World Health Organization, 2010). This ratio indicates that there may currently be an oversupply of physicians that could eventually lead to increased healthcare costs. Physicians working in office-based practices act as gatekeepers for institutionalized care. If they wish to be reimbursed by sickness funds, physicians have to qualify and apply for accreditation with a regional association of physicians. Germans have freedom of choice of physicians. If a patient wants to switch physicians, however, he or she has to wait 3 months before selecting another office-based physician.

Germany has a well-developed pharmaceutical industry, with significant drug development occurring in the country (Spivey, Wertheimer, & Rucker, 1992). In 1995, Germany was the world's fourth largest producer of pharmaceuticals (Jacobzone, 2000). Medications are covered through the sickness funds and are available from both hospital and retail pharmacies. Retail pharmacies in Germany have to be owned by pharmacists, and each pharmacist can own only one pharmacy (Ulrich, 1999).

Financing

The statutory health system is financed primarily through payroll taxes; employers and employees make equal contributions to this system. The contributions represent a percentage of the employees' income up to a certain threshold. Sickness funds are financed to a lesser extent by pension funds, local unemployment offices, and welfare organizations (Hoffmeyer, 1994). Sickness funds with a high share of chronically ill participants receive a high-risk pool supplement, aimed at compensating them for 40% of their expenses for specific types of patients, over a certain limit (Busse, 2004).

Hospitals and most physicians negotiate their fees with the sickness funds. Physicians working in hospitals, however, are salaried employees. Payment for office-based physicians follows a fee-for-service point system; that is, each service is assigned a number of points and a conversion factor translates these points into German marks (Hoffmeyer, 1994). Each state has a union of physicians that provides services to the sickness funds that are in charge of negotiating budgets (Jost, 1998). Hospitals' payments have shifted from per diem rates to prospective cost-per-case payments. Patients are charged a co-payment for some benefits, but the majority of services are free at the point of delivery.

Sickness funds also provide reimbursement for approved medications. Reference pricing, whereby drugs with similar properties would be reimbursed at the same level, was introduced in 1989. When a more expensive pharmaceutical is prescribed, the patient pays the difference. Prices for medications across the country are uniform because regulation determines the markup allowed to wholesalers and retailers. Patients pay co-payments reflecting the package size for the particular prescription drug (Ulrich, 1999).

Current Status

The 1993 Health Care Act introduced reforms to Germany's healthcare system, some of which are still being implemented. Among the short-term measures included in the reform package were ceilings on expenditures for office-based physicians and hospital services and on budgets for medicines prescribed by office-based physicians (Hoffmeyer, 1994). These measures were aimed at controlling two of the healthcare system's biggest problems—overutilization of health services and increased spending on drugs. Germany also implemented a diagnosis-related group payment system for hospital services and medical devices (Wood, personal communication, June 19, 2003).

Perhaps the biggest problem with Germany's health system relates to the country's high unemployment levels over the decade of 1990–2000. The slowdown in the German economy has created revenue problems for the sickness funds because their financing is based on wage-based premiums (Jost, 1998). Despite the pressures brought by reunification of East and West Germany, high unemployment rates, and the large percentage of elderly citizens (who account for approximately 16% of the population), the country has been successful in managing its healthcare system (Reinhardt, 1999).

In recent years, it has become apparent that some reform of the sickness funds will be necessary, and the following two different strategies have been proposed: citizen insurance and flat-rate premiums (Saltman & Dubois, 2005). Citizen insurance would require all Germans to buy a standard benefit package regardless of whether they participate in a sickness fund or a private insurance plan. The flat-rate premium would entail the implementation of a modest premium for all adults. Experts believe that citizen insurance would help perpetuate the existing system, whereas the flat-rate premium might erode the solidarity concept upon which the German healthcare system was developed.

After Germany's 2009 election, the new governing coalition agreed to fundamental health reform aimed at adjusting the Health Fund, the key component of the country's 2007 healthcare reform (Facts about Germany 2011; Zander, Kimmerle, Sundmacher, & Bäumler, 2009). Since January 2009, the Health Fund has become the new central entity in charge of collecting and allocating a nationwide uniform contribution fee from all sickness funds. As of October 2009, this fee conformed a rate of 14.9% of the contributory income (employee, 7.9% and employer, 7%). The government also contributes a subsidy to the fund. The payments are allocated based on a risk structure compensation scheme that adjusts for age, gender, and well-defined morbidities for each sickness fund member. "This ensures a fairer allocation of financial resources with respect to the risk-structure of the sickness funds" (Zander et al., 2009, p. 4). It has been estimated "that the health fund in its current form and the sickness funds will face a 7.5 billion euro deficit by the end of 2010" (Zander et al., 2009, p. 6).

The United Kingdom's Healthcare System

The movement toward the United Kingdom's current healthcare system started after World War I (Harrison, 1988). In 1939, only half of the nation's population had insurance coverage (Allen, 1984), and people were concerned about creating a more rational and comprehensive health service. Planning for a comprehensive healthcare delivery system continued during World War II, although major disagreement existed between different players regarding the system administration, funding, and physicians' roles in the system.

The National Health Service Act was finally passed in 1946 (Harrison, 1988). The National Health Service (NHS) presented the following three innovations: (1) universal comprehensive service, (2) financing through general taxation with little or no charge at point of service, and (3) nationalization of the country's hospitals (Allen, 1984). This system can be defined as socialized medicine whereby most of the services are provided by practitioners who work for the government.

Since the implementation of the NHS, the United Kingdom has experienced longer life expectancy rates and concomitant changes in disease patterns. In 2008, life expectancy was 78 years for men and 82 years for women (World Health Organization, 2010). Infant mortality was less than 5 deaths per 1,000 live births in the same year (World Health Organization, 2010).

Structure: Healthcare Facilities and Workforce

The United Kingdom's healthcare system includes the following three major components: hospitals, community services, and primary medical and dental care (Harrison, 1988). All of these services are available to the entire population, and only hospital care requires referral from a primary care physician. Primary care is delivered by a wide range of health professionals, including family practitioners, nurses, dentists, pharmacists, and opticians (National Health Service, 2006).

Physicians work mainly in the following two settings: government hospitals and office practices. Physicians who work in NHS hospitals are salaried employees. Senior medical staff members, however, are allowed to hold contracts for private practice that account for as much as 10% of their gross income (Booer, 1994). General practitioners (GPs) are in charge of primary care and act as the gatekeepers for hospital and specialty care. Patients have to register with a GP practice but are allowed to change GPs whenever they like. The government controls the establishment of primary care practices.

Secondary and tertiary care is provided by hospitals. Secondary care includes maternity care, pathology, radiology, and emergency care. Tertiary care deals with highly specialized services such as organ transplants and treatments for rare diseases.

In 2002, physicians were organized into approximately 300 primary care trusts (PCTs) (Bindman & Weiner, 2000; National Health Service, 2006). These groups include about 50 GPs each and are in charge of managing primary health services budgets for their patients (Enthoven, 2000). In 2006, the existing PCTs were merged into 152 as part of an NHS overhaul (BBC News, 2006). As of 2010, there were 151 PCTs (National Health Service, 2010).

PCTs control 80% of the total NHS budget. Given that providers are paid based on quality incentives rather than the quantity of care provided, physicians in PCTs have incentives to work as part of a primary care team along with other healthcare providers, including nurses, midwives, and pharmacists. Pharmacists, for example, are currently being trained to prescribe some medications and/or approve patient refills and other primary care roles. Community trusts are in charge of those community services not provided by GPs, such as specialized mental health services.

Patients are not charged for their visits to health providers who work as part of the NHS system (National Health Service, 2006). Patients can also choose to receive care from private providers, but these services are not reimbursed by the NHS.

All drugs available through the NHS are reviewed by the National Institute for Clinical Excellence, which confirms the drugs' clinical efficacy and cost-effectiveness (Morgan et al., 2006). The NHS creates a negative formulary that lists drugs that are excluded from coverage and then determines which drugs it will provide on a subsidized basis to the regional populations in its trusts (Morgan et al., 2006). Almost 70% of the medications prescribed in the United Kingdom are generics (Jacobzone, 2000). Most medications are dispensed for free, though there is a charge per prescription dispensed of approximately $10 (Reid, 2009c). Prices for pharmaceutical products are negotiated by NHS and drug manufacturers (Jacobzone, 2000). Drug development in the United Kingdom is significant, and the U.K. drug industry continues to be one of the largest producers of pharmaceutical products worldwide (Spivey et al., 1992).

Financing

All health care through the NHS is free at the point of delivery to anyone who is a U.K. resident. All taxpayers, employees, and employers contribute to the system. Approximately 87% of the cost of health services is paid by the government. Employers and employees pay most of the rest through premiums and out-of-pocket payments (KaiserEDU.org, 2011).

Hospitals have to provide care within their annual contract constraints. Most contracts are specified as an annual block payment or budgeted amount. Hospitals are then paid a lump sum that covers a specific range of services and facilities for which PCTs contract. This reimbursement amount includes services such as inpatient hospital care, dialysis treatments, and day surgeries.

Primary care funding is provided through an annual budget assigned by the Department of Health to each PCT. GPs have independent contracts with the PCTs for which they work. Their payment is based on a complex equation involving a mix of capitation (60% of financing) and fee-for-service payments, with additional fees being mandated for special situations (such as working in deprived areas, night visits, and minor surgeries). Generally, physicians in the United Kingdom earn half of the amount earned by U.S. physicians (Keeler, 2006).

Additional trusts have been established to provide specialized or specific services. For example, mental health trusts serve people with mental health problems, care trusts combine social care and healthcare services, and ambulance trusts respond to life-threatening emergencies. All trusts operate within an annual budget allocated by the federal budget and based on the region and the size of the population they serve.

Current Status

The NHS is facing severe budget constraints, and it is feared that the program will prove inadequate to respond to increased technological advances and the aging of the U.K. population. Although a guaranteed healthcare package exists, it is not properly codified, and differences remain in various parts of the country (Booer, 1994). Because of these financial difficulties, treatments commonly available to patients in the United States, such as dialysis for individuals older than age 65, intensive care, and aggressive cancer treatments for terminal patients, are generally unavailable in the United Kingdom. Lack of facilities in some areas has resulted in waiting lists for certain hospital services, albeit not for emergency cases, pregnancy, or planned treatments such as chemotherapy (NHS A to Z HelpDirect, 2000). Some recent reforms aimed at improving the NHS include the creation of national clinical standards and external performance monitoring of NHS hospitals and PCTs.

In 2000, the NHS released *The NHS Plan*, a 10-year plan intended to increase the efficiencies of its services. This plan's publication was followed by two documents, *The NHS Improvement Plan* and *Creating a Patient-led NHS,* which outlined the goals of giving patients more choice about their providers and health, increasing the country's health spending, increasing preventive care, expanding patient education for chronic conditions, creating new urgent care strategies, making healthcare services more convenient, and improving coordination of social and healthcare services (Partnership Development Team, 2011). Other reforms included the establishment of NHS Direct, a free nursing phone line, and future online appointment services through NHSnet, a computer-based network linking NHS organizations (Dobson, 1999). NHSnet has been replaced by N3 (N3, 2011). The United Kingdom has also stressed the removal of waiting lists by imposing its own form of diagnosis-related group payments, called healthcare resource groups.

Although there is general dissatisfaction with waiting lists and restricted access to certain services, the United Kingdom has been able to achieve health outcomes that exceed those found in the United States (World Health Organization, 2010). However, when faced with long waiting lists in their own country, many British individuals travel to foreign countries such as India and other parts of Europe to seek treatment if they can afford to do so (Rai, 2005). Overall health spending is set by the British Parliament, which has defined efficient use of resources as a policy goal.

A 2002 survey of sicker adults in five health systems (the United States, the United Kingdom, Canada, New Zealand, and Australia) found that sicker British adults reported problems with waiting time and other nonfinancial barriers to care but were the most satisfied with their health system (Blendon, Schoen, DesRosches, Osborn, & Zapert, 2003). In the same survey, sicker U.S. adults were most likely to be concerned about costs and coverage and to report access barriers due to costs; consequently, they were more likely to forgo medical care or not get the recommended follow-up treatment, including skipping medications (Blendon et al., 2003). The government's current financial commitments to the existing U.K. system may mean that the country will continue to achieve high health outcomes at a fraction of what the United States spends on health care.

Cuba's Healthcare System

Cuba's current healthcare system is the product of the socialist transformations that have occurred in this island nation since the revolution of 1959. This system can be classified as socialized medicine. Cuba's healthcare system is ruled by the following five basic principles:

1. Health care is a right.
2. Health care is the responsibility of the state.
3. Preventive and curative services are integrated.
4. Everyone participates in the function of the healthcare system.
5. Healthcare activities are integrated with economic and social development (Santana, 1987).

Two main programs have been instrumental in achieving Cuba's basic healthcare principles: the Medicine in the Community program (1975) and the Family Physician program (1985) (Santana, 1987).

By the end of the 1960s, Cuba's healthcare resources had been aggregated into a single system. The Cuban Ministry of Public Health was established in conjunction with polyclinics (discussed in detail in the next section) that provided primary care services at the local level. The Medicine in the Community program was proposed in 1975 to promote, maintain, and improve individual and community health through individuals' participation in the functioning, organizing, and use of the system. The polyclinics were restructured to become responsible for the total health services of a geographic area and population, as well as teaching and research activities. However, the polyclinics' staffs were not able to integrate fully with the communities they served. Moreover, the number of persons assigned to a community team was sometimes too high, and continuity of care was not easy to achieve (Santana, 1987).

The Family Physician program of 1985 changed the way primary care was delivered by increasing the number of family physicians and changing the role of the polyclinic. Under this program, a physician–nurse team works in a small office in charge of the medical and public health needs of a geographical area consisting of roughly 600–800 persons. In 1990, 50% of the population was covered by the Family Physician program (Roemer, 1993). The program now claims to have enough family physicians to cover almost every neighborhood on the island (Sanchez, 2009). This goal proved difficult to reach, however, given Cuba's economic crisis, which continues to this day.

The restructuring of Cuba's healthcare system after the Cuban revolution of 1959 clearly improved the health of the nation's population. Cuba's health indicators are better than those of all other countries except those with industrial capitalist economies (Nayeri, 1995). Life expectancy is now 76 years for men and 79 years for women in Cuba (World Health Organization, 2010). Since the 1980s, in the Western Hemisphere, only the United States and Canada have ranked better than Cuba in terms of infant and child mortality indicators (Susser, 1993). The health profile of the majority of Cubans resembles that of their counterparts in developed societies; the leading health problems are chronic and degenerative diseases, including heart disease, cancer, and diabetes (Santana, 1987).

Structure: Healthcare Facilities and Workforce

The Family Physician program (*Médico de Familia*) currently constitutes the backbone of Cuba's healthcare delivery system. Family physicians and nurses are assigned to an office-consultation room (*consultorio*) in a given community. Living quarters either in the same building or nearby are provided for these caregivers (Ramers, 2001). Family physicians hold office hours during the mornings. In the afternoons, they follow patients in the hospital, make visits, and inspect community facilities such as food stores, pharmacies, and day care centers (Santana, 1987). Thus the family physician is in charge of the complete well-being of the whole community rather than just the health of a given number of patients.

Patients in need of additional services are referred to a polyclinic (*policlínico*). The polyclinic has evolved into an ancillary facility that provides laboratory and emergency services as well as specialty consultations. In addition, it serves as a setting for physician residency training. Each polyclinic serves 30–40 *consultorios* (Dresang, Brebrick, Murray, Shallue, & Sullivan-Vedder, 2005). Hospital services are also available, but they focus on tertiary care. In 1995, there were 400 polyclinics and 263 hospitals in Cuba (Veeken, 1995).

Cuba prides itself on the advances it has achieved in medically related scientific endeavors. Resources have been allocated to training for primary care and to improving research into and knowledge of new diagnostic and treatment techniques (Santana, 1987). For example, computed tomography scans, organ transplants, and other high-technology facilities are all available in Cuba (Nayeri, 1995).

The healthcare workforce in Cuba has grown dramatically to fulfill the goals of the Family Physician program. According to Cuban government statistics, Cuba had 71,000 physicians by November 2005 (Rios, 2005). This represents the highest family physician per capita ratio in the world (Dresang et al., 2005). A physician trained through the Family Physician program spends 6 years learning medicine with a preventive, prophylactic, and epidemiologic view. The majority of family physicians and medical students in Cuba are women. Also, the proportion of male nurses has increased, reflecting a change in traditional gender roles in the medical professions. Physicians' salaries remain modest, however (Santana, 1987).

A unique feature of Cuba's healthcare workforce is its internationalist focus. A number of Cuban physicians participate in a program that sends them abroad for 2 years of service to another country in Latin America, the Caribbean, Africa, the Middle East, or Asia (Nayeri, 1995). Cuba is also involved with the education of foreign doctors. The *Escuela Latinoamerciana de Medicina* (Latin American School of Medicine), which is sponsored by the Cuban government, was originally established to train doctors of poor origins from Latin American countries affected by Hurricanes George and Mitch in 1998. It currently has 7,200 students from 24 countries, including 4 African nations and the United States (*Escuela Latinoamericana de Medicina*, 2011). U.S. students in the program are exempted from the U.S. government's ban on travel to Cuba (Mullan, 2004).

Financing

The government controls health care in Cuba, so financing for health care is entirely public. Even providers' medical education is paid for by the state, which provides additional financial aid to students with dependents (Nayeri, 1995). National budgets established for healthcare services are an important part of the country's expenditures.

Current Status

Cuba has been facing an economic crisis originally driven by the following two external factors: the fall of the Soviet bloc and the U.S. economic embargo (Nayeri & Lopez-Pardo, 2005; Nayeri, 1995). Before the Cuban revolution, most of the country's pharmaceutical products were imported; more than 80% came from the United States. Importation of goods, including drugs, shifted to the Soviet Union and Soviet bloc nations before the dissolution of this Soviet alliance in 1991. With the downfall of the Soviet bloc, Cuba lost the main supplier of its basic needs.

Cuba's situation is unique, in that a trade embargo imposed by the United States has influenced Cuba's healthcare system by affecting the flow of medical supplies and related materials to Cuba. This embargo has been in place since the 1960s and is one of the world's few sanctions that explicitly includes both food and medical supplies (Williams, 1997). The embargo was strengthened in the United States by passage of the Cuban Democracy Act of 1992, which prohibited foreign subsidiaries of U.S. companies from trading with Cuba (Barry, 2000). This measure effectively banned Cuba from purchasing half of the new world-class drugs available on the market (Barry, 2000; Williams, 1997). The lack of medical supplies and equipment has also reduced surgical rates in Cuba as well as the country's use of laboratory and radiologic services such as mammography and other diagnostic tools (Williams, 1997).

The Cuban government has tried to preserve both education and healthcare services, despite the ongoing economic crisis. For example, the use of alternative medicine (called traditional medicine in Cuba) has increased (Dresang et al., 2005; Quick, 1997). The Family Physician program has not appeared to be affected by the economic pressures so far (Nayeri & Lopez-Pardo, 2005; Nayeri, 1995). However, only half of the family physicians live in the geographic area they serve due to a housing shortage (Nayeri & Lopez-Pardo, 2005). Some health problems may be related to the scarcity of food supplies. Nevertheless, the infant mortality rate has remained low, at 7 deaths per 1,000 live births in 2006 (World Health Organization, 2010). Restrictions relating to the U.S. embargo on Cuba were further tightened in 2004 (Garfield, 2004); however, the Obama administration seems to favor a different policy toward Cuba (Drain & Barry, 2010). Despite the Cuban population's satisfaction with the gains in health care delivered by the socialist regime, the future success of this nation's healthcare system remains uncertain.

INTERNATIONAL HEALTHCARE SYSTEMS: IMPLICATIONS FOR THE UNITED STATES

The United States has a fragmented, multiple-payer healthcare system that makes it difficult to reduce inefficiencies and inappropriate spending (Keeler, 2006). Interestingly, the United States does not have a single health system model; it actually has elements of all four healthcare models—different models for different segments of the population, including:

1. Working Americans who receive insurance benefits through their employment characterize a Bismarck model.
2. Veterans, the military, and Native Americans receive health care through systems that resemble the Beveridge model.

3. The elderly and disabled participating in Medicare and the medically indigent covered by Medicaid are participating in a national health insurance model.
4. Uninsured Americans exemplify the out-of-pocket model representative of most developing nations (Reid, 2009a).

After discussing the health-related issues of developed and developing nations and the major features of four healthcare systems representing a variety of models of healthcare delivery, Jane (introduced in the case scenario at the beginning of this chapter) has been able to extract several lessons. The same pattern is evident in each of the countries examined—namely, a cycle of unsustainable spending growth, followed by implementation of numerous cost-containment strategies (Anderson et al., 2005).

Policy makers continue to try to determine whether prices, technology, aging, waste, inefficiency, the legal system, new disease patterns, corporate consolidation, or too many consumers and providers are to blame for rising costs (Anderson et al., 2005). In the United States, recent cost-containment strategies have focused on increased cost-sharing requirements in an effort to decrease demand for services, albeit so far with negligible results. In comparison, both the United Kingdom and Canada have sought to limit the supply of services, resulting in waiting lists for elective procedures.

In 2007, the United States spent $7,285 per capita on health expenditures, whereas Germany spent $4,209 per capita, Canada spent $4,049 per capita, and the United Kingdom spent $3,867 per capita for health care (Anderson et al., 2005; World Health Organization, 2010). The United States continues to pay more per capita for health care than any other country. While one might expect the dollar amount spent on health care to be higher in the United States because of higher incomes, the United States still has the highest expenditures when looking at healthcare costs as a percentage of total gross domestic product (GDP)—the total value of all final goods and services produced in a country during a given year. For the United States, the percentage of GDP devoted to health care in 2007 was 15.7%, which was 50% greater than healthcare expenditures in Canada, Germany, or Cuba (10.1%, 10.4%, and 10.4%, respectively) and almost twice that of the United Kingdom (8.4%) (World Health Organization, 2010).

Some important lessons can be learned by comparing how health services are structured in the various countries. Both Canada and the United Kingdom set annual budgets that restrict reimbursement and tend to limit supply of certain services, especially elective procedures. By contrast, both the United States and Germany have a plentiful supply of physicians, technology, and health resources. While this ready supply has been cited as a cost driver for these systems, it has also meant that many U.S. residents cannot afford basic medical services. In the United States, resources are distributed in a decidedly nonegalitarian fashion. People who have the ability to pay for services, either through income or insurance, can enjoy the best possible health care in the world. An increasing number of individuals, however, lack access to even the most basic primary care services. This system stands in contrast to the U.K. system, where approximately 80% of the annual healthcare budget is spent on primary care services but spending on heroic end-of-life technology is limited.

Another interesting component in the comparisons of systems is the role played by government in financing the systems of care. In this regard, the United States is unique in its reliance on private systems and funding for health care. Generally, as most countries achieve a high per capita income, the government assumes a greater role in financing healthcare services through public expenditures. In the United States, expenditures on health care represented about 45% of total public spending in 2007, compared with about 87% of total public expenditures in the United Kingdom, 70% of total public expenditures in Canada, and 77% of total public expenditures in Germany. These contrasts in public funding reflect a strong ethos in the United States that emphasizes the private sector's role and responsibility in the healthcare delivery system. This preference also leads to a pluralistic, fragmented delivery system with unique opportunities to shift costs between public and private payers.

While a high per capita income is generally associated with improved health outcomes, both the United States and Cuba, in their own ways, demonstrate that increased expenditures alone cannot improve health outcomes. In Cuba, which has a low per capita income, health outcomes are comparable to those achieved in many developed countries. In contrast, in the United States, having a high per capita income and health care expenditures that exceed those in all other countries has not improved health outcomes considerably. Clearly, how fairly and equitably health resources are distributed is an important consideration when comparing health systems.

CONCLUSION

Although healthcare systems may differ from nation to nation, they enable us to compare and contrast those characteristics that move a system toward the goals of providing affordable, accessible, and equitable health care for all populations. As pointed out by the case scenario at the beginning of the chapter, lessons can be learned from both industrialized and developing countries. Healthcare systems constantly evolve and change. Many factors—including consumer activism, political change, and public and private financing efforts—influence these complex processes. The distribution of healthcare resources both globally and within a particular country has a profound impact on how healthcare services will be delivered and used.

The need for health personnel in a healthcare system, in terms of both the number of providers and the mix of skills, is directed by policy decisions within a particular country. If policies direct greater involvement of pharmacists or other allied health professionals, then significant resource planning must be undertaken to ensure the availability of appropriately trained personnel. Appropriately trained personnel may be among the many constraints that planners face when developing healthcare policies. The disparities in the distribution of healthcare resources will continue to strain all healthcare systems, but particularly those in developing countries where competing social and economic programs are equally justified for funding.

QUESTIONS FOR FURTHER DISCUSSION

1. Are there components or features of the healthcare delivery systems discussed in this chapter that should be adopted to improve healthcare delivery in the United States?
2. Are there components or features of the pharmaceutical sector of the countries discussed in this chapter that should be adopted to improve healthcare delivery in the United States?
3. Should a national drug policy be developed and adopted in the United States? If so, what should its goal be and how should it be structured?

KEY TOPICS AND TERMS

Beveridge model
Bismark model
Decentralized national health program
Developed nation
Developing nation
Gross domestic product (GDP)
Infant mortality rate
Life expectancy
National health insurance model
Out-of-pocket model
Portability
Sickness funds
Social partnership
Social solidarity
Socialized health insurance
Socialized medicine
Universality

REFERENCES

Allen, D. (1984). Health services in England. In M. W. Raffel (Ed.), *Comparative health systems* (pp. 197–257). University Park, PA: Pennsylvania State University Press.

Anderson, G., Hussey, P., Krogner, B., & Waters, H. (2005). Health spending in the United States and the rest of the industrialized world. *Health Affairs, 24*(4), 903–914.

Anis, A. H. (2000). Pharmaceutical policies in Canada: Another example of federal–provincial discord. *Canadian Medical Association Journal, 162*(4), 523–526.

Barry, M. (2000). Effect of the U.S. embargo and economic decline on health in Cuba. *Annals of Internal Medicine, 132*(2), 151–154.

BBC News. (2006). *Local health bodies face shake-up.* Retrieved from http://news.bbc.co.uk/go/pr/fr/-/2/hi/health/4987430.stm

Beske, F. (1988). Federal Republic of Germany. In R. B. Saltman (Ed.), *The international handbook of health-care systems* (pp. 93–106). Westport, CT: Greenwood Press.

Bindman, A. B., & Weiner, J. P. (2000). The modern NHS: An underfunded model of efficiency and integration. *Health Affairs, 19*(30), 120–122.

Blendon, R., Schoen, C., DesRosches, C., Osborn, R., & Zapert, K. (2003). Common concerns amid diverse systems: Health care experiences in five countries. *Health Affairs, 27*(3), 106–121.

Booer, T. (1994). The health care systems in the United Kingdom. In U. K. Hoffmeyer & T. R. McCarthy (Eds.), *Financing health care* (pp. 1071–1145). Dordrecht, Netherlands: Kluwer.

Boyes, W., & Melvin, M. (1999). *Fundamentals of economics.* Boston, MA: Houghton Mifflin.

Busse, R. (2004). Disease management programs in Germany's statutory health insurance system. *Health Affairs, 23*(3), 56–67.

Canadian-healthcare. (2006). *Canadian health care.* Retrieved from http://www.canadian-healthcare.org

Canadian Institute for Health Information. (2010). *Figure 1: Number of family medicine and specialist physicians by province/territory, Canada, 2008.* Retrieved from http://www.cihi.ca/cihiweb/en/smdb_2008_fig1_e.html

Chidley, J. (1996). Radical surgery: Cuts in public funding imperil Medicare's future. *Maclean's, 109*(49), 44–48.

Dobson, F. (1999). Modernizing Britain's national health services. *Health Affairs, 18*(3), 40–41.

Dresang, L. T., Brebrick, L., Murray, D., Shallue, A., & Sullivan-Vedder, L. (2005). Family medicine in Cuba: Community-oriented primary care and complementary and alternative medicine. *Journal of the American Board of Family Practice, 18*, 297–303.

Drain, P. K., & Barry, M. (2010). Fifty years of U.S. embargo: Cuba's health outcomes and lessons. *Science, 328*, 572–573.

Enthoven, A. C. (2000). In pursuit of an improving national health service. *Health Affairs, 19*(3), 102–119.

Escuela Latinoamericana de Medicina (ELAM). (2011). *Nuestra Universidad - Historia.* Retrieved from http://www.elacm.sld.cu/historia.html

Evans-Cuellar, A., & Wiener, J. M. (2000). Can social insurance for long-term care work? The experience of Germany. *Health Affairs, 19*(3), 8–25.

Facts about Germany. (2011). *Medical care for everyone.* Retrieved from http://www.tatsachen-ueber-deutschland.de/en/society/main-content-08/medical-care-for-everyone.html

Garfield, R. (2004). Health care in Cuba and the manipulation of humanitarian imperatives. *Lancet, 364*,1007.

Harrison, S. (1988). Great Britain. In R. B. Saltman (Ed.), *The international handbook of healthcare systems* (pp. 123–143). Westport, CT: Greenwood Press.

Harvard School of Public Health. (2000). *Burden of disease unit.* Retrieved from http://www.hsph.harvard.edu/organizations/bdu/index/htm

Health Canada. (2006a). *Access to Insurance Coverage for Prescription Medicines.* Retrieved from http://www.hc-sc.gc.ca/hcs-sss/pharma/acces/index-eng.php

Health Canada. (2006b). *2003 First Ministers' Accord on Health Care Renewal.* Retrieved from http://www.hc-sc.gc.ca/hcs-sss/delivery-prestation/fptcollab/2003accord/index-eng.php

Hilts, P. J. (2000, June 21). Europeans perform highest in ranking of world health. *The New York Times*, p. 9.

Hoffmeyer, U. (1994). The health care system in Germany. In U. K. Hoffmeyer & T. R. McCarthy (Eds.), *Financing health care* (pp. 419–512). Dordrecht, Netherlands: Kluwer.

Iglehart, J. K. (2000). Revisiting the Canadian health care system. *New England Journal of Medicine, 342*(26), 2007–2012.

Jackson, J. (1997). The German health system: Lessons for reform in the United States. *Archives of Internal Medicine, 157*(2), 155–161.

Jacobzone, S. (2000). *Pharmaceutical policies in OECD countries: Reconciling social and industrial goals* (Vol. 40, pp. 1–98). Paris, France: Organization for Economic Cooperation and Development.

Jost, T. (1998). German health care reform: The next steps. *Journal of Health Politics, Policy and Law, 23*(4), 697–711.

KaiserEDU.org (2011). *International Health Systems–UK.* Retrieved from http://www.kaiseredu.org/Issue-Modules/International-Health-Systems/UK.aspx

Krauss, C. (2004, September 12). *Canada looks for ways to fix its health care system.* Retrieved from http://www.nytimes.com/2004/09/12/international/americas/12canada.html

Krauss, C. (2005, June 10). *In blow to Canada's health system, Quebec law is voided.* Retrieved from http://www.nytimes.com/2005/06/10/international/americas/10canada.html

Morgan, S., McMahon, M., Mitton, C., Roughead, E., Kirk, R., Kanavos, P., & Menon, D. (2006). Centralized drug review processes in Australia, Canada, New Zealand, and the United Kingdom. *Health Affairs, 25*(2), 337–348.

Mullan, F. (2004). Affirmative action, Cuban style. *New England Journal of Medicine, 351*(26), 2680–2682.

N3. (2011). *The N3 Story.* Retrieved from http://www.n3.nhs.uk/TheN3Story/TheN3Story.cfm

National Health Service (NHS). (2006). *About the NHS—how the NHS works.* Retrieved from http://www.nhs.uk/england/AboutTheNhs/Defalut.cmsx

National Health Service (NHS). (2010). *Primary care trusts.* Retrieved from http://www.nhs.uk/nhsengland/thenhs/about/pages/authoritiesandtrusts.aspx#primary

Nayeri, K. (1995). The Cuban health care system and factors currently undermining it. *Journal of Community Health, 20*(4), 321–334.

Nayeri, K., & Lopez-Pardo, C.M. (2005). Economic crisis and access to care: Cuba's health care system since the collapse of the Soviet Union. *International Journal of Health Services, 35*(4):797–816.

Naylor, C. D. (1999). Health care in Canada: Incrementalism under fiscal duress. *Health Affairs, 18*(3), 9–26.

Newman, D. (2010). Health-care reform, Canadian-style. *CBC news.* Retrieved from http://www.cbc.ca/canada/story/2010/04/15/f-vp-newman.html

NHS A to Z HelpDirect. (2000). Retrieved from http://www.nhsatoz.org

Organization for Economic Cooperation and Development. (1994). *The reform of health care systems.* Paris, France: Organization for Economic Cooperation and Development.

Partnership Development Team. (2011). *Latest information and useful resources.* Retrieved from http://www.pdteam.org.uk/news/nhsimprovementplan.htm

Quick, R. (1997). A health care revolution. *Nursing Times, 93*(29), 17.

Rai, S. (2005, April 7). *Low costs lure foreigners to India for medical care.* Retrieved from http://www.nytimes.com/2005/04/07

Ramers, C. (2001). Medicina Cubana: A fresh perspective. *The Western Journal of Medicine, 175*(2), 129.

Reid, T. R. (2009a). Different models, common principles. In *The healing of America; a global quest for better, cheaper and fairer health care* (pp. 16–27). New York, NY: The Penguin Press.

Reid, T. R. (2009b). Germany: Applied Christianity. In *The healing of America; a global quest for better, cheaper and fairer health care* (pp. 16–27). New York, NY: The Penguin Press.

Reid, T. R. (2009c). The UK: Universal coverage, no bills. In *The healing of America: A global quest for better, cheaper and fairer health care* (pp. 103–124). New York, NY: The Penguin Press.

Reinhardt, U. (1999). Mangled competition and managed whatever. *Health Affairs, 18*(3), 92–94.

Rios, A. (2005). 40 years after the first graduation on Pico Turquino, Cuba now has 71,000 doctors. *Granma International online edition.* Retrieved from http://www.granma.cu/ingles/2005/noviembre/juev17/47turquino.html

Roemer, M. I. (1993). Primary health care and hospitalization: California and Cuba. *American Journal of Public Health, 83*(3), 317–318.

Rozek, R., & Mulhern, C. (1994). The health care system in Canada. In U. K. Hoffmeyer & T. R. McCarthy (Eds.), *Financing health care* (pp. 255–344). Dordrecht, Netherlands: Kluwer.

Saltman, R. B., & Dubois, H. F. W. (2005). Current reform proposals in social health insurance countries. *Eurohealth, 11*(1), 10–14.

Sanchez, R. (2009). Army of Cuban doctors hunt for possible swine flu carriers. *Sun Sentinel*.com. Retrieved from http://www.sun-sentinel.com/news/nationworld/sfl-cuba-swine-flu-051309,0,1198204.story

Santana, S. M. (1987). The Cuban health care system: Responsiveness to changing population needs and demands. *World Development, 15*(1), 113–125.

Schieber, G., & Maeda, A. (1999). Health care financing and delivery in developing countries. *Health Affairs, 18,* 193–205.

Spivey, R. N., Wertheimer, A. I., & Rucker, T. D. (1992). *International pharmaceutical services: Drug industry and pharmacy practice in 23 major countries of the world.* New York, NY: Haworth Press.

Susser, M. (1993). Health as a human right: An epidemiologist's perspective on the public health. *American Journal of Public Health, 83*(3), 418–426.

Ulrich, V. (1999). Health care in Germany: Structure, expenditure, and prospects. In W. McArthur, C. Ramsay, & M. Walker (Eds.), *Healthy incentives: Canadian health reform in an international context.* Vancouver, Canada: The Fraser Institute. Available at http://www.fraserinstitute.ca/admin/books/files/Healthy%20Incentives%20(all).pdf

UNICEF. (1995). *The Bamako initiative: Rebuilding health systems.* New York: UNICEF.

Veeken, H. (1995). Cuba: Plenty of care, few condoms, no corruption. *British Medical Journal, 311*(7010), 935–937.

Williams, R. (1997). In the shadow of plenty: Cuba copes with a crippled health care system. *Canadian Medical Association, 157*(3), 291–293.

Woolhandler, S., Campbell, T., & Himmelstein, D. (2003). Costs of health care administration in the United States and Canada. *New England Journal of Medicine, 349,* 768–775.

World Health Organization. (2000a). *The world health report 2000, health systems: Improving performance.* Geneva, Switzerland: WHO.

World Health Organization. (2000b, June 21). France, Italy provide best healthcare. *Reuters.*

World Health Organization. (2010). *World health statistics, 2010–Part II: Global health indicators.* Retrieved from http://www.who.int/whosis/whostat/2010/en/index.html

Zander, B., Kimmerle, J., Sundmacher, L., Bäumler, M. (2009). *Health policy in Germany after the election.* Health Policy Monitor. Retrieved from http://www.hpm.org/en/Surveys/TU_Berlin_-_D/14/Health_Policy_in_Germany_after_the_election.html

CHAPTER 21

Healthcare Reform

Catherine N. Otto and Thomas E. Buckley*

LEARNING OBJECTIVES

Upon completion of this chapter, the student shall be able to:

- Describe the effects of lack of access to health care in the United States
- Compare and contrast demand and need with respect to healthcare delivery
- Identify potential outcomes of proposals addressing the insolvency of the Medicare program
- Discuss the federal government's provisions to support health care as a right: Kerr-Mills Act, Medicare, Medicaid, and Patient Protection and Affordable Care Act
- Summarize the key components of federally proposed cost-containment methods for health care
- Explain the key concepts of uncompensated care pools, employer mandates, and Medicaid waivers
- Compare and contrast Hawaii's Prepaid Health Care Act, the Oregon Health Plan, and TennCare
- Discuss methods to increase access to health insurance in Massachusetts and Vermont
- Define employer and employee mandates, sin taxes, health savings accounts, and portability of health insurance coverage

CHAPTER QUESTIONS

1. Why is healthcare reform an issue in the United States?
2. What state and federal healthcare reform efforts have been introduced in the past?
3. What solutions have been proposed in the healthcare reform debate?
4. How can pharmacists influence healthcare reform? What responsibility do pharmacists have? Why is pharmacist participation in the healthcare reform debate important?

---

*With acknowledgment to Craig A. Pedersen.

INTRODUCTION

An in-depth discussion of the topics covered in this chapter could fill an entire book. In many ways, this chapter integrates material from other chapters of this text as well as information on history, politics, financing, and the structure of the U.S. healthcare system. It discusses the problems of the U.S. healthcare system, the politics of healthcare reform, past landmark efforts to reform the U.S. healthcare system, current reform efforts, and pharmacy's role in reform efforts. This chapter can serve as an introductory guide to this textbook or as a capstone to the information provided elsewhere in this text.

This chapter does not endorse any particular side on any of the controversial issues, nor does it hold the answers to the complex problems the United States faces today regarding health care for its citizens. Instead, this chapter seeks to outline the issues, suggest questions for debate, and stimulate readers to look deep within themselves and their core values to come to a reasonable and rational opinion on these issues. Finally, it suggests that pharmacists have the opportunity and responsibility to work proactively to ensure that the profession of pharmacy plays an integral part in the future of health care in the United States.

IDENTIFICATION OF THE PROBLEM

The people and the government of the United States are unique in their approach to health and health care. The United States is the only developed country that does not ensure access to health care through guaranteed coverage. This structural uniqueness of the U.S. healthcare system fragments the financing system and makes it difficult for the poor and the sick to seek preventive care. Thus expensive safety nets that drive up costs and aggravate the problem of cost shifting are required.

As discussed in Chapter 20, which covers international health care systems, the United States spends more of its gross domestic product on health care and has higher per capita expenditures on health care than any other industrialized nation (Anderson & Poullier, 1999; *OECD Health Data 2009,* 2009). The cost of health care in the United States has been increasing since the early 1960s. This rise can be attributed to multiple factors, including an aging population, patient demand for the best care available, technological advancements, increasing therapeutic options, and general and health care inflation.

Yet, although the U.S. levels of spending exceed those of other industrialized nations and cost increases outstrip the growth of other components of the U.S. economy, researchers report that Americans are generally dissatisfied with the healthcare system (Donelan, Blendon, Schoen, Davis, & Binns, 1999; Smith, Altman, Leitman, Moloney, & Taylor, 1992). This dissatisfaction is rooted in the high cost of health care, lack of universal access, and lack of demonstrated gains in life expectancy. Life expectancy at birth for female Americans was 80.4 years in 2007. The United States ranked below the Organization for Economic Cooperation and Development median of 82.3 years for women, and behind Japan (86.0 years), France (84.4 years), Sweden (83.0 years), Germany (82.7 years), and Canada (83.0 years). At birth, males have considerably shorter life expectancies of 75.3 years in the United States, compared with the Organization for Economic Cooperation and Development median of 77.2 years (*OECD Health Data*

2010). Meanwhile, the United States has spent a considerably larger percentage of its gross domestic product on health care than these other countries. Clearly, the United States has not gained in life expectancy from the additional money spent. Therefore, a crisis appears to exist in U.S. health care.

AN ISSUE OF ACCESS

In the United States, access to health care is often determined by age, economic status, and race/ethnicity. The enactment of Medicare and Medicaid in 1965 addressed some of the access issues for the elderly and the indigent. Even so, the number of uninsured Americans has increased from 27 million in 1977 to about 46 million in 2008, which is 17.3% of the population. Seventeen states have uninsured rates exceeding 17.3% for their residents younger than age 65 (Kaiser Commission on Medicaid and the Uninsured, 2009b).

Adults are more likely to be uninsured than children, comprising 80% of those uninsured. (Kaiser Commission on Medicaid and the Uninsured, 2009b). Approximately two thirds of uninsured individuals are in families where one or more individuals are employed full time (Kaiser Commission on Medicaid and the Uninsured, 2009b). Nonwhite Americans—Hispanics (32%), African Americans (21%), Native Americans (28%), and Asians (19%)—are more likely to be uninsured compared to white Americans (13%) (Kaiser Commission on Medicaid and the Uninsured, 2009b).

Lack of access to health care in the United States has become a high-profile issue for several reasons. First, health insurance coverage is an important determinant of access to care. Second, lack of adequate health coverage puts individuals at risk for high medical expenses. Third, everyone ends up paying for costs shifted because of uncompensated care (Brown & Wyn, 1996).

THE BEST HEALTH CARE?

Does the United States have the best health care system in the world? Many say yes—we are the leaders. We have the latest and best treatment available anywhere in the world. Fuchs (1992) agrees that the United States is the leader in technological advances related to medicine. Physicians come from around the world to receive the most advanced training. Very wealthy patients come from around the world to receive care in the United States. At the same time, Fuchs suggests other dimensions in which the United States may not be the best: public health, service, efficiency, and distribution equity.

The United States ranks below average among developed countries in most public health measures. Frequently, access to providers is limited, and many providers lack the caring nature that patients desire. If the U.S. healthcare system were efficient, it seems that we should be able to spend amounts comparable to those spent by other countries to achieve the same level of public health. Also, the distribution of health care in the United States is clearly not equal. The large number of uninsured and underinsured Americans is evidence of this fact. Thus, Fuchs suggests, for the United States to claim to have the best healthcare system, improvements in efficiency (controlling the high cost of care), distributional equity (providing universal coverage), service, and public health are necessary (Fuchs, 1992).

The United States clearly has made judgments about the nature of access to its health-care system. Structurally, health care is a privilege in the United States and not a right. Nevertheless, many question the wisdom of not providing universal health coverage for all Americans.

DEMAND VERSUS NEED

In the late 1960s, economists began analyzing demand versus need—an important component to understanding access to medical care in the United States. Needs are normative judgments concerning the quantity of medical services that ought to be consumed (Jeffers, Bognanno, & Bartlett, 1971). Frequently, needs are fixed by policy makers. An example is the need for prenatal care. Society and policy makers believe that every pregnant woman needs prenatal care. It is difficult to object to this position because, without such care, the health of the unborn infant can be at risk.

Need is often criticized by economists as being too mechanical, as denying the individuality and autonomy of the patient, and as characterizing the human body as a machine that needs fuel in the form of food and repairs in the form of medication or surgery. Demand, by comparison, implies patient autonomy, choice, and tailoring inputs to individual preferences (Boulding, 1996). Demand, therefore, is the quantity of medical services that patients think they ought to consume based on their perceptions of their healthcare needs (Jeffers et al., 1971). Individual tastes and preferences determine utilization (see Chapter 13 for further discussion of demand).

GOVERNMENT TRUST FUNDS

Medicare and Social Security trust funds are frequently cited in discussions about healthcare reform. The concern over these trust funds stems from widespread confusion about their function and about the organization and purpose of the Medicare and Social Security programs.

Only recently has the disposition of trust fund moneys become a concern. When Social Security was created in 1935, the Roosevelt administration was aware that the amount of money collected would exceed expenditures for many years. The solution was to create a trust fund to account for the receipt and disposition of these funds.

The first source of confusion centers on the money in these trust funds. By law, the Social Security Administration is required to invest the surplus funds in special U.S. Treasury bonds (Peterson, 1996). Therefore, the taxes collected flow into the U.S. Treasury, just like all other tax collections. And like most taxes collected, these revenues become part of the general fund, available for any use (e.g., roads, infrastructure, and defense). No special savings account exists that surplus funds are deposited into and thus saved for future obligations. In essence, the trust funds are a bookkeeping device.

Of recent concern is the question of what happens when the Social Security trust fund is exhausted—an event projected to occur in 2037. However, tax revenues are predicted to fall below program costs in 2010 and 2011 due to the recession. Tax revenues will exceed program costs in 2012 through 2014 and then fall below program costs beginning in 2015 due to the retiring baby boomer generation (Social Security Trustees, 2010).

Perhaps the greatest source of confusion related to Social Security is the common belief that the Social Security Administration functions like a private pension fund, when, in fact, it does not. In a private pension fund, funds are collected and invested to provide retirement income to participants when the time comes for them to retire. Social Security does not work that way. Taxes collected from an individual for Social Security benefits are not designated for that individual upon retirement. Instead, these taxes are paid to current beneficiaries. Thus the Social Security system allows for an intergenerational transfer of funds between the working population and those eligible for Social Security benefits.

Maintaining these trust funds becomes a major challenge as members of the baby boomer generation (born between 1946 and 1964) reach retirement age beginning in 2011. Although U.S. citizens expect to use Medicare and Social Security when they retire, they are concerned that these programs will be difficult to maintain because of underfinancing and changing demographics. Substantial reforms will be required to ensure long-term solvency of the programs.

The year that the Hospital Insurance trust fund (Medicare Part A) has been projected to become insolvent has fluctuated over the past 25 years. For example, in 1982 the trust fund was forecast to become insolvent in 1987—only 5 years later. From 1987 to 1995, the projected year of insolvency ranged from 1999 to 2005 (O'Sullivan, 1996). Currently, the Hospital Insurance trust fund is projected to be exhausted in 2017 (Medicare Trustees, 2009). Medicare taxes covered 88% of costs in 2009; however, estimates indicate that they will cover 81% of the costs in 2017 (Medicare Trustees, 2009). Although the potential insolvency of this trust fund is not a new issue, the recession, the aging baby boomer population, and the effects of the 2010 Patient Protection and Affordable Care Act have made it a more critical matter for the president and Congress to address.

A number of approaches have been suggested to reform the Medicare program, such as lowering provider fee schedules, increasing patient cost-sharing requirements, increasing premiums, changing eligibility requirements, and promoting health savings accounts.

HEALTHCARE REFORM EFFORTS BY THE FEDERAL GOVERNMENT

In an effort to eliminate some of the economic barriers to medical care for the elderly and medically indigent, the federal government has addressed the notion of health care as a right and not a privilege, at least for some people in the United States. Enactment of the Kerr-Mills Act and establishment of the Medicare and Medicaid programs in the 1960s paved the way for health care to be perceived as a basic human right.

Kerr-Mills Act

Amendments to the Social Security Act in 1960 provided healthcare coverage to elderly indigent individuals. This landmark legislation, known as the Kerr-Mills Act, was the first to provide health care to elderly or indigent persons on a broad scale. Many critics were concerned that the states would not implement this legislation in a timely manner. These predictions were confirmed. Many states had failed to adopt Kerr-Mills by 1963, when 90% of the funds were received by the five largest industrialized states (Starr, 1982).

Kerr-Mills did not provide healthcare coverage to the nonindigent elderly or the indigent nonelderly. These groups were not covered until amendments to the Social Security Act in 1965 established Medicare coverage for elderly persons (regardless of income) and Medicaid coverage for the poor.

Medicare and Medicaid

Medicare and Medicaid were significant healthcare reform programs (see Chapter 18). Before 1960, many elderly people in the United States lacked any kind of health insurance coverage. The Kerr-Mills Act and its successor, Medicare, addressed this need. Medicare Part A covers hospitalization, and Medicare Part B covers outpatient and physician bills. The third layer of reform was Medicaid, which covers indigent persons.

These programs reflected contrasting traditions. Medicare had popular support, and Social Security had made it acceptable for the elderly to receive government retirement benefits. Medicaid, however, was burdened by the stigma of public assistance (Starr, 1982). Medicare had uniform national criteria for eligibility, whereas Medicaid allowed states to determine the breadth of their programs. These differences persist today.

The Cost-Containment Era

By the early 1970s, Americans understood that their healthcare system was in a financial crisis. One survey in 1970 found that approximately three fourths of heads of households agreed with the statement, "There is a crisis in health care in the United States" (Starr, 1982). Terms used to describe costs included *skyrocketing* and *runaway inflation*. Medical care had become very expensive, and costs were exceeding inflation at an alarming rate. Coupled with worries about high prices for medical care were concerns about access, such as the diminishing number of primary care practitioners and patients' inability to obtain care from a physician on the weekends or in the evenings (Starr, 1982).

During this era, cost containment became a primary concern. Several strategies were implemented to control rising costs. They included voluntary hospital planning, wage and price freezes, changes in the amounts and methods of reimbursement for services, development of more cost-effective healthcare delivery systems, and regulatory programs such as utilization review and controls on hospital capital expenditures. Ultimately, most of those strategies proved unsuccessful in controlling costs.

Another significant healthcare reform effort was the 1972 amendments to the Social Security Act, which established professional standards review organizations. Professional standards review organizations were a national network of utilization review programs that had dual responsibility for medical cost containment and quality assurance. This program did not work, however, and it was replaced in 1983 by peer review organizations with a local focus.

Yet another cost-containment program was Section 1122 of the 1972 amendments to the Social Security Act, which required states to review proposed capital improvement expenditures of healthcare organizations and to provide authorization through a certificate of need at the state level. The certificate-of-need program was intended to reduce unnecessary duplication of services but was unsuccessful in meeting this goal. Some states have since eliminated the certificate-of-need requirements for capital improvements.

In 1973, President Richard Nixon signed the Health Maintenance Organization (HMO) Act. The HMO Act encouraged the use of these lower cost healthcare delivery systems and provided financial assistance for development of nonprofit HMOs. This act constituted the federal government's first effort to develop an alternative to fee-for-service medicine (Iglehart, 1982). Healthcare reimbursement would be forever changed by this act.

Diagnosis-Related Groups

These cost-containment efforts did not appreciably restrain the growth of healthcare costs in the United States. By contrast, the 1983 implementation of diagnosis-related groups (DRGs)—a type of prospective payment system for hospital services—was a landmark effort to control hospital reimbursement under Medicare. Medicare established a fixed schedule of fees to be paid to hospitals, where the fee varied for each diagnosis. If the actual cost to the hospital is less than the set fee, the hospital keeps the difference; if the service costs more than the set fee, the hospital absorbs the loss.

The objective of DRGs is to promote rational use of healthcare dollars and to stimulate competition among hospitals. Under this system, hospitals are reimbursed on an episode-of-care rather than a fee-for-service basis, placing the hospital at risk for inpatient healthcare costs.

DRG-based reimbursement has substantially slowed the growth of hospital expenditures, but physician expenditures, which are not uniformly subject to prospective payment incentives, continue to grow. Concern also exists about hospitals dumping patients and discharging patients early (Epstein, Bogen, Dreyer, & Thorpe, 1991). Inappropriate use of these mechanisms without proper controls has the potential to hurt quality of care. (For further reading on hospitals, see Chapter 7.)

Portability of Coverage

The Health Insurance Portability and Accountability Act of 1996 (HIPAA) addressed the following three issues in the healthcare reform debate: (1) preexisting condition exclusions, (2) elimination of health discrimination applications to eligibility rules, and (3) guaranteed renewability for plans that cover more than one employee. Later, HIPAA was expanded to address patient confidentiality issues.

Under HIPAA, individuals cannot be denied coverage because they have a preexisting medical condition if they agree to an exclusionary period (also known as an elimination period) for that condition, which cannot exceed 1 year. After 1 year, the policy holder can no longer be denied coverage for the preexisting condition. As long as the policyholder remains continuously enrolled in a plan, with breaks no longer than 63 days, the exclusion period cannot be reimposed. In short, HIPAA guarantees that policies and benefits available to a specific group cannot be withheld if an exclusionary period has already been met.

The second part of the act addresses the discriminatory practice of eliminating individuals and groups from the insurance market based on risk, preexisting conditions, or utilization history. In the past, the practice of "cherry-picking," or selecting the healthiest groups, was commonplace in the insurance industry. Now, however, insurance companies are required to sell coverage to small employer groups and individuals who lose coverage without regard to their health history. This issue is especially important to employers with fewer than 50 employees. Previously, one employee with a high risk factor could jeopardize the coverage of all members of the small group (Cantor, Long, & Marquis, 1995). A significant component missing here is controls on insurance prices for these small groups and individuals.

The third component of HIPAA is that insurers must renew policies they sell to groups and individuals. Previously, insurance companies were allowed to eliminate costly individuals or groups from their policies by denying renewal of coverage.

Health Savings Accounts

The Medicare Prescription Drug, Improvement, and Modernization Act of 2003 included a provision creating health savings accounts (HSA) (Remler & Giled, 2006). HSAs are a type of medical savings account (MSA)—a pilot project Congress created in 1996 for self-employed individuals and employers with fewer than 50 employees as a method of paying for medical care expenses. Under the Medicare Prescription Drug, Improvement, and Modernization Act, an employer of any size may offer an HSA as a health insurance option to its employees (Minicozzi, 2006). Like MSAs, HSAs are tax-free savings accounts that are used for the out-of-pocket medical expenses for those individuals who select a high-deductible health insurance plan (e.g., $1,000 to $5,000 per individual or $2,000 to $10,000 per family). Contributions from pretax income are limited to the amount of the deductible ($2,600 for an individual or $5,100 for a family) and may be made by either the employer or the employee. Total out-of-pocket spending is capped at $5,000 for an individual and $10,000 for a family; after this point, the health insurance will cover all healthcare expenses. Balances in HSAs do not expire, but rather accumulate over time, even if a person is no longer covered by a high-deductible health insurance plan (Remler & Giled, 2006).

MSAs and HSAs are designed to create price sensitivity among healthcare consumers. Patients with traditional health insurance coverage are largely unaware of the cost of medical care services. Economists suggest that this lack of knowledge is one of the reasons why health care costs have risen so dramatically over the years (American College of Physicians, 1996). Unlike most health insurance plans, MSAs and HSAs do not shield the consumer from the cost of medical care. The consumer becomes directly responsible for dollars spent on health care and thus becomes more price sensitive. Consumers are at partial risk for expenditures, because money comes from their MSAs or HSAs to pay for care. As a consequence, they have an incentive to avoid medical care that is not worth the cost (Goodman & Pauly, 1995). Proponents of MSAs and HSAs have suggested that these accounts will reduce wasteful utilization of resources and hold down healthcare cost inflation rates (Hsiao, 1995).

Critics of MSAs and HSAs remain concerned about the prospect of adverse selection with these accounts. As discussed in Chapter 15, adverse selection occurs when insured individuals can accurately predict their future need for health insurance coverage (Folland, Goodman, & Stano, 1997). Consumers know more about their health than the insurance company, so sick people are more likely to enroll in a health plan in higher proportions than individuals who are well. With these types of plans, the fear is that healthy individuals would drop their low-deductible health insurance in favor of MSAs combined with high-deductible plans. Premiums in the low-deductible plan would then skyrocket because only the sick would participate in the plan (Gardner, 1995).

Although access to health care in the United States may not be significantly altered by either MSAs or HSAs, the growth of healthcare spending may be slowed by their adoption. However, consumers may be unwilling or unable to determine the appropriateness, quality, and cost of healthcare services given the specialized nature of healthcare delivery and thus do little to decrease spending. Also, consumers who have limited resources may forgo necessary care, potentially resulting in increased spending to compensate for their delays in seeking treatment.

HSAs represent a radical change in healthcare reform—moving away from the concept of collective responsibility and toward the notion of individual accountability (Robinson, 2005). Their consequences—intended and unintended—to healthcare delivery systems, employer health insurance costs, and individual health outcomes are unknown.

Patient Protection and Affordable Care Act

The Patient Protection and Affordable Care Act, P.L. 111-148 (referred to as the Affordable Care Act [ACA]), was signed into law by President Obama on March 23, 2010. Not since amending the Social Security Act in 1965 when Medicare and Medicaid were created has Congress passed legislation this comprehensive impacting all aspects of the healthcare delivery system—patients, healthcare providers, insurance companies, state and federal governments, as well as the Medicare and Medicaid programs. Due to vast changes and infrastructure that must be developed prior to implementation, a majority of the provisions begin in 2014; however, a number of programs, reforms, and requirements took place in the first year (Kaiser Family Foundation, 2010b). When the law is fully implemented in 2019, it is predicted that 32 million previously uninsured individuals will have health insurance (Kaiser Family Foundation, 2010c).

The purpose of the ACA is to expand access to healthcare services using an individual mandate requiring U.S. citizens and legal residents to purchase health insurance. Individuals who do not enroll in a health insurance plan will be assessed a tax penalty. However, this is balanced with premium credits (a subsidy) based upon the individual's income for those who do not have access to an employer-based plan and subsequently purchase health insurance on their own (Kaiser Family Foundation, 2010c).

Coupled with mandating individuals to enroll in health insurance plans are requirements placed on employers. The incentive for employers to offer health insurance is balanced with the risk of paying penalties for failing to offer this benefit. Requirements and penalties placed upon employers are determined according to its number of employees. Large employers—those with more than 200 employees—are required to automatically enroll employees into health insurance plans offered. Most large employers currently offer health insurance, thus this requirement will appear seamless to these employees. Employers with 50 or more employees who do not offer health insurance to their employees and who have at least one full-time employee who receives a tax credit for purchasing health insurance will be assessed a $2,000 fee per full-time employee after exempting the first 30 employees (Kaiser Family Foundation, 2010c).

ACA expands the health insurance infrastructure by authorizing the development of state-based insurance exchanges and nonprofit health insurance companies. Individuals and small businesses that have 100 employees or fewer may purchase health insurance through state-based health benefit exchanges and small business health options programs (Kaiser Family Foundation, 2010c). These exchanges will be administered by a nonprofit organization or government agency. Opportunities to purchase health insurance plans are further expanded by the creation of a consumer-operated and oriented plan to develop nonprofit, member-run health insurance companies in each state. Current health insurance companies will be ineligible to create a consumer-operated and oriented plan (Kaiser Family Foundation, 2010c).

Medicaid will be expanded to non-Medicare eligible individuals under age 65 with incomes up to 133% of the federal poverty level (Kaiser Family Foundation, 2010a). It is estimated that half of the newly insured under ACA will receive their coverage from Medicaid and the Children's Health Insurance Program because ACA has essentially changed the eligibility requirements for the Medicaid program (Rosenbaum, 2010). To assist with the increased cost, states will receive 100% federal funding for the expansion of the Medicaid program beginning in 2014. By 2020, federal support will be reduced to 90% (Kaiser Family Foundation, 2010a), although significant financial support from the federal government will be provided for the Medicaid expansion, an increase estimated at $443.5 billion. State budgets will increase an estimated $21.1 billion between 2014 and 2019 (Kaiser Commission on Medicaid and the Uninsured, 2010). Many states that are already struggling to provide education, social services, and police protection during the economic recession will find it difficult to increase Medicaid spending. State legislatures will consider the trade-offs involved in decreasing the number of uninsured individuals with costs incurred for uncompensated care by hospitals and other providers and increased health insurance premiums if Medicaid is not expanded in their state.

Insurance companies will have to comply with a number of new regulations. Access to health insurance has been improved in the first year of implementation for two populations—adult children until age 26 and individuals with preexisting health conditions (Kaiser Family Foundation, 2010c). Health insurance companies must provide dependent coverage for adult children up to age 26 for individual and group policies. This will be of great benefit to recent college graduates having difficulty finding jobs during the recession. For individuals with a preexisting medical condition who have been uninsured for at least 6 months, a temporary national high-risk pool will be created to provide health insurance (Kaiser Family Foundation, 2010c).

Multiple funding sources were created to finance increased access to health insurance through ACA. In addition to employer and individual tax penalties, some of the provisions to pay for increased access include imposing an excise tax on insurers of employer-sponsored health plans with high costs, reducing the amount allowed for contributions to flexible medical spending accounts, increasing the threshold for itemized deductions for unreimbursed medical expenses, imposing a tax on nonprofit hospitals for failing to comply with new requirements, and annual fees on both pharmaceutical manufacturing and health insurance sectors (Kaiser Family Foundation, 2010c).

Modifications and adjustments to Medicare focus primarily on changes in reimbursement mechanisms. In an effort to slow the growth of Medicare spending and to reward the provision of quality care, payments to hospitals will be reduced for preventable hospital readmissions and for hospital-acquired conditions. Once a hospital value-based purchasing program is developed, hospitals will be paid based on performance on quality measures (Kaiser Family Foundation, 2010c). Value-based purchasing programs are also expected to be developed for ambulatory surgical centers, skilled nursing facilities, and home health agencies. An independent payment advisory board will be established to make annual recommendations for reducing the growth rate of Medicare spending (Kaiser Family Foundation, 2010c). These recommendations will be nonbinding, as Congress has final authority for appropriating funds for federal programs (Jost, 2010b).

Improving healthcare quality was an important focus of ACA by establishing a national quality improvement strategy and the nonprofit, independent Patient-Centered Outcomes Research Institute. The quality improvement strategy will identify processes to develop and use quality measures to improve healthcare delivery, patient health outcomes, and population health (Kaiser Family Foundation, 2010c). The Patient-Centered Outcomes Research Institute is expected to identify and conduct comparative clinical effectiveness research of medical treatments. Both of these provisions will incorporate input from stakeholders including that of patients.

Provisions specific to pharmacy practice and Medicare reimbursement policies for the Medicare Part D coverage gap include its gradual elimination by 2020, a phase-in of federal subsidies for generic prescriptions filled, and the requirement for pharmaceutical manufacturers to provide a 50% discount on brand name prescriptions provided (Kaiser Family Foundation, 2010c).

Politicians in at least 11 states were concerned about the constitutionality of ACA, specifically the individual mandate (Richey, 2010). Virginia's Attorney General filed a suit in federal court challenging the constitutionality of the ACA based upon a bill passed by its General Assembly stating that its residents were not required to obtain individual health insurance (Helderman, 2010). Thirty states proposed legislation that opposed various concepts of healthcare reform in 2009 and 2010. However, many of those bills were created to oppose single-payer or public options types of reform (Jost, 2010a). Arguments in support of constitutionality are based upon the notion that ACA is not a mandate, but it is a tax (Balkin, 2010). Furthermore, this tax is on a behavior. If an individual does not enroll in a health insurance plan, a tax penalty of an equitable amount to purchasing health insurance is imposed (New York Times, 2010). Arguments in support of unconstitutionality are based upon several aspects of the Constitution. The first considers the 10th Amendment which prohibits the federal government from forcing states to carry out federal programs such as the expansion of Medicaid described in ACA (New York Times, 2010). However, Medicaid is a voluntary program; states do not have to participate in the expanded program. The second argument questions whether Congress exceeded its authority to use an individual mandate in ACA. Lastly, supporters of unconstitutionality perceive that the ACA and its individual mandate expands federal powers and sets a precedent for further expansion of its powers into other aspects of Americans' lives (New York Times, 2010). The United States Supreme Court may determine whether the ACA is constitutional (Oberlander, 2011).

Although the full impact of the ACA will not be felt for more than a decade, all stakeholders will have reactions and input into its implementation and the healthcare delivery system will look like something other than it did in 2010.

HEALTHCARE REFORM EFFORTS BY THE STATES

Reforms at the state level have primarily consisted of adjustments to the financing of healthcare delivery. A number of states, however, have developed unique approaches intended to expand access to health care for their citizens. These approaches include uncompensated care pools subsidized by taxes on acute care services, employer mandates to provide health insurance for employees, and a federal waiver allowing states to expand access to the Medicaid program.

Uncompensated Care Pools

The American Hospital Association estimates that U.S. hospitals provide more than $16 billion of uncompensated care each year (Weissman, 1996). States have set up uncompensated care pools, also referred to as free care pools, to reimburse hospitals for a portion of these uncompensated services delivered to uninsured and underinsured individuals who meet some means test, usually based on level of income. Uncompensated care pools are primarily financed by placing a tax on the hospital bills of individuals who have health insurance, but they may also be supported by funds from general tax revenues. Hospitals apply to the pool for reimbursement for those patients who are unable to pay for their hospital care.

Unlike the expansion of Medicaid programs, uncompensated care pools do not increase access to healthcare services. These programs simply finance acute care received in a hospital setting. However, the existence of an uncompensated care pool creates an incentive for hospitals to offer care to the uninsured. In the current competitive market, without the availability of an uncompensated care pool, many public hospitals may close or reduce the care offered to indigent individuals (Weissman, 1996). An uncompensated care pool is only one aspect of financing health care for a state's citizens. It is most effective when used in conjunction with other state programs that increase access to primary care services.

Employer Mandates

In 1974, long before there was a national debate about universal access to health care, Hawaii passed the Prepaid Health Care Act, a type of legislation referred to as an employer mandate (Budde, Patrick, & Budde, 1995; Lewin & Sybinsky, 1993). The Prepaid Health Care Act requires all employers to provide a standard, state-established health insurance package for their employees who work 20 or more hours per week. The program requires both employers and employees to share in the cost of the health insurance package. The employers pay at least 50% of the cost of the insurance. Employees pay up to 1.5% of their monthly salaries toward the monthly health insurance premium (Lewin & Sybinsky, 1993).

The Prepaid Health Care Act mandates a minimum set of basic services: hospitalization, emergency treatment, surgical services, physician office visits, laboratory tests, radiology services, and maternity services (Lewin & Sybinsky, 1993). Within the state, the options for health insurance include fee-for-service and managed care plans.

Health insurance in Hawaii is less expensive than it is in the states on the mainland. Considering that the cost of living in Hawaii is significantly higher than in most of the United States, one might expect that the cost of health insurance would also be higher. There are two explanations for this phenomenon (Lewin & Sybinsky, 1993). First, because the employer mandate requires all employers to provide health insurance, there is less need to subsidize health care for uninsured individuals; this allows health insurance companies to use community rating rather than experience rating, which is frequently used when insuring small businesses. Thus small businesses and large employers are offered similar rates. Second, because Hawaii has experienced a lower rate of hospitalization and a subsequent higher rate of outpatient physician visits than the rest of the country, health insurance premiums can be reduced.

Health outcomes for Hawaiian citizens have been better than those for the rest of the U.S. population with respect to extended longevity, low infant mortality, and low premature morbidity and mortality for cancer, cardiovascular disease, and pulmonary disease (Lewin & Sybinsky, 1993). One might think that the environment—the sunshine—and perhaps a healthy lifestyle cause these outcomes. In reality, these factors do not appear to significantly affect health outcomes in Hawaii. Although Hawaiians exhibit health risk behaviors common to all Americans, their commitment to outpatient care and prevention—instead of hospitalization—has improved health outcomes and decreased costs. Hawaiians visit their physicians twice as often and are hospitalized half as often as the national average (Lewin & Sybinsky, 1993). With less costly outpatient care and the use of preventive measures, expensive hospitalizations are used less frequently; this allows health insurance to remain at a lower rate than in other states.

From Hawaii's experience, it appears that an employer mandate could eliminate the largest percentage of uninsured individuals in the United States. However, since Hawaii's Prepaid Health Care Act was passed in 1974, several other states have passed employer mandate legislation. These states have been unable to implement their laws because of the Employee Retirement Income Security Act (ERISA), which restricts the types of mandates that states can impose on the benefits that employers offer their employees. Because Hawaii's Prepaid Health Care Act was enacted before ERISA was passed in 1974, it was not initially affected by ERISA. Yet, since ERISA has been enacted, no amendments have been made to Hawaii's Prepaid Health Care Act. Changes that might improve Hawaii's program, such as requiring coverage of dependents or adjusting the employer and employee contributions to the health insurance premiums, cannot be implemented because they would violate ERISA.

The intent of ERISA is to protect employees' retirement plans. Under ERISA, the federal government is solely responsible for regulating employee benefit plans, with its authority superseding any state laws (Gostin & Widiss, 1993). ERISA does not apply to the regulation of insurance. However, one half to two thirds of employers provide healthcare benefits for their employees with self-insurance. Self-insurance, also referred to as self-funded arrangements, involves setting aside money specifically to pay for employees' medical expenses rather than purchasing an insurance policy to protect them against financial loss. Employers that use self-insurance for their employees' health benefits are exempt from state employer mandates under ERISA.

Employer Versus Employee Mandates

Frequently, discussion about federal healthcare reform turns into a debate over employer versus employee mandates. Employer mandates place the burden for financing on the employer. Employee mandates place the burden on the employee.

Economists argue that benefits are a component of reimbursement. Direct payments and benefits are both considered employee compensation. For example, the Medicare contribution for employees and employers is set at 1.45% each. If the employer did not have to pay this Medicare tax, he or she could afford to provide a higher wage to the employee. Either way, the employee pays the tax—whether directly through taxes or indirectly through lower compensation.

Thus the distinction between employer and employee mandates matters in the sense of the wage a worker receives, although total compensation remains constant. When the employee is forced to participate through payroll deduction, he or she is more likely to realize the true cost of the mandate. However, employer mandates shield the employee from the true cost. This price sensitivity is at the core of theory behind cost sharing. For this reason, increasing patient cost sharing is always a component of healthcare reform.

Medicaid and State Requests for Waiver

Medicaid program costs have increased annually since the program went into effect in 1966. They are now the fastest-growing state expenditures, often limiting the ability of states to support higher education and other social programs. The increasing proportion of state budgets—as much as 20%—devoted to Medicaid has prompted states to look at methods to limit the growth of this spending (Holahan, Coughlin, Ku, Lipson, & Rajan, 1995). The federal government allows states to enroll Medicaid patients into managed care plans and to experiment with other cost-containment programs through a Medicaid waiver procedure. (See Chapter 18 for a discussion of the Medicaid waiver procedure.) Examples from two states, Oregon and Tennessee, that received Medicaid waivers and used managed care to expand access to Medicaid are presented next.

Oregon Health Plan

One of three pieces of legislation for Oregon's Basic Health Services Act of 1989 expanded Medicaid to 120,000 uninsured low-income persons. Instead of determining who will be covered, the Oregon Health Plan (OHP) assumed that everyone will receive coverage and addressed what will be covered based on values assessed in town meetings, ratings for health states, subjective judgments about treatment effectiveness, and reprioritization based on commissioner judgment (Kaplan, 1994). Using this information, a prioritized list of diagnoses and treatments was created. Once the budget was determined, a line was drawn on that list of diagnoses; the diagnoses above the line were funded, and those below the line were not covered (Bussman, 1993). To obtain its Medicaid waiver from the Centers for Medicare and Medicaid Services (CMS) the Oregon Health Services Commission had to revise this plan by eliminating the quality-of-life component and resubmitting its waiver application to CMS. The revised proposal is considered to be more subjective than the original proposal and to lack its most scientifically justifiable and reproducible portion (Kaplan, 1994). A key component of the OHP, in addition to its ranking protocol for funding care for only a specific number of conditions from the prioritized list of disease processes, is its use of managed care as a delivery and financing system to control costs. The success of the OHP, in terms of its ability to enroll more individuals, was linked to the availability of numerous MCOs throughout Oregon. At the time of the plan's implementation, one third of the Oregon population was already in HMOs, and 31% of Medicaid recipients were already in capitated health plans (Gold, Chu, & Lyons, 1995).

Although there was considerable debate about the explicit rationing program proposed in the OHP, the plan has functioned more as a mechanism for defining the benefits package rather than as a rationing instrument. The OHP has been funded through an increase in state funding and a cigarette tax—frequently referred to as a sin tax—and by moving recipients into managed care plans rather than by rationing care from the list of approved services. These changes in funding were manageable because of Oregon's growing economy in the 1990s and because Medicaid expenditures were already relatively low before the program started. When the OHP began, Oregon ranked 46th in Medicaid spending as a proportion of the state budget (Jacobs, Marmor, & Oberlander, 1999).

The OHP was successful in extending health care to an additional 130,000 low-income individuals. The percentage of uninsured Oregonians fell from 17% to 11% in 1996, and the percentage of children without health insurance fell from 21% to 8%, each less than the national averages of 15% (Jacobs et al., 1999).

Although the OHP was considered a success at improving access to health care in its first 10 years of existence, its record has been marred by two recessions and Oregon's high unemployment rate, which combined, produced budget deficits. Increases to premiums and co-payments, reductions to provider reimbursements, and limits on provided services were instituted to the approximately 100,000 people who qualify for the expansion portion of the OHP (Colburn, 2003a). Given continued reductions in state income tax receipts, the Oregon legislature instituted cuts to enrollment (Steves, 2003). Changes to the OHP resulted in hospitals incurring large budget deficits due to reductions in reimbursements (Rojas-Burke, 2003), hospitals filing a lawsuit to block payment reductions (Colburn, 2003b), and pharmacies losing revenue because they could not require patients to pay co-payments before filling prescriptions (Colburn, 2003c); and the percentage of uninsured Oregonians has risen to 20% (644,300 individuals) (Kaiser Family Foundation, 2011).

TennCare

In 1993, Tennessee, motivated by problems similar to those in Oregon (an increasing portion of the state budget allocated to Medicaid and an increasing proportion of the population being uninsured), expanded its Medicaid program to include previously uninsurable and uninsured individuals through a program called TennCare. The foundation of the TennCare program was the enrollment of recipients in managed care plans.

Like other states that were expanding access to their Medicaid programs, Tennessee based its program on using managed care as the key component to improve access and contain costs. However, because only 2 of the state's 9 established HMOs and 20 preferred provider organizations (PPOs) chose to participate, 10 new managed care organizations were then created specifically for TennCare participants (Mirvis, Chang, Hall, Zaar, & Applegate, 1995).

Cost sharing was a key element of the TennCare program. It required premiums, co-payments, and deductibles using a sliding scale based on income (Mirvis et al., 1995). Cost sharing was not required for individuals who qualified for Medicaid; it was required only for individuals who were enrolled in the expanded portion of the Medicaid program. Throughout its history, TennCare has experienced numerous problems. The inception, development, and implementation of the TennCare plan were extraordinarily fast paced. The new managed care organizations created specifically to serve the program recipients had little time to organize their delivery systems (Weil, 2007). Potential TennCare participants did not know which providers were associated with which managed care organization or even which managed care organizations were participants in TennCare (Mirvis et al., 1995).

Initially, TennCare expanded both the number of recipients eligible for healthcare services and the quantity of services recipients could obtain (Mirvis et al., 1995). Yet, it has also periodically closed enrollment to new enrollees in the uninsured and uninsurable categories. Since the program's implementation, more than 200,000 people have lost their healthcare coverage through TennCare—the largest reduction in U.S. history (Hurley, 2006). Benefits were altered to match those offered by private health insurance, and the program imposed limitations on the number of prescriptions or refills per month for adults (Weil, 2007).

TennCare's lack of long-term success can be attributed to both the imposition of a managed care model in a state with limited experience in this delivery system and state budget deficits.

Other State Initiatives to Increase Access to Health Insurance

Legislation to provide universal access had not been attempted since the late 1980s, but two states—Massachusetts and Vermont—passed sweeping legislation intended to increase access to health insurance in 2006. Both accomplished this feat with bipartisan support from Republican governors and Democrat-controlled legislatures. The primary focus of these reforms is a requirement that individuals purchase health insurance policies. Both states also require employers to pay an assessment to help finance the programs. Massachusetts passed an individual health insurance mandate in April 2006, requiring all residents 18 years and older to purchase a minimum level of health insurance by July 1, 2007 (Steinbrook, 2006). Failure to comply with the law will result in a fine of 50% of the cost of an affordable insurance premium. Although this program is not an employer mandate, it does have an employer financing component, requiring businesses with 11 or more full-time employees that do not provide or contribute to health insurance to pay a fee of $295 per employee per year. The state subsidizes premium payments for families who earn less than 300% of the federal poverty level. The law also expanded Medicaid to include the children of families who earn up to 300% of the federal poverty level (Steinbrook, 2006).

Since implementation began in 2006, it is estimated that 430,000 previously uninsured people have insurance coverage, representing two-thirds of the estimated 650,000 who were previously uninsured in Massachusetts. By November 2008, the Massachusetts Division of Health Care and Policy estimated that 2.6% of Massachusetts residents remained uninsured, the lowest rate in the country (Kaiser Commission on Medicaid and the Uninsured, 2009a). Other key features of the Massachusetts program include the creation of the Commonwealth Health Insurance Connector to administer the insurance components of the laws. This organization serves as a clearinghouse to link individuals and businesses with fewer than 50 employees with insurance products. Health insurance is portable for individuals who purchase health insurance through the Commonwealth Connector (Steinbrook, 2006). By December 2008, 57% of the newly insured were enrolled in public coverage, and the remaining 43% were enrolled in private coverage through the Commonwealth Connector (Kaiser Commission on Medicaid and the Uninsured, 2009a).

As part of the state's cost containment efforts, the legislature created a Special Commission on the Health Care Payment System. In July 2009, the Commission recommended that the state shift from a fee-for-service system in which healthcare providers are paid per encounter to a system where providers work together to share responsibility for the patient's care. These accountable care organizations receive a global payment for all services patients receive (Kaiser Commission on Medicaid and the Uninsured, 2009a).

Three years after enacting comprehensive healthcare reform, Massachusetts has been successful in expanding coverage to the uninsured through a public-private approach. Nearly half of the newly insured have enrolled in private coverage through their employer or purchased an individual plan. As a result of the employer role in health reform, Massachusetts did not experience a decline in employer-based coverage. The state's experience demonstrates the viability of an individual mandate (required insurance coverage), when combined with affordable health coverage options, as a method to reduce the number of uninsured. The Massachusetts initiatives of mandated insurance coverage and payment system options (accountable care organizations) were the basis of many recommendations for federal healthcare reform (Robert Wood Johnson Foundation, 2009).

In May 2006, Vermont passed the 2006 Health Care Affordability Act, which created Catamount Health. It is available to anyone who has been uninsured for the previous 12 months effective October 1, 2007 (Vermont, State of 2006). Premiums were subsidized based on income for persons with incomes at or below 300% of the federal poverty level, both for those who enroll in Catamount Health and for those employed with comparable employer-sponsored health insurance (Vermont, State of, 2006). Employers were assessed a fee—$365 per year per full-time equivalent—for each uninsured employee. Exemptions for 8 employees were allowed in 2007 and 2008, for 6 employees for 2009, and for 4 employees in 2010 and thereafter (Vermont State Legislature, 2006).

Vermont's Health Care Affordability Act also created a chronic disease management plan called Blueprint for Health, which incorporates early disease screening, promotes patient self-management tools, and financially rewards healthcare providers for using proactive chronic care management tools (Vermont, State of, 2006).

Since 2006, several bills have been enacted to further the implementation of the 2006 Health Care Affordability Act (Vermont State Agency of Administration, 2008). In April 2010, the Vermont legislature passed a bill directing the State Health Care Reform Commission to prepare three financing options and implementation plans for three new healthcare financing systems (Cheney, 2010). The bill would require the three options to include a single-payer option, a public option, and an option based upon that created by the ACA (Cheney, 2010).

The Pharmacy Profession and Information Technology

Prior to the historic health reform act of 2010, the following two laws were enacted in 2009: the Children's Health Insurance Program Reauthorization Act and the American Recovery and Reinvestment Act. The Children's Health Insurance Program Reauthorization Act is expected to provide access for 4 million children by 2013, while the American Recovery and Reinvestment Act provided an unprecedented level of healthcare spending on health information technology, comparative effectiveness research, and wellness and prevention activities (Reynolds, 2009).

The American Recovery and Reinvestment Act contained $1.1 billion in funding for comparative effectiveness research (Steinbrook, 2009), an amount nearly 37 times the annual federal spending on comparative effectiveness research (Schumock, 2009). The Congressional Budget Office defined comparative effectiveness research as "a rigorous evaluation of the impact of different options that are available for treating a given medical condition for a particular set of patients" (Bertagna, 2009). Its goal is to provide patients, healthcare professionals, and payers with evidence to support treatment decisions.

Combining investments in health information technology for implementing electronic health records in more hospitals and physician offices, comparative effectiveness research has the potential to provide clinical decision support tools for clinicians. Comparative effectiveness research will impact policy decisions for formularies and provide opportunities to implement evidence-based decisions in pharmacy practice.

The $1 billion spending provision from the American Recovery and Reinvestment Act in wellness and prevention may also impact pharmacist services and represents the largest allocation of funding to prevention activities in American history (Steinbrook, 2009). With substantial new spending on clinical and community-based prevention activities toward chronic disease, immunizations for low-income communities, and initiatives to reduce healthcare–associated infections, pharmacists are well positioned to play a more active role in coordinated care activities.

The Pharmacy Profession and the Patient Protection and Affordable Care Act

Several provisions included in the Patient Protection and Affordable Care Act (ACA) were designed to promote coordination among healthcare providers and will improve the quality of pharmacy practice. The Patient-Centered Outcomes Research Institute provides pharmacists with opportunities to apply for grants for medication therapy management (MTM) services to chronically ill patients. Under the newly created Innovation Center within the Centers for Medicare and Medicaid Services, pharmacists may participate in pilot projects to examine and evaluate payment mechanisms to reduce expenditures and quality improvement protocols to enhance healthcare quality (Kaiser Family Foundation, 2010c). Working with community health teams to provide transition care, pharmacists may work with other members of the healthcare team to provide medication reconciliation and discharge planning with MTM services.

Expanding payment for pharmacist-provided MTM services has been a key objective of pharmacy organizations' lobbying efforts for many years prior to ACA enactment. The MTM grant program through the newly created Patient-Centered Outcomes Research Institute will provide grants to pharmacists employed by organizations that are involved with collaborative, multidisciplinary care of chronically ill patients.

In anticipation of this provision, pharmacists in many states advocated for collaborative drug therapy management legislation to be applicable in any practice setting in their state. The combination of protocol-driven therapy through collaborative drug therapy management authority and MTM provides a new paradigm of pharmacy practice. Hospitals, through their MTM subsidiary, could provide pharmacist-driven MTM services to a local public health agency or a health insurance company, or to patients discharged home after an acute-care episode. Initially, MTM services would be reimbursed as part of the grant, with the opportunity for the development of new payment mechanisms from health insurance companies or public health agencies.

The statutory definition of pharmacist-driven MTM services is ground breaking, because prior to the enactment of the ACA, MTM services were loosely defined and no specifications for pharmacist oversight were delineated. Identification of the true value of pharmaceutical care services may be identified because MTM programs will be required to evaluate their clinical effectiveness. Although Congress acknowledged the potential benefit of MTM services by incorporating them into the law, an annual funding authorization was not defined. Therefore, funding of the program will be determined by future appropriations bills.

Additional MTM opportunities are available through the ACA requirement of an annual pharmacist review of medications for patients receiving Medicare Part D. While Medicare beneficiaries are allowed to opt out of the service, the annual review would provide a foundation for follow-up services for covered patients. Pharmacists may also provide MTM services in demonstration projects that include medical home models, a Medicaid health home, and a community transition program for high-risk Medicare patients who are discharged from the hospital, all components of ACA.

The 2009 American Recovery and Reinvestment Act and 2010 ACA provide vast opportunities for pharmacists to incorporate comprehensive pharmaceutical care services into the healthcare delivery system, work collaboratively with other healthcare providers, and demonstrate improved patient outcomes.

THE PHARMACY PROFESSION AND HEALTHCARE REFORM: A CALL FOR ACTION

The pharmacy profession is in a unique position to influence healthcare reform efforts. Pharmacists have more contact with the general public than do other healthcare professionals. Community pharmacists have ample opportunities to interact with patients who receive a prescription or who are visiting the pharmacy to pick up an over-the-counter drug product or other products stocked on pharmacy shelves. Whether dispensing a prescription to a patient or helping a customer in the store, pharmacists have direct and frequent contact with the public.

Although insurance coverage for prescription drugs has broadened in recent years, it still lags behind coverage for other components of medical care. Consumers are less sheltered from the burden of paying for prescription medications than from the burden of paying for other medical care services because of the higher utilization of prescription services coupled with the higher percentages of cost sharing they are forced to bear. Pharmacists are in the position to understand the patient's perspective, and they also have the opportunity to manage reimbursement from the third-party payer's perspective.

Pharmaceutical care offers members of the pharmacy profession an opportunity to move from providing a product to providing true service and securing a more important role in the changing healthcare marketplace. A pharmacist who becomes a disease state manager, for example, will be better able to influence public policy and healthcare system change. Pharmacists should get involved in their professional associations, in community groups, and in insurance plans. They should understand the perspectives of different players so that they can address the concerns of others as well as promote their own perspective.

Healthcare system reform should not frighten pharmacists. It should provide a challenge and an opportunity to carve out a niche in tomorrow's healthcare system.

CONCLUSION

Reform of the healthcare delivery system has been accomplished in many ways, such as requiring a certificate of need prior to building a new hospital, creating the Medicare and Medicaid programs, requiring Medicaid patients to receive their care in a managed care setting, and requiring that all citizens obtain health insurance either through their employer or purchased themselves. All balance access with financing and cost containment and effectiveness of care. At the core of healthcare reform is people's willingness to pay for changes to the healthcare system.

Healthcare reform is far from being completed. Provisions and requirements delineated in the Patient and Affordable Care Act require many years for implementation. Stakeholders will continue to voice their opinions and concerns to impact these processes.

QUESTIONS FOR FURTHER DISCUSSION

1. Which healthcare reform solutions are most viable?
2. What should be done to save Medicare?
3. Should the United States move toward a basic health benefit for all?
4. Should the Oregon Health Plan pay for treatment of diseases that consistently get better with self-treatment (such as colds)?
5. What are the intended and unintended consequences of the individual and employer requirements under the Patient Protection and Affordable Care Act?

KEY TOPICS AND TERMS

American Recovery and Reinvestment Act
Children's Health Insurance Program
Comparative effectiveness research
Cost containment
Diagnosis-related groups
Employee mandate
Employee Retirement Income Security Act
Employer mandate
Health Insurance Portability and Accountability Act
Health savings account
Kerr-Mills Act
Managed care
Medicaid
Medicaid waiver
Medicare
Medication therapy management services
Oregon Health Plan
Patient Protection and Affordable Care Act
Sin tax
Social Security
TennCare
Trust fund
Uncompensated care pool

REFERENCES

American College of Physicians. (1996). Position paper: Medical savings accounts. *Annals of Internal Medicine, 125,* 333–340.

Anderson, G. F., & Poullier, J. P. (1999). Health spending, access, and outcomes: Trends in industrialized countries. *Health Affairs, 18,* 178–192.

Balkin, J. J. (2010). The constitutionality of the individual mandate for health insurance. *New England Journal of Medicine, 362,* 482–483.

Bertagna, L. M., & Dreyer, N. (2009). *Comparative effectiveness research: Coming soon?* Retrieved from http://pharmexec.findpharma.com/pharmexec/Regulatory/Comparative-Effectiveness-Research-Coming-Soon/ArticleStandard/Article/detail/589172?ref=25

Blue Boulding, K. E. (1996, October). The concept of need for health services. *Milbank Memorial Fund Quarterly, 44,* 202–223.

Brown, E. R., & Wyn, R. (1996). Public policies to extend health care coverage. In R. J. Anderson, T. H. Rice, & G. F. Kominski (Eds.), *Changing the U.S. health care system: Key issues in health services, policy, and management* (pp. 41–61). San Francisco, CA: Jossey-Bass.

Budde, J. C., Patrick, W. K., & Budde, M. T. (1995). Hawaii HealthQUEST: A managed care demonstration project. *Hawaii Medical Journal, 54,* 720–722.

Bussman, J. W. (1993). The Oregon Health Plan: A rational approach to care for the underserved. *Journal of Health Care for the Poor and Underserved, 4,* 203–209.

Cantor, J. C., Long, S. H., & Marquis, M. S. (1995). Private employment-based health insurance in ten states. *Health Affairs, 14,* 199–234.

Cheny, T. (2010, April 23). Vermont house passes comprehensive health care reform bill. *Vtdigger.* Retrieved from http://vtdigger.org/2010/04/23/vermont-house-passes-comprehensive-health-care-reform-bill/

Colburn, D. (2003a, April 30). 10,000 low-income Oregonians will be cut from state health plan. *The Oregonian,* pp. B1, B4.

Colburn, D. (2003b, March 18). Oregon hospitals sue state over cutting low-income health plan payments. *The Oregonian,* p. B7.

Colburn, D. (2003c, January 8). Oregon pharmacies plan co-pay suits. *The Oregonian,* p. B2.

Donelan, K., Blendon, R. J., Schoen, C., Davis, K., & Binns, K. (1999). The cost of health system change: Public discontent in five nations. *Health Affairs, 18,* 206–216.

Epstein, A. Z. M., Bogen, J., Dreyer, P., & Thorpe, K. E. (1991). Trends in lengths of stay and rates of readmission in Massachusetts: Implications for monitoring quality of care. *Inquiry, 28,* 19–28.

Folland, S., Goodman, A. C., & Stano, M. (1997). *The economics of health and health care* (2nd ed.). Englewood Cliffs, NJ: Prentice-Hall.

Fuchs, V. R. (1992). The best health care system in the world? *Journal of the American Medical Association, 268,* 916–917.

Gardner, J. (1995). Medical savings accounts make waves. *Modern Healthcare, 25*(9), 57.

Gold, M., Chu, K., & Lyons, B. (1995). *Managed care and low-income populations: A case study of managed care in Oregon.* Washington, DC: Mathematica Policy Research, Inc.

Goodman, J. C., & Pauly, M. V. (1995). Tax credits for health insurance and medical savings accounts. *Health Affairs, 14,* 126–139.

Gostin, L. O., & Widiss, A. I. (1993). What's wrong with the ERISA vacuum? *Journal of the American Medical Association, 269,* 2527–2532.

Helderman, R. S. (2010, May 25). Obama administration asks judge to dismiss Virginia suit against health-care law. *The Washington Post.* Retrieved from http://www.washingtonpost.com/wp-dyn/content/article/2010/05/24/AR20105240473.html

Holahan, J., Coughlin, T., Ku, L., Lipson, D. J., & Rajan, S. (1995). Insuring the poor through Section 1115 waivers. *Health Affairs, 14*(1), 199–216.

Hsiao, W. C. (1995). Medical savings accounts: Lessons from Singapore. *Health Affairs, 14,* 260–266.

Hurley, R. E. (2006, April 25). TennCare—a failure of politics, not policy: A conversation with Gordon Bonnyman. *Health Affairs, 25*(3), w217–w225.

Iglehart, J. K. (1982). The future of HMOs. *New England Journal of Medicine, 307,* 451–456.

Jacobs, L., Marmor, T., & Oberlander, J. (1999). The Oregon health plan and the political paradox of rationing: What advocates and critics have claimed and what Oregon did. *Journal of Health Politics, Policy and Law, 24*(1), 161–180.

Jeffers, J. R., Bognanno, M. E., & Bartlett, J. C. (1971). On the demand versus need for medical services and the concept of "shortage." *American Journal of Public Health, 61,* 46–63.

Jost, T. S. (2010a). Can the states nullify health care reform? *New England Journal of Medicine, 362,* 869–871.

Jost, T. S. (2010b). The independent payment advisory board. *New England Journal of Medicine, 363,* 103–105.

Kaiser Commission on Medicaid and the Uninsured. (2009a). *Massachusetts health care reform: Three years later.* Publication No. 7777-02. Retrieved from http://www.kff.org/uninsured/7777.cfm

Kaiser Commission on Medicaid and the Uninsured. (2009b, October). *The uninsured: A primer, key facts about Americans without health insurance.* Report No. 7451-05. Retrieved from http://www.kff.org/uninsured/7451.cfm

Kaiser Commission on Medicaid and the Uninsured. (2010). *Medicaid coverage and spending in health reform: National and state-by-state results for adults at or below 133% fpl. May.* Publication No. 8076-ES. Retrieved from http://www.kff.org/healthreform/8076.cfm

Kaiser Family Foundation. (2010a, May). *Financing new Medicaid coverage under health reform: The role of the federal government and states.* Publication No. 8072. Retrieved from http://www.kff.org/healthreform/8072.cfm

Kaiser Family Foundation. (2010b). *Focus on health care reform: Health care reform implementation timeline.* Publication No. 8060. Retrieved from http://www.kff.org/healthreform/8060.cfm

Kaiser Family Foundation. (2010c). *Focus on health care reform: Summary of new health reform law.* Publication No. 8061. Retrieved from http://www.kff.org/healthreform/upload/8061.pdf

Kaiser Family Foundation (2011). *Oregon: Nonelderly uninsured.* Retrieved from http://www.statehealthfacts.org/profileind.jsp?cat=3&sub=40&rgn=39

Kaplan, R. M. (1994). Value judgment in the Oregon Medicaid experiment. *Medical Care, 32,* 975–988.

Lewin, J. C., & Sybinsky, P. A. (1993). Hawaii's employer mandate and its contribution to universal access. *Journal of the American Medical Association, 269,* 2538–2543.

Medicare Trustees. (2009, May). *2009 annual report of the boards of trustees of the federal hospital insurance and federal supplementary medical insurance trust funds.* Washington, DC: U.S. Government Printing Office.

Minicozzi, A. (2006). Medical savings accounts: What do the data tell? *Health Affairs, 25,* 256–267.

Mirvis, D. M., Chang, C. F., Hall, C. J., Zaar, G. T., & Applegate, W. B. (1995). TennCare—Health system reform for Tennessee. *Journal of the American Medical Association, 274,* 1235–1241.

New York Times editors. (2010, March 28). Is the health care law unconstitutional? *New York Times.* Retrieved from http://roomfordebate.blogs.nytimes.com/2010/03/28/is-the-health-care-law-unconstitutional

Oberlander, J. (2011). Under siege—The individual mandate for health insurance and its alternatives. *New England Journal of Medicine.* Retrieved from http://www.nejm.org/doi/pdf/10.1056/NEJMp1101240

OECD health data 2009: A comparative analysis of 30 countries. (2010). Paris, France: Organisation for Economic Cooperation and Development. Retrieved from https://stats.oecd.org/index.aspx

O'Sullivan, J. (1996). *Medicare: Financing the Part A Hospital Insurance program* (95–650 EPW). Washington, DC: CRS Report for Congress, Congressional Research Service, Library of Congress.

Peterson, W. C. (1996). Those Social Security trust funds. *Omaha World Herald,* p. 15B.

Remler, D. K., & Giled, S. A. (2006). How much more cost sharing will health savings accounts bring? *Health Affairs, 25*(4), 1070–1078.

Reynolds, S. (2009). *Obama's crusade to make U.S. healthcare work efficiently and effectively.* Retrieved from http://about.datamonitor.com/media/archives/1893

Richey, W. (2010, March 22). Attorneys general in 11 states poised to challenge healthcare bill. *Christian Science Monitor.* Retrieved from http://www.csmonitor.com/layout/set/print/content/view/print/289261

Robert Wood Johnson Foundation State Health Access Reform Evaluation. (2009). *The secrets of Massachusetts' success: Why 97 percent of state residents have health coverage.* Retrieved from http://www.shadac.org/files/shadac/publications/SecretsOfMassSuccessLongPaper.pdf

Robinson, J. C. (2005). Health savings accounts—the ownership society in health care. *New England Journal of Medicine, 353*(12), 1199–1201.

Rojas-Burke, J. (2003, January 28). Spending cuts, recession puts state's hospitals under pressure. *The Oregonian,* pp. C1, C3.

Rosenbaum, S. (2010). A "customary and necessary" program—Medicaid and health care reform. *New England Journal of Medicine, 362*(21), 1952–1955.

Schumock, G. T., & Pickard, A. S. (2009). Comparative effectiveness research: Relevance and application to pharmacy. *American Journal of Health-Systems Pharmacists, 66,* e2–e10.

Smith, M. D., Altman, D. E., Leitman, R., Moloney, T. W., & Taylor, H. (1992). Taking the public's pulse on health system reform. *Health Affairs, 11,* 125–133.

Social Security Trustees. (2010, August). *2010 annual report of the board of trustees of the federal old-age and survivors insurance and federal disability insurance trust funds.* Washington, DC: U.S. Government Printing Office. Retrieved from http://www.ssa.gov/OACT/TR/2010/tr10.pdf

Starr, P. (1982). *The social transformation of American medicine.* New York, NY: Basic Books.

Steinbrook, R. (2006). Health care reform in Massachusetts: A work in progress. *New England Journal of Medicine, 354*(20), 2095–2098.

Steinbrook, R. (2009). Health care and the American Recovery and Reinvestment Act. *New England Journal of Medicine, 360*(11), 1057–1060.

Steves, D. (2003, July 11). New figures may force cuts in Oregon health plan. *The Register Guard,* pp. A1, A9.

Vermont, State of. (2006). *A summary of the 2006 Health Care Affordability Act.* Retrieved from http://www.csgeast.org/Annual_Meeting/2006/healthchen2.pdf

Vermont, State of Agency of Administration. (2008, October). *Overview of Vermont's health care reform.* Retrieved from http://hcr.vermont.gov/sites/hcr/files/Revised_Vermont_HCR_Overview_October_08__0.pdf

Vermont State Legislature. (2006). *2006 health care reform initiatives, quick overview. State of Vermont.* Retrieved from http://www.leg.state.vt.us/HealthCare/2006_HC_Affordability_Act_Leddy_Summary.htm

Weil, A. (2007). Next steps for Tennessee: A conversation with governor Phil Bredesen. *Health Affairs, 26*(4):w456–w462.

Weissman, J. (1996). Uncompensated hospital care: Will it be there if we need it? *Journal of the American Medical Association, 276,* 823–828.

Glossary

Academic detailing: a tool used by managed care organizations in which a health plan representative (or the contracting pharmacy benefit manager) visits targeted physicians to provide information regarding the most cost-effective use of selected drugs and to encourage physicians to prescribe in ways that will reduce overall costs while maintaining program quality. The targeted physicians are usually identified by the practice profiling program as ones with higher than average costs or unusual prescribing patterns.

Accreditation: the formal review process that institutions, such as schools and colleges of pharmacy and hospitals, periodically undergo to ensure that they are meeting predetermined quality and standards.

Accrediting agency: independent organization that develops standards for entities such as hospitals, home care providers, and colleges and universities, among others. Accrediting organizations are not federal or state agencies.

Activities of daily living (ADLs): activities that are performed during the course of a normal day, such as bathing, toileting, dressing, and eating.

Activity–passivity model of care: as described by Szasz and Hollender, practitioner–patient communication in which the patient is passive. This interaction can be compared to a parent–infant relationship.

Actual acquisition cost (AAC): the price that pharmacies pay for drug products after subtracting all discounts.

Actuary: an insurance company employee who conducts a statistical analysis of an insured population to estimate the income (premiums) that must be earned to cover the estimated expenses, usually expressed as cost per member per month.

Adjudication: the process of reviewing or screening claims to determine payment.

Administration on Aging: a DHHS agency that works to provide services that enable elders to live independently—especially those who are disadvantaged.

Administrative agencies: units of executive branch that promulgate and enforce regulations needed to implement laws.

Adulterated: made impure by adding extraneous, improper, or inferior ingredients.

Adverse drug reaction: an undesirable or harmful reaction to a drug that occurs at doses normally used for the treatment, prevention, or diagnosis of a disease.

Adverse selection: a situation in which individuals or companies purchase insurance only when they expect a loss.

Agency for Healthcare Research and Quality (AHRQ): a DHHS agency that supports research regarding the organization, financing, delivery, quality assessment, and improvement of the health delivery in the United States.

Aging-in-Place: a concept where older adults do not have to move from their present residence in order to secure necessary support services in response to changing needs.

Alternative health therapy: nontraditional sources of health care, such as use of herbal and nutritional supplements, acupuncture, support groups, meditation, and massage therapy, among others.

Ambulatory care: healthcare services provided to a patient who is not an inpatient in a healthcare institution (e.g., a nursing home or hospital) and can walk or move about to obtain these services.

Ambulatory patient group (APG): a type of prospective payment for outpatient services that is based on diagnosis.

American Hospital Association: a national organization composed of hospitals, healthcare organizations, and individual members. It provides education to the public and its members and advocates for and represents its membership in legislative and regulatory issues.

American Recovery and Reinvestment Act (ARRA): also known as the "Stimulus Act of 2009," it was enacted by Congress with the intention to create jobs and to promote investment and consumer spending during the recession.

Analysis of extremes: a sensitivity analysis method conducted by reassigning values of both cost and effectiveness variables concurrently to their highest and lowest extremes in order to determine the robustness of the conclusions in the best and worst case situations.

Asepsis: a practice introduced in the late 19th century that consists of washing hands and using sterilized instruments for surgery in an effort to stop the spread of infectious diseases.

Assignment: the payment of a healthcare service directly to the provider rather than the beneficiary; usually requires a participating provider agreement between the health plan and the provider.

Average manufacturer's price (AMP): a proposed method for estimating pharmacy acquisition costs that is based on actual costs charged by manufacturers rather than the wholesale list price.

Average wholesale price (AWP): the list price established by the manufacturer. AWP is higher than the actual acquisition cost (AAC) that pharmacies pay for drug products and is discounted by the payer to arrive at the estimated acquisition cost (EAC).

Balanced Budget Act: law enacted in 1997 that required the implementation of a prospective payment system (PPS) for home health services, reductions in reimbursement rates for home medical equipment, and implementation of competitive bidding processes. Under a PPS, a home health agency is paid a flat rate to care for a Medicare recipient.

Benefit-to-cost ratio: a method of representing outcomes in a cost-benefit analysis whereby total benefits are divided by total costs.

Beveridge model: socialized medicine program developed in United Kingdom. Named after the British social reformer who inspired United Kingdom's National Health Service.

Biologic: a very complex drug that is designed to mimic a human protein or is a monoclonal antibody.

Biopsychosocial model of care: a model of care in which the social, emotional, and psychological aspects of the patient are taken into account, as is the patient's physical status, in understanding his or her health or illness.

Biosimilar: a copy of a biologic drug.

Bismarck model: decentralized national health program developed in Germany. Named after the German Chancellor who instituted this social health insurance system.

Blue Cross and Blue Shield: originally a nonprofit health insurance established in 1929 offering comprehensive plans. Most Blue Cross and Blue Shield plans switched to for-profit status in the 1990s.

Brand-name drug: the original product first developed, marketed, and made available by a pharmaceutical company; contrast this with a *generic drug product.*

Break-even point: the point found in a threshold sensitivity analysis where two alternative treatment options have the same outcome and there is no advantage between the treatment options. The break-even point is determined by varying a single assumption in the threshold sensitivity analysis until the outcomes are the same for both options.

Bricks and mortar: the situation in which an establishment's (usually a business establishment's) operations are conducted in a physical space, as opposed to online. Many establishments have both online and bricks-and-mortar presences.

Budget impact analysis: an estimation of the financial impact of adoption and diffusion of a new healthcare intervention within a specific healthcare setting. For example, budget impact analyses can predict how a change in the formulary mix of drugs used to treat a disease state will affect healthcare spending for that disease state, and therefore, can be used for budget planning.

Capitation: a type of prospective payment in which providers are paid a fixed amount each month for each enrolled patient, regardless of the number of healthcare services actually provided.

Catastrophic hazard: a situation in which an insurance company incurs excessive losses due to widespread and catastrophic events such as hurricanes, acts of war, and earthquakes. Companies that provide casualty insurance limit their exposure for catastrophic events by trying to avoid insuring large numbers of policy holders in the same geographic area.

Centers for Disease Control and Prevention: a DHHS agency that works to prevent and control infectious and chronic diseases, injuries, workplace hazards, disabilities, and environmental health threats.

Centers for Medicare and Medicaid Services (CMS): a DHHS agency that oversees Medicare, state Medicaid programs, and the Children's Health Insurance Program (CHIP), and regulates self-insured employers.

Centralized pharmacy services: pharmacy services that are provided from a single location within the hospital.

Certification: process by which a nonregulatory agency recognizes an individual who has met certain qualifications, such as successfully completing an examination following an intensive course of self-study.

Certified pharmacy technician (CPhT): an individual designated and recognized for completing the certification requirements administered by the Institute for the Certification of Pharmacy Technicians or the Pharmacy Technician Certification Board.

Chain pharmacy: a retail pharmacy that serves the general public and that is owned by a larger corporation (e.g., Walgreens, CVS, Rite-Aid).

Change in demand: a shift in an entire demand curve such that the quantity demanded changes even though price remains constant. An increase in demand is represented by a rightward shift of the demand curve; a decrease in demand is illustrated by a leftward shift of the demand curve.

Change in quantity demanded: a movement along a given demand curve caused by a change in price. The demand schedule shows that as the price charged increases, the quantity demanded decreases. Therefore, a change in quantity demanded is caused solely by a change in the price charged to customers.

Change in quantity supplied: a movement along a given supply curve caused by a change in price. The supply schedule shows that, as the price that customers are willing to pay increases, the quantity supplied increases. Therefore, a change in quantity supplied is caused solely by a change in the price charged to customers.

Change in supply: a shift in an entire supply curve such that the quantity supplied changes even though the price customers are willing to pay remains constant. An increase in supply is represented by a rightward shift of the supply curve; a decrease in supply is illustrated by a leftward shift of the supply curve.

Charitable hospitals: Medical care facilities in the 19th century that housed impoverished patients who had no friends or relatives to care for them. These institutions provided patients with only the bare necessities. The public generally perceived these institutions as places to die; professionals saw them as places to develop clinical experience.

Children's Health Insurance Program (CHIP): a program that expanded health insurance to at least half of the 11 million U.S. children lacking health insurance.

Chronic disease: illness that lasts a long time, affecting patients either continuously or episodically. Chronic illnesses such as heart disease and cancer began to appear with greater frequency in the early 20th century.

Clinical testing of new drugs: the phase of testing required by the FDA in which the drug entity is first used in human subjects to determine its safety and efficacy.

Clinical trial: study conducted to evaluate potential new drugs.

Co-payment: a form of patient cost sharing that requires patients to pay a specified dollar amount every time a service is received (e.g., $50 per hospital admission or $5 per prescription).

Coinsurance: a form of patient cost sharing that requires patients to pay a specified percentage (usually 20%) of the cost of covered services; the plan pays the remainder.

Commissioner of insurance: a state agency that monitors health insurance companies and the products they sell, including financial reserves, marketing and enrollment activities, rates, and services covered.

Community-based health care: healthcare services provided for individuals within a community who need healthcare assistance at home.

Community health center: federally supported health center that provides primary care services (e.g., physicians, physician extenders, laboratory services, dental services, social services, and pharmaceutical services) to underserved areas in urban and rural areas of the United States.

Community pharmacy: any independent, chain, or supermarket-based pharmacy that provides pharmaceutical products and services to ambulatory patients.

Community rating: a method of setting insurance premiums based on the insurance company's overall expenses for a specific geographic area during the previous year.

Comparative effectiveness research (CER): designed to inform healthcare decisions by providing evidence on the effectiveness, benefits, and harms of different treatment options. The evidence is generated from research studies that compare drugs, medical devices, tests, surgeries, or ways to deliver health care.

Complement: product that tends to influence the purchase of other related products, such that an increase in the price of one good can cause a decrease in the demand for another good.

Comprehensive: characteristic whereby essential healthcare benefits are covered.

Comprehensive health reform: extensive reform legislation that would broadly and fundamentally change the healthcare system in reference to financing and delivery.

Congressional Budget Office: an office of the U.S. Congress that is designed to help Congress formulate budget plans, stay within those plans, assess the effects of federal laws, and estimate the impact of proposals on the federal budget.

Consultant pharmacist: a pharmacist who provides advice on individual medication use, institutional-based medication use, and/or institutional pharmacy services.

Consumer drug use: the act of using medications by the general public.

Consumer model of care: a practitioner–patient model of care in which patients have a greater autonomy in decision making and are somewhat skeptical buyers of medical care.

Consumer Price Index: an economic indicator published by the Bureau of Labor Statistics that measures increases in the price level (i.e., inflation) of a set of goods and services purchased by consumers. Data can be used to determine inflation rates for many types of consumer goods and services such as medical care or prescription drugs.

Continuing care retirement community: a retirement community that provides a continuum of independent living, assisted living, and skilled nursing care on a single campus.

Coordination of benefits: a provision in insurance contracts that is designed to prevent duplicate payments by more than one insurance plan for the same medical care by limiting total reimbursement from all insurance plans for the same event to the amount of the actual loss. Health insurance policies usually pay after automobile, homeowners', or workers' compensation insurance policies have paid their portion.

Cost-benefit analysis (CBA): a method used to evaluate two or more alternatives where the input and outcomes are measured in dollars.

Cost-consequence analysis (CCA): a method used to evaluate two or more alternatives where the inputs are measured in dollars and the outcome is measured using a variety of methods, including natural units of effectiveness, quality-adjusted life years (QALYs), or dollars.

Cost containment: concept considered to either decrease healthcare spending or restrain the growth of healthcare spending. It has become the focus of much of healthcare reform since the 1970s.

Cost-effectiveness analysis (CEA): a method used to evaluate two or more alternatives where the inputs are measured in dollars and the outcome is measured in natural units of effectiveness.

Cost-minimization analysis (CMA): a method used to evaluate two or more alternatives where the inputs are measured in dollars and the consequences or outcomes of the alternatives are identical.

Cost-of-illness analysis (COI): a type of pharmacoeconomic analysis that estimates the magnitude of resources needed for a specific disease state in a defined population. The resources needed include both direct and indirect costs associated with prevention, treatment, and disease-related morbidity and mortality. This type of analysis can provide insight into the value of disease prevention or treatment of an illness or to compare the relative economic burden of one disease state compared to another to aid decision makers in allocating limited healthcare resources and research funding monies. Also commonly referred to as *burden-of-illness analysis.*

Cost sharing: a provision in managed care plans requiring patients to share in the cost of services received. Cost sharing attempts to optimize utilization of health services by making patients more cost conscious. It can take many forms, including co-payments, coinsurance, deductibles, out-of-pocket limits, or maximum benefits.

Cost-to-charge ratio: the ratio of the cost of providing services and the reimbursement obtained for those same services. This calculation is sometimes used in retrospective claims analysis to adjust available charge data to better reflect actual costs.

Cost-utility analysis (CUA): a method used to evaluate two or more alternatives where the input is measured in dollars and the outcome is measured as life years saved or patient-preference weighted outcome.

Counterdetailing: see *academic detailing.*

Counterfeit drug: fraudulently created medical product passed off as the real thing.

Cyberpharmacy: see *Internet pharmacy.*

Data exclusivity period: period of time when a generic or biosimilar manufacturer cannot rely upon the clinical trial data of the drug they are copying.

Decentralized national health program: a type of healthcare system where the administration of healthcare delivery is divided among various groups, usually the government and private agencies.

Decentralized pharmacy services: pharmacy services that are provided from satellite locations in patient care areas, or specialized areas, such as the operating room or emergency department.

Decision analysis: a systematic approach to decision making under conditions of uncertainty. This approach uses existing data and models the outcomes based on the best available data.

Decision tree: a type of decision analysis whereby all possible consequences of a decision are mapped in a branching or tree shape.

Deductible: a form of patient cost sharing that requires patients to pay their own healthcare expenses until a specified dollar amount has been paid out of pocket during a given period of time, usually a year.

Demand: the ability and willingness of a consumer to pay for a good or service.

Demand curve: a graphic representation of a demand schedule.

Demand schedule: a table or chart that shows the amounts of a commodity consumers are willing and able to purchase at each specific price charged in a set of possible prices during some specified period of time. The following two variables exist: (1) the price charged by the supplier (independent variable) and (2) the quantity demanded by the consumer at each given price (dependent variable). It is assumed, for the sake of simplicity, that all other variables are held constant.

Department of Health and Human Services: a cabinet-level federal agency with numerous branches that are engaged in the delivery of health services and directly involved in the formation of health policy. Some DHHS offices and agencies provide social services or deliver administrative and support functions. DHHS also assumes a significant role in the research and development activities of the healthcare system, by conducting and sponsoring fundamental research, assuring the safety of food and drugs, and monitoring the adoption of information technology.

Developed nation: any country with a high standard of living that is characterized by high per capita incomes, strong health infrastructures, and positive healthcare outcomes. Also known as an industrialized country.

Developing nation: any country with a low standard of living that is characterized by low per capita incomes, weak health infrastructures, and poor healthcare outcomes.

Diagnosis-related group (DRG): a categorization of diseases or conditions created initially by the federal government as a means to reimburse hospitals prospectively for services provided to patients.

Direct medical cost: the medical input or resource consumed that is directly related to the product or service being evaluated.

Direct nonmedical cost: a consumed nonmedical resource that is directly related to the product or service being evaluated.

Direct-to-consumer advertising: the act of advertising prescription medications to the general public through a variety of media.

Disability-adjusted life years: a measure developed by the WHO that represents the loss of 1 year of full health.

Discounted fee for service: a retrospective reimbursement rate in which healthcare providers are paid a negotiated fee each time a service is provided. The agreed-upon rate is lower than the providers' usual and customary charges to cash-paying patients.

Discounting: the process of converting dollars, either paid out or received over time periods of more than 1 year, to their present value. The purpose is to incorporate the time preference for money into the analysis.

Disease management: a system of coordinated healthcare interventions and communications for populations with conditions in which patient self-care efforts are a significant component of care.

Disease state management: a continuous and coordinated process that seeks to manage and improve the health status of a patient population over the course of a disease.

Dispensary: separate, freestanding institutions in urban neighborhoods designed to provide medical care for the poor, usually employing a physician and/or pharmacist.

Dispense as written (DAW): a provision in the participating pharmacy agreement that allows full reimbursement for the higher cost multiple-source drug product if the pharmacy indicates on the prescription claim that the prescriber demanded a brand-name product instead of its generic equivalent.

Dispenser: points of distribution for medications through the pharmaceutical supply chain (e.g., manufacturer, wholesaler, pharmacy).

Drug therapy monitoring: verifying drug, dose, and route of administration and monitoring for medication-related problems to optimize drug therapy.

Drug use control: the system of knowledge, understanding, judgments, procedures, skills, controls, and ethics that assures optimal safety in the distribution and use of medications.

Drug use evaluation: see *drug utilization evaluation*

Drug utilization evaluation (DUE): an evaluation of the use of one or more drugs prescribed for one or more diseases or conditions within the context of quality assurance and risk management procedures.

Drug utilization review (DUR): the review of physician prescribing, pharmacist dispensing, and patient use of drugs with the goal of ensuring that drugs are used appropriately, safely, and effectively. A DUR may be conducted prospectively or retrospectively.

Drug wholesaler: a company that buys pharmaceuticals directly from manufacturers and then resells those drugs to individual pharmacies.

Duration of treatment: a measure of how long patients continue receiving treatment. For hospitals, this means length of stay; for physicians, the episode of care; and for pharmacies, the number of prescription refills.

Earned discount: the difference between the average wholesale price and the pharmacy's actual acquisition cost.

Economic resources: land, including all natural resources; labor; and capital, including physical resources produced by labor. Economists refer to these three basic economic resources as factors of production because they are used to produce those things that people desire (commodities).

Economics: the study of how individuals and societies allocate their limited resources in attempts to satisfy their unlimited wants.

Effectiveness: the ability of a product to produce an effect in real-world practice, typically outside of the well-controlled setting of clinical trials.

Efficacy: the ability of a product to produce an effect, typically demonstrated in randomized controlled clinical trials.

Efficiency: the goal of producing the greatest output for the lowest net cost.

Elastic demand: a situation in which consumers are relatively sensitive to price changes, such that an increase in price will result in a decrease in total revenue.

Elasticity: an economic concept that measures the responsiveness of consumer demands to a change in price.

Electronic data interchange (EDI): the transfer of data between organizations using networks or the Internet.

Elimination period: a restriction found in group insurance policies that is aimed at reducing adverse selection by restricting coverage for preexisting health problems until after the policyholder has been covered for a given period of time. Expenses related to pregnancy and childbirth, for example, may not be covered for the first 9 months of a new policy. Elimination periods are often waived when new employees are hired and during open enrollment periods.

Emergency services: a wide range of emergent and urgent services provided in hospital emergency rooms to emergency medical services (e.g., 9-1-1, emergency medical vans, paramedics, trauma centers, and emergi-centers).

Employee mandate: a requirement usually set by a state law requiring all employees to purchase health insurance.

Employee Retirement Income Security Act (ERISA): a federal law designed to protect employees' benefits, including health insurance and retirement plans. Self-insured plans are exempt from state employer mandates under ERISA.

Employer mandate: a proposal that would require employers to provide health insurance for all their workers or pay a tax that would create an insurance pool for the uninsured.

Epidemiology: the study of the factors that determine the frequency and distribution of disease in human populations.

Equilibrium point: the point where a demand curve intersects the supply curve. The coordinates for the equilibrium point are the equilibrium price and the equilibrium quantity.

Equilibrium price: the price corresponding to the point where the demand curve and the supply curve intersect; the price where the market can rest without a natural tendency to increase or decrease price.

Equilibrium quantity: the quantity corresponding to the point where the demand curve and the supply curve intersect; the quantity where the market can rest without a natural tendency to increase or decrease the quantity supplied or demanded.

Estimated acquisition cost: the amount paid by a pharmacy benefit manager for drug ingredient costs, calculated as a percentage of the average wholesale price.

Exclusive provider organization (EPO): a form of preferred provider organization in which no coverage is provided for care received outside the provider network.

Experience rating: a method of setting insurance premiums based on the insurance company's overall expenses for a specific subset of insured individuals—usually an employer group—based on the group's experience from the previous year.

Factors explaining changes in mortality rates and life expectancy: improvements in public health measures (e.g., garbage collection, pure water, clean air, sewerage disposal), improvements in lifestyle (e.g., domestic sanitary practices, diet), and therapeutic interventions (e.g., anesthetics, antibiotics, surgical procedures).

Federal Medical Assistance Percentage: the portion of Medicaid program costs that is paid by the federal government for provider services. Each state's portion is determined annually through the use of a formula that compares a given state's average per capita income to the national average. By law, the percentage can be no greater than 83% and no less than 50% for any given state. States that are wealthier in terms of average per capita income have a smaller share of their Medicaid costs paid by the federal government than do relatively poorer states. There are some exceptions that limit the portion of a state's administrative costs that are paid by the federal government and other exceptions that allow the federal government to reimburse states at a higher rate for family planning services and for healthcare services provided through Indian Health Service facilities.

Fee-for-service (FFS): reimbursement in which a fee is paid to a provider for each service performed. FFS was the predominant reimbursement mechanism before managed care; some managed care organization contracts still allow a discounted FFS. FFS provides incentives to increase the quantity of services provided.

First-dollar coverage: a reimbursement mechanism in which there is no provision for patient cost sharing.

Fiscal intermediary: an organization that facilitates exchanges between healthcare payers and healthcare providers by underwriting and/or administering healthcare benefit programs.

Flat of the curve: a point where additional healthcare expenditures produce relatively little incremental benefit to the patient.

Flexner report: a report on the state of medical education in the United States sponsored by the Carnegie Foundation and prepared by Abraham Flexner in 1910. The report examined such factors as entrance requirements, teaching, labs, financing, and clinical status. Recommendations of the report resulted in closure of inadequate medical schools and new emphasis on scientific, lab-based medical education.

Floor-stock distribution: a drug distribution system that involves supplying the nursing staff units with a predetermined number of dosage forms, which are stored in a separate drug room on each patient care area. Nurses dispense the medications to any number of patients from this supply, and then they reorder from the pharmacy as needed.

Food and Drug Administration: See *U.S. Food and Drug Administration.*

Formal care or caregiving: care that is provided by healthcare workers in an institution or offered by other organizations.

Formulary: a list of medications compiled by a hospital or pharmacy benefit manager that contain either those drugs approved for use within the hospital or for reimbursement by the pharmacy benefit manager. Medications are included based on the relative clinical benefit and cost of the medication as compared to other agents within a similar therapeutic class.

Full-time equivalent (FTE): a unit of labor supply equal to one person working full-time, approximately 40 hours per week.

Gatekeeper: a central component of most health maintenance organizations in which primary care physicians must coordinate and authorize all medical services, including laboratory services, specialty referrals, and hospitalizations. In many gatekeeper systems, a patient must receive a referral from his or her primary care physician to receive coverage for a specialist's care. The rationale underlying this approach is that it avoids unnecessary and often expensive referrals to specialists. The gatekeeper may be financially at risk—not only for the services that he or she provides, but also for the medical services provided by specialists to whom a patient is referred.

Generic drug: a drug product manufactured by a company other than the one that originally developed the product, after the original product's patent has expired.

Government Accountability Office: the investigative arm of Congress charged with evaluating federal programs and activities, examining the use of public funds, and providing analyses, options, and recommendations to Congress.

Gross domestic product (GDP): the market value of all final goods and services produced within a country within a given period of time.

Gross margin: the difference between the selling price and the cost to the pharmacy for the product that was sold.

Group-model HMO: a type of HMO characterized by contracts with large, multispecialty medical groups offering services exclusively to the HMO on a capitated basis.

Group policies: insurance plans sponsored by employer groups for employees and their dependents. Group policies are usually less expensive than individual policies because they are less subject to adverse selection and because they are less expensive to sell and administer.

Guidance cooperation model of care: as described by Szasz and Hollender; practitioner–patient communication in which the patient is active in the interaction, but defers to medical expertise. This interaction can be compared to a parent–adolescent relationship.

Health: a state of physical and mental wellbeing, not merely the absence of disease or infirmity.

Health belief model: a health behavior theory that describes the likelihood an individual will take action to change a behavior. Components of this theory include susceptibility and severity of disease, perceived benefits and barriers, cues to action, self-efficacy, and demographic, sociopsychological, and structural variables.

Health department: a public health agency at the federal, state, or local level that is established to identify and manage health problems that affect individuals and population groups (e.g., environmental sanitation, communicable diseases, chronic diseases, immunizations, maternal and child health clinics, and prevention services).

Health disparities: differences in the overall rate of disease incidence, prevalence, morbidity, mortality, or survival rates.

Health insurance: a situation in which individuals or employers buy a plan from a company to assist them in paying for healthcare costs incurred. Insurance coverage varies but often includes physician visits, hospitalizations, laboratory tests, and other medical expenses.

Health Insurance Portability and Accountability Act (HIPAA): a law enacted by Congress in 1996 that limits the amount of time a preexisting condition may be excluded from coverage to 1 year, requires insurance companies to sell health insurance policies to small employers and individuals who lose coverage without regard to their health history, requires insurance companies to renew policies they sell to groups and individuals, and outlines standards for patient confidentiality.

Health maintenance organization (HMO): a type of managed care organization that shares risk with a network of healthcare providers by requiring that the providers assume some risk, either directly or indirectly, and that generally does not provide coverage for medical care that is received outside the network. The risk arrangement can take many forms, such as capitation or risk pools. The gatekeeper is a central component of most HMOs. The four basic types of HMO models are staff models, group models, network models, and independent practice associations.

Health Maintenance Organization Act: a federal law enacted in 1973 that set standards and provided start-up funds for health maintenance organizations—specialized insurance plans that involve restrictive provider networks and primary care gatekeepers that are responsible for referrals to other healthcare services and risk sharing with providers. This act also required employers with more than 25 employees to offer an HMO plan.

Health-related quality of life (HrQoL): a measure of an individual's well being; often used to determine how an individual's well being is affected over time by a given health condition or by treatment of that condition.

Health savings account (HSA): a provision of the Medicare Prescription Drug, Improvement, and Modernization Act that established tax-free savings accounts to be used for out-of-pocket medical expenses for those individuals who select a high-deductible health insurance plan.

Health Security Act: a Clinton administration proposal that would have imposed an employer mandate and established managed competition in which health providers would compete for patients based on cost and value.

Healthcare employer data and information set (HEDIS): a group of performance measures developed by the National Committee for Quality Assurance (NCQA), which gives plan sponsors objective information that they can use to evaluate managed care organizations.

Heroic medical therapy: an aggressive type of patient care that used depletive and strengthening measures to return the patient's diseased body to equilibrium. Methods used included leeches, tonics, medical instruments, and medicines to bleed, purge, puke, or sweat patients.

Hill-Burton Act: see *National Hospital Survey and Construction Act.*

Home care: provision of healthcare services in a patient's home that are intended to restore and maintain the patient's optimal level of well-being in a familiar environment.

Home care standards for pharmacists: standards established by the American Society of Health-System Pharmacists that apply to activities pertaining to home care pharmacy practice. These standards establish a minimum level of pharmacy services within this component of pharmacy practice.

Home health services: services usually associated with nursing care provided through a home health agency. They may also include speech and physical therapy or other types of rehabilitation therapies, homemaker services, social services, and hospice care.

Home infusion therapy: the parenteral administration of drugs, solutions, and nutrition to patients in their homes.

Horizontal integration: integration of two or more hospitals—frequently a large, urban, tertiary care hospital and a small community hospital—to provide a larger number of services and increase the hospitals' managerial efficiency.

Hospice: care provided for individuals who are terminally ill or close to death.

Hospital clinics: ambulatory care clinics in hospitals that range from family practice and internal medicine (e.g., general medicine, cardiology, dermatology) to surgical clinics (e.g., general surgery, urology, orthopedics, plastic surgery).

Hospitals at the turn of the 20th century: hospitals in which orthodox physicians and trustees sought private paying patients from the middle and upper classes. These institutions implemented the germ theory of disease and introduced new aseptic and antiseptic techniques and new technology such as X-rays. The architectural design focused on private and semiprivate rooms rather than the ward arrangement prevalent in charitable hospitals.

Human capital approach: a method used to value lives saved in terms of the income that the person could have earned the remaining productive years of his or her life.

Human trials—Phases I, II, III, and IV: scientific studies required by the Food and Drug Administration for the approval of an investigational new drug. Phase I trials generally include 20 to 100 healthy volunteers, with the goals of assessing safety, studying drug metabolism and excretion, and documenting pharmacologic response. Phase I results are used to calculate the sample size and length of testing needed to establish efficacy in the next phase of clinical studies. Phase II trials include several hundred individuals who are representative of the patients the drug is intended to treat. Response to most new drugs is compared to placebo and less often to existing treatment. Various doses are compared, and additional safety data are gathered. Phase III trials are controlled clinical studies that are conducted with several hundred to thousands of persons and are intended to demonstrate that the drug has statistically significant safety and effectiveness. Information gathered through these clinical trials determines the content of the product label and package insert required by the FDA. Phase IV trials, known as postmarketing surveillance, are conducted after a drug is marketed to the public. Their purpose is to monitor for and report any uncommon, yet serious, adverse reactions that were not found in the clinical trial phases but become evident when the drug is used in a broader population.

Humoralism: Galen's second-century concept that saw the human body as interrelated and in natural balance. Health equaled a human body in balance; disease meant the body's system was in disequilibrium.

Incidence: the rate of new cases of diseases occurring in a population over a specific time period.

Incremental cost-effectiveness plane: a chart that illustrates the decisions to be made when two alternative treatments are compared when one treatment is both more expensive and more effective than the other.

Incremental cost-effectiveness ratio: a ratio comparing the additional cost incurred to the additional benefit provided by one alternative relative to another option.

Incremental cost-utility ratio: a ratio comparing the additional cost incurred to the additional quality-adjusted life years provided by one alternative to another option.

Incremental healthcare reform: step-by-step, slow passage of individual pieces of health legislation.

Indemnity: a form of insurance that traditionally required patients to submit claims for reimbursement. Today the term is often used to refer to any health insurance plan with fee-for-service reimbursement and few cost controls.

Independent pharmacy: a retail pharmacy that serves the general public and that is independently owned, usually by a pharmacist.

Independent practice association (IPA)-model HMO: a type of HMO in which physicians form a separate legal entity, usually a corporation or partnership, that then contracts with the managed care organization. The IPA usually shares risk with the managed care organization and individual providers are paid by the IPA for services provided to enrolled patients for a negotiated fee. The IPA may reimburse physicians on a discounted FFS basis or may share some risk with them. These physicians typically have their own private practices and are allowed to provide services to patients enrolled in other managed care organizations.

Indian Health Service (IHS): managed by the U.S. Public Health Service, the system of hospitals and ambulatory care centers that provides health care and pharmacy services to nearly 1.5 million American Indians and Alaska natives living on or near reservations.

Indirect costs: those costs indirectly associated with the product or service under evaluation. Examples of indirect costs include the cost of lost productivity associated with an illness and the costs borne by caregivers.

Induced demand: the increased demand for healthcare services that is created by the availability of insurance payment. Healthcare providers, especially physicians, can increase utilization of health services by creating more demand for the services they provide.

Inelastic demand: a situation in which consumers are relatively insensitive to price changes, such that an increase in price will not result in a decrease in demand.

Infant mortality rate: the number of children younger than 1 year of age who die during a particular year divided by the number of live births during the same year.

Infectious diseases: communicable, contagious diseases that historically killed large numbers of people. These diseases are always present (endemic) or appear occasionally with great intensity (epidemic). They include pneumonia, gastritis, measles, small-pox, and scarlet fever.

Inflation: an increase in the price level of specified goods or services over time; often measured by the Bureau of Labor Statistics (BLS) as the Consumer Price Index (CPI).

Informal care or caregiving: care provided by family or friends to an individual.

Inpatient prospective payment system (IPPS): the reimbursement or payment mechanism used for Medicare beneficiaries receiving hospital care. Payment is based on the patient's diagnosis and is determined prior to the patient receiving care. Also referred to as the DRG payment method.

Inputs: as related to pharmaceuticals, all resources—including but not limited to human capital and supplies—that are needed to produce optimal outcomes.

Institutional pharmacy: the practice of pharmacy usually found in hospitals and larger healthcare systems and organizations.

Instrumental activities of daily living (IADLs): activities that are required for independent living but are not necessarily performed on a daily basis, such as meal preparation, housework, balancing a checkbook, driving, and using a telephone.

Insurable hazard: a type of pure risk that can lead to specific, measurable, and substantial losses that are unanticipated for an individual, but that are anticipated and relatively predictable for the group as a whole.

Insurable interest: a situation in which the individual who will receive payment for an insurance claim actually experiences a loss when an insurable hazard occurs.

Intangible costs: those costs that cannot be measured or tracked easily or are not associated with a medical or nonmedical resource. Intangible costs are often associated with the pain and suffering due to illness or disease.

Intellectual property rights: regulations that allow for innovators to have market exclusivity in order to recoup development costs.

Intensity of services: a measure of the types and numbers of services provided. It includes the service mix (types of services), the quantity (per capita use), and the quality of services.

Interdisciplinary: involving those professionals who work together for the patient's good and who also communicate effectively among themselves and with the patient.

Internet pharmacy: a retail entity in which consumers can purchase pharmaceuticals via an Internet website. Also known as a cyberpharmacy.

Investigational new drug: a chemical entity that shows promise as a potential new drug and has been approved by the FDA for clinical testing.

Joint Commission: a nonprofit organization that sets standards of practice for, evaluates, and accredits more than 15,000 healthcare organizations and programs in the United States. Formerly known as the Joint Commission on the Accreditation of Healthcare Organizations.

Kerr-Mills Act: a 1960 amendment to the Social Security Act that provided healthcare coverage to poor, elderly individuals.

Law of demand: an economic principle that states that, as the price charged for a product or service falls, the corresponding quantity demanded rises; alternatively, as the price charged increases, the corresponding quantity demanded falls. In short, an inverse relationship exists between the price charged and the quantity demanded.

Law of diminishing marginal utility: an economic principle that states that the value of any additional goods declines as one consumes more of it. In other words, the more we have of a good, the less we desire it.

Law of large numbers: an insurance principle that states that the larger the number of insured persons, the more accurate the predictions regarding losses. With losses being more predictable, the risk of this loss actually decreases.

Law of supply: an economic principle that states that, as the price customers are willing to pay falls, the corresponding quantity supplied falls; alternatively, as the price customers are willing to pay increases, the corresponding quantity supplied increases. In short, a direct relationship exists between the price customers are willing to pay and the quantity supplied.

Legend drug: one of a class of drugs created by the Durham-Humphrey Amendments in 1952 that were required to bear the legend, "Caution: Federal law prohibits dispensing without a prescription."

Length of stay: the amount of time a patient stays in the hospital, calculated from admission to discharge.

Licensure: permission granted by a regulatory body to an individual meeting predetermined qualifications, allowing him or her to practice in a particular occupation or profession.

Life expectancy: average number of years remaining for a person of a given age to live.

Locus of control: a health behavior theory that refers to whether an individual feels the attainment of a particular outcome is within his or her control (e.g., internal locus of control) or outside of it (e.g., external locus of control).

Long-term care services: a set of services—whether health, personal, or social—that is provided over a period of time to individuals who have lost some aspect of functioning.

Mail-order pharmacy: the practice of pharmacy in which consumers mail in their prescriptions to a pharmacy to be filled and mailed back.

Major medical insurance: a type of insurance policy designed to help offset expenses incurred by catastrophic illness or injury. These policies usually have high deductibles and are not designed to cover minor expenses.

Managed behavioral health care: specialty managed care organizations that attempt to reduce the costs of health care by carving out mental health services and using mental health practitioners at discounted fees, thus reducing the length of mental health treatment, decreasing the use of hospital treatment, and increasing the use of ambulatory mental healthcare treatment.

Managed care: the application of cost and quality controls to health care by controlling patient demand and provider supply. The defining feature of managed care is the use of provider networks through a contractual arrangement specifying the types of services to be provided and the reimbursement to be received in return.

Managed care organization (MCO): an organization designed to manage the cost and quality of a health insurance program. The differentiating feature of managed care plans versus fee-for-service plans is the use of a provider network. MCOs are categorized according to their degrees of (1) risk sharing, (2) provider exclusivity, (3) out-of-network coverage, and (4) physician autonomy and organization.

Managed competition: a provision of the Health Security Act that would have organized healthcare providers into health alliances that would compete with one another for patients based on cost and value.

Mandated categorically needy: groups of Medicaid recipients that the federal government requires state Medicaid programs to cover as a condition for receiving matching federal funding. The groups included are individuals who meet the eligibility criteria for Aid to Families with Dependent Children (AFDC), those receiving government cash assistance through the Supplemental Security program, pregnant women and children under the age of 6 in families with incomes of less than 133% of the federal poverty level, children under the age of 19 in families with income less than the federal poverty level, and certain groups of low-income Medicare recipients.

Manufacturing and distribution: the production of prescription drugs that meet FDA standards for best manufacturing practices. Prescription drugs are sold and distributed by the drug manufacturer to the pharmacy via a direct or wholesale route. In the pharmacy, the drugs are dispensed by the pharmacist for the patient, via the prescription, and are ultimately taken or consumed by the patient.

Marginal utility: the additional utility received from consuming one additional unit of a particular good or service.

Market structure: the categorization of firms based on attributes such as the numbers of buyers and sellers, product differentiation, pricing behavior, and so on. The four types of market structures are perfect competition, monopolistic competition, monopoly, and oligopoly.

Markov model: a type of decision analysis suited for those situations in which the patient may transition from one state to another. The simplest example of a Markov model features a three-state transition—from well to ill to dead.

Maximum allowable cost: the amount paid by a pharmacy benefit manager for the drug ingredient cost for a multiple-source drug. The maximum allowable cost is usually set at the price of a low-cost generic product without regard to whether a brand-name or generic product was actually dispensed.

Means testing: a requirement that participants in a program have less than a specified level of income or assets before enrollment or benefits would be granted. Such a requirement may also mandate using a sliding-scale payment mechanism for participation in a program, such that individuals with higher incomes would pay a larger amount than persons with lower incomes.

Medicaid: Title XIX of the Social Security Act; a joint program between the federal and state governments that pays for medical care for individuals who receive case assistance through the Supplemental Security Income program and certain low-income pregnant women, children, and other vulnerable groups.

Medicaid waiver: a provision established by the Omnibus Budget Reconciliation Act of 1981 that allows states to apply for exceptions to federal Medicaid guidelines for the purpose of either establishing Medicaid managed care plans or creating new initiatives to curb costs or improve delivery of Medicaid services.

Medicalization: redefining or relabeling of a personal or social problem as a medical condition, thus necessitating treatment for it in the healthcare system.

Medically needy: a group of individuals who would be eligible for Medicaid under one of the mandated or optional groups except for the fact that their income and/or assets are higher than allowed by the state. Such individuals become Medicaid eligible under the medically needy provision if their medical expenses reduce their net income to the Medicaid eligibility threshold or less. Thus, the medically needy consist of families and children, or elderly, blind, or disabled individuals, who spend down to Medicaid eligibility by incurring high out-of-pocket medical expenses. States may elect to cover these individuals and may qualify for federal matching funds.

Medicare: Title XVIII of the Social Security Act; a federal social health insurance program for individuals 65 years of age and older, individuals who receive disability benefits from Social Security or the Railroad Retirement Board, or individuals with end-stage renal disease requiring dialysis or kidney transplantation.

Medicare Advantage: see *Medicare Part C.*

Medicare Catastrophic Coverage Act: a 1988 proposal to expand Medicare Part B coverage to include outpatient prescription drug coverage.

Medicare Part A: the component of Medicare that pays for inpatient hospital, skilled nursing facilities, and home health care, and is financed by a payroll tax levied on employees and employers. Also called Hospital Insurance.

Medicare Part B: the component of Medicare that pays for physicians' services, outpatient hospital care, and a variety of other medical services not covered under Part A. Financed through premiums and patient cost sharing. Also called Supplemental Medical Insurance.

Medicare Part C: originally known as the Medicare + Choice program, but now is called Medicare Advantage. It expanded beneficiaries' ability to participate in a wide variety of private health plans, including health maintenance organizations (HMOs) and preferred provider organizations (PPOs).

Medicare Part D: a provision that created a new voluntary outpatient prescription drug benefit for Medicare recipients; it became available in 2006.

Medicare supplement (Medigap) insurance: insurance available to Medicare recipients that is designed to cover the cost for healthcare services not covered by Medicare.

Medication adherence: successfully following a specified medication treatment regimen.

Medication assistance program (MAP): program that provides low-income patients with access to brand-name prescription products from pharmaceutical companies at little or no cost to patients.

Medication delivery: a delivery system for prescription drugs in community and institutional settings that ensures medications are used safely and effectively.

Medication Regimen Review (MRR): a thorough evaluation of the medication regimen of a resident with the goal of promoting positive outcomes and minimizing adverse consequences associated with medication. The review includes preventing, identifying, reporting, and resolving medication-related problems, medication errors, or other irregularities, and collaborating with other members of the interdisciplinary team.

Medication therapy management services (MTMS): a broad range of activities within the scope of practice of pharmacists and other qualified healthcare providers intended to ensure that patients with multiple diseases and on many medications get the greatest benefit possible from their medication regimen.

Medication use evaluation (MUE): an objective evaluation of selected drug use in the hospital, which is compared to specific criteria established for these medications.

Mental health: functioning at a satisfactory level of physical, mental, and social well-being; a harmonious balance between the individual, his or her social group, and the larger environment context.

Monopolistic competition: a market structure similar to perfect competition except that it does not have standardized and interchangeable products.

Monopoly: a market structure that has only one seller of a product for which there are no close substitutes.

Monopsony: a market structure that has only one buyer, but several competing suppliers.

Moral hazard: a situation in which patients with insurance coverage overconsume healthcare services to the extent that the additional health benefits achieved from consuming additional health services are not really worth their full costs. Nevertheless, because the enrollees are paying only a fraction of the costs, they still want to use the services. Overconsumption of health services owing to moral hazard increases total health expenditures and insurance premiums.

Morbidity: rates that report the number of instances of a particular disease in an area per year.

Mortality: rates that report the number of deaths in an area per year.

Mutual participation model of care: as described by Szasz and Hollender, a practitioner–patient communication in which the patient assumes an active role and is equally powerful to the practitioner. This model is most commonly seen with patients who have chronic diseases and can be compared to a parent–adult child relationship.

National Committee for Quality Assurance: an independent, nongovernment agency that promotes performance standards, quality assurance, review standards, and accreditation for health maintenance organizations.

National health insurance model: any healthcare system characterized by a socialized health insurance plan.

National Hospital Survey and Construction Act (Hill-Burton Act): a federal law passed in 1946 that established hospitals in rural, town, and city areas that were previously underserved and provided renovations and extensions to already-existing hospitals. This act contributed to the growth of major medical centers, which are now widespread in the United States.

National Institutes of Health: a DHHS agency that supports health research, especially in cases where economic incentives are lacking or risky.

National Library of Medicine: an office within NIH that serves as the world's largest medical library and provides Internet access and services such as *PubMed* and worldwide access to peer-reviewed literature.

Naturalistic designs: an approach to pharmacoeconomic analyses in which patients are recruited and randomly assigned to treatment groups with follow up care being representative of routine clinical care.

Net benefit: a method used to represent outcomes in a cost-benefit analysis where the time frame of the analysis is less than or equal to 1 year.

Net present value: a method used to represent outcomes in a cost-benefit analysis where the time frame of the analysis goes beyond 1 year.

Network: a defined group of providers, typically linked through contractual arrangements, who supply a full range of primary and acute healthcare services. Managed care enrollees who use providers outside the network may receive reduced coverage or even no coverage.

Network-model HMO: a type of HMO characterized by nonexclusive contracts with large medical groups. While networks typically bear risk, the nonexclusivity of the arrangement reduces the influence of the risk on the physician's behavior.

New drug application (NDA): the application submitted by a pharmaceutical manufacturer to the FDA for approval of a drug product that has completed the FDA's clinical testing requirements.

Nonprescription (over the counter, nonlegend): pharmaceutical products that can be purchased without a prescription.

North American Pharmacy Licensure Examination (NAPLEX): an examination created by the National Association of Boards of Pharmacy and used to determine, along with a state's jurisprudence examination, an individual's eligibility to acquire licensure to practice pharmacy.

Office of the Inspector General: a DHHS agency that conducts nationwide audits, investigations, and inspections, reports to both the secretary of the DHHS and Congress about program and management problems, and makes recommendations for improvements.

Off-label drug use: use of drugs for an indication for which they do not have formal approval from the FDA.

Older adults: individuals who are at least 65 years of age.

Oligopoly: a market structure that consists of a few sellers and many buyers. Firms in oligopolies are often interdependent, and a dominant firm can exert influence through price leadership.

Oligopsony: a market structure that consists of only a few buyers but several competing suppliers.

Open enrollment period: a short period of time when employees are allowed to join the employer's health insurance plan. Open enrollment, without restrictions for pre-existing conditions, is usually available to new employees immediately upon being hired and to incumbent employees during a short period of time (i.e., approximately 2 weeks) each year.

Opportunity cost: the value of a resource based on its highest valued alternative use or market value.

Optionally categorically needy: groups of needy individuals who do not meet the requirements for mandated coverage but may be covered at the option of a state Medicaid program, which then receives federal matching funds. Many of those considered optionally eligible are children or pregnant women.

Oregon Health Plan: expanded Medicaid program in Oregon covering previously uninsured citizens as a result of the Oregon Basic Health Services Act of 1989. To determine what was covered, the program evaluated treatment options based on their effectiveness and their cost.

Orphan diseases: disease that affects very few people every year, typically less than 200,000 per year.

Orthodox (allopathic, regular, or mainstream) physician: physician who possessed some didactic medical education and underwent apprenticeship to develop his or her clinical skills. He or she practiced heroic medicine.

Outcome: the impact or effect of drug therapy.

Out-of-pocket model: any healthcare system characterized by no insurance coverage.

Pandemic: widespread epidemics of infectious or contagious diseases that affect one or more countries or continents contemporaneously.

Participating pharmacy agreement: a contract between a pharmacy and a pharmacy benefit manager that specifies the rights and duties of each party with regard to prescription drug coverage.

Patent: the right for an innovator to be the exclusive producer for a period of time.

Patent medicine: cheap concoction in tonic or pill form that was widely advertised in newspapers and popular magazines and sold in pharmacies or by traveling tradesmen.

Patent registration: the period of time during which a manufacturer has exclusive rights to develop, market, and produce a product without competition from other manufacturers.

Patient-centered care: a model in which the focus of the practitioner shifts from disease orientation (the body) to the person as a whole. Practitioners are encouraged to view the illness from the patient's eyes.

Patient cost sharing: a provision in health insurance plans that provides financial incentives for patients to avoid using unnecessary healthcare services by making them pay a portion of the cost of the service. Patient cost-sharing methods include co-payments, coinsurance, deductibles, out-of-pocket limits, and maximum benefit limits.

Patient-induced demand: an increase in the quantity of services demanded resulting from insurance coverage that lowers patients' out-of-pocket expenses. By isolating patients from the true cost of healthcare services, health insurance has encouraged patients to consume more healthcare services than they would if they were bearing the full cost of the product or service themselves.

Patient Protection and Affordable Care Act (ACA): also referred to as the Affordable Care Act of 2010. The largest reform passed by Congress to the healthcare delivery system since Medicare and Medicaid were passed in 1965. The law expands Medicaid to cover more individuals, expands access through the creation of state based insurance exchanges and non-profit insurance companies, and creates a Patient-Centered Outcomes Research Institute.

Per diem: a type of prospective reimbursement in which hospitals are paid a flat rate for each day of hospital care provided to covered individuals without regard to the actual costs incurred.

Perfect competition: a market structure characterized by (1) many buyers and sellers, (2) freedom of entry and exit, (3) standardized products, (4) full and free information, and (5) no collusion.

Personalized medicine: treatments for diseases that are tailored to each individual based on genetic and diagnostic test results.

Perspective: the point of reference (typically the decision maker) from which a pharmacoeconomic analysis will be conducted.

Pharmaceutical care: the responsible provision of drug therapy for achieving specific outcomes that improve a patient's quality of life. A pharmacy's mission in taking responsibility for patients' medication-related outcomes.

Pharmaceutical manufacturer: a company that participates in the manufacturing of drug products.

Pharmaceutical marketing: techniques used to publicize pharmaceutical products to prescribers and users of those products.

Pharmaceutical research and development: the process through which a pharmaceutical company discovers and develops new drug entities.

Pharmaceutical Research and Manufacturers of America (PhRMA): a U.S.-based organization that represents the interests of research-based pharmaceutical companies.

Pharmacoeconomics: the evaluation of the inputs and outcomes associated with pharmaceuticals or pharmacy services.

Pharmacoinformatics: the field of informatics that focuses on the creative use of computers and other technologies in support of pharmaceutical services, including patient care, education, and research.

Pharmacotherapy: the use of drugs to treat illness.

Pharmacy benefit manager (PBM): a specialized company that adjudicates prescription drug claims and manages the prescription drug coverage for a third-party payer by containing costs and influencing the quality of services provided.

Pharmacy education: the education that a pharmacist receives in the United States that leads to a doctor of pharmacy degree (PharmD). The PharmD replaced the baccalaureate degree as the entry-level required degree in 2004.

Pharmacy information services: provision of drug and health information by using textbooks, library, and web-based sources to answer questions and provide information to patients and health professionals.

Pharmacy practice: practice settings where a pharmacist may work, including a community pharmacy (e.g., independent, chain, supermarket, and megastore pharmacy), an institution (e.g., hospital, nursing facility, home care, and community health center), or in education, government, or the pharmaceutical industry.

Pharmacy practice residency: an organized, directed, postgraduate training program designed to develop competencies in a defined area of pharmacy practice. The program may be for 1 or 2 years.

Pharmacy technician: an assistant to a pharmacist whose roles and functions include medication preparation, customer service, and other activities as deemed appropriate by the employer within the context of state law.

Pharmakon: the Greek term for *drug*, meaning remedy, poison, or magical charm.

Physician profiling: a tool used by managed care organizations to analyze the practice patterns of physicians on cost and quality dimensions. Measures are generally expressed as a rate over a specific period of time within the physician's patient population (e.g., the average dollars spent per patient per month).

Point-of-service plan: a type of managed care organization that is a hybrid of a health maintenance organization and a preferred provider organization. As with a PPO, when care is received from a provider outside the network, partial coverage is provided. As with a health maintenance organization, physicians may be at risk or contract exclusively with the plan.

Population effects: a measure of the number of patients and the mix of various demographic factors within the group (e.g., gender, age, socioeconomic status, and other factors) that affect utilization. For hospitals, this means the number of hospital admissions; for physicians, the number of new patients; and for pharmacies, the number of new prescriptions.

Portability: a characteristic whereby healthcare benefits are readily transportable when individuals change their jobs or place of residence.

Postmarketing surveillance: the act of collecting information about a drug's use after it has been on the market for some time and is used more widely in the population.

Preclinical testing phase: a part of the FDA drug approval process that involves animal testing in order to study the chemical and physical properties of a molecular entity. Dosage forms are designed and tested, and chemical engineers develop optimal ways to manufacture adequate quantities of the drug product. Patents are filed to protect the intellectual property rights of the inventor. This testing is conducted prior to human testing.

Preferred provider organization (PPO): a type of managed care organization that creates a network of providers who agree to discount their charges for services delivered to enrolled beneficiaries. Beneficiaries are free to see any provider they choose, but have a financial incentive (i.e., lower out-of-pocket expenses) to receive care from providers in the preferred network.

Prescriber: a healthcare professional who is licensed to prescribe medications.

Prescription: an order written by a prescriber for a patient that describes therapy that a patient should receive.

Prevalence: the proportion of a population affected by a disease at a specific time.

Prevention: In a public health model, there are three successive stages to prevent pathologies, to initiate therapy, and to assist in the social reintegration of patients. Primary prevention covers all activities designed to reduce the instances of an illness in a population and to reduce the risk of new cases. Secondary prevention covers activities aimed at reducing the prevalence of an illness in a population and its duration. Tertiary prevention tries to reduce the incidence of chronic incapacity or recurrences of a disease.

Preventive health care: performance of activities or behaviors for the purpose of avoiding or deterring disease and maintaining health.

Primary care: ambulatory services for common ailments provided by primary care (first-order or gatekeeper) providers, who include physicians (e.g., those in family practice, internal medicine, pediatrics, obstetrics, and gynecology), nurse practitioners, and physician assistants.

Probabilistic sensitivity analysis: a type of sensitivity analysis in which researchers assign plausible ranges for variables and an estimate of the distribution of the data points for each variable. The most common type of probabilistic sensitivity analysis is Monte Carlo simulation, which uses computer simulation to randomly assign values from inputted variable ranges and estimating outcomes from models with large numbers of hypothetical patients.

Professional: a person who possesses specialized technical knowledge, is licensed to practice, and is motivated by a desire to be of service to others.

Prospective drug utilization review: see *drug utilization review.*

Psychopharmacology: the treatment of mental disorders with the use of prescription drugs.

Psychotherapy: a variety of treatment modalities for treating and evaluating individuals with mental and/or emotional disorders.

Public health: The practice of preventing disease and promoting health in communities of people. Public health professionals rely on policy and research strategies to understand issues such as substance abuse and chronic disease in particular populations.

Public policy: health or drug policy (e.g., a political position, statement, or viewpoint) that affects the public (community or population). Public policy is often determined at the community, state, and/or federal government level.

Pure risk: a type of risk in which there is a possibility of a loss but no possibility of a gain. This type of risk is insurable.

Quackery: false medical knowledge or credentials used to defraud the public; manufacture or sale of nontherapeutic nostrums or medical devices that generally cause harm.

Quality-adjusted life year (QALY): an outcome measured as life years gained adjusted for patient preference or another means of weighting/adjusted gains in life years.

Quality assurance: quality of care considerations that typically include both assessment of care and a feedback loop to the healthcare organization that recommends either a continuation or a change in care.

Randomized controlled trials: a research design model in which the unit of analysis (typically a patient) is randomized to one of multiple study arms (typically treatment and control or placebo).

Rebate: payment received by a pharmacy benefit manager from a pharmaceutical manufacturer in return for putting a specific drug on the pharmacy benefit manufacturer's formulary or giving the drug preferred status. The amount of a rebate may be based on performance (e.g., a certain level of prescribing) or market share (i.e., the percentage of all prescriptions within a given therapeutic class that are dispensed for the company's product).

Regulatory agency: a federal or state agency that regulates components of the healthcare industry, such as the Department of Public Health, the Drug Enforcement Administration, or the Food and Drug Administration.

Reinsurance: a type of insurance that protects insurance companies from extraordinary, unexpected losses. Insurance companies are willing to accept some risk of having claims exceed income, but obtain reinsurance to protect them from catastrophic losses. The reinsurance company pools the risks faced by many insurance companies together.

Report card: a periodic report sent by a managed care organization to inform providers about how their general performance and compliance with plan guidelines compared with the same characteristics for their colleagues or to the managed care organization's standards. Typical information on report cards includes cost per patient per month, number of prescriptions per patient per month, percentage of brand-name versus generic prescriptions, compliance with formulary guidelines, and prescribing patterns for selected prescription drugs.

Residency program: an organized, directed, post-graduate training program designed to develop competencies in a defined area of pharmacy practice.

Retrospective claims analysis: analysis that relies on paid administrative pharmacy or medical claims data. It is retrospective in the sense that researchers are typically evaluating events or measuring associations that have occurred in the past.

Retrospective drug utilization review: see *drug utilization review.*

Risk bearing: the amount of risk borne by the providers, which can range from full risk to no risk. Physicians typically accept risk in the form of capitation and risk pools; hospitals accept capitation as well as per diem and diagnosis-related group reimbursement.

Risk pool: an arrangement in which a health maintenance organization places a portion of payments in a pool as a source for any subsequent claims that exceed projections, with the provider and the health maintenance organization sharing in the surplus (or loss) from the risk pool at the end of the year.

Roemer's law: reflects the historical tendency for healthcare providers to increase hospital admissions and the use of healthcare technology when excess capacity exists.

Sectarians (irregular physicians): rivals to orthodox physicians who sought education or training outside the orthodox medical educational system. They represented various beliefs, therapies, or medical systems that competed with the orthodox practice of medicine and included homeopaths and eclectics.

Self-care: the act of consumers selecting and using products or processes to treat health ailments without the supervision of a healthcare professional.

Self-dosing: do-it-yourself medicine. It uses traditional practices, family recipes, and folk and herbal medicines to treat oneself and one's family.

Sensitivity analysis: a methodological approach whereby assumptions made in modeling are tested to determine how sensitive the results are to changes in key assumptions within the model.

Service benefit: a form of health insurance plan in which healthcare providers submit claims and are paid directly by the insurance plan.

Shortage: a situation that occurs when the market price is below the equilibrium price, resulting in a quantity supplied that is less than the quantity demanded.

Sickness funds: the common name for the quasipublic, third-party payers characterizing Germany's healthcare system.

Simple sensitivity analysis: a pharmacoeconomic analysis that involves varying study assumptions (either cost or outcome) within the range of plausible values to determine if the original conclusions remain sound. A one-way simple sensitivity analysis allows only one variable to be changed at a time while a multiple-way simple sensitivity analysis allows more than one variable to be changed at a time.

Sin tax: a tax applied to nonessential items, such as alcohol and tobacco products.

Single-payer plan: a plan in which the government is the primary financer in one, all-inclusive healthcare system.

Skilled nursing facility (SNF): a facility that provides basic medical and nursing care, as well as additional services or therapies, that can include restorative, physical, and occupational therapies.

Social cognitive theory: a health behavior theory that describes an individual's expectations in relation to changing behavior. The model includes two main components: (1) outcome expectations, or the individual's belief that a behavior leads to a specific outcome, and (2) efficacy expectations, or the individual's belief that he or she has the ability to perform this behavior.

Social healers: usually female healers who treated friends and neighbors in rural and small-town communities in the 18th and 19th centuries. Patients sought simple medicines and treatments for boils or wounds as well as advice. Social healers were often also midwives.

Social partnership: characteristic whereby both the employer and the employee contribute funds to the healthcare system.

Social Security: a program created by the Social Security Act of 1935 that provides a minimum level of income for qualified individuals who are 65 years of age or older or who are disabled.

Social solidarity: a characteristic whereby some members of a country subsidize other members' healthcare costs.

Socialized health insurance: a type of healthcare system where the government provides health insurance to all citizens. Healthcare providers and facilities are private.

Socialized medicine: a type of healthcare system where the government participates in or enforces participation in the country's healthcare system, employs healthcare practitioners, owns healthcare facilities, and administers the healthcare system.

Speculative risk: a type of risk in which there is the possibility of either a gain or a loss. Business ventures and gambling are examples of activities in which there is speculative risk. This type of risk is not insurable.

Staff-model HMO: a type of health maintenance organization characterized by direct ownership of healthcare facilities and direct-employment physicians. Physicians in a staff-model health maintenance organization typically bear no direct risk, but the health maintenance organization can influence the physician through utilization review (the review of the necessity and efficiency of patients' utilization patterns).

Subrogation: the process in which an insurance company enforces a coordination of benefits provision by determining which insurance company is required to pay first if a particular patient has duplicate coverage.

Substance abuse disorders: disorders related to the use and abuse of various substances, both legal and illegal. Also referred to as addictive disorders and chemical disorders.

Substitutes: related products that may be interchanged by consumers. When the price of one good increases, the quantity demanded for that good decreases and the demand for its substitute increases.

Supplier-induced demand: an increase in demand created by the service provider. Physicians may induce demand for their own services by ordering follow-up care or referring patients to physician-owned laboratory, pharmacy, radiology, or other diagnostic or treatment services.

Supply: the ability and willingness of a supplier to provide a good or service.

Supply curve: a graphic representation of a supply schedule.

Supply schedule: a table or chart that shows the amount of a commodity suppliers are willing and able to supply at each specific price that customers are willing to pay in a set of possible prices during a specified period of time.

Surplus: a situation in which the market price exceeds the equilibrium price, resulting in a quantity supplied that is greater than the quantity demanded.

Taxonomy: the classification of objects or phenomena into an ordered system that indicates natural relationships.

Technology: the technical means that a person uses to improve his or her surroundings by extending user capabilities and performing repetitive tasks.

Telehealth: health care provided at a distance, through the use of technologies, including medical, pharmacy, and public health.

Telepharmacy: technologies used to support and deliver pharmaceutical services at a distance, most often in rural areas.

Temporary Assistance for Needy Families: a federal government program that provides block grants to states to be used for time-limited cash assistance. TANF generally allows a family to receive cash welfare (income maintenance) benefits for no more than 5 years and allows states to impose other requirements related to employment.

TennCare: Tennessee's program to extend Medicaid coverage to include previously uninsured citizens in managed care plans.

Theory of planned behavior (TPB): a health behavior theory that is an extension of the theory of reasoned action. It includes an additional component relating to the degree an individual has control over the behavior, such as knowledge, time, money, and opportunity.

Theory of reasoned action (TRA): a health behavior theory that hypothesizes an individual's behavior is related to his or her behavioral intention or the likelihood that the person will perform a behavior. According to the model, the following two main factors contribute to this intention: (1) attitude toward performing the behavior (beliefs and outcome), and (2) the subjective norm (what important individuals think of the behavior and the motivation to comply) associated with the behavior.

Threshold sensitivity analysis: a type of sensitivity analysis in which a single assumption in the analysis is varied until the alternative treatment option has the same outcome and there is no advantage between the treatment options. The value determined by conducting such an analysis is often referred to as a break-even point.

Tiered co-payments: a type of patient cost sharing that specifies multiple co-payment levels that are designed to encourage the use of preferred drug products, such as generics and lower cost brand-name drugs.

Total revenue: the average price charged per unit multiplied by the quantity demanded ($TR = P \times Q$).

Transtheoretical model: health behavior theory that theorizes that a patient progresses through five stages before a change in behavior occurs: (1) precontemplation,

(2) contemplation, (3) preparation, (4) action, and (5) maintenance. Often referred to as stages of change or readiness to change model.

TriCare: an agency of the Department of Defense that provides medical services to active-duty members and retired personnel of the armed forces, their dependents, and their survivors.

Trust fund: a fund that accounts for the moneys collected as Social Security and Medicare taxes.

Uncompensated care pool: an account financed by a tax on hospital bills or general tax revenue that establishes a pool of money used to reimburse hospitals for a portion of the cost of providing medical care to underinsured and uninsured patients.

Underwriting: the process of insuring. Underwriters attempt to calculate the amount of financial risk that they assume for insurable events, estimate losses and administrative expenses (with the aid of actuaries), and set the level of premiums needed to cover expenditures and provide for a reasonable profit.

Unit-dose distribution: a drug distribution system in which each dose of medication is separately packaged and labeled with the drug name, strength, lot number, and expiration date in a ready-to-administer form.

Universality: characteristic whereby all healthcare benefits are provided for all citizens of a given country.

U.S. drug approval process: the process identified by the Food and Drug Administration and by which pharmaceutical manufacturers must abide, for products to be approved for use in the United States.

U.S. drug development process: the process of creating and testing new drugs according to regulations set by the FDA in the U.S.

U.S. Federal Trade Commission (FTC): the federal agency that governs unfair business practices.

U.S. Food and Drug Administration (FDA): the federal agency that is responsible for assuring the safety and effectiveness of many food and drug products.

U.S. Pharmacopeia (USP): a nongovernmental, national, public agency responsible for setting standards for all prescription and over-the-counter medicines, dietary supplements, and other healthcare products manufactured and sold in the United States.

Utility: the satisfaction obtained from purchasing a particular good or service.

Utility score: a measure of patient preferences elicited from patients by a variety of means, such as analog scales, validated questionnaires, or standard gamble or time trade-off game theories. Scales typically range from zero to 1.0 with the assumption that patients will prefer those health states with higher utility scores.

Utilization review: a tool used by managed care organizations to review the necessity and efficiency of healthcare services, with the aim of decreasing costs and enhancing the safety and quality of services. See also *drug utilization review*.

Vertical integration: the provision of a continuum of healthcare services. For hospitals, it entails expanding healthcare services beyond traditional acute medical care to include nursing home care, home health care, and outpatient and rehabilitation services.

Veterans Administration: a Department of Defense agency that provides clinics and hospitals that treat injuries and provide rehabilitation services for disabilities resulting from military service, as well as care to veterans with low incomes or special health-care needs.

Waiver: see *Medicaid waiver.*

Web-based pharmacy: see *Internet pharmacy.*

Wholesale acquisition cost (WAC): The manufacturer's list price for drug products sold to wholesalers or direct purchasers as reported in wholesale price guides or other publications of drug pricing data. WAC prices are used as one method of calculating reimbursement of drug ingredient costs by some states' Medicaid programs.

Willingness-to-pay approach: a method used to value lives saved and/or the intangible benefits and health risks associated with a product or service, whereby individuals express their willingness to pay to reduce a health risk.

Workers' compensation: a system operated by states and funded by employers that provides health insurance coverage for employment-related injuries and illnesses, compensates workers who are disabled and unable to return to work, and provides benefits to survivors in the event of an employee's death.

Index

Note: Italicized page locators indicate a figure; tables are noted with a *t*.

G

J